Prevention

The Critical Need

Newly Revised

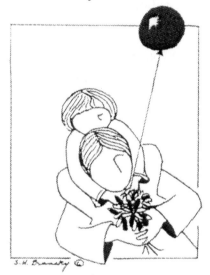

Jack Pransky

Burrell Foundation,
Nehri Publications
&
1st Books Library

The initial publisher of this work, the Burrell Foundation was established to advance the development and availability of options for personal growth.

We are proud to play a role in bringing this important book to those who continue to struggle with the problem of how to bridge from what is ... to what can be.

Whether in the role of educator, public official, student, practitioner or concerned citizen, one can find assistance here in defining a path to effective prevention of a wide variety of personal and societal ills.

Prevention is a book that helps us focus not simply on avoiding what we don't want, but also on promoting positive and viable alternatives.

— **Todd Schaible**, Ph.D.
President
Burrell Foundation

Table of Contents

Acknowledgments

I can't begin to thank enough all the people from whom I've learned so much over the years, and all the practitioners across the country who every day are doing exceptional work in the name of prevention. Without all of you this book would not have been written.

Thank you to those who helped me obtain information for this book and those who helped me along the way: Dr. George Albee, Dr. Kerby Alvy, Bonnie Benard, Jacqueline Bode, Vicky Church, Pam Crown and the Council for Children of Charlotte, N.C., Dennis Gallagher (wherever he may be), Dr. Steve Glenn, Fay Honey Knopp, Dr. Jane Nelsen, Glenn Lambert, Bill Lofquist, Sherrill Musty, David Pines, Harriet Russell and Heather Weiss.

Thanks to Prevention Unlimited for its support, especially Elizabeth Lawrence and Peter Perkins.

Thanks to all those who spurred me on, to Sas Carey for pointing the way, to Rob Langone, D.C., who kept me together physically during this time, and to Sherelee Cooper for her early volunteer work.

Special thanks to all those who contributed interviews.

Extra-special thanks to my pre-publication editors–Peggy Sax, Walter Crockett, George Brown, M.D. and the editorial help on a few chapters from Richard Wilkinson, Ph.D.–and to my publication editors: David Robinson and Evanne Weirich.

Extra extra-special thanks to Todd Schaible, Ph.D. and the Burrell Foundation.

And most of all, thanks to Judy, David, and Jaime for putting up with me and sacrificing income during the time of my writing this.

-Jack Pransky

Author's Note ~ Preface to the Second Edition

I have been so gratified by the response to this book. So many people from around the country—and world—have told me how valuable this book has been to them; that they continually use it as a resource and reference, that it helps them write grants, that it helps them with prevention program development, community development and prevention policy development. A review in *New Designs for Youth Development* called it "a prevention classic that will guide the field into the 21st century"; that *Prevention* would "inspire...its readers to push beyond current accepted theories and practices in the human services arena" (Miller, 1991, p.28). It has been used as a prevention text in over twenty-five colleges and universities, and in many state-sponsored prevention courses.

So much has happened within the past decade in the field of prevention, though, that parts of this book had begun to get a bit dated.

Since *Prevention: The Critical Need* first appeared at the end of 1990 the prevention field has undergone some dramatic changes. When I began writing this book in 1987, the public knew very little about prevention. Very few politicians spoke of it. No book existed that presented an overview of the prevention field. No book existed that compiled research-based, prevention-related results and attempted to translate them for practitioners in the field. No prevention practitioners had prevention credentials; they were low-paid and most served in the field because they loved the work or believed in its importance.

Now, in the year 2000, the general public is reasonably familiar with the concept of prevention, if not how it works. Politicians, including an entire presidential administration, regularly speak of it, if not putting enough money where their mouths are. The field is guided by research. Many packaged prevention programs abound, some highly marketed. Prevention credentialing is in full swing in many states. And pay for prevention professionals is still low.

Yet the fundamental approach to prevention as practiced in the year 2000—that is, the fundamental approach to "outside-in prevention," which nearly the entire field practices and which this book primarily is about—has not changed. Nothing has come along to alter the basic tenets of the prevention field as currently practiced. Nothing has come along to prove wrong the "conceptual framework of prevention," the "prevention wheel," or "prevention strategy pyramid" that appeared in the first edition of this book. While the terms, "risk," "resiliency" and "assets," and "outcomes" and "research-proven approaches" have become the guiding forces in the field over the past decade, the prevention practices these suggest are really no different than the practices promoted in the first edition of this book. This is because this entire book is a resiliency-focused approach in terms of building healthy conditions that promote well-being, and it is also a risk-focused approach in terms of changing detrimental conditions that contribute to problem behaviors.

So what does this mean for the prevention field now, compared with when the first edition appeared? In short, **we now know about more programs that work, but what we know works has not changed.**

In the year 2000 what *is* dramatically different is an understanding that the field knows very little about as yet, and which the first edition naively presented as simply another effective approach to prevention. I, myself, had only been exposed to this new understanding immediately before the first edition went to press—if fact, it was the last thing I added to the book. At the time, I did not realize that this approach—now often referred to as "Health Realization"—represented an entirely different paradigm for prevention, an *inside-out* approach. This new paradigm, however, cannot be given adequate presentation within this volume to the depth it deserves. Thus, a new volume will appear, hopefully in 2001, called [working title] *Prevention (II) From the Inside-Out*, that will hold vast implications for the prevention field.

Until then, does that make what appears in this book obsolete or irrelevant? Not at all! This book is about prevention from the outside-in, and despite where the field has evolved in my view it can gain a great deal from what appears here. Many people have told me that despite the evolution of the field, Section I, Chapters 1-6, and Section VI, Chapter 44, still provide as relevant an overview of prevention and a conceptual framework for operating within it as can be found. Sections III and IV, Chapters 32-39, still provide as relevant and necessary supports for practitioners as can be found. To my knowledge, there is still no other book that covers the scope and breadth of prevention that this book does.

The question has been whether Sections II and V, Chapters 7-31 and 40-43 are still relevant, now that the field has begun to be guided by research-proven strategies and that much new research has come to the fore. Yet if one looks closely, as suggested above, this new research offers little more than we already knew, little more than what appeared in these chapters in 1991. [However, Chapters 4, 24, 33, 42, and the Appendix have been substantially revised from the first edition.] Plus, the detailed interviews with prevention practitioners on the inner workings of various facets of prevention are still as relevant and instructive as they always were. These chapters can be thought of, then, as providing much of the original prevention research, the initial model research, and important lessons learned from it—which in this book are sometimes called "principles" and sometimes "elements" of effective programming, and are the same lessons as the new research shows. Unlike a decade ago, because "research-proven programs" are now discussed adequately in a number of other publications, the need no longer exists in the 2000s to highlight all the newly-researched programs here. Instead, at the beginning of Section II, I point the reader to sources where detailed, updated information can be found.

One important caution is in order. The value lies not in replicating these research-proven programs, but in learning from them, learning what makes them work, learning what specific elements contributed to their effectiveness, so no matter what program we implement we will have the best chance to be effective. Unfortunately, in my view, in the year 2000 various agencies of the federal government have misinterpreted, albeit with the best intentions, the value of these programs for funding direction. To achieve the best results the idea is not to limit funding to only these programs that have had large research grants behind them so we can replicate them, but instead to apply the elements of effectiveness learned by these programs about what makes them work to whatever approaches we develop in creative partnership with communities.

Now that the prevention field has begun to be guided by what this book originally pointed to, I was faced with a decision. Should I let this book die on the vine? Should I completely revise it, even though my personal interests now lie in inside-out prevention? I decided on a third possibility, to keep this book pretty much as it was, while culling out some outdated and nonessential material and providing an update of the more compelling new directions in the field that appeared in the past decade.

I still feel blessed to be part of this incredible and essential prevention field.

Jack Pransky
Cabot, VT
8/1/2000

Author's Note ~ Preface to the First Edition (Edited)

My intent was to provide the field of "prevention" with a book that could serve as a guide for its effective practice. I had no idea what I was getting into. This field is huge! Yet when so many people around the country told me how much this book was needed, I had to complete it.

Prevention is my life. It began for me in 1964 when I worked with kids from Harlem and the Lower East Side of New York City. It escalated in 1968 when I joined VISTA, living and community organizing in a Black community in Centralia, Illinois, and later training and supervising VISTA volunteers throughout New England. I have been a federal and a Vermont State bureaucrat. I was the prime mover behind the development and passage of the first state prevention law of its kind (Vermont's Act 79 of 1983). I helped establish the model Vermont Juvenile Court Diversion system. I helped develop the first "school climate" improvement projects in Vermont. I disseminated Steve Glenn's Developing Capable People course throughout Vermont (the first state to do so), and I trained course instructors. I helped organize two parent-child centers. I helped found and am co-director of Prevention Unlimited, a national prevention consulting corporation, which created the (for-a-while-annual) Spirituality of Prevention conference. I attempted to develop national prevention policy. Yet for the first ten years I spent in this field—even while in a position of funding prevention projects—I had no real knowledge of what really worked. It makes me shudder to think about it!

My search began in 1978. It led me through a morass of research conducted in many different fields. In the process I became aware of the acute connections between the "causes" of all problem behaviors and what works to prevent them. This led me to develop a conceptual framework for prevention in 1983, tying it all together (published in *New Designs for Youth Development* in 1985). My own research into the research of what contributes to problems and what works to prevent them has continued. Much of what I have learned is in this book.

This book attempts to cover much of what is known about the prevention field as the new millennium begins. I had to gather information from a wide and diverse number of sources to locate what is presented here. No doubt there is still more to know.

The information comes from three sources: my personal experience, the research, and interviews with top Vermont prevention people who are reflective of the top prevention work being conducted across the country. I tried to put it all together in a simplified way that makes sense.

The book consists of six basic parts: I. Understanding Prevention; II. Community Prevention Strategies That Work; III. Prevention Policy; IV. Behind the Strategies; V. Personal Prevention/Health Promotion; VI. Conclusions. The book focuses largely on "primary prevention" and emphasizes strategies that affect children and young people, for I firmly believe that the best hope for prevention lies in effectively reaching young people.

One final note: The prevention field attracts caring, optimistic, thoughtful, hardworking, dedicated people who work without expecting much in return. It is a joy and an honor to work alongside people like this. Separately, yet together, and against many odds, we have joined to make a difference in the world because we believe humankind can reach a higher potential. It is for you—for us—that I write this.

Jack Pransky
Cabot, VT
8/1/1990

Foreword
George W. Albee

I am delighted that Jack Pransky asked me to write a few pages as a foreword to his book on primary prevention. I have known Jack for several years inasmuch as we are both Vermonters and we are both dedicated to the ideas, strategies, and importance of primary prevention. We have had long discussions about prevention and we have given workshops and talks at the same conferences around the country. Jack has taken a couple of years off the daily demands of the world of work and has closeted himself with his word processor. He has produced a monumental book, not only in size, but in content. I commend it to anyone who is genuinely concerned about doing something effective about preventing behavioral problems and mental disorders in this country.

Anyone who has examined the situation has to be aware of the futility of attempts at providing individual treatment for the great majority of mentally disturbed people. The facts and figures are simply too clear to delude ourselves with the hope that we will someday have enough practitioners to offer service to those who are suffering. (This is not to say that we should not do everything possible to intervene where we can, to help those that are most likely to benefit from our intervention).

Back in 1959, as director of the Task Force on Manpower [sic] of the joint Commission on Mental Illness and Health, I spent the better part of a year collecting data on the nation's needs and resources in the field called mental health. I wrote a book-long analysis of this subject, in the course of which I was brought face-to-face with reality. The number of persons with serious emotional problems in our society far exceeded our resources to help. Both in terms of mental health personnel and mental health institutions, I discovered we were never going to have the resources to treat individuals. The final report of that joint commission, titled *Action for Mental Health*, published in 1960, partially recognizing the problem, urged the development of short-term psychotherapy and short-term treatment of other kinds. It urged the preparation of more nonmedical therapists who could be rushed into the gap created by the chronic and irremediable shortage of psychiatrists. But short-term treatment was not the solution, as the intervening thirty years have demonstrated so clearly.

Back in 1984 the results of a massive epidemiological study coordinated by the National Institute of Mental Health (see Regier, Myers, Kramer, Robins, et al., 1984) found that something like 19% of the adult population of the United States could be diagnosed as having a mental disorder represented in the Diagnostic and Statistical Manual of the American Psychiatric Association. The study did not include institutionalized persons, homeless people, nor persons with sexual problems (not included in the standardized interview). As the study was concerned with adult Americans, it did not include children and adolescents (who are estimated to have mental disorders at a rate of something like 12%). When we realize that in any given year only six to seven million separate persons are seen anywhere in the entire United States mental health system, both in public institutions and in private care, we can begin to appreciate the hopelessness of our present treatment efforts. The lion's share of funds still goes to support mental cases in nursing homes and other public institutions. Very little of it is spent (perhaps 5%) in treatment programs of tax-supported community mental health programs.

Clearly all of this logistical information supports the demand for increased efforts at primary prevention of mental disorders. But logic and common sense clearly do not guide the formulation and development of public social policy. The mental health establishment is largely controlled by interests that find the "causes" of mental disorders to be biological and biochemical, or otherwise organic and genetic. Because these organic models do not require social change they're very popular with groups that support the status quo.

Primary prevention efforts in the field of mental health, as a general rule, require efforts at creating a more just and equitable society. Some of the major stresses in our culture include poverty, powerlessness, and hopelessness. Indeed, it is people who are powerless and hopeless who have the highest rates of practically every form of mental and emotional disorder. The Carter Commission's four massive volumes documented over and over again the devastating consequences of sexism, racism, exploitation, poverty and powerlessness. But the strategies for changing these injustices mean a redistribution of power, a change in the distribution of tax revenues, and a whole different value system than that which currently dominates the American scene. So primary prevention continues to be underfunded and undersupported...

At the root of the disagreements over primary prevention is the conflict between the humanists and the anti-humanists. Those who espouse a humanistic view argue that human beings can act to save themselves and their societies, that any society is improvable if not perfectible. The anti-humanists argue that poverty, powerlessness, and human suffering are a result of the natural inequality that exists between the haves and the have-nots, the upper classes that control the world's resources and the lower classes that are doomed to lives of toil and suffering.

Humanism is clearly opposed to authoritarian political and social positions. The humanists continue to stress the critical importance of human freedom, especially the freedom to change people and society, and they emphasize the interrelationships of human beings and nature.

Humanists are inclined to focus their efforts on improving the human condition through societal change. They view people as malleable and societies as capable of changing and developing as a consequence of positive human values and actions. They see human psychopathology as a consequence of normal learning processes that occur in pathological social environments. And so their focus is on improving the social environment.

Most people, if asked to rank order Albert Schweitzer, Mother Theresa, John Snow, and Ignaz Semmelweiss would put the first two names at the top and confess ignorance about the latter two. Yet in term of contributions to humankind, like the number of lives saved, human anguish prevented, and accomplishments for the betterment of people throughout the world, Snow and Semmelweiss tower over the other two.

It may seem subversive, or mean-spirited, to fail to praise Schweitzer and Theresa as recent-day saints, but I greatly prefer the canonization of Snow and Semmelweiss.

As B. F. Skinner pointed out at his last public address at the APA Convention in Boston, Schweitzer was trying to save humanity one person at a time. Similarly, Mother Theresa, with a heart full of compassion and kindness, is also trying to save the world one person at a time. It simply can't be done. By way of contrast, John Snow figured out that cholera was a water-born disease long before the noxious agent causing cholera had been identified. He observed that the pattern of cholera infection was related to where drinking water came from; in the most famous act in the history of public health he removed the handle from the Broad Street pump in London and stopped a cholera epidemic. Semmelweiss puzzled over the high rate of childbed fever and death in women in the public obstetrical wards of hospitals in Budapest. (In those days physicians didn't wash their hands, but wiped them dry on the lapels of their frock coats, so the more experienced physicians had stiffer and smellier coats.) Semmelweiss decided that somehow medical students and obstetrical trainees were carrying some unknown poison from the dissecting rooms of the anatomy lab to the women giving birth. He ordered all of his medical trainees to wash their hands for ten minutes before they delivered a baby. Suddenly and precipitously the rate of childbed fever and death dropped to almost zero. Of course the great experts of the day did not believe either Snow or Semmelweiss. But, fortunately, as Freud was wont to point out, "The captains and the kings depart, truth remains."

The point here is that Snow's and Semmelweiss's work illustrates the truth of the dictum, "No mass disorder afflicting humankind has ever been eliminated or brought under control by attempts at treating the affected individual." These two public health saints have saved millions of lives, while Schweitzer, full of heart and compassion, was treating suffering individuals in his jungle hospital in Africa and while Mother Theresa was administering to the poor and the hopeless in Calcutta. Individual treatment has no effect on incidence!

One cannot help but admire and respect those selfless people who reach out in humanitarian concern to support suffering individuals. But at the same time, if we respect evidence, efforts at primary prevention are even more humane and admirable if our criteria include the reduction of mass human suffering.

The American public is being educated to believe that anxiety, phobias, obsessive compulsive behavior, depression, bipolar disorders, schizophrenia, alcohol and other drug abuse, and juvenile delinquency are all caused by bad genes or bad brains. The advantage of this organic model is that it means that no social changes are required to reduce the stresses of sexism, racism, homophobia, and exploitation of the poor and homeless. Prevention efforts are opposed as woolly-headed idealism.

The prevention of mental and emotional disorders must involve social change efforts at creating a more egalitarian and just society. This is not to say that we should oppose research into health psychology, biology, physiology, or other organic investigations. What I am talking about is the premature application of preliminary, tentative findings which some claim have resolved fundamental questions about the causes of emotional disturbances.

Last spring I offered a couple of bright undergraduate students the opportunity to attend our annual conference on prevention, this one titled Improving Children's Lives: Global Perspectives on Prevention. After some agonizing they both decided that they would rather go to Alaska and volunteer to scrub oil off rocks on the beach. Somehow this symbolized for me one of the critical intellectual conflicts in our field. Should we sit around and scrub oil off rocks after the oil spill or should we demand that safer tankers be required by international law? Treatment or prevention? Schweitzer and Theresa, or Snow and Semmelweiss?

Clearly Jack Pransky belongs with Snow and Semmelweiss group. He is not a rock scrubber This book will establish him among the stars of public health and primary prevention.

Introduction

People will generally do the right thing,
but only after they've exhausted all other possibilities.

- Winston Churchill

If "an ounce of prevention is worth a pound of cure," what would a pound of prevention be worth?

"Prevention" is the single most important domestic activity this nation can engage in today. A bold statement! But it is not made lightly, for if we do not prevent the destruction of our resources—human and environmental—it will lead to our downfall. This book concerns itself with the human side.

This nation has adopted a "pay-me-later" approach to problems, and it has taken its toll. We are just beginning to recognize that we can no longer afford to continue this path. Business leaders have begun to recognize that the educational system is not producing a work force that will enable us to compete successfully with Japan and other industrialized nations. While most Americans have been able to turn a deaf ear to inner-city problems, they can no longer be ignored, for it is costing billions of our tax dollars to pick up the pieces. Many families and children are forced into poverty even during this new age of welfare reform. Despite the recent trend of diminishing crime rates, crime and violence have spilled over inner-city boundaries, making everyone less safe. Schools are less safe; children are now killing other children and teachers. Prisons are overflowing. Treatment centers have waiting lists so long that there is less chance that the addicted and troubled will get treatment when needed, and timing is critical. Despite slightly reduced rates, problems such as alcohol and drug abuse, teenage pregnancy, teenage suicide, child abuse, sexual abuse, domestic violence, crime and delinquency, emotional disorders, eating disorders, and AIDS are still killing and damaging and emotionally harming our children. We cannot afford to sweep these problems under the rug.

Fortunately, there is also a growing interest in promoting general health and well-being. People want to lead healthy, balanced lives. They want their children to reach their full potential. A concerted effort toward prevention can help accomplish this.

Prevention reduces social problems that tear this country apart and drain its resources. Prevention helps people become more productive citizens. Prevention makes the nation healthier. Prevention saves money. So why has prevention not become a top priority? Why has it not been made the driving force behind our domestic policies?

One reason is that many people still do not understand how prevention works. The fact that prevention works can be proven, but such proof is still not known by the general public or by its policy makers. Another reason is that preventing something doesn't have the dramatic appeal of tragedies or disasters, nor the political appeal of prisons and enforcement. Perhaps some may even have a vested interest in maintaining the status quo.

The Prevention Movement

Despite not enough political interest and leadership—although no matter what else people think of President Bill Clinton we have to applaud him and his entire Administration for making prevention far more of a priority—a movement is growing across the country and is picking up steam. It is called "prevention," in many different fields of work. It is called health and "wellness" promotion. The family support movement is part of it. The child welfare advocacy movement is part of it. Whatever people call it, it is all part of the same trend. It is exciting, and it is here.

No longer is prevention known and practiced by a dedicated few. Now the word prevention is on many people's lips. Not long ago prevention was seen as little more than a myth (a nice idea but...). Finally, it is becoming recognized as an idea that can make a real difference in people's lives and behaviors, "an idea whose time has come" (Klein & Goldston, 1977). In the 1980s and 1990s the progress has been remarkable.

Suddenly, the image of prevention is everywhere. Never in American history have more newspaper and magazine articles, more television specials, or more commission reports been devoted to the grave problems faced by the children and families of this nation. While those of us who have worked in the field of prevention—of many different social problem behaviors—have understood this and fought to gain this attention for years, prevention now stands starkly before the American public.

When I began writing this book in late 1987, we saw little of this national attention. Prevention was buried deeply on the back burners of the nation's agenda; in fact, it wasn't even on the stove.

Then an odd thing happened. The well-respected Lisbeth Schorr wrote a book suggesting that solutions to these problems were "within our reach" (1989), that the nation could change the course it had set. While other books had been written on this subject, this one received fairly wide attention.

Around that time, the corporate community began making public their concerns about the lack of preparedness for employment of young people coming out of our schools, and their fear that the United States was beginning to fall behind other nations. This gave new impetus to the "school restructuring" movement that had begun with little more than a whisper in the early-mid 1980s.

Then in the 1990s the Clinton Administration became the first presidential administration in history to truly make public the need for prevention, and this truly propelled the prevention effort. Heretofore, this rapidly advancing interest in preventing problems among our most precious resource, our children, had never been seen. Yet the political-governmental response still amounts to little more than a ripple.

Prevention as Logic

No health-related problem has ever been solved by treating only the symptoms. Something must prevent those symptoms from appearing in the first place. Prevention is our only hope for reducing the incidence of new problem "cases."

Most social conditions are learned. If they are learned, they can be prevented. Prevention is inherently optimistic. It changes destructive conditions that create social behavior problems. That is what prevention is all about. That is what this book is about.

This book is for everyone remotely concerned about these social-behavior problems. It is for practitioners who work in the field. It is for policy makers who want to know what works. It is for students learning how to prevent problems and promote well-being. It is for anyone with the desire to make a difference.

A Field Without a Guidebook?

Back in the mid-1980s, I was startled to realize that this complex, rapidly growing field had no book to help guide the workers who practiced it. Volumes had been written about prevention in the academic world, yet these works rarely made it into the field where practitioners could use them. The one exception was an insightful book by William Lofquist (1983), *Discovering the Meaning of Prevention*. Yet, Lofquist's book covered primarily the community development approach to prevention, only one important aspect of a far more complex picture.

Prevention: The Critical Need attempts to fill this void. It consolidates a large amount of what the prevention field has learned to date and translates it into a practical, down-to-earth, informative guide—a resource/reference guide for effective prevention practice. It should also inspire support for prevention.

The Prevention Field: In a State of Adolescence

The prevention field has grown gradually and fitfully over the years, blowing with the wind of whatever problem was most politically appealing at the time. Recently the field has undergone a growth spurt. It has moved out of infancy into (now-mid) adolescence. It is on an emotional roller coaster, undergoing massive changes in hormonal balance in the form of studies and data about what does and doesn't work, yet steadfastly it still clings to what it knows, doggedly insisting on doing things the old, comfortable way. It is striving to become independent, a force to be reckoned with, all the while trying to overcome an identity crisis [through credentialing?] and understand what it is all about. Sounds like a lot of adolescents I know and love.

Practitioners of prevention have been forced to swim in a barrel of contradictions. Alcohol and Drug Abuse Prevention funds appear to have increased dramatically, yet prevention still receives a drop in the bucket compared with treatment and enforcement. Delinquency prevention still receives a drop compared with incarceration. Psychopathology prevention receives a drop compared with treatment and institutionalization. In all problem-based and health promotion fields combined, prevention receives a mere fraction of the resources it needs to make a noticeable difference. Thus, those with the money and power to bolster the field haven't been able to observe or recognize its true importance.

This becomes prevention's double bind. Some say prevention wastes money because it is impossible to prove that problems haven't occurred. Yet we can show that problem behaviors have been reduced as a result of many different prevention programs. Some say prevention programs have not shown community-wide reductions in problem behaviors. Yet prevention programs have rarely if ever been funded adequately enough to show community-wide reductions. This book, and now others, have demonstrated that we in fact have clear research that shows significant reductions in problem behaviors among participants within prevention programs. If prevention were given the necessary resources to affect everyone in a community who needs it, prevention would clearly be able to demonstrate community-wide, statewide, and nationwide reductions in problem behaviors.

Internally, the field grapples with other contradictions:

- Prevention should work, but we don't readily see results.
- Prevention should involve changing systems and environments, but we often don't because it's the most difficult thing to do.
- Prevention needs more research and better evaluations, but we now seem to be so locked into known, highly-evaluated, "research-proven programs" that creativity is stifled.
- Prevention should be fun, but it's hard, and the problems are deadly serious.

Despite its rocky soil, prevention remains one of the most hopeful fields for humankind. It builds people's strengths. It improves destructive conditions. It improves behavior. It promotes good health and well-being. It reduces problems that are troubling for others.

The Prevention Challenge

Our challenge in helping this field grow smoothly into adulthood is to know how to achieve the best possible results. We now know enough about prevention to know it works. We can see the results. We must continue to expand our knowledge and understanding and translate what we already know Into useful, practical actions so we can be even more effective, without stifling creativity. To do so would mean that everyone would see broader and more tangible outcomes.

If prevention were conducted on a wide-enough scale, it would save much money and aggravation for many. This desired result is worth supporting. Prevention is an investment that we all must make in our future for our own and our country's well-being.

I. Understanding Prevention

1. What Is This Thing Called Prevention?

The Basics

"Prevention" is an odd beast. At one level it is motherhood and apple pie. Most everyone understands the wisdom of "an ounce of prevention is worth a pound of cure."

At another level is practical application. How does one actually do prevention? Here, prevention becomes difficult to understand. Here, many seem to lose interest. They begin to question its value, as if the concept is somehow worth less if they don't personally understand how prevention works.

Many people still believe that prevention is nebulous and unclear. It isn't. Too much research shows it works. Chapters 8-31 demonstrate how clear and practical prevention can be. But the reality is that most people do not know how to apply prevention concepts.

Prevention of What?

"What do you do?"

"Prevention."

"Prevention of what?"

Many prevention workers have been involved in conversations like this. After all, the response is thoroughly logical. On one level, the rest of the world does not fathom human services jargon. At a higher level however, our one-word answer is right on target. I usually answer, "Of everything bad."

My quip may be too cute, but we have now come to understand the similarities among all the social behavior problems we want to prevent, and I want people to consider the implications.

Definition

Not long ago, prevention practitioners used to spend hours trying to agree on a definition of "prevention." It was something the field apparently needed to get out of its system. Still, it would have been easier to have simply consulted the dictionary—with one crucial caveat. In most recent dictionaries, prevention carries a definition that has strayed far from its original intent. To discover the real meaning of the word one must consult an old twenty-five-pounder and examine its roots. Depending on the specific edition, it will say something like this:

3

"Prevent" comes from the Latin word, *praevenire*. "Venire" means "to come." "Prae" means "before." Prevention means, *to come before.*

To prevent is to act in anticipation of, to act ahead of, to precede. So, prevention is the act of anticipating by action—the act of coming before.

Somewhere along the way, prevention has come to be defined as "stopping something from happening." This is such a narrow interpretation, such a tiny facet of its original meaning, that it appears nearly its opposite. We are not trying to stop things from happening so much as we are anticipating what might happen and acting to create or build or unveil something that comes before it, that precludes it. It is a principle of physics that two objects cannot occupy the same space at the same time. If we build something constructive, we preclude the destructive.

Because of today's dictionary definition, many people in the field still believe that the very word, "prevention," has negative connotations (stopping something) and wish it could be changed to something more positive, such as "promotion" or "development." The true definition of prevention, however, is entirely positive. If one promotes or creates a state of Health, it makes ill-health, disease, destructiveness, disruption, pain and misery less likely. If we want to prevent something, we need to take constructive action beforehand so something more constructive will occur instead. Instead of bemoaning the narrowest interpretation of "prevention," and risk dividing the field, we ought to be proclaiming to the public *all* of what prevention *really* means in all its glory.

In its landmark prevention legislation of 1983 [Chapter 32] the State of Vermont chose a strictly results-oriented statement to define "primary prevention": "Primary Prevention" means efforts to reduce the likelihood of juvenile delinquency, truancy, substance abuse, child abuse, and other socially destructive behaviors before intervention by authorities.[*]

This wording was carefully chosen so as not to confuse the concept of prevention itself with the wide variety of methods that can be applied in its name. The statute focuses strictly on what prevention strives to accomplish, believing that workable strategies should be discussed apart from definition.

Most definitions of prevention do include methods but are certainly worth noting. Bill Lofquist offers what I believe to be the best definition of this type:

> Prevention is an active process of creating conditions and personal attributes that promote the well-being of people (Lofquist, 1983).

That, in a nutshell, is what should "come before." If we find little children falling off a cliff into a river, we could keep fishing them out downstream, or we could build a fence upstream at the source of the problem—or better, help them learn how not to get so close to the edge in the first place.

Primary, Secondary, and Tertiary Prevention

To further complicate matters, it seems necessary to distinguish between different types of prevention. To help with this distinction, the prevention field has adopted terms from public health: primary, secondary, and tertiary prevention. Many practitioners do not like these terms,

---

[*] T. 33 Vermont Statutes Annotated §3301; Note: This definition originally included, "...and the promotion of health," but it was knocked out by a legislator who believed it clouded the meaning.

but we seem to keep using them or other terms even less fathomable to the general public. The question is, do the terms help people understand the different levels at which prevention can be conducted?

Instead of trying to define prevention and its component parts, many have found it helpful to delineate the boundaries. What fits, and what doesn't? The chart in Figure 1-1 may be helpful in distinguishing among primary, secondary, and tertiary prevention.

Primary prevention is what happens for everyone, before there is any sign of a problem. Conditions are created that build a state of health and well-being—for everyone.

Secondary prevention or early intervention happens at the earliest signs of a problem, or whenever a person or group can be identified "at risk" of developing a problem.

Tertiary prevention is not really prevention. It bills itself as preventing people from getting into trouble again, or getting sick again, but for any tertiary prevention program it is important to ask, "What is its prime purpose?" If the answer is "to treat" or "to punish," its purpose is not prevention at all. The concept of preventing recidivism and relapse, however, is still important. In addition, intervention in the family cycle of violence may well be primary prevention for a fetus or a young child.

The chart below implies a continuum from prevention through intervention to treatment and rehabilitation. All points on this continuum are equally important. Thus, primary prevention should be accorded effort and resources equal to the other parts.

Figure 1-1. Prevention Boundaries*		
Prevention	**Intervention**	**Treatment**
Primary Prevention	Secondary Prevention	Tertiary Prevention
Purpose to promote: • healthy individuals • resistance to disease • law-abiding and nontroubled behavior	to intervene at early signs of problems to stop disease to reduce crises to change troubling behaviors	to rehabilitate to reconstruct to treat
Target everyone nontroubled individuals community conditions	"at risk" individuals people in crisis "high risk" groups	troubled people diseased people clients
Strategy change environments promote health build skills promote awareness provide supports	assess level of problems and recommend solutions respond to and defuse crises; short term provide skills to change responses to situations change situations one responds to	treat symptoms: • detoxification • therapy • residential treat injuries and illnesses provide skills to rehabilitate

*Chart by Rufus Chaffee and Jack Pransky

Helping People Understand Prevention

Those who work in the field of prevention could also be helping others to understand what prevention is all about. People will not support what they cannot understand and, right now, most people do not understand prevention. If others do not support this field, we will never be able to achieve the level of results we and others want.

People often understand the prevention of social problems most readily if the connection is made to the prevention of disease. Smallpox, for example, never would have been eradicated had we only treated those afflicted with the disease. If we had been 100% successful in treating smallpox patients, we still would have had throngs of new people continually struck down with smallpox. Only when an inoculation was devised that prevented the disease from occurring in the first place were we able to virtually eliminate smallpox. An inoculation is, essentially, giving someone a small dose of a disease under controlled conditions to help the body build resistance so that when the real disease comes along the body won't succumb to it. The same concept can be applied to preventing social ills. If people are given a "social inoculation" [Chapter 23], they are less likely to succumb later to social problems such as substance abuse, unwanted pregnancy, or sexual abuse. This is one type of prevention: building people's resistance to problems they are likely to encounter.

Another type of prevention relates to how we eliminate malaria epidemics in certain parts of the world. Again, we cannot simply treat victims of malaria and expect to make a dent in the disease. Instead, we have to ask ourselves what causes the disease. Malaria is carried by mosquitoes. To wipe out mosquitoes we have to drain the swamps in which they breed (or spray poisons all over the environment). Draining the swamps is changing an environmental condition which, through a complex chain of events, does not allow the disease to materialize. The same holds true for preventing social problems. If we change environmental conditions that breed problems, through a complex chain of events we prevent or reduce those problems.

Another type of prevention relates to how we minimize the risk of lung cancer or heart disease. Probably the greatest contributing factor to the cause of lung cancer or heart disease is smoking. To minimize the risk of acquiring those problems, we can make a personal decision not to smoke. Helping people make sound individual decisions is another form of prevention, in both the public health and social-problem fields.

The Agent, the Host, and the Environment

Others have found it helpful to understand prevention through the public health model of the "agent," the "host," and the "environment." The National Association of State Alcohol and Drug Abuse Directors and the National Prevention Network suggested that this model be a guide for all alcohol and other drug abuse prevention (1989). In this model, the *agent* is the drug or disease, the *host* is the body in which it resides (with its particular susceptibilities, knowledge, and attitudes), and the *environment* is the context or setting in which It occurs (for example, peer pressure). The peculiarities of any of the three elements ultimately affect what transpires. It follows that to successfully prevent substance abuse or disease, it is necessary to affect all three elements.

This model is less helpful in understanding prevention of other problems like delinquency and child abuse. In these fields, the "host" and the "environment" are pretty clear, allowing similar conclusions to be drawn, but the analogy of the "agent" probably has to be stretched beyond the point of helpful clarity.

Pay Me Now or Pay Me Later

Fram Auto Filters understands prevention. They advertised, "You can pay me now, or pay me later!" True! If we don't put in enough resources up front to prevent these problems, it will be more costly later to pick up the pieces.

This nation either still does not understand the "pay-me-later" philosophy, or we consciously decide it isn't politically expedient for enough concern. The Clinton Administration began to look in the direction of prevention, and there is much more to be done. If we go back to the old path, if we do not go much further on the new path, we will likely drown in our own mess, just as we're doing with garbage and the hole in the ozone layer. We must continually ask ourselves, "What kind of a country and world do we want for our own children and grandchildren?" Just as Eastern European communist dictatorships were only able to be brought down from within despite our enormous military build-up, our nation is not immune from toppling itself from within if we do not invest more in our future.

There is no mystery to prevention. It is as much common sense as the saying about an ounce and a pound.

Achieving Results Is What Prevention Is All About

Prevention should achieve results. If it doesn't, what are we doing? This is the level at which prevention must be understood: knowing how to get results. Otherwise, what we do may not amount to very much.

Achieving results is the focus of this book.

2. The Big Picture

A Lesson From the Sea

One day as I was walking along a beach by the sea, becoming lost in the salt air and pounding surf, I looked down just in time to avoid slicing my foot on the jagged glass of a broken bottle. Cautiously I stepped around it[*] and proceeded to the ocean. I spotted a shining jewel in the wet sand, left behind by the tide. I moved closer. It was a beautiful, smooth, frosty piece of seaglass.

Here was a lesson. Who are the young people who cause so many problems? Like jagged pieces of broken glass, they lash out at the world around them or at themselves. Can these same children also be beautiful seaglass, lovable to all, appreciated, cherished, and respected?

Something happens within the ocean turbulence that changes the jaggedness into smoothness, into something to be appreciated. The only difference between the two pieces of glass is the environment itself.

Our behavior appears to be shaped by conditions in our environment, particularly as we grow. This is an essential piece to the puzzle. The way our children are treated within their important environments appears to largely determine the shape they will be in and how they will be

Beware of Partial Prevention

Before proceeding too far, an important issue should be considered. Many types of strategies can be applied in the name of prevention. Some are more effective than others; some are more complete and far-reaching. The methods we choose will largely determine the results we get. If we are not acutely aware of the results we ultimately want and how they match our selected strategies, at best we can waste a lot of precious time and energy. At worst we can do some harm.

The first question to ask ourselves is this: "To what end are we engaged in prevention work?" Each of us may have a different, legitimate answer. When I ask myself this question, then try to match various prevention strategies to the answer, I find myself dissatisfied with certain types of prevention strategies.

---

[*] my father told me I should have picked it up.

9

I am not satisfied with some types of assertive discipline strategies in schools [Chapter 13]. While they may squelch classroom disruptions, they may also breed resentments or build aggression that could later be taken out on the weakest link in the system. With some methods we may well achieve a limited desired outcome, but in terms of the big picture we may inadvertently promote other undesirable behaviors.

I am not satisfied that an effective neighborhood watch campaign protects a neighborhood. If the neighborhood wants it, I'm all for it. But I know people are still running around out there who have chosen committing crimes as their lifestyle. They will simply go elsewhere to commit their crimes.

I am not satisfied that a child learns how to ward off sexual advances. I am very happy for the child; it may be invaluable if she or he is ever attacked. But we cannot put all the responsibility on the child, for some people have chosen child sexual abuse as a lifestyle, and they will simply find other easier targets.

I am not satisfied that kids learn the facts about drugs and abuse and are told to "just say no," or "no use." I'm happy they know the facts, and I'm happy if they can say no to what they don't want to do. But if they still feel a hole inside that needs filling up because, for example, they are being beaten at home, they will find some other destructive way, externally or internally, to fill that void.

I am not satisfied that I learn to wear my seatbelt when there are drunk drivers all over the road. If I get hit and my seat belt saves my life, I may be quite happy about it, but why the *@#* might I have to get hit by one of those guys in the first place?

I am not satisfied to learn that we need to use condoms to protect ourselves from AIDS. I am happy to know this in case I ever get myself in that situation. But much of AIDS is being spread by needle-sharing drug addicts who have given up all hope except to get that next high, and they don't care a damn about anything else. They will still be spreading AIDS to others.

I am not satisfied that students participate in classroom curricular activities designed to increase their self-esteem. I am happy they have that opportunity. But if their sense of self-worth is being wiped out in other ways by other important interactions in the school, these activities are likely to have little effect. I am not satisfied until those conditions are changed.

In the name of prevention we cannot do half the job. We cannot kid ourselves. If we do not prevent perpetrators from needing to do bad things in the first place, we will lose the battle. If we do not prevent young people from needing to feel fulfilled through destructive means, we will lose the battle. If we do not develop a prevention strategy to overcome all important aspects of a problem, we will lose the battle.

Even if we could get parents and school systems to behave perfectly toward children, and get their supportive peers to pull them in constructive directions, as beautiful as that would be, I still would not be satisfied. This appears to truly be "big picture" prevention! But if people still live in poverty and despair and in conditions that breed so much hopelessness they don't much care what they do, our job is still not done. And if one's thinking doesn't change, our job is still not done.

Is What We're Doing Related to the Big Picture?

Most efforts conducted in the name of prevention are worthwhile, although research and experience suggest that some have more impact than others. This book will examine many of these. Most prevention strategies are all parts of the big picture and have a place for application, provided they do no harm.

We would do well to be continually asking ourselves, Are the methods we choose achieving our end? Is what we're doing aligned with the big picture?

Keeping the big picture in front of us so we always know where we are heading is fundamental to prevention, although we can't let it overwhelm us, and we must take one step at a time.

3. The "Technology of Prevention" Revisited

Bill Lofquist, one of the leaders and original thinkers in the field of prevention, has a chart that reads:

The technology of prevention = concepts + tools + skills + strategies + values (Lofquist, 1983: 1989)

This in itself is an important concept. Prevention does in fact have a technology. It can be learned. It should be applied. The question is, What are the concepts, tools, skills, strategies, and values that one needs to know to build a thorough prevention effort? A more detailed itemization of this technology might look like this:

The technology of prevention = understanding and putting into practice–

1. *a framework for conceptualizing prevention* (understanding what contributes to problem behaviors)

+

2. *a community development process* (understanding how to make prevention happen, how to bring people together to solve problems and change conditions)

+

3. *a focus on desired behavioral results* and indicators of success (guiding the proper direction)

+

4. *a range of model strategies*, including principles of effectiveness of why they work (knowing what makes programs show behavioral results)

+

5. *understanding what makes people behave as they do*

+

6. *a mandate through policy* (having authority to act and the time and resources to make prevention happen on a large enough scale to make a real difference)

13

Understanding the Component Parts (a quick overview)

1. *A Framework for Conceptualizing Prevention.* To promote the behaviors we want, we need to understand what contributes to both problem and healthy behaviors. A fair amount of research has been conducted in many problem behavior fields. While not able to show direct cause and effect, the research does suggest that certain critical factors appear to place people more at risk of engaging in these problems, and certain critical factors make people more resistant to these problems, and relationships exist between the various problems we seek to prevent. A conceptual framework should show these interrelationships and point to areas where we might have the best chance of achieving results. Such a framework should guide prevention strategies and show how what we are doing fits into a larger whole. An effective framework should help to clearly explain the practical realities of prevention to those unfamiliar with it.

2. *A Community Development Process.* It does little good to understand prevention unless people come together to make it happen. If the research-based conceptual framework suggests that certain conditions are contributing to the problems, and certain conditions create resilience, people must be brought together to change conditions. These are community organizing principles applied to prevention, helping us understand why and how people come together, and being able to draw upon tools for bringing people together to solve the problems they care about. We can learn how to ask the right questions so people will reach the best conclusions for themselves and be able to take the most beneficial action.

3. *Keeping the Focus on Desired Behavioral Results.* We can bring people together to solve problems, but the direction they choose may not prevent anything. How do we guide them in the most constructive direction? We can help identify what is ultimately important, and figure out how to know we are getting there, by identifying behavioral outcomes and indicators of success, and measuring our progress toward those results. By so doing, we can engage in planning and, at the same time, frame a simple but meaningful "evaluation" of our programs.

4. *A Range of Model Strategies.* A number of prevention programs have demonstrated success. We need to know what those programs are, and why they are effective. Our interest should not be in replicating models—for we can rarely duplicate the exact conditions that caused a program to be successful—but in extracting and learning the principles that made those programs successful. We can then apply those principles to similar efforts, in varying circumstances.

5. *Understanding what makes people behave as they do.* This has been the least understood aspect of prevention, and until we understand it, we will have hit-or-miss success. In fact, it is such a huge subject that this book cannot do it justice; we will have to wait for *Prevention (II) from the Inside-Out* [Chapter 4 of this volume touches on it]. Here we can only say, briefly, that people's behavior is created from the inside-out, through their thinking. Thought brings people to well-being or obscures it. Here we can understand the inner workings of our minds, first for ourselves, then we can help others see the power of thought to create our various experiences of life, out of which we then think, feel, and act. We can see principles

that guide healthy relationships. We can to learn to treat others in ways that draw out their health and well-being, to help yield the behaviors we desire.

6. *Mandated Policy, Time, and Resources.* If we want to effect prevention on a large-enough scale to make a difference, we need policy on the national and state levels that promotes, encourages, insists on, provides adequate resources for, and allows adequate time for prevention. Without it, the field will continue to be relegated to second-class status. We need a mandate for prevention. We need to know how to create the kind of policy that would be most helpful to advance and support the field.

A wholly effective prevention strategy embodies this entire technology. There may be other components (feel free to add to the list)—Lofquist himself offers six useful tools to assist communities with this technology (1989)—but these are the minimum necessary to do the job successfully on a wide enough scale to make a real difference in behaviors. We would do well to thoroughly learn all aspects of this technology.

This is not to suggest that prevention workers cannot be successful within the scope of, say, one prevention program. They can! But until we can demonstrate community-wide, statewide, nationwide results, we will not convince the public of prevention's worth. We cannot be satisfied until we do because only then will important changes in conditions take place on a large-enough scale.

This is prevention's greatest challenge. The rest of this book is devoted to assisting people with many of the parts of this technology.

4. The Key to Behavior

Prevention is about changing behaviors. It is not about information or skills we can impart to people. It is not about feelings or attitudes they may acquire as a result of our efforts. All that may be part of it, but individuals can have all the information and skills they need, can have apparently satisfactory feelings and attitudes, but if they still behave in destructive or unhealthy ways, it doesn't amount to very much. **Behavior is ultimately how we can tell if prevention is effective.**

As we try to affect behavior in a constructive way, whether it be reducing child abuse or drug abuse or generally promoting health and well-being, we cannot expect to be completely successful until we understand what makes people behave as they do.

In the first edition of this book, I focused on an enticing and instructive theory by Dr. William Glasser and scientist William T. Powers on how and why the brain makes us behave (Glasser, 1983). I suggested that their theory held valuable lessons for all prevention work. Glasser and Powers stated unequivocally that we do not behave because of some stimulus that happens to us out there in the environment, to which we then respond; instead, we behave because we have some internal perception that makes us want to behave as we do—usually to meet some perceived, unmet basic need *to belong*, *to give and receive love*, *to feel worthwhile*, *to have power*, *to have freedom*, or *to have fun*, or some combination thereof. Glasser suggested that these basic needs somehow got translated into specific needs, and when we perceive that a need is not getting met, an "error signal" occurs, which we experience as some kind of pain or discomfort, and we will behave in any way we can to close that gap. And, **each of us acts from a different frame of reference, based on our own perceptions**.

I stated that the implications for prevention work were that to change someone's behavior, we must first try to understand what needs they might be trying to fulfill, and to understand their perceptions. If we can come close to this understanding, then we can try to help create a different perception within them. I offered a couple of examples: A parent whose perception is, "This kid is in my way," is not likely to behave toward that child in a particularly constructive way. That parent's brain is interested only in closing that perceptual gap between (perhaps) her need for freedom and being tied down to a crabby child. The parent's perception is the key to her behavior toward that child. If we expect to help her deal better with her child, or help her not neglect or abuse her child, we must work with her perception. If we do not, we will not see results, unless by accident. A young person who has a need to belong but doesn't feel wanted at home and doesn't fit in at school has a huge "perceptual error" that he may try to correct by gaining that

17

sense of belonging through a peer group, often not a constructive one. If, as school teachers, we want to intervene in that process, we need to try to understand the student's perception. If we can come close to understanding it, we can try to create conditions in school where the young person might feel he fits in more. If we can catch it early enough, we may have a chance. In sum, unless we are able to help people to change their perceptions, when needed, we will not be wholly effective in prevention.

A New Understanding: Three Principles that Create All Behavior

Glasser and Powers were onto something. They were pointing us in a critical and still largely unpracticed and untapped direction in prevention. However, thanks to philosopher Sydney Banks (1998), and psychologists George Pransky (1998) and Roger Mills (1996), I now understand that there is something even more fundamental and profound than how the brain makes us behave.

It is how the Mind makes us behave.

Neuroscientist Candace Pert (1997) states unequivocally that the Mind is beyond the brain. It appears that it may be connected to a spiritual realm [Chapter 42].

Banks realized that all behavior, in fact all perceptions, are the result of the interplay of three universal principles. Together these show how our experience of life is created. I am in the process of writing an entire book [working title, *Prevention (II) From the Inside-Out*] on how these principles inform prevention. Because it is so different from most of the rest of this book I recognize that it may be more confusing than helpful to barely touch upon it here. However, to give a little taste: **Once people see the inner workings of how they create within them an experience of well-being—or not—they seem to gain a handle on life that protects them internally from the ravages of the external world**.

"Principle" used here refers to a force that always exists and is always at work, irrespective of people's awareness of it. In the world of nature, gravity is such a force. In the world of psychological functioning, the forces are ***Mind, Consciousness, and Thought*** (Banks, 1998; Pransky, G., 1998). Universal *Mind* refers to the energy or intelligence behind life; the life-force which is the source of all things, including Consciousness and Thought. *Thought* is the power to create. *Consciousness* is the power to experience. Banks asserts that people are capable of experiencing only what their thoughts create. We experience our thoughts within our consciousness as "reality." In turn, we then think, feel and act based upon the "reality" we see. Glasser is correct to say that we can never perceive the real world directly through our senses; that whatever comes through our senses is always and automatically filtered through our thinking. **Consciousness picks up those thought-perceptions and makes them come alive for us, giving us an experience that looks "real." But this "reality" is being created by our own thinking combining with consciousness, and because everyone has different thinking, everyone exists in a different "reality," out of which they then behave.**

Does this mean that if someone is being beaten at home it is not real and that we are "blaming the victim?" Of course not! First, it means that the person giving the beating is only doing so because he *thinks*, based on his "reality," that that is what he must do, and unless we are able to help him see that he is making up that angry, horrible view of the world or of the person he is beating, he will always be controlled by that thinking and at best will always have to be fighting against it. Second, it means simply that, beyond the bruises, the person getting beaten will take that situation in through her thinking in a wide variety of possible ways, anywhere from "This has ruined my life," to "I'm going to kill him," to "I guess I deserved it," to "I'm worth more than this; I've got to take care of myself and get some help" and many, many, many others. **The way we take in any experience is determined solely by our thinking. No one view is necessarily "right," but each is determined by different thinking. It is all an internally-generated affair.**

People can be helped to see how the three principles are continually at work within them creating new experience, and that a new experience can and will be created with the next thought. Thus, they are never "stuck" where they are; there is always hope. People can also be helped to understand that when their thinking quiets down, it appears to get healthier or wiser. Conversely, the path to an unhealthy existence or dis-ease and problems is a mind full of muddied, agitated, compelling thinking that accompanies low moods, highly charged emotions, or a busy mind—-unless people realize that these are only passing thoughts.

When people realize that life happens to them "in their heads" and not "out there" in the outside world, to which they then react or respond, their life experience seems to change for the better. As an illustration, no matter what we attempt to do from the outside to reduce substance abuse, unless people have some kind of shift in perspective, short of external controls their behavior will not change because their compelling feelings will not change. In other words, if one believes, "I need to drink to do okay," unless that perspective shifts to something like, "I can do okay without drinking," the accompanying feelings and behaviors that compel that person to act will not change regardless of what is done in the name of prevention. **Ultimately, change occurs within people's consciousness.**

People change their feelings and behaviors because they have new thoughts—often in the form of new insights—that alter the way they experience life. Life never again looks as it did, therefore they cannot go on as they have. This change occurs from the realization of their power within to create the internal life they then experience. From this new understanding, they view their relationship to their problems and problematic behaviors in new and healthier ways.

See Chapter 42 under the heading, *Health Realization,* for a bit more on this subject.

In summary, if, as Glasser says, perception is the key to behavior, then *thought* is the key to perception. **The key to our relative success in dealing with people lies in our own understanding of how Thought works in us in conjunction with Consciousness and Mind to create our and others' behaviors.**

As preventers, this means our goal becomes not only to create external conditions that help promote healthy perceptions and therefore behaviors, but to also help people understand how they can create internal conditions within their own minds that bring them to their health and well-being—or its opposite. If we only try to change external conditions we only do half the job, and we will be only half as effective as we could be.

However, for now, we move to the external, to "outside-in" prevention—for that is what most of this book is about.

5. A Conceptual Framework for Prevention

Many social-behavior problems plague this country. Our response has been to treat them as separate entities, to attempt to prevent them one at a time. Yet, research demonstrates that the apparently diverse problems of alcohol and drug abuse, child abuse and neglect, delinquency, domestic violence, eating disorders, emotional disorders, teenage suicide, sexual abuse, teenage pregnancy, chronic welfare dependency, and others all stem from the same general contributing "causes." We can do more than just respond to these symptoms. We can ensure that common factors that contribute to the creation of each of these problems are reduced or eliminated and that a set of healthy conditions is built that will serve to prevent them all.

The significance of this cannot be understated. **One conceptual framework appears to explain the origins of most problem behaviors, and what prevents them all is essentially the same**.

A Synthesis of Contributing Factors

Most of the early research into causal theories of social problem behaviors focused on demographic, epidemiological, or physical conditions. These studies suggest that we are continually barraged by an abundance of stimuli that affect us in unhealthy ways, and over which we appear to have little control. The more we're subjected to these harmful stimuli, the more our behavior is affected. What should have been clear long ago—that these behaviors are related—has been muddied because the terms used by the various fields to describe such forces vary widely. An analysis of the research across many problem-specific fields makes it clear that we experience these stimuli in, generally, four ways:

1. through our culture, as expectations
2. through our social environment, as stressors
3. through organic factors that become problems
4. through perceived opportunity or lack of it

Culture: Behavioral Expectations

American culture maintains certain values, beliefs, and norms that are passed from generation to generation. Much of what our culture transmits can be considered standards of behavior or expectations for what is considered proper. Our culture essentially tells us how to behave.

Many of these behavioral standards are communicated to us through the media. Television, for example, demonstrates that violence is an appropriate way to solve problems, that consuming alcohol is the proper activity for almost any occasion, that it is advisable to self-medicate problems away and not endure a moment's discomfort, that sexual activity is commonly practiced by virtual strangers and rarely results in any difficulties. These are but a few examples of the types of values and beliefs about our behavior that American culture communicates and models.

To complicate matters, our culture also teaches norms for accepted behaviors that may conflict with the above—for example, it is okay for parents to hit their kids but not okay to cross over that line called abuse. The line is confusing to many. It is okay to drink but not too much. It is okay to consume some drugs but not others. It is okay to have sex but only under proper circumstances. It is good to be thin but not too thin—and we must eat well. All this can be quite confusing.

To add to the confusion, we are a multicultural society. Different subcultures and neighborhoods hold and transmit different sets of expectations. For example, while "White American culture" suggests that it is good to look someone in the eye and give a firm handshake, in some other cultures this is considered an insult. To varying degrees we are presented with messages of racism and sexism—some subtle, some not so subtle.

Our own families propel some of these messages. The family models acceptable behaviors that are learned by children and younger siblings. All these messages from many cultural sources model to us how to think and act.

In addition, if a person or a people is torn away from a longstanding and rich cultural heritage, serious problems can develop. This has happened with Native cultures, African-American cultures, and some Hispanic cultures. The import of this was eloquently and powerfully stated by Howard Weaver in a series called "A People in Peril" from the *Anchorage Daily News* (1988):

> Culture is not an item-an artifact to be lost or pawned, or a memory that might be forgotten like the words to an old, no-longer-popular song. It is the anchor that holds each individual to his or her place in a vast and otherwise uncaring universe. When the culture is gone, the individual stands face-to-face with apocalypse.

Together these expectations or learned ways of behaving define the boundaries, if in a blurred way, of what is considered acceptable and unacceptable, appropriate and inappropriate. The more we are exposed to cultural messages that intimate problems, and the more we are separated from cultural messages that provide a solid anchor, the more likely we are to experience problems.

Social Environment: Stress

Many of the stimuli in our environment affect us in unhealthy ways. These stimuli appear to cause stress. Stress can frustrate us and act upon us emotionally and physically to produce still more stress. When feeling stressed it is difficult to experience a sense of well-being. Too much stress often causes a breakdown in healthy functioning that can manifest itself in many ways.

Some of the stress we feel appears to arise from the environment in which we find ourselves. Our thinking tends to be stressed the more we live in overcrowded conditions or in social isolation. We can feel stressed by living in substandard housing, by being unemployed, or by living in poverty. Stress can be physical; an inadequate diet or lack of sleep can impair one's ability to function adequately. We can be affected by stressful events across the life span, many of which can involve changes in life patterns—moving, having children, changing jobs, getting divorced, getting married, losing someone close—and by transitions in our lives, such as moving from elementary school to high school, or from school to work. Traumatic events can stress us or less pronounced difficulties can eat away at us over long periods of time.

One of the most powerful sources of stress can be our own families. A family that is in conflict, that confuses adult-child roles (disorganization), or that has a member who is chemically dependent or experiences some other powerful dysfunctional behavior, is a family that appears to create stress.

The more stress we encounter, the more we're affected. No matter how it is experienced or what the cause, stress affects healthy functioning, which in turn affects behavior.

Organic Problems

The environment can also interact with us in ways that harm our being. Organic problems such as brain damage can be caused by the fetal alcohol syndrome, ingesting lead-based paint, chemicals in the environment, head injury from automobile accidents or being shaken violently as babies, and other ways.

Experiencing traumatic head injury as a child, in fact, may have implications well beyond the bounds of what we normally consider. Internal bleeding into the frontal lobe of the brain, for example, may cause lack of controls over behavior (Savage and Allen, 1986). Dorothy Lewis (1979) found that serious delinquents were more likely than nonincarcerated delinquents to have sustained traumatic head and face injury early in their histories. This may be because central nervous system dysfunction is associated with difficulty in modulating feelings effectively, controlling emotions, stopping impulsive behaviors, and envisioning consequences of dysfunctional acts (Lewis, 1987).

We now know why this is likely true. Arguably the most important new research with relevance to prevention that occurred in the past decade is brain research. It has been found that both traumatic head injury and bad experiences such as being abused as a child can detrimentally affect behavior in at least two important ways: 1) the overactivation of hormones such as cortisol and noradrenaline can set up aberrant connections in the neural network between brain cells which, depending on the severity and persistence of the event(s), can become patterns that can imprint mislearning instead of clear signals between cells; this can lead to maladaptive responses to stress such as violence and even learning disabilities; 2) the underproduction of seratonin can activate genes that have been linked to bad feelings, depression, and other mental problems. These are also linked to lack of control, irritability, loss of temper and explosive rage [Note: alcohol also lowers seratonin levels.] Further the understimulation of a young child's brain such as when parents neglect or do not read to their children can inhibit important synapse connections that can inhibit learning ability at other ages (Kotulak, 1997).

Mental retardation, even mild mental retardation, may also affect behavior. We may also suffer from other types of health problems that affect us physically and in turn affect our behavior.

We can also experience organic problems through genetic inheritance. It has been postulated (though not proven) that genetic factors may increase one's predisposition to alcoholism, to depression, or to schizophrenia. If true, obviously such factors could affect behavior.

To rely primarily on biological factors to explain causes of socially maladaptive behavior, however, treads on dangerous ground. Genetics are very difficult to sort out. On one hand, it may be helpful to know if one is genetically predisposed to alcoholism. It may be very helpful to know if someone has an internal chemical imbalance causing depression. It may be that someone could have an organically based sexual preference for children. On the other hand, to connect genetic factors with symptoms such as delinquency raises serious concerns. As Johnson, Bird and Little (1980) concluded in a thorough study of delinquency research, "many years of biogenic exploration of delinquency have not yielded any valid generalizations about genetic inheritance and deviance." Even in the field of psychopathology, "[I]t is clear...that old-fashioned, simplistic ideas about reducing mental illness by discouraging reproduction in the psychiatrically ill, or even by legislating it, are bound to fail...[for] the patterns of transmission of psychiatric disorders are complex and are modified by other familial influences" (McGuffin and Katz, 1987). In the year 2000, even the human genome project had not yielded proof that genes create behaviors.

At another level, could increases in suicide rates in some areas be related to nuclear fallout? Does a substance called cesium get into the bloodstream, then accumulate in and damage the thyroid gland, causing organic depression? Does cesium irradiate the reproductive organs? Have depression and suicide rates significantly increased in the vicinities of nuclear tests and nuclear power plant accidents like Three Mile Island? In Kotzebue, Alaska, where the suicide rate is ten times the national average, is it true that cesium levels were found in blood samples of North Alaskan Eskimos? Is it a coincidence that the Soviet Union on Halloween, 1961, detonated the largest-ever hydrogen bomb at Navaya, Siberia, very close to Kotzebue, and from the direction of the prevailing winds?[*]

Whether problems are caused genetically or stem from the environment, or both, organic factors can act upon us and cause problems.

Lack of Opportunity

Our society places great value on achieving certain success goals. If we perceive that we lack the opportunity or means of fulfilling desired personal goals or needs, and if the value placed upon them by society is very high, we may seek to fulfill those needs in ways unacceptable to society. Advertisers exploit this tendency by attempting to substitute for success goals products such as alcohol or cigarettes, by equating their use with sex, love, money, fame, or status.

The perceived difference between where one is and where one wants to be can "strain" an individual and thus affect behavior. The more people experience this strain, the more they may feel a sense of hopelessness and helplessness, and display destructive behaviors (Johnson, Bird, Little, 1980).

---

[*] Note: I struggled long and hard whether to include this. On one level, it is irresponsible of me to report it because I cannot find the reference. (It appeared as a series of newspaper articles by Daniel C. Cole, who used to live in Rutland, Vermont. I was unsuccessful in tracking him down.) On the other hand, it would be irresponsible of me not to report it. These questions need to be researched, and I hope this will inspire it.

Figure 5-1. Conceptual Chart of Prevention

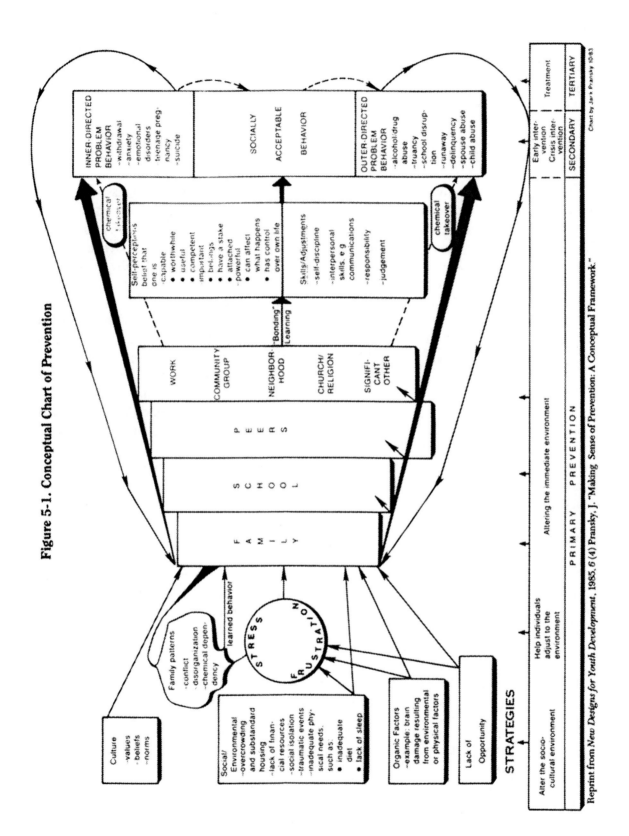

Reprint from *New Designs for Youth Development*, 1985, 6 (4) Pransky, J. "Making Sense of Prevention: A Conceptual Framework."

In many Native Alaskan cultures when someone dies, the survivors say "It was their time to go." This saying once reflected the natural order of life. Now, with the increased use of alcohol and other drugs and rising suicide, the natural order has been tampered with. The statement is now one of hopelessness.

The more of these stimuli we're exposed to, and the more fierce they are, the more we are placed "at risk" for developing problem behaviors [Chapter 24].

Social Institutions: The Filtering Mechanisms

The early research into "causes" of problem behaviors neglected to ask an extremely important question. Many people are bombarded by the same stimuli. How is it that after growing up side-by-side in apparently similar difficult environmental conditions, some people will display various problem behaviors and others will not? Some other dynamic must be involved that absorbs these forces and filters them, transforming them into individual behaviors. By the late 1970s and early 1980s, researchers were beginning to extract what made this difference (Johnson, Bird, Little, 1980; Glenn and Warner, 1983).

From the time we are born we are almost never in complete isolation. We live within a social context, our immediate environment, which mediates between the cultural-social-environmental forces that bombard us and our individual behavior. First we enter some type of family environment; second, we move through school; third, we become influenced by our peer group; and fourth, we are shaped by the rest of the community in which we live and work. These social institutions determine the context through which we receive the outside stimuli. As our most proximate environments, they have a powerful effect on our lives: They are able to filter out how we receive and absorb the outside forces and, ultimately, how we react to them. Thus, they can protect us from or build our resistance to those outside forces [Chapter 24]. For a graphic depiction of these forces, see Figure 5-1. For a specific breakdown for some of the different problem areas, see Figure 5-2.

The Development of Healthy Self-Perceptions and Life Skills

Preventionists have researched different types of socially destructive behaviors. Although this research is incomplete and somewhat disorganized, their conclusions are remarkably consistent about what contributes to and has the best chance of preventing each of these problems.

> ... after years of seeing teenage pregnancy as one issue, delinquency as another, and dropping out and underachievement as another..., we have found that the chronic forms of all these problems reflect the very same set of issues. People who are chronically dependent on alcohol and drugs ... are very much the same as those who are chronically dependent on crime, delinquency, vandalism. And they are very much like those who are chronically dependent on the educational system (they express it by underachievement, absenteeism, disciplinary referrals), and they are very much like the chronically dependent family member or the chronically dependent unemployable person...
>
> That we have not seen this relationship earlier is in part a result of the "special interest" approach we take in solving problems. Each approach to the problems has been ... designed to solve a very specific problem (such as drug abuse)...the behavior we see is dependency—the inability to manage the freedom and resources available to us in our socioeconomic system. Until we

approach the problem of dependency as a type of behavior, it is not possible to solve the range of specific problems which are actually different manifestations of the larger problem of dependency (Glenn and Warner, 1983).

Again, the terms used by researchers in the different fields vary considerably—yet they describe remarkably similar phenomena. To ensure the best chance of healthy functioning and reduce the likelihood of problem behaviors, research concludes that certain essential self-perceptions and skills must be present. These perceptions and skills are primarily what build resilience and set apart "high-risk" and "low-risk" individuals. These have been consolidated into three healthy self-perceptions and four life skills by Steve Glenn (Glenn and Nelsen, 1988). This adapted version includes a few terms used by other researchers.

Healthy Self-Perceptions

1. belief that one is ***worthwhile and competent, capable*** of making it in the world without being dependent on others
2. belief that one is an ***important*** contributing part of or has a stake in things greater than oneself-, that one belongs; that one's life has meaning, purpose, significance
3. belief that one has ***power*** or control over one's life; that one has the ability to affect what happens in life

Social/Life Skills

4. skills to control oneself from within—***self-discipline***, self-control, self-assessment
5. skills to communicate with others—***communication***, cooperation, negotiation, empathy, listening
6. skills to deal with the world around us—***responsibility***, flexibility, adaptability; understanding limits and consequences, privileges and responsibilities
7. skills to apply abstract concepts to the decisions we make—***judgment***, moral and ethical reasoning; understanding concepts as safe-dangerous, fair-unfair, right-wrong, appropriate-inappropriate; values

Figure 5-2 again provides specific examples from various problem-based fields.

As young people grow and develop, they acquire these self-perceptions and skills largely through the immediate environments in which they live. It is within this context that they gain the means for healthy functioning.

The Influence of Family

In their early years the most powerful influence on children's lives is the family. From the very beginning families either build healthy perceptions in their children or unintentionally destroy those perceptions. Families either promote skills for acceptable behavior or they do not. If the family provides a solid foundation, supplying the young person with the tools needed to survive and be successful in a difficult world, that child will have the best chance of growing up displaying socially acceptable and nontroubled behavior. In contrast, if the family—through the environment it creates and the way it responds to problem behaviors—wipes out a young person's feelings of worth, capability, belonging, and sense of power, that child will be at greater risk of displaying one or more problem behaviors. We have no sure way of knowing what specific behavior pattern will emerge, although this technology has been attempted by Fred Streit (1983). Chances are, at least one of many inner- or outer-directed problem behaviors will materialize. Parents can learn many ways to help build healthy self-perceptions and skills in their children.

The Influence of School

If the child does not gain needed self-perceptions and skills through the family, all is not lost; in the early-mid elementary school years, school often takes over as the most powerful influence in a child's life. The school can structure its environment or "climate" to promote learning and respond to student behavior problems in ways that help the child gain what was not developed in the family. Because the child returns to the home environment every day, it can be difficult at this level to have as potent an impact; but research indicates that the school can have a very powerful effect (Johnson, Bird, Little, 1980). It is often easier to alter a school's environment than a family's, and doing so is likely to be less costly. Unfortunately, because of the way most schools in this country are structured, many children are often unintentionally affected in counterproductive ways.

The Influence of Peers

In early adolescence, peers often take over as the most powerful influence in a young person's life. In fact, association with delinquent and drug-using peers was found to be the greatest factor contributing to delinquency and drug abuse (Elliott et al., 1982). This same research showed that if a solid foundation was built within the family and school, however, the influence of such peers was minimized. In other words, **if children have not assimilated a set of healthy self-perceptions and skills by the time they become strongly influenced by peers, they will often attempt to gain their sense of worth, belonging, and power from these peers.** This process can happen in constructive ways, but more often, this kind of peer influence is in socially unacceptable directions. In brief, peers rule by default. Negative peer pressure can be changed to positive peer influence. It is just more difficult to impact behaviors at this level.

The Influence of Community

Parts of a community can have a constructive influence to turn around young people who have not gained what they need from family, from school, or from constructive peers. Meaningful work or community service, participation in a meaningful community group, a strong sense of neighborhood pride, strong spiritual or religious beliefs, or a significant person in someone's life, can make up for earlier deficits. At this stage, however, picking up the pieces is quite difficult. We need inspiration and support to move beyond our plight. Support is especially difficult for people to do without. Without it, we are at high risk for developing problems.

Felner and Felner (1989) suggest that we must also focus on the nature of the relationships and progress of interactions between an individual and each of these systems throughout the developmental process. The Felners believe that disorder results from a "deviation in normal developmental processes" and "from the contexts in which a pattern of behavior evolves"; that "what might appear to be deviant outcomes may be those that any healthy child or adolescent would exhibit in the environments and systems that define the contexts of their lives." In other words, in attempting to respond to "developmentally hazardous circumstances," children often react predictably, but in ways that are also problematic.

The more we are "bonded" to a community or to society (or to school or family), the less likely we are to engage in delinquent and probably other disruptive behaviors. In other words, the more we are involved in and committed to acceptable activities or lines of action, the more we attach ourselves to "conventional" others (according to the general community), and the more we believe in the moral and legal order, the less likely we are to get into trouble (Gilmore et al., 1989).

In summary, referring again to the conceptual framework chart (Figure 5-1): The bombardment of cultural expectations, stress from the social environment, perceived lack of opportunity, and organic problems are filtered through the powerful influences of the family, school, peers, and community. Where healthy self-perceptions and necessary skills are developed, young people will generally grow up displaying reasonably socially acceptable, nontroubled behavior. If those healthy self-perceptions and skills have not been developed—particularly if the barrage of other influences is strong—young people will likely display a range of behaviors outwardly destructive to society or inwardly detrimental to themselves.

Pictorially, this allows for a research-based alteration of George Albee's (1980) landmark prevention formula:

$$\text{rate of problem behavior} = \frac{\text{cultural expectations} + \text{lack of opportunity} + \text{stress} + \text{organic problems}}{\text{healthy self-perceptions} + \text{life skills} + \text{awareness} + \text{supports}}$$

If we are serious about reducing the problems about which our society is concerned, we must decrease the negative factors and increase the positive factors in this equation.

Detour

Referring again to figure 5-1, in at least one circumstance this process of developing socially acceptable, nontroubling behaviors can be diverted. Drug experimentation and resultant use can for some individual body constitutions reach a point where a physical or psychological dependency begins to occur. For example, certain chemicals may act differently upon alcoholics and other addicts that may cause them to be more affected by a particular drug. The person becomes overtaken by that chemical. This can happen even though from all appearances it seems as if the individual is progressing well through the process of healthy perceptual and skill development. This dependency is less likely if a solid foundation has been built in family or school, but chemicals can have a powerful enough effect over some people, perhaps because of genetic predisposition, to divert into problem behavior what would normally have been socially acceptable.

Figure 5-2. The Conceptual Framework by Problem Area	
Contributing Factors	**Alcohol and Other Drug Abuse**
Cultural Influence	• cultural perception: alc/drug use is normative, expected, as portrayed on TV • cultural ambiguity about what is and isn't acceptable • subcultures/ethnic groups define varying patterns of use • subcultural shift in acceptable norms, e.g., in low-income subcultures, drug dealer is seen as "making it" while others suffer financial hardship • easy availability and accessibility
Social Environment-stress	• related to a social environment replete with stress and other "negative aspect," particularly deprivation and abuse • related to financial status, but found in all social classes
Organic Factors	• genetic predisposition to alcoholism possible • earlier the use the more likely youth will abuse and harder to break habit • Fetal Alcohol Syndrome affects 1 out of 3 live births, due to drinking in first trimester
Lack of Opportunity	• related to lack of access to legitimate opportunities for status • profit motive drives both corporations and pushers • alc/drugs often replace something felt missing in life
Family Dysfunction	• alc/drug dependency in family causing confusing adult-child roles • learned patterns from parents' use • the less constructive the influence of parents, the stronger peer influence • marijuana use related to lack of rule enforcement and rebellion against mother
The factors below, built within the family, school, peers and community, build resistance to the above	
Healthy Self-perceptions	• healthy self-concept/self-esteem • belonging • competence
Social Skills	• affective skill development, self-understanding, self-improvement • responsible decision-making and choices • resisting peer pressure and "saying no" • positive peer selection; peer participation • self-discipline • communication and assertiveness • values clarification and judgement • stress reduction and coping • problem-solving and critical thinking • "social inoculation"
Awareness	• consumer awareness of drugs, effects, short and long term consequences • knowledge, attitudes, behaviors influencing alc/drug use • reasons to delay onset of first use • sanctions against use
Support	• social support networks and groups • peer expectations of non-use/abuse • opportunities for nurturing relationships and friendships • supportive community

Contributing Factors	Figure 5-2. The Conceptual Framework by Problem Area (cont'd)
	Child Abuse and Neglect
Cultural Influence	• media: violence is appropriate for resolution of conflict • physical punishment accepted as disciplinary practice • children viewed as property of parents; few rights, low status • what happens in families is private
Social Environment-stress	• reported abuse higher among lower incomes, blue-collar, and part-time employed, but found in all social classes • hitting out of frustration related to stressors like job dissatisfaction, lack of money, larger families in overcrowded conditions, substandard housing, social isolation/loneliness, poor diet, insufficient sleep, trauma, social alienation • most apt to occur during times of crisis
Organic Factors	• may be related to personality characteristics like depression • related to alcohol abuse (lowering of inhibitions) • conditions like handicap may lead to increased victimization • small percentage related to psychiatric disorders • related to mother's illness during pregnancy or prolonged and difficult labor and delivery • related to congenital malformations • related to premature birth and lower birth weights • related to mentally slow parents
Lack of Opportunity	• perceived lack of opportunity to reach socio-economic success goals or ideal family vision: sometimes projected onto children • perceived impotence related to abuse
Family Dysfunction	• history of abusive or neglectful parents; background of emotional and physical deprivation: observation and modeling • abusive parents grew up with images of themselves as "bad" • disordered and disruptive family roles • marital and interpersonal conflict • unsupportive spouses • child unrealistically perceived by mother as unlovable, difficult, disappointing • blaming babies and children for causing the parents trouble or not living up to expectations
The factors below, built within the family, school, peers and community, build resistance to the above	
Healthy Self-perceptions	• self-esteem • power • unconditionally loved
Social Skills	• caregiving, nurturing, parenting(what to do when children cry) • self-control, what to do with anger; coping • human interaction/communication • empathy (abuse/neglect related to poor ability to empathize)
Awareness	• child-rearing and child development • basic family interaction patterns • available resources for help for child: "It's not your fault."
Support	• social supports to overcome isolation • support groups, like Parents Anonymous • natural helping networks

31

Contributing Factors	Figure 5-2. The Conceptual Framework by Problem Area (cont'd)
	Delinquency
Cultural Influence	• violence of society/American image of lawlessness, as portrayed on TV • alienation from/not attached to conventional norms • social learning favorability toward violating law comes to outweigh favorability toward respecting it
Social Environment-stress	• police contact, arrest and incarceration rates (but not delinquent acts) related to "social class" or "ethnic group" • more prevalent in lower and working class neighborhoods, but not among individuals of different social status within those neighborhoods
Organic Factors	• no valid generalizations about relationship of biogenic factors and deviance; although adoption studies support that genetic factors are related to "anti-social personality," does not mean predisposition for delinquency • no supportable assumption of personality differences between delinquents and non-delinquents • questionable causal link to learning disabilities; more likely that those with learning disabilities are less able to communicate with authorities, thus better chance for adjudication
Lack of Opportunity	• blocked legitimate conventional opportunities lead to "strain" (a dysfunction between aspiration and perceived opportunity)
Family Dysfunction	• in girls, related to family rejection and alienation; in boys, related to unsatisfactory father-son interaction • related to constant family disharmony and crisis • involvement in nonviolent crime related to family history (modeling?)
The factors below, built within the family, school, peers and community, build resistance to the above	
Healthy Self-perceptions	• self-worth • usefulness • competence • belonging • having a stake in (attachment to) something worth protecting • having power or control over own life • being seen by others in those ways • commitment to conventional lines of action • belief in validity and legitimacy of the social order • perception of self as successful (real or anticipated failure is related to delinquency, as is external attribution of blame)
Social Skills	• communication • problem-solving • responsibility • judgment • coping • finding rewards in legitimate opportunities • social skills training • resisting negative peer pressure/promoting positive peer pressure • parenting
Awareness	• of law and criminal justice system, coupled with moral/ethical examination • realities of gang involvement
Support	• law-abiding supportive peers (access and exposure to delinquent groups is related to delinquency)

Contributing Factors	Figure 5-2. The Conceptual Framework by Problem Area (cont'd) Domestic Violence
Cultural Influence	<ul><li>violence promoted in society, especially through media</li><li>social learning theory: violence is learned</li><li>belief that marriage license is hitting license (1 of 4 men and 1 of 6 women approve of husband slapping wife under certain circumstances)</li><li>sexism and sex</li><li>role socialization: male dominance; inequality of pay; girls taught to play secondary roles</li><li>belief in implicit right of family members to influence behavior of other family members, c/w belief in family privacy</li></ul>
Social Environment-stress	<ul><li>related to stress produced by low education, lack of job, low-income</li><li>related to social isolation</li><li>related to psycho-social experiences that devalue people</li></ul>
Organic Factors	<ul><li>related to alcohol abuse</li><li>no sound evidence that those committing family violence are more likely to be mentally ill, but related to lack of emotional control</li></ul>
Lack of Opportunity	<ul><li>when people desiring dominance lack resources, they may resort to ultimate resource (force) to attain or maintain it</li></ul>
Family Dysfunction	<ul><li>high level of family conflict</li><li>family is primary training ground for violence; often child's first exposure; learn those who love you are often those who physically hurt you</li><li>violence observed and experienced as child related to violence used as adult</li><li>related to difficulty in expressing thoughts and feelings verbally</li><li>male dominant marriages</li></ul>
The factors below, built within the family, school, peers and community, build resistance to the above	
Healthy Self-perceptions	<ul><li>healthy self-concept (including enhancing women's self-esteem)</li></ul>
Social Skills	<ul><li>interpersonal communication and assertiveness skills</li><li>job training and skills to increase financial resources to reduce stress</li><li>alternatives to violent behavior</li><li>stress management</li><li>problem-solving and conflict resolution; negotiation and compromise</li><li>interpersonal skills</li><li>employability skills</li><li>parenting skills</li></ul>
Awareness	<ul><li>accurate information on incidence and prevalence</li><li>help victims understand how their behaviors may have contributed (this in no way constitutes an excuse or justification)</li><li>options in leaving an abusive relationship</li><li>resources for getting immediate and concrete help to victims</li><li>arrest as deterrence</li></ul>
Support	<ul><li>support groups for victims</li><li>education groups for batterers</li></ul>

Figure 5-2. The Conceptual Framework by Problem Area (cont'd)	
Contributing Factors	**Eating Disorders**
Cultural Influence	• cultural demands for/image of thinness • shows up predominantly in women (10:1 ratio) • most show up in adolescence, a time of developmental pressures, identity and boundary searching in world that gives mixed messages about future productive roles, particularly for female adolescents
Social Environment-stress	• show up during transition and separation periods, like entering high school or college • external avoidance behaviors • weight gains shown during stress, particularly life stress situations • poor diet increases stress on the body
Organic Factors	• difficulty recognizing hunger/disturbance in hunger awareness • constitutional impulsivity/self-regulation difficulties • perfectionistic, overly compliant and overconscientious personality • may be constitutionally heavy but try to fight it with constant dieting • binge-purge or excessive dieting produces imbalance (blood-sugar roller coaster) • serotonin deficiencies, related to depression
Lack of Opportunity	• perception of lack of opportunity to make major life decisions • feelings of helplessness • related to being overachiever
Family Dysfunction	• difficulties in maternal bonding (hostile-dependent mother-child relationship) • forced feeding based on other than biological needs, often present in infancy • obesity related to disturbances in family relationships • overrestrictiveness (especially around food); parent makes most decisions • "best little girl in the world" syndrome • poor boundary definitions • characteristics of enmeshment, overprotectiveness, conflict avoidance, and rigidity
The factors below, built within the family, school, peers and community, build resistance to the above	
Healthy Self-perceptions	• capability and success (related to sense of failure; not in step with others) • self-worth (related to low self esteem and belief worth depends on weight) • control over life (related to lack of control in life) • self image (related to distorted perception of self and negative self-statements)
Social Skills	• getting in touch with feelings • impulse control • self-motivation • self-evaluation • alternative ways of achieving relief and comfort (instead of gaining it through substitute of binging and vomiting)
Awareness	• knowledge that don't have to live up to others' expectations • effects of lack of food and binging • vomiting cycle effect on body
Support	• eating disorder support group

Figure 5-2. The Conceptual Framework by Problem Area (cont'd)	
Contributing Factors	**Emotional Disorders**
Cultural Influence	• media: it's good to be driven by impulse and comfort • practices of excessive power: it's okay to pollute and degrade environment, to exploit the weak • racism, sexism
Social Environment-stress	• stressful life events, including life changes; trauma connected to birthing process or other life events • sudden overwhelming stressors or chronic, long-term stressors deplete body's immune system, leading to physical and emotional vulnerability • environmental factors, e.g. inadequate housing, poor nutrition, unemployment, poverty, overcrowding, low social status • discrimination on the basis of race, sex, age • social isolation
Organic Factors	• genetic predisposition to illness or disorder • biological or constitutional vulnerabilities • hormonal imbalance • depletion of body's immune system • brain damage resulting from head injury or environmental interaction like lead poisoning • fetal alcohol syndrome can cause mental retardation • major medical illnesses
Lack of Opportunity	• feelings of hopelessness and powerlessness
Family Dysfunction	• history of early parental loss and childhood bereavement • severe marital and family discord • paternal criminality • maternal psychiatric disorder • related to family alcoholism, sociopathy, depression, mental ilness
The factors below, built within the family, school, peers and community, build resistance to the above	
Healthy Self-perceptions	• competence to deal with life's problems • power or control over one's life • self-esteem
Social Skills	• coping skills: adaptability in crises • goal setting, problem-solving, and decision-making • time management • parenting and child-raising practices • communication • conflict resolution • assertiveness • stress-management • self-discipline • self-affirmation • also, cognitive skills
Awareness	• options and alternatives • how and where to acquire resources • public information about causes so people don't view mental illness as sign of moral/spiritual weakness
Support	• social supports where people feel cared for and valued as individuals • support groups around issues of common concerns • mutual-help organizations

Contributing Factors	Figure 5-2. The Conceptual Framework by Problem Area (cont'd)
	Teenage Pregnancy
Cultural Influence	• sex-oriented media erroneously portrays sex as meeting intimacy needs and that sex is enjoyed frequently with few consequences; c/w if parents aren't around, TV becomes substitute parent • contradictory messages about sexuality and parenthood in media • related to limited access to affordable, confidential contraceptive services • changing social mores concerning out-of-wedlock pregnancy • denial of sex education and contraceptives because of puritanistic attitudes toward sex • creating a child is subcultural means for feeling valued; • subcultural value: belief that at a young age is when people should have first sex
Social Environment-stress	• poverty is greatest single predictor; related to disintregrated neighborhoods • related to unemployment, including that of parents • related to welfare dependency • related to forced, unwanted sexual experience some time in life; sexual abuse
Organic Factors	• alcohol/drug use lessens judgement • tendency toward egocentric, impulsive personalities (if organic based) (note: low birthweight contributes to leading cause of death for children under five, increased mental retardation, developmental delay, learning disabilities, vision and hearing defects)
Lack of Opportunity	• low sense of opportunity and aspirations: believe life options limited • feelings of helplessness, fatalism, and being unprotected • related to low educational expectations and achievement • only way some perceive they can feel valued and needed
Family Dysfunction	• related to weak early attachments to parents • related to negative family relationships and family problems • related to mother or sister being teen parent, especially if intergenerational pattern • single parent if parent is modeling irresponsible sexual behavior
The factors below, built within the family, school, peers and community, build resistance to the above	
Healthy Self-perceptions	• self-esteem, self-identity • belonging • motivation to prevent early sexual activity and pregnancy
Social Skills	• self-control • responsible decision-making • resisting peer pressure • socialization and communication • positive parenting skills • basic educational and work skills • providing safe, nurturing child care
Awareness	• realities of teenage pregnancy: the earlier the pregnancy, the greater problems of marital separation and divorce, the greater regrets about marriage, lower average birthweight and associated problems, lower educational/occupational attainment, higher economic distress, increased welfare dependency, children of poorer health • sex education and family planning, including knowledge about contraception • responsibilities of parenthood • relationship between teenage pregnancy and sexual abuse • incidence, causes, and effects of child sexual abuse • available community resources
Support	• staying with parents after having baby=more likely to be employed, graduate from high school, and not be on welfare • supportive atmosphere to discuss feelings about pregnancy and teen parenthood, and to disclose sexual abuse

Figure 5-2. The Conceptual Framework by Problem Area (cont'd)	
Contributing Factors	**Sexual Abuse**
Cultural Influence	• many men have difficulty acquiring intimate, interpersonal relationships because not raised to get emotional needs met through touching and closeness; do so only later through sexual relationships, thus equating intimacy with sex; girls encouraged to get intimacy needs met other than through sex • men trained to feel that weakness and subordination have erotic quality, leads to inappropriately sexualizing relationships, as with children; many male child sexual molesters speak of children in very sexual, erotic terms • not deterred by social norms • many men don't see their roles as caretakers of children • children taught to comply, no matter what • children and women viewed as objects
Social Environment-stress	• social isolation • related to lower socioeconomic status, but may only be inequality in ability to avoid courts (conflicting studies) • related to trauma: victims are at higher risk for depression, acute mental health problems, psychological treatment, alcohol/drug problems
Organic Factors	• when assault is by stranger, related to sexual preference for children (may be organic) • perpetrator is usually either passive-ineffective-introvert or strong-authoritarian-controlling type (whether organically caused is debatable) • more likely to occur under alcohol intoxication
Lack of Opportunity	• social and normal heterosexual relationships are perceived blocked
Family Dysfunction	• history of sexploitation in family, 75-95% of abuse occurs by parents, stepparents, or relatives • re-father-daughter incest: emergence of daughter as central female figure in household; sexual incompatibility of parents and father unwilling to seek sexual relationship outside family; fears of abandonment or family dysfunction; unconscious sanction by mother
The factors below, built within the family, school, peers and community, build resistance to the above	
Healthy Self-perceptions	• self esteem and positive mental image • empowerment (sexual abuse, particularly rape, is believed to be a "power" issue even more than a sexual issue) • feeling unconditionally loved (abusers may be attempting to fulfill unfound needs for love, affection, attention, loyalty; child victims may be attempting to fulfill needs that aren't met in other ways)
Social Skills	• self-protection (how to avoid at risk situations, rehearsing specific, workable responses) • developing and implementing personal safety plans • intuitive skill development • critical analysis • coping with/responding well to pressure situations • communication • stress relaxation and "centering" • for parents, how to question a child sensitively
Awareness	• retaining right to be safe, strong and free • for children: what sexual abuse is, who are potential offenders, "appropriate" vs. "inappropriate" touch, body awareness • for parents: potential warning signs; how to respond if abuse suspected; also should receive training that children receive so they can understand it • educating public about nature and dynamics of sexual abuse (NOTE: No information found in literature on info or skills needed to prevent potential perpetrators. Apparent assumption: Victims of sexual abuse, through modeling and trauma, are at increased risk of becoming perpetrators, so if victims are prevented that is all the awareness needed.)
Support	• supports groups for victims • support/therapy groups for perpetrators

Figure 5-2. The Conceptual Framework by Problem Area (cont'd)	
Contributing Factors	**Teenage Suicide**
Cultural Influence	• modeling: suicides often imitated, even when seen in news reports, TV shows, films and books
Social Environment-stress	• stress-induced problems with perceived uncertain consequences; examples: rejection (often boyfriend-girlfriend), humiliation, school failure, failure to find work, getting into trouble • teen mothers attempt suicide seven times more than adolescent females without children
Organic Factors	• alcohol/drug use often plays role in attempt; alcoholic youth 58 times more likely to commit suicide • related to (predisposition to?) intense moods, depression, aggressive outbursts, over-anxiety, perhaps due to biochemical abnormalities • related to learning disorders • possibly related to high cesium levels found in blood after exposure to nuclear fallout
Lack of Opportunity	• hopelessness, coupled with feeling overwhelmed • lack of meaningful social roles for adolescents
Family Dysfunction	• related to close family member attempting or committing suicide
The factors below, built within the family, school, peers and community, build resistance to the above	
Healthy Self-perceptions	• self-concept/self-esteem • importance or significance • having power to affect life's outcomes
Social Skills	• coping • stress management • problem-solving • decision-making • personal responsibility • communication and assertiveness • values clarification • for others; handling confidences, what to do if warning signs
Awareness	• adolescent stressors (without making a connecting link to suicide; linking suicide to depression may actually increase rate of suicide) • labeling suicide as a deviant response • for others, realities about teen suicide, early warning signs, longstanding mental health symptoms • available resources
Support	• peer supports • support students with alcohol/drug problems, failing grades, parent problems • peer counseling
Figure 5-2. The Conceptual Framework by Problem Area (cont'd)	

Contributing Factors	Chronic Welfare Dependency
Cultural Influence	• American culture: "them who has (power), gets"; the rich get richer and poor get poorer • Poor seen as out of mainstream
Social Environment-stress	• Lack of money • Unemployment/underemployment • Lack of connection to community resources (c/w fear and suspicion of agencies) • Overabundance of stress • Living in violent neighborhoods, surrounded by alcoholism and drugs • Isolation
Organic Factors	• Individual incapacity to work, emotional or physical • Alcohol/drug impairment
Lack of Opportunity	• Inadequate employment opportunities • Unequal opportunity • Welfare policy makes it easier and financially more beneficial to be "on" than "off," leading to little motivation and incentive for self-sufficiency; no hope/aspiration of eventually getting self/children out of poverty • Ambivalence to autonomy • Feelings of deprivation; see selves as "worse off" than others; fatalistic view of life, unable to change anything; self-devaluation; hopelessness
Family Dysfunction	• Family instability • Associated with pattern of matriarchal family structure, children from many different fathers, childbirth by mother at young age, lack of employed male role models • Welfare policy that excludes men from the subsidized family • Child-raising orientation that lacks authority and purpose, and is generally disorganized, confused, inconsistent; over-reliant on physical punishments, lacking verbal relationships • Present-time oriented life pattern that promotes impulsive behaviors • Family pattern (brothers and sisters) and among friends of welfare dependency • Apathy about schooling, leading to failures and drop-outs • Older children pushed into the streets in search of more attractive and exciting role models and to help "take care of" family (e.g. gang memberships, having babies to bring more welfare money home)
	The factors below, built within the family, school, peers and community, build resistance to the above
Healthy Self-perceptions	• Self-esteem • Empowerment • Building emotional strength
Social Skills	• Preparation skills (for entry into mainstream activity) • Job and job readiness skills • Financial management • Meshing coping skills with coping skills already learned from streets and survival • Planning • Self-discipline • Problem-solving
Awareness	• Importance of staying in school to ensure grounding for life career • Postponement of child-bearing until work or career preparation; having additional children while on welfare vs. waiting until financially self-sufficient • Sexual associations vs. mutual lasting commitments; unprotected sexual activity vs. dependable, reliable, regular and informed birth control • Early marriage vs. marriage postponement until economic productivity of at least one partner is assured • Belief in welfare as temporary condition vs. welfare as a right • What to buy, what not to buy, and when
Support	• Altering perception of dependency to empowerment among peer group • Organizing to make needed changes • A welfare policy that doesn't promote system dependency

What About the Individual?

People do have individual characteristics that may affect behavior. Are these characteristics inherited? Are they shaped within our environment? Do they come from the stars and planets (if one believes in astrology)? Is it all or part of the above?

On December 1, 1986 the *New York Times* (Tellegen, 1986) reported on a study conducted at the University of Minnesota of 350 pairs of twins, 65 of which were reared in different families. The study, which measured personality traits, concluded, "the genetic makeup of a child is a stronger influence than the family." More than half the personality traits measured were influenced by heredity; less than half were determined by parents, the home environment, or other experiences in life. The authors did admit that a family might tend to make an innately timid child more timid or less so, but the family would be unlikely to make a timid child brave.

At first glance, this may seem to refute what the conceptual framework suggests. But there is a huge difference between the personality one has and what one does with that personality. "A masterful, forceful leader" can be a corporate executive or a gang leader. A timid person can be a successful librarian or a drug addict. What one does with his or her personality, no matter what it is, makes the difference. This is where one is influenced by the factors represented in the conceptual framework.

I now see something far beyond this at play. People's thoughts are the ultimate mediating variable [Chapter 4]. Nothing is more powerful than an individual's creative power of thought to determine his or her experience. Thought is where most individual differences arise. In that sense, **every variable presented in the entire framework is *always* filtered through one's own thinking**.

Strategies to Prevent Problem Behaviors

In summary, the research in all these fields makes it apparent that no matter what specific socially destructive behavior we target, similar factors affect the proliferation of that problem. Social-institutional conditions contribute, often unintentionally, to many different types of problem behaviors. This is true for behaviors directed outward, such as truancy, school misbehavior, runaways, child and sexual abuse, and domestic violence. It is also true for behaviors directed inward, such as withdrawal, anxiety, suicide, or problems such as underachievement, chronic welfare dependency, teenage pregnancy, and many more. The same factors contribute to each of these problems; only the behaviors emerge differently, depending on the individuals involved and perhaps the specifics of what happens to them along the way. Contributing relationships have also been found between many of the different problem behaviors (see Figure 5-3).

Behavior	found linked to:									
	a/da	ca	del	dv	eatd	emod	tp	sxa	ts	wd
alcohol/drug abuse	-	X	X	X	X	X	X	X	X	X
child abuse	X	-	X	X		X	X	X	X	X
delinquency	X	X	-			X		X		X
domestic violence	X	X	X	-		X		X	X	X
eating disorders	X	X			-	X			X	
emotional disorders	X	X	X	X	X	-		X	X	X
teen pregnancy	X	X				X	-	X		X
sexual abuse	X	X	X	X		X	X	rape	X	
teen suicide	X	X		X	X	X		X	-	
welfare dependency	X	X	X	X		X	X			-
AIDS/STDs	X						X	X		X

Figure 5-3. Research-indicated Relationships Among Social-Behavior Problems

Note: This chart indicates that there is some relationship among these social behavior problems for which I have seen a specific reference in the literature. There may well be additional relationships.

The implications for human services work are staggering. **Since the same factors contribute, to truly prevent all these problems the various disciplines must collaborate to affect all contributing factors. Without this cooperation it is unlikely that any of the problems will be adequately prevented**—as is still the case today. **To achieve substantive results, prevention strategies in all fields must be directed at the contributing causes—at what research says works.**

The question is, where should we begin?

Primary Prevention: Affecting the Socio-Cultural Environment

At the "primary" prevention level, we could choose to attack the source of the stimuli—the outside forces that model inappropriate behavior, produce stress, promote lack of opportunity, and minimize organic risks in the physical environment. In this set of *environmental strategies* we would find media campaigns or attempts at neutralizing the effects of the media. Here, too, would be the Native "staking down" ceremony [Chapter 30] that aims to reclaim and rekindle Native cultures to prevent problems such as alcohol and drug abuse, and strategies to recapture pride in, for example, African American and Hispanic cultures and respect for cultural diversity. To counteract potential organic problems one might try to influence a mother's smoking, drinking or drugging habits that could organically affect her fetus. In this set of strategies we would find New Orleans businessman Patrick Taylor who offered new hope to low-income, inner-city high school kids by offering to pay their college tuition if they maintained a certain grade average and graduated from high school. Within this strategy we try to affect a

41

communities' attitudes or values about, for example, alcohol. At a deeper level, we might organize to eliminate social injustices, restructure the country's economic system, halt pollution of the physical environment, and other seemingly "radical" approaches.

Focusing on this set of strategies is extremely important. For many people, however, functioning on the shallower levels does not go far enough, and functioning at the deeper levels of radical social change seems nearly overwhelming, for to truly have impact requires changes in the very fabric of society and culture in which we live.

Primary Prevention: Stress Reduction

We could choose to focus on reducing stress associated with those forces. We could use stress management and stress reduction techniques such as biofeedback or meditation. These methods usually target an individual or a group of individuals.

Though these techniques may be useful, they do little to change the conditions that caused stress in the first place and will continue to cause the stress. We simply help individuals to adjust or cope.

One approach that includes changing conditions that contribute to stress is focusing on critical "transition" points in one's life. For example, we could structure, ways to ease the transition for students moving from small, rural elementary schools into large union junior high or high schools [Chapter 20].

Primary Prevention: Altering Immediate Environments

We could also choose to focus on changing the conditions of the local institutions that have such a powerful influence over young people. We could assist the family and school in creating an environment conducive to building healthy self-perceptions and needed life skills, as in teaching parenting skills [Chapter 12], or in school "climate" improvement [Chapter 13], or in establishing early childhood education programs [Chapter 10]. We could attempt constructively to influence the peer group, as in "teenage institutes" [Chapter 21], or gang prevention strategies [Chapter 16]. We could devise strategies to affect other segments of the community, as when citizens reclaim an inner-city neighborhood from drug dealers block by block [Chapter 30], involve people in spiritual endeavors [Chapter 42], or create meaningful work or community service opportunities [Chapter 26]. This set of strategies, particularly at the level of families and schools, is where we can expect to have much impact (Johnson, et al., 1980; Glenn and Nelson, 1988; Schorr, 1988).

Primary Prevention: Helping People Gain New Perspective on Their Thinking and the Source of their Well-Being

We could help people see the true source of their experience and their health [Chapters 4 and 42], thereby shifting their perspective and causing them to think, feel, and act in healthier ways. This inside-out prevention approach could be done, not as a separate activity, but throughout the entire framework.

Secondary Prevention: Intervention

We could also use secondary prevention or intervention strategies with so-called high-risk groups or at the first sign of a problem. Intervening early with families at risk is a critical strategy for affecting a wide range of symptoms. For example, because "relationships...[have been found]...between abuse and delinquency, an integral part of prevention of antisocial behavior in youth should include efforts to reduce physical violence and abuse among family members" (Wolfe, 1987). Many of the efforts to prevent child abuse and neglect focus on the early identification of mothers who immediately before and after giving birth display certain "warning signs" in their own histories or in their perceptions of the birth or the child, or in interaction with their new infants. Then a special system of close observation and supportive visiting is arranged, coupled with skill-building and referrals to support groups so the abusive tendencies are less likely to become manifest (Kempe and Kempe, 1979).

Tertiary Prevention

One could also focus on tertiary prevention—treatment or relapse prevention after the problem behaviors have become serious. Much of the work in preventing sexual abusers happens after an abuse has already occurred and the abuser has become part of "the system," in hopes that he (or she) won't abuse again.

Intervention and treatment are essential but do little if anything to change the conditions that initially caused the problem (the exception being some types of family therapy and relapse prevention)—conditions to which the clients usually return. Once "treated," these individuals again face the same difficult situations. If they have gained those missing self-perceptions and skills from the rehabilitation process, they have a chance of recovery. If they have not, once they return to their old environment, they will often begin to manifest the same or a different problem once again, for the conditions have not changed.

> To speak of rehabilitation is misleading. To rehabilitate someone involves restoring them or returning them to a former state of excellence. Yet most of these people have never been capable, productive or independent. Because of this ... these people who need so-called rehabilitation, in reality need primary habilitation. Habilitation is the process by which people develop the primary skills for living ... [What young people need to become fully functioning, capable adults ... (are] seven basic skills and attitudes ... if they are to be successful people (Glenn and Warner, 1983).

Treatment and rehabilitation are also more costly.

Unfortunately for us all, the vast percentage of the resources allocated toward combating these problems is spent on the remedial end of the spectrum. The earlier something is learned and the more it is reinforced, the better. It would follow that the earlier we use prevention strategies, and the more often, the more successful we will be at preventing and reducing problem behaviors. Ideally, to be fully successful, we must conduct prevention strategies across the entire conceptual framework. If we have limited time, energy, and resources we should be guided by what researchers believe has the best chance of working; namely, attempting to construct environments that build healthy self-perception and skills, and help them unveil their own internal health from within—and concentrate our efforts accordingly.

Jack Pransky

6. The Prevention Wheel and the Community Prevention Strategy Pyramid

In practical terms, the purpose of a conceptual framework is to help guide us toward strategies that have the best chance of preventing problems. Another way to approach this is to begin with the premise that problem behaviors are the result of the decisions people make, and certain factors are essential to responsible decision-making.

Individual Decisions

All social-behavior problems, with the possible exception of emotional disorders (and a few theorists would even dispute this), are the result of individual decisions. Everyone makes his or her own decision to become involved with or abuse anyone or anything. These decisions are the direct result of people's own thinking. No matter how forcefully we tell young people not to take drugs, not to have sex, or not to commit crimes, ultimately they decide for themselves—whether we like it or not. They also may be confronted with such decisions when we are not around to guide them, so it would be wise if they were prepared.

To make a responsible decision, one needs-

- accurate *information* (awareness)
- decision-making *skills* reflecting self-discipline, good judgment, responsibility, and to counteract harmful pressures
- *perceptions* of self and of the world *that build resistance* to inappropriate pulls
- *supports*
- *opportunities* to get needs met legitimately

When young people (or anyone) have correct and accurate information, skills, supports, and a healthy perception of self, they are in a more favorable position to make an appropriate decision.

Information

If a young person is confronted with a decision to have sex, it would be best for that person to have knowledge about his or her body, how new human life is created, what it means to bring new life into the world, the kind of caring and nurturing and time commitment this new life

45

needs from the parent, implications for the lives of the parents, options for preventing the bringing of new life, diseases one could contract in having sex, the effects of alcohol and other chemicals on the fetus, and so forth. Without such information, how can he or she make a fully informed, responsible decision?

If a person is considering putting a substance into her body, it would be best if she knew everything possible about what that substance is, its possible effects and side-effects, how one might be affected physically and mentally, socially and spiritually. If the substance is injected, she should know about implications for AIDS.

If a person is considering committing a delinquent act, he should at least have information about the law and its consequences, what it means to harm or take from another, and implications for society.

If a teenager is considering not eating so she can be the thinnest she can imagine, she at least needs to know the detrimental affects it will have on her health and body.

Each potential problem has its own specific information. Without full awareness of each issue, people don't have all the cards in their decks to make a knowledgeable, responsible decision. To give inaccurate information exacerbates the problem (example: using scare tactics as in the film *Reefer Madness*), for as soon as someone discovers that a piece of information is wrong, he will likely discount the rest of the information given and will lose trust for the giver. The outcome may be the opposite of what we would desire.

Responsible Decision-Making Skills

People can have all the information they need, but if they don't have the skills to use it, that information is meaningless. The minimum skills needed are self-assessment, self-control and self-discipline, responsibility, problem-solving, judgment–also, skills to communicate with others, listen, negotiate, and resist peer pressure.

To learn skills takes practice. We need feedback on how well we're doing. We need to experience in a safe setting what it is like to try to resist when the pressure is on.

It is not good enough for people simply to have general skills. They must learn these skills in the context of the specific problems and issues they will face (Schaps et al., 1978). Young people who may be pressured to do drugs need to practice making decisions specific to drug use. Young people who may be pressured to have sex need to learn and practice the skills involved in making decisions about having sex.

Many of these problems require skills and information that should be communicated to children by their parents, but it is unrealistic to expect that all parents are adequately equipped to teach children and teenagers all they must know. It would be wonderful if parents could, but we cannot afford to leave it to chance. Thus, schools can play an important role by providing comprehensive health and law-related education.

Peer Support and Influence

Just because we have the information and skills to make appropriate decisions does not mean we will. When pressures are great from our peers to do things we may not want, but when we also want to be accepted, it is very difficult to resist. Negative peer pressure must be transformed into positive peer influence. "It's good to do drugs" must be turned into, "It's not cool to do drugs," and "We don't get into a car when the driver is drunk, period"; or, "We're not going to have sex until we're mature enough to handle all the emotions involved." This transformation is not so easy.

Teenagers and preteenagers must have opportunities to deal openly with issues important to their lives. Young people can be trained to help each other. For example, support groups like those for children of alcoholics can help them know they're not alone, and so they can understand together why they act the way they do, learn that it is not their fault, learn how to best cope, and learn how to break out of the trap. Support from people experiencing similar problems make it a little easier to survive in a seemingly uncaring world.

Healthy Self-Perceptions and Changing Environmental Conditions

Research in the alcohol and drug field shows that if people only receive information about substances, their use either will remain the same or will slightly increase. If they also learn the skills to make responsible decisions, their use will decrease slightly. If in addition they develop healthier self-concepts, their use and abuse will substantially decrease (Schaps et al., 1978). This has implications for other problems as well. People can have the best information, skills, and supports available but if they feel worthless, incompetent, unimportant, and powerless, they will still say, "Why should I bother trying anyway?"

Building healthy self-perceptions must be the central effort of prevention [Chapter 4]. The California Task Force to Promote Self-Esteem and Personal Responsibility (1990) found that "lack of self-esteem" was at the root of most problem behaviors.

Self-esteem is the likeliest candidate for a social vaccine, something that empowers us to live responsibly and that inoculates us against the lures of crime, violence, substance abuse, teen pregnancy, child abuse, chronic welfare dependency, and educational failure. The lack of self-esteem is central to most personal and social ills plaguing our state and nation ... (p. 4)

This proved a controversial assertion. If they had substituted the words "healthy self-perceptions" for "self-esteem," it would not have been so controversial. Bandura (1989; 1982) found that perceived "self-efficacy" or "the self as agency" was an even more important variable than self-esteem. For example, how a person sees his or her abilities was found to be more important than the person's actual abilities.

As children, we are surrounded by a particular "climate" in our homes, schools and neighborhoods, where how we are treated appears to affect our perceptions/our thinking. Out of what we see, we then think, feel and behave accordingly.

Often we mistakenly believe that we can build self-esteem or self-efficacy in young people through activities found in many health education curricula or through special programs designed to help them feel good about themselves. These activities certainly do no harm, are often fun and sometimes helpful, but if we want to truly build healthy self-concepts, we would do better to alter the conditions within families, schools, and communities that help to mold self-concept in the first place. Parenting courses such as *Developing Capable People* and school climate improvement efforts work because parents and teachers see how to create healthier conditions within their homes and schools. They begin to treat their children and students differently, which in turn produces healthier self-perceptions. **To change external and internal conditions that detrimentally affect people, and to draw out people's health, is the hub of the entire**

47

prevention wheel. Without it our prevention strategies have no center and the wheel collapses.

Using the Prevention Wheel

No matter what symptom we want to prevent, if we want to succeed we need to consider the total picture. By looking at the wheel [Figure 6-1], one can see it is important to provide information and skills specific to the problem and the opportunity for constructive peer influence and supports. **It is also critical to work within the hub of the wheel, with others who share the central core, to create healthier conditions within families, schools, communities, and within one's own mind, so that healthy self-perceptions can emerge.**
For example, those who wish to focus on child abuse must provide information, skills, and supports specific to child abuse, but they also could join with preventers concerned with other symptoms to change conditions to ensure healthy environments. If we were to color in the parts of the wheel that relate to child abuse, it looks like an old-fashioned keyhole [Figure 6-2]. To prevent child abuse, then, the key is to cover all parts of the child abuse keyhole. For other problems, each key is specific to that problem but also intersects in the center with all other keys. **Together it makes a whole. An incomplete wheel cannot get people where they want to go. A wheel without a center collapses.** Only if people involved with each of these problems collaborate and act together to prevent them will we see community-wide reductions.

The Primary Prevention Pyramid

The center of the prevention wheel contains a set of prevention strategies found by research to work in changing behaviors. **If we truly want to see community-wide reductions in problem behaviors, a "pyramid" of prevention strategies must be in place in every community.**
A pyramid is a structure with a square base and four triangular faces culminating in a single apex. A pyramid is solid. A pyramid forms its own stability. Its image is of indestructibility; the pyramids of Egypt and Mexico have withstood centuries of pounding by the elements, yet they still stand as the most powerful constructed monuments on earth. It is this kind of power, this kind of solidity, that prevention seeks within each community and each individual.
Each level of the pyramid represents a prevention strategy that works [Figure 6-3]. All must be in place to build a solid, healthy community that has the best chance of preventing problem behaviors. To build our structure we must begin at its foundation, at the bottom.

Pre- and Postnatal Care
What kind of start do we want for a baby born into this world?
Prenatal Care. Before a baby is born, it exists in an environment created for perfection. Left to its own healthy integrity, this biological system usually produces a baby healthy and whole, with a minimum of problems. No matter what the inherited traits, no matter what the inherent personality, the uterine environment surrounding this baby-to-be can either nurture it or harm it. Deprive this environment of adequate nutrition and the fetus suffers. Add chemicals such as alcohol, cocaine, or heroin to this environment and the fetus suffers. Deprive this environment of oxygen through smoking, and the fetus suffers. Add a disease like AIDS to this environment, and the fetus suffers destruction of basic immunity. Prevention at this level means efforts to ensure or

Figure 6-1. The Prevention Wheel

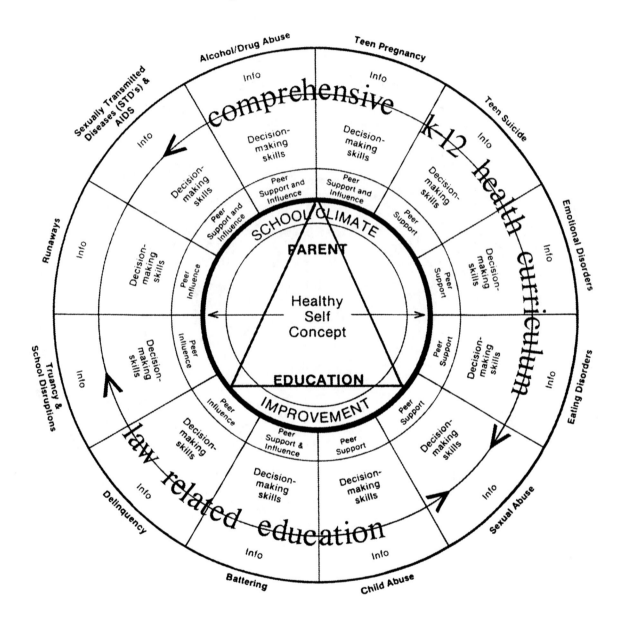

Chart by Jack Pransky. Rendition by People Against Sexual Abuse, Brooklyn , New York.

Figure 6-2. The Prevention Wheel

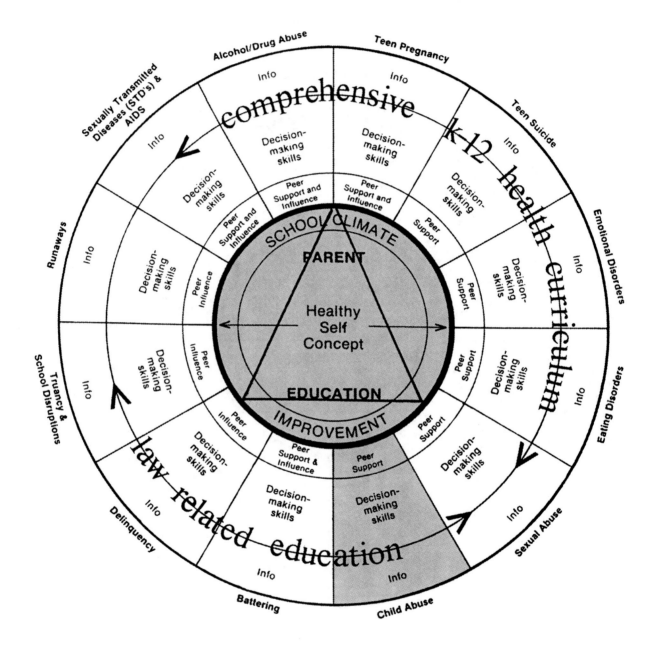

Chart by Jack Pransky. Rendition by People Against Sexual Abuse, Brooklyn , New York.

improve the health of the mother and her fetus prior to birth (and the father to ensure healthy sperm), to give a baby the healthiest emergence into life and to ensure that the parents have the best possible perception of this new life, and are adequately prepared for it. The process may even begin before conception to be certain that a pregnancy is appropriately planned.

Mother-Infant Bonding. At birth a baby is transferred from a once-comfortable environment into a new and formidable world. What would we wish her first perception of this world to be? Coldness, harshness, distance, and discomfort? Or warmth, caring, comfort, safety, protection, and love? Prevention at this level is helping a mother and baby feel a strong bond and attachment with one another. It means ensuring touching and closeness immediately after birth. It means teaching parents how a newborn communicates, and what to look for and how to respond. In the case of premature or "difficult" birth it may mean helping the parent feel more support under the circumstances, helping her move forward without feeling guilty.

Postnatal Care. A baby is in a continual process of becoming. When s/he leaves the hospital or birthing room, s/he enters another environment where s/he will often spend the next years of his life. This is the world in which the child will grow and develop. In this environment a child is either helped to be healthy or is harmed. Prevention at this level means building a healthy, mutually satisfying relationship between parents and child, and improving the parents' capability to care for their child. It means helping parents read and respond to the infant's cues. It means helping parents create a stimulating, caregiving environment responsive to the child's needs and encouraging of "self-regulating behaviors." It includes ensuring good nutrition, helping parents understand and appreciate the stages of child development, helping parents respond well to child-caused stress, ensuring child health, and more.

Parenting Education. Once a child grows into toddlerhood and beyond, becomes mobile, and begins to communicate verbally, she again finds herself in a different and very exciting world. There is so much to do, so much to discover, so much to touch and experience. The child has entered a growth process that continues through the teenage years. For parents this process is challenging, rewarding, and exciting—and often quite difficult and trying. Unfortunately, few parents are taught how to raise children in ways that build healthy perceptions and produce constructive and healthy behaviors. Thus, prevention at this level is helping parents learn necessary skills and gain self-confidence so the home environment can be a nurturing place that builds healthy self-perceptions and life skills. Parents also need adequate knowledge of child development. If this level is not sound, the pyramid can collapse. If this level stands solid, it can stabilize the rest of the structure.

Quality Child Care. If parents go off to work (or elsewhere) the child enters yet another environment where a good portion of her early life can be spent. Available, affordable child care enables both or single parents to work, preventing their dependence on welfare. Child care also gives parents much-needed respite from stress. While a very beneficial prevention practice for parents, however, there is little about child care, per se, that is inherently good for children—except socialization—(in a few child care settings some children have even been physically and sexually abused). "High-quality" child care is a different story, giving children new opportunities to socialize, improve their social skills and master the environment. Prevention at this level is not only ensuring available, affordable child care for the parents, but is also fostering healthy and supportive child care climates and ensuring skilled child care workers.

Early Childhood Education. Children need adequate preparation for the world they will enter. Are they prepared for school, the next major environment of their lives? Do they have problems that may impede them? Prevention at this level is screening all children to identify developmental and cognitive delays, and then designing specific early education strategies to address those delays. Prevention at this level is the development of constructive preschool education programs or "educational-play groups," ideally in conjunction with quality child care centers that include opportunities for positive interactions between children and parents. It is ensuring that nursery schools with healthy climates are in place. The purpose is to help children get off to a solid start and be developmentally ready and socialized for school, so they can have successful experiences from the start.

School Climate Improvement. When children enter school, they enter another environment that will have a major impact on their lives. Conditions in schools can have a powerful affect on subsequent behavior. Students can be treated in ways that produce either healthy or unhealthy self-perceptions. The way discipline and teaching are practiced, the relevance of school to life, the degree of student governance, the attitude and structure of the school—all can make a huge difference in the way students feel and behave. Prevention at this level is the process of improving a school's total environment or "climate" so that students' healthy selves can emerge and learn. It is the process of restructuring schools for higher performance. If the pyramid's base collapses but this level stands strong, the rest can remain supported.

Comprehensive Health Education. Within the school environment, the content of what students learn is also important. When young people get out of school, they should be prepared for life. A comprehensive K-12 health curriculum should offer an age-appropriate process of providing the information and building the skills students need to contend with their physical, mental, emotional, and social health. Prevention at this level includes helping young people understand and deal with issues they may encounter during their growth and development: sexual issues, teenage pregnancy, sexual abuse, alcohol and other drugs, eating disorders, marriage and divorce, family life, family dysfunction, social skills development, self-esteem building, and so on. Prevention at this level provides accurate information about health-related issues and develops skills so that young people can make informed, responsible decisions.

Educational/support groups such as Early Drug Abuse Prevention (EDAP). Programs such as EDAP complement school health education programs and provide an often missing ingredient. These are structured, educational/support group experiences within schools but in comfortable, small-group settings designed to develop healthy self-concepts and build life skills. Ideally, such programs should be an integral part of a comprehensive school health curriculum because its small-group format encourages sharing in an informal, supportive atmosphere. Where a school has no comprehensive health curriculum or has an inadequate one, a program such as EDAP can be a program unto itself. The same may be said of programs such as QUEST at the high-school and middle-school levels, and of other programs that provide similar opportunities— but few are constructed as well as EDAP.

Figure 6-3. Primary Prevention Pyramid

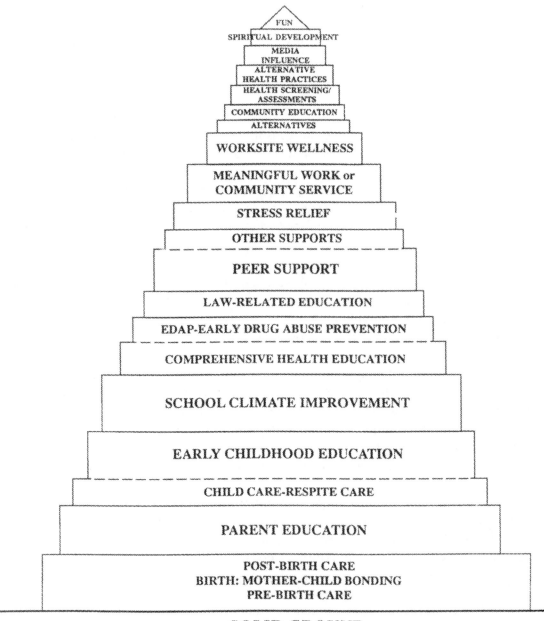

FUN

SPIRITUAL DEVELOPMENT

MEDIA INFLUENCE

ALTERNATIVE HEALTH PRACTICES

HEALTH SCREENING/ ASSESSMENTS

COMMUNITY EDUCATION

ALTERNATIVES

WORKSITE WELLNESS

MEANINGFUL WORK or COMMUNITY SERVICE

STRESS RELIEF

OTHER SUPPORTS

PEER SUPPORT

LAW-RELATED EDUCATION

EDAP-EARLY DRUG ABUSE PREVENTION

COMPREHENSIVE HEALTH EDUCATION

SCHOOL CLIMATE IMPROVEMENT

EARLY CHILDHOOD EDUCATION

CHILD CARE-RESPITE CARE

PARENT EDUCATION

POST-BIRTH CARE
BIRTH: MOTHER-CHILD BONDING
PRE-BIRTH CARE

SOLID GROUND
SOCIAL CHANGE

"If you want to get high, build a strong foundation." - Neil Young, "Like an Inca"

Law-Related Education. Law-related education (LRE) covers aspects of social living that do not fall within the realm of a comprehensive health curriculum. LRE is a reality-based curriculum that helps young people explore issues related to reasons for law, principles and values underlying law, justice, fairness, the legal and enforcement systems, the Constitution, and so on. Part of this education includes visits from members of the law enforcement and justice communities, and visits to correctional facilities. This category also includes gang-related education, where appropriate.

Teen-Peer Support. The peer group is an extremely influential subenvironment existing within a larger environment. For teens and preteens in particular, it can play such a powerful role that its negative pressures can undercut what all other levels of the pyramid are trying to build. Prevention at this level tries to turn potentially negative peer pressure into positive peer influence, especially around issues that are important to teenagers. Some strategies to accomplish this task include "teenage institutes," peer-to-peer counseling/support programs, and teen discussion groups such as Alternatives for Teens which are especially effective when combined with meaningful community service.

(Other) Supports. The more that people move out into the world and experience its difficulties, the more they need supports to help them cope or thrive. Prevention at this level ensures that an individual has access to nurturance and security from others. This could be in the form of support groups: for children of alcoholics, for victims of child or sexual abuse, for children of broken homes, for those with eating disorders, around bereavement, for single parents, for teenage mothers, and many more. To ensure a primary prevention focus, such groups could be open to anyone interested. Supports can also take the form of mentoring programs such as Big Brother/Big Sister/friends. They can be groups like Alanon, Alateen, or Parents Anonymous, which are most often used as secondary and tertiary prevention but can also be used for primary prevention. Supports can occur naturally among family members, neighbors and friends; at other times they have to be deliberately organized.

Stress Relief. One of the problems people encounter most often is the effect of stress on their lives. Too much of it, or the inability to respond well, can impede healthy functioning. Prevention at this level is reducing distress within individuals or reducing the stressors within the environment that cause distress. These efforts often involve teaching stress management, stress reduction, or relaxation techniques.

Meaningful Work/Community Service. If people do not have satisfying and meaningful work experiences, as they perceive it, they can face difficulties. Likewise, if people are not connected in meaningful ways to their community, they are not as invested in what happens there. Prevention at this level promotes attachment to the world of work and to the community. It ensures opportunities to earn adequate income and to perform meaningful functions for the community that can build feelings of worth, competence, and significance and allow people to be seen by others in those ways. It is essential that the work or service also be meaningful to the worker or nothing will be prevented except attendance.

Health Promotion in the Workplace. The environment of the workplace is critical to good health. Is the worksite safe? Do employer policies and practices ensure the best production, satisfaction, and enthusiasm of the workers? Prevention at this level is examining the workplace for conditions and practices that are detrimental to employees' emotional and physical health, and then altering practices as necessary.

"Alternatives" to Problem Behaviors. Opportunities should be available for young people so they will not feel they need to resort to drug use, delinquency, and other problem behaviors to get their kicks. Prevention at this level is ensuring that there are such opportunities. Recreation, the arts, and other alternatives may excite people enough to divert them from engaging in problem behaviors. This strategy works best in combination with others.

Community Education. When people do not know the facts about a problem they are unlikely to take constructive action. Some of the information young people learn in school about critical life issues should also be learned by the rest of the community through community-wide educational efforts. Many of these can be in conjunction with the school. A fairly common prevention practice is to educate the community about symptom-specific problems. A less common practice is to educate the community about how all such problems are interconnected, and what constitutes effective prevention. Community education becomes an "environmental" approach when it attempts to change community norms or values. Advocacy for particular concerns can be part of the community education process.

Health and Educational Screening/Assessments. Health and educational problems caught early can often save much trouble. Good prevention practice provides the opportunity to screen and assess everyone in the general population to identify any existing problems. Screening everyone is primary prevention even though by itself it doesn't prevent anything. What one does with those identified problems is secondary prevention.

Media Influence. Television has come to dominate many children's and families' lives. It brings the world, in all its craziness, right into people's homes. Other media have influence too, but probably less than TV. The most common prevention practice here is to present alternative messages to what is broadcast or printed. The problem is that such alternative messages amount to a drop in the bucket compared to the messages of big businesses to sell products and garner high ratings. Less common practice is the transmission of messages that teach us to become immune to the messages we get bombarded by all the time, such as "drinking will make you sexy."

Alternative Health Practices. The extent to which we understand and take care of ourselves and recognize how we fit into a larger scheme influences our experience of personal health and well-being. Much of the medical establishment practices a form of medicine that falls within the bounds of intervention and treatment. Little instruction and practice is done to promote health and prevent future health problems. For the primary prevention of health problems we often have to look outside the medical establishment. Alternative health practices such as chiropractic, acupuncture, and reflexology are designed not only to ameliorate problems but also to keep the energies of the body aligned and flowing. Bodywork such as Rolfing, the Alexander technique, and various forms of massage have a similar intent. Yoga, aikido, and t'ai chi combine this intent with spiritual attunement. Exercising and aerobics also fall within this category, as does good nutrition, high-fiber diets, macrobiotics, and more. The number of different approaches is enough to make one's head spin, yet common principles underlie all. Common to all, including traditional medicine, is the creation of health care teamwork between persons and professionals for health promotion.

Spiritual Development. Many people believe there is a spiritual dimension to life. We exist in some relationship with this spiritual realm, even if we are nonbelievers. Prevention at this level means efforts designed to connect the individual to the spiritual. People define this differently for themselves. Some see it in terms of traditional religion; others see it in many other forms: universal love, peace, oneness, however they define God for themselves. To be fully connected spiritually is to experience well-being, and to love and treat one's neighbor as oneself. If everyone lived that way, little prevention would be needed. Practices such as meditation, prayer, attending official places of worship, and freeing the body's energy centers can all be used to help people reach a more spiritual state. Ultimately, to see as spiritual gifts the source of one's "health" and the creative power one has to create his or her experience of life with the power of thought appears to be most instructive and helpful and can lead to a change in consciousness.

Fun and Excitement. It is strange to find "fun" here because it is not meant to be an endpoint; rather, it appears here only to illustrate that it should trickle down through all the strategies below it. The more that fun permeates any of the prevention efforts in the pyramid, the more receptive to those efforts young people and others will be. William Glasser identified fun as one of people's basic needs. Norman Cousins virtually laughed his way out of a terminal illness. Sociologist Walter B. Miller (1959) identified the need for excitement as one of the prime motivating forces of delinquency. When people have legitimate opportunities to have fun and excitement they are less likely to fulfill these needs in illegitimate ways. Prevention should help provide those opportunities, based on helping to alter individual perceptions and removing the barriers at the bottom of the pyramid.

Social/Environment Change. On what base does our pyramid rest? Suppose we have created a solid pyramid but the ground on which it sits is weak and collapses under it. Our structure may not survive. No matter how well we've constructed this pyramid of strategies, it may not be worth so much if it cannot be supported by the ground beneath it. The ground may not be solid because many people may feel too overwhelmed by poverty and despair to care. Day-to-day living may be so difficult they can't even bother. Prevention at this level means ensuring that people's basic needs are met for food, clothing, shelter, having enough income to survive, to be safe. Thus the foundation of our pyramid relates to the bottom of Maslow's hierarchy of needs—the "basic survival" and "safety" levels. Prevention at this level is changing conditions in the social structure or physical environment to improve the quality of life: reducing poverty and social injustice, ensuring basic economic opportunity, jobs, and adequate housing, and preventing the environment from harming human beings and other creatures. It also means efforts to counter racism, sexism, and elitism.

The levels of strategy that form this pyramid are not merely ideas that sound logical and promising. Each of these strategies is based on research demonstrating that problem behaviors are reduced as a result. Generally, there is more evidence supporting the lower half of the pyramid; also, the taller the level depicted the generally more indispensable the prevention strategy, according to research. Even the narrow levels, though, have some research basis.

In 1986, the American Psychological Association Task Force on Promotion, Prevention, and Intervention Alternatives in Psychology identified 14 research studies that they believed held up under intense scrutiny in demonstrating beyond doubt that these programs worked to prevent problems. Their findings were subsequently published in a volume called *14 Ounces of Prevention* in 1989. The chapters that follow cite much of this research, along with evidence from other highly regarded programs, to build each level of the pyramid in every community. In the late 1990s this approach was picked up by the Federal government which identified a number of "research-proven programs" to be replicated.

My intent is not to identify model programs to be replicated, but to extract the principles that make each program effective, to ensure the best chance that an approach will work at any level of the pyramid. Organizations that offer similar programs may want to check these research-identified principles against their program operations. These principles can also be valuable as a guide in developing new programs. **An examination of what makes these programs work will reveal that the key variable is nearly always the relationships that are built and the connections that are made to the participants—at least as a starting point. Thus, this pyramid is not meant to suggest that programs are the answer to prevention; it *is* meant to suggest that the answer to outside-in prevention lies in ensuring that preventive efforts establish healthy connections with others at *all* of these levels and to ensure that principles or elements of effectiveness are in place at each level.** These principles or elements are presented throughout this book. Also, the more people who are affected by these efforts in a given community, the greater the chance for community-wide change.

Communities may also want to use the pyramid as a "reverse needs assessment"— comparing the preventive efforts they now have in place to the types of programs proven to be successful. If a community does not have a preventive effort at any level that serves all people who need it, the community could together consider developing such an effort or expanding what they have. This is best accomplished through a community development process [Chapter 34].

To have the best chance of reducing the behavior-related problems, this entire pyramid of preventive strategies should be in place in every community.

II. Community Prevention Strategies That Work

Some sources where updated information can be found on programs that work are-

- *Blueprints* (Muller & Mihalic, 1999). Office of Juvenile Justice and Delinquency Prevention
- *Here's Proof Prevention Works: Understanding Substance Abuse Prevention—Toward the 21ˢᵗ Century.* (Center for Substance Abuse Prevention, 1999)
- *New Directions Guidance* document (1998). Vermont Office of Alcohol and Drug Abuse Programs, Vermont Department of Health
- *Preventing Drug Use Among Children and Adolescents.* (National Institute on Drug Abuse, 1998)
- "Resilience: Status of the Research and Research-Based Programs" (Davis, 1999). Substance Abuse and Mental Health Services Administration
- "Replicable or Promising Approaches for Safe and Drug Free Schools" (undated). U.S. Department of Education
- *What Works* series (various combinations of Brooks, Jimerson, Downey, & Murphey, 1999) from the Vermont Agency of Human Services.

No doubt there are others. Examples of programs highlighted in these publications but not included in this book are-

Across Ages—intergenerational mentoring, community service & life skills curriculum
Adolescent Alcohol Prevention Trial—5ᵗʰ and 7ᵗʰ grade resistance skills & normative education
The Bullying Prevention Program—school-based identification and school environment restructuring
Midwestern Prevention Project—comprehensive, community-based w/ mass media, school, parents, community organizations, and health policy change to combat drug use among middle school students.
PeaceBuilders—school-wide violence and substance abuse program
Promoting Alternative Thinking Strategies—elementary school program to promote emotional and social competence
Project Alert—7ᵗʰ & 8ᵗʰ grade classroom program: peer pressure, resistance, countering pro-drug messages
Project Northland—school-based curriculum, parent involvement, peer leadership, community task force
Quantum Opportunities— high-risk, high school program: academic skills, service activities, sustained peer group and caring adult relationship.
Reconnecting Youth—high school, high risk, life skills, personal growth, social, school bonding, crisis response
Resolving Conflict Creatively Program (RCCP)—comprehensive school-based conflict resolution and intergroup relations
Seattle Social Development Project—grades 1-6, teacher training classroom management, interactive teaching, cooperative learning, parent training
SMART—Boys/Girls Clubs, social skills, parent involvement
Strengthening Families Program—parent training, children's skills training, (together) family skills training

The value lies not in replicating these research-proven programs but in learning from them, learning what makes them work, learning what specific elements contributed to their effectiveness, so no matter what program we implement we will have the best chance to be effective. Unfortunately in my view, in the year 2000 parts of the federal government have misinterpreted, albeit with the best intentions, the value of these programs for funding direction. To achieve the best results the idea is not to limit funding to only these programs that have had large research grants behind them so we can replicate them, but instead to apply the elements of effectiveness learned by these programs about what makes them work to whatever approaches we develop in creative partnership with our communities. (from Preface)

7. Getting Off to the Right Start: Prenatal and Early Infancy Care

Would any of us want our own baby to have a strike or two against it before it even emerged from the womb? It would be unimaginable. What about other people's babies? It is a frightening thought, but the choice is made often—usually unintentionally.

Why would anyone make such a choice? Could it be through ignorance—not knowing the correct information? Could it be because a parent doesn't have the skills? Could it be because a parent has such unhealthy self-perceptions that she doesn't even care? Could it be because a parent doesn't have supports to help her through? Could it be too much stress? Could it be mental incapacity? It sounds like the parts of the conceptual framework. No matter what the answer, the question for preventers is, "What can we do to ensure that all babies have the best possible start in life?"

The research here is exceptionally clear, and it became even more clear in the 1990s through new brain research. Even despite maladaptive neurological patterns developed within the brains of abused and neglected children, those patterns can be changed through new learning experiences. For example, "The wiring that gets established in the brain and makes a child fearful and hesitant may be undone, then formed again into networks that make the child more outgoing and trusting" (Kotulak, 1996, p.62). New learning experiences and new thinking change the pattern of brain activity. A newly supportive and educationally-stimulating environment can turn around what had looked like a poor prognosis.

This is likely what occurs within the well-researched prevention efforts at this important level. The American Psychological Association (APA) selected a longitudinal study by David Olds (1984; 1988) as one that could hold up under the most intense scrutiny, to show that prevention works at this level. Olds's *Nurse Home Visitation Program: The Prenatal/Early Infancy Project* will be used as a base, supplemented by other programmer-researchers.

Following them for seven years, Olds's Nurse Home Visitation Program used a combination of prenatal and early infancy care with program mothers to produce the results shown below.

Item	*Program Group*
• cigarettes smoked per day by mothers	20% less than controls
• inadequate weight gain of mothers	0% vs. 15% of controls
• premature delivery among smokers	3% vs. 11%
• preterm delivery for young teenagers	75% less

- child abuse and neglect by mothers .... 6% vs. 20%
- child abuse and neglect for poor, very young teen mothers .... 75% less
- emergency room and doctor visits, first year .... 50% less
- children hospitalized .... 80% less
- repeat pregnancies .... 40% less
- length of time on public assistance by mothers .... 50% less
- poor unmarried teen mothers completing/returning to school ...... 89% vs. 52%
- older unmarried women obtaining employment by second year .... 66% vs. 27%

Program mothers generally viewed their children's temperaments more positively and reported that their children were easier to care for. There were fewer instances of conflict and less scolding, and less restriction and punishment of babies.

This group was again studied 15 years after the initiation of the project (Kitzman et al., 1997). Significant results were found in-

- Perpetrators of child abuse and neglect: 0.29 for intervention group compared with 0.54 of controls.
- Months receiving AFDC: 60 compared with 90 of controls
- Behavioral impairments due to use of alcohol and other drugs: 0.41 compared with 0.73 of controls
- Arrests (self-report): 0.18 compared with 0.58 of controls
- Arrests (NY state records): 0.16 compared with 0.90 of controls
- Significant reductions in adolescent cigarette and alcohol use
- Significant reductions in adolescent runaways

Other similar programs found similar and additional results:

- increased school attendance as children grew
- reduced need for special school services related to educational and behavioral problems

(Greenspan, 1986)

To achieve these impressive results, these programs were carefully designed to span both prenatal and postnatal care, and to influence parental attachments in early childhood.

Prenatal Care

Prevention starts before birth, as the unborn fetus grows and develops inside the mother's womb. Prevention can begin even before that by ensuring that appropriate decisions are made to have a child, and that a healthy egg meets a healthy sperm.

The mother is the source of fetal nourishment. Her blood runs through the placenta to nourish her fetus. Digested food in the mother's bloodstream passes through the fetus. Drugs and chemicals ingested by the mother run through the fetus. Substances are first absorbed by the fetus; what is left passes back into the mother. To tamper with the natural system can produce problems.

Premature Birth

Tampering with the system increases the chance of premature birth, which can be the source of many other health problems. These include-
  Sudden Infant Death Syndrome
  Failure to Thrive Syndrome
  Minimal Brain Dysfunction (Attention Hyperactive Deficit Disorder)
  learning disabilities
  hearing deficits
  cerebral palsy and epilepsy

Premature infants who were followed through school showed evidence of-
  language problems
  cognitive problems
  developmental problems
  behavior problems
  visual-motor deficits
  perceptual-organizational skill deficits
  speech and language deficits
  poor reading skills
  poor arithmetic scores as late as age thirteen
  marked hyperactivity at ages two and three

Distressingly, premature birth is also related to child abuse. Twenty-five to 35% of abused children were born prematurely; 40% were among the most severely abused. Why? Some reasons may be that the physical characteristics and vocal cries of premature infants are experienced by parents as more unpleasant, that mothers who delivered prematurely suffered greater postpartum depression and anxiety and had more negative perceptions of their infants, that preterm infants are often less responsive, and that parents of premature infants spend less time face to face with their infants and talk to them and touch them less (Searight and Handal, 1986).

The single greatest prevention of premature delivery is good prenatal care. Obtaining this care at any stage of pregnancy significantly reduces the chance of premature delivery, but it is especially beneficial during the first trimester.

Other birth conditions have been linked to abuse and related problems: lack of preparation to have children, limited supports, and high life stress and change during pregnancy, especially among anxious, ill-prepared mothers who were not knowledgeable about children (Wolfe, 1987).

"Needs" of the Unborn Infant

The research appears to show that a fetus has the best chance of emerging healthy when its environment provides at least six essential ingredients:

1. biological integrity
2. adequate nutrition
3. adequate weight gain
4. absence or minimum of harmful chemicals
5. absence of sexually transmitted and other infectious diseases

6. absence of accidental or nonaccidental injuries

1. *Biological Integrity.* Biological integrity means a fundamental genetic and congenital soundness that will not lead to physical or mental abnormality. From a preventive point of view, little can be done about ensuring biological integrity short of the ethically challenging practice of genetic screening before conception. Yet, rapid advances in genetics and fertility now promise prevention of some organic conditions.

2. *Adequate nutrition.* This refers to the type of food intake of the mother. Crayton (1986) shows that malnutrition has been found to decrease the number of cells in the brain and the size of individual nerve cells (in experimental animals); to affect brain biochemistry, neurotransmitters, and the brain functions mediated by them; to affect body and head size; and to affect stillbirths and neonatal deaths. Poor nutrition and inadequate diet have been linked to-

anxiety and depression
insomnia
eating disorders
violence (but with inconsistent results in human populations)
congenital malformations or mental retardation.

Nutritional intervention can successfully reduce premature births. If the mother was underweight at the start of pregnancy and had less than an average weight gain or a weight loss, the incidence of prematurity was 23.8%. Giving protein and vitamin supplements to prospective mothers before pregnancy reduced the prematurity rate to less than 2%.

3. *Adequate weight gain of the fetus.* This relates to the amount and type of food ingested. Low birth weight babies are susceptible to intracranial hemorrhages, are at increased risk for rehospitalization in the first year of life, and may suffer delayed or abnormal development (Minde, 1986).

4. *A minimum of harmful chemicals.* It is commonly accepted that alcohol intake causes— Fetal Alcohol Syndrome, characterized by smaller and lighter babies with abnormally small heads, facial irregularities, joint and limb abnormalities, heart defects, poor coordination, and often, hyperactivity, extreme nervousness, poor attention spans, and mental retardation. People argue over how much is okay to drink. Minde (1986) contends that anything more than an ounce per day is dangerous. Alcohol travels through the bloodstream in the same concentration, so what is in the mother's blood is in the fetus's blood. Because fetal systems are still developing, it isn't nearly so equipped to handle alcohol. Because of unexplained variations of individuals, and even with different pregnancies in the same individual, no alcohol use during pregnancy is the safest rule. Intake of other drugs by the mother may cause similar symptoms. Smoking reduces the amount of oxygen that gets to the fetus; this lack can cause lower birth weight and prematurity. Obvious now, but apparently not in the past, is that Thalidomide causes fetal abnormalities. There are drugs today about which we don't yet know enough; they may also cause dangers in pregnancy.

Since the mid-1980s, there has been an alarming increase among babies born addicted to drugs such as heroin and cocaine because of a mother's habit. The Fetal Alcohol Syndrome and—Fetal Crack/Cocaine Syndrome are causes of an immense number of mentally retarded children, of children with birth defects, of children with learning disabilities, of children with behavior problems. Learning problems can even materialize at age nine or ten if there had been drinking in the third trimester, even if there had been no previous physical or other outward signs. And it is 100% preventable.

Not only is it preventable but, as Michael Dorris (1989) points out in a heart-rending, extremely well-written and informative book, *The Broken Cord*, we don't even know what works once the syndrome appears. Yet we spend hundreds of millions of dollars on medication, on Special Education, on treatment, on incarceration—all in an attempt to pick up the pieces. Many of these children will pursue a life of crime without being able to understand the nature of their crime. Many are incapable of empathy. And there is a 75% chance that those who give birth to FAS and FC/CS babies will give birth again to babies with the syndrome, and those babies will grow up to have their own FAS and FC/CS babies.

5. *Freedom from sexually transmitted and other diseases.* If it is possible, perhaps even more alarming are the number of babies born with preventable diseases such as AIDS, herpes, syphilis, rubella, and Cytomegalic Viral Disease. These have very detrimental, sometimes fatal, effects on the fetus.

6. *Freedom from accidental or nonaccidental injuries.* Accidents can damage the fetus. Domestic violence against a pregnant woman can damage the fetus. An attempt at abortion without proper medical care can severely damage both the fetus and the mother.

Societal Intervention?

For a baby to emerge from the womb the healthiest it can be, the mother can provide an environment with these six qualities. If she does not, for whatever reasons, should society intervene?

In part, this is an ethical question. Whose business is it if the mother does not provide a healthy environment? My answer is, if society must pay for the results of an unhealthy maternal environment, it then has the responsibility to prevent such destructive outcomes. How can society ensure that a mother provides a healthy maternal environment?

Ensuring a Healthy Maternal Environment

Olds (1984) and others conclude that the best way for mothers to gain the knowledge, skills, supports, and desire to create a healthy environment is by establishing a system that includes the following components:

1. extensive home visits with specialized nursing care
2. available and appropriate medical care
3. nutritional guidance
4. maternal supports

Adequate home visiting is the key, for most other components can be included within it or arranged through it. Home visiting is one-to-one personal contact. It often helps put first-time prospective parents at ease. This strategy appears to work even better for "high-risk" groups than for the general population, and high-risk women are unlikely to take advantage of classes and groups. Home visiting should ideally begin in the first trimester of pregnancy, when the fetus is most vulnerable to nutritional and chemical intake.

Home visits at the prenatal stage should offer-

- help in improving diet and monitoring weight gain

65

- help in eliminating the use of cigarettes, alcohol, and drugs
- teaching to identify the signs of pregnancy complications
- encouragement of regular rest, appropriate exercise and good personal hygiene related to obstetrical health
- preparation for labor and delivery
- preparation for the early care of the newborn
- encouragement of appropriate use of the health care system
- encouragement to make plans about subsequent pregnancies, returning to school, and finding subsequent employment

In addition to home visits, **accessible medical clinics** could be available to pregnant women, open at times additional to regular working hours, and staffed with providers who are sensitive to potentially hazardous circumstances.

Once the services exist, it is important that prospective mothers use them. A few ways to enhance this possibility are-

- canvassing neighborhoods to be sure people know about the service
- providing financial incentives for pregnant women to follow nutritional and other prenatal care recommendations (paying a mother $60 to attend a prenatal clinic is far less expensive than the $150-200 minimum that governments must pay to subsidize Medicaid or other health care costs)
- providing transportation as needed

Birth, Attachment, and Bonding

Besides preventing obstetrical or other accidents that may occur during the birthing process, **the prime prevention intent at and immediately after birth—the neonatal period, from birth to two months—is to ensure attachment and bonding between mother and child.** Attachment refers to "the infant's behaviors, cognitions, and feelings towards the mother." Bonding refers to "mother's earliest feelings and behaviors towards her new infant" (Minde, 1986).

The attachment relationship between infant and parent appears to be the most important contributor to the infant's growth and development. Infants reared in residential nurseries without the opportunity to develop attachment became children who were attention-seekers, restless, and unpopular in school. This was true even for children adopted after infancy (Minde, 1986). Securely attached infants were found to display more social sophistication and higher social competence, more positive affect, greater popularity, more empathy and caring, better attachment to others, and less dependency.

A responsive mother builds in her child feelings of security and expectations of her ready availability; from this base a child can explore the world safely and gain opportunities to acquire competence. Loving and nurturing feelings can develop over time, but the sooner they develop the better. Stressors in early childhood, such as marital discord, can teach a child that the mother is emotionally unavailable and increase his sense of vulnerability (Minde, 1986).

T. Berry Brazelton (1974; 1988), a widely known proponent of mother-infant attachment and bonding, says every parent gets feedback from her baby that tells her, "You are important." The trick is for parents to recognize it. The baby and the parent must become locked into each other so they recognize the signals and subtle cues each gives. Brazelton teaches a system of recognizing these cues, which both the mother and father can learn together. Mothers have said that learning this system helped them better understand their baby and themselves.

Other ways to increase attachment and bonding are through regular handling of infants (Searight, 1986) and breastfeeding (Pascoe and French, 1988).

The attachment and bonding process cannot be accomplished by simply going through the motions. It must occur with feeling. Emotional signals are the language of the baby who cannot talk. Crying, smiling, or a bright alert look express feelings and readiness for interaction that the infant can communicate in no other way. Expressions of fear, anger, and sadness are equally important. Through this emotional/communications process the infant begins to perceive how it is being perceived (Osofsky, 1987).

Researchers have found an association between the mother's perception of her infant during first months of life and the child's later development. The importance for prevention is that we can affect that perception. The early maternal perception of an infant is fluid; it can change during the first months. The time immediately before birth is when mothers most need support and guidance, yet this is precisely when the present care system skimps on professional support for new parents.

Mothers at Risk

A woman without healthy self-esteem can view her own infant as defective. After all, it came from her. If that mother is also unable to gratify her child's needs, her difficulties are evident.

Another emotional crisis for parents can be premature birth. Immediately after giving birth, mothers need emotional support to offset depression, anxiety, and guilt. After these intense emotions have subsided somewhat, parents can then learn about the development and special needs of preterms. They can learn methods of early stimulation, how to establish emotional attachment with the infant during the critical 24-48 hour period immediately after birth, and how to interact productively with the premature infant (Searight, 1986). They also can use help to meet their own needs.

When preterm infants receive early tactile, kinesthetic, visual and auditory stimulation, they usually show clear benefits: increased weight gain; neurological maturation; increased motor, cognitive, and social development; and a greater activity level.

Ideally, this help should begin within the hospital or near the birthing room, provided by carefully selected, trained staff. It should be a comfortable place where parents can be alone with their infants and with any siblings. A primary care nurse assigned to the new mother and her infant could meet or arrange for all their needs. Group support meetings should be available.[*] The care should include comprehensive follow-up to monitor the infant's growth and development.

Attachment and bonding could be enhanced if hospitals would take the responsibility to promote it. Televisions in hospital rooms, for example, could be used to provide information needed by new parents and to demonstrate skills. This can significantly increase mothers' positive perceptions of their infants (Searight, 1986). Now that VCRs have become so popular, we can begin this process in the birthing room, and carry it on in a person's own home.

---

[*] Note: Parents who participate in self-help groups for their prematurely-born infants were more securely attached one year later.

Infant and Young Child Care

The baby has now emerged from the womb and has returned home from the hospital or birthing center. The young child soon enters a period (from two months to one year) when he or she learns to meet the world, forms perceptions of it, finds his or her place in it, and reacts toward it.

The aim of prevention during this period is to create conditions in the home that give the child the best chance of developing soundly and securely. An infant raised in a warm, generally consistent, loving, physically safe, and interactive environment feels secure; he is ready to relate to others and feel close and trusting. Conversely, an infant lacking this, and surrounded by parental anger and rejection and failure to adjust to its changing developmental needs, has a lessened chance of growing into childhood able to cope effectively, both socially and intellectually (Greenspan, 1989).

Infant Needs

During the infancy periods, an infant's primary needs are-

1. to be cared for and loved
2. to be healthy: to receive adequate nutrition adequate health care, including screenings appropriate immunizations
3. to be safe: from chemicals from injuries, accidental or otherwise (car, shaken baby syndrome), from sexual abuse
4. to be developmentally, cognitively, and socially stimulated in a nurturing environment

While "to be cared for and loved" needs little explanation, others may:

Nutrition. Children's brains appear to actively develop and be sensitive to disruption well into their second and third year and beyond. Nutritional supplements can improve children's cognitive and physical growth. Children re-nourished before age three had significantly better cognitive development than those rehabilitated later, although environmental enrichment may have equally contributed (Crayton, 1986).

Chemicals. On January 10, 1990, CBS News reported a study that children exposed to lead in the environment were seven times more likely to drop out of school and be truant. Other studies found that acute and chronic exposure to low levels of lead-based paint can lead to learning disabilities and serious brain dysfunction later in life. (Other studies have found an increase in lead and cadmium levels in violent criminals.) Other chemicals can have effects: for example, infants inhaling the smoke-filled air or PCP-laced marijuana in a poorly ventilated room suffered convulsions. Alterations in levels of copper appear to affect the brain's neurotransmitters and schizophrenia. Certain food dyes and preservatives may disrupt the behavior of approximately 5% of children, probably in interaction with individual body chemistries (Crayton, 1986). This is a controversial area. The problem is that only a few of these chemicals have been adequately tested (Jacobson, 1981).

Environmental deprivation. An infant may be victimized by the results of poverty, or by the feelings and actions brought about by unplanned or unwanted children, or because a parent feels overwhelmed. "When taken together, familial, psychological, and interactive variables and social class variables can predict a 25% increase in the probability of having a poor developmental outcome at age four" (Greenspan, 1986).

What Parents Need to Meet Infants' Needs

A baby is born completely dependent. It is the caregivers' responsibility to provide the kind of environment that meets those needs and creates independence. This is not so simple. Some parents seem able to meet their baby's needs naturally; others need to learn how.

Again, the Olds project (1984; 1988) is our model, supplemented by information from Osofsky (1987) and Greenspan (1986). What specific information, skills, perceptions, and supports does a home visiting model try to impart to parents?

At a minimum, parents need information on the following:

- *Routine health care*: the need for routine care, diet, bathing, umbilical care, taking temperature, managing common problems, preventing accidents (safety seats and belts, locks on cabinet doors, falls from beds, shaken babies), nutrition, immunization, well-child care, recognizing and responding to illness
- *Infant and child development*. infant temperament (types of crying and its meanings, sensitivity to the child's way of responding to the world); that a passive infant may need extra stimulation and an irritable one calming and protection from hordes of relatives; coping with a colicky infant and recognizing that a child's later temperament can't usually be predicted from early infancy
- *Cognitive development*. the need for appropriate cognitive stimulation in the home (being talked to, read to, stimulated but not overstimulated), the need for progressively more complex motor, social, and intellectual development
- *General parenting*: that parents' behavior affects the child's well-being, handling various forms of infant behavior, modeling appropriate, responsive caregiving

Parents need child-caring skills related to this information, and skills related to the following:

- *Managing family life*: ensuring that parents can meet basic needs
- *Communications skills*: demonstrating responsiveness; ensuring secure emotional attachment; holding, singing, playing interactive games; responding to infant's cues; turning routine care into opportunities for play and communication; communicating with others on the infant's behalf
- *Crisis skills*: interpreting and dealing with infant crises

Parents need to build healthy self-perceptions in their infants.

- *Developing a healthy emotional climate*: creating a climate that is attentive, warm, affectionate, nonrestrictive, stimulating, responsive, sensitive to needs; accepting the infant's limits as an immature person, viewing the child's temperament positively; believing that infants can see, hear, and understand things early; creating an environment with few emotional upsets, depression, conflicts, disorder; building the perception that the environment is safe and free of harm

69

Parents need support in their efforts to raise infants.

- *Surrounding themselves with supportive people*: encouraging friends and relatives to help with the household, be responsive, and help care for the child

Parents need help in reducing the stress in their lives.

- *Successfully dealing with life changes*, difficult circumstances, and everyday hassles: Difficulties in parenting or marital problems can result in an infant "symptom" like a sleep or eating disorder, which is usually alleviated when family stress is reduced (Osofsky 1987).

If parents, for whatever reasons, are unable to provide what an infant needs and ensure a healthy environment, preventers can provide the opportunity for all parents to receive what they need, so they in turn can provide what their infants need. To ensure more lasting success, the work need not only be with the infant but also with the parents.

Methods

Again, the best way to reach parents of infants is through a series of home visits at regular intervals. Olds used the following intervals in his model program:

> 1 month-6 weeks = 1 visit per week
> 6 weeks-4 months = 1 visit every 2 weeks
> 5 months-13 months = 1 visit every 3 weeks
> 14 months-20 months = 1 visit every 4 weeks
> 20 months-24 months = 1 visit every 6 weeks
> plus availability for crises
> visits average 1 hour and 15 minutes

To ensure that appropriate topics are covered with each parent, it may be best for home visitors to use an "infancy curriculum," focusing on all developmental periods of the infant. Here are a few examples of curricular items to help parents promote good emotional and mental health, and prevent emotional maladjustment and underachievement:

- Try to relax and enjoy the child; do not become too anxious.
- Recognize that the best form of stimulation is not toys or mobiles or a fancy crib, but interaction with parents and other caregivers; a commitment should be made to set aside some portion of the day exclusively to the child, even if both parents are working.
- Recognize that the child does not need constant care and attention; after ensuring that the infant is fed, changed, played with, and loved, for a reasonable amount of time, it is probably best to assure the infant that we love her and that we're around but sometimes it's important that the child learn to be with and entertain herself for reasonable periods.
- Recognize that child care should not be separated from child development. Changing a diaper, for example, is a perfect opportunity to look at the child's face and smile; dressing

is an opportunity to rub a tummy, feeding is an opportunity to talk. These may be simple but they're extremely important to the child's development and are not done enough. (Gordon, in Yahraes, 1977)

Perhaps even more important than curricular content are suggested *operating principles for working with prospective parents and parents of infants during home visits*. Some are-

♦ Visits and services are provided by a single, consistent, responsive, well-trained caregiver.

♦ One of the first tasks of the visitor is to organize service systems in behalf of the parents' and infants' survival needs around food, housing, clothing, and medical care.

♦ A regular trusting relationship is established between the parent(s) and at least one member of an intervention team to provide a constant emotional relationship with the family. Because mistrust is often ingrained, the staff needs the ability and fortitude to deal with patterns of avoidance, rejection, anger, illogical and antisocial behavior, and substance abuse. It may be difficult to get in the door. At first the visitor should work with what seems most to interest and concern the parent.

♦ Quality care is provided that not only offers information but demonstrates how to prepare for and care for a baby so that the physical, sensory, motor, cognitive, and emotional challenges of each developmental stage are met.

♦ Parents are provided with easy-to-understand information describing developmentally appropriate activities to be conducted in the visitor's absence and discussed during the following visit.

♦ Parents are helped to understand their sometimes maladaptive coping strategies. They are helped to deal effectively with their own needs, as well as those of the infant.

♦ Parents are encouraged to build a natural support system to aid in preparing for and dealing with their new baby, encouraging friends and relatives to visit and help with household responsibilities. Parents are encouraged and helped to complete their education.

♦ Parents are connected with service providers as necessary, including ensuring visits to health professionals for comprehensive, preventive health care, and referral to sources such as Planned Parenthood, WIC (Women, Infants, and Children Program), legal aid, mental health, and Medicaid.

♦ The longer and more intensive the visits, the better the chance that the parents will adopt the promoted behaviors.

It is also advisable to have clear written protocols, focusing on specific goals to be achieved by parents, and careful record-keeping of progress toward goals, but this may depend upon the "client" population being served. In addition to home visits, Osofsky's (1987) program also provided a twenty-four-hour "warm line" where mothers could call to receive information, help or advice with problems. A weekly "drop-in center" provided the same and also aided in breaking social isolation. Other successful programs such as the Yale Child Study Center and Infant Development Unit add a therapeutic day care center to supplement home visiting. The Yale program also uses an intervention team consisting of a social worker, a primary pediatric worker, and a developmental examiner (in Greenspan, 1986).

71

Pierre the Pelican

> Let me introduce myself. I'm Pierre the Pelican, and my special interest is in that brand new baby of yours... I want your baby to grow up happy and friendly, able to do his part in the world, and be a fine person. I know you do, too. Some people call this mental health. So I will sometimes talk about how the baby grows and develops as a person... (Rowland, 1976).

These words greeted thousands of new parents. Once a month for the first year of the child's life, every other month for the second year, and gradually diminishing thereafter for six years, a four-page newsletter called Pierre the Pelican has been sent by the American Medical Association Council on Mental Health to all new parents in given geographical areas, explaining what they could do to promote good mental health at each stage of early development.

The first issue covers the new and different world that the baby experiences, nursing, how often to feed, how much the baby cries, the importance of being gentle, who should handle the baby, the necessity for parents to take "time out" for themselves, what to do if the mother has to go it alone, and family planning.

At eight months, the issue includes the baby's sitting up, crawling, feeding himself with a spoon, cleanliness, how everyone has bad days as a parent, what to do when the baby is sick, parental consistency, talking with the baby, and loving the baby as she is. Under each topic is a discussion. This is a way of reaching parents who may not let us in the door, or to supplement home visiting. Since Pierre the Pelican, many other similar publications have been developed—written by many organizations all across the country—that assist parents in dealing with their new infants and young children. An excellent publication sent to all new parents in Vermont is the *Vermont Parent's Home Companion*, published annually or biannually by Prevent Child Abuse-Vermont. It covers many similar topics to Pierre... in an abbreviated but useful way, and extends its information all the way into adolescence under the heading of "knowing what to expect" (at different developmental stages). It also gives a very useful resource directory of available services for parents. Other programs may want to adapt their own for special populations. The topics are invaluable.

Such publications are important for prevention. For the parents who read them there at least will be less chance of abuse and neglect occurring out of ignorance because they now know what to do and know what to expect.

Early Parent-Child Interaction and Its Relationship to Child Abuse

All parents make mistakes. Most are not harmful. We all have our good days and bad days. When difficult interaction patterns become the norm, however, problems can develop. Relationships indicating high risk for being abusive often have the following qualities:

- low parental involvement/more passivity with infants (especially in intimacy, speech, and stimulation)
- parental reliance on punitive child-rearing methods or restrictive control
- aggression as a response to stress
- developmental deficiencies

The following prevention and early intervention strategies can help combat potentially abusive situations:

- behavioral parent training that increases positive physical contact with infants and that increases the frequency and quality of positive experiences while reducing aversive control
- anger control training
- stress and anxiety management; desensitization to perceived stressors
- parent-mediated developmental stimulation
- peer support and increased social interaction
- involvement in nursery school and community activities
- supportive visiting, providing crisis relief, parent nurturing, and family counseling

Children who have established a strong, positive relationship with at least one birth parent are more likely to adjust to family adversity. To help prevent child abuse, we can strengthen children's adaptive abilities, improve parental competence, and help parents experience pleasure in dealing with their young children (Wolfe, 1987).

Prebirth and Early Infancy Programs Save Money!

Prevention of difficulties during prenatal and infancy periods saves money:

- $1 for child immunization saves $10 in medical costs
- $1 for WIC saves $3 in short-term medical costs
- $1 for prenatal care saves $3.38 in care for low-birthweight infants
- $1 for prenatal care for Medicaid recipients saves $2 in first year care
- $1 for prenatal care saves $4-6 in newborn intensive care
- $1 for family planning saves $2 in health-care costs Each publicly assisted teen birth prevented saves more than $7600 in medical and welfare costs the first year

What is the cost of not putting such programs into effect?

- Low-birthweight babies whose mothers received no prenatal care needed intensive care for an average of 18 days costing $18,000. Nationally, the cost of treating high-risk babies in intensive care units is approximately $1.5 billion.
- Nationally, it cost approximately $19 billion for all families started by teenagers in 1987.
- Nearly 66% of daughters of single women later go on welfare.
- In South Carolina, 20% of low-birthweight babies incurred rehabilitation costs averaging $20,000 per year. (Note: South Carolina estimated that if it could reduce its low-birthweight babies to just the average national rate, it would save $12,744,576 In initial hospital costs alone.)

Compare these to the cost of providing high-quality prenatal care, averaging $706 for "high-risk" infants and $476 for "low-risk" infants (Child Welfare League of America, 1989; Dollars and Sense, 1987).

The costs of not responding preventively are staggering, and are draining our system.

Where to Concentrate: "High-Risk" Families or All Families?

It is a crime that we hear debates about whether to provide prenatal and early infancy programs to "high risk" families or to all families. The debate would be unnecessary if we were provided with adequate resources. All new and prospective parents should have equal opportunity to take advantage—if they want it—of prenatal and postpartum services. Those who want to reduce the incidence of subsequent problems and pay fewer tax dollars to pick up pieces later will see the wisdom in this type of prevention.

Where a choice must be made about to whom limited services should be available, given extremely limited resources, it is probably worth identifying high-risk populations. Rather than single out high-risk individuals, though, it would be best to identify areas with the highest rates of poverty or teenage pregnancy, and serve all families within those areas.

How much better it would be if the care most people demonstrate for their own children could be broadened to include caring for everyone's children (Green, 1980).

8. Family Support and Education Programs

What is the best mechanism for ensuring that pre- and postnatal services are in place in every community? The probable answer is community-based family support and education programs.

Family support and education programs are difficult to define; they do not operate by one model. Since their intent is to meet local community needs with respect to family issues, such programs vary according to local needs. In Vermont, most of these programs are called parent-child centers, yet these too are structured differently in different communities. Heather Weiss (1988; Weiss and Halpern, 1988) attempted to define general characteristics of these voluntary programs. They-

- provide social supports for families in a secure, accepting climate
- sustain relationships with families over a long period
- allow families a voice in shaping the programs, based on local concerns
- promote and enhance healthy parenting practices
- assist in combating outside forces that impinge upon parenting
- promote and strengthen ties among young families in the neighborhood
- advocate for improved services
- reach out to families unwilling or unable to seek support
- often use community members to work with families
- respect cultural preferences in childrearing promote healthy development rather than remediate problems

Family support and education programs are usually community agencies that employ lay or professional family workers to provide sustained support to families during pregnancy, infancy, and childhood. Their general goal is to improve family conditions, parental competencies, and behaviors that contribute to maternal and child health, maternal personal development, and healthy family and child development.

Program content often includes-

- information about child development, parenting, and adult development
- feedback and guidance on childrearing
- joint problem-solving
- information and referral to other community agencies

- encouragement and emotional support to families with young children
- strengthening family supports in the neighborhood or broader community advocacy and crisis intervention

This content is most often provided through some combination of-

- home visiting peer support groups
- parent education classes drop in centers
- child care, providing both respite and/or a "playgroup" format where parents participate
- developmental preschool activities
- health and developmental screening
- special services for particular populations
- toy and book lending
- adult education counseling newsletters

The programs emphasize family strengths; they help parents gain power and control over their lives. Parents are considered partners whose strengths, knowledge, and experience contribute to the program. Parents learn from each other as well as from program staff.

Family support and education programs also help children improve their educational motivation and achievement, producing sustained gains as children move into and through school. (Note: The *Coleman Report* of 1966 stated that family factors accounted for more variation in school achievement than even school structure and quality (Gordon; Gary and Klaus; Coleman; in Weiss, 1988). Here are the family attitudes and practices that were found to contribute consistently to young children's subsequent achievement in school:

- high parental educational and occupational expectations and aspirations for the child
- warm, affectionate relationships between parent and children, much encouragement
- firm control over children's behavior, with consistent standards
- quality verbal interaction between parents and children
- much time spent playing, talking, and responding to children, with more advanced thought and language used (Weiss, 1988)

These are precisely what family support and education programs try to affect.

A schoolteacher who served for a while as a home visitor in one such program told me she would never again look the same way at kids acting out in school. Instead of responding to students' problem behavior with "What's going on with you," she now seeks to find out what's going on in the family to make the child act that way.

Unfortunately, "evaluation-based knowledge about these programs is somewhat narrow and shallow. It does not reflect the richness, complexity and potential of these programs. Program development is ahead of program evaluation in this sphere" (Weiss, 1988).

So how can we tell that these programs are successful?

I helped organize two such programs in the state of Vermont: the Washington County Parent Child Center in Montpelier and the Family Resources Project in St. Johnsbury. It became very clear to me and the staff that many families who had never before been effectively "reached" by any other "service" responded extremely well to this type of program, and they began to improve their behaviors in relation to their children.

The oldest and largest of these programs in Vermont, the Addison County Parent Child Center, commissioned the University of Vermont to conduct a three-year study of its effectiveness. In addition to the high number of services and contacts provided to families that would not have occurred in any other way, the evaluation found that-

- 21 "center" families got off welfare rolls while only 4 became welfare clients
- 33 became employed for the first time and only 4 who had been previously employed became unemployed.
- The study concluded, "the state will realize a saving of from $189,000 to $297,000 in one year. Projected over the next 40 years in 1988 dollars, this figure becomes very significant ($11,888,000)."
- In addition, 49 "cases" improved their educational level, while 29 remained the same (Meyers, 1987).

Another APA-approved program, the *Houston Parent-Child Development Center*, bridges the gap between a family support and early childhood education program (Johnson and Breckenridge, 1982; Johnson, 1988). Their intent was to improve the later school competence of Mexican-American children and to promote the mental health of participating families.

The Houston center works with children from birth to three, trains mothers to be effective teachers of their children, and provides comprehensive services to counter the effects of poverty. When the child is one year old, the center provides biweekly home visits, several weekend group sessions, English-language classes for mothers, medical examination of children, and assistance in accessing other community services. Through in-home visits, many issues related to infant development are uncovered. Mothers are helped to become sensitive to the child's cognitive development, to learn the value of songs and word games, and to become sensitive to the child's developmental level and emotional states.

By the second year, activities shift to a center-based program; they include homemaker lessons in sewing, buying strategies, and health and safety in the home. Mothers are taught principles of child development and have the opportunity to practice childrearing skills. They are encouraged to express affection toward their children. The entire program involves participants for approximately 500 hours over two years.

The Houston program began with 214 families and 244 controls. Unfortunately, about half of the program families dropped out during the two years, mostly because they moved and/or mothers went to work.

However, those who remained at the end of program saw real benefits. Follow-ups in grades two to five, five to eight years after program completion, found-

- fewer behavior problems among program children, including: less destructiveness, less overactivity and restlessness, less negative attention seeking and disruptiveness, less impulsiveness and obstinacy, less often involved in fights, less withdrawn, moody behaviors (approached significance), less hostility, less dependence, more emotional sensitivity and considerateness
- four times as many in the control group were referred for special services,
- a small but significant increase in IQ among program group children

- program parents' behavior toward children to be more affectionate, more full of praise, less critical, less rigidly controlling, more encouraging of children's verbalizations, more educationally stimulating

The use of praise, lack of criticism, and flexible control displayed by mothers promotes secure attachments in infants. Insecure attachment at age one is associated with behavior problems at age six.

There were also benefits for the program parents:

- increased work motivation
- improved self-esteem
- increased feelings of security
- greater sense of group belonging
- a diminished belief that physical punishment was necessary for discipline

Johnson and Breckenridge believe that the following *elements* were *crucial to the program's success*:

- Intense program participation extends for two years (550 hours), beginning when the child is one.
- Parents are highly involved in the program and participate jointly with their children.
- All aspects of the program promote parents' efficacy and autonomy.
- The program begins in the parents' home and moves to the center sequentially.
- The entire family is included.
- Supportive services help families cope with acute financial, medical, childrearing, and other problems.
- Early positive mother-child interaction is developed, with parent training in child management and positive discipline skills, including maternal sensitivity to the child's emotions and developmental stages.
- Learning occurs in groups of mixed sizes and in varied settings.
- A variety of educational methods is used.
- A support system is developed among parents.
- Bilingual communication is encouraged. Bilingual professionals are used.
- The program is culturally sensitive.

Another program, the *Ounce of Prevention Fund* in Illinois, is probably the largest organized state system of family support and education programs in the country, serving 60 Illinois communities, with 6000 adolescent families "enrolled in the system." Examining long-term effects, while admitting to some problems with their tracking system, they report that-

- 58% of participants who stayed in the program 12 months or more had graduated from or are continuing in high school
- 25% of program participants became employed full time or part time.

These are higher percentages than among the general population. Most impressive is that only 3% of these families are now considered at high risk of abuse and neglect, a far lower percentage than in the general population (Rubino, 1987).

Among the most telling data supporting a family support and education system comes from the Scandinavian countries. To varying degrees Sweden, Finland, and Denmark all have nationwide systems that look very much like an expanded, broadened version of family support and education programs. Additionally, they have the benefits of universal insurance (sickness, disability, unemployment), free tuition for academic and vocational training, paid maternity leave, paid educational leave for those wanting to upgrade their skills, yearly cash allowances for each child up to age 16 and for nonworking mothers for six months during pregnancy, maternal child health services, subsidized primary health care, and others. They believe families should not be penalized economically for having children, and that high quality services should be accessible to all community residents regardless of problem, geographic location, or income level. They believe a major emphasis should be placed on prevention.

Results from these countries show:

- 95% of pregnant mothers start prenatal care before the end of the fourth month, compared with less than 85% entering care by this time in the United States
- fewer than 4% of mothers are under 20 at the time of their first birth, compared with 10% in United States
- an abortion rate of 12-18 per 1000, compared to 27 per 1000 in United States infant mortality rates and births of low-weight babies among the lowest in the world
- an infant death-from-respiratory disease rate of 22-67 per 100,000, compared with 107 per 100,000 in the United States
- prevalence of mild mental retardation 8-10 times lower than in the United States
- rates of child abuse about 8 times lower than in the United States

And, "In spite of (or because of) providing comprehensive subsidized health service, expenditures for health care as a percent of the gross national product are less in the Scandinavian countries than in the United States (7-10% vs. 11%). The percent of GNP spent on social services is greater, however ... (25-35% vs. 18% in the U.S.)" (Chamberlain, 1988).

The Political Appeal of Family Support

Family support programs can have political appeal. These programs achieve aims often expressed by conservatives: strengthening and promoting well-functioning, independent, self-supporting families that produce children who, in turn, will become independent, self-supporting adults.

9. Reflections on a Parent-Child Center

Cheryl Mitchell *co-founded and co-directed the Addison County Parent-Child Center, arguably the most successful family support and education program in Vermont. The program has many of the components identified in the previous chapter. Cheryl also co-founded the Vermont Children's Forum, a statewide children's advocacy group, chaired the Governor's Task Force on Teenage Pregnancy, and as of this edition is Deputy Secretary of the Vermont Agency of Human Services. She is appreciated by families, co-workers, and advocates throughout the state, especially in her own community.*

JP: What do you have to offer us about prevention?

CM: Well, we've had ten years of making mistakes, so we've probably learned a couple of things. I was real naive in getting into it, thinking that everyone was automatically a good parent. But for a lot of people, especially if they didn't have nurturing when they were kids, it's hard to figure out what to do to become a good parent.

JP: What kind of mistakes did you make?

CM: Our major mistake at the beginning was trying to teach people things. **We've learned to keep our mouths shut more and listen to what people are saying about the kind of help they need, because they're usually a lot more accurate than we are.** We started with an educational mindset, thinking that we should teach nutrition, basic exercises, budgeting, child development. We finally realized, especially in our work with teenagers over the years, that this was not a useful way to approach people. It was important to hear what they wanted to know, and try to help and support them with what they wanted.

JP: What made you want to get into this business in the first place?

CM: The belief that we could provide infant day care for the entire working population of Addison County [laughter]. I was working at a day care center, and we always had a huge waiting list for infant day care. We also had a pretty huge group of parents who'd show up at the end of the day freaked out, whose kids would throw themselves on the floor and scream and not want to go home. It was real clear that people were asking for help, but we never had any more than three to five minutes to talk in that kind of setting. It wasn't conducive for helping people feel more competent as parents. A lot of people said they wanted help with parenting. Most of our initial referred families came from Adult Basic Education, and the tutors said the parents weren't asking, "Please help me learn how to read," it was, "I'm losing it with my kids, what can I do?" or, "I'd like to learn how to read but I can't because my kid is demanding too much attention." The community had good prenatal health care and childbirth services, but nothing in the way of services after the babies popped out—no support between delivery and when your kid was three, when they were old enough for day care or Head Start.

JP: So, with that gap, what was happening to them?

CM: I think people felt insecure about what they were doing as parents and didn't know if what they were doing was okay. This was at a time when mothers were starting to go back to work after having their children, and there were feelings of guilt that they weren't doing the right thing for their kids, but they didn't have any choice economically. They didn't want to go on welfare. Divorce was becoming more and more accepted, so a fair number of single parents were feeling torn between their need to make a living and their desire to do a good job for their kids, suspecting they probably weren't. We were also seeing statistical increases in child abuse and neglect and in adolescent pregnancy, and more teens were keeping their babies and staying single. So there were increasing numbers of parents of young kids incapable of handling childrearing on their own.

JP: So you assumed that they needed certain things?

CM: We assumed what they needed was education about parenting and child development, child care, and some kind of social support network. It turned out many of those things were true, but our approach was, "Here's what you need," instead of doing what a good outreach worker does: "I'm here to help. What do you want?" People were very receptive to being asked. It was amazing. We had one or two families at the beginning stand behind their door and not answer it, but by and large it was what people had been asking for.

We did the home visiting part right; the mistake we made was to start offering classes in child development at the center right off the bat. People didn't come, or they'd come once or twice then stop. And when we asked, people said they wanted parties [laughter]. That seemed to us professionally inappropriate in the beginning. But it turned out that parties were what people needed to overcome feelings of social isolation, so we started doing picnics and spaghetti suppers where everyone showed up and had a great time. And we saw that **people were learning a lot from watching other people handle their kids**, even in that setting. So we started doing more and more social stuff. And after people felt comfortable, then they would start asking for formal classes. Then the classes were much more effective.

JP: Do you operate now only with what people ask for?

CM: Because we've been going long enough we have a basic menu of things that people have asked for in the past. And now any time somebody says, "This is what I want," we consider it much more seriously than we used to. We're more apt to say, "Let's try it," instead of kicking and screaming, saying that's not our job. And if it doesn't work we can say, "At least we tried." We try to do it two ways—both what the parents want and what the staff are excited about doing—and hope there's a match. **The most effective interaction goes on between somebody doing something they want and somebody getting something they want.** It's fairly useless to tell a staff person to teach something they don't want to teach, and its fairly useless to give people something they don't want. We also have enough parents who've been part of the program long enough that they're our resource in making things happen.

Our classic example was teaching people to drive. We were doing cooking classes, exercise classes, nutrition classes, homemaking-type classes, but we'd ask parents what they wanted, and they said, "We want to learn how to drive." We had an elaborate van transportation system all over the county and Drivers Ed. is there, and we said, "That's not our business at all." But parents kept saying that was really important. Finally one staff said she'd take them out on her lunch break with her own car. She did that for about a year before somebody asked, "Did you tell your insurance company?" It had never occurred to me. So when we did, they said, "You're going to have to have a certified Drivers Ed. teacher," and someone else on the staff said, "I can get certified to do that," and did. What we found was the parents were exactly right: Driving was one of the most empowering things that could happen for an isolated family, for a mom at home alone with kids depending on others to take her grocery shopping and get her kids to the doctor. In a county like this there's no way you can hold down a job without a car, unless you happen to live in town within walking distance. So, parents will say, "We really want this." We'll say, "We can't do it." They'll say, "But this is what we want." And we'll say, "Okay, we'll try it," and usually it works out really well.

JP: What other mistakes have you learned from?

CM: Our other major mistake was with teenage pregnancy prevention. A lot of us thought that many high-risk girls could get the desire to have a baby out of their system by having a chance to take care of babies. We invited young women, mainly girls who had dropped out of school, to work with our babies. Not only did it not get it out of their system, it made it appear really easy, because this place is set up for taking care of babies, and when you're here all you have to focus on is the babies. You don't have to focus on making a living or cleaning your house or anything else. So the first year we did this, two girls got pregnant and said to us, "It didn't look so bad."

JP: That must have been a shocker.

CM: It was a theory we tested, and it wasn't a good way to prevent pregnancy. Then we started having the girls work with the toddlers. And we've never had anyone who's worked with toddlers become pregnant [laughter]. It's such hard work! They're demanding. They talk back. They're not sweet and cuddly; they don't look up at you with adoration in their eyes. They look at you and say, "No."

JP: How did you get from one to the other? Did somebody wring their hands together and say, "Hey, maybe we should put them in with toddlers, ha ha!" [laughter]

CM: We had high school students working with both, and after the first young woman got pregnant we were talking about how difficult it was to raise a baby, and I said, "Gosh. Didn't you think of that when you decided to get pregnant?'" She had deliberately decided to get pregnant. And she said, "Well no, because it seemed so much easier than I thought it was going to be." Then we asked the people on the toddler side what they thought, they said it was exhausting.

JP: Did you start your program with the day care center?

CM: Yes. We started in the basement of the First Congregational Church. All programs for children start in the basement of a church [laughter].

JP: Were you doing that to fill a day-care need, or was it a hook to get the parents involved in other things?

CM: We thought it would fill the infant day-care need for the community, which clearly it didn't. We also thought it was the way teenage parents could finish school, because they would need day care. It was only gradually that we learned how to use day care effectively as a way for people to learn how to take care of kids. We hadn't thought of it in terms of parenting, except peripherally. We thought of parenting more as teaching people through classes, but we found that **parents learned better by doing it hands on, and then having a chance to talk about what they were doing and what they were learning**.

JP: How did they have the chance to talk about it?

CM: We had **support groups**. That's still pretty much the model we use. The people work three mornings a week in the day care, and the afternoons are classes and supervision and support groups.

JP: What are the support groups generally about?

CM: Relationships with men is probably the thing that gets talked about most, because mostly it's not working out well. It's been interesting to watch people give each other increasing support, especially about getting out of abusive situations. We see people supporting each other in their expectations of how they should be treated by other adults; that not only is it not okay for people to be beating and raping you, it is also not okay for people to be calling you stupid and putting you down all the time; that often when things go wrong, it's not your fault.

JP: It sounds like the support groups have a staff person involved who offers this kind of information as well. People with similar experiences come together in a support group, all they can do is support each other. But if someone is also able to impart information and skills—

CM: That may be. We do assertiveness training here, and self-presentation—how to talk to people, look somebody in the eye, how to say hello. And now we can bring years of experience in the form of stories of people who have made changes, with that certainty of knowledge that things can be different, and it's been different for Sally and it's been different for Susan.

JP: Tell me some of those stories.

CM: One went on here yesterday. We started a transitional housing project with Community Action in December. There had been a lot of problems with one of the young parents in the program. A boyfriend had moved in, and increasingly friends were visiting and being loud. It was creating a lot of turmoil within the house because the other women living there were saying it was keeping their kids awake at night. They were feeling threatened because they came from backgrounds where drunkenness usually led to some kind of abuse, like getting molested. They were worried. So the meeting yesterday was to tell this young mom that she needed to leave; she couldn't be there anymore. The meeting started with saying there had been a lot of complaints by neighbors about the noise, that it had been talked about for two months and the problem was escalating instead of getting better. She responded by saying, "Why doesn't everybody just leave me alone! It's my life! I'm not going to stay here anymore anyway because you're all just butting into my affairs."

It then evolved from people being angry at her, to saying, "Is that what you want to have going on?" And first she said, "Well I told them to stop, but they wouldn't stop!" Then she said, "No, I don't want it going on, but I don't know how to stop it!" So they asked, "What would happen if you asked all these friends creating the noise and drinking to leave?" She said, "Then my boyfriend would be angry at me, and he would hit me and throw things at me."

Then it flipped for most of the women there to, "I was in that situation, and it took me five years to get out of it." And instead of being angry at her, it turned to, "If it's something you want out of, and maybe you don't, we're here for you." It took about 45 minutes, but there was a great transition from the other three women being ready to kick her out, to working out a whole game plan for how the friends would be told they had to leave.

She finally agreed that it wasn't just that she wanted the friends to leave; she was petrified of this guy she was living with but didn't want to be lonely and was even more terrified of that. And with the other women talking about their experiences, how long it took to get out of it, what happened, what kinds of support finally helped them get out, and that they were still lonely—it doesn't automatically become better overnight—but things are much better, then by the end saying, "We're there for you." It was pretty dramatic.

84

JP: How did they know to move from the initial anger to questions that began to move the conversation?

CM: Some of it was staff asking the questions. Then the other women started changing their perspective and orientation.

JP: What would have happened in that meeting if the staff hadn't been there?

CM: My guess is there probably would have been a blow-up and a fight, and she would have moved elsewhere and had that situation continue without a support system around her.

JP: Do you train the staff to ask questions like this?

CM: Most of the people who are drawn to this field are pretty good about asking those kinds of questions. We have also done a huge amount of formal counseling training, and we talk about it a lot at staff meetings and individually.

JP: As formal or informal counseling?

CM: Both. Originally we said we didn't do formal counseling because of insurance issues, but some of the people on staff said that's how they feel most comfortable working, and that's what they're doing. Others provide more support and listening, or re-parenting. Each staff member has a different relationship with the families they deal with. Some are mothers, some are older sisters, some are professional counselors. The relationships are all pretty different. You sometimes find a family where your and their style just don't fit, and people are pretty flexible in saying, "It's not working with me, but maybe it would if you saw her." People have learned a pretty wide repertoire of skills over the years.

JP: What do you look for in a staff person?

CM: People who have a pretty solid sense of their own worth, so they're not needing to get something from the families they work with. We look for people who really enjoyed raising kids, who can listen, who are nonjudgmental, people who have a huge amount of energy, who have a sense of humor, who really enjoy being around teenagers and other kids, who have a pretty high tolerance for chaos and randomness, a lot of flexibility and inner-resourcefulness, who are real open to continual teaming—and people whose cars can work [laughter].

JP: Besides the domestic violence you've talked about, what kinds of problems does the parent-child center prevent?

CM: The long-term effects of people's lack of confidence in themselves. **One of the nice things is beginning work with women when they're pregnant and helping them feel positive about what they're doing as parents. It has a ripple effect in many areas of their lives**. People feel, "Gee, I had a healthy pregnancy. I have a great baby. Things are going well between me and my child. Maybe I could go back to school. Maybe I could hold down a job. Maybe I could get off welfare. Maybe I could have a mutually loving relationship with somebody. Maybe I could work things out with my family. Maybe I deserve an apartment that's got running water. That's real exciting! Working with people during the time their children are very young is exciting for both them and their kids because **the patterns of parent-child interactions get set early. It is a lot easier to learn to feel positive about your child and learn positive behavior guidance, than to later re-learn to stop thinking about your kid as a monster, or to stop hitting your kid. Child abuse and neglect are things we can prevent**.

We're also in a position to prevent a lot of health problems by **helping people have healthy and much lower-stress pregnancies than they would have otherwise**. Also, teenage pregnancy. The teen parents have gone back into the schools to talk to the students about what it's really like to have kids. They have gotten us more and more involved in the school, so we've been able to help out with some alcohol and drug abuse issues. And they said that one of the reasons they got pregnant was because, other than sex, there wasn't a whole lot to do around here. So we got into developing activities for kids.

JP: What makes you think what you're doing is working?

CM: We did a longitudinal study with families involved in this program, so we have outcome data that showed significant reductions in child abuse, domestic violence, welfare dependency, negative birth outcomes (low-birth-weight babies or infant mortalities). The other thing is looking statistically at what's happening in a county. **If you're going to say that a community-wide, community-based program like this is making a difference, you have to look at the whole community. Otherwise you'll be tempted to just pull in people who will make your program look good. Looking at the reductions in this county's adolescent pregnancy rate and the reductions in child abuse make us feel pretty confident that this kind of program makes a difference**.

JP: Did you know the program was making a difference before you had a large evaluation done?

CM: Yes, because. people were saying, "Thanks, this wouldn't have been possible without you." Like going back to school. A woman in the program our second year said that she was the first person in her family ever to finish high school. She'd been initially referred to us by the mental health service. She had agoraphobia, where you're afraid to go out in public. She was absolutely terrified and thought she was dying all the time, severe anxiety attacks all the time. She was 17 when we first met her and had a two year old. And through working with a home visitor and getting her involved with a small group of other parents where she felt pretty safe and knew somebody was there all the time, and spending hours with her at home and on the phone, and holding her hand initially, we watched her confidence build to the point where she said, "Now I'm going to go to school. I'm ready to do this." It was real exciting going to her graduation.

Then she said, "Okay, I've done that, now I'm going to go to college." So she went to a school for cosmetology and became employed. The anxiety attacks didn't go away entirely, but she learned how to cope with them, and her calls in between would start coming in less. Instead of needing to talk to us three or four times a day, it would be once a day, then maybe twice a week, then three or four weeks at a time. Now she'll call maybe once in awhile to say, "Things aren't going well, I just need to talk," and she'll talk for an hour or stop by and just hang out.

We've been grateful both to the parents who've said, "You guys are really screwing up," and the parents who've said, "You really, really helped me. I felt like you cared about me." One of the foster grandmothers downstairs said, "Never in my life was I ever told when I did something right, only when I was being stupid or when I made a mistake—and it was really nice to come here and hear, 'You did a really nice job.'"

JP: How often do you see things like that?

CM: Constantly.

JP: How many people have you served?

CM: Somewhere around 3000. That includes high school kids. We've probably served 1000 parents. Not only teenagers. Some are older parents who were having a hard time with their kids.

JP: Out of those 1000, what percentage can you feel some success with?

CM: The real successes? The stories of people finishing high school for the first time, or somebody who's come from a real abusive situation who's now doing a beautiful job with their kids? Maybe 25% of those parents. I would say we've only really lost, not been able to reach, just about 5 percent. There have been about 15 to 20% who I don't think have changed at all. The others pretty much say, "I feel much better about myself and the job I'm doing with my kids."

JP: What else do they say the parent-child center has done for them?

CM: **The most dramatic change is with parents who were hitting their kids and not liking it, saying, "You taught me another way that really works."** Each time a new group of parents starts here, we have three basic ground rules: no hitting, no yelling, and no name-calling. At the beginning people are always appalled at those. "How do you expect a child to mind?" or "How do you think you're going to keep a child safe if you can't do those things?" or "That's the way I was brought up, and it was good enough for me! Are you saying that I'm not a good parent?"

JP: How do you respond to that?

CM: I say, "Sorry, but these are our rules here. The way you interact with your child is pretty much your business at home, although we happen to know some other ways that might work better, but here the other children can't differentiate between whether you're the parent of that child or not. If they see you yelling at or hitting your kid, they'll be afraid you might do that to them. This is an environment that's safe for the adults and its safe for the kids, so we just can't allow it."

So people grudgingly say, "Okay." It's a requirement, in the same way you can't smoke and drink on this job, and you have to be here on time, and you have to take your shoes off [laughter]. Then people find out that it works. Not only does it work, but it works so much more easily and comfortably than what they've been used to. The process takes anywhere from two days to six months. It's not as if people change dramatically overnight—although some do. Others learn to do it here but don't transfer it to their homes for a long time. The people we lose never transfer it.

JP: What happens with the people you lose?

CM: We're still seeing them ten years later [laughter]. It's usually parents who are so heavily drug- and alcohol-involved that we're not reaching them on any rational level, where there's been some kind of dependency that we haven't been able to help them break.

JP: Do you think you would have been able to get as far with the rest of your program without your **home visiting component**?

CM: No. That **is probably the absolute key piece in being able to provide the support someone needs who's under stress and feels isolated. A lot of the families we work with have never had a strong, positive connection with another adult. That's what home visiting does**. It's when you know the person you're with respects you and cares about you, no matter what kind of weird things you're doing. It gives people the confidence to try new things, to take classes, to get involved in groups. Without home visiting I don't think this would work at all.

JP: Take me through the process. How does anybody know that a home visitor should show up at someone's door?

CM: Well, it's loose. Most people will show up for a pregnancy test, or someone will have a friend who's pregnant and ask, "Could you go and visit her?" Or the mother calls and says, "My kid's pregnant." Or a guidance counselor will call and ask, 'Will you come and do a pregnancy test and talk to somebody? Either the two nurses on the staff or I will go and talk to them about maternity counseling and pregnancy testing, and say, "I'm available to do home visiting. How about if I come and see you at home—would that be okay?' We don't ask anymore if they'd like us to come. We say, "When would you like us to come?" Then we might do an intake and take a pretty formal history and let them know about other things that go on at the parent-child center.

For awhile everyone had to come here for an intake, but now we'll usually go to them, and the nurses will let me know who they're visiting.

JP: These are nurses who go visit?

CM: Yes. We initially started with people whose backgrounds were in counseling and family planning. Then we decided there are important medical and health issues where we felt much more comfortable having nurses there. We also found in working with teenagers that people were much more likely to follow suggestions made by someone with the title, nurse, than by a home visitor. Since we end up doing labor support for people, it was acceptable to the obstetricians in town that nurses from the parent-child center would be there to do labor support. People seem to be more accepted with medical training.

The first thing a home visitor does is listen a lot. We encourage people to talk. We try to find something funny that's going on in their lives, to find the strengths that are in their family, to hear their hopes and dreams for themselves and their children. Then we ask what kind of assistance they would like. The nurses will visit for as often as they feel needed, sometimes once every other week, sometimes two to three times a week. If people need a lot of support, we'll try to get them involved in the center. A lot of what goes on is helping people find a place to live, helping them get hooked up with WIC, with ANFC, with Medicaid, with other support services. There is also a pregnancy class so they get a chance to meet others in the same situation. And they're there. We may see people 40 hours a week, others for an hour every week.

JP: Forty hours a week?

CM: They're here 20 hours a week in the Parent Training Program and come in as volunteers on Thursdays and Fridays. It sounds like a lot, but this place is warm and sunny. There's food. It's safe. There are happy people around who give a lot of positive recognition. People who need a lot of time can get it. That's one of the ways our outreach workers keep from burning out. They've got the resources of all the rest of us. If someone needs more attention, there's a pile of other people here. We have vans to help get them here. We teach them how to drive. The other big hook is money. People get paid for coming here.

JP: They do? How's that?

CM: If they make a commitment to be part of the Parent Training Program, there's a stipend that goes along with it.

JP: What goes on in the Parent Training Program?

CM: People work with the kids in our day care center three mornings a week. Then they have an hour a week with whomever the caregiver is in the room they work in. They have classes and support groups. They have time to hang out. All the parents meet together each morning, so there's a lot of social contact.

JP: How can you afford to pay them?

CM: We've now had 15 different funding sources for this particular program [laughter]. It changes every year, We live in a society that gives financial recognition, yet somehow we assume it's not important for low-income single moms. But it's important to us to say, "The effort you're making to do a good job in taking care of your kids is as valuable as most anything else." The reason the stipend is small is so it won't interfere with people's ANFC checks.

JP: What advice would you give to people who want to start programs like this?

C M: They should do it! [laughter] They shouldn't worry about where the money's going to come from, and believe it will show up somehow. It shows up because you have to work real hard to make sure it shows up. They should welcome making mistakes, and welcome the creative tension that comes when people work together. We used to have a terrible time here at the beginning. We used to end our staff meetings in tears a lot. The caregivers would be absolutely clear about what needed to be happening with these babies, and the parents weren't doing it, and they'd be really angry at the parents. Outreach workers would be seeing the young parents as teenagers who needed support to continue their own growth and development and not to have to suspend it to take care of others. It took us quite a while to work towards an approach that could balance the needs of those parents and kids.

JP: So why doesn't that happen anymore?

CM: We listen to each other. Sometimes one person needs attention, and we give it. It takes recognizing that it's not always going to be fair. And part of it is just time. For me, when I start something, everything has to happen immediately, and if it doesn't, something's wrong. Getting older and slowing down means having enough time to see that things do happen over time. The goal you had for next week may take until next month, but if you really believe it will happen, it eventually will.

7/89

10. Quality Child Care and Early Childhood Education

While the debate rages on about whether preschool is a necessity or a luxury, evidence mounts that early and adequate preparation for school can be critical to a child's subsequent school success, and that early school failure can begin a downward spiral resulting in a wide range of problems.

...[It] has become clear that many children with fine potential are already educational failures by age four because the critical establishment of learning capacity that occurs in the first three to four years of life has been defective, or its development has been ignored... Such basic behavior as paying attention and concentrating, trusting and relating to others, controlling impulses and actions, being imaginative and creative, distinguishing fantasy from reality, having positive self-esteem is either learned or not learned for the first time during the first three to four years of life. If children have not learned to act and interact in these specific ways before formal schooling begins, they will be impulsive, without hope, distractible, and irrational... The child who cannot focus his attention, who can't decode simple sounds, much less read letters, who is suspicious rather than trusting, sad rather than optimistic, destructive rather than respectful, and...is [not]...grounded on a foundation of reality...has little opportunity at all, let alone equal opportunity (Greenspan, 1989, pp. 131-134).

This does not imply that the pieces can't be picked up later, nor that kids can't be turned around. But to do it later is far more difficult, and far more costly. Who should be responsible for ensuring readiness for school? It would be wonderful if school readiness could be guaranteed within the home, but reality dictates that we cannot count on it from all families. Most parents are no longer even present for a substantial portion of their children's upbringing: out of economic necessity, they're off working. So what are our choices? Would we rather have our children placed in a holding tank for often more than 2000 hours per year until they begin school? Or, during this time, would we rather have our children being adequately prepared for school?

Many of the better child care operations include an early education component. Most of the research I could find supporting child care as an effective prevention strategy included early childhood education as a major part of the program.

Logically, most people believe that day care or child care (the two terms are often used interchangeably) must be an essential component for prevention—at least for the parents. If a parent is stuck at home with her kids, she obviously can't be out working. If a parent can't afford the costs of day care, short of leaving her children at home alone, she can't be out working. If a parent does not trust that her children will be cared for lovingly in a child care setting, she can't feel confident enough to be out working. Available and appropriate child care prevents chronic unemployment and welfare dependency.

For children, the issue is not so clear. Day care centers are like schools: there are good ones and bad ones. I could find no evidence that child care, per se, is automatically good for children and therefore should be required as an essential part of normal healthy growth and development. If every day-care center and home met minimum licensing standards and had trained caretakers, there would still be a question about the overall effects of placing very young children in day care. According to some researchers, day care can have a highly positive effect, especially on children's social development. Others see day care—if it meets minimum standards—as benign.

> And still others argue that separating mother and infant can have lasting negative effects, even when quality day care is provided... Even those who find day care harmless say there should be no more than three infants per caretaker, and this standard doesn't exist yet (Zigler, in Trotter, 1987).

Some child care experiences have even been detrimental to the well-being of children—witness day care centers where children are physically or sexually abused. Thankfully these are rare exceptions rather than the rule, but it underscores that the term "high-quality" should always precede child care when referring to its importance for prevention. The "climate" of a child care center (even the "climate" created by a baby-sitter) must promote the healthy development of children—physically, mentally, emotionally and socially—for it to be a bona fide prevention strategy.

Yet, because this society must pick up the high costs of illness, death, court, and jail for the multitudes of infants deprived of a bonding, loving, mother-child relationship, we could ensure a caring bonding-like relationship, at least for those children so deprived.

The Need for Quality Child Care

High-quality child care is an essential prevention strategy. It allows parents the opportunity to work confidently and become self-sufficient. It provides respite. For single parents, there is little opportunity without it.

Today nearly half of American households headed by a single mother are poor. Single mothers raising one or more children younger than age six have a median income of $6595 (as of 1986). The average cost of child care for one child would eat up half their income (Children's Defense Fund, 1989). I am reminded of the movie, *Popi*, one of Hollywood's most underrated films, where Alan Arkin, portraying a single Puerto Rican father of two children, had to hold down three jobs just to make ends meet, only to have his kids subjected to the brutality of the inner-city streets whenever he wasn't around to watch them. This state of affairs is becoming increasingly real for families where both parents must work to stay financially afloat. For more and more families, the second paycheck is essential.

Half of all mothers with babies one year old and younger are working. Yet nearly half the women who went back to work four to seven months after childbirth faced significant problems finding child care. Infant care costs are especially high, and the choices are few. Parents whose three- to four-year-old children are lucky enough to attend a preschool find that preschools only run for half a day.

After-school care presents an equal problem. In Los Angeles for example, nearly one-quarter of seven to nine year olds are left on their own after school. A Harris poll study in 1987 found that teachers cited "isolation" and "lack of supervision after school" as the two major reasons children were having difficulty in school. Fifth and sixth graders describe fears of being left home alone, mostly when their parents are away working (Children's Defense Fund, 1989).

Thus to have child care exist at all is critical. This care must also be available, affordable, responsive to family needs, and of high quality.

What Is "Quality" Child Care?

The Children's Defense Fund (1989) defines quality" child care as "care that makes a positive and permanent difference to a child's development. High-quality child care has the following features:

Structure:

- **small group sizes**, few children per adult caregiver
- **well-trained caregiver staff**
- **low caregiver turnover** (meaning, for one thing, that employees must earn decent wages. Two-thirds of daycare providers earn below poverty level wages, and 87% of home providers earn below the minimum wage.)
- **serves children from all** social, economic, and educational **backgrounds**

Content:

- **appropriate to the child's stage of development**, educationally, emotionally, and socially
- provides **positive attention**
- provides **opportunities to improve cognitive, social, and language skills**
- has **resources** available for families at **risk** of abuse and neglect
  (Children's Defense Fund, 1989; Vermont Agency of Human Services, undated)

These qualities cannot be assumed. In 1990 in a community near Chicago, forty-seven youngsters—half of them younger than two—were discovered being cared for in a basement by only one adult. At $25 a week, the program was one third the cost of most child care in the community. When the state closed this "center," many of the parents objected. No concerned parent would happily put a child in this care situation. But the parents could afford no better. When parents cannot afford decent child care, children suffer and often are placed in child care that is dangerous (Children's Defense Fund, 1989).

As of 1988, it cost an average of $3500 to send one child to full-time child care. A single parent of two preschool children earning $15,000 per year can pay up to 43% of her income for regulated child care. Child care is the fourth-largest budget item to a working family after food, housing, and taxes.

A two-tier system thus exists: those who can afford good-quality care and those who can afford only mediocre (sometimes even dangerous) care. This is inequality. It is unfair. And it exacerbates future problems that we all must pay for.

To complicate matters further, most child care centers can barely afford to do business. If these centers were to charge parents what it costs to care for their children, the centers would put themselves out of business. Nationally, 90% of private household childcare workers and nearly 60% of center workers earned wages at or below the poverty level. Animal caretakers, bartenders, parking lot attendants, and amusement park attendants all earn more than child care workers, who typically have higher levels of education. Does this suggest what we value as a society? It also leads to inordinately high staff turnover rates: "42% of all child care workers in household settings and 59% of all childcare workers in household settings will need to be replaced each year just to maintain the current supply of child care workers" (in Youngwood, 1990).

Worksite Day Care

One place the research is clear about the benefit of child care is at the worksite. In *a study of 195 firms nationwide offering child care benefits*, the following results were observed:

- Reduced turnover—65%
- Reduced absenteeism—53%
- Increased recruitment—85%
- Increased morale—90%
- Increased productivity—49%
- Increased quality of workforce—42%
- Increased scheduling flexibility—50%

Businesses that offer child care relieve parents of worries and reduce the amount of time and attention lost on the job. A day care policy for employees increases the likelihood that an employee will be happy at his or her position and have closer ties to and stay with the company (Kuntz, 1988). For on-site day care to work well, it must meet the needs of the employer, by helping to solve management problems (absenteeism, turnover, and so on) the community, so services are not duplicated and public and private sectors can together provide quality experiences for children the workers (assessing employee child care needs). Child care is also cheaper when provided by employers.

Because of tax benefits, employees can save 30% to 50% in annual child care costs. "When employees pay for child care out of their disposable income," said Jacques Simon (president of the Voucher Corporation of Scarsdale, NY), "they're paying with more expensive after-tax dollars." The savings on federal income taxes, FICA taxes, and state taxes add up significantly. If, for example, a married couple with a combined household income of $35,000 takes a $5,000 pretax salary reduction, in 1987 they would save a total of $2,008, compared with the $480 deduction they would get under the conventional tax credit for child care expenses (North, 1987).

A variety of child care options is available for businesses. Some are-

- on-site day care, where a facility is operated near or on site
- consortium center, where employers collaborate in starting a center at a location convenient to the work sites

- contracting with an existing center or neighborhood person(s) to provide child care
- voucher system, where the employer gives the employee a voucher worth a specified amount toward the purchase of child care from any provider (as practiced by the Ford Foundation and the Polaroid Corporation)
- flexible benefits, where employees select from a variety of benefits that suit their individual needs, including child care (as practiced by Procter & Gamble and the Educational Testing Service)
- resource and referral, which matches employee needs with existing community child care resources

For businesses considering the child care option, I recommend *Employer-Supported Child Care: Investing in Human Resources* (Burud et al., 1984). Among other things, this book substantiates effects of child care assistance programs on employee turnover, recruitment, morale, productivity, absenteeism, and for the company's public image and community relations, while providing cost-benefit and cost-effectiveness analyses.

Opposition to Child Care?

It is important to understand the root of much of the opposition to childcare. To quote an editorial from the *Caledonian Record* in St. Johnsbury, Vermont (November 4, 1986):

"This newspaper believes it is time for more people to accept responsibility for their own lives. When a couple chooses to get married and have children, they should be willing to make the necessary changes in lifestyle that enables one of the parents to stay home with their children or be willing to provide for their own children's day care arrangements. It should not be the responsibility of the taxpayers, the . . . bureaucracy, or employers to pay for the day care of their people's children."

If only the world were that ideal! I doubt if this editor was ever faced with the dilemma of having to spend half his family's income for childcare or remain on welfare. People who argue this point believe their argument is entirely logical. They simply do not have all the necessary information. Many, perhaps most, families would choose to have only one parent work if they could afford to. Most parents would rather be home with their small children.

A Child Care Solution

Ed Zigler, one of the founding fathers of Head Start, has proposed what he calls "a practical, affordable solution to the number-one problem of American families."

We must convince the nation that when a family selects a child-care center, they are not simply buying a service that allows them to work. They are buying an environment that determines, in large part, the development of their children.

Zigler says there may be as many as 5 million children who go home to empty houses after school. These so-called "latch-key" children represent 50% of the child care problem. Zigler's solution lies with the school.

We have to open schools earlier in the morning, keep them open later in the afternoon and during summer... Don't think of school as an institution... Think of it as a building—one that is already paid for, one that is owned by taxpaying mothers and fathers who need day care for their children. Part of the school building would be used for teaching, and the rest of it for child care and supervision. This kind of system...could provide working parents with good developmental child-care services. And it should be available to every child over age three.

For children 6 to 12 there would be before-school, after-school, and vacation-care for those who need it. In Zigler's scheme, teachers would not be asked to provide this child care. They are trained as educators, they have enough to do and they are expensive. What we need is something called a "child development associate (CDA)," a person trained to work with children-but one we can afford to pay. Someone with a degree would run the system, but CDAs, with on-the-job training, would do the bulk of the work (Trotter, 1987).

To pay for opening schools earlier and later Zigler advocates adding a small amount to local taxes, with a realistic fee system built in.

Some people complain about paying higher taxes to keep other people's children in day care, but Zigler says we are in the same situation now as when we started universal education. It is something we decided to pay for the good of the nation. We don't want children to be damaged. We don't want them to grow up becoming criminals or have other problems that are also such for the society... Prior to age three, he believes this should be handled by paid pregnancy and infant-care leave.

People have got to realize that there is a connection between leaving children unsupervised after school...[for] such problems as teenage pregnancy, juvenile delinquency, and the use of drugs... We are really precipitating those problems if we do not provide adult supervision for children and allow them to socialize themselves and each other (Zigler, in Trotter, 1987).

Early Childhood Education/Preschool Research

For assurance that prevention at this level works in changing behaviors and saving money, I refer again to programs approved by the American Psychological Association. One of the best known of all successful prevention programs is the *High/Scope/Perry Preschool* program of Ypsilanti, Michigan (Berruda-Clement et al., 1984; Schweinhart and Weikart, 1988). When the first edition of this book came out in 1990, even with this program's popularity, few prevention practitioners knew about it, and likely it is still unknown to the average person.

The Perry Preschool program began in 1962 and followed the lives of 123 Black children of low socioeconomic status from ages three to four through age 19. "Experimental group" children received 2 ½ hours of "high-quality early childhood education" five days a week for one or two years (depending on age). Others were assigned to a control group that received no preschool.

The overall objective of the Perry Preschool was to prepare children for success in school. It is grounded in Piaget's principles of child development and focuses on:

- cognitive development
- language development
- broadening of information and experience
- development of social and behavioral skills
- active learning
- problem solving
- a high degree of interaction between and among the children and adults

At the beginning of each day, the children plan their work for the day, estimate what they think they can accomplish, and take responsibility for carrying out whatever they decide. The children thus act as planners who have some power over their lives.

The program also consists of home visits for 90 minutes each week to promote parents' interest in their children's learning. Parents are also encouraged to be involved in their children's classrooms.

At the time these data were collected, this longitudinal study had lasted 16 years. The children have been periodically followed and tracked. Here are some of the results for these kids at age 19, comparing the preschool group to controls:

- decreased mental retardation (15%-35%)
- decreased delinquency and crime (31%-51%)
- decreased use of welfare assistance (18%-32%)
- decreased teenage pregnancy (teen pregnancies per 100:64-119)
- decreased school dropouts (33%-51%)
- increased literacy (61%-38%)
- increased enrollment in post-secondary programs (38%-21%)
- increased employment (50%-32%)
- higher overall satisfaction with work at age 19 (42%-26%)
- higher median earnings at age 19
- decreased years in special education (16%-28%)

The researchers also found:

- improved cognitive performance during early childhood, higher scores in competence in everyday life skills (at age 19)
- improved performance on initial IQ tests (diminished over time)
- improved academic achievement during the school years (slightly better grades, fewer failing marks, higher standardized test scores)
- fewer absences in elementary school
- more favorable attitude toward high school, placed higher value on schooling, stronger commitments to school
- improved social and emotional maturity (as rated by teachers)
- greater competence in life skills (as measured by Adult Performance Level Survey)

A follow-up (Schweinhart & Weikart, 1997) to age 23 of this preschool comparison study found that children in the High/Scope program committed fewer crimes, had better success on the job, and maintained healthier relationships than controls.

Similar program effects were found in six other longitudinal studies on various forms of preschools (combined average estimates): reduced special education placements (7.5%-19.4%); reductions in grade retention (31%-45%); reduced high school dropouts (36%-55%).

The Head Start program showed similar results (compared with controls):

- 59% graduated (compared with 32%)

- 31% were arrested (vs. 51%)
- 18% went on welfare (vs. 32%)

Head Start also showed less use of special education and increased IQ upon entering school, which Zigler attributes to improved motivation more than to increased intelligence. Families involved with the program also saw their children better nourished and happier (Zigler, 1986; 1987).

That both the Head Start and the Perry Preschool results were realized in low-income neighborhoods makes the findings all the more exciting. Furthermore, the benefits appear lasting. For example, school failure in the first grade has been linked to subsequent substance abuse and delinquency (Kellam, 1982).

At least as exciting are the cost savings of the Perry Preschool program to society. The average cost of education for preschoolers was compared with the cost for non-preschoolers, and controlled for "dollar value" by year. The results show a lower cost of putting a child through school ($38,813 for a preschooler compared with $41,895 for a non-preschooler), thus reducing the cost of elementary and secondary education by $7,082 per child (approximately 20% of the annual cost of elementary and secondary education), largely because proportionately fewer children who attended preschool needed special education, and received it for fewer years.

On average, each preschool participant showed:

- reduced cost of special education by $5,000
- reduced cost of crime by $3,000
- reduced cost of welfare assistance by $16,000

One child-year of the Perry Preschool program cost about the same as one student-year in special education, and less than half of the costs of imprisoning a criminal for a year. Yet the Perry Preschool is an expensive program because it maintained a teacher-student ratio of 1:5-6; other similar programs demonstrated nearly as good results with ratios of 1:8-10, which would reduce the cost of one child in the program from $5000 to $3000.

Subtracting the average value of per-child preschool cost for one year of preschool ($4,818) from the estimated benefits in combined savings of preschool attendees in education, earnings, welfare, and crime ($1,233 observed through age 20, not including victim costs) we arrive at average savings of $28,933 for one year of preschool and $23,769 for two years.

The High/Scope researchers claim these conservative estimates: $1 for one year of preschool saves $6 in costs to society, $1 for a two-year preschool saves $3.56 in costs to society, or savings of between $18,000 and $24,000 to the taxpayer per child. For each $1 of Head Start, $7 in savings were projected.

The authors project higher lifetime earning projections and reduced Social service program costs for those attending preschool. Savings in welfare approximate $16,415 for each person attending preschool. With projected additional tax revenues generated by increased earnings ($25,948 in increased lifetime earnings) and the amount saved in welfare reduction, it is approximated that the benefit to the taxpayer is $21,155. That benefit alone means that the two-year Perry Preschool program pays for itself.

Preschool programs were found to be particularly beneficial for poor children.

Implications: Creating an Upward Spiral of Success

Preschool better enables children to carry out their first school-related tasks. Because this performance is visible to everyone (the teacher, the parents, other children, and themselves), children begin to realize that they have a capacity for better school performance, and they believe and act accordingly, leading to a stronger commitment to schooling. The school reinforces this and thus becomes a source of encouragement and inspiration, improving performance for children who otherwise would have had a relatively poor prognosis for school success. Success in school strengthens the belief that one can be successful elsewhere.

Early education improves motivation and ability. Preschool develops new social and physical skills and intellectual thought that the children can demonstrate in new settings. They appear to have an increased willingness to try new things they can display to others, improving the prognosis for overall life success.

Principles of Program Effectiveness

Some key ingredients of a successful preschool program appear to be-

- a part-time program, lasting a year or two (not more) (Note: child care can be provided for the other part of the day)
- parent involvement (Note: the most successful preschool programs combined their programs with voluntary home visits where teachers worked with both parents and children.)
- competent administrative leadership and supportive staff supervisor
- teacher-student ratio of 1:5-9
- a high-quality program
- a curriculum model that guides program operations (Note: Originally the researchers believed that the specific curriculum used appeared unrelated to program effectiveness, but their new research suggests that the best preschools offer a child-directed curriculum in which teachers let children's interests guide the learning.)
- ongoing planning time and in-service training for staff
- compatible staff relationships
- ongoing evaluation

Preschool is recommended for all three and four year olds. As of 1984, 37% of this age group was not attending preschool, but for families with incomes under $10,000, 81% of three year olds and 61% of four year olds were not in preschool programs. What kind of a future do we want?

Interpersonal Cognitive Problem-Solving Skills

Substantial evidence exists elsewhere that besides a child-centered curriculum, certain other curricula applied to early education programs can make a large difference in the behavior of children. Therefore, if we also employ a highly successful curriculum on top of the general pre-school base, we may be able to realize even greater results.

Another APA-approved study was conducted by Shure and Spivak (1982; 1988), in a long line of similar work extending over 20 years. Their premise: that teaching interpersonal cognitive problem-solving skills at early ages can improve behavior; that even the very young can learn to solve everyday problems involving others; that children with these skills are likely to be better adjusted than those without them, and they act accordingly.

Interpersonal cognitive problem solving skills (ICPS) involve the cognitive or "thinking process." Children develop the ability to think through and solve typical everyday problems that arise with peers and authority figures.

Poor interpersonal cognitive problem solving skills are characteristic of-

- psychiatric patients and the clinically depressed
- delinquents and criminals
- teenage girls with unwanted pregnancies
- battered women
- suicidal children
- the learning disabled
- impulsive children; and
- the overly impatient and inhibited

Children competent in these skills, when confronted with conflict, are able to generate more alternative solutions from which to draw, think of possible consequences before taking action and, as they get older, identify necessary steps in problem solving and carrying out a plan.

The ICPS program teaches these abilities. Sets of problems are presented to children: for example, "how one child can get to play with a toy another child has," or "how to avert a mother's anger after having broken an object of value to her." The better-adjusted youngsters were able to think of more nonforceful ways to solve these problems. This improves peer relations and reduces negative impulsive and inhibited behaviors. Here is an example of this process.

T: Billy, why did you push Michael off that bike?
B: I want it.
T: What might happen if you push him like that?
B: He might fight.
T: Is pushing him off a good idea?
B: Yep!
T: Why?
B: He won't give it to me.
T: Pushing is one way to get the bike. Can you think of a different way to get him to let you ride the bike?
B: (turns to Michael): Can I have it when you're finished?
   (in Shure and Spivack, 1988)

This skill is learned by asking, "What might happen next?" and "Can you think of a different way?" The idea is to get the child to say to himself, "If I grab the toy from Johnny, he might ... grab it back... tell the teacher ... he might not be my friend. Maybe I can try something else instead."

Through this process children develop a set of thinking skills that help them solve their problems in their own way. The authors insist that this is even more important than helping a child know what is right and wrong. "Dialoguing" is the key to helping children associate how they think with what they do, and therefore how they behave. The problem solving steps are-

- identify a problem
- look back and consider what led up to the problem
- consider alternative solutions or plans (taking the perspective of others into account)
- look forward in anticipation of possible consequences of an act
- change solution or plan, if need be (Shure, 1988)

The program format begins with daily 20-minute lessons in game form, consisting of simple word concepts to be used later in association with problem-solving. For example, the word "or" helps children think there is more than one way to solve a problem ("I can do this or I can do that") and the word *different* helps children think of options. To help understand the effect of behavior on others, a game focuses on why a child might feel as he does: "He's mad because ... [I took his toy]."

After mastery of these skills, generally in about eight weeks, children are presented with pictures and puppets depicting interpersonal problem situations and are asked for all the ways they can think of for the portrayed child to, for example, "get another to let him feed the hamsters." All solutions are accepted equally, even such forceful ones as "hit" or "grab the food," and nonforceful ones as "say please," "I'll be your friend," or offering a toy. This approach helps them see that there is more than one way to solve a problem. Reinforcement comes not for "good" solutions, but for "different" solutions. In subsequent games, the children evaluate whether an idea is or is not a good one, and why (Shure and Spivack, 1979).

In the APA-approved study, these interpersonal cognitive problem solving skills were offered in nursery school or kindergarten or both for three months to Black four to five year olds in a low socioeconomic area. One hundred thirteen youngsters were trained and 106 followed as a control group. The program was evaluated over two years. As part of the program, teachers were taught to help children with problem-solving skills when actual problems arose outside of the formal lessons and to "role play" solutions.

Results (equal for both nursery school and kindergarten):

- 50% of those who began the program as impulsive became adjusted (compared with 21% of controls)
- 75% of those initially inhibited became adjusted (compared with 35%)
- 86% of already-adjusted children displayed no behavior problems when they entered the more demanding primary grades (compared with 58 percent)
- program children were more concerned about children in distress and were better liked by their peers

The results held over time. Children trained in both years did significantly better (85%) in social adjustment and interpersonal competence than those trained once, but one exposure to the program was sufficient.

With a three-month exposure to this program, many nursery school children with beginning signs of behavioral problems stop displaying these behaviors. Other nursery school children are

101

less likely to begin high-risk behaviors. For preschoolers, the impact lasts for at least two years; for second and fourth graders, at least one year (as long as the program was measured).

When parents of nursery school children were taught the skills to then teach their children, results were similar and carried over into the school.

Parents who neglect their children show substantial deficits in these skills. Neglectful and abusive parents have distorted beliefs about what they can expect from their children, particularly about family responsibility and care of siblings. Most of these parents were themselves never positively parented, and some, emotionally, are still like children. Yet, when older abused youngsters (ages 6-16) were exposed to this program, parent-reported behavior problems decreased (Shure, 1988).

Principles of program effectiveness:

♦ The focus is on the process, not the solutions (not what to do).

♦ Participants must have age-appropriate prerequisite skills (before preschoolers could learn these skills they had to learn key language. concepts and perspective-taking skills).

♦ The program must provide for practical application when real problems arise during the day (there can be no discrepancy between what they're learning and the way they're being treated, thus creating confusion); problems are turned into learning experiences.

♦ Problems that arise are role-played if they're not happening in front of the teacher at the time.

♦ Any intervention is only as effective as the agent who conducts it; they must believe in it, be sensitive, and be a good model.

♦ Periodic reinforcement is needed (especially for fifth graders on up).

Results suggest much benefit would be realized if this program were implemented as a standard part of early childhood education programs and in elementary schools.

Early Compensatory Education

Two other APA-approved programs attempt to bridge the gap between child care and early childhood education.

The first is the *North Carolina Abecedarian Project* (Ramey and Campbell, 1984; Ramey et al., 1988), a program of early compensatory education: preventing developmental and intellectual underdevelopment. This program attempted "to modify the environments of 'disadvantaged' children" and provide experiences during the preschool years that teach skills required for school success. This program too suggests the importance of a specific curriculum.

Children were enrolled as young infants in a stimulating educational program designed to support optimal development throughout the preschool years. The program followed 107 mostly Black families, mostly with female heads of households with less than a high school education. Approximately half were assigned to a control group. Nearly all began attending a full-time, high-quality day care program at three months for five days a week, with a staff ratio generally of 1:6, and 1:3 for infants. Free transportation was provided. All children in both experimental and control groups received excellent nutrition, pediatric care, and supportive social work services. In addition, the children of program families were exposed to a curriculum-

- consisting of language, motor, social, and cognitive development for the first years of life, presented individually for young infants and as age increased, in small groups (curriculum by Sparling and Lewis)
- after age three, augmented by the Peabody Early Experience Kit (by Dunn); Bridges to Reading (by Greenberg and Epstein); GOAL math program (by Karnes); My Friends and Me, a social skills program (by Davis); a prephonics reading program (by Wallach and Wallach); communications skills programs (by Tough; by Blank); a language curriculum (by McGinnis and Ramey) (for all citings, see Ramey, 1984; 1988).

Results:

- There was a 79% reduction in the risk of borderline or low-functioning children. More than 8.3% of the program group (compared with 36% of controls) scored 84 or below in IQ; By 48 months the control group was six times more likely to receive scores classified as "mildly mentally retarded."
- From 18 to 54 months, the program group was consistently and significantly superior to the control group on all full-scale scores of mental development, including general cognitive index, memory, motor, perceptual-performance, quantitative, and verbal skills.

It is interesting that this intense early educational experience did not produce scores in the superior range on standardized tests; rather, the program group remained at or near the national average while the controls dropped six times below. In other words, Ramey's "data suggest that the 15-point IQ differences typically reported between blacks and whites in the United States can be effectively eliminated during the preschool years and that high-risk, socially disadvantaged children can perform at least at the national average on tests of intelligence if they and their families are provided additional education and family support services" (Ramey et al., 1988).

Effective program principles and components:

- The prime concern: to provide a healthy, intact, well-nourished child
- The more intense the program, the greater the gain
- Developmental day care: systematic and daily exposure to people/staff who are affectionate, involved, responsive, and nonpunitive, and who provide healthy developmentally appropriate experiences that challenge motor-development and stimulate social interactions
- Cognitive and fine motor curriculum: awareness of object permanence, awareness of positions in space, puzzle skills, sorting skills, matching skills, awareness of cause and effect

- ◆ Social and self curriculum: awareness of self-image; skills in sharing with an adult, interacting with other children, imitating gestures; self-help skills; awareness of needs and feelings
- ◆ Motor curriculum: skills in rhythm, balance, throwing, pushing/pulling
- ◆ Language curriculum: dialogue, using books, talking about pictures with concepts, action, objects, relationships
- ◆ Skilled adult teachers who create and prepare materials for child-learning activities, model appropriate language and problem-solving, show support with smiles, encourage the steps a child takes toward mastery, revise a task that is too difficult, or add challenging elements to a completed task
- ◆ Skill-Toy lending library that provides parents with opportunities for choosing toys that extend into the home the skills the child learns
- ◆ Home visiting (parent-focused care yields even greater results than just child-focused care): providing interaction with parents, information about child development and resources, emotional support, help in learning ways to facilitate their child's cognitive and social development, help in learning to problem-solve
- ◆ Parent support groups

In summary, intense and comprehensive "early compensatory education" has a broad-based impact on cognitive development. It can begin within the first year of life and be sustained over the preschool period. It can prevent developmental and intellectual delay in high-risk children, and subsequently enhance children's later school success.

Combining Early Childhood Education with Pre- and Postbirth Care and Family Support and Education

In a longitudinal study through Syracuse University (Lally, 1988) beginning in 1969, 82 mostly young, Black, low-income families who were jobless and without a high school diploma were provided education, health, and counseling services. The program began in the last trimester of pregnancy and continued until the child reached age five. At age six, the children started going to an *intensive enriched day care program at the Syracuse University Children's Center*. Compared to a control group, the 65 children who received the day care and family services during their first five years showed the following results:

- • 6% had delinquency records (compared with 22% of controls)
- • three-quarters of the girls had C averages or above with none failing (compared with half the controls, with one-sixth failing), but little educational difference was found in the boys
- • 53% of program participants said they expected to be in school five years later (compared with 28%)
- • program participants expressed greater pleasure with their physical or personal qualities than did controls
- • program mothers were more affectionate, used more praise, were more encouraging of their children's verbalizations, provided more appropriate play materials, were

more emotionally and verbally responsive, used less restriction and punishment, and were more involved

Partnerships can be formed between the schools and community-based agencies. This is being done very effectively in programs like the Missouri *Parents as Teachers* program. Based on the belief that parents are the first and primary teachers of their children, the program in both home and school group settings beginning before the child is born attempts to help parents become effective teachers of their children by helping to build their self-worth, teaching them skills to help optimize the child's physical, social, and intellectual development, to reduce their own stress, and to promote the pleasures of parenting.

- A four-year follow-up study found that children in the pilot program consistently scored 20 points higher on intelligence, achievement, and verbal language abilities than controls, regardless of environmental factors
  (in National Governors Association, 1987).

Cognitive Development and Social Competence

Garbarino (1989) offers insights that help explain why these programs show positive results. He first cites Sternberg, who speaks of three basic kinds of real life intelligence:

componential intelligence—analytic power; brain functions that make sense of perceptions, solve abstract problems, and process information

experiential intelligence—the ability to combine knowledge and ideas creatively and insightfully, creating new arrangements out of what one has experienced or learned; the ability to see relevant information in a situation; the ability to put facts together in a consistent way

contextual intelligence—the ability to understand a particular situation, to know what the environment's expectations are, and to arrange or meet or change those expectations, understanding how to make realities work toward one's goals.

Cognitive development allows these aspects of intelligence to flourish, nurture, and prosper.

The major threats to intelligence are early physical and sensory deprivations that suppress componential intelligence; repressive environments that stultify creativity and foster rigid thinking; and being sidetracked and dead-ended into social settings that are lacking in opportunities for dynamic and positive Interaction...
Child development is the process of becoming a fully functioning human being. A child's experience combines with a child's biological givens, and from this mixture emerges an adult person, one who will face the challenges of day to day life—as student, worker, friend, family member, and citizen. If they are to succeed in these roles as adults, children need to be rooted in the basic skills of modern life. They need to become socially competent. They must come to know who they are. They must have acquired a secure and positive sense of their own identity. In addition they must become proficient in thinking and speaking clearly. They must learn to understand the many ways people communicate with one another...

The child's capacity to experience trust depends upon an ability to recognize continuity and regularity in care and caregivers. To feel the world is a regular and safe place, the child must be able to know the basic behaviors required for mastery...

Beyond the demands of everyday social competence, children need a sense of curiosity to sustain cognitive development. They need to appreciate the fun experience of being alive. They should do more than just learn to read; they should be able to understand and enjoy literature, to take pleasure in reading, to want to read. They need to do more than just cope with human relationships. They should learn about a range of positive feelings, including love and friendship, as well as competition, anger, fear or dislike. In sum, they need to be able to do more than just exist. It is not impossible for any child to experience the emotions and perceptions associated with success, with creativity, with the sight of a blue sky, or the sound of a poem, with the rush of a dance, or the peace of reflection, or the satisfaction of helping someone else. To know all this, to have even a chance to develop fully, children need to spread their wings and fly, as much as they need to take root and live socially responsible lives. They need to develop in all three domains of intelligence (Garbarino, 1989, pp. 26-30).

Early attachment relationships form the foundation and are the training ground for subsequent relationships. Problems in early attachments lead to social problems, cognitive deficiencies and emotional difficulties.

If the home environment does not provide what the child needs or if destruction is done in that environment, we now know that this will not only be harmful to the child but also costly to society. If the family does not provide adequate cognitive and social stimulation, problems will also develop. Again, if we have to pay to later pick up the pieces, it means we would do well to intervene early, and to prevent. Because social relationships need to be developed outside the home, and because most children benefit from increased developmentally appropriate challenges, high quality socially based early childhood education could be available to all children. If it is not, many children will be behind before they even start. I remember Jesse Jackson's classic analogy of the late sixties, that if two people started out in a race, and one had on shackles and chains, would we think that fair? If children do not have an equal beginning in life, it is unfair.

11. Reflections on Quality Child Care and Early Childhood Education

Judy Pransky developed one of the first and longest-lasting "early compensatory education program in Vermont, the Caledonia Rural Early Education Program (CREEP), through the Caledonia Central Supervisory Union. She also began one of the first and largest Vermont employer-assisted day care centers, Cabot Playcare, through the Cabot Farmer's Cooperative Creamery. Judy now directs her own child care center, Emerson Falls Playcare in St. Johnsbury, Vermont, a center that includes an early education component, and during the summer a day camp in Cabot called Camp Laughing Turtle. Formerly, she served as teacher-principal at the Ira Allen Elementary School in Roxbury, Mass.

JP: Define "quality child care."

JuP: A registered day care center where a child is in a safe, nurturing environment; where the caregiving is focused on the needs of the child; where it's consistent and in tune with the values of a strong family.

JP: Is day care, per se, good for kids?

JuP: It can be excellent. Day care affords opportunities for many children who, without it, and because of rural isolation and the pressures of two working parents, would rarely socialize with children their own age, or gain experiences that help them get ready for school. When they're with other people they're learning how to share time and space. They're learning how to respect. They have opportunities to interact with their teachers, with their peers, and with different program materials, so they're becoming more able to perform the tasks awaiting them at school.

JP: Are you talking about day care itself, or day care with an early childhood education component?

JuP: I don't think there should be child care without an early education component.

JP: But many don't have it.

JuP: True. Lots of kids are in "day care," but that doesn't mean they're in registered, certified or licensed programs. Are you talking about a child who is with their next door neighbor or with grandma? That might be just as fine. It depends what's going on, and what kinds of opportunities there are for the children. Are they involved? What kind of thought goes into in making sure they're not sitting in front of the television all day? Is there guided interaction?

JP: Have you seen behavior changes as a result of kids being in your center?

JuP: Sure, but it depends who you're talking about. Children come into care for different reasons. The majority of kids are probably in care because their parents are working, and they need a place for their children to be. Most of those parents want the best setting for their kids that they can afford, but they don't have a lot of time to check the places out. Other kids are there because their parents are aware that they're not having any opportunity to interact with kids their own age and it's important for them to develop more language and social skills so they're not delayed for lack of experience when it's time for kindergarten or preschool. Then there's a much smaller group of kids who are in care because they've been determined to be in need of some kind of family support services, or because the children are at risk of neglect or abuse. It's with those kids that you see tremendous strides, because a lot of them arrive in pretty tough shape. They usually have very limited social skills and have a real tough time adjusting to other kids and to a setting that demands interaction, because they come from pretty unstimulating or needy home environments. For the kids who have been abused—the custody cases—you see tremendous changes because you may be the first stop for the two or three year old who's been in a really difficult home situation and is out of control.

JP: What kind of changes do you see?

JuP: Children begin to thrive in a situation that provides opportunities to learn and socialize. They begin to be in control of their own behavior. They get a sense even at a very early age that this is a fun place to be, but it's not so much fun if you're being outrageous or hurting others. So you learn how to cope with your feelings and how to be with other kids without being out of control or hurting them. They also benefit tremendously from the positive warmth and consistency of our care. We've had a number of children that come from really marginal situations and usually it takes them longer to adjust than it does for kids from a normal home, but once our center becomes their real anchor, they seem to be most secure with us. These are kids who have been bouncing around in the system, in foster placements. But all kids thrive here. **We see tremendous increases in language development and social skills. They learn to care for and respect each other**. It's very rewarding.

JP: Is it the child care or the early education component that makes the difference, or can they even be separated?

JuP: I think they're impossible to separate. The whole experience at Emerson Falls focuses on early childhood development and maximizing opportunities for positive interaction and learning. We provide a strong home-like atmosphere, along with a preschool. It's one total experience.

JP: Give me an example of some of the behaviors you've seen kids come in with, and what happens to them.

JuP: We see kids come with really antisocial behaviors like kicking, biting, pinching, screaming, throwing tantrums constantly—way beyond the typical two- or three-year-old craziness. They're filled with fear. They're often not well bonded to the person they're leaving, although sometimes even a child that's been abused is bonded to the mother in a real negative way. But we get kids who don't have healthy, secure, trusting relationships; and not only do we care for them, we can also help influence the mother or their primary caregiver to provide a secure, safe, positive, and supportive environment for the child. So we're at once trying to train the mom, and meet the child's needs.

JP: At the end of it, what do they do that they weren't doing before?

JuP: It takes a long time to gain the trust of a four year old, and sometimes we don't have a lot of time with at-risk kids because they get bounced around so much. But we've had some longer-term kids—infants and toddlers—that we've really had a powerful impact on. We've seen one child change from an angry, hurting, overweight, unhealthy baby who was not capable of even interacting on a momentary basis—no trust at all, didn't want to be held or cuddled, didn't want any kind of nurturing—to a child who just blossomed and became not only happy, but we discovered in there a child who wasn't tremendously deficit. He was incredibly bright. With a lot of work and a lot of focus he left us really happy, healthy, and whole. He went to an adoptive family, and I don't know that he would have been adopted by anybody when he came to us [laughter]. He was really a struggling little guy expressing incredible anger all the time, throwing things, hitting people, hurting, "don't touch me—don't get near me," and he turned out to be a bubble—a lot of fun. At two years old he could say the names of everyone in the center. He really became involved in "the family" aspect, the real closeness. Everybody absolutely loved him. And that's what he needed: a lot of security and a lot of loving.

JP: What does your staff actually do to help the kids change like that?

JuP: First, the staff members really care about what they do. Number two, they're there 100%. They're not with their heads somewhere else. The staff aren't making a lot of money, but they're really happy at what they're doing. They're really committed to the kids and their needs, no matter what those needs are, whether it be changing a diaper or wiping a nose or helping kids sort out conflicts. We work hard to be "up" and positive, nurturing, supportive, fair, consistent—making sure that all the kids get a sense that they really count and they're important and everyone is the center of attention. We try to meet each kid's needs, and each kid is different.

We have an older child right now who's really struggling. Dad's an alcoholic. Mom's finally kicked him out—for the last time, she says. And this kid's been bounced back and forth for years. She's seven years old and she's hurting. She can hardly conform to what's going on. But the way to support her is not to make her constantly conform, but to help her believe in her strengths and abilities...

JP: How do you do that?

JuP: She throws tantrums a lot, and spends a good deal of time in what we call "time out." If the children aren't able to cope with the group at the time, the teacher can say, "It's time for you to leave the group for a few minutes. Think of what's going on here, and come up with an idea of how you can do it differently, so you can come back and be with us and not be disruptive. If you're going to be here you need to help us to do this project," or whatever we're doing. Often, you can see her reaching a burnout place emotionally, and now she'll make this choice herself to go to time out and go through her tantrum, which she will do in a really loud and outrageous manner. Then she'll say, "I'm ready to talk to you now." Then she'll want more time to do something alone and, boom, she's ready. She goes back to the group, is real positive, is real happy about being there, really contributes to what they're doing, is helpful to everybody. She's beginning to get under control. Now she's not waiting for someone to say "You've had it." She's beginning to say, "I need to do this."

You have to handle each child differently. If we were to confront her, it would just escalate. But she's allowed the freedom to do it in her way. Other kids wouldn't be as productive on their own yet. I can see the difference in kids who've been with us a long time. They're at a different level of self-correcting their behaviors. If it isn't working with the group, those kids realize and haul their little buckets out of there and give it a break. It's rare for our teachers to be giving time-outs to the older kids, unless it's a sudden kind of conflict that gets a little physical. But the kids are able to learn this over time because of the consistency of our staff.

JP: How are you able to keep your staff around?

JuP: One of the things I do initially is really know the people I hire. The couple of times I've gone against my inner judgment, I've regretted it. Then, as a director, I may not be able to offer as high a salary or as many benefits as a lot of businesses, but I have a lot of respect for the people who work for me. I don't have to take credit for all the good ideas that happen. It's a team effort. Together we share the responsibility, we share the blame, we share the credit. We share everything.

JP: What about money? Why are day care providers paid so little, and you and many day care centers always in danger of going under?

JuP: **That's the real negative thing about child care: the pay and benefits are so low. It's a struggle to be in a profession that has such little regard for you that people leave it as soon as they can—figure out some way of making money. Part of it is, you cannot charge what it costs, because it's totally unaffordable.** I figure it costs at least $85-$90 per week [in 1990] to care for a child—just to break even, to pay everyone there, to pay the director. Most of the people who direct child care centers don't get paid. They put in their time and their services— many of them work 10 or 11 hours a day and do all the bookkeeping and all the accounting and all the business management and all the curriculum development, all that stuff—and they don't get paid. If I were doing what I do here for some corporation, I'd be making a bundle. That's not going to happen in this business. There are fixed costs for renting a building, paying the utilities, running a program, paying for the food, paying for the administrative and office expenses. Then there are educational materials and supplies (which is where most programs take a beating), and repair and maintenance and upgrading the facility. Then there's salaries and payroll expenses, which is the greatest expense. A lot of programs go out of business because they can barely meet the costs, which are almost 100% of income, and they can't approach the costs of buying the materials and supplies they need, so they're struggling all the time to meet the expenses, scrounge materials, forego that piece of special equipment, and they don't feel good about what they're doing. So the creative end of the educational experience for kids never gets fulfilled. Along the way, people are being paid fairly low salaries...

What can I offer to offset that? I try to offer benefits far beyond what most day care centers offer. Most of our staff are able to get two to three weeks paid vacation and ten paid holidays. And their time is flexible. If anyone comes in saying, "I'd like to have the day off, I'm having company over," or "my kid is sick," or "my kid is playing in a basketball game," whatever, we all cooperate in finding a way to switch people around. Everyone understands. Everybody's really happy with that.

JP: How much of a difference do the subsidies make that come from the state for family support day care, and federal lunch subsidies?

JuP: **Right now the federal food subsidy is what's between us and falling apart.** I don't take a salary. I take what I can to get by on. The center itself, given its income against expenses on a weekly basis, is in the black by about $26. If anything breaks or goes wrong, we've had it. Our income from the federal food program is close to $750 per month. That's the money that's between us and disaster. When we don't have to spend other money on food, we can afford to maintain things and do unforeseen repairs. Recently we had a freeze-up in our water system that had to be dealt with. Where would that $200 a month come from? It gives us flexibility to buy program materials, and it affords me some kind of compensation, so I'm not absolutely starving, but sometimes it's close.

JP: What about for the kids?

JuP: I've always been committed to serving tremendously nutritious, well-prepared, well-thought-out meals. A lot of these kids need it. They get shuffled in early in the morning. They haven't eaten much of a breakfast. They have their best meals, I think, at the day care. Many of the kids at first have a hard time getting used to the fresh foods and whole foods they get at the center, because they're used to Spaghettios and hot dogs. That's what's on the table at night when you pick up your kid from a hard days work and land home at six and have to do everything and get kids in bed by seven because you've got to get them up at six the next day. We're giving those kids the benefit of a good solid start that they wouldn't get anywhere else. We have one of the best health records around, and we're really proud of it. We're always cleaning and disinfecting. Our procedures are focused that way. Our food program is solid nutrition all the way. Because we're on the federally subsidized food program we haven't had to raise our rates, which is really important because folks are at the limit of what they can afford to pay for child care, even though we're always at the edge of it ourselves.

JP: What does it mean when the state comes along and suddenly takes away your "family support child care?"

JuP: These are kids whose families qualify because there's an index of risk. There may be alcoholism in the home, or marginal care. It's not an open, "protective services" case, but **these families have been identified as needing services. These kids are going to be at risk. They are the future problems that the state is going to have to take care of.** There may not be room for them in the Head Start programs. The state …[in 1990]…eliminated or froze those funds— I'm not sure which—because of a budget crunch. It means two things. For some centers it's meant a 20% loss in income, or else the percentage wasn't as high but it meant something— probably a couple of hundred dollars a week. That really hurts, because you're talking about programs right on the edge. Centers need to replace that income somehow.

But what it means to the kids is even more important, because these kids are now at home, back in those marginal situations, not having an opportunity to experience a healthy environment. The families aren't having the same kind of contact on a regular basis with the outside world. They don't have to maintain a level of care or a standard of nurturing, because nobody's supporting and assisting them, so the kids are thrown back into a risky situation with no monitoring at all. I think the day care has played that critical role, but the center has suddenly lost income. A lot of families, children and child care centers have suffered.

JP: What should parents look for in choosing a child care center?

JuP: Number one, the qualifications of the people who will be providing care. They should know whether they're looking at a state-licensed facility that is, whether the state is overseeing the program and the health and the environment of the center or home. They should be aware of the policies, like nurturing the child. What kinds of experiences are available there? How does center discipline work: is there corporal punishment? Are they in a safe environment: is the place well-maintained and clean, are there dangers around, is the door locked? To what extent can the center meet their needs? To what extent are they encouraged to participate? What happens if the kids get sick? A lot of kids are in care where none of this has been taken into consideration. There's been a real push to register private homes.

JP: You worked in early compensatory education. What's important about that?

JuP: When I was developing that program **I discovered that many of the kids who suffer from delays: language delays, visual-motor delays, fine and gross motor delays as young children, will later, without some kind of intervention, experience failure in school or will at least not have a positive school experience.** Those kids are everywhere in Vermont. It has as

111

much to do with being isolated as having a lack of opportunity within the environment itself. These kids aren't interacting with other kids in many instances. So across the board, instead of having maybe 20% with language deficits, you have 43% with developmental-languagedeficits. And these kids are really going to have a tough time when they get to school. They're going to be behind. And they're going to be unsuccessful at doing whatever task is required of them. So they're not going to have a positive first experience with school, and that will be the benchmark for the rest of their experiences at school. Early compensatory education allows for early identification and intervention for kids with those needs. Even the most normal kids, or the kids who have every opportunity available to them, have those needs because they can still have developmental delays. Without support, these kids will have insurmountable problems when they get to school.

JP: Should early compensatory education be required everywhere for all kids?

JuP: **There should be a system of universal screening or assessment to identify children who need early intervention**.

JP: If they then find that a kid has a problem, what should happen?

JuP: **The optimum would be a combination of home-based and center-based experiences to assist the parent with parenting and work with a child to provide the experiences he or she needs, because most of what kids need enhancement in are things they could be doing right within their own homes**—counting and sorting silverware, playing with pebbles and egg cartons, stacking cans. Those things are all available. Then the children need to experience situations where they have an opportunity to interact with other kids and learn social skills and language skills, and hear stories with a group of kids and act out "Three Little Pigs" with puppets.

JP: Are the parents in attendance for that?

JuP: It's very beneficial for the parents to be there, for two reasons. First, they can see more things to do with their kids. Second, they can have some time themselves to socialize with other parents, and be in a setting that says, this is a really positive and valuable experience for everybody, including you and your child. The parents get a chance to share concerns and needs, which doesn't happen as much anymore because 70% of the moms are at work.

JP: What could you see that told you that program worked?

JuP: There was a quantifiable drop in the number of kids requiring education Title I services. In the past, these kids weren't identified. They would come to kindergarten and be struggling and might stay back or be shoved on to first grade and not quite make it. Once the program began, all sorts of things suddenly started happening. The school system realized they needed to raise the entry age to school so kids didn't have to come when they weren't developmentally ready. By pushing that date back to September instead of January, it allowed kids to be more developmentally ready when they arrived at school. People began to understand children's needs in terms of development, not in terms of Special Ed., not in terms that this kid is deficit or mentally retarded. This kid just lacks experiences, so we can address it in a different way. There's less entry into Special Ed.. Through their screening Special Ed. picked up right away that kids who would have ended up in Special Ed. in third or fourth grade were having positive school experiences; they felt good about themselves; they were willing to struggle harder to get it together; their families were willing to participate in the struggle to a greater extent than they had before; and there were lower numbers in our Special Ed. programs. The percentage of kids with needs didn't change, but they were addressed at an earlier age, so they didn't enter school with big deficits. They came ready.

JP: Give me an example of a situation that particularly stands out for you..

JuP: In one family of three children, I screened the middle child. There was a two-year-old, a four-year-old, and a handicapped eight-year-old who had never attended school. The four-year-old was incredibly language deficient, very shy, didn't know colors, didn't know concepts, had low cognitive skills. But her mother was pretty articulate, and I couldn't put the two together. I met her father and he was okay. Mom was pretty together but really nervous. I got to the home and saw the eight-year-old sitting in an old straight back chair like you see in the old mental institution movies. She'd been totally paraplegic, mentally retarded since about nine months old when she had a misdiagnosis of some illness, was mismedicated, and became severely brain damaged. Mom is attending to her every need and trying to cope with two toddlers with virtually no contact outside the home. The kids had no contact with children their own age.

I did an intervention with the family for a year, on every aspect of what was going on. Then I got them to the center-based program and continued to deliver services twice a week in the home. The mother had never been informed about ways and strategies to deal with the issues, like getting respite care, a modern orthopedic chair that mom could get in and out of her car so she could take the kids out and go shopping or go to church with the whole family. The four year old had a struggle for the first couple of years because she was really shy and lived a very limited and isolated life stuck out in the boonies, but today she's in the seventh grade, she's a top honors student, she plays basketball, they've become active and involved socially. Both younger children were ready to go to school and not struggle. Their first in-school experiences were positive where, otherwise, they may have been extremely negative. They continued to develop positive self-images.

JP: Have you seen a lot of kids blossom who were questionable, now that they've gone through school?

JuP: Yes, and become really successful. The program itself is the longest-running early compensatory education program in the state. When it came time to cut programs due to budget cuts, the towns wanted to keep this one, because they knew it worked.

JP: What do you actually do with the kids in the program?

JuP: Pretty much the same thing that happens in our day care early childhood education program, plus screening all kids in a district. We provide a whole array of integrated experiences and language and motor development that address the specific learning delay of that kid.

JP: So the only difference between general early education and compensatory education is you screen the kids, get to know what's wrong, then design something based specifically on what their deficit is.

JuP: Yes. And seeing the results of this approach is very rewarding. I sometimes question why I'm in this crazy business, and it's because of the rewards I see with kids and their families. It's very rewarding to help parents acquire the skills to assist their children through the early developmental stages. It's extremely rewarding to see children and families having positive early educational experiences and not having negative and isolating first school experiences that are so easily avoided by early identification and intervention strategies. **You find some people who are very resistant. Some people aren't willing to hear that their child has a deficit. This is hard for me, because they eventually experience the results when their kids have to stay back or aren't able to function well in school.**

9/90

113

12. Parent Skills Education[*]

We all want our children to behave as we wish, but very often they drive us crazy. We don't want teenagers to use alcohol or other drugs, become pregnant, commit delinquent acts, develop eating disorders or commit suicide. Yet they do—in staggering numbers. We don't want them to become child abusers and sexual abusers, yet if trends continue, many of them will. We want our children to become healthy, capable human beings who reach their full potential.

It is difficult to believe we can change things when we often feel powerless—where so many forces are waiting to direct our children into unhealthy activities.

However, research has shown that parents can make a difference in the way their children behave, The problem is, rarely have they been taught how. From the moment they bring their baby into the world everyone mistakenly assumes that parents automatically know what to do. Most of what parents know was learned from watching and experiencing their parents. Ironically, this seems to have become part of us, whether we liked it or not.

It is rare these days to live in an extended family where we can watch generations participate in bringing up children and learn from that experience, thereby preparing us for parenthood. Nothing has replaced this, yet we are still expected to perform our parental roles perfectly and raise children who do not cause problems.

Unfortunately, when we have so much to do and so little time, we sometimes unintentionally cause our children to feel bad. We may not even be aware of what we're doing, but if negative feelings grow, behavior problems could develop. It's not our fault that we don't know how to produce desired behaviors in our children, but if we want anything to change it is our responsibility. These days we must go out of our way to compensate for what used to happen naturally.

Thanks to people who formulated the basis for and authored parent education programs, a set of principles has recently become clear about how to effectively guide young people to develop constructive, healthy behaviors. If we want our children to behave as we wish, we would be more likely to succeed if we follow certain principles of interacting with and disciplining them.

---

[*] Note: Parts of this chapter originally appeared as "Skills for Parents" papers, Pransky, 1989.

115

The Research

In 1987, Dr. Kerby Alvy performed a great service to the parent education field by pulling together much of what was known about parent training up to that time. He reviewed many of the popular programs and available research and cited many studies that showed ineffective parenting to be an important contributing factor to many social and health problems, among them-

- abused and neglected children
- substance abusing children
- delinquency and crime
- poor academic performance
- poor social and school adjustment
- emotional disturbance

While many factors contribute to the way parents function (such as parental attitudes and skills, knowledge of child development, parents' and children's unique characteristics, cultural and religious values, stress and supports in the parent's life including household, marital, and job-related factors), extensive studies by Belsky, Macoby and Martin, Coopersmith, Rohner, Wolfe and others helped Alvy (1987) identify two dimensions of parenting that appear to be most important in child-rearing. These are:

* a large amount of love, acceptance, warmth of the parent toward the child

- satisfaction (with the child's abilities and characteristics)
- high involvement (seeking out and enjoying the company of the child)
- high responsiveness (providing positive reinforcement)
- sensitivity to the child's needs (add: perceptions and feelings)
- open communication (listening to the child's point of view as well as expressing one's own)

* a moderate to high level of restrictive control

- clear standards of behavior
- rules and consequences for violations rules firmly and consistently enforced
- coercive demands rarely given in to
- mature behavior expected (at the appropriate developmental level)
- independence and individuality encouraged
- good modeling of parental behavior and how parents resolve conflicts

"Study after study reflects that this pattern is associated with" children who display-

- high self-esteem and self-confidence
- emotional stability
- independence
- competence in social and academic areas

- appropriate self-assertion social responsibility
- ability to control aggression

Macoby and Martin (in Alvy, 1987) state that this style of parenting can be generally distinguished from three other patterns associated with inappropriate child behaviors:

1. *Authoritarian/autocratic* parenting: strict, unbending limits, edicts, and suppression, coupled with fairly severe, and often physical punishment—was found to contribute to withdrawal or out-of-control behavior, lack of spontaneity and social initiative, low motivation for intellectual performance (in boys), low self-esteem, a feeling of lack of control over the environment.

2. *Indulgent/permissive* parenting: tolerant and accepting of child impulses, few demands for mature behavior, few rules, overly indulgent—was associated with impulsive behavior, aggressive behavior, lack of responsibility.

3. *Indifferent/uninvolved* parenting: detached, emotionally uninvolved and psychologically unavailable, self-absorbed—yielded impulsive behavior, aggressive outbursts, lack of frustration tolerance, inability to concentrate, moodiness, hedonism, lack of long-term goals, truancy, drinking, smoking, and dating at earlier ages, and drinking to excess, arrest records.

Children from these homes are more likely to be anxious, hostile, insecure, or emotionally unstable. These children often feel inadequate and generalize those feelings, seeing the world as unfriendly, hostile, and unpleasant.

A critical issue for prevention, then, is how to build constructive patterns and minimize destructive patterns within the home environment.

Parent Training (or "Parent Education" or "Parenting") Programs

"Parent training" courses use a small-group format to teach parents how to deal with a wide range of child-rearing problems and challenges. They use a variety of role-playing and multimedia techniques to improve parental performance. Parent education courses help parents appreciate their children's unique qualities and to recognize their similarities. They help parents teach children how to relate successfully to others, including the parents. They attempt to promote and teach parenting patterns associated with healthy child development and functioning, high self-esteem, and stable social adjustment (Alvy, 1987).

Do Parent Training Programs Work?

In a comprehensive review of studies on results of parent training programs, Alvy concluded that they are "a critical strategy in preventing mental-emotional disabilities, delinquency, alcohol and drug abuse, and abuse and neglect."

Unfortunately, research in this area is quite muddy. Parent training programs cannot claim with certainty that they lead parents to assume the healthier patterns, nor can most demonstrate that behavior changes in children are the result of parents training. Yet, successful outcomes have been reported by many families, even dysfunctional, abusive, underclass families of different cultures. Evaluation studies have been generally positive but have left many unanswered questions.

The overall pattern of results, emerging as it does from such a wide range of programs and with such varied populations of parents, is very encouraging in light of the...inherent limitations of short-term programs, the complexity and costliness of conducting outcome studies, and the multiple determinants of parenting behavior, and child development. When these programs are used by themselves they are up against great odds in terms of being able to demonstrate measurable and sustained effects on parental functioning and child development. Yet the majority of outcome studies provide evidence that all of these programs produce some effects, though different programs seem to produce different effects... There need to be more and better research studies, studies where booster sessions or other forms of continued involvement are used... (Alvy, 1987a, pp. 128-29).

It is clear...that some parents in some programs appear to gain a great deal from participating. We know from our own studies that some parents transform their relationships with their children in very dramatic ways, while others do not (Alvy, 1987b, p. 138).

Although results of outcome studies on parent education courses are inconsistent, it appears that the majority of parents change their attitudes and behavior in the direction of the "authoritative/reciprocal" parenting model. There is enough evidence of effectiveness to warrant their use as a prevention strategy for parents.

Without the luxury of longitudinal studies to determine effectiveness over time, the true test of a parenting course's effectiveness lies at the most basic level: Is the behavior of children improving for parents involved in the program? This is relatively easy to assess through before/after measures based on parental perceptions of children's behavior. Unfortunately, few parent training programs ask participants this question as a standard part of program evaluation.

I needed to learn this for myself when embarking on teaching the *Developing Capable People* course (Glenn, 1983;1988). 1 needed to be sure the course would change children's behaviors for the better, so I insisted on before/after measures. Before the class started, I asked the parents to list the three behaviors of their children that troubled them most, what the parent's usual response was, the usual outcome, and approximately how many times per week those behaviors occurred. At the end of the course I asked the same questions about those troubling behaviors. When I began to train instructors for Developing Capable People, I collected their data on the same questions.

I collected data on 45 Developing Capable People courses affecting 409 parents. Results showed a 72% reduction in the number of times per week these most troubling behaviors for parents occurred. In addition, 92% of these parents stated that their children's behavior improved as a result of the course, and 91% of the parents said that their own behavior in dealing with their children had changed. While not thoroughly scientific, when similar results are repeated over time, one can surmise that it has something to do with the content and process of the Developing Capable People course.

Other parenting courses have yielded data that imply effectiveness. A "meta-analysis-of *Parent Effectiveness Training (PET)* programs showed measurable effects on parental behavior and on children's self-esteem (Levant, 1983). In a similar evaluation of *Systematic Training For Effective Parenting (STEP)*, 80% of the participants said the course helped them improve their communication with their children, and 61% said the course lessened conflict (Dinkmeyer, 1981). A study comparing STEP and PET said behaviors considered to be problems for parents decreased significantly in both courses (in Dinkmeyer and McKay, 1988). STEP was also found to work for parents from Korea (Huang, 1988).

Course authors have produced other data through their own "field tests" or "pilot studies." In results from 35 groups of participants in the *Active Parenting* course, 84% of parents reported improvement in their children's behavior, and 97% reported positive behavior changes in their own parenting (Popkin, 1984). For the *Nurturing Program*, 58% had been involved with child abuse or neglect prior to participation; one year after the course only 16% were still receiving child abuse/neglect-related services. There was also a significant increase in age-appropriate behaviors, gains in empathy, and use of methods of punishment other than corporal punishment (Bavolek et al., 1983).

In the *Confident Parenting* course, a longer-term evaluation showed that 52% of participants were still using the techniques at 6 months, 47% at 12 months, and 39% at 24 months. Significant correlations were also found between performance on outcome measures and parental attendance (Alvy, 1987). Alvy also provides evidence that the standard courses show positive effects for poverty-level Black and Mexican parents, for whom they were not originally designed. The courses were perceived to be very helpful for many attending parents. However, courses specifically designed for these populations would be better [Chapter 30].

The Parenting Courses

The first modern parenting course was probably-

- *Parent Effectiveness Training* (PET), created by Thomas Gordon (1971) and based on Rogerian psychology.

Other early courses were:

- *Systematic Training for Effective Parenting (STEP)*, created by Dinkmeyer and McKay (1976), based on Adlerian psychology and Rudolph Dreikurs
- A few early behaviorally-oriented courses, among them work by Patterson (1971, 1975), and *Confident Parenting* by Aitchison (1976), based on the work of B. F. Skinner.

A number of other courses have since sprung up, particularly in the past few years. Notable among them are (in approximate order of their creation):

- *Developing Capable People* (originally called *Developing Capable Young People*) (Glenn, 1983), research based, but drawing upon works of Dreikurs, Gordon, and others.
- *Active Parenting* (Popkin, 1983), based on Dreikurs and, to a lesser extent, Gordon's work
- *The Nurturing Program for Parents and Children* (Bavolek and Comstock, 1984), based to some extent on principles of Behaviorism
- *How to Talk So Kids Will Listen, How to Listen So Kids Will Talk*, based on the work of Chaim Ganot (Faber and Maslisch, 1984)

- *Preparing for the Drug-Free Years* (Hawkins et al., 1985), based on "risk factor" research
- *Effective Black Parenting* (Alvy et al., 1987), based on Confident Parenting. *Los Ninos Bien Educados* (Alvy et al., 1987), based on Confident Parenting
- *Positive Discipline* (Nelsen, 1981; Nelsen, 1988), based on Dreikurs

There are lesser-known courses and many other combinations too numerous to list.

Subsequently, many authors of these courses came out with further packages for specific populations, and some revised their original packages. To cite a few, PET updated itself and called itself *Parent Effectiveness*. STEP came out with *STEP Teen, the Next STEP* (a postparenting course), and *New Beginnings for Single Parents*. Active Parenting developed *Active Parenting for Teens* and *Family Talk* (for home-based "self-study"). The Nurturing Program put together ... *Birth to Five Years. . . Parents and Adolescents*, and ... for *Teenage Parents and Their Families* courses. Some of the courses have been translated into Spanish, like STEP's *PECES*.

There is no perfect parenting course. The courses cited above are all pretty good. My personal favorite has been Glenn's *Developing Capable People*, provided it is taught with a minimum of tape listening and a maximum of role playing. It is grounded in research, and many have found it the most personally challenging of all the courses. [Now I am partial to courses based upon my own work (no surprise there!), *Parenting from the Heart* (Pransky, 1997) which operates without a curriculum and therefore tends to be more flexible than the rest, and points parents to their own innate wisdom in raising kids and dealing with problem behaviors in lieu of techniques.]

All parenting courses have been criticized for one thing or another, whether it be too White middle class, too cerebral, too many big words, too complex for use with highly dysfunctional and abusive families, geared for too young an age group, too long, too sexist, or too stilted. I am not one for throwing out the baby with the bath-water; after all, there is so much of worth in these courses. I suggest cutting out the few objectionable parts and making them be what the instructor wants. No matter what the course, most of the learning takes place during role plays, practicing the new techniques on the kids back home, and receiving feedback on how it worked. Beware of programs that don't provide opportunities for hands-on work with the concepts, or ones that are insulting to kids (which is a matter of perception, but parts of the *You've Got to Be Kid-ding* program strike me that way).

How does one make sense of all this? **First, what works in raising children is basically the same, no matter what one calls it or how it is packaged.** Second, certain courses may work better for parents of younger or older children. Third, parents have different learning styles, and some courses may fit some parents better. This implies that a variety of courses, available periodically within a geographical area, may be the best approach.

Alvy (1987) offers a summary review of many of these programs but does not include Developing Capable People, How to Talk So Kids Will Listen..., Preparing for the Drug-Free Years, or Positive Discipline. Rather than repeat Alvy's review, it may be more productive to identify some common and important parental practices toward children that are promoted in these courses.

Karol Kumpfer (1998) concluded that "comprehensive family programs that combine social and life skills training to children and youth to improve their social and academic competencies with parent skills training programs to improve supervision and nurturance are the most effective in impacting a broader range of family risk and protective factors for drug use" (p.5). She claims there is no single best family intervention program. For providers to select family programs for implementation, she suggests that the following criteria are useful:

♦ Comprehensive interventions are more effective in modifying a broader range of risk or protective factors and processes in children.
♦ Family-focused programs are more effective than child-focused or parent-focused only.
♦ Sufficient dosage or intensity is critical for effectiveness.
♦ Family programs should be long-term and enduring.
♦ Tailoring the parent or family intervention to the cultural traditions of the families involved improves recruitment, retention, and outcome effectiveness.
♦ Addressing developmentally appropriate risk and protective factors or processes at specific times of family need when participants are receptive to change is important.
♦ Family programs are most enduring in effectiveness if they produce changes in the ongoing family dynamics and environment.
♦ If parents are very dysfunctional, interventions beginning early in the lifecycle (i.e., prenatally or early childhood) are more effective.
♦ Components of effective parent and family programs include addressing strategies for improving family relations, communication, and parental monitoring.
♦ High rates of recruitment and retention are possible with families if transportation, meals or snacks, and child care are provided.
♦ Videos of families demonstrating good and bad parenting skills helps with program effectiveness and client satisfaction.
♦ The effectiveness of the program is highly tied to the trainer's personal efficacy and characteristics.
(Kumpfer, 1998, pp. 9-14).

Kumpfer and Szapocznik co-chaired a panel of experts who determined that there is sufficient research evidence to conclude that for prevention only Behavioral Parent Training or Family Skills Training have a "strong level of evidence of effectiveness" (Kumpfer, 1998, p. 6). Family skills training involves behavioral parent training, social skills training for children, behavioral family therapy, and family role plays with coaching by the trainer. These programs usually target high-risk families, and they tend to have a positive impact on a large number of family and youth risk and protective factors. Examples of family skills training programs are:

- *Strengthening Families Program* (Kumpfer, et al., 1989; Kumpfer, et al., 1996; Kumpfer, et al., 1997)
- *Focus on Families:* For physically and sexually abusive families (Haggerty et al., 1991)
- *Families and Schools Together (FAST):* For high-risk students in school (McDonald, et al., 1991)
- *Family Effectiveness Training (FET):* To prevent drug abuse and problem behaviors in Hispanic adolescents. (Szapocznik et al., 1989a)
- *The Nurturing Program* (Bavolek, et al., 1983).

Other programs cited were more family therapy-related and treatment-related programs.

Does this mean that other parenting programs do not cut the mustard and should be rejected in the name of prevention? Absolutely not! It may only mean that they have not been as well-researched. Further, some new parenting approaches such as *Parenting from the Heart* (Pransky, 1997) were not examined by Kumpher's expert panel; in fact, this inside-out approach is too different to be included in the review below, as well.

Parenting Course Differences and Similarities

My conclusion is that most of the principles of effective parenting espoused in these courses are basically the same. Some may offer more than others, but no matter what the different emphases and general philosophic underpinnings of the different programs, they ultimately offer similar principles of effective potential behavior. Alvy (1987) tends to emphasize more differences in the courses than I would, and no doubt the authors and instructors of the various courses would be quick to point out the unique qualities of their own programs.

Before emphasizing the common principles, a few key philosophical and other differences are important to note. One of the most important distinctions lies between programs based on Behaviorist principles (Confident Parenting and its culturally relevant stepchildren, Effective Black Parenting and Los Ninos Bien Educados, and to a lesser extent The Nurturing Program), and most other programs. Behaviorally-based programs espouse that parents should manage their children's behaviors through use of rewards and punishment and attention withdrawal. Other courses frown upon this or ignore it.

A second, more subtle distinction concerns the use of praise. Some courses such as The Nurturing Program push the use of praise; others like Confident Parenting suggest using "specific" praise (telling the child specifically what s/he is being praised for). Others like STEP make the distinction between praise and "specific encouragement," and Developing Capable People says general praise can actually do harm because the child is left with the insecurity of now knowing how to produce that feeling again. Semantics? Perhaps. But the distinctions are important.

A third major difference among the programs is that the Parent Effectiveness model shuns the use of what they consider to be "control-based" methods of dealing with young people (including even "logical consequences," as used by STEP, Developing Capable People, Active Parenting, and Positive Discipline). PET favors a "no-lose, mutual-problem-solving" approach, and "natural consequences" (as used in other courses). They object to the imposition of consequences that they see as "controlling." Others would disagree that they are controlling—it depends how they're used. Most other courses use a problem-solving approach similar to PET, in addition to logical consequences. Developing Capable People insists that the decisions be in the child's hands, because when consequences are understood in advance, the young person then decides how she or he will act, accordingly.

Most other program differences are largely structural: length of course (6-21 sessions), target audience (parents of younger kids vs. older kids vs. mixed), type of presentation (audio/video/film strip/instructor), use of instructor "script" vs. a more general structure, and packaging (from the slick productions of Active Parenting at one extreme to the loosely structured Developing Capable People, which is usually reflected in the price). These all relate to parent learning styles and instructor preference.

Breaking Old Patterns

Old patterns are hard to break. But **by learning common principles inherent in these parenting skills courses, and how to apply them, we can make a difference in our children's behaviors**.

As parents, we are faced with two important questions:

1. How can we help our children achieve what we want for them?
2. How can we help our children behave the way we want them to?

Our Children Need a Set of Healthy Self-Perceptions and Skills

The answers lie in developing the critical perceptions and skills in children outlined in Chapter 5. The list below states these in a slightly different way, and also incorporates Glasser's "basic needs" from Chapter 4.

Healthy self-perceptions:

1. I am a worthwhile and competent person, capable of figuring things out for myself. I can make it without being dependent on others.
2. I am important. I belong. I am a significant contributing part of, or have a stake in, something greater than myself. My life has meaning.
3. I have power to affect what happens to me. I have control over my life. I have freedom.
4. I am loved and cared for. I have support
5. I have fun in my life. I can have fun in legitimate ways.

Plus, the *skills* to:

6. handle ourselves from within, as in self-discipline
7. interact with others, as in communication, cooperation, negotiation
8. deal with the world around us, as in responsibility
9. deal with abstract concepts (safe-dangerous, right-wrong, appropriate-inappropriate, good-bad, values), as in judgment

Babies are born completely dependent. Left on their own they will die. As children grow and develop, they have to acquire these self-perceptions and skills. Our job as parents, if we want our children to behave appropriately and be reasonably successful in the world, is to help these healthy perceptions and skills emerge.

The healthy perceptions and skills and the principles of behavior that follow are the same no matter what one's culture. Different cultures only apply the principles differently, based on their unique cultural styles, beliefs, and values. However, beyond the principles, these may be additional cultural content that could enhance the effectiveness of the course, for example, in Effective Black Parenting (see Chapter 30).

123

Remembering That Perception Is the Key

If we want to change our children's behavior, we must first try to understand their perceptions. Once we come close to this understanding, we can work with their perception.

In any given situation, or with any problem, if we have the presence of mind to ask ourselves, "What are all the choices I have in dealing with this? What will my kid's perception likely be for each action I could take?" we will usually do okay in dealing with them. This is probably the most important thing we can keep in mind in raising children.

Each of us has a choice about how we deal with our children. How they behave depends largely on the choice we make.

Modeling

Contrary to popular opinion, children learn very little from what we tell them; they learn almost everything from the behaviors we model. If we want them to behave in ways we want, we would do best to set the examples we want to see. If we demand that our child keep a clean bedroom, we would do well to keep our own bedrooms clean. If we want our kids not to yell and scream, we would do well not to yell and scream. If we want our kids to treat others in a respectful and caring way, we would do best to relate to them in a respectful and caring way. If we want our kids not to smoke cigarettes, we would do well not to smoke.

Seeing Every Problem as an Opportunity

People often dislike hearing this, but every problem or situation that presents itself is an opportunity to build any one or a combination of the healthy self-perceptions and life skills.

Although we cannot always think this clearly at the time, whenever a problem arises we have a choice. We can either respond by treating our kids in ways that build healthy perceptions, or we can wipe them out (usually not intentionally). But by adhering to the parenting principles listed in this chapter, we will come closer to building healthy perceptions than destroying them. The payoff is, our kids will usually treat us better and do better in return.

Using the Right Moment to Teach—But What Do We Do When We're Angry?

Not every moment is the right moment to teach. Obviously, when danger is present is not the time to stop and analyze. At those times the first order of business is to avoid harm or control the situation. Another inappropriate time to teach is when emotions are high, either our kid's or ours. This is especially true when we're angry.

When angry, we can express that anger and say or pound anything we feel like, so long as no one else is around—especially our kids. The idea is to gain control so we don't take our frustrations out on them. No one is at his or her best when angry, and we can often unintentionally do harm at these times. It helps to step back and gain some perspective.

If we must say something right then, it would be best to say, "I'm too angry to talk right now; we'll talk later." Or, "I'm really upset about this; we'll discuss it in the morning." We should also do the same when our child is upset: "I can see you're upset; we'll talk later."

All of us get angry. It is a legitimate and real emotion. It is healthy to express it. But others shouldn't have to suffer just because we're out of control.

The Appropriate Response at the Appropriate Age

As parents we need to understand that kids are simply incapable developmentally of doing certain things at some ages. Knowing helps us deal with them. Consider these brief, general rules of thumb:

Ages 0-4. These children operate by instinct. They respond to immediate stimulus-response. It is natural for little children to explore their world and get into things. If what they are doing is inappropriate, we need to show them by saying something like, "Honey, that's something you shouldn't do. If you do, here's what will happen... "And, "I like it when you do that."

Ages 5-6. These children are able to delay their responses a little. They can deal with immediate implications (What will happen to me now if I do this now?). At this stage it's appropriate to give a cue and delay the negative response a bit. "If you're doing something you shouldn't, I'll count to three and if you're still doing it, here's what will happen."

Ages 6-8. These children can begin to understand cause and effect (What could be possible outcomes for me?). "If you don't pick up your toys, you can't be in here playing."

Ages 8-12 and on up. These kids are usually capable of dealing with abstract concepts, and can understand how someone else might feel. They can begin to deal with values and morals. They can respond to reasonable consequences.

Ages 13-17. Sometimes it seems like teenagers forget everything they've ever learned. Their bodies and minds are undergoing extreme, rapid change. They become selfish because they're trying to figure out who they are. This is natural; we shouldn't take it personally.

At every stage its natural for kids to push the limits to see how far they can go. Within certain clear limits, kids need to explore and learn for themselves, provided there is no danger. Taking responsibility for them can only go so far; eventually they will have to be off to living their own lives.

There's No Such Thing as a Perfect Parent

Raising children can be the hardest job any of us will ever do if we have never been taught parenting, and most of us have not. Under these circumstances it is a wonder most of us do as well as we do. There is no reason to think parents should be perfect. We aren't. We all blow it with our kids sometimes. But Jane Nelsen says, "Mistakes are wonderful opportunities to learn." And as Steve Glenn says, "If we can just do one of these things one time during the course of the year, it is 100% better than not doing them at all." However, the more we use them, the better off we will be.

Learning New Skills Takes Practice

As parents we each have our own natural behavioral responses. It is possible to learn other ways of responding, but we must also have the opportunity to test out and practice our newly learned responses, preferably in a safe environment. Then we can practice enough so these new ways become our natural response. [Note: I now realize that when parents' minds calm down they generally know what to do because they access their own wisdom, and it becomes unnecessary to practice or even to remember the principles listed below. For those interested in this new, inside-out approach, which makes it much easier for the parents, see *Parenting from the Heart* (Pransky, 1997, 2001)].

Creating Conditions in the Home That Promote Healthy Behavior

As parents, we all want children to behave as we want. Most of us want them to be responsible, not embarrass us in public, be self-disciplined, use good judgment, and generally do what we tell them to do. We can increase this probability by developing the kind of atmosphere or conditions in our home where children will be most responsive to our disciplinary practices. If we ensure that our children gain healthy perceptions, they will be more likely to act in desirable ways.

In the first edition of this book, I listed what I called the principles of effective parenting, gleaned from the aforementioned parenting courses, and I then provided an explanation for each. Here I will only list the principles and point readers to the appendix of *Parenting from the Heart* (Pransky, 1997; 2001) If they are interested in the detail. The reason: This is not the type of book that people seek out when they want information about parenting.

Principles of effective parenting

- *Begin with the child's perception (then share ours)*
- *Help young people explore and analyze situations, and make plans*
- *Encourage (for little things done well)*
- *Communicate unqualified love and respect*
- *Give clear, specific feedback about the good and bad one does by using statements that include: I feel... about... because...*
- *Check to be sure both parties understand each other correctly and understand the realities of a situation*
- *Help children better understand their own feelings (particularly when they experience a problem) and treat all feelings as legitimate*
- *Structure opportunities for the child to contribute significantly to others*
- *Establish and maintain family rituals and traditions*
- *Spend quality time with children, so they know they are listened to and taken seriously, by engaging them in meaningful dialogue.*
- *Set reasonable limits and consequences (where possible) in advance (and plan for what might go wrong)*
- *Follow through with respect and caring, being sure the child understands how s/he made the decision*
- *Structure opportunities (and allow for opportunities to occur) where children can experience either the natural rewards or the pain and consequences of their decisions*
- *Remove children from situations where they can't control themselves to take time out or cool off*
- *Offer choices*
- *Provide nonthreatening opportunities for the young person to understand why and how we make the decisions we do*

- ***Be certain children understand why we hold certain values that we want them to adopt***
- ***For young children especially, ignore the bad behavior as much as possible, and attend to the good behavior***

By adhereing to these principles, we can handle most behavior problems that arise with children. One rule of thumb: First we should be sure the child is "capable" before resorting to principles that "control" a situation.

If parents feel overwhelmed, there are supports out there, and free help is available. If anyone feels he or she has out-of-control abusive tendencies, it's too hard to deal with alone. Parent's Anonymous is an organization that can be of great comfort and help.

It is much harder to do any of this alone. We need to talk to each other and give each other support. After all, we've all got one thing in common: We all have some difficulties with our children. But again, *Parenting from the Heart (Pransky, 1997; 2001)* can make it all so much easier and enjoyable.

13. School Climate Improvement/Restructuring Schools

The crisis has finally been recognized. Business leaders became frustrated that the school system was not adequately preparing young people. Many officials are now realizing that our school system has not changed with the times, and we are beginning to suffer because of it.

When I first became involved with "school climate improvement," and still six years later when I wrote the paper that formed the basis for this chapter (Pransky, 1985), it was one of the least practiced of all effective prevention strategies. Except for small pockets of successful activity that produced impressive results, "school climate improvement" never really took hold. Neither did the parallel "school effectiveness" movement. For some reason these movements were unable to get people excited about what school could really be like.

In the latter part of the 1980s, a new movement emerged known as "school restructuring." Led by some of the best educational minds in the country, its leaders cry out for educational reform and propose revolutionary strategies. Small changes will not do, they say; rather, the entire way schools conduct their business must be restructured. As San Diego Superintendent Thomas Payzant says, "it involves fundamental questioning of traditional assumptions about the best way to organize our schools for teaching and learning" (in Lewis, 1989). This school restructuring or educational reform movement now presents the prevention field with a much stronger footing from which to launch school improvement efforts.

Schools Are Critical for Prevention—But Are We Overburdening Them?

Nearly half of children's waking hours are spent in school and related activities. Thus, school today has nearly the influence on children that families do. This influence is so powerful that school can even make up for deficits in the home by its practices toward students. And because it is generally easier to affect a large number of young people through schools than through an equivalent number of families (schools have, essentially, a captive audience), the school setting is fundamental to any comprehensive prevention strategy.

Yet schools are overloaded and overburdened. Society is looking increasingly toward schools to help it solve its ills. Teachers are complaining legitimately that they have less and less time to teach the material they should be teaching. Are we now asking schools to take on additional prevention activities as well?

No! And yes. Schools cannot afford to take on school climate improvement and school restructuring as an additional activity. They can, however, take it on as an additional goal.

129

"School climate improvement should be a different way of conducting the same business—an alternative way of using the same time and energy. The only additional burden would be the time it takes the school to set the process in motion, for example, to conduct an initial "assessment" of its "climate," decide how it wants to respond, and provide any training needed for new approaches. This extra burden should be weighed against the potential results: usually a substantial reduction in behavior problems and an improvement in learning.

Most schools want to increase academic achievement and learning, to enhance school spirit, and to reduce truancy, dropouts, classroom disruptions, suspensions, school vandalism, and the use of drugs (at least in school and at school functions). Most schools also profess in their philosophy and mission statements to want to help students reach their full potential and become responsible members of society. Any or all these desires can motivate a school to engage in school climate improvement.

What Is "School Climate"?

"School climate" refers to the way the total school environment affects those within it. A climate is an atmospheric or environmental condition. Climates can be warm, cold, hot, turbulent, peaceful. Climates affect people's health and people's behavior.

Institutions have internal climates. Each school as an institution has a different feel to it, a different atmosphere. As Eugene Howard (1980), one of the leading proponents of school climate says, like people, institutions can be either sick or well. Mostly they are somewhere on a continuum between the two.

"School climate" can be defined as: Those qualities of the school and the people in the school that affect how people feel while they are there. Schools with positive climates are places where people care, respect, and trust one another; and where the school as an institution cares, respects, and trusts people. In such a school, people feel a high sense of pride and ownership which comes from each individual having a role in making the school a better place (Howard, 1980).

"Unrigging" the Schools

How people believe they are being treated in school affects their perceptions and, in turn, their behaviors. If we are serious about preventing and reducing problem behaviors, we should be examining how all actions of a school toward its students (and staff) affect their perceptions. These actions can be in the form of policies or practices, or even the way school is structured.

Sadly, many schools in this country are unintentionally structured in ways that are not conducive to building healthy perceptions in all students. Eugene Howard (1978) says, **"Schools are unintentionally rigged like gambling casinos against a certain percentage of students."** What does he mean?

When a bell-shaped curve is used for assigning grades, a certain percentage of students are guaranteed to be losers. No matter how well the class does as a whole, some students either fail or receive poor grades. This doesn't do wonders for the perceptions of those at the bottom.

When standardized tests are used to measure academic achievement, students learn that at least 50% of them are below average. I'll never forget when one of my junior high school teachers lined us up around the room according to the score each of us received on a standardized test. I was in the bottom third—I never could take those tests!—and was never more humiliated in my life. The kids at the top felt great. My teacher did not do this to hurt me intentionally, but that did not change how it made me feel.

When grouping and ranking practices are used to classify students in accordance with their academic ability, a select group of students becomes known as the "dummies" and the "losers." The theory isn't bad for students at similar levels to advance at similar rates, but what are the consequences for the students at the bottom? A school does not have to treat this group as dummies and losers for them to feel that way, they know they're at the bottom. It is no coincidence that these are often the students who cause the most problems.

Grading practices can be a serious problem. In most schools, students who improve from an 88 average to a 92 move from a B to an A, while other students who improve from a 20 to a 50 move from an F to an F. One student improves by 4 points and jumps a whole grade. Another improves by 30 points and still fails. Nothing reflects her improvement (Durham, 1983). This only helps to destroy that student's perception of capability.

Other school policies and practices can be problems as well. When academic requirements are used for participation in extracurricular activities, the opportunity is denied for some students to experience school success through nonacademic means. While it is true that some students don't try as hard as they might and need motivation, what are the consequences of using this form of external motivation for students who have real academic difficulty? They have no impetus to attach themselves to school in ways that make them feel good and no way to perceive they're an important contributing part of school. Then they behave accordingly. Nonacademic activities may be the only way some students can experience success.

When others set school rules for students, and especially when those rules are inconsistently enforced, it is difficult for students to experience an internal locus of control. I was consulting in one school that had a rule, "No sitting on the heaters." I walked into a classroom and saw five students and a teacher sitting on the heaters. Why have a rule if it is not enforced? It may be an unnecessary rule. If so, change it. If not, enforce it! That way students will be able to predict what will happen and act accordingly. Teachers also vary in the extent to which they enforce the same rules. This confuses students, encouraging them to guess at what they might be able to get away with. Further, when a school says, "If you get caught with drugs, we'll kick you out," then catches some kids with drugs and doesn't kick them out, it sets up the perception in the minds of students that it must be fate, chance, or luck if someone gets nailed (Glenn, 1983).

When largely "bad" messages are sent home to parents and they hear little about what might be going well with their kids in school, they gain a negative perception. How people believe they are seen by important others affects their behavior (Johnson, Bird, Little, 1979). Is it a coincidence that parents who show up enthusiastically in early elementary school stop coming around by junior or senior high school? As George Durham (1983) says, "schools punish parents."

These are but a few examples of how school structure, policies, and practices tend to negate the perceptions of worth, competence, importance, and power so critical to building healthy self-concepts and producing desired behaviors. Yet schools do not do this intentionally! On the contrary, most schools have the best of intentions. Their structure and practices could use some serious examination, to match their intentions.

Before the school restructuring movement, it was both frustrating and nearly overwhelming to try to affect schools at the level of structure. It is not much easier now. Little makes school officials more resistant than a suggestion to tamper with their grading, testing, grouping, or ranking practices. Schools are disinclined to make structural changes of this magnitude. Yet it is terribly important for schools to ask themselves a very difficult question: Are our methods getting in the way of our desired results?

Other aspects of school climate are far easier to tackle than changing school structure, and these aspects can still make a big difference in the behavior of students. Sometimes changing less-threatening practices can even counter some of the behavioral consequences of detrimental structures. **Schools that claim to be serious about improving student behavior and performance and still adhere to some of the problem structures must go out of their way to ensure that all other interactions within the school promote healthy self-perceptions in all students.**

Characteristics of Healthy and Effective Schools

What are the characteristics of a school with a healthy school climate? What are the principles of an effective school? A restructured school?

Through both formal and informal research, experts have reached remarkably similar conclusions.[*]

Schools successful at both reducing problem behaviors and improving learning and other desirable behaviors tend to have these similar characteristics:

- ◆ *clear school goals, shared expectations and vision*, including specified, desired results, and measured progress toward achieving those results
- ◆ *equal treatment for all students*; no group singled out for special treatment (Note: This is meant to imply, when a school has a group of "problem" students, it is usually best not to design a special program for that group, because no matter how good the program, the students tend to get negatively labeled and reinforce each other. It is better to change school conditions in ways that affect all students constructively. An exception might be made for Special Education, but some would even argue this.)
- ◆ *clear rules, perceived as fair* by students
- ◆ *consistent enforcement* of those rules
- ◆ *demonstrated interest in and caring for all students*; school structured so all students can be successful
- ◆ *curriculum relevant to life and work outside the school*, in which students are taught life skills, learn fewer things more in depth, and develop higher-order thinking and analyzing skills
- ◆ *high expectations for all students'* achievement and success
- ◆ *students become active learners*, partners in the learning process
- ◆ *student involvement in the governance* of the school
- ◆ *involvement of parents*
- ◆ *a pleasant, stimulating working environment* for both students and staff

---

[*] Note: The conclusions listed here have been consolidated and paraphrased from the following sources: my own assessment of school-based delinquency prevention projects funded through the Vermont Commission on the Administration of Justice (1982); the Phi Delta Kappa Commission on Discipline (Wayson, 1982); a summary of "school effectiveness" literature (Hersh, 1981); a summary of "school climate" literature (Van Buskirk, 1980); a summary of "school restructuring" literature (Lewis, 1989).

◆ *flexible structures* to accommodate different content goals, learning rates, interests, and styles; removal of unnecessary, time-consuming barriers to innovation

◆ *enthusiastic commitment, involvement, and leadership of the school principal* (in the school improvement process, and otherwise)

◆ *teachers empowered* to become involved in school decisions, especially concerning organization of instruction

◆ *a core group of staff* (at least one-third) *committed to school improvement* who become trained in and practice new skills (coupled with an overview for the rest of the staff)

Applying These Principles Well Can Yield Impressive Results

School climate improvement is the process of ensuring that these principles of effectiveness are in place in a school. The goal of school restructuring is to open the process of learning/teaching and human interaction so students and teachers assume greater responsibility for improving the way students learn, the way teachers teach, and the way people in the school interact.

These principles have support in high places. The National School Boards Association supported many in their report, *Toward Better and Safer Schools: A School Leader's Guide to Delinquency Prevention* (1984). Former President Reagan, specifically endorsed this report, and therefore the principles. Albert Shanker, former president of the American Federation of Teachers, supported serious school restructuring in a written statement (in Lewis, 1989). Many of these principles were supported in reports by the National Institute of Education/RAND Corporation's (1988) *Steady Work* and the Carnegie Corporation's (1986) *A Nation Prepared*. The principles are underscored in Goodlad's (1984) *A Place Called School*, Sizer's (1984) *Horace's Compromise*, and Boyer's (1986) *High School*.

These are not pie-in-the-sky ideas. They can make a real difference. Using these principles, Champlain Valley Union High School in Hinesburg, Vermont, under the leadership of former Principal Jim Fitzpatrick, instituted a school-wide Reality Therapy discipline system that reduced behavior problems and subsequent office discipline referrals, suspensions, and expulsions by 85%, and reduced vandalism costs from $15,000 per year to $1500 per year. The entire grant to bring in a consultant to assist them and to pay for training time cost $8500 (Pransky, 1981). This is a school that once had security guards patrolling the hallways. In subsequent years, by adding individualized "learning styles" and "accelerated learning," the school reduced the dropout rate from 7-8% per year to 0.5% per year [Chapter 14].

At Cleveland High School in Seattle, Washington, former Principal Bill Maynard reduced absenteeism from 35% to 5.6%, reduced the dropout rate; reduced office discipline referrals by 50% and increased the number of students sent to college by 35%. He accomplished this by building school pride and student pride and self-concept ("Each and every one of you is special"), by taking security guards out of the school, by revising the discipline code down to six rules, by instituting a staff training program to improve decision-making and problem-solving skills, by decorating school walls with original student paintings, by expanding course curriculum with mini-courses more relevant to life outside school, by modifying the grading policy to eliminate failing grades, by involving staff in decision-making, and more (Howard, 1978).

In the Widefield-Security School District in Colorado Springs, Colorado, a district-wide school climate improvement effort was established in 11 schools. As a result of comprehensive planning and implementation, when 1975-77 rates of behavior were compared with 1979-80 rates, discipline referrals were reduced by 30%, "serious" discipline referrals by 73%, thefts during school hours dropped by 55%, the absenteeism rate was cut by 20%, and school vandalism by 98%, cutting vandalism costs from $19,272 to $365 (Howard, 1982).

In the Colville and Washington Schools of South San Francisco's Unified School District (13), vandalism was reduced by 78% and 90% respectively through implementation of a financial incentive program. The school agreed to pay funds to the student body for activities in accordance with the amount saved in school vandalism costs (Howard, 1978).

Williamstown Junior-Senior High School reduced office discipline referrals by 53%, suspensions by 38%, and vandalism costs by 64%, through instituting the LEAST Approach to Discipline (Pransky, 1981).

Ridgewood High School in Norridge, Illinois, Apollo Elementary School in Bossier Parrish, Louisiana, Nueva Day School in Hillsborough, California, and the Wilson School in Nankatom, Minnesota, all reduced discipline problems considerably and improved academic performance by individualizing learning and reducing failure through elimination of school grades (Howard, 1978).

These are but a few of many, many examples of how improving school climate can make a huge difference. Many more examples are listed in the *School Discipline Desk Book* (Howard, 1978), *Restructuring America's Schools* (Lewis, 1989), and other sources. Many of these approaches can actually save money. Teachers usually report being better able to handle students' disruptive behavior, and they experience less of it. They often report that students get along better with one another and with teachers, resulting in calmer classrooms, happier students, and improved staff morale (Pransky, 1981; Wilson, 1981).

Each of these schools had to put itself through some sort of process to determine what was best for it at the time. All had to learn how to implement effectively the approach they selected. But how do schools put these principles into effect?

Critical Elements of a School Climate Improvement Process

First, it is important to understand that the following elements (adapted from Maynard, 1977) are critical to the school climate improvement process:

- agreement by staff on a school philosophy and mission that reflects educational quality and individual self-worth
- development of trust through promoting open and honest communications among administration, staff and students
- sharing leadership, with high involvement of staff and students
- assessment of all actions of a school (school rules, approach to discipline, approach to teaching, and so forth) against the agreed-upon school philosophy and mission statement, and against how practices are affecting all students' self-perceptions
- acquiring skills to accomplish the above, and making changes as necessary—effective staff development

Building Healthy Student Self-Concepts

Before we embark on the actual process to assess a school's climate, it is important to respond to a common concern. If school climate improvement is to build healthy student self-concepts, why not simply design a course to promote self-esteem as part of the school health curriculum? Why go through all the bother of changing school conditions?

The answer is that a healthy student self-concept is gained from all that happens within school toward a student. How one is treated within the school can negate even the best classroom activities designed to build self-esteem. This is not a concept that can be learned primarily through curricular activities.

School systems do reasonably well at building self-esteem in the majority of students. They do not often do so well with the others. Twenty percent of students usually cause 80% of the school's discipline problems and absenteeism (Maynard, 1977). Schools need to find ways of effectively reaching this segment of students as well.

Subtle practices can sometimes make the difference. At an elementary school in which I was consulting, I attended a meeting about a truant student who had been absent for three weeks. The staff and administration were trying to be responsive but didn't know what to do. I asked, "What will happen to the truant student if he returns to school?" Their answer: "He'll have to make up the work he missed, stay after school for as long as it takes." I said, "Then this kid is never coming back. As soon as he takes the first encouraging step to walk back in the door, he'll get nailed, and he knows it."

The chronically truant student sees himself getting further and further behind. He cannot dream of catching up. The first order of business should be to help him feel safe enough to return. Later the school can worry about getting him caught up. The first step with a troubled student should almost always be to try to rebuild some semblance of healthy self-perceptions, at least in terms of his interaction with school. Otherwise it is unlikely anyone will be able to get anywhere with him.

Often, more is going on in a student's life than meets the eye. A school sees a legitimately troubling behavior, but it is often a symptom of far more serious problems. A strictly behavioral response may not work. A kid who makes inappropriate sexual overtures to another may be sexually abused at home. To simply punish him for his inappropriate behavior may not help him stop that or other disturbing behaviors. A kid who punches another without apparent reason may be abused at home. This does not excuse the behavior, it only suggests that other means are needed. The same holds true for withdrawn students.

Schools might ask themselves, "How can we help students feel okay enough in school so they want to respond appropriately?"

A few years ago I witnessed an incident concerning my own daughter. In her third-grade class, she was unable to settle down or concentrate, particularly during silent reading when she was all over the room. Her teacher called her "lazy" and "uncooperative." Luckily, her mother, who coincidentally knows about such matters, thought she spotted a perceptual problem and insisted that the school test her. We discovered she has a fairly rare form of dyslexia where letters and words on a page seem to move in and out of her field of vision. It is not easy to read under those circumstances. She had been driving the teacher nuts—but she was also feeling terrible about herself because she could not do the work her friends were able to do. The solution involved getting her special corrective glasses, coupled with Special Education assistance. It worked wonders. I shudder to think what might have happened if her teacher had continued to

135

pay attention only to the presenting behavior and continued to see her as lazy and uncooperative. What would have happened to her self-esteem and probably to her behavior?

Why do some teachers respond inappropriately? Expediency? Not having the skills to recognize these types of problems? Teachers have a very difficult, often thankless job, but there is no excuse for this kind of inappropriate response because of what it can mean for a child. When confronted with a difficult child, we have to: (1) figure out what is behind their presenting behavior, and (2) try our best to build them back up. Otherwise, we have little hope of reaching them, and we all lose.

Students who fear failure, or who believe they will fail, cannot become constructive learners (Durham, 1983). To get through to these students, teachers can learn promising ways of rebuilding healthy student attitudes toward themselves and toward learning, so they can regain excitement about learning. But currently, an estimated 80% of classroom teaching is based on competitive strategies (Johnson and Johnson, 1975). School systems are locked into a standard mode of operation. It is time to recognize that business-as-usual means problems-as-usual.

A major longitudinal study found that first graders who failed to learn, to deal with school rules and authority, and to participate socially in the classroom showed increased substance abuse, delinquency, and dropping out of school ten years later (Kellam, 1983). This underscores the necessity of ensuring school success, particularly in the early grades.

How to Begin a School Climate Improvement Process

How does one begin to open a school to the possibilities of embarking on a school climate improvement process? Here are four approaches to consider:

1. If a school system is concerned about a problem (for example: vandalism, an inordinate number of office discipline referrals, drop-outs, truancy), the primary goal should be combating that particular problem. As a first step, the school administration should pull together the various segments of the school community to work together creatively to solve that problem.

2. If a school is experiencing no apparent, major problems it may want to consider generally improving itself. No matter how well any of us is doing, we can always improve. The administration could pull together the various segments of the school community to ask itself the following:

- What are we doing well now that we should be doing even better?
- What are we not doing that we should be doing?
- What are we doing now that we should not be doing at all? (Shaheen, 1981)

With respect to what? Building healthy self-concepts? Improving learning? The school philosophy and mission statement? All are good reasons to improve. All are good starting points.

3. If a school is offered an incentive to improve or restructure itself, the school may be more inclined to try to change. Such an incentive might be a grant through the state department of education or some other source, an increase in teacher salaries, with negotiations for what might be expected in return.

Shortly after the release of the 1986 Carnegie Report, *A Nation Prepared*, the Rochester, New York, school system decided to make many of the changes recommended in the report. The superintendent, Peter McWalters, had to negotiate with the president of the Rochester Teachers

Union, Adam Urbanski. McWalters wanted to hold teachers accountable for student achievement and wanted them more closely involved in the students' lives. He also wanted more control over the assignment of teachers "to remedy the old problem of inexperienced teachers facing the toughest students," and "the right to dismiss weak teachers if peer mentoring and other intervention didn't work." In return, Urbanski wanted more money, a professional career ladder, and a much greater role in deciding what and how to teach. The result was an agreement to raise teacher pay an average of 40% over three years, with a new category of "lead teacher" able to earn as much as $70,000. In exchange, the pact had the teachers working longer hours and extra days, giving up automatic pay increments for years of experience and extra education, and waiving seniority rights (so that deadwood could be culled). The teachers also had to become involved in "home-based guidance," where each is a mentor for a group of 20 students. Ultimately, the teachers would be held accountable. As David Kearns, chairman of Xerox, said, "Teaching is the only profession I know of that, if you do well, nothing good happens to you, and if you do poorly, nothing bad happens to you" (in Lewis, 1989).[*]

4. If a school has a directive to assess its climate and make changes accordingly (as through the Vermont School Approval Standards), schools have a built-in reason to embark on a school climate improvement process.

Vermont's School Climate Standard

States without a standard of operation pertaining to school climate may find Vermont's school climate standard a useful example.

The Vermont Department of Education included "School Climate" as Standard 2140 of the *Standards for Approving Vermont's Public Schools* (1984). The standards "are intended to stimulate school personnel to engage in reflective self-examination and to embark on vigorous school improvement efforts" (Approved Standards Self-Assessment Guide, 1984). The school climate standard requires evidence that the school is a bright and inviting place as characterized by positive relations among staff and students, and between the school and community it serves...

The standard requires further that the faculty and administration participate in a review of school climate on an annual basis. Where deficiencies are found, improvements are made after consultation with parents and students.

Among the facets of a school's climate required to be assessed are-

- student and faculty satisfaction
- community involvement in school
- student participation in extracurricular activities
- recognition of student and faculty excellence
- disciplinary actions
- student dropouts
- student problems including substance abuse
- student promotion and retention

The school climate standard also emphasizes that the central purpose of the school's programs is the "intellectual development of students." Even if such development were a school's

---

[*] Note: Apparently Kearns isn't familiar with working for the government, but his point is well taken.

only goal, it would be good reason to improve its climate. Intellectual development is directly related to improving motivation and achievement, which is largely accomplished through building healthy self-perceptions and skills (Glenn and Nelsen, 1988).

Typically, the clarity of the standard, and the enforcement mechanisms, aren't nearly as good as the intent, but it is a step in the right direction.

School Leadership and Followship

School principals and the behavior they model largely determine what happens in schools, just as teachers and the behavior they model determine what happens in the classroom.

Some principals resist change—for many reasons. Their jobs are replete with pressure. The enormity of their task can feel overwhelming, particularly in inner-city schools. Substantive improvements are always difficult, but they can be especially difficult to realize under the reign of a resistant principal. Yet, teachers or community members who want to make a difference still can do so. They can exert pressure from within or from without. Anyone with initiative and persistence can make change happen [Chapter 34].

Resistance can also come from teachers. These people who devote their lives to teaching and being with our children for at least seven hours every day have some of the toughest of all jobs, and departments of education and lawmakers keep handing them additional responsibilities. If teachers are frustrated these days, it is with good reason. Now, on top of all that, we are asking them to conduct their business differently. New ways of operating are as difficult for teachers as they are for administrators—as they are for any of us who are asked to change how we operate.

School improvement efforts do not necessarily need the support of all staff. A core group of those interested (hopefully one-third, but even one-fifth or fewer) can begin. If they are successful, others will come around.

The training teachers receive often does not prepare them for how learning and discipline best occur. Primarily, teachers learn curricular content. Colleges that prepare teachers to teach are therefore in need of change. To learn new techniques after we become comfortable is difficult for any of us. That some teachers feel threatened is understandable. However, learning new, effective practices can also be very exciting. The way these practices are presented can make a big difference.

For any of us to change our behavior, we need the information, the skills, the opportunity to practice in a safe setting, and feedback on how well we're doing, so we can learn from our successes and from our mistakes. We are all students in a continual process of learning.

The more that teachers are involved in decisions that affect them, the less threatened they will feel. In the Mansfield, Connecticut, schools, Superintendent Bruce Caldwell instituted a "shared leadership" approach where teachers conceived and wrote curricula, helped to screen and nominate professional staff, helped prepare the budget, and brought recommendations to the board of education. The teachers conferred with the superintendent and heard his thoughts and cautions, but the proposal was theirs. This plan required that the parties trusted each other, that they were willing collaborators with common goals, and that the sharing process was continuous. As one veteran teacher put it, "The damn thing works!" (Weingast, 1983).

Recommended School Climate Assessment Process for Schools

The following process is a combined adaptation of Eugene Howard's work (1978; undated; 1987) and my own (1985). If a school follows these steps and adheres to the principles and critical elements cited previously, it will almost always improve its climate and therefore improve student behaviors:

1. School officials and interested parties examine the principles of a healthy school climate and any related requirements for which a school is responsible.
2. The school administrator makes a clear, enthusiastic statement that the school will be undergoing a school climate improvement process.
3. The school administrator asks for volunteers and appoints a "school climate improvement committee" whose job will be to periodically assess the school's climate and set up a mechanism for improvement. Administrators should serve on the committee, along with teachers and other school staff, school board members if possible, and interested parents and students.
4. The committee elects, or the administrator appoints, someone to chair the committee.
5. The committee learns about school climate improvement principles, theories, and strategies, either through a presentation or reading materials.
6. The committee examines its school philosophy and mission statement. The committee either reaffirms what is stated and holds it up as the guide for all school actions, or suggests revisions. If a revision is necessary, the statement should present whatever formal process is required by the school system, including circulating it to the rest of the school for their comments. [Note: School philosophy and mission statements are very often indicative of a healthy school climate. Once such impressive statements are written, however, they often gather dust on a shelf and are rarely used to guide the direction and actions of the school. These statements should reflect the school's aims for its students. The more every action of the school toward young people is geared toward making this statement a reality, the more a school will reduce its problems with students and increase their academic achievement.]
7. The committee and administration set a date for a school-wide school climate assessment, and decide upon the best process. Options might include interviews, a questionnaire, a full staff meeting where the assessment is conducted all at once, or some combination of these. School staff, students, and parents should all participate in the assessment.
8. The committee develops a draft school climate assessment form. The form asks how well the school is doing at living up to its school philosophy and mission statement, following the principles of schools with effective climates, and, if applicable, meeting any existing requirements for school climate/effectiveness/restructuring. It presents questions on a scale from one to five or one to ten, with spaces for comments and suggestions for improvement.
9. The committee finalizes the assessment form.
10. The committee and administration assess the total school community on the date scheduled.
11. The committee reconvenes and analyzes the results; from the survey, the committee determines the top one, two, or three priorities for improvement.
12. The administration and the committee appoint or ask for volunteers from the rest of school community to work on task forces for the specific priorities. At least one committee member sits on each task force.
13. The committee establishes a mechanism for gathering base-line data on the frequency of student behaviors that the school wants improved, deciding what information will be gathered and who will gather it.
14. Each convened task force follows a recommended process. It-
     - examines the results of the assessment with respect to particular issue

- determines the desired results and indicators of success (what it would like to see happen and how it will know when it gets there), and the goals/objectives for the aspect of climate to be improved
- finds out if any other schools (in state or elsewhere) have worked on the particular problem
- where possible, visits those schools, and/or invites representatives to meet with the task force and perhaps with the entire school
- determines whether an outside consultant is needed to help the school deal with the issue
- develops a plan for recommended action to change or improve that aspect of the school's climate
- if training is necessary, searches out a qualified consultant and designs the training with assistance of the administration

15. The committee and administration consider all task force recommendations, and makes changes or improvements in the school accordingly.

16. Where needed, the committee and administration arrange for training of appropriate staff.

17. The administration and school climate committee set up an annual review process for school climate improvement, including a way to periodically gather data on student behavior to measure success.

Strategies for Improving School Climate

Once a school has done its climate assessment and knows where to focus, it should learn about all the available strategies. It is very tempting to pick a good-sounding strategy and run with it. What sounds best, however, may not be the most productive approach. Doing the formal assessment should guide the school toward the best strategies.

Many creative strategies for improving school climate and effectiveness are listed in the following sources:

- *School Discipline Desk Book* (Howard, 1978)
- *Handbook for Developing Schools with Good Discipline* (Wayson, 1982)
- *Delinquency Prevention: Selective Organizational Change in the School* (Little and Skarrow, 1981)
- *Restructuring America's Schools* (Lewis, 1989)

The strategies cited in these and other related works can be generally categorized into strategies to-

- improve the way school staff work to cooperate in solving problems
- improve school discipline improve instructional practices make the curriculum more relevant to life outside school
- empower students to make decisions about how school affects their lives
- reduce status differences among everyone in the school
- strengthen the interaction among school, home, and community
- provide personal supports to students
- change the school structure to enhance students' self-concept

As usual, these categories may overlap. Some approaches within each follow.

Improve the Way School Staff Cooperate in Solving Problems

The intent here is to have a staff with a shared sense of purpose and commitment acting together to achieve that purpose (Wayson, 1982).

The very process of joining the various segments of the school community to solve problems (or improve situations) often improves a school climate. In a school assessment, colleagues focus on shared goals and values. They reflect together, analyze, and work to improve all aspects of the school in an atmosphere of trust, respect, and caring.

Few factors related to successful schools are fixed by external constraints; most are open to modification by staff. In the least-successful schools teachers were often found to be isolated, and vice-versa. A school should empower its staff to work together in an organized fashion to make the changes they feel are needed, or plan together what needs to be planned (Rutter, 1979).

Improve School Discipline

The goal here is for teachers to spend less time disciplining students, so more time can be spent on teaching. If practiced well, a good discipline system builds student perceptions of power, self-discipline, and responsibility. The best systems also help students learn a planning process to solve their problems, which helps them become more capable in the process. The practice of discipline can be considered part of a school's entire learning process.

No matter what the discipline system, its foundation should rest on two principles cited earlier: (1) conducting discipline in an atmosphere of caring, friendliness and respect; and (2) setting forth clear rules, perceived as fair by students.

Regarding school rules, it is best if the number of school rules is kept to a minimum. Long lists of specific rules only confuse students. One elementary school had its students develop its rules (that's good), but the little pupils came up with a long list of items like "no hitting, no biting, no pinching, no scratching..." and they left out "no tripping." If a student stuck his foot out and tripped someone, he could point to the rules and say, "It doesn't say that!" (Not good.) Contrast this with the five rules developed at Champlain Valley Union High School (CVU):

1. We will respect and be considerate of the rights and responsibilities of ourselves and others.
2. We will respect and be considerate of our own property and the property of others.
3. We will be responsible for following our designated class and/or time schedule.
4. We will respect the rules for specific areas such as library and cafeteria.
5. Student traffic will be end of the period only except for prearranged appointments with DUO, guidance, and so on.

These are rules young people can remember. They are stated in positive terms. They are broad enough to cover a lot of ground. If a student is violating a rule, she usually knows it. In CVU's Reality Therapy discipline system, the teacher can ask, "Is what you're doing against the rules?" and have confidence that the students usually know whether it is. If they don't know, the teacher can easily remind them: "Well, I saw you..., and that's against the rules."

Within the context of clear rules—firm and consistent limits for students—many canned discipline systems have been used effectively in many schools. But for the approaches to work as intended, all stated principles must be followed. There is no room for short-cuts in applying discipline models.

Some of these models are-

- *Reality Therapy/Ten-Step Discipline System* (Glasser, 1969; 1986)
- *Developing Capable Young People* (Glenn, 1983; 1981)
- *LEAST Approach to Discipline* (Carkhuff, 1978)
- *Behavior Management* (Bushell, 1973)
- *Psychology in the Classroom* (Dreikurs, 1968)
- *Assertive Discipline* (Canter and Canter, 1976)
- *Developmental Discipline* (Watson, 1982; Ellsworth and Monahan, 1987)

A worthwhile discipline system includes at least these five components:

1. *Setting up a caring, supportive atmosphere in which discipline can be conducted.* Reality Therapy (RT), Developing Capable Young People (DCYP), and Dreikurs insist on becoming involved with all students on a friendly and caring basis, and eliminating criticism. Developmental Discipline (DD) builds in a means for establishing warm and supportive social relationships and helps the students understand the reasons for norms and rules. Assertive Discipline (AD) also encourages each students need for warmth and positive support. Behavior Management (BM) uses prompts" to reinforce good behavior. The LEAST Approach suggests first leaving the disruption alone because most disruptions will go away by themselves.

2. *Providing an effective initial response to the inappropriate behavior.* DCYP begins the interaction with the student's perception. RT deals with the present behavior only: "What are you doing now?" "Is what you're doing against the rules?" and accepting no excuses. In AD, upon seeing disruptive behavior, the teacher may write the student's name on the board without stopping the teaching, then place a check mark by the name for each further disruption. BM eliminates "prompts" to "extinguish" inappropriate behavior, and encourages statements like "Walk!" instead of "Stop running!," thereby defining the behaviors one wants to see. In LEAST, if the disruption won't go away by itself, the teacher is to "end the action indirectly" (example: move closer to the student) before giving a verbal response, then "attend more fully" to find out what is really going on within the student. DD may draw the student's attention to the behavior by calling out his or her name, stating the relevant rule, and demanding compliance.

3. *Responding with immediate, clear action.* DCYP and Dreikurs use logical and natural consequences in an atmosphere of firmness, dignity and respect, with limits and consequences understood in advance, and follow-through. LEAST spells out specific directions. In AD, a second check beside a name on the board often means that the student will have to stay after school for a set (brief) period of time; a third check may mean a longer set time and a visit to the principal's office. In BM, the student will often be given a certain period of time (maybe five seconds) to follow a directive or the teacher will take some specific action, often "time out" for a specified period of time. RT also uses a form of "time out," but the length of time depends on how long it takes the student to come up with an acceptable plan. In DD, the student may be asked to leave the classroom for a time, but the model takes great care to ensure that the demands are adjusted to the student's developmental capabilities.

4. *Including a way for students to learn a more appropriate behavior.* RT requires that a student set forth a specific plan to do better. If the student doesn't come up with a reasonable

plan, she is sent to a "planning room" (a last resort) where she stays until she completes one, but she is assisted in the process. DCYP uses the "what," "'why," and "how" questions (EIAG) to help students understand how to avoid the difficulty next time. DD teaches social skills and techniques for self-control, and involves students in decision-making and problem-solving. BM uses a series of prompts and reinforcers to move students to the desired behavior. LEAST and DD pay attention to the reasons behind the presenting behavior.

5. *Following through*. BM has a detailed, sophisticated way of measuring student progress, too complex to cite here. LEAST tracks student progress. Developing capable young people is an on-going process. In RT, if it fails, try again; never give up.

In comparing these approaches, I have only skimmed the surface to illustrate the principles involved. Before selecting any approach or combination, examine each thoroughly. The specific model may not matter so much as using a clear, consistent approach school-wide. Different approaches may fit different school personalities better than others. My personal preferences are Reality Therapy and Developing Capable Young People; I have seen them used most effectively, and they have a strong teaching component as part of the discipline process. Training is needed for effective use of any of these approaches.

A caution: Assertive Discipline has received mixed reviews. On one hand, many teachers love it because they have found it to reduce classroom behavior problems and allow more time on task (Barrett, 1985; McCormack, 1987). It views all classroom disruptions as getting in the way of what the teacher wants to accomplish. Teachers are trained to intervene with problem behaviors in a way that takes the least time from teaching. On the other hand, the approach has been criticized because it can overemphasize the negative at the expense of the positive (particularly if used improperly). With its largely teacher-centered focus, it pays little attention to the child's perception and does not teach the student a new way to behave. While AD may squelch disruptive behaviors, the student frustrations that caused the disruptive behavior may still be present—in fact, some believe they may even be promoted within the model—and that frustration may simply be displaced outside the classroom (Gantrell, 1987).

Improve Instructional Practices

Rutter (1979) concluded that students' behavior seems to rise or fall in accordance with teacher expectations. If students are treated as responsible people, they tend to behave accordingly. Children treated as intelligent and capable of learning do so. A classic example of this was portrayed in the fact-based movie, *Stand and Deliver*, when teacher Jaime Escalante took a class of students that everyone had written off as losers and misfits and helped them become among the top calculus students in the nation.

How can we make learning more productive and at the same time build healthy self-perceptions? How can every student achieve in school? Many "canned" instructional approaches have been used with great success in many schools. However, the same cautions hold as for discipline approaches. By myopically latching onto a particular model, we may divert ourselves from what really makes the difference in learning. Certain principles have been found by researchers to increase learning in both the cognitive and affective domains. These principles should guide the use of any instructional approach.

Research by Malcolm Knowles on what contributes to effective adult learning is very pertinent to effective learning in children. The four critical ingredients are-

- *Respect*—learners must feel heard, honored, respected as people, not for what they know, but for themselves.
- *Immediacy*—learners must see how they can use their new knowledge, skills and attitudes immediately.
- *Experience*—learners learn best when what they are learning is directly related to their own life experience.
- *Our own discovery*—We can use 20% of what we hear; 40% of what we hear and see; 80% of what we discover for ourselves. (Vella, 1989[*])

Considerable evidence exists that using external incentives undermines students' own motivation to learn. Instead, children need to have activities that they find inherently interesting (in Battistich et al., 1991). The teaching/learning process can be active, engaging students physically and mentally and keeping the amount of lecturing and explaining to a minimum. The learning environment can be varied, avoiding a single, standard mode of instruction (Fox, 1975).

Students need to be taught the skills to give effective input, and they need opportunities to see if they are mature enough to handle it. Students are going to make mistakes; that is part of the learning process. But we should not assume too quickly that students are incapable. Sometimes we'll be amazed at their responsiveness when given the opportunity to be responsible for their learning. The real question is whether cognitive and affective learning is enhanced.

Here are some creative instructional practices that have been found to enhance learning:

- *Cooperative Learning* (Johnson and Johnson, 1975)
- *Student-Team Learning* (Center for Social organization of Schools, Johns Hopkins University) (Slavin, 1987; Hawkins, 1981)
- *Mastery Learning* (Bloom, 1971, in Taylor, 1983)
- *Individualized Learning Styles* (Dunn and Dunn, 1978)
- *Suggestive Accelerated Learning* (Bancroft, 1978; Asher, 1982; Schuster, 1976; Levin, 1988; Cullen, et al. 1987)
- *"Capability-building learning"* (Note: I coined this term, based upon some of Glenn's (1983) principles in Developing Capable Young People.) This method appears related to building "higher-order thinking skills."

Schools and teachers should ask the following questions to determine whether they are using practices that promote the most effective learning.

Does the model engage all students in a cooperative work atmosphere where they can learn from, instead of compete with, each other?

In Cooperative Learning, students perceive that they can realize a goal if, and only if, the other students with whom they are linked also obtain their mutual goal. If the task is to list the factors that influence the time a candle burns, the goal is reached when the group generates the list. To be successful requires interaction, communication, trust, acceptance, support, use of each other as resources, and no comparison of self with others. Teachers prepare students for

---

[*] Note: Jane Vella's book, *Learning to Listen/Learning to Teach*, from the Save the Children Federation of Westport, Connecticut, is loaded with excellent suggestions an improving the way learning occurs.

cooperative lessons by describing the academic task, helping them see reasons for doing it, sometimes assigning specific roles to group members, discussing the norms and values that should guide them, and explaining the specific skills they need to achieve their academic and social goals. The students see that they are each personally responsible for the functioning of their group, and that they should rely on one another for help as much as possible. The teacher's role is to observe interactions and assist only when groups are unable to solve problems themselves. When the groups have completed the lesson, the teacher helps the children think about and discuss both their academic and social learning. Research shows that when the classroom is structured in a way that allows students to work cooperatively on learning tasks, students benefit both academically and socially (Johnson and Johnson, 1975; Slavin, 1987; Hawkins, 1981; Nederhood and Hawkins, 1986).

Student-Team Learning is a subset of Cooperative Learning. In it, heterogeneous groupings of students are assigned to different teams, each of approximate ability, which then engage in learning "games." There is no individual recognition—only team recognition for achievement, and a collective reward structure that contributes to motivating lower-achieving students. There can be competition between the teams, but not at the expense of any student.

Even Individualized Learning Styles works best when coupled with small-group instructional methods like team learning and "circle of knowledge" to review and reinforce learned information. In "circle of knowledge," for example, five or six chairs are set up in a circle. The teacher then poses a single question or problem for which the group comes up with as many answers as possible. (Examples: Name all 50 states./ What are the causes of war?/ Name as many American poets as you can./ Develop as many analogies as you can in four minutes.)

Learning can also be enhanced through the cooperation of students tutoring their peers or younger pupils—even using tutors who are having difficulty in a subject—which appears to enhance learning in both the tutees and tutors [Chapter 20].

Does the model assume that virtually all students can learn all the material, progress at their own pace, and set their own learning goals?

In Mastery Learning students learn at different rates, and they must accomplish or "master" each learning task before moving on to the next, creating the foundation for further learning. Time becomes the variable. Task complexity and degree of difficulty is gradually extended as the student progresses. Success in Mastery Learning requires that learning objectives be well defined and behaviorally specific, that students understand exactly what's expected of them, that teachers regularly check student learning and give immediate feedback to provide positive reinforcement, that teachers use a variety of teaching strategies with guided practice, and that a system allows students as well as teachers to regularly monitor their own progress and success. Results show that these students are more highly motivated to learn, that their learning is increased (often by 72-93%), and that they have better feelings about themselves as learners (Guskey and Cates, 1986; Dunkelberger and Heikkinen, 1983).

Does the model increase student time on task?

In Accelerated Learning the amount of learning that takes place within a given time period is increased. The goal is to raise achievement substantially beyond what it would normally be. To successfully accomplish this requires increasing the capacity of the child to learn (even by ensuring optimal health through nutrition and health care, and so on), increasing the attractiveness of learning activities and the rewards for putting effort into learning, and improving the way time is used (Levin, 1988). (Note: The Direct Instruction Model, not highlighted here, which works best for reading and math, also keeps time-on-task high by expecting much work in a business-like atmosphere. The teacher explores reasons for incorrect responses.)

Does the model take into account individual differences?

Individualized Learning Styles identifies students' personal learning styles through a carefully designed, complex inventory that explores what aids and blocks their communication and learning abilities. They are matched with a teaching style (also determined through an inventory) that is consonant with the ways they learn. The "classroom box" is then broken down into a multifaceted learning environment with dividers; and by clearing the floor the students can set up "learning situations" that correspond to their learning needs. Students use various activity packages as well as sequenced programs of learning that match individual learning styles with various programs, methods, and resources.

Does the model teach students how to be learners, and to be excited about learning?

"Capability-building Learning," creates an atmosphere where students are encouraged to think for themselves, because their perceptions are valued no matter what they are. For example, a teacher might say, "I'd like each of you to write down the most important thing to you [or what you learned] about what we're studying." Once the task is completed, ask, "What does it say on your paper? What made you choose it? Why was that important to you?' And then, "Thanks; does anyone have something different?' Everyone's response—whatever a student finds important—is equally valued because it is based on individual perception. Once a teacher has heard from everyone who wants to share (most do in this atmosphere), the teacher says, "Now that I understand what each of you had, here's what I saw…, and it was important to me because…" These questions promote higher-order thinking skills.

Does the model focus on increasing the enjoyment of learning?

Suggestive Accelerated Learning seeks to provide a "whole-brain" approach to learning by using music, relaxation, visualization techniques, and an integration of the two hemispheres of the brain to promote maximum receptivity to learning. The purpose is to increase enjoyment and tap otherwise-unused learning reserves through the power of suggestion. In using this model for foreign languages, students have covered 5 to 50 times as much material as with traditional instruction, with equal or superior rates of retention (Levin, 1988). The intent is to work with real objects in the here and now and apply the FIRM principle: Fun, Imagination, Relaxation, with a background of Music, using anything to get the whole self involved in the learning process.

Cullen (1987) describes what may take place in this type of classroom: The student enters a pleasant, colorful, well-lit atmosphere with music playing in the background, chairs often in a semicircle on a carpeted floor. Students are encouraged to change chairs during the class, often many times, so they can see all the material presented around them. The class begins with a relaxation exercise designed to remove stress, in which students are asked to remember a pleasant learning experience from the past. Next comes a movement exercise where students visualize a "money tree" before them and try to pick dollars from high on the tree. Using "Total Physical Response" developed by James Asher) the teacher gives commands in the foreign language while doing what she says; then the students do it. Commands are repeated numerous times. Students are then asked to pretend to be a different personality and choose a new name (in the language being taught). They have to sound out the name, thereby inadvertently learning the alphabet. They then might pretend they're at a party and must meet each other in that language. Finally (for that session) the class reads two special readings of text material, the first guided by background music. The students read along with the teacher. In the second reading, the teacher uses in a normal, idiomatic tone. Students are invited to relax and experience the flow of words and music, visualizing the events and ideas about which the teacher reads.

These are but a few creative teaching/learning models that can have exceptional influence on the amount and quality of what students learn. These models may well be used best in conjunction with one another. Compare these methods to the lecture-discuss in large group-test-approach still practiced in most high school classrooms today.

Effective teaching practices still are not used to the extent that results suggest they might. Some teachers understandably tend to shy away from "canned" approaches. But the models themselves are not the essential ingredient; the principles are. Effective teaching could be maximized if teachers approached learning from a different starting point. If teachers asked themselves three questions, they would be well on their way toward enhancing learning for all:

1. If the students were to leave at end of the year carrying with them only one thing, what should it be?
2. How might they be able to learn this best? What creative, engaging ways can I use to excite them about learning it, so they'll carry it with them for the rest of their lives?
3. How will I know they're getting it?

To ask these questions with 25 of the most important concepts could be the major part of a year's work. After all, how much of what we learn in school do we carry with us as adults? What if schools went out of their way to ensure that students learned those things that best prepared them to be responsible and successful in the world?

Make the Curriculum More Relevant to Life Outside School

School success often appears to have little to do with life success. Some students who excel in school later find themselves ill-equipped for the world of work. At the opposite extreme is Einstein who had great difficulty in school and later became the world's leading scientific genius. Between 60% and 80% of what children learn in school is unrelated to their later lives (Carkhuff and Berenson, 1976). Schools could do more to incorporate real-life experiences into the curriculum.

The business community could do much to stimulate school restructuring if many of the top business leaders in each state were to get together and publish the general types of skills that their businesses would require in the 1990s and beyond. When the Cabot, Vermont, school system received a grant from the Vermont Department of Education to restructure its school for higher performance, the principal invited some major employers to address this issue at a community meeting. Bill Davis, former chief executive officer of the Cabot Farmers Cooperative Creamery, suggested that these abilities were needed (paraphrased):

- to think critically
- to problem-solve
- to make decisions
- to work with a team
- to communicate and cooperate with others (social skills)
- use high-tech equipment, such as computers
- to read and comprehend
- to compute, as in mathematics

The other business leaders echoed this list. Might these abilities be what schools should concentrate on?

To connect course work with the world of work, individuals from the private sector could bring reality into the courses, as in law-related education where probation officers, police, officers, attorneys, judges, and inmates conduct relevant parts of the course [Chapter 19]. Students could go into the community to apprentice with employers for work-study credit. Math exercises could be actual calculations needed for managing a household, including budgeting. Students could become involved in environmental improvement activities, or in big brother/big sister programs. "Discovery units" could help students to explore their career choices.

Meaningful community service could be built into the curriculum. School service clubs could participate in community involvement projects or school fix-up projects. Student-produced news programs could cover important community issues. The school cafeteria could be opened to the elderly, with students assisting.

Leitenberg (1987) and others have proposed that every student take a course on parenting and child raising as a requirement for graduation. This course could be conducted in conjunction with child care, early childhood education, or after-school daycare services being provided to the community.

Social skills training [Chapter 24] could be an integral part of the curriculum. Throughout their lives young people will find themselves in situations that call for skills in problem-solving, decision-making, conflict resolution, and resisting peer pressure. They can learn to analyze situations, define alternative courses of action, identify likely consequences, and make decisions. A well-conceived curriculum gives them this opportunity.

The QUEST Skills for Living Program [Chapter 16] is an excellent example of a combined social skills and life issues program that could be considered an essential part of the school curriculum. It explores marriage, divorce, family, peer relationships, and other personal issues important to students.

A school curriculum can also help students explore values and morals and ethical bases for actions. The *Character Education Curriculum* teaches 15 "consensus values common to major religions and cultures throughout the world": courage, conviction, generosity, kindness, helpfulness, honesty, honor, justice, tolerance, sound use of time and talents, freedom of choice, freedom of speech, good citizenship, and the right to be an individual. School administrators using the program have reported dramatic improvements in student attitudes and attendance, and 87% of teachers report improved student behavior (Brooks and Paull, 1985).

The school can reexamine the purpose and methods of studying literature. Teachers could choose books to help students see that others who differ from them in age, religion, national origin, or other characteristics share essential human qualities. They could choose books that widen and deepen students' personal understanding of important values.

Literature can help students to appreciate situations and experience feelings they have not encountered in their own lives, and to experience familiar situations in new ways. Books can enhance students' interpersonal understanding and concern for others (Battistich et al., 1991). A comprehensive annotated bibliography of children's books organized by social themes and identified by grade level is available from the Developmental Studies Center, under the title *Good Books for Good Kids* by Watson, Tuck and Morris (1986).

Courses can also help students learn how to handle the stress in their lives. Pupils could identify sources of stress and learn to relax, to express feelings, and to make appropriate decisions.

An innovative approach is George Richmond's Micro-Society School, as practiced at the City Magnet school in Lowell, Massachusetts. Essentially, the school is run as a society in microcosm, complete with an economy and the institutions that keep the economy and society running. The students operate everything, with teachers as advisors. Students are able to earn "money" and spend it for various goods and services. There are banks, stores, and other businesses, a government, a legislature, police, courts, media, a tax structure complete with the IRS, and other essential parts of a standard American community. The students decide how to run their micro-community, what laws to pass, what taxes to levy to keep the government in operation, and so forth. Classes connect to the "real world" of the micro-society. For example, American history students studying the Whisky Rebellion might discuss the justification for a government levying taxes, then the reasons for taxes in the micro-society, and what's fair and isn't fair. Those who graduate from this system are well prepared for making real-life decisions. In addition, since this system was set up, learning has improved and discipline problems have declined. A student court, complete with judge, jury and lawyers, handles each discipline "case" and determines the appropriate consequence. Many exciting, creative things can be done within the curriculum that make learning more relevant—and more fun [Chapter 14].

Empower Students to Make Decisions About How School Affects Their Lives

"What you have to say is appreciated here! You can make a difference here!" Many schools seem reluctant to say this, or to allow students the power to make real decisions about their school lives. Yet school authorities could define the boundaries, then guide students to use power responsibly within them. This concept is used quite effectively in Teenage Institutes [Chapter 21]; students feel empowered even though a few rules are nonnegotiable. A similar approach could also work in schools.

Schools usually view the student council as its contribution to student empowerment. But often only popular students are elected, and the council rarely has authority to make decisions that affect the operations of the school. Instead of selection through voting, could the council be open to anyone interested, or to anyone who has ideas on how to improve the school?

In some schools students become involved in enforcing school rules through "student courts," where students are trained in rules of evidence, conducting hearings, passing judgments, and so on.

The student empowerment process doesn't have to be threatening. Students could brainstorm ideas that they believe would help the classroom or school run smoothly. At class meetings they could discuss these or other issues. Students could describe how school affects their attitudes toward learning and toward themselves, or how they think other kids are affected by the school. They could then negotiate with the faculty and the administration. Such a process would teach students how to be effective within an established system.

A school could ensure that each student believes he or she is cared about equally, that each is special. All students could be commended in some meaningful way. All could have a day where they demonstrate what their best talent is and try to teach it to others. Student artwork could be the only decoration on school walls.

Reduce Status Differences Among Everyone in the School

Schools are often filled with student cliques that don't interact well. Whenever I have asked groups of students how they wish school could be changed, they surprised me by saying they wish the students would be more accepting of one another and not be so hung up about status. School structure can either contribute to this separation or help students interact in cooperative, nonthreatening ways.

As cited earlier, Cooperative and Student-Team Learning evenly distributes students throughout team memberships. A school could also invite the leaders of the different clique groups to participate in improving the school or assessing school climate. The school could create a forum for discussions of cliques and peer pressure after watching a movie like *The Breakfast Club*.

Schools could develop special programs that help students better appreciate each others' cultural differences and ensure that these differences are respected in discipline and teaching.

Students could tutor other students not only in academic courses, but in sports, shop, home economics, art, music, auto mechanics, or wherever someone has a special skill [Chapter 20]. This tutoring can be of special value in bilingual schools.

Provide Personal Supports to Students

Many students need personal support. Many live in difficult family situations. Many have emotional problems. Most teenagers are struggling with their hormones and the meaning of their lives. Schools could arrange for students to receive personal supports in nonthreatening ways.

One approach is peer-to-peer counseling, where trained students receive structured supervision to assist others with problems. This practice is often even more helpful to the "peer counselors" than to those being helped because the counselors usually form a tight-knit support group [Chapter 20].

Other educational support groups could form around different subjects: children of divorced parents, children of alcoholics, victims of abuse, and so on. Some of these are touchy subjects. It is not the school's responsibility to provide group therapy. Yet these and other issues concern many students, who often have no other forum to deal with their feelings. Schools could sponsor educational support groups on such issues and open the groups to anyone interested [Chapter 18]. Group facilitators could come from mental heath centers, youth service bureaus, parent-child centers, or school faculty. Begin where the students are most interested. But remember, students need to feel they can trust a situation before they will open up.

Strengthen the Interaction Among School, Home, and Community

Logic dictates that there be powerful connections among the most powerful influences on a young person's life. Yet sometimes there is powerful antagonism.

> It is time to break the cycle where teachers point to the failings of parents, parents fault the schools, teenagers blame everyone but themselves and politicians accuse the university of recruiting misfits and graduating incompetents. Each believes the real power lies with the others and that the really important factors are beyond their control . . . The strengths of the major participants must be mobilized, their roles expanded, and their contributions recognized if effective approaches are to have a chance to take root. (Monahan, et al., 1989)

It is interesting that, amid the blaming and antagonism, most often all parties want what they believe to be best for children, and what they want is often the same.

Schools should encourage parents and the interested community to help make the school a better place. Teachers could interest parents by calling them or writing notes home with something good to say about the student: "You've got a great kid!" or "She's really showing improvement in these ways. I just thought you'd like to know." These contacts would help heal negative feelings that parents may have. The school must convince parents that their presence is wanted and encourage them to help out if they have the time.

Parents and interested community members could be asked to help set the goals and mission for the school. They could even sign an agreement that clarifies these goals and defines the responsibilities of all involved. For the parents this might mean encouraging their children to attend school regularly and punctually, to read daily, to show an interest in the child's experience, to set high educational expectations, and to ensure that assignments are carried out-all in partnership with the school. The school could offer training for parents in actively working with their children, and in adult basic education (Levin, 1988).

The school could enlist all community resources at its disposal to accomplish its mission; for example, it could provide adult tutors, give assistance to teachers, have senior citizens come into the school to share their expertise, have local businesses provide personnel and other resources to assist the schools, have social service agencies address the basic needs of families, and set up after-school support and enrichment programs for students (Levin, 1988).

Among the many creative programs that he instituted at the Apache Junction Unified School District in Apache Junction, Arizona, Superintendent William F. Wright initiated a Home/School Visitors program, which provides a liaison between the family and school to identify environmental conditions that may have an adverse effect on children and their education. If there are issues of truancy, health, or other social problems that may affect the ultimate success of the students, the home visitors look into the situation and follow up by lending a helping hand, providing transportation, delivering food, providing access to medical services, making referrals to community services, monitoring and enforcing attendance for chronically truant children by checking the places they are likely to congregate, and more. The parents become more open and responsive and open to the school, and problems are able to be caught early.

Change the School to Enhance Students' Self-Concepts

151

The overall intent is to change the basic structure of the school to enhance students' self-perceptions. The school might eliminate class blocks and ability groupings. It might set up innovative grading systems that eliminate failure, perhaps substituting a listing of strengths and areas for improvement, or a listing of competencies demonstrated. A school could make learning the constant and the time it takes to learn the variable.

These and other practices fall within the realm of major school restructuring. Teachers and administrators need to be freed from needless regulations and reporting requirements so they can concentrate on what's really important: helping students learn and creating better citizens.

A school can use any combination of strategies; each will help improve some aspect of its climate. It should simply select a strategy using a logical process that fits the needs of the particular school.

Combining Approaches Toward a Comprehensive School Improvement Effort

At the Child Development Project in San Ramon, California, Victor Battistich, Eric Schaps, Marilyn Watson, Daniel Solomon, and Judith Solomon combined several of these approaches into a comprehensive school improvement effort. Building upon what research said would improve attitudes, motives, behaviors, and promote consideration of others' needs and feelings, they designed a program to create a "caring school community" and to enhance "the social and moral development of children." Their program was used in three elementary schools in San Ramon and Hayward. Students were monitored throughout their elementary school careers and compared with those in control classrooms.

The program consistently achieved significant results in-

- greater demonstrated "prosocial" behavior toward other students (more helpful, cooperative, concerned for others' needs and feelings, affectionate, supportive, and encouraging)
- greater social problem-solving skills (program students were better able to express their own position and to maintain equal participation and representation among members in group decision-making).
  (Battistich et al., 1991)

The program required extensive teacher training, yet it enjoyed good results despite "the trainers' judgment that most teachers had assumed only an 'adequate' level of program implementation by the spring of their year with the cohort children." Plus there was "considerable variability in implementation among program teachers," so students' reinforcement of these principles varied from year to year. Still, compared to observations before the start of teacher training, the teachers had become-

- more sympathetic, warm, and personal toward students
- more enthusiastic in their teaching
- more responsive to differences among students in needs, feelings and abilities
- more inclined to give their students autonomy, choice, and opportunities to make decisions in the classroom
- less reliant on lecturing as a teaching technique (Battistich, 1989)

The program required the schools to make systematic changes to help students internalize values of fairness, concern, respect for others, and social responsibility. Program components (followed by examples) included opportunities for collaboration with others in pursuit of common goals:

- asking students, "What kind of school do we want to have?"
- asking students, "How can we solve [this problem] together?"
- sponsoring "goals assemblies" to decide/reflect on values for the school
- reflecting these values in school handbooks
- sharing responsibilities with students for putting on school events
- experiencing "a caring school community"
- fostering warm relationships
- training the entire school staff, including janitors, bus drivers, cafeteria workers about the values, norms, and rules of the school
- providing activities that help the students get to know each other; welcoming newcomers
- randomly selecting a class member each week for special recognition, where they're given special responsibilities and a chance to tell others about themselves
- promoting social understanding, highlighting "prosocial" values and learning how to resolve conflicts in a fair way
- reflecting upon their own and others' behavior as it relates to values
- reflecting upon the experiences of others to gain an understanding and appreciation of others' feelings, needs, and perspectives (such as through selected literature that promotes understanding of others)
- developing and practicing social skills and competencies
- discussing social and moral dilemmas and trying to resolve different points of view according to moral principles, ultimately leading to taking a responsible role with others and in the community
- assigning "special buddies," where for that week students and staff do nice things for their buddies
- pairing older with younger students for tutoring, and buddies (as for field trips)
- using school-wide helpers for the various functions in a school, classroom chores, and maintenance and beautification projects .
- participating in community service activities, such as "adopting" a needy child or family, "trick-or-treating" for UNICEF, responding to disasters

With this as a backdrop, the program used a school-wide system of developmental discipline and cooperative learning. These and other means set a tone of care and trust, where each person was asked to live up to the ideals of kindness, fairness, and responsibility. An environment was created where students could experience being helpers, so they could experience the pleasures of being helpful, learn the needed skills, and come to think of themselves as generous people (Developmental Studies Center, 1989; Battistich et al., 1991).

Despite the success of the San Ramon program, we should note that program results did not generalize outside the classroom into improved interpersonal behavior in small-group activities to the extent the researchers had anticipated: "Observed differences have generally favored program children ...but they have often been weak and occasional inconsistencies have been observed over the years" (Battistich et al., 1991). This may indicate that prevention works best when reinforced throughout all the systems and environments affecting children.

Special Programs for the Most Difficult or Needy Students?

Even if a school establishes a healthy climate that provides all students with successful experiences, some may still appear to need remedial work to make up for basic skill deficiencies. While this group may need special approaches, limiting a program to a select group of students also labels them and places them in a position where they reinforce each other's negative behavior. A better approach might be to develop programs that include motivated students as well.

Certain traditional instructional practices like lecturing, large group discussions, and reading-based activities have proven unsuccessful for the needy or difficult student. But if the alternative approaches would benefit almost all students, why separate a special group from the rest? After making structural changes, see who remains with extra-special needs. The numbers—and therefore the costs—would be cut considerably.

Still, the good of the one versus the good of the many is a critical issue. The good of the many must ultimately prevail. The problem has been that the one is usually given up on too quickly, and usually only traditional methods are tried, and these rarely work.

Subtleties of School Climate Improvement

Just because a school goes through a school climate improvement process and carefully considers the best possible strategies does not necessarily mean that the climate will improve. Though its intentions may be grand, the school's subtle practices may still interfere. For example, I witnessed a student punch another on a school playground. Punching was against school rules, so something had to be done. Later, I walked into the office to find Slugger being punished by copying a page out of a dictionary. We would do well to remind ourselves of some principles from Chapter 12. First, this punishment was not predictable in advance; it was something the principal dreamed up on the spot. Slugger could perceive it all as someone else's fault. (Use of punishment often creates that perception.) Second, this incident occurred in what was allegedly a Reality Therapy school. When schools use Glasser's ten-step school discipline approach, a "planning room" is supposed to be a last resort for the student to make a reasonable plan to do better. Copying a dictionary is not at all what Glasser intended. If the school were using "logical consequences," the logic of copying a dictionary as a consequence for hitting someone escapes me. Because a school adopts a particular approach does not mean it will be used correctly. The school needs to question continually whether it is adhering to all principles of an effective school.

Dealing with the Toughest Kids

Sometimes, even when school staff are trained in an effective discipline approach, very tough kids tax even the best of them. This is probably why even a tough incoming principal like Joe Clark (as depicted in the movie *Lean on Me*) booted out all the "troublemakers and miscreants" as his first move. His approach certainly worked to improve the school, and he was very helpful to the students who remained in school, but it is likely that he merely pushed the problem out into the streets.

Yet some school staff seem to be able to handle these kids more adroitly than others. Why? Often these are teachers who seem to have a natural rapport with students or who are themselves seen as the toughest. These are teachers who naturally put into practice principles that work.

If there is any "trick" to dealing with these kids, it is practicing these principles over a long enough time to make a difference. And even this doesn't always work. These kids aren't called the toughest for nothing. They are usually the ones with a long history of reacting to difficulties in a destructive way, based upon the way they perceive themselves and the world. These young people should have been reached early in their school career, but we're often faced with them when they haven't been. It sometimes seems like a miracle to get through to some of them, but I believe this is the rare child. I think we have a tendency to write off many kids long before we might.

Our first task is to try to create such a safe, exciting, and stimulating environment that the student would be so successful that he wouldn't even want to act out. Our every action should build his perception of capability, importance, and power. But if we have done everything we can think of, and he is still disruptive, Steve Glenn (1981) suggests an effective discipline procedure.

In our classrooms at the beginning of the year, we discuss together how we must have an atmosphere conducive to learning and respect for others. So if anyone causes a disturbance that disrupts learning or is disrespectful to others, it will not be allowed. We remind them one time of what we agreed to, but if the behavior continues, we say, "You will have to leave the class for the rest of the period (or until you can control yourself), then we'll have to come up with a plan for how your behavior will have to change to get back in. We want him to perceive that by choosing to disrupt the class by pushing over the desk, he is also choosing to leave the room. If he knows this beforehand, the decision is his. We are merely carrying out what was agreed.

If he won't leave, then we might say, "It'll be a lot easier for everyone if you leave on your own. But either way we're respecting your decision to leave."

"You gonna make me?" he may respond.

"It would be much easier for you to leave on your own now, but if you insist I'll have to get the principal, assistant principal, the coach and the three janitors in here to haul you out." If we have to, we'll call the police. But long before that point we allow him the opportunity to escape with some of his dignity still intact. We want him to know he has alternatives, but only within the established school limits, just as with the laws of the land. We try to avoid a power struggle, but when it comes down to it, it is either him or the class, and the class has to prevail. If students want to negotiate a change in the rules, we should be open to that, but in its proper place and time.

Of course we might then get ready to go home and find our tires slashed, or worse—these days teachers can even get shot, as frightening as that is—but so long as we deal with dignity and respect, do not scream at him, and structure the encounter so he realizes that it is his decision to get thrown out, such retaliation is unlikely. At the same time we should communicate that we are open to working it out whenever he is willing to, given our schedule. We must create a plan for how we can coexist peacefully.

If a student chooses to keep getting thrown out, we might consider reversing the system on him, and give little rewards for staying around and being reasonable, such as getting out of class five or ten minutes early. Don't forget these are extreme situations. If other kids want to do the same, we could say, "We designed a specific plan for him, based upon particular problems he has. If you would like me to draw up a specific plan for you based on your problems, I'll be happy to." Usually they won't want anything to do with it (Durham, 1983).

Our challenge is to use every possible school and classroom situation as an opportunity to build healthy self-perceptions and skills. We can shape the environment so we are more likely to get the behaviors we want. A little preventive action up front, time-consuming though it maybe, will cut down problems at the other end, and in the long run save time and our sanity.

Classroom Climate Activities

It is frustrating sometimes to look at the big picture. It is sometimes overwhelming to try to solve school-wide problems. Still, even if the school is resistant to restructuring or improving its climate, teachers can exercise considerable control over their own classrooms. Even if nothing else occurs in the school, substantive results can occur at the classroom level. Little things done well can make the difference.

As teachers, we could ask ourselves if all students in our class are receiving an equal amount of positive attention. This includes troublesome ones who receive a lot of negative attention, and the quiet, withdrawn ones who rarely receive any kind of attention. We could ask ourselves if we are demonstrating to all students that we are interested in them and that we care about them, particularly when they have done nothing special to deserve it. We could devise a system of recognition where an increase in the number of correct responses is recorded as improved performance, no matter how low or high the number. We can ensure that we are building the perceptions we want, despite the craziness elsewhere. If our students' behavior and learning improves, we know we're doing something right.

In these ways we can set prevention and climate improvement as additional goals, and consider our actions a different way of doing the same business.

School Restructuring from the Outside

While the schools themselves can accomplish much school improvement and restructuring, some cannot. Support for changing schools can occur elsewhere. Many schools need reasons and incentives for improving.

One now-popular recommendation in some circles is for a "voucher system" that would allow children to attend any school they want, no matter in what town or district they live, thus creating a system where schools would essentially compete for students. To attract students, the schools would have to become places young people would want to be. Setting aside for a moment the potential busing nightmare, and the drastic changes that some towns would be forced to make, schools would ultimately have to become wonderfully creative in attracting students. Simply making schools compete could make a huge difference. Many people oppose this idea when it involves including private or parochial schools, but have no problem with the idea of school choice among public schools. Unfortunately, in my view, when voucher system proponents want private and parochial schools included, it clouds the issue, because many people become infuriated when public tax money is spent on private and religious institutions, and the initial reason for school choice becomes lost.

Another recommendation is that the colleges and universities that prepare teachers and administrators be restructured to emphasize the changing needs of today's schools. These institutions of higher learning could form a partnership with schools, in every community where feasible, to match the schools' needs closely with what people are trained and educated to do. In-service training could also become more relevant to what teachers need to know, emphasizing more creative and effective teaching and discipline practices. As Goodlad said (in Lewis, 1989), "for schools to get better, they must have better teachers. To prepare better teachers, and all professional staff, including administrators, universities must have access to schools that exhibit the best practices. Therefore, to assure the best practices, schools must have ongoing access to alternative ideas and knowledge..." Therefore such a partnership is essential.

Another recommendation is that state departments of education offer grants or other incentives for schools to restructure themselves for improved performance. State officials could also pass new regulations for schools to improve. However, new regulations may be counterproductive, as Ernie Boyer explained to the Business Roundtable in Washington, D.C., in June, 1989:

> Thus far over 40 states have adopted tough new regulations. But all too often, these mandates focus on bureaucratic procedures rather than on the outcomes of education, forcing teachers and principals to spend more time with paperwork and less time with their students... State officials should set goals, provide equitable support, and hold every school accountable for its performance. Here the leadership of governors is crucial. But within this framework, principals and teachers should be given full authority to choose textbooks, shape curriculum, hire teachers, organize the school day, and have discretionary funds to introduce bold innovations (in Lewis, 1989).

It is extremely important to free teachers and administrators from unnecessary bureaucratic paperwork.

Testing as School Restructuring?

For testing to be used as a school restructuring effort is to put the emphasis in the wrong place. First, it is after the fact. Secondly, schools and administrators and teachers often feel pressured to produce, and the classroom and school climate can actually be harmed in the process. Third, curricula often become geared to "teaching to the test," and much creativity in teaching may become diminished. Testing may result in students having an even worse experience in school, especially poor test-takers. If we want to know how well schools are doing, if we want schools to have report cards, all we have to do is ask the students. They know who the best teachers are, and they are usually the most challenging teachers that expect a lot from them but who also have a great attitude, and inspire students to learn. This inspiration will likely result in higher test scores—if the tests measure the right things.

Will Schools Ever Change Substantively?

In early September, 1990, Roger Mudd hosted an ETV program called, "Learning in America: Schools That Work." Sponsored by the Chrysler Corporation, the program highlighted four schools that are setting a standard for the future. The next night brought a CBS special hosted by Charles Kurault titled, "America's Toughest Assignment: Solving the Education Crisis."

Each of the exemplary schools cited as examples from the ETV program—the Northview School in Kansas; the Columbia Park Elementary School in Landover, Maryland; the City

157

Magnet School in Lowell, Massachusetts; and the Lorenzo Special Emphasis School in Corpus Christi, Texas—applied many of the principles described in this chapter. Each of these schools showed a dramatic reduction in school discipline problems and a dramatic increase in learning and test scores. For example, the Columbia Park School, based on James Comer's principles [Chapter 30], showed an increase from 50% to 95% in the number of children performing at or near grade level and a 93% drop in suspensions.

These schools owed a major part of their success to innovative principals—Dan Young, Pat Green, Sue Ellen Hogan and her predecessor, and Maggie Ramirez, who showed the courage and skillful leadership to involve and empower others and turn around difficult situations—and to the many wonderful teachers who showed extraordinary caring for the children and creativity in building a learning process that excited and motivated them to excel.

My hat goes off to these folks, and to whoever is involved in performing this creative work in scattered schools and classrooms throughout the country. They are the new American explorers, the innovators, who can help bring America back as an educational force. What they are accomplishing is true prevention!

But ten years later their fine work is still the exception, and as Ernie Boyer said at the end of the CBS program, "We've got to make the exception the rule." When will we catch on and institutionalize what works, instead of focusing after the fact on cosmetic practices such as testing? When will all schools practice what we know works?

Still, I highly recommend that tapes of programs such as these could be shown at community meetings, with school staff, the school board, students, parents and other interested community members present, to serve as an inspiration. Together, people could decide which practices they might consider adopting and adapting for their school in their community.

A New Innovation: Student Aspirations

The National Center for Student Aspirations (NCSA) of the University of Maine in Orono, through the innovative work of Russell Qualia, has gained national and international recognition for its approach to helping schools and parents incorporate students' perspectives and needs into educational reform efforts. Two decades of research allowed NCSA to identify eight conditions that foster aspirations and impact the development of student achievement. Couched in language that students can understand, the eight conditions are 1) belonging; 2) heroes; 3) sense of accomplishment, 4) fun and excitement; 5) curiosity and creativity; 6) spirit of adventure; 7) leadership and responsibility; 8) confidence to take action.

In the year 2000, NCSA surveyed over 100,000 students, finding that students believe in their abilities to improve and with hard work can reach their goals but today are uninspired to recognize options and extend the necessary effort to reach their goals. Their conclusion is that students need inspiration, encouragement and support to target and work purposely to reach the ends they envision. NCSA works with schools to help shape student aspirations.

Two independent organizations, Acu Poll and Eureka Ranch, conducted research finding that children with high aspirations-

- are significantly more excited about learning
- have significantly greater ambition and overall happiness.
- are significantly less likely to do drugs and alcohol or cheat.
- are significantly better able to resist peer pressure.

Their research also found that school aspirations programs conducted by NCSA have shown-
- 72% reduction in discipline problems
- 25% reduction in absenteeism
- 150% increase in national proficiency test scores
- 50% increase in grades with a 43% increase in A's and B's
- report card increases in demonstrating self-control, cooperating with others, following directions, and showing respect.

NCSA achieves these results through this general process: First, students take the "student speak survey." Second, NCSA provides data analysis and consults with both the students and the school about what the survey shows are the "hot issues," Third, with students and others they help develop activities and programs that meet student needs and fit within the culture of their school. NCSA involves all parties that work with kids (teachers, coaches, administrators, parents, community members, as well as students). Whatever specific program or activity that emerges is determined from the inside, through the needs of the students and the school. One example is providing monthly training to volunteers in the school around the eight conditions, and those volunteers are assigned a student or two to be their "Aspiration Advocate," an adult friend for those who may or may not have a significant adult in their lives. Another example is working directly or behind the scenes with a school's leadership team to help school staff implement the eight conditions. The NCSA says its greatest success comes when all players come together with students around one table over time to identify and discuss what these eight conditions mean to them, and what they can do collectively to make a difference. From their experience, when it comes to realizing the eight conditions in action, communication and understanding of one another are the two key ingredients for success (Qualia & Fox, 2000).

14. Reflections on School Leadership and School Change

*We see it happen from time to time (but all too rarely): A new principal enters a difficult school where, historically, kids have been bouncing off the walls. Suddenly the school is turned around, discipline is under control, students who could not get along are suddenly doing well, everyone seems happier, more learning is taking place—almost everything is going better. This happened when **Jim Fitzpatrick** took over as school principal of Champlain Valley Union High School in Hinesburg, Vermont. He has subsequently moved on to become a private consultant, but not before leaving a legacy as one of the country's most successful principals in providing leadership to improve a school's climate.*

JP: If you could design the ideal school, what would it look like?

JF: First of all, it would be a school that was competing with other schools, either private or public, either through the voucher system or with private enterprise running it-

JP: Competing for students?

JF: Yes. It would be designed for students and their parents. It would be open year round. It would be open early in the morning so that parents who worked could have their kids dropped off, and it would end probably six or seven o'clock at night. The kids would not necessarily have to be there all day long, but during that time you would do everything—your athletics, your music, your drama, your "core curriculum." It would be completely individualized in terms of individual growth and learning and academic and social progress, coupled with group learning. High use of technology to assist kids and keep track of them. Interactive satellite communication so you'd be touching other parts of the world and truly bringing it in for global studies. The teacher would be a manager and resource of instruction, prescribing, diagnosing, and providing learning environments and activities for that student's learning style. There would be a lot of opportunities for kids to go outside the building for learning, perhaps they wouldn't even have to come to school every day; they might go somewhere else for a day or so. Kids would progress as they went along. We wouldn't have grade levels, arbitrary gates for kids to go through. The whole thing would be geared to, "How do I get the kid to succeed at this." That's sort of where it should be. You see, we have that knowledge now, but we're not using it, we're not putting it into practice—

JP: How do we know it?

JF: We know that people have different learning styles from research. We know kids don't learn through a scope and sequence, even though that's how the state Department of Education and others tell us to design a curriculum. Kids—everyone—learn in the most chaotic ways and through many other means besides just reading a book and listening to someone talk. We've got to get away from that. Someone may indeed learn decimals before they learn fractions. But if you talk to math teachers, they're convinced you've got to have fractions first. Same in English. It's crazy that we do that as educators. No wonder we're so stressed out. We lay out a curriculum. We get it all organized in September, and then they send us the wrong kids. The kids they send us don't fit our curriculum at all. And that's the problem. **We blame the kids, when it's the curriculum that's screwed up. We've designed a curriculum for a majority, middle-of-the-road curve of kids, and a lot of them do okay or even very well, but there's a awful lot of kids that don't do well**.

JP: So how do you take a school and move toward your ideal?

JF: I hate to say it, but I'm giving up.

JP: What? You are?

JF: Only because people want to do it incrementally. It seems to me that too many people in education are looking for the right arrangement of curriculum, the right arrangement of the organization, that will allow them to somehow teach all the kids the same way again. And the mass production factory model is not for education anymore. Superintendents, principals, board members, everybody, get very nervous about changing this stuff. So they want to do it incrementally. Then what happens is what's been happening to schools for a long time. We swallow it up, and we keep doing what we're doing.

JP: So are you saying there's no hope?

JF: **Oh, there's hope, but you've got to blow the walls apart. Figuratively, you need to just blow the current thinking away, the whole mess, and start over**.

JP: Okay now, if you walked into a situation where everyone was willing to cooperate with you, how would you start the process?

JF: I'd try and get an agreement that we're not going to take the kids for awhile. "We'll guarantee that we will do better than the kids did before [sic], but you've got to give us some time to get it together, to change our thinking, to work out the kinks, work out the mechanics." If you go to a completely individualized instructional method, you need some tools; you're going to have to rely heavily on technology. So we'd say, off the top of my head, "We'll take the kids in November, and we'll spend September and October getting ready." And then we'll run it in a similar way to what to what I was describing. The teachers would have a lot of control over what happened instructionally with the kids and with the schedule. **The focus would be, how are kids doing? How are kids learning? Setting goals for the kids**. With a heavy awareness of the use of language, and how we prepare kids for this new learning experience.

JP: I'm not sure what you mean by that.

JF: Okay, I watched a teacher who was introducing James Fenimore Cooper say, "You're going to hate this book, but it's good for you and we're going to go through it. "Language—sounds in the air—changes people's behavior. When you stop and think of the way we use language in school—all the messages, verbal and nonverbal, that we send to kids—we have to stop and set it up right, be conscious of the messages we're sending. We send different messages to different kinds of kids. In a union high school it could be the town they're from, it could be their last name: we make incredible prejudgments. If a kid comes from a family where there have been behavior problems in the past, there are preconceived notions. "Don't be like your brother." We have to pay attention to the way we present things. We should at least spend September and October talking about that. So I would start there.

JP: A lot of the things you're mentioning, like the use of language, could be done without blowing the whole system apart, so it seems some things would improve a school situation markedly, even if people were reluctant to make massive structural changes. What would discipline look like?

JF: **If you changed the school structurally I don't think you'd have many discipline problems.** That's what I mean. **Most school discipline problems stem from the messages that get sent to kids. When they walk in the door, when they wake up in the morning and are heading out of the house for school, what is the picture in their minds of school? Is it a happy place? Is it a place where people are going to help me? Is it a place where I experience success? Where people have those kinds of experiences, there aren't discipline problems. If there are, it would be handled individually so the kids learn a new behavior in place of the old one that is not very functional or is antisocial.** That doesn't mean you shouldn't have disagreement, or even civil disobedience—in fact I think that's important and it would be part of the curriculum—but if there was a problem I'd follow the Glasser model, Reality Therapy. No one's convinced me that there's something better yet.

JP: Well, it worked for you.

JF: Yes it did. And other things are working for other people. But what I like about Reality Therapy is that it truly honors the individual as having an incredible amount of power, and it doesn't take it away from them. So there's the utmost respect for each individual in that method, which I have a hard time finding with some of the others. Reality Therapy is a nice mix because it says, when people need help, then you go help them. You don't keep being nondirective to the point where they destroy themselves. You help them out, and you teach them a new behavior. Someone who has a skill helps out someone who doesn't or who's having trouble. We do that in all other facets of life, and that's really what we're doing there.

JP: What about the most difficult kids? Was Reality Therapy successful in dealing with them?

JF: One of my best experiences with that was when a student, who dropped out of school and was very difficult to deal with, said to me, "Mr. Fitz, the only thing I learned to help me in school was Reality Therapy. That was the only thing that really helped me." So there's the most difficult kid. Now, he didn't change his behavior a whole lot in our school, but at least he went away with an understanding about behavior, so he knew it was up to him, and he had stopped blaming the school for his problems. He decided to get out and do something else. He went into the service I think, and, for him, maybe that was a good decision because he wasn't experiencing academic success here, and he had other problems, drugs and alcohol and so on. But even the most difficult kids, you don't give up on, and you recognize the context they're coming from. You look for growth, you look for success, so you don't judge a difficult kid against a "good" kid's standards and say, 'You're not a good kid," or "you're too difficult for us because everyone should be like so and so—"

JP: How would you judge them?

JF: On their individual growth, where they're going academically, where they're going socially, and so on. And that model I described for a school would be the best way to get them there.

JP: Now, in that model, your emphasis is on individualized learning. Do you mesh that with group activities somehow or is it all individual?

JF: If you look at learning styles, some people learn better with others, so those people would be learning with others. Another thing is, we've got to teach kids how to communicate, and you can't communicate alone. People-to-people interchange is an important skill to have, so I think that has to be part of the curriculum too, within and apart from academics. **Too many times we communicate in school where the purpose is to come up with the right answer. So you have a lot of kids who won't enroll in that process because they're afraid of being wrong. You have to let kids talk about things where they can simply share opinions, where there is no danger of getting marked off for it. School should be a place where people can do that**.

JP: You were probably the most successful principal in the state in terms of turning around a difficult situation in a school, where you could see the results in front of you. You accomplished a great deal, but here you are, saying you're going to give up because you can't do enough. You did plenty.

JF: Well, I did a lot with discipline and school climate, and I think achievement grew, but it didn't require a real change in the organization. Everybody still had their pecking order and, curriculum-wise, it was still a teacher-centered process. The reason I liked the school climate part was that we were able to turn it into a student-individual program in terms of discipline, and in some cases, learning too. We did a lot with learning styles—at least there was a recognition of that. But when it came time to change the real structure of the school and turn it into a student-centered school, people backed away from that in droves. That's because the system is built on teachers having an incredible amount of control and power over knowledge, over information, over how it will be delivered. The territorial aspects of that are so strong, and you just can't do it incrementally. You'd have to do it the way we changed the discipline system. You'd have to walk in and say, "We will not have departments; we will have interdisciplinary learning. We are going to do it this way. And we're going to agree to do it!"

JP: And you get a lot of people mad at you by doing it that way.

JF: That's right. The reason we didn't get a lot of people mad at us about the discipline thing is because, typically, a lot of people aren't very happy about the way they deal with kids. It's very frustrating, and they're willing to change that. But that's the first layer. That's an outward symptom of what's really going on in a school. And we took care of that first layer. When we peeled that back, **the real reason a lot of these kids were acting out is because of the dead-end courses they were in.** We took a look at the variety of teachers that the low-level and mediocre kids have versus the variety of teachers the college prep kids have in a given high school. Incredible! The curriculum, the number of teachers to choose from—I mean, many kids see the same English teacher for four years while other kids see a variety of teachers and have a wider choice of electives, and I would say, "No!" An assumption was made, for example, that these kids couldn't learn Shakespeare, that they couldn't learn algebra.

The one I went through the roof on was when the state said everyone ought to have three years of mathematics. One could argue about that, but the math people said, "Oh, that means we're going to need a third year of general math." That's like being sentenced to another year in purgatory. That is absolutely unforgivable! General math is unforgivable in the first place, but to have three years of it? It's a holding tank for kids. If you get out of the general math strand, the assumption is that you need algebra and geometry, then maybe calculus, and you have to have Algebra I before you have chemistry, and all that garbage—but there again it's the departments that control information and learning. It's not kid-oriented. But when God predicts you'll be in general math, it seems like there's an infinite strand of general math in this universe that a kid is never able to break out of.

So I said, "What the hell do we need a third year of general math for? Maybe by that time they ought to experience a little bit of algebra. Get them out of that Godforsaken place!" The focus isn't kids and learning; the focus is, how do we label kids.

In Pre-Algebra 1 one year, the kids went into class the first day and the teacher said, "We should really have this class divided into Pre-Algebra 1a. and Pre-Algebra 1b. All of you don't belong here, and I'm the one that has to teach this class, but I really think we ought to split it." Now, that's a hell of a way to start any class, but how many times do you have to split the thing? What they're trying to do is get the class to where they can teach all of the kids the same way and don't have to do any individualization, or they're recognizing that what we really ought to have is individualized instruction.

JP: What puzzles me is, if a teacher is going to make a statement like that anyway, no matter what method he or she is teaching in, that teacher is probably going to make inappropriate statements anyway. Isn't it as much someone's actual teaching skill as it is the structure?

JF: Yes, except that the structure right now eats up a lot of people, and the organization isn't designed now to do what the research says we ought to be doing. Most corporations in this country, for example, have changed with the times in terms of being more sensitive to people. We still have a system that is controlled by people who want to stand up in front of the room and talk and dispense information. The good teachers—the ones I think you're referring to—know that, and they try their best under very difficult circumstances and burn themselves out of education because they can't do what they really want to do, because the structure's wrong. Or they get criticized for it sometimes by their peers, by their colleagues.

JP: When you say the teachers control what happens, do most teachers want to teach the way things are now?

JF: Well, I think they're comfortable doing that. They might give lip-service to the fact that— and I'm probably not being very nice here—in my experience, people will talk about the way it should be, but when it comes to changing it, there is an incredible risk, and that's where the administration and community has to be ready to support them. The risk is that the teacher doesn't control what goes on; the kids are in control because they're learning at their own rates now. And I'm going to have to take care of that situation by prescribing learning experiences for a number of kids, and I've only got fifty minutes a day to do it, and then tomorrow I'm going to have to reevaluate and do it again. The current structure really prevents that.

JP: So is it harder for teachers to teach in this new way?

JF: Under the present system it is. It's very difficult. They only see the kids for 50 minutes and you only get halfway around the room. School is a conservative institution, and parents don't like risks taken with their kids. They're aware of what today's parameters are. They know the definitions. They know the pluses and minuses. If we move to this new way, there aren't a lot of knowns. In fact the ones that have tried it have sometimes backed off from doing it all the way because of this pressure, then basically tried to do it within the old structure. But the joy of success comes after you take the risk, not before, and it's going to be a big one.

JP: You describe what you did at CVU as "peeling back the layers." Is it worth it to peel back the layers?

JF: Oh sure. We were peeling back the next layer at CVU. We literally restructured the school by taking the offices and breaking them up separately. We took the guidance department and the main office and split it up and sent the secretaries to these offices. We put a special educator, a curriculum person, and a guidance counselor in each office, so the kids and the parents went to one place for four years, and when they called the school it was that office's responsibility to get an answer back to the parent or address whatever the concern may be. So we got one office and secretary following the kid through school, knowing the school, knowing the parents, friendly voices all around, the kind of language that says, "We're glad you're here. How are you doing?" And when a student has been out, there are people who are aware you've been out of school. A large school broken up into parts can be like a small school in those ways. The Glasser stuff and some of the stuff we looked at in terms of self-concept was important. The next step would have been to actually have three schools within the school. But that was where we were getting terrible resistance, overt resistance, at board meetings and everywhere.

JP: From parents?

JF: No, not parents, just the teachers. They collectively came to the school board en masse one night and said, "You can't do this. We've done our own survey and here's what the teachers say." It was threatening the whole science versus math versus social studies. Where's the pecking order now? If I don't have a department called science, where do I belong? I suppose people could argue that we were not meeting the needs of the faculty, but it was done to meet the needs of kids.

JP: So when you break things up, how does the science curriculum get defined?

JF: It's still met by the curriculum director. There's an interdisciplinary curriculum director for each of the three houses. **The idea was to promote interdisciplinary learning, because when learning is interdisciplinary, kids learn it; it gets internalized**. You used to hear from a chemistry teacher, "You should know that! You guys had it last year in Algebra 2—what's the matter?" Well, the problem was, it was learned in isolation, and unless you apply it, just like in other learning experiences in life, you lose it, because it doesn't have any meaning. It's not relevant.

JP: So, as an administrator, how do you deal with resistant teachers?

JF: Well, we went through a lot of things that the human relations people tell us you have to do. You have to involve people. You have to give them the opportunity to make decisions. They have to be involved in the decisions. And we did all that, but there was a reluctance to get involved in decisions because people wanted to reserve the right to throw stones afterwards.

JP: Out of fear?

JF: Probably. And power. We had a strong union there. It was strong and survived because it took adversarial positions. You co-opt that by becoming part of the decision-making process. If it doesn't turn out, you're part of the problem. That was threatening. They had their structure, they knew what it was, and they liked it that way. Individual teachers would tell us they wanted to be involved but would change their mind on a daily basis, as soon as they got back into the power structure of the school.

JP: So teachers were cooperative only to a certain point. Some were cooperative when you instituted the discipline system, but others remained resistant. As I recall, one-third were for it, one-third were neutral, and one-third were against it. Then when people saw it worked, the third that was neutral became supportive and the resistant third became neutral. That's not uncommon. Did the same breakdown occur when you instituted learning styles?

JF: We didn't try to do that school-wide. We went with people who wanted to do it because I didn't want to mess with people who were content and doing things well. That's pretty much the way we did Reality Therapy. It's interesting that most of the changes I've done in education have been with people who want to try it; sometimes you get more people than with others. Then we got involved with Accelerated Learning. I called it "Superstart." Accelerated learning started in Bulgaria. It's a way of learning things very quickly, like in a week someone can learn a language.

They're using it in athletics now. It's the whole business of imaging, putting pictures in your mind, which goes along with what Control Theory says, "You put pictures in your mind of being successful, and you use music and a supportive environment so you can assimilate things you learn much more quickly. I moved from learning styles to that because people don't learn when they're not feeling well. There's a thing called SuperCamp, which is pretty commercial, but it's based on these learning principles. Like Outward Bound, it has a lot to do with overcoming obstacles and challenges and the belief about yourself of what you can and can't do.

So I was going to take the freshmen—I started fundraising and everything—to Smuggler's Notch for the first two weeks in September, and teach them computer skills, study skills, speed reading skills, note-taking skills, do a ropes course, hike up the mountain, have learning teams, have discussions at night through closed-circuit TV, have parents there over the weekend if they wanted to, all this stuff. I had some teachers that wanted to do it. My thing was, freshmen come into the school and we ought to let them start off fresh. We put them into a school building and they frig around with their lockers, they're worried about this and that, and they very quickly learn from upperclassmen about what goes on in the school. I wanted to tell the kids that they could be the first class to change the school completely, and every kid could succeed. I wanted to have the kids broken up into teams so everyone was working with all kinds of kids, 'cause that's what the real world's about. The goal was to make them the most productive young people, and send them off after four years just blowing out the gates. I absolutely believe it could be done, but you've got to get away from that damn content—we-gotta-finish-the-book-by-the-end-of-the-year idea—and give the kids learning skills, not content. A lot was accomplished by telling kids that we cared about them and that they could make a difference through Reality Therapy, so I thought we were giving the kids some power, but with that, if you change the curriculum, the content, the delivery system, and put those things together, then bring in some of the research about behavior and motivation, and bring in some exciting speakers for them to hear and to make them feel good, it'll work. It'll work.

JP: So did you ever take them?

JF: I never quite got there. It was at the time I was also getting a lot of resistance. There were a lot of union power struggles going on. Supporting me, being seen with my ideas, was the kiss of death. Not that they didn't agree with me; I never had anybody question that. But it was somehow giving me power if people supported those ideas. As I look back, I think what happened was that the union had literally held that school together through many past difficulties. Then along comes this guy with all these ideas and it's, "Wait a minute, where do we stand?' I used to invite them to be part of it, but there's a line. And it's too bad. You don't have the freedom to say, "Get on board, guys or you can work somewhere else." In fact I called one person in one day who used to complain about me all the time, and I said, "You know, you don't have to stay here. You're unhappy here."

JP: What was the response?

JF: A grievance.

JP: On what grounds?

JF: Harassment. So I did what I could. The thing I really feel good about is that I left without compromising my beliefs. I was afraid I was doing that. We were settling for the lowest common denominator, settling for what was good for the teachers, the administration—not what was best for the kids. The community was just looking to settle the conflict. "Settling" became the most important thing—clean up the files so there's no record that this teacher ever harassed anyone. Put it in a separate file, so if anyone wants to know they could ask." But no one knows the file exists. Or, "The principal will put a letter of apology in the teacher's room." And I just got tired of it.

JP: Sounds like it was hard.

JF: Oh yeah. It was. I went out and bought a convertible. It was cheaper than going to a psychiatrist. [laughter]

JP: So was it worth it?

JF: Oh yes. The more change we created toward building successful students and the more we used the language of trust and the more we were committed to how we could be helpful, the more we helped people take responsibility for and control of their lives. When we talked that way we never had to say' "It's time we did something to that kid." That's worth it.

JP: What are you proudest of?

JF: **The dropout rate. When I got there it was 7 to 8%, which is high for Vermont. After the first year it dropped to 2.4%, and when I left it was one-half of 1 %. Plus, we had 95 to 98% return to CVU to get their diplomas—after they had dropped out**. Kids generally stopped blaming school. I could ride down the street and kids would wave to me, "Hi, Mr. Fitz." That's compared to the way it used to be when I would ride down the road and they'd give me the finger. [laughter]

JP: Sounds like something happened right.

JF: Yes, but we could have done even more—if most people weren't only interested in spreading ointment on so they won't have to change what they do.

12/88

15. Reflections on a Creative Teaching Practice

Sharon Behar *is a consultant who teaches teachers how to teach elementary-level science in an exciting way that builds student feelings of worth, significance and power. Initially I went to ask her about her approach, to cite it in a paragraph for the school climate chapter. In the process, I found what she had to say so impressive that I decided to interview her on the spot.*

JP: Describe what you do.

SB: It's hard to describe, but generally I try to help teachers create hands-on, exciting, and open-ended learning experiences for kids.

JP: They don't do this naturally?

SB: Most don't.

JP: Why?

SB: They were not taught this way themselves. Also, a lot of teachers have issues of control, in that when you give more power to children, you're letting go of some of your control, and it's scary. Plus, you have to worry about what your principal will think when he walks into the classroom and every kid is doing something different and the noise level is way up.

JP: Is this approach something you use just with the science curriculum?

SB: I do it just with science, but my science is not just science. It's basically a questioning technique, setting up an inquiry that works with any model. With the curriculum I designed for the Chittenden East school system, everybody's reading it and going, "Why is this just for science?" And it's not. It's a way to learn everything. So a lot of my teachers are starting to take the way I work with kids and incorporate those sorts of questions into other topics.

JP: Give me an example of the type of questioning in your curriculum.

SB: Okay. Let's say I set up a bunch of experiences at different learning stations where the kids do something with water. At one station they might put pennies in a glass until the water gets to the top of the cup, and keep putting pennies in until the water starts to overflow, and **I'll ask, "Why do you think this is happening?" And most of them will look at you like, "What's the right answer?" But I'm not interested in a right or a wrong answer. I ask kids, "Why do you think? Come up with an idea. What do you want to know about this? What's your opinion? Think of something you'd like to explore. How could you relate that to what you did today?"** Those sorts of questions.

JP: Is this a standard set of questions you have for most activities?

169

SB: No. But they basically all fall into higher level thinking skills, as in Bloom's taxonomy. Most teachers teach by having a child read or hear something then repeat back what they read or heard. Rote learning; the "banking method." And science doesn't have to be that way, especially if teachers aren't that familiar with the material. Teachers don't like to teach things they don't know, because they don' t have the answer. **In our educational system, the teacher is supposed to be the expert. There's little analysis, little synthesizing, little working together. It's repeating back; it's memorization. What I try to do is bring the process of how you go about being curious into the learning situation—with those higher level skills that create creativity.**

JP: Is that what you're trying to do, build kids' ability to be creative?

SB: I'm trying to do a number of different things. Yes, build creativity. But basically, **I'm trying to stimulate them to think about what's going on around them, empower them to believe that they have an opinion worth hearing. And just by doing that, I hope that will be enough respect to build their self-esteem and affect the way they look at the world.**

JP: How do you know it works?

SB: Lots of different ways. Wherever I walk, kids come up to me and say, "Are you coming to see us today?"

JP: Is that you, or is it what you're doing with them?

SB: Both. Another way I know, though, is by what the kids do when I'm with them. Usually the kids that do best with me are the ones that either act out or just sit there with the regular teacher. Then when I work with them, they're the ones that are, like, "Whoooh, Miss Sharon, do you think ... (this or that)?" And it may be a far-out idea, but they have a connection in their head. But nobody ever asked them. They're the ones with their hands in it. They're the ones asking the questions, trying different things.

Kids come up to me all the time and tell me things that I did with them years ago that they're still doing. I adopted trees with second graders, and I was in a sixth grade class yesterday and this boy came up to me and said, "You know, I still visit my tree every day." Another kid who's an absolute pain in the neck to all the teachers—the kid that sits in the "time-out" room all the time—when we did a water lab and were mixing water and learning about miscible-immiscible he went off with all these amazing ideas to try. So I just gave him the materials. He decided to try to mix oil and detergent and found out that they didn't mix. So he says to me, "Is that why detergent doesn't get out oil stains?" Whooh, where did that come from? It's those little things that make me know I'm succeeding.

The teachers are also starting to tell me things. I was designing an in-service on questioning skills last week, and one teacher said, "What do you mean questioning skills? You only ask one question, Sharon." I said, "What question is that?" And she said, "You always say, 'What do you think?' Ever since I've been working with you, I'm really aware of how I talk with the kids, and I'm changing the way I ask them things." One teacher now does all learning centers. She doesn't even need me to come in any more, but I'm helping her design them. She's doing the process on her own. So not only does it work for the kids, it helps the teachers too. It takes the burden off them. They don't have to be the expert. They don't have to know the answer.

JP: What do you think are the **principles of effective teaching**?

SB: First of all, **respect**. That we respect each student as an individual. Not being afraid to say, "I don't know." **Setting up experiences that are open-ended, that there isn't a right or a wrong all the time. Incorporating a lot of different techniques** into what you do, like having the kids work sometimes in groups, sometimes alone. Paying attention to the process of what you're doing as much as the product.

JP: What about the process do you pay attention to? What are you looking for?

SB: **Helping the kids develop skills. There is a sequence of skills**. Skills in observing. Skills in categorizing and classifying things. Skills in experimenting, thinking about something, trying an experiment, coming up with an idea of why you think that happened, and using your own language to explain it. Skills in applying it. Taking what you learned in one area and seeing how it connects to something else. Skills for stepping back from the process and looking at it and being able to say, "I did this well," synthesizing it, creating something new from something you learned. And within that, skills of communicating and working together.

JP: What's the highest grade you do this with?

SB: Me personally? All grades, but most of my time is with K-8. You can do this at any level. The problem is, in a school system, the more you advance in grade, the more rigid the structure gets, to the point where the curriculum is written so teachers are locked into being specific, like teachers that teach for the SATs. That's why evaluation in this method is different from usual. The old way is that kids will know four characteristics of a reptile, or tell you five parts of the body—

JP: Do you care whether kids know that stuff?

SB: No. I care that they're stimulated to start to think about the world around them and make connections.

JP: Isn't it valuable to know the parts of the body?

SB: Yeah, but that will happen.. That shouldn't be the end point. That should be the tool for the process. You can teach the parts of the body through a process. What happens is that those facts become everything.

JP: **So you're trying to get them to be continual learners—**

SB: **And empower them with that gift that learning isn't something you only do at school**. I had one mother call me up, saying, "What's going on? My son has been staring into the refrigerator for three hours." [laughter] I had a bet with the kids that they couldn't find a food we eat that could not be traced back to plants, and if they did I would eat my shoe—just so they'd realize the importance of plants. So for months this kid was driving his mother crazy.

The content is important, but what happens too often is the kids aren't learning the concepts. Research is showing that our teaching is ineffective, that there is little conceptual change going on, at least in science. This kind of teaching gets at concepts better. There's this so-called "new" approach—Paolo Friere talked about it—that we are all constructors of knowledge in our own lives, and that whenever we come to a learning situation, we have concepts of what we think are the reasons for things. And if somebody just talks at you, you walk away holding the same concept you came in with. Just by talking with children and respecting them as learners, you come to understand where they're at; you know how to develop things that touch them where their concepts are and figure out what concepts they may need to develop.

I'm helping a teacher design a month-long unit on gravity, force, and motion. We're setting up a series of learning stations every day where we're not telling the kids our reasons for what we're doing. **At all the learning stations, the kids are communicating with each other: "Why do you think this is happening? What do you think is going on? Predict what will happen. Talk with each other. Share theories."** In another class on a similar unit, the kids were doing a experiment, and I asked the kids, 'Why is that happening?" and immediately all 20 kids said, "Every action has an equal and opposite reaction." And I said, "What does that mean?" And they

171

didn't really know. **They had been taught a pat response. They were doing an experiment and knew this pat thing was the reason for the experiment, but they didn't have a conceptual understanding—**

JP: Did your kids understand it?

SB: They might not know exactly what you want them to know, but they'll begin to see. They won't tell you in those words. They'll say, "Wow, what I think is happening is that when I push on this, the other thing goes the other way." Then you ask them to come up with why they think that's happening. And at the end you can say, 'Well, this guy Newton found out that in most situations this happens." But even if you don't ever say that, that's okay.

JP: Why would a school be interested in having you help them out?

SB: Just today a teacher said to me, "You're the best thing that ever happened in this district. How did you ever get to be here?" I basically sold myself to the district, and they decided to try it out, and they liked it. The feedback was positive and it just kept going. A lot of what I do now is modeling. I work in the class with the teacher, and I help them set up stuff. I'm now finding a lot of changes in the district with the teachers. Most teachers don't get the support or chance to work with each other and try new things and have available resources. It seems like one thing on top of another keeps being piled on top of them. Someone in my position can make it a lot easier. Teachers are grabbing me and excitedly showing me what they're doing in science and asking me for ideas on other things. I had one teacher call me up last night at nine o'clock because she tried something I showed her, and she was unbelievably thrilled and wanted to ask me about trying something else today and she said, "I knew you were going to tell me that. I just needed to ask you anyway." I'm the stimulator. I go from place to place and help people to create and spark them.

As I go around I find that many good people are getting frustrated and leaving the system. It's a sad state of affairs. But there are some incredible things going on in some classrooms. I was just in a school today where the teachers are great, but the climate of the school is terrible because of the administrator. So you have these amazing resources who don't communicate with each other because they're so frustrated with the system. Everybody goes into their individual classrooms and closes their door. The educational system doesn't seem to have a good way of dealing with poor teachers and poor administrators.

JP: How did you get interested in all this?

SB: I was always interested in the environment. I always wanted to be a teacher. I believe that if you really want to effect change you have to do it where people are at, where they live, where their beliefs are. So I decided I wanted to work with school systems in a way that turns kids on to being excited about the world around them, to help them be better caretakers. Because that's what helped me in life. The earth would help me through all my bad times. It's kind of a spiritual thing. I figured if kids had a way of believing in themselves somehow—it didn't have to be the earth for them—I use the environment because that's what works for me, and I believe in it because that's where you can see connections real clearly to teach you things that help you. But I teach things now other than the environment. I teach physics. I teach chemistry. If you can stimulate connections for, kids that help them, then they'll have a tool they can use when they're getting beaten or abused, or when something's happening to them—

JP: Whoa! Wait a minute! Out of physics? How do you make the connection between physics and knowing how to handle being beaten at home?

SB: It's not the content. Physics is something you can take outside of yourself. It's something you can touch. It's something where you can try things and get excited. You have something in your life to get excited about. If, as a teacher, you can work with a kid in a way that's positive, they have a positive interaction with an adult. You share that excitement together. They start to think, "What I have is worthwhile." They begin to believe they have something to share that's worthwhile. And it's something you can connect to the outside world. Physics is connected to everything else, so the kid begins to see the interconnectedness. So just between those two things, you've built self-esteem and you've got connectedness around us all. It's prevention.

JP: Okay, a kid is being beaten at home. How does your process of teaching physics help in a situation like that?

SB: **I think that if one part of you doesn't get totally crushed, then you've helped a kid. If they walk out of a horrible experience with a shred of knowing that at least they have some valuable ideas, that might be the spark to help them make it through**. When you're eight years old, in those situations, what's important is how to survive. If you can survive with some spark, then you've got those tools to build on. Then not all of you is squashed. If I can help facilitate that in anyway—I only use science because I'm more comfortable in that realm. It could be done with anything.

They're doing it now with writing, It's called "process writing." Kids are becoming their own editors, deciding what they want to write about. They write, go through the editing process, use all the correct terms, and when a teacher is reading it, the teacher doesn't say, "Your story is this or that." She asks, "Does your story say what you want it to say? Is there anything that you want to change in the story? How do you feel about this?" That's a very different style of teaching. Teaching it is difficult. Each kid might have three different stories he's working on, one that he's writing for the first time, one that he's editing, and one that he's doing the final draft on. And they conference with each other: One reads it to the other and they give opinions. So the teacher has to make sure she knows what each kid is doing. It's a lot of work for the teacher, but the kid is involved all the time and is excited. It's the same thing. It builds kids' power. They can write what they want to write about, and what they have to say is worth hearing.

2/90

16. Comprehensive Health Education Curriculum

Young people need information and skills to make responsible decisions about many potential problems. Preventers are confronted with how to best impart these. Short of all parents being able to provide accurate, up-to-date information and skills on all preventable problems, it is logical to try to reach young people while they are gathered in the one place where they are, essentially, a captive audience, at least until age 16.

A comprehensive K-12 school health education curriculum appears to be the best vehicle for ensuring that young people receive accurate and up-to-date information on all physical, emotional, and social aspects of health, and about problems they may encounter as they grow. It is also the best place to ensure that they acquire skills to make responsible decisions and to counteract pressures to become involved in uncomfortable activities.

The Special Interest Approach

Unfortunately, nowhere is the special interest approach to prevention more evident than in our symptom-by-symptom approach to school-based health education curricula.

This is not the school's fault. While it used to be that many schools were resistant to teaching anything other than "standard" school curriculum—the "three Rs," science, and social studies (in its narrowest sense)—in recent years many schools have become open to nontraditional curricula, including health education. Some states, like Vermont, have even passed regulations or legislation requiring that schools provide K-12 comprehensive health education.

But while some schools may have made it tough in the past for preventers to get in the door, most of the problem now lies with us. The alcohol and drug abuse prevention field has been pushing alcohol and drug abuse education curricula. The teenage pregnancy field has been pushing "Family Life" curricula. The sexual abuse field has been pushing personal safety curricula. Mental health and other fields have been pushing self-esteem curricula. Schools have become overwhelmed. They see people flying at them from all directions with different curricula, all claiming that schools should add theirs to what they already do. To make matters worse, within each of these fields there is a variety of "canned" curriculum packages, each with a different name. Schools that are already overwhelmed with the volume of work they are being asked to do thus become resistant all over again.

There is no need for this, when all these curricula could be combined into one. The different symptom-specific fields could get together, stop using different terms to describe what is essentially the same, and start saying with a unified voice that **schools need a K-12 comprehensive health education curriculum that includes self-concept development, skill building, and specific information about all the major issues that young people are likely to encounter as they grow and develop.**

To accomplish this, some of us may have to give up use of some of our favorite terms, such as "Family Life curriculum." This will be difficult, but we must keep in mind our desired result. All schools could have an effective comprehensive K-12 health education curriculum. We can best achieve this if we all work toward this end, while advocating that information and skills about each specific prevention problem be included, so all our needs get met.

Definition and Goals

The purpose of a comprehensive health education curriculum is to promote the health of school-age children. Its intent is to help individuals optimize their health and quality of life. As Michael McGinnis, former director of the U.S. Office of Disease Prevention and Health Promotion for the Department of Health and Human Services, said:

> What is very clear is that education and health are inextricably intertwined. A student who is not healthy, who suffers from undetected vision or hearing defect, or who is hungry, or who is impaired by drugs or alcohol, is not a student who will profit from the educational process. Likewise, an individual who has not been provided assistance in the shaping of healthy attitudes, beliefs, and habits early in life, will be more likely to suffer the consequences of reduced productivity in later years (Allensworth and Kolbe, 1987).

Curricular Content

A comprehensive health education curriculum is "the process of learning experiences which favorably influence understanding, attitudes, and conduct relating to individual and community health" (Lohrmann et al, 1987). The goals of comprehensive health education are:

- to champion health as a value, along with responsibility, honesty, worthy citizenship, and quality of life
- to provide students with the knowledge, skills, and power to choose and sustain personal health behaviors; to motivate health maintenance and promote "wellness"
- to foster students' ability to gain, evaluate and use new information to make the best health-related decisions; to develop decision-making skills related to healthy behavior

The content and methodology must be developmentally appropriate. The term "wellness" is used to denote that the intent is not merely the absence of sickness or disease, but rather optimal health. Wellness is **the integration of social, mental, emotional, physical, and spiritual health at all levels.**

Content about substance abuse pervades much comprehensive health education. This is unavoidable because not long ago the surgeon general said it was the major problem in the United States. In 1983 1 conducted an analysis of the then better-known "canned" substance abuse education curricula. My intent was to identify common concepts at each grade level for schools to include in developing a substance abuse curriculum. I examined 12 different curricula and found many common elements. I outlined subject areas to be included, with learning objectives for each subject by grade. I keyed suggested classroom activities for each learning objective to each curriculum source. Since then, the number of available, marketed curricula has vastly increased, but the basic outline remains intact. Major portions of the outlined substance abuse curriculum bear remarkable resemblance to curricula from other fields, and to comprehensive health curricula. Following is a breakdown of the subject areas identified:

I. Self-Concept Development
    a. Everyone is Separate, Unique, and Important
    b. Recognizing, Understanding and Accepting feelings
    c. Encouraging and Developing Capabilities
    d. Needs
    e. Self-control/Expressing Feelings
    f. Growing Up
    g. Taking Responsibility for One's Behavior
II. Self in Interaction with Others
    a. Families
    b. How people Affect each other—Empathy
    c. Communications Skills
    d. Building Trusting Relationships
    e. Giving and Receiving Feedback
    f, Citizenship and Laws
III. Introducing Foreign Elements into Self
    a. What Gets Put into the Body Affects Health
    b-f. (drug-specific information)
IV. Issues related to Use/Misuse/Abuse
    a. General: Reasons for/Signs of
    b. Health
    c. Stress
    d. Risk
    e. Social Pressures
    f, Peer Pressure/Assertiveness
    g. Values
    h. Decision-making
    i. Problem-solving
    j. Alternatives
V. Chemical Dependency
    a. Process of Dependency
    b. Characteristics
    c. Enabling
    d. Treating
    e. Resources
VI. Chemical Dependency in the Family
    a. Effect of [Alcoholism] on Family Members
    b. Constructive Responses to the Problem
    c. Resources

(Pransky, 1983)

When Vermont's alcohol and drug abuse prevention-education law was passed (Act 51 of 1983), an *Alcohol and Drug Education Curriculum Plan* (authored by Chaffee, Simpson, and others, Department of Education and the Agency of Human Services, 1983) was developed to help schools with their response to Act 51. This plan corresponded closely to the above outline (see Figure 16-1). Massachusetts subsequently adopted the Vermont State Curriculum Plan as a major part of its own approach to substance abuse prevention.

A similar approach to curriculum was used when the Vermont State Department of Education published its *Standards for Approving Vermont's Public Schools* (1984), which included "comprehensive health education" as one of its standards. In 1988, these standards were expanded as a new legislative act (270) required the Department of Education to "offer assistance to school districts and supervisory unions to provide teacher instruction in comprehensive health education." *A Framework for the Development of a Health Education Scope and Sequence* (Simpson et al., 1988) was published as a guide for schools. The framework lists concepts and skills believed to underlie all "strands" in a comprehensive health education curriculum, to guide learner outcomes:

Concepts
1. Whole Person Concept: self-awareness, physical, emotional, social, mental, spiritual
2. Importance of Self-esteem
3. Responsibility for Personal Well-being
4. Responsibility to Others
5. Necessity of an Accurate Base of Information

Skills
1. Decision-making: gather information, explore alternatives, predict consequences, act on the decision, evaluate the results
2. Communication Skills
3. Examination of Values and Attitudes
4. Location and Evaluation of Health-Related Information
5. Practical Application of Information
6. Interpersonal Skills
7. Coping Skills

Subject areas to be covered in age-appropriate ways are:
Body structure and function
Human growth and development
Family and mental health
Nutrition
Prevention of disease
Safety
Personal health habits
Consumer health
Community health
Drugs and alcohol

This framework, which lists objectives in each subject for each grade, is available from the Vermont Department of Education, Montpelier, Vermont.

A comprehensive health education curriculum should tackle issues like anorexia and bulimia, excessive calories, drinking and drug abuse, sex, personal safety, suicide, use of seat belts, sufficient sleep and exercise, anxiety, obsessiveness, apathy, withdrawal, hyperactivity, depression, coping with stress, family life and others.

SOCIAL SKILLS INFORMATION
Figure 16-1. Alcohol and Drug Education Curriculum Plan

EFFECTS OF DRUGS ON BODY FUNCTION	1. Identify the effects of alcohol and other drugs on behavior 2. Identify substances containing alcohol and other commonly used drugs.	1. Recognize the short and long term effects of alcohol and other drugs on an individual. 2. Identify classification systems, for alcohol and other drugs.	1. Understand the short and long term effects of alcohol and other drugs on body functions. 2. Understand classifications of drugs and their general effects. 3. Discuss the influence of alcohol and other drugs on risk taking behavior.	1. Discuss the short and long term effects of alcohol and other drugs on body functions and behavior 2. Classify alcohol and other drugs according to their effects on body functions.
USE OF ALCOHOL AND DRUGS IN SOCIETY	1. Identify rules for the use of medicines and toxic substances. 2. Recognize the purpose of medicines and drugs. 3. Identify terms commonly used in discussing drugs.	1. Recognize laws pertaining to alcohol and other drug use. 2. Identify how alcohol and other drugs are marketed and sold.	1. Understand the laws pertaining to alcohol and other drug use. 2. Recognize advertising and marketing techniques for alcohol and other drugs. 3. Recognize cultural differences regarding the use of alcohol and other drugs.	1. Explain the laws and standards pertaining to the use, sale, and possession of alcohol and other drugs. 2. Discuss the impact of the marketing of alcohol and other drugs on the use of these substances. 3. Discuss cultural differences in the use of alcohol and other drugs.
MISUSE AND DEPENDENCY	1. Recognize the relationship between accident and the consumption of alcohol and other drugs.	1. Comprehend the relationship between accidents and alcohol and other drug consumption. 2. Recognize the signs and symptoms of alcohol and other drug misuse, and dependency. 3. Comprehend the terms: use, misuse, abuse, and dependency as applied to alcohol and other common drugs.	1. Identify the effects of alcohol and other drugs on driving skills. 2. Identify medical procedures related to alcohol and other drug misuse and dependency. 3. Identify community treatment resources for alcohol or other drug dependent persons and their families.	1. Evaluate the effects of alcohol and other drugs on driving skills. 2. Identify procedures to help in alcohol and other drug emergencies. 3. Discuss excessive or problem drinking and drug use. 4. Discuss community treatment resources for alcohol or other drug dependent persons and their families. 5. Understand the relationship between the use of alcohol and other drugs and fetal development.
SELF-CONCEPT Self-Assessment Self-Esteem Self Discipline	1. Recognize and experience capabilities. 2. Understand that my behavior affects others. 3. Recognize different common human feelings. 4. Recognize that everyone is separate, unique and different 5. Identify personal likes and dislikes	1. Recognize personal strengths and areas for improvement. 2.Recognize the concept of responsibility for one's behavior. 3. Identify own and others' feelings. 4. Recognize personal needs and ways to meet these needs without drugs.	1. Understand personal strengths and areas for improvement. 2. Recognize the concept of adulthood and one's own development toward adulthood. 3. Practice enhancing self-concept. 4. Recognize the relationship of self-concept to health.	1. Practice assessing strengths and weaknesses. 2. Identify and analyze positive adult role models. 3. Practice enhancing self-concept and thus achievement.

INTERPERSONAL SKILLS	1. Recognize roles and interactions of families and how families differ. 2. Recognize that others' feelings affect their behavior.	1. Recognize the effects of alcohol and other drug use on family interaction. 2. Recognize how groups function and one's changing role in groups.	1. Recognize the influence of the family on decisions to use alcohol and other drugs.	1. Discuss the influence of alcohol and other drugs on risk taking behavior in social and family situations. 2. Understand the skills needed to build close, trusting relationships. 3. Understand the role of parenting in prevention of alcohol and other drug abuse.
COMMUNICATION SKILLS	1. Identify and use good talking and listening skills. 2. Recognize and demonstrate appropriate ways to express feelings.	1. Understand the use of interpersonal skills in talking, listening, assertiveness and conflict resolution. 2. Practice appropriate ways to express feelings.	1. Understand use, and evaluate active listening skills. 2. Demonstrate assertiveness with peers when pressured to use alcohol and other drugs. 3. Identify way to support others in their decisions not to use alcohol and other drugs.	1. Demonstrate skills in active listening, conflict resolution, an giving and receiving helpful feedback/criticism. 2. Demonstrate the ability to question assertively anyone recommending or prescribing drugs, and ask for alternatives to their use. 3. Demonstrate techniques for supporting others in their decision not to drink or use other drugs.
COPING SKILLS	1. Identify the concept of peer pressure. 2. Identify groups of trustworthy adults. 3. Recognize how and why rules are made.	1. Recognize the role of peer pressure on the use of alcohol and other drugs. 2. Recognize the major pressures to use alcohol and other drugs. 3. Identify groups of trustworthy peers. 4. Recognize the need for laws regarding alcohol and other drugs and their limits. 5. Identify sources of stress and the beneficial and harmful effects of stress.	1. Understand the role of peer pressure and its influence on our decision to use or not use alcohol and other drugs. 2. Understand and evaluate the reasons for the misuse of alcohol and other drugs by peers and adults. 3. Practice ways to relieve stress through non-drug involved means.	1. Practice and evaluate alternatives to the use of alcohol and other drugs. 2. Demonstrate practical personal DWI countermeasures that teenagers can employ.
RESPONSIBLE DECISION MAKING Gather Information Explore Alternatives Predict Consequences Act on the Decision Evaluate the Results	1. Recognize the relationship of values and goals and decisions about substance abuse. 2. Recognize the steps of a problem-solving process. 3. Recognize habits as part of behavior. 4. Identify safe behaviors in situations involving medicine and poisons.	1. Understand values and goals as they pertain to decisions regarding substance use. 2. Describe the application of a problem-solving process as a non-chemical method of dealing with personal problems. 3. Recognize how and why people use drugs. 4. Recognize ways to reuse alcohol and other drugs.	1. Demonstrate an awareness of personal values and goals as they pertain to decisions regarding substance use. 2. Demonstrate a problem-solving process in situations involving substance use. 3. Understand reasons why people use drugs. 4. Demonstrate ways to refuse alcohol and other drugs.	1. Analyze the influence of community values and attitudes on decisions regarding substance use. 2. Practice a problem-solving process in situations involving substance use. 3. Discuss how individual responsibility and decisions determine a person's use/misuse/abuse. 4. Practice ways to refuse alcohol and other drugs.

State of Vermont Department of Education
And
Agency of Human Services, Alcohol and Drug Abuse Division

If someone has not already done so, it is time to examine thoroughly all curricula related to comprehensive health—including alcohol and drug curricula, family life education curricula, sexual safety curricula, mental health curricula, self-esteem curricula, social skills curricula, and others—to build a framework for schools to see, in as much detail as possible, what concepts should be included, so they can adapt a health curriculum that best suits their needs.

Curricular Integration

A comprehensive health education curriculum should be planned and taught in careful coordination and integration with other school subjects.

Besides providing exercise and improving cardiovascular and respiratory efficiency, motor performance, and aerobic capacity, physical education can provide the opportunity for self-expression, social development, relief from stress, and provide meaning to movement in the life of a child. Home economics can provide help with decision-making, and social issues. Science can help provide information on physical and biological implications of health-related issues. Social studies can provide information and discussions on their historical and social contexts and implications. Math can provide opportunities to calculate items like blood alcohol content.

The school nurse can provide health promotion activities, remediation of specific health problems, first aid, health counseling, and health instruction. The guidance department can provide programs to promote the mental and emotional health of students, assertiveness training, life-skills training, peer-led discussions, problem solving, self-esteem building, internal locus of control, resisting peer pressure, and adolescent emotional development. Special education can provide information on handicapping conditions and how to prevent and cope with them.

The curriculum should be continuously assessed by students, teachers, the school district, and the community to ascertain whether its goals are being met.

Integration with the Rest of the School

For a health education curriculum to realize its goals, it should be reinforced throughout the school and achieved within the context of a comprehensive school health education program. It should extend beyond curriculum into the total physical and social environment of the school. It should be **related to the type of food the kids eat in school** (nutrition education would be far more effective in reducing dietary risks for cancer and cardiovascular disease if the school food service reduced the availability of foods that increased such risk and replaced them with nutritious foods).

The health curriculum should also be **related to the physical school structure and its health and, of course, to the school's climate. The school should model healthy ways of treating others to reinforce what is being taught.** It should be connected to other health-related services like nursing and counseling, and extend beyond prevention into intervention and referral.

A school team could be responsible for planning and implementing all aspects of a comprehensive health program. Learning about children of alcoholics can be connected to the guidance department's sponsoring or running a group on the subject. The same holds for sexual abuse, coping with family issues, and all other important issues. In learning about chronic health problems like asthma, students can learn techniques from the school nurse for managing attacks.

181

Students could use principles learned in health classes to develop their own personal fitness programs, tied in with physical education. All this magnifies the benefits of a curriculum.

In the study of safety, students can do a safety check of school grounds as an assignment, and recommend changes. They could examine school environmental hazards (asbestos, use and disposal of cleaning fluids and chemicals from chemistry labs, safety features). They could examine the school's physical effects on persons, layout, temperature and humidity, noise, lighting.

A comprehensive health program could include programs like Early Drug Abuse Prevention (EDAP) [Chapter 18] to complement the curriculum.

Comprehensive health education could provide opportunities to understand health in its larger social context, exposing students to an array of local, state, national, even international priority health concerns. The curriculum can include bringing in practitioners and going out to observe the realities of health practices. Schools do not exist in isolation. Much of what students learn occurs outside the formal classroom. Students can develop community health programs, with the school providing support.

Effectiveness

What basis is there for suggesting that comprehensive health education makes a difference in young people's lives?

In 1985, a massive *School Health Education Evaluation* was undertaken involving more than 30,000 children in grades four to seven in 1,071 classrooms in 20 states (Connell et al., 1985). Besides the expected increases in health knowledge (particularly substance abuse), findings were as follows (compared to controls that started at near-equal pretest scores):

- healthier attitudes
- improved health skills and practices (the greatest difference was in decision-making skills)
- one-third as many students reported smoking at the beginning of seventh grade

With a second exposure in the fifth and sixth grades, students' attitudes and practices improved, suggesting cumulative gains through several grades.

The following factors appear to make the difference in *health curriculum effectiveness*:

- ♦ the more classroom hours, the more significant the attitude change; health knowledge gains were visible after only 50 hours of exposure
- ♦ the higher its priority for the teacher, the greater the gains for students
- ♦ the more fully implemented the program, the greater the general and specific knowledge gained, the attitude change; and self-reported, practices [In another program, where fully implemented, effects were 90% greater for attitude and 85% greater for practices (Fors and Dostar, 1985)]
- ♦ the greater the amount of teacher in-service training, the greater the percentage of the program taught (fully trained: 85%; partially trained. 76%; not trained: 70%)[*]

---

[*] Note: "Both teachers and administrators must be forewarned that teachers for this program, virtually none of whom are trained health educators, must be given time to develop and implement modifications

♦ the greater the school resources allocated to health curricula (classroom time, support materials, learning resources to carry out the program), the greater the gains for students

♦ the more sensitive the curriculum to ethnic, geographical, and environmental factors and the sensitivity to various levels of interest, ability and skill among students, the better

♦ the greater the administrative program support demonstrating that the curriculum is important, the greater the program continuity

♦ the better the planning, the more effective the program

♦ the more sequential the program (beginning at entry into school and continuing through completion) with specific delineation of age/grade-appropriate content areas, the greater the changes over time
(Fors and Dostar, 1985)

Special Substance Abuse Curricula and Programs

Most of the evidence that health education curricula can affect behaviors comes from curricular programs that deal with parts of a comprehensive curriculum, largely in the substance abuse field, particularly when combined with other efforts that enhance curricular effectiveness.

Here's Looking at You, 2000

Evaluations were conducted on the extensive and thorough K-12 substance abuse education curriculum, *Here's Looking at You, 2000* in grades 4-12 in rural Marion County, Oregon (Bubl, 1988), and in grades 1-6 at an inner-city elementary school in Philadelphia (Swisher, 1989). While preliminary results of both studies showed that students increased knowledge and skills related to decision-making and "refusal," the Philadelphia evaluation also showed-

- an increase in self-esteem, grades 1-3 (This was particularly significant because "the control group slightly decreased over the same period.")
- a decrease in use of chewing tobacco, grades 1-3

This is an improved version of the original *Here's Looking at You* curriculum where Kim (1983) found no differences from controls in attitudes about drinking or drugging patterns. Training in the use of this curriculum is available through Roberts, Fitzmahan, & Associates, Seattle, Washington.

Project SMART and *Project STAR*

Some programs are designed as small, complete packages but may be considered as a part or unit of a comprehensive health curriculum. Such a program is Project SMART, developed by the Institute for Health Promotion and Disease Prevention Research at the University of Southern

---

to the program so their local needs are best met." The training should consist of use of appropriate methods and materials for the specific curriculum, and of basic principles of health and wellness and health education (Connell and Turner, 1985).

California in Pasadena. The program focuses on teaching refusal and resistance skills in grades six to nine. In 11 sessions this program targets the use of cigarettes, alcohol and marijuana, specifically in resisting peer pressure to use. A program conducted in seventh grade had the following results:

- onset of first marijuana, alcohol, and cigarette use delayed
- 48% less tobacco use, 22% less alcohol use, 38% less marijuana use than controls (at post-test in eighth grade); smoking reduced by 32%, alcohol by 6% and marijuana use no different from controls (at post-test in ninth grade)

The Irvine Unified School District in Irvine, California adapted this program for grades six to eight, expanding it to 50 sessions and calling it Project STAR (Social Thinking and Reasoning). Added or expanded upon were social skills (how to begin conversations, how to handle criticism), assertiveness skills (how to identify passive, aggressive, and assertive behavior, how to say no), personality styles (recognizing one's own needs and strengths, appreciating. differences in others), stress management (relaxation skills, imagery). Activities include discussions, stories, role-plays, short workshops, games, and imagery.

STAR results for middle school students included.

- higher grade point averages
- better classroom behavior better school attendance
- improved attitudes toward health
- 51% reduction in cigarette smoking among sixth and seventh graders, but less dramatic changes in marijuana and alcohol use

The Project STAR program has been packaged and can be purchased with a one-day training plus follow-up consultation back at the school (STAR: Irvine Unified School District, Irvine CA; SMART: Institute for Health Promotion and Disease Prevention Research, U. S. C., Pasadena, CA).[*]

QUEST

One of the earliest packages is the *QUEST: Skills for Living* high school curriculum. Students are helped with four major competencies: self-discipline, responsibility, good judgment, and the ability to get along with themselves and others. It allows for exploration of common adolescent concerns about friends, feelings, attitudes, self-concepts, family, marriage, parenting, careers, finances and life planning. It includes reading, group and family activities, contact with community resources, field activities and personal reflection, and consists of mini-lectures, discussions, awareness sessions, role playing, and skill building. The curriculum includes 94 different sessions, but one need not use them all.

Results from several evaluations find statistically significant gains on the following measurement scales:

---

[*] Note: Crime Prevention Center California Office of the Attorney General (1987). Schools and Drugs: A Guide to Drug and Alcohol Abuse Prevention Curricula and Program. Sacramento, CA.

- improved locus of control (feeling responsible for and in control of one's life)
- improved feelings about self and family
- improved communication with others
- improved interpersonal relationships

As of 1987, QUEST had been used in 900 school systems in 44 states and seven countries.

QUEST saw the need for a similar program at the middle school level and created the *Skills for Adolescents* program for grades six through nine. This program focuses on communication and other social skills, decision-making, goal-setting, self-concept, and family relationships. It includes learning about emotions and self-discipline, improving peer relationships, developing critical thinking skills for decision-making, and setting goals for healthy living. It includes an introductory session on "the teen years." The facilitator encourages student participation, use of role playing, personal reflection, and (added later) peer refusal skills.

Results of evaluation included significantly higher scores on self report measures (compared with a control group) of-

- improved relationships with others
- improved resistance to peer pressure
- improved attitude toward teachers and authority figures
- improved assertiveness
- improved communication

Teachers reported observable positive changes in-

- improved self-worth
- improved responsibility
- improved respect for others
- improved problem-solving, decision-making, critical thinking
- improved ability to see oneself as responsible for and in control of one's life

As of 1990, over 2,000 schools throughout North America and Great Britain had used this program.

A *Skills for Growing* program was later added for grades four to six. The QUEST programs are fairly expensive and require three days of training, but I have seen it in action, and it appears worth it (Contact: Quest International Center, Columbus OH).[*]

Combining Curriculum with Supports: Tribes

The Tribes program combines curriculum with "A Process for Social Development and Cooperative Learning." In this K-8 program, students work together in peer groups called "tribes" that create a supportive, cooperative environment for growth and learning, build self-esteem and a sense of belonging, caring, trust and respect for self and others. All students are included in classroom activities that teach communication, problem-solving and decision-making

---

[*] Note: Crime Prevention Center (1987).

skills, and an appreciation of individual differences. Each group of five to six students is encouraged to support and take responsibility for each other in activities focusing on trusting, sharing, being assertive, cooperating, and being comfortable with oneself.

In a program evaluation, positive affects were found in-

- improved self-concept
- improved attitudes toward school
- decreased disruptive behavior (at primary level)
- increased academic achievement

These materials are fairly inexpensive but an extensive four-day training is required.[*]

An Innovative Curriculum Idea: *In My House*

A prevention program that applies somewhat of a cognitive approach is *In My House*, from Responsible Decisions, Inc. of Denver, Colorado. This program is designed to help young people ages 10 to 13 make positive choices and reduce at-risk attitudes and behaviors. It uses an innovative approach called "Interactive Journaling,"[®] created by The Change Companies, which is an experiential writing process designed to motivate and guide participants toward responsible lifestyle change. A composite of five studies involving over 2500 users of Interactive Journals in both inpatient and outpatient sites and in correctional facilities showed that 74% said their journaling helped them "to stay clean and sober today." For *In My House*, this approach has now been adapted for primary prevention. Built on a spirit of action, it uses a house as a metaphor for a person's life, and nine different rooms (topics) are explored: Alcohol, Tobacco, and Other Drugs; My Feelings; My Self-Image; Respecting Others (violence prevention); Relationships; My Body; My School; Having Fun; My Future. The journaling in each topic is designed to draw out and organize people's thoughts and feelings about their lives, and help them set goals and establish positive habits. As of this writing, a study of effectiveness was being conducted but results were not yet in.

Combining Curriculum with Meaningful Community Service: Ombudsman

The *Ombudsman* program of the Drug Education Center of Charlotte, North Carolina, combines meaningful community service with a fifth and sixth grade school drug abuse curriculum that focuses on self-awareness, communications skills, refusal and decision-making skills, group interaction skills, and helping relationships. The program is named after the Swedish concept of helping a person. Ombudsman is certified by the U.S. Department of Education as "a program that works." The intent is for the students to apply the insights and skills that they learned by planning and implementing projects within their own school or community; for example, making drug abuse prevention videos, anti-drug PTA presentations, peer helper projects, "Just Say No" clubs, school or community clean-up, sponsoring alcohol/drug free events, etc. Students are often exposed to the local news media, community leaders, and to the satisfaction that stems from commitment and responsibility.

---

[*] Center for Human Development, Lafayette, CA

Ombudsman graduates showed-

- less self-reported drug use
- less display of "high risk correlates of frequent drug use" (Kim, 1981; Kim, 1983)

If the program was implemented without the community or school project phase, the program was found to be less successful.

A manual is available for program implementation called *Ombudsman: A Classroom Community* (Williams, 1980). Teachers are trained to conduct the program.

A nine-session program called *I'm Special* covers many of the same topics as Ombudsman, but geared to students in the fourth grade. The program began in 1978, and students were surveyed as they progressed through the 5th through 12th grades. Results for grades 5 through 7, compared with controls, showed-

- significantly lower proportions of substance users among I'm Special graduates
- significantly lower incidence of problem behaviors like stealing, school absenteeism, and school suspension. However, the impact of the program seemed to diminish significantly in and around the ninth grade (Kim, 1989)

I'm Special also has a training manual available through the Drug Education Center of Charlotte, North Carolina.

A Truly Comprehensive Program: The San Juan Unified School District

The San Juan Unified School District's K-12 Substance Abuse Prevention Project is one of the best and most extensive in the country. It combines use of an integrated substance abuse education curriculum with other prevention and intervention programs affecting peers, their parents, and the community.

Their curriculum consists of the following:

- *ABCs of Prevention* (K-3), concerned with attitudes, behaviors, coping skills, stress reduction, personal safety, and self-esteem
- *DIS'N DAT* (Designated Instructional Services In Drugs, Alcohol, Tobacco) (4-6) concerning decision-making, peer pressure, self-esteem, feelings, and drug/alcohol information
- *Tribes* (K-6)
- *Quest: Skills for Adolescence* (7-8)
- Physical education substance abuse prevention mini-units (8-9)
- *Here's Looking at You, 2000* (K-12)

It is complemented by a wealth of other prevention/intervention programs:

- *Just for Kids* (K-6), which provides one-on one "special time" for "high risk" students with a trained paraprofessional counselor;
- *Prevention/Intervention* (7-12) small group classes focusing on problem-solving, self-esteem, drug and alcohol information, values;

-   *Student's Reaching Out* (9-12) trains peer leaders to make presentations and facilitate discussions with (4-8) feeder schools on issues such as decision-making, peer pressure, refusal skills, and drug/alcohol info.;
-   *Student Support Groups* (K-12) providing group support for chemically dependent students maintaining sobriety, students concerned about the drug/alcohol involvement of family and friends, and use-focused groups called "Insight";
-   *Teen Leadership Conference* (9-12), a summer leadership training event to get involved in meaningful activities that promote personal growth and positive self esteem;
-   *Students Against Driving Drunk*;
-   *Parent Rap Programs* (9-12) where students have the opportunity to discuss a variety of problems with trained parent volunteers;
-   *Youth Advisory Committee on Substance Abuse Prevention* where student and faculty representatives from 25 student groups meet monthly to share ideas on substance use and abuse, and plan district-wide campaigns to combat problems;
-   *Developing Capable People* course for parents and teachers;
-   *Preparing For the Drug Free Years*, for parents;
-   *Student Assistance Programs* to help students having substance related or emotional problems;
-   *Employee Assistance Program* to assist staff with substance abuse or emotional problems;
-   *uniform policies and procedures* for discipline and substance use;
-   *PIECES* (Prevention/Intervention Education Classes for the Enlightened Student)(6-12) for students who violate school district drug/alcohol policies for the first time;
-   *Community Forums* that provide awareness weeks for the community and "Be Smart/Don't Start" community education campaign;
-   *BASE* (Businesses Actively Supporting Education) (9-12) where "at risk" youth have lunch with an visit the work places of various business people, emphasizing the importance of education and staying in school;
-   *Natural Helpers* (9-12) determining the school's natural leaders who are provided with extensive training on effective helping strategies, resources, and school climate improvements;
  ...and much more.

An annual survey of all seventh and tenth graders in the district shows:

- 50% reduction in substance-related suspensions
- reductions in problem behaviors

Even with all these components, the cost of running this project is less than $3.50 per student.[*]

DARE (Drug Abuse Resistance Education)

It is sometimes easy to latch onto a particular curriculum as the "be-all and end-all" of programs, but this is rarely the case. DARE (Drug Abuse Resistance Education) has special appeal because it is promoted and conducted by police for schools and thus has become quite popular in recent years. Reviews, however, have been mixed. While reports from various

---

[*] San Juan Unified School District, Carmichael, CA

programs have generally been positive, a journal-published study using control groups found that DARE had no impact on student attitude or self-concept, and no impact on student intentions to use drugs in the future. There was an increase in the use of refusal skills. Self-reports showed that cigarettes and hard liquor were used less frequently, but beer, wine, marijuana, speed, downers, PCP, and inhalants were not (DeJong, 1987). This does not make DARE an undesirable program; it only suggests that it would be best if other forms of prevention education were used in conjunction.

Child Sexual Abuse Curricula

Another important segment of a health curriculum concerns itself with the specifics of sexual abuse. Two of best and the most innovative curricular-like programs are those developed by CAP (the Child Assault Prevention Project) in Columbus, Ohio, and PASA in Brooklyn, New York. For these and perhaps some other components of a comprehensive health curriculum, it may be best for trained, skilled workers to be brought in to run certain sessions.

CAP: The Child Assault Prevention Project

Some child sexual abuse curricula have been criticized for increasing children's fears as they attempt to decrease their vulnerability. CAP believes that children can be taught to protect themselves without being made fearful or being taught that they are victims.

CAP begins with an explanation of "rights": the right to be safe, the right to be strong, the right to be free. This includes the right to talk about anything that makes children feel frightened or confused or that hurts them. The focus is on providing children with practical skills while building confidence in their own abilities to solve problems, even in crisis situations.

The curriculum is run as a hands-on workshop. Children are trained to recognize potentially dangerous situations and to make effective use of options available to them. They are taught to distinguish between affectionate touching and sexual or exploitive touching. Adults who exploit children rely on children's passivity and obedience to adult authority, thus, CAP teaches that children have a right to say "no" to an adult.

The core of the curriculum revolves around three scenarios acted out by workshop leaders chosen to reflect the ethnic makeup of the local community. The "stories" show different kinds of dangerous situations: first, a child who is bullied and robbed by a bigger child; second, a child who is enticed and grabbed by a stranger; and third, a child whose uncle insists that she kiss him, directing her not to tell anyone. After each scenario, workshop leaders discuss options the child might use to protect herself and retain her right to be safe, strong, and free. The first time the scenario is acted, the CAP leader playing the role of the child acts confused, frightened and passive. After a discussion where the children are involved in coming up with potential solutions, the scene is then reenacted, with the child successfully thwarting the attack. In the last scene, the, leader might say, "The uncle told his niece to keep the kiss a secret. But good kisses and touches don't make us feel frightened. Is this a good secret?" (Cooper, undated).

Workshop leaders are available for individual conversations after the session to deal with any intense feelings that may have been dredged up.

CAP also offers workshops for teachers, covering information on the children's workshop, an overview of child sexual assault, identification of sexually abused children, crisis intervention guidelines, community resources and referrals for reporting abuse, legal rights and responsibilities of reporting, information to consider when they suspect that a child is being abused, and talking with a child in crisis. In workshops for parents, the emphasis is on prevention and communicating with children.

Sally Cooper, the driving force behind CAP, says, "There is the wrong notion out there that prevention is karate-chopping somebody in a dark alley at 3 A.M. It's much more a mental attitude, consisting of being aware of potentially threatening situations, assessing what you could do to protect yourself in the situation at hand, and being prepared to use what tactics you decide are best" (Weaver, 1987).

PASA, Brooklyn, NY

PASA takes sexual abuse prevention curriculum a creative step further. Kathy Dee Zasloff, the driving force behind PASA, questions common assumptions of many child sexual abuse curricula that can be confusing for kids. The first is the emphasis on "good touch" and "bad touch," which can be particularly confusing for incest survivors, many of whom report liking the touch. What they didn't like was the force or the secrecy. "We didn't want young people growing up with an aversion to being touched. Touch is an important and essential part of people's lives." The second is the theme of "No-Go-Tell," that children have the right to say no to bad touch, then they should go and tell someone they trust. The problem is, many offenders are known and trusted by the victim, so this message can be confusing.

PASA concluded that the better one gets at developing one's intuition and catching potentially dangerous or uncomfortable situations early, the less one need use strategies for getting out of difficulties. It is therefore important to help children build their inner strength and intuitive skills so they will be less likely to find themselves in a dangerous situation. PASA focuses on the "core characteristic" of many symptoms: low self-esteem. The idea is for children to feel good about, have respect for, and be in control of their bodies.

In developing their training curriculum, PASA examined many theories and programs of personal improvement, physical development, eastern philosophies, spiritual consciousness, New Age thinking, and other techniques to create an innovative approach to building personal strength in children. They created "an active viewing, critical-analysis, media program" called *Communivision* that provides "a common ground where people can discuss their perspectives, opinions, and feelings about a variety of issues." Communivision helps people acquire skills to challenge media messages and their influence in their lives. PASA observed that people began to apply these critical analysis skills in other areas of their lives. They began to challenge authority, take an active role in the determination of their lives, and feel better about themselves.

PASA's "risk reduction education and training program" consists of the following: personal safety training, communications skills, critical analysis skills, law-related education, energy awareness skills training, stress relaxation and centering techniques, holistic health concepts, use of sound and music on and with the body, and guided imagery. It attempts to combine people's experiences and emotions with specific information, causing a "perspective shift" that enables them to look at situations more completely and understand experiences differently. It therefore promotes understanding that there are strategies they can use to reduce the risk of being sexually abused, victimized, and exploited.

The program helps children to be sensitive to experiencing "funny body feelings" and to implement a personal safety plan. They improve their ability to relax in high-stress situations so they can keep their heads and know what to do. "Energy awareness" helps people learn how to relax and master their fear and rage that can immobilize and make them feel powerless. It helps develop intuitive skills that allow the wisdom and knowledge of their bodies to assist children in implementing personal safety plans. Children find that they can apply these techniques to other stressful times, such as test-taking (Zasloff, undated).

I have seen no research that concludes whether these sexual abuse prevention programs change children's behaviors. To my knowledge, such research has not been conducted. It needs to be. Yet the programs sound promising and, because this field is so new, it would seem best to try these promising strategies and at the same time insist that researchers conduct the needed studies.

The problem with most sexual abuse prevention curricula is that they are only intended to prevent victims from being victimized—not to prevent sexual perpetrators. Fay Honey Knopp, who before her death was one of the top sexual abuse experts in the country, through the Safer Society in Bradford, Vermont, wrote probably the first book on this subject. In fact, the Safer Society has many excellent publications pertaining to sexual abuse.

Family Life Education

Another component of comprehensive health education is Family Life Education. Fewer than one in ten American teenagers currently takes a separate, comprehensive and timely course in human sexuality and relationships. Courses that do exist are rarely introduced below the ninth grade, and the emphasis is often placed on physiological facts about reproduction, not on emotions and feelings, decision-making, confidence, and values (Wilson, 1985).

Besides increased student knowledge about sexuality, sex education programs have been found to yield-

- increased use of contraception
- lower rates of pregnancy and out-of-wedlock births
- fewer abortions

Sex education in tandem with school health clinics where contraceptives are available reduces the pregnancy rates further. This has been the experience of many countries in Western Europe. Yet compared to other industrialized countries, little contraception education occurs in American schools (in Wilson, 1985).

Though many believe otherwise, no evidence exists that sex education increases young people's sexual activity, or that it increases the likelihood that they will begin sexual activity earlier. In fact, in no other area of prevention is it more apparent that ignorance of basic facts contributes to problems, in this case pregnancy. Many teens do not know at what time of the month they are fertile. Many believe they are too young to become pregnant. Many think that pregnancy is impossible "the first time."

Opponents of sex education in schools commonly believe that parents should be the ones to provide information about sex to their children. But most adolescents report that they have never been given information about sex by either parent. To fill the void children have turned to their peers and the media. The media exploits sex. Kids witness thousands of scenes of suggestive sexual activity on television and have no effective means of processing the information. Many parents admit that they lack confidence in talking with their children about sex and they welcome assistance.

191

Opponents of sex education also believe that the school has no place pushing moral issues and family values. Most proponents agree, believing that students have the right to information, and that families and religious institutions should more properly impart morality. But in school, as part of the information people need, all viewpoints on the subject and reasons different people feel the way they do can be presented and discussed.

Most opponents and proponents also agree: the less young people engage in sexual activity the better, and the fewer abortions the better. One group believes that sex education will aid in reaching these ends; the other group believes it will hinder. In Omaha, Nebraska, a poll indicated that 66% of residents favored required sexuality education. In New Jersey, a statewide poll showed that 87% of parents with school-age children supported sex education programs. Only 9% were opposed.

The state of New Jersey was probably the first state to require that Family Life Education be taught in schools. The state policy requires "instruction to develop an understanding of the physical, mental, emotional, social, economic, and psychological aspects of interpersonal relationships; the psychological and cultural foundations of human development, sexuality, and reproduction, at various stages of growth; the opportunity for pupils to acquire knowledge, which will support the development of responsible personal behavior, strengthen their own family life now, and aid in establishing strong family life for themselves in the future, thereby contributing to the enrichment of the community" (New, Jersey Administrative Code, Title 6:29-7.1).

Among the subjects discussed in Family Life Education are-

- anatomy and physiology
- puberty and its changes
- contraception
- pregnancy and childbirth
- dating
- sexuality and personality
- abortion and alternatives
- avoiding unwanted sex
- masturbation
- love and marriage
- family planning
- homosexuality
- rape
- sexually transmitted diseases
- drugs, alcohol, and sex,
- sex and the law,
- chastity, morals and values—a discussion of all views
- fertility
- fetology
- sexual dysfunction
- sexual exploitation
- sex and the media
- teenage pregnancy
- child sexual abuse (Wilson, 1985)

All these subjects can be incorporated in a comprehensive health education curriculum, at age-appropriate levels.

AIDS/HIV/STD Prevention Education

One of the most critical of subjects pertaining to health is the subject of AIDS/HIV. Since HIV (Human Immunodeficiency Virus) is transmitted through sexual contact, to combine this with information on other sexually transmitted diseases (STDs) is appropriate. Because AIDS is also transmitted by sharing needles, it also relates to drug abuse. Learning about these diseases must be viewed as an integral part of teaching young people about their lives, their bodies, and their safety.

Even when the cause of a problem is clearly organic, as with AIDS, organic solutions may not be the solution. Medical scientists still are not certain that the virus will ever be able to be killed or that a vaccine will be found to protect a host. But, as Albee (1989) points out, "AIDS is the first epidemic in human history in which we have learned so quickly that the identified noxious agent can be kept from spreading by specific behavioral changes." Whether it be transmitted by the blood transfusions of an infected donor, by shared needles and paraphernalia among infected intravenous drug users, by unprotected sexual intercourse where bodily fluids containing the virus enter another's bloodstream, or by infected mothers prenatally or postnatally through breastfeeding to their infants, all means of transmission are through behaviors, and behaviors can be changed. But it's not that easy. Besides those strung out through intravenous drug abuse who aren't particularly concerned about whether they're spreading the disease through needles or through sex, what about the spread by infected gay or bisexual men who cover their sexual orientation with the trappings of marriage and family or through frequent enough sexual contact with women? (Osborn, 1989). What about when it is transmitted through rape or other sexual abuse? Here, it is clear that education alone won't be enough. Why is AIDS spreading disproportionately among Black and Hispanic populations? Could it be because of the conditions they are forced to live in that affect behavior? Until such conditions are changed, there is little hope of overcoming AIDS.

As always, students need clear, accurate, and thorough information, honest and open discussion, and skills to make informed, responsible decisions. Perhaps more than any other subject, discussions about AIDS bring up complex medical, ethical, social, and scientific questions. As former Surgeon General Coop stated, "We are fighting a disease, not people. This country must face this epidemic as a unified society. We must prevent the spread of AIDS while at the same time preserving our humanity and intimacy" (U.S. Department of Health and Human Services, undated).

Students need to come to terms with the impact that AIDS and STDs will have on their lives. The infection rate in the inner cities is becoming alarming. It is insidiously spreading into the suburbs and elsewhere. The world situation is particularly frightening, especially in underdeveloped nations.

This portion of a comprehensive health education curriculum should also begin as early as possible. In grades K-3, the foundation can be laid by presenting basic concepts of disease prevention, human development, sexuality, interpersonal relationship development, and decision-making. We can begin to allay children's fears about contracting the disease. We can prepare them for the possibility that they could have an HIV-positive schoolmate at some point.

Among the subjects to be covered include-

Grades K-3:

- illness and wellness
- germs and viruses
- diseases that can be spread through blood
- definition of AIDS; that it is caused by a virus, that it's a serious disease that some adults get but that it's rare in children so there's no need to worry about getting the disease from friends
- how to stay healthy and prevent the development of disease
- effects of alcohol and other drugs on behavior
- safe behaviors in situations involving medicines and poisons
- risks of nonmedical blood exchange with another person, such as blood brothers and sisters

Grades 4-6:
- the ten major body systems; recognizing that they all work together
- influences, such as heredity and environment and personal health habits that affect growth and development
- defining personal boundaries, physical and emotional privacy
- communicable and noncommunicable diseases; that AIDS is hard to get except by persons who engage in certain behaviors; that it is transmitted by sexual contact with an infected person, by using needles and other injection equipment that an affected person has used, by an infected mother to her infant before or during birth; that it is not transmitted through coughing, sharing drinking glasses, mosquito bites, toilet seats, hugging or friendly kissing, donating blood, masturbation, shaking hands, or eating in restaurants
- how to avoid contact: not engaging in sexual intercourse, not sharing needles (tattooing, ear-piercing, nonmedical use of drugs)
- appropriate procedures for dealing with another's blood in emergency situations
- discussion of fears about becoming infected

Grades 7-8:
- interrelationships among all body systems, how HIV affects all body systems, specifically the immune system
- sexual orientation: homosexuality, bisexuality, homophobia
- major risk factors and major causes of death in the United States
- physiological, biological, chemical and mechanical means of controlling and preventing disease
- testing procedure for HIV infection
- risks of certain sexual practices
- how to avoid contact
- ways people are contributing to the spread of the disease
- responsible actions to prevent the disease
- personal desires and social pressures related to risk-taking
- assertive responses to sexual situations
- relationship between drug/alcohol behavior on risk-taking behavior
- discuss ways to identify, respond to, and prevent sexual abuse
- responsibilities friends have for each other
- fear surrounding AIDS and how rational thinking may be difficult under some circumstances

Grades 9-12:
- decisions accompanying conception, the prenatal period, and birth
- risks of HIV and STDs
- critical phases of the prenatal period
- levels of infection

- more on how AIDS and STDs are transmitted: oral sexual contact included
- avoiding the virus: abstaining, using latex condom with spermicide, refraining from injecting drugs, seeking HIV counseling if concerned
- the decision to engage in sexual activity
- feelings about the extent and spread of AIDS

(Vermont Department of Education, 1988)

An AIDS/HIV curriculum affords students the opportunity to grapple with the critical issues surrounding this important topic.

Some Mental Health-Related Curriculum Issues

Spivak (1986) suggests, "there appears to be at least speculative evidence" that other skills are important for behaviors and should therefore be considered for inclusion in any comprehensive health education curriculum, beginning in the earliest grades possible.

Perspective-taking and empathy: the ability to infer and adopt another's perspective and understand another's feelings. These can be built by affording the child the opportunity to enact different roles and to switch roles quickly within a dramatic scene. Deficiencies in these abilities were found related to aggression, unpopularity, and delinquency. Teaching these skills was found to-

- reduce aggressive behavior
- reduce delinquent acts (18 months later)
- increase positive social behavior
- enhance positive self-concept

"Delay of gratification" and "future time perspective": The ability of four year olds to tolerate waiting for something they want predicts 10 to 12 years later adolescents' reasonableness, competence, playfulness, ability to cope with stress, and social competence. Children are taught skills to distract themselves from the needs or motives they feel at the moment and to shift their orientation from immediate rewards to more long-term goals.

"Coping" with stress: A range of cognitive and related behavioral responses can help a person deal with stress and unpleasant feelings or allow an altered perception of a situation to make it more bearable. What are one's choices when faced with stress? How can the situation be confronted and resolved? Can its importance be minimized? When faced with interpersonal stress, it is best to have a variety of coping mechanisms from which to choose. Enhancing coping skills in children was found to-

- reduce their use of cigarettes
- reduce their use of alcohol

Principles of Effective Comprehensive Health Education Curriculum Development

The following is a composite of some of the common principles in developing health curricula, gleaned from the health, substance abuse, sexual abuse, HIV/AIDS and mental health fields.

195

- The curriculum should be developed in the local school district, with appropriate consultation and participation of teachers, school administrators, parents, students in grades 9-12, and representative members of the community.
- The curriculum should be comprehensive, sequential, and age/growth/maturity-appropriate.
- The curriculum should be taught by a qualified teaching staff (from biology and science, elementary, health education, physical education, home economics, the school nurse, guidance/psychology).
- In-service training should be provided, preferably by the state department of education, and drawing upon the expertise of those in health, alcohol and drug abuse, and sexual abuse fields.
- Procedures should be established where students whose parents object to a program because of conscience or sincerely held moral or religious beliefs shall be excused from participation.
- The curriculum and related policies should be adopted by each local school board.
- Each school system should understand that it is responsible for implementing, by a given date, a completed curriculum that corresponds to certain guidelines.
- Procedures should be established for instituting a support and referral system for students.

The Wellness Conference

Initiated in Oregon, Wellness Conferences had been held in 24 other states as of 1988. These conferences are usually five-day teacher in-service trainings, usually set in beautiful locations. There participants learn to incorporate a "wellness life-style into their personal and professional lives, and to improve peer and student health-related behavior. School staff gain skills and knowledge to initiate health promotion in their school curricula, including issues such as nutrition, physical fitness, stress-management, self-help, and drug abuse. The goal is to transform participants into change agents who become advocates for a school-wide emphasis on health.

An analysis of the Wellness Conference was conducted in 1980. Of participants-

- 96% report enhancing some aspect of their personal health
- 72% decreased intake of saturated fat, salt, and sugar
- nearly 50% of smokers decreased cigarette consumption
- 63% reduced caloric intake
- 66% increased exercise
- 40% reduced weight
- 58% reported feeling an increase in energy
- 56% increased self-esteem
- 51% improved ability to relax
- 41% improved concentration levels
- 27% decreased blood pressure

A carry-over evaluation measured the conference's impact on the school system:

- schools adopted a wellness curriculum model
- schools increased and improved their health education curriculum
- schools increased financial support for health-related activities
- schools increased wellness activities before, during, and after school
- students and teachers reported more positive classroom experiences
- insurance premium refunds were offered as incentives for reduced sick-day absenteeism
- increased parent involvement in school health-related activities
- school site health promotion programs instituted

The School as a Model Worksite Promoting Health

Comprehensive school health programs can also have impact on staff. Worksite health promotion [Chapter 27] can provide health benefits for the district and improve the productivity of work personnel. Such programs have been found to reduce weight, body fat, blood pressure, anxiety, depression, smoking, to increase exercise; and to promote a more balanced diet. Such programs can cut costs by decreasing absenteeism, decreasing health care claims, and decreasing the need for substitute teachers. These programs have also improved teacher morale and productivity.

Teachers who participated in school health promotion programs report improved attitudes about their personal health, perceptions of improved general well-being, decreased absenteeism, improved morale, and an improvement in their quality of instruction. Also, healthy teachers serve as role models.

After a ten-week health promotion program, teachers reported (compared with controls)

- less energy expenditure in physical activity
- weight loss (4.3 lbs.); body-fat loss (4.1%)
- better ability to handle job stress (self- and principal rating)
- better general well-being and self-concept
- better job satisfaction
- improvements in dietary behavior (68%)
- improvements in lifestyle (49%); improvements in physical fitness
- decrease in smoking (18% of smokers quit)
- less absenteeism (1.25 days per year per employee. The adjusted mean difference at $47 day for substitute teachers, saved one school district $150,000, but a complete cost-benefit analysis was not performed.) (Blair et al., 1987)

These benefits were achieved through a combination of classes, written and audio-visual materials, counseling, health screening, fitness assessments, community resources, facility modifications and other environmental changes, employee assistance programs, and policy changes. The intent of the program is to promote awareness, build skills, and provide motivation, supports, and intervention.

We could conclude that a comprehensive health education program should be more than just a curriculum. It can be a total health education program concerning itself with all aspects of people's health. But the curriculum is the central core.

17. Reflections on Developing State Prevention-Education Initiatives

Steve Gold is now the Commissioner of the Vermont Department of Employment and Training. At the time of this interview he was chief of prevention and treatment services for the Vermont Office of Alcohol and Drug Abuse Programs (ADAP) and a founding member of the Vermont Prevention Training Team. He was the driving force behind the implementation of Vermont's Act 51 of 1 983, which required all schools in the state to institute an alcohol and drug abuse education program, including a K-12 curriculum. Steve has a reputation in Vermont and across the country as being among the best prevention program implementers. I interviewed him to gain insights into successful statewide program implementation.

JP: Let's talk about Act 51. From your perspective, what does it really do?

SG: From my perspective, Act 51 was an opportunity to get schools to deal much more seriously with alcohol and drug issues.

JP: Was that the intent of the law?

SG: No. The legislature expected that the schools would be teaching alcohol and drug abuse prevention, become trained to do so and coordinate with community alcohol and drug resources. But the Act could have been whitewashed, with nothing much happening as a result. The Act gave me and the people I work with the opportunity to mount a major effort. It provided the leverage through a statutory mandate to say to schools, "You really have to pay attention to us. You have to let us in. You have to listen to what we say, and you have to get going on this business."

JP: Isn't that what the legislature expected?

SG: I have no idea what the legislature expected. The legislature passes all kinds of statutes. Some of them generate a lot of activity and others generate little. The actual law charged the Department of Education with doing the training, providing assistance to the schools, and developing a curriculum plan. There was very little mention that the agency I work for would have any direct responsibility with the schools.

JP: So, then, how did you end up taking the lead, working for Alcohol and Drug Abuse?

SG: We had the money, and we had an "Act 51 Council" charged to us under the law. That caused the Agency of Human Services secretary and the commissioner of education to have a historic meeting where they hammered out a letter of agreement as to how we would jointly approach implementing Act 51.

JP: So because the law put responsibilities in two different places, that provided the impetus–

SG: That provided another opportunity. The situation was also fortuitous in that, before Act 51 was passed, Governor Snelling and his newly appointed secretary of AHS had already told us to get an effort like this going, causing us to implement a pilot program in the Chittenden East Supervisory Union. We made a lot of mistakes in developing that pilot project but learned a tremendous amount about how to be more effective in working with schools.

JP: What did you learn?

SG: We learned that we had to involve school people in an active way in planning the program. We learned what made for an effective training. We learned the kinds of issues teachers would raise, and we began to plan for the concerns we would run into in the schools. We learned that it had to be a comprehensive program; it couldn't just be a curriculum. It had to be complemented with support and referral, written policy, teacher training, and community involvement. So when Act 51 came along we really began to think through what we had learned. We looked at the research and saw what that had to say—which wasn't much at the time, but we relied heavily on the Schaps analysis of 127 programs in our design.

We also had to figure out where our statutory authority lay. It actually lay in our 1979 school drug policy law, Title 16 V.S.A. 1165, in some ways even more than in Act 51, because Act 51 was a very vague piece of legislation. The other was more precise, requiring that there be written school policy, education, discipline, and referral for treatment, rehabilitation, and counseling. So we could insist that schools had to have written policy and procedures for those.

JP: Why wasn't that being done before, if it had been the law since 1979?

SG: That's a perfect example of what I'm talking about. When the 1979 law was passed, there was a major battle between the Alcohol and Drug Abuse Division and the Department of Education health education curriculum coordinator at the time. The health education person had won in terms of who would be responsible for implementing the 1979 law, and she drafted a relatively poor model policy, with not much to back it up, sent it out to the schools, and waited for the schools to send in their policies. And every school sent one in. But there was no real effort to work with the schools to help them grasp what they needed if they were really going to implement the program. So most schools didn't bother to use their policy, or do much, because the policies didn't really deal with what the law called for. So that was a good example of a law being passed where nothing happened.

JP: So Act 51 caused something constructive to happen because?

SG: Act 51 gave us a mandate that school administrators couldn't brush off. They had to give it some attention. How seriously they were going to take it, and whether they were going to really implement a program, became a shared responsibility of the Act 51 Assistance Team, which consisted of members of the Department of Education and ADAP.

JP: If any of those parts didn't exist, would you have gotten where you did?

SG: It would have been a lot harder. I personally had been involved since 1973 in trying to get into schools and get them to work on written policy and curricular programs. In ten years we had made very little progress. There was no overall statewide effort. It was a matter of wheedling, and cajoling, and persuading. A lot of what we did was respond to crises. Schools would be going along not paying any attention, and then some kid would get killed in an alcohol or drug-related car accident, or show up at school drunk, and the school would get all excited and call us up and say, "You've got to come in and deal with this. We're very concerned."

Our technology stunk too. We'd go into the school for a day or two, or a week at times and run assemblies and workshops for everyone in the school, show all these films, and walk away thinking, "Boy, weren't we great! We really took that place over and shook 'em up." And it was all baloney. We had some impact in terms of short-term awareness-raising, but did nothing about changing the institution or the policies and programs or behaviors of people in it.

JP: How does it make you feel to know that what you were doing in those days was baloney, when you thought it was so good at the time?

SG: I don't feel particularly good about it. When I got into a position where I could do something about it, one of the first things I did was say, "We're not going to do that anymore. No more glory trips into schools!" It was real hard for some of the people who were then prevention specialists to accept. Some of them overtly resisted by scheduling more. When I confronted them, they would throw up their hands and say, "This is what the school wants! They really insisted. We can't say we're not doing it!" That was the year before Act 51 passed, and because we had such little success getting in the door in the first place, we were spending a lot less time with schools and a lot more time working with community groups and state workers.

JP: So passage of Act 51 allowed you to make more headway with the schools than all your previous work.

SG: True, and two other key things were at play: Governor Snelling had made the issue of alcohol one of his inaugural address issues, and I happened to have an overwhelming, long-term commitment to try to impact the schools—

JP: Why?

SG: Purely personal. In 1969 1 was casting around without being certain what direction my life would go in, and I decided that what I wanted was to have an impact on public education. I got a Master of Arts in teaching and ended up in Vermont, getting involved with the alcohol and drug field. In 1983 they happened to pass this law, and I happened to be in a position where I controlled a fair amount of resources and could say, "We're going to make this our major emphasis." I remember having one of the more intense discussions I've ever had with my boss about who was going to be the lead person in ADAP to follow up on Act 51 and be involved in planning for it—

JP: So you kind of forced your way into the position of being in charge?

SG: Right. I had a powerful interest in being involved in a very strong way.

JP: Because of what you went through in 1969?

SG: I didn't realize it at the time, but I got so intensely involved in it personally that first year—I mean, we were planning it and trying to do it at the same time: We were writing the curriculum plan, having meetings between the Department of Education and ADAP, forming the planning group, meeting with them on practically a weekly basis. We were starting to involve the schools—it was very, very intense—that at the end of the 1983-84 school year I thought I was completely lost or in over my head. I decided to take a two-month leave of absence that summer, and it was then that I finally got enough distance to figure out why I was so incredibly driven and putting out so much more energy than I had ever put out before in my work. I mean, I was really committed in a personal way and had to stop and figure out what was going on. That's when I realized, "Geez, this is a culmination of a goal you set for yourself a long time ago. That's why it means so much to you."

JP: Well, it wouldn't have happened the way it did without you! It probably wouldn't have happened very successfully. You took the ball and ran with it. Are there **principles** that you can pull out of how you made it happen that can be applied to others in pulling off a huge prevention project like this?

SG: Well, one important thing was the **availability of some directable resources**. In other words, it wasn't like we said, "We're going to do something like this, let's look around for the resources." The legislature had created some funding to support the Act, which was somewhat unusual, and I was in a position where I actually commanded a fairly sizable level of resources (for Vermont). I had two or three central office staff and nine field staff to whom I could say, "This is what we're going to do!"

JP: So **being in the right position**—

SG: Yes, and knowing I could direct a considerable amount of person-power and some financial resources at the problem. **Having the support of the system vertically** was very important, in terms of my boss and his boss and all the way up to the governor. Then a really important thing was **hammering out a specific working agreement with the other state department that was involved, which provided very clear guidance about how we were going to operate**, at least through the first year. That document described shared responsibility, shared planning, even down to the level that there would be teams consisting of a member of ADAP and a member of the Department of Education to work with each of the 50 schools we wanted to enroll in the first year.

That letter of agreement, signed by the commissioner of education and the agency secretary, set the agenda for the year—and it was a powerful agenda. It said we would enlist 50 schools, and we would have a team of people out there delivering technical assistance and training. It said we would have a **central working group to oversee the program and do whatever necessary to implement a thorough program**. The linkage formed there was critical, because it broke new ground. Prior to that agreement there had been not only an ineffective but a negative working relationship between the Department of Education and ADAP.

JP: Just because there's an agreement doesn't mean things will happen.

SG: Right. It still goes back to the fact that I and Rufus Chaffee, who for years before this had led the effort to get into the schools and who had previously written policy direction papers—it wasn't just me—were very instrumental in pushing this thing and making sure it had substance to it.

JP: How did you move it from the discussion stage to making it happen?

SG: When the letter of agreement defined a planning group, I pushed for who would be on it, and we got some very responsive people from the department.

JP: So it takes **commitment from some group** of people—

SG: Yes, we certainly had the commitment. But when we started the process, after receiving applications from 80 to 90 schools and whittling it down to 50, it became clear that the Department of Education didn't have nearly enough human resources to devote to this, and we knew they didn't have the financial resources. That became a real problem for our prevention specialists, feeling that the Department of Education was always shirking its responsibility.

JP: Before you get into that, another principle seems to be that **you started where the interest lay**. Schools applied to you. You didn't try to plow in—

SG: Yes, we made the Act 51 assistance program voluntary, meaning that you would get technical assistance, training, and funding support from the state. That remained voluntary throughout the four years of the implementation period. It wasn't until the last year of implementation that we went to the state Board of Education and said, "You've got to change your regulations to reflect more accurately what the schools are required to do under Act 51. The implementation period is ending. Here is what schools now need to do." So in the last year of the program we finally got the state board to be more specific in directing all schools to **develop thorough written policy that dealt with education, discipline, referral; that the curriculum plan we had developed in the first year was being followed; what the teacher training**

needed to consist of; that there needed to be community involvement; there needed to be a referral agreement with a community agency. So we waited four years before we set up a means for enforcement.

JP: What do you have to have in your own head to pull off such a huge project?

SG: One of the most important feelings that I dealt with again and again was **maintaining a clear perspective on whose responsibilities were whose.** The prevention specialists felt responsible for ensuring that the schools they were working with developed a good, solid program, and that the teachers were actually teaching it in the classroom. Sometimes that happened and sometimes it didn't. If the school didn't do what it was supposed to, the prevention specialists got involved in a lot of guilt and self-blame, and I would repeatedly have to sit down with them and say, "Look, let's be sure we're clear on responsibility here. It's the school's responsibility under the law. They have to implement the program. We can't do that. All we can do is to offer them the best assistance and training and funding support we can to assist them in developing and implementing their program." So that was really important, to **figure out what you can do and what you can't.**

JP: Did you have **a vision of what you wanted to see done?**

SG: Yes.

JP: I think that's critical. If you have a picture of what you think should be done, it means you can direct whatever you have to make it come out that way.

SG: What I had in my head was not specific. I knew that schools had to have a competent response in certain required areas. I didn't know what a given school would exactly have for a program. One school might have a health educator who would have the major responsibility for a lot of the learning activities. Another school system might have to make sure that all elementary school teachers went through the training program so they could integrate it into their classrooms. I had some models in my head of how it could look. It was our responsibility to say to the school, "Here are three or four ways you could do this. You may come up with something else. You're going to have to show us that it works for you and for the kids." So I didn't have a specific model program in mind, but I knew what schools needed to work through to effectively implement the different parts. For the teacher training, we came up with a minimum of 15 hours, plus three hours of orientation for everyone. Schools threw up their hands and said, "We can't possibly do that!" Yet somehow or other 280 schools did, and they did it a number of different ways. For the community involvement piece, we probably gave the schools the least direction, and the result was that they did the least effective job with that part. Maybe that's the way it should be because the community should probably be knocking on the school's door saying, "We want to be involved," not the other way around. The places in the state where the most exciting community involvement is happening are where parents have said, "This is serious business. We've got to get involved."

JP: I want to get back to something. To reach your vision, your desired result, other people have to contribute. What happens if they don't? What happens if they don't see it the way you do?

SG: One of the critical pieces is doing your best to **provide leadership to exhort the key people who are doing the implementing to take it seriously and do the best job they can.**

JP: How do you do that?

SG: That's a good question. I'm not really sure how you do that. Leadership is a tough thing to define. I think you do it by **showing your own commitment.** You do it by **providing them with clear guidance** about what's supposed to go on, and how they can carry out their work—

that kind of **support**. I'm talking about the program planning group in general, and me in particular as the head of the prevention program. I'm not prescribing. I may have my ideas about how I would do it, and in some cases I might go in and work with them and show them how I would go about it, but also give them the opportunity to develop their own working style and figure it out for themselves in accomplishing the end. Sometimes it works and sometimes it doesn't.

JP: When do you step in?

SC: Mostly where I was asked, or where major problems occurred. But where major problems occurred, it was more that the school was totally screwing up, and it wouldn't have mattered much who went in there.

JP: Whether or not the Department of Education took its responsibility, you **made sure that the people you controlled took their responsibility**.

SG: Yes. That's important. We were going to do it anyway, even if they didn't come through. And in some cases they didn't. Even though they were supposed to be working in teams, it ended up with the prevention specialist essentially working alone with the school. You might remember being in that situation. [laughter]

JP: Yes I do. It wasn't easy. What are other states doing in this regard?

SC: I think a lot of other states have passed laws like this, and there have been a variety of responses out there, but I don't know of any state that's had a statewide mandate where they've marshaled a proportionate level of state resources to address it in this way. Other states have run training programs. Utah is an example. New York passed a law and spent a lot of money to invent and publish their own curriculum and send it out to the schools with a bit of in-service, but they didn't have the same level of specific, directed, on-site attention and technical assistance that we did. Maine has been working for years on the federal government's school-team approach, building school-community teams.

JP: Ultimately, was what Vermont did successful?

SG: Well, we definitely created a space on schools' agenda for alcohol and drug education in a major way, which is not to say that every school is doing a responsible job teaching it, but I don't think there's a school in the state that isn't taking it relatively seriously at this point. On its heels, the Feds passed the 1988 anti-drug law that provides new resources to the schools, which came at a perfect time for us, because suddenly at the end of our five year start-up program, there's almost $20 per kid available to the schools to continue to enhance their programs.

JP: I hate to bring this up, but so what? So what if all the schools are teaching alcohol and drug education?

SG: That's a major question that we're taking a look at. I am anxious to see if we can say, "So this..." One of the ways we're trying to do that is through a biennial high school survey. We're getting ready to take the survey a third time. From the data we have so far, we're seeing more positive attitudes.[*]

JP: But you don't know whether it would have gone up anyway. You didn't have control schools.

---

[*] Note: After this interview, when the 1989 and 1990 surveys were conducted, comparing results from the 1987 survey, 12th and 10th -grade self-reported monthly use of alcohol had dropped approximately 20% and 12% respectively. Marijuana and cocaine use had also dropped. Eighth grade use of alcohol and other drugs remained about the same (Data Base, 1991; White and Swisher, 1989; Swisher, 1987; 1985).

SC: That's right. This was a random sample of students in schools across the state, but we believe we're seeing some progress.

JP: Were these trends similar to what was going on across the country?

SC: One of the problems is that the only national survey we have for any kind of comparative data is information on high school seniors. There's nothing on anybody else, although individual states are surveying kids at younger ages.

JP: What about the trends for high school seniors?

SG: With only two points in time, you can't say you have a trend, but we're doing better than the national comparisons with the high school seniors.

JP: At least you know you weren't doing worse. This is important! [laughter]

SG: Yeah. But that's only one measure. You have to look at other things like growth in the level of involvement among high school students in prevention activities, the growth of Project Graduation as a viable activity in nearly every high school in the state. Now that's not the result strictly of Act 51.

JP: Right, the Green Mountain Teen Institute had a lot to do with it—

SG: Yes, but the point is, in prevention you can't point to any one thing and say this is the cause of that. We're working with a constellation of strategies that together are pushing from a lot of different places, and that's exactly what I see going on. There's more prevention activity, and more kids are getting involved in a variety of ways. Alternatives for Teens began as a little local project, and this year it's going into four other sites around the state. Probably a dozen schools are planning on using their Drug-Free School dollars to get involved in the Junior High Peer Prevention Project that Green Mountain Prevention Projects runs. Winooski is doing its own junior high project for the entire school, with 300 kids sleeping on the gym floor. These kinds of things were just not happening five, six, or seven years ago. And people are beginning to understand that prevention is broad-based, that when you're working on self-esteem issues and on communications and decision-making, you're affecting a lot more than just alcohol and drug issues. You're affecting how kids behave in their sexual behavior, in their attitudes of respect for themselves and for others—a whole range of stuff.

JP: What's the difference between implementing Act 51 and implementing…Act 79 [Chapter 32]

SG: It's interesting that you should ask about comparing the two. One major difference is there were no major resources that could be directed… There…isn't the same level of commitment from the top down…and Act 79 flopped around for years after it was passed in an attempt to get people to buy into it.

JP: The committed people weren't in a position of authority to make it happen.

SG: That's right. And with Act 79, you were trying to get people to focus away from remediation and intervention that people get so caught up in, and get them to move toward prevention. It's interesting, the more I think about it, with educators, what they're about is the prevention end. Remediation is what keeps getting added on to the school's agenda through things like special education and all the stuff that's come at them over the years. It's a different headset. But what really needs to be improved with Act 79, and the Vermont Prevention Training Team that evolved from it, is the level of commitment in direction and resources coming from the state… We really need someone in a position to direct resources and command people's attention.

6/89

205

18. Early Drug Abuse Prevention (EDAP) and Drug Abuse Reduction Training (Project DART)

*EDAP (Early Drug Abuse Prevention) is a supportive small group experience, within an elementary school setting, that improves self-perceptions and life skills among students. In a two-month follow-up evaluation, using pre- and post-tests, 91 out of 124 EDAP participants, or 73%, showed significant increases in self-esteem on the Rosenberg self-esteem scale. The Elks Clubs of Vermont adopted EDAP as an early drug prevention mode, and since the first edition of this book, EDAP won the 1990 OSAP Exemplary award. Both EDAP and its predecessor, Project DART (Drug Abuse Reduction Training) were created by **Peter Perkins** through his work with the Washington County Youth Service Bureau in Montpelier, Vermont. Instructive manuals for both programs are available through the Bureau. Peter is one of the truly inventive prevention program innovators (he also helped create the Vermont Prevention Group and Prevention Unlimited). It is sometimes more instructive to examine the reasons an effective program is created, and the principles involved in developing and running it, than to simply report facts about the program. Peter is now a private prevention consultant and trainer.*

JP: What made you think a program like EDAP was needed?

PP: Well, EDAP grew out of Project DART, so I should really talk about DART first. I was on the Washington County juvenile Court Diversion Board [a program to divert first-time juvenile offenders who commit nonviolent crimes from the court system], and we didn't have any appropriate referral sources for kids that committed a crime under the influence of or in connection with alcohol and other drugs. So Jim Cleamons [Diversion Coordinator] and I talked about it and he asked me, "Why don't you create something?" So I did. We got a grant from OADAP [Vermont Office of Alcohol and Drug Abuse Programs] to develop it in 1984.

JP: What made you go in the direction you did?

PP: I wanted to work with groups of teenagers emphasizing peer interaction. I knew that was successful—

JP: How?

PP: Because kids are more apt to respond to a peer confrontation than an adult intervention. I also wanted to make it experiential and safe. I didn't want it to be like a school experience. I wanted to create a special environment catering to the needs of the kids.

JP: Why experiential?

PP: Because I learn best through experiential. In most of my educational experiences, I learned most and was more open where I was involved and where I felt respected. That's when I was hooked in. Any other time was a major struggle, and my resistance was terrible. I knew these kids were going to come into DART with a lot of resistance because they were busted. Diversion has a contract that you have to sign or you go to court. So what opens you up? What helps to engage you? To feel respected. Then I can maybe get some learning to happen. I know now that that's been verified by research by Malcolm Knowles on learning theory [Chapter 16]. But I had been working with kids for nine years, and I knew experiential stuff seemed to take hold more. So this was developed with kids in mind.

JP: As opposed to, with "the information" in mind?

PP: Or with adults in mind. Or schools. This means not just the way I presented the information. **The environment needed to be casual, away from the school. It needed to be safe and confidential**. We used couches, soft chairs, a little carpet in the room, not a very fancy looking office, that's all pretty intentional—not to mention restricted by budget [laughter]. And often, the kids will respond. After the first session they'll say, "Hey, this is pretty cool in here," or they'll say, "This is great. I thought it was gonna be like a classroom." Or "I thought there'd be a hundred people." The group size is maximum eight, so the intimacy level is much higher. Also, intensity was essential, so we designed it in two-hour sessions three times a week. It only lasts for two weeks, but it's an intense injection of information, interaction and involvement. By the third session, most of the kids' basic assumptions are gone and it moves into a task-oriented group where they become very close, to the point where they don't really want to end sometimes.

JP: What about the content?

PP: I only chose things that I believed in. I only chose things that I felt could make sense for this age group. I only used information that they could integrate somehow into their lives. I looked at what was already out there for kids: the Green Mountain Teen Institute, some of the early alcohol and drug education curriculums. I had been collecting things for years. Now, though, almost nothing is the same as the way I originally designed it.

JP: Does that mean you were wrong?

PP: No. It means I was able to improve it [laughter]—based on trial and error. I knew right from the beginning I was going to make mistakes. I wasn't going to create the perfect group the first time. For one thing our curriculum was too similar to things they'd had before. They knew the words. **What was missing was integrating that information into their lives**, and that's the way we ended up changing DART altogether, so they could integrate it into their lives more, **by connecting it to their feelings, the way they communicate, the way they make decisions and understand what those decisions are based on**.

JP: Give me an example of how you take a concept like "drinking and driving" and integrate it into their lives.

PP: It's spread throughout. After creating a relaxed and trusting atmosphere in the group, we focus on their own drug-taking and other behavior. We break down into small groups and talk about creating the drug-dependent person, and about myths and misconceptions. We use as much of their information as possible, and we correct the misinformation. Then we move into peer pressure. We try to turn it all back to them: "How are you responsible for that?" A kid might say, "There's no such thing as peer pressure." And I'll say, "Okay, so what'll you do when somebody wants you to drive them home and you've been drinking too much? What are you going to do?" "Well, if I haven't been drinking much I'll take them home, but if I drink too much, I'll tell him no." And I'll say, "Well, aren't you responding to peer pressure?" So we integrate it like that. Just by talking about peer pressure, we've brought in what drinking and driving is about, especially if a decision is made. But then we'll take that a little further and say, "How would you feel if in the morning you wake up in the hospital," or "How would you feel in the morning if you decided not to take him home, knowing you didn't drive?" "How would you communicate to this person that, no, you're not going to drive?" "What kinds of commitments do you make to yourself?" Any of those sorts of questions.

JP: What do you do if a kid says, "It can't—or won't—happen to me?"

PP: "I don't have a problem!" "Did you ever get in any trouble 'cause of your drinking?' "No!" "Then how come you're here?" That usually shuts 'em right up [laughter]. The other thing we can do is point out what we see happening. They're going to take it or leave it, but the best thing we can do then is turn it over to the other kids. "Anybody see any bullshit going on here?" It depends how confrontive we can be, how long they've been together and whether or not we're at a stage when we know we can call on the group to do some confronting. Often we sit back and let it be silent until another group member says something. In almost every group it happens. Kids are not comfortable with silence. Somebody's eventually gonna talk. Often you can count on the fact that there's a caretaker in the group, because a lot of children of alcoholics come into DART. But you're not going to make a kid not do something. All we want to do is raise their consciousness, that they can't keep it hidden no more 'cause everybody knows now—at least in that circle and we want them to try to use that circle to be honest with themselves.

JP: So how do you know this works?

PP: We identified that about 70% of the kids needed a referral. Remember, DART is an early intervention group, so the idea is to intervene. Of that 70%, about 50 to 60% actually accepted the referral. So **one of the things DART does is identify kids with a need that would have probably gone undetected until it got worse, and at least half of those identified actually entered treatment**. Now, whether that actually changed their lives, we have no control over. We got 'em there. We intervened, and we were successful at that. That was one of the main purposes. The other is to increase the awareness, the consciousness, and we have shown that 100% of the kids have increased their awareness—

JP: So what if they know more?

PP: It doesn't guarantee anything, but at least they can't make a decision out of ignorance.

JP: Was there anything that indicated their behaviors had changed at all?

PP: Only from what they said on their evaluations: 75% of the kids said that they would change something in their life as a result of attending DART, which usually was "cut back" or "stop" their drug use. Now, there's a self- report, and whether they did it, I don't know…A lot of that comes from modeling by the facilitator. A lot of it comes from role playing situations that exist in their lives, with feedback from the group. And if they're talking about someone in the group, "Don't talk to me, tell, him."

JP: From just watching the groups, how did you know DART was worthwhile?

PP: **Lots of kids come in totally resistant in the initial interview, denying that they have any problem with a drug or anything in their life, and they think this is bullshit. So I say, "Well, you've got to be here so you may as well give it a try, be open to learning something." And they say, "Aw, all right." Then it turns out after a couple of sessions that they start sharing a lot of information about themselves, and you can see in their affect that they're feeling this stuff for maybe the first time—that it hurts—and they start breaking down the lies, and they're admitting to certain aspects of their drug use, or a family history that's painful or unhealthy, and they admit, "Yes I have a drug problem," and they place**

themselves on the personal drug use chart up as far as "dependent," and they say now they're "abusive" and "harmfully using."—"Yeah, I need to change that. I see that really clearly now." When those kinds of things happen, it's incredible. Because it would not have happened anywhere else. Some of these kids just need some caring time, and some of the group's time.

JP: Okay, so how did you get from there to EDAP? That's really what we're supposed to be talking about here [laughter].

PP: Well, we were writing a DART manual and we were saying, "Wouldn't it be nice to have a DART for younger kids!" Right around that time, the Elks Clubs came along with this initiative of drug abuse prevention with kids. We presented DART to them, and they said, "No, we want it for fourth to ninth grade." So we said, "Why don't we do it!" and we proposed EDAP, and they bought it. They gave us a grant for $18,000 to develop it. I spent a whole year developing it, including piloting it around in a few places. The focus needed to be significantly different. I wanted this to be a primary prevention program, not an intervention program like DART. I assumed most of the kids in EDAP weren't going to be drug users at present, and being fourth to ninth grades, I wanted to develop a curriculum that could be modified to meet those different ages. To make prevention work, I decided to focus on developing perceptions and basic life skills because of the research and because I felt it was right. I tried a lot of experiments and combinations in developing this program too.

JP: What were your basic principles in setting up this program?

PP: I didn't want to teach a lot of information because I didn't think information alone was enough, and I knew they'd be getting information eventually through Act 51 [Chapter 17]. I saw EDAP as a complement to Act 51 and developed it with that in mind. The next step beyond it—

JP: Or, what should be an integral part of it—

PP: Yeah, right, but it isn't—

JP: Yet! Okay, so where did you come up with the curriculum for this? What did you think would work for these kids?

PP: I didn't exactly know when I started, but I had some hunches. My hunches were that if I gave kids an opportunity in a small, intimate, comfortable, safe setting—the same kind of environment as with DART, but within schools now (and with this age group it works fine)—if I controlled the make-up of the group, and the number and genuineness of the facilitators, it would work. I didn't want it to be a labeling group. I wanted it to be voluntary, because if it's forced it won't work, I wanted these perceptions and skills to be things people wanted to learn. And, at this point, we find in fourth to sixth grades that about 60% of the kids want to be in the group.

JP: Which kids are these?

PP: It's a mixed bag. We get high-risk kids, and we get low-risk kids. We get screwed-up kids, and we get really together kids, and middle-of-the-road-kids. We get behavior problem kids and non—

JP: So who doesn't volunteer?

PP: I don't know. I would guess the same. But I think there's a group of kids that don't volunteer, who don't like to share things, who like to take care of everything themselves. They're not willing to even consider asking for anything, let alone listen. But we get a real cross-section. It depends on the size of the school. It depends what the incentive is to be in the group. Most of the groups are during school time, so there's an automatic incentive. If it's considered a cool thing in the school to do something like this, you get a high percentage. If it seems like a lot of kids are interested, that creates more interest.

JP: So how did you decide on the different topics in the curriculum?

PP: I decided to focus on some themes I felt were really important in creating a whole person, based around self-perceptions and basic life skills. What do these kids need that I feel is important, based upon my experience and reading and interaction—everything I've learned.

JP: It's a good thing you've had a lot of experiences or you could have been way off base [laughter]. Take me through it piece by piece and tell me why you came to the conclusion you did about each.

PP: Okay, session two, after people get to know each other, is *trust building*. You've got to build trust or you're not going anywhere. Everyone in the group asks each other if they trust them, and why.

JP: That puts it right on the line.

PP: Sure does. That was developed by a fourth grader in Lyndonville Graded School. We were trying to do another activity and it wasn't working, and this kid just said, "Wait a minute, do you trust me? Do you trust me? Do you trust me? "Wow! "You try that." "All right!" Okay! From then on, that's what we did. It's so simple and it's very direct communication. Then, once you feel trust can be established, feelings can be expressed honestly and clearly.

The third session is *feelings*. We spend a whole session figuring out what feelings are, drawing them, identifying them, expressing them, because the trust and the feelings set the pace for the whole rest of the group.

Then, although this can change, depending on the needs of the group, we usually move into *peer pressure*—finding out what they know about peer pressure, what it is, what it means, what tools they use, teaching a tool we have, and role playing.

JP: What makes kids want to resist peer pressure in the first place?

PP: One of the problems with the peer pressure thing is that we're creating robots. Like "just say no." They're being told to just resist peer pressure without a whole lot of understanding about themselves and why it has any relevance to their life. And it's going to mean nothing to them in the future. Besides, there's a lot of good peer pressure too. What's important about peer pressure is that a kid can identify what's important, what's right and wrong for them, and if somebody wants them to do something they don't want to do, they can feel okay to say they don't want to do it. If they can be clear about who they are—that means having a sense of their value system, knowing how they see the difference between right and wrong, knowing how to communicate their feelings about something—then it means something.

Next we go to *building relationships*. What it's about to make friends. What relationships are. Different kinds of relationships. Understanding how you fit into a relationship. Identifying who in the group has a lot of friends, and who doesn't. Who gets picked on. And we work with it. We might set it up as a problem to solve, and role play to help the person identify what it's like to be picked on.

JP: And since some of the kids in the group are likely the ones that are picking on them, what happens there?

PP: It's great! Those kids never realized that picking on the quiet kids had such an impact on them. It's amazing when that happens. When we check in with them two months later, they've said, "I don't pick on kids the same way I used to. I realize that it affects their feelings." It can be really powerful. And the quiet kids are always the ones that benefit the most, because they start to make friends. They've made a connection to six other kids in the group. They've been listened to, they've talked, they've been leaders. At every group we do a check-in. It's an opportunity twice a week for every kid to say how they're feeling with no strings attached. And they love it.

211

They're empowered that way. But, what happens depends a lot on who's there. We get a lot of information on the kids in the group before we start, like from teachers, so we can probe issues they might have.

JP: **So your intent is to get as personal as possible—**

PP: **Absolutely, because we want them to be touched enough for it to be real**. Then from relationships we move on to *cooperation and sharing*, a session where we give them a task to build a board game, however they want to do it, with three rules: They must agree on every decision made, everyone must participate, and everything about the game has to be connected to EDAP. The facilitators observe, take notes about the behavior and interactions, and throw out process comments occasionally: "It appears that one of the members of your group is not participating," "It appears that one member of the group is pushing their opinion"—only observations of what's going on. We give them a time crunch. We let them struggle. We try not to help them until the time's running down. And they get really pissed off and frustrated with the process. And if the game gets finished, great. If it doesn't, as a group they have to decide what they want to do about it. Because in the next session they're supposed to play the game. So if they don't get it done in that session, it has to go into the next session, and they have to figure out how much time they need to use, and all that stuff. We really let them struggle through as much of that process as possible. When that's all done, we give each kid feedback within the group on what we saw each doing, as leader, as follower. Oh, at the end of the first day we had them write whether or not they thought they were leaders or followers, so we can compare their perceptions to our perceptions. We give feedback like, "I saw you listening in the group." "I saw you wanting to be involved in all of the activities." We try to make it as nonjudgmental as possible. Then we play the game, which is centered around EDAP, so that's where some drug questions come in, and all sorts of feeling questions. So that's that session.

JP: And from there?

PP: We have two sessions devoted to *family stress*. It starts out with drawing a picture of your family, describing your family to the group, and a check-in with how you're feeling about your family today. The next session takes it a little further. If there's alcoholism in the family, or a lot of family stress, we'll do a piece on the different characteristics of the roles of children in families of stress, and we have them role play what those roles might look like and the purpose and meaning of those roles. Then we have a *problem-solving* session, where we brainstorm some possible problems or have the kids identify their own problems. We figure out a system for solving problems in the group. Either they throw out a problem and the group works with the kid to solve the problem, or the kid directs two or three other kids in a little play that solves their problem. We might do a theater game—whatever works best at the time. The session following that is an open session that's usually a catch-up because we've gone over with everything else, or it can be used for anything the kids want to focus on. Then it's *closure*.

JP: How do you know EDAP works?

PP: Because it's a-maz-ing! [laughter] The feedback we get from the kids, the feedback we get from the parents, the feedback we get from teachers. I've got a letter on my desk right now from a parent whose kid was in EDAP. They had an alcoholic grandfather who they never told anybody about, and it became real apparent at a family gathering. So the parents decided to talk to the kids about it. When they started, the kid started talking about it to them, and they had such a constructive conversation, the parents were blown away. They asked him, "How did you know about this stuff?" and he said, "EDAP." So she wrote me a letter saying, "Thank you. It really helped him understand what alcoholism is about." That's one example.

JP: Do you ever get the opposite from parents?

PP: I've had a couple of parents pull their kids out because we were talking about feelings, and they said that wasn't drug abuse prevention. They wanted us to show them bags of marijuana and tell them, "Don't do this!" But I think only three kids have been pulled out. I remember one time we had a real behavior-problem kid in our group. It was so much work, but we kept her in and really worked hard with her to put on the table what was going on with her. She was always pulling and tugging on the facilitator, getting up talking, making jokes, fiddling around, really acting out. We knew there was a lot of stress at home—her mom was blind, she had an alcoholic father who was not in the family anymore, and no friends, and didn't know how to interact. She got a lot of feedback from the kids about her interaction, about how they didn't feel respected by her. She didn't know that about herself. In the group she said, "You're all full of shit." But two months later when we had the follow-up session she came back, and her behavior in the group was incredibly more controlled. We found out from teachers that her behavior in the classroom had changed significantly. We said to her, "Tell us if you learned anything from EDAP, and if so how did you use it." And she said she learned to be nicer to people, to listen to people, and that she's made a lot more friends. So that was incredible. Powerful. Tons of those kinds of things happen. About 90% of the kids report a positive experience, that they learned something and use it.

JP: Give me some other examples of what kids have said that you remember.

PP: That they learned to control their temper. They don't get into fights as much. They talk about it before they get into a fight. They go to the teacher. They talk to their parents. The relationship with their parents has improved. They look people in the face when they talk. They feel more comfortable saying no in a peer pressure situation. Things like that.

JP: Now, take a typical health education curriculum in a school. Let's say it covers some of these very same topics. Somehow I get the feeling the kids don't walk away with the same kinds of impact. What's the difference?

PP: **Intimacy, and facilitator skill. There's a serious amount of skill needed to make it happen. I used to think anybody could do it. It's not true**.

JP: So how do you maintain quality control?

PP: We co-facilitate. I've trained my staff here. **We have a two-day training. We practice doing it. We give feedback. They see themselves on the video. The people trained get to co-facilitate a group with our staff.** The way the training is designed now, it's very good.

JP: If you do say so yourself [laughter].

4/89

213

Jack Pransky

19. Law-Related Education

"But to live outside the law you must be honest."

-Bob Dylan[*]

Comprehensive health education does not usually cover the problems of crime and delinquency, child abuse and neglect, truancy and school disruptions. Another set of information is needed. If we expect young people and others to exist as responsible citizens in this democracy, they must also have another kind of awareness.

It takes a special kind of knowledge and skill to appreciate our form of government, and to interact with this society in ways that respect and preserve it. Under a democratic government, it is perhaps easier to get away with breaking laws and to disregard society's rules than under any other except anarchy, for a government founded on the principles of trust and respect for its citizens goes out of Its way to protect their rights and ensure that they're innocent until proven guilty. Dictatorships and other repressive governments find it far easier to keep the lid on illegal behavior. They do it out of fear. The U.S. government is supposed to be "of the people, by the people, and for the people." As such, the people are supposed to decide what is and isn't acceptable and tolerable. *We the People* define the norm.

Those whose behaviors fall outside the norm at best challenge it, and at worst threaten its very existence. People need to be part of this society without causing a basic collapse of the structures we chose, unless we deem that structure to be no longer relevant, and we change it. This government was set up under some basic ideals and principles. It set up a structure we thought could best foster and preserve those principles. It was founded on the assumption that every citizen could understand it as our founding fathers did, and therefore fully appreciate It and desire to respect it as much. If everyone did, perhaps there wouldn't be so many problems.

But many citizens do not come close to gaining this understanding and appreciation. In many cases, it may be that it appears that this "system" is not preserving and protecting everyone equally. It appears to work against some people. Whole communities—entire subcultures—can feel this way. The people in charge haven't taken very good care of them. They don't feel part of the "we." If the smooth functioning of the system depends on the respect and appreciation people have for it, in many cases it is not something that can readily be appreciated, especially if one is

---

[*] Note: *Absolutely Sweet Marie* c. 1966.

born into poverty and surrounded by crime and drugs and lack of hope. Somehow, the system is supposed to be preserved at least to the extent that other people's lives, liberty, and property will be respected. These are issues for law-related education.

Law-Related Education Curriculum

Law-related education is "education for citizenship in a constitutional democracy" (Pereira, 1988). It is learning to respond effectively to the law, learning about legal issues, and learning about one's place in relation to it. Generally included in a law-related education curriculum is the following:

- development of citizenship: knowledge, skills and attitudes necessary for informed, responsible participation in a constitutional democracy
- knowledge of the justice system, government, and rights and responsibilities of citizenship
- development of skills of civic participation
- decision-making
- critical thinking
- positive attitudes about the law, justice system, and responsible citizenship (Hunter, 1987)

It includes discussions about-

- sources of law
- functions of law
- legal processes
- legal roles
- legal principles (justice, equality, authority, freedom, order)

Effectiveness

Controversy was generated when *Scared Straight*, a program to bring young people into Rahway Prison in New Jersey and "scare them straight" by talking to convicted criminals, received a positive evaluation, showing reduced delinquent acts after the visit. This prompted many officials to begin promoting this type of program. Many others, however, pointed to flaws in the evaluation design. Their concerns were corroborated a couple of years later when a new study on a similar program showed no differences in problem behaviors and even suggested that the program did more harm than good to some students, causing nightmares and other anxieties. In their extensive study of delinquency prevention programs and research, Johnson, Bird, and Little (1980) concluded that this mixed evidence made programs like Scared Straight questionable without further study. However, visits to correctional facilities and even discussions with inmates, given appropriate controls, can have a place within the context of a complete law-related education program.

Besides making a difference in knowledge, skills and attitudes, when law-related education (LRE) is properly conducted, it has been found to-

- reduce tendencies toward delinquent behavior
- reduce association with delinquent peers
- reduce the use of violence as a means of resolving conflict
- improve a range of attitudes related to responsible citizenship
- increase reporting of criminal behavior to authorities

Law-Related Education has also been found to increase the relevance of the social studies curriculum for students. Students generally become more interested in and appreciative of social studies because it is more directly related to their lives. "Students...value LRE classes as relevant, useful, and interesting, that the classroom interaction is rewarding—offering students who had difficulties in other courses opportunities to participate successfully" (Hunter, 1987).

Principles of Effective Law-Related Education

Periera (1988) identified characteristics of effective LRE programs, and Hunter and Johnson (1987), in their study of programs implemented at 12 schools in eastern Colorado, identified features of the most successful classes. Their findings were quite similar and are combined as follows:

- extensive interaction among students—active student participation and involvement, including use of opportunities for interactive or cooperative team learning, small-group work, simulations, role-plays, mock trials
- realistic, fair, and balanced treatment of issues—critical thinking about all sides of controversies; promoting understanding that our legal system is not flawless and infallible, nor is it a failure; teaching that law is a positive tool for maintaining the social order; balance between the respect for law and constructive criticism; judicious selection and presentation of illustrative material
- use of outside resources as co-teachers—lawyers, judges, police, legislators, probation/parole workers, correctional officers, and so on are strongly associated with increased student interest in LRE, and with positive responses to teachers and the school; caution: whoever is brought in must be adequately prepared and must exhibit behaviors sought in students
- strong support by the principal and administration—providing classroom resources; facilitating field trips (such as to a courthouse); providing justification for inclusion in curriculum and dealing with concerns voiced by teachers or community; organizing opportunities for peer support and staff development
- high instructional quality—knowledgeable and skilled teachers with positive attitudes
- use of mastery strategies of stated learning objectives and thorough checking of understanding of one topic before moving on to the next, with systematic and extensive staff development that includes successful teaching strategies
- professional peer support for teachers, preferably from persons teaching LRE in the same building or district
- at least 30-40 classroom hours devoted to LRE

217

In Colorado, the strongest programs were found in schools where a team of building administrators, teachers, and police attended a week-long training seminar in LRE and citizenship education at the University of Colorado.

> Schools whose efforts were limited to improvements in instructional strategies or other aspects of the educational process experienced considerably less impact on students' citizenship than schools whose programs included a normative component as well... Normative or moral content...emerged from nonthreatening interaction between students and representatives of law enforcement and justice and from a more accurate understanding of the judicial processes than that conveyed by the media... After learning firsthand that police and other symbols of authority were human beings with tough jobs to do, students came to share some of their concerns and to value their approval. After learning that rules were not just oppressive intervention by adults, but were necessary and could work to their advantage, students came to see more merit in obeying them (Hunter, 1987).

LRE Curriculum Materials

Classroom and teacher training materials are available from the *Center for Civic Education: Law in a Free Society Project*, Calabasas, California. These contain multimedia instructional units: "Authority, Privacy, Justice, and Responsibility, including a "Leader's Handbook," "Casebook: Selected Readings for Teachers," "Curriculum Guide" and "Lesson Plans" for grades K-12.

The *Constitutional Rights Foundation: National Delinquency Prevention Education Project* of Los Angeles, California has other materials, including: "Criminal justice in America," a "Law and Social Studies Series" ("The Purpose of Law," "The Crime Question: Rights and Responsibilities of Citizens," "The Development of Law," and others), "Bill of Rights in Action," "Business-in-the-Classroom," a quarterly publication on ethical, legal, and economic issues affecting business decisions, simulation games such as "Police Patrol," "Jury Game," "Kids in Crisis," "Halfway House," and "Managing School Conflict," and others.

The *National Institute for Citizen Education in the Law (NICEL)* of Washington, D.C. offers training and mentoring programs, and audiovisual materials including the award-winning "Street Law—A Student's Guide to Practical Law" and "Current Legal Issues." It also has materials on mock trials, such as The Street Law Mock Trial Manual, which includes sample trials.

The *Phi Alpha Delta Law Fraternity, International: Phi Alpha Delta Public Service Center* in Bethesda, Maryland provides support for community LRE projects. Its publications include "A Resource Guide on Contemporary Legal Issues for Use in Secondary Education," and others that assist different law and justice personnel in preparing to participate in LRE programs.

Gang-Related Education—The Paramount Plan: Alternatives to Gang Membership

A subset, or perhaps the antithesis, of law-related education is gang-related education, which should be considered a needed part of the educational process in those geographical areas infested by or about to be infiltrated by gangs. The idea is to prevent gang membership by showing young people its realities This is education that dispels myths and gives young people the tools to resist the pressures to join. Nowhere is this practiced more successfully than in the city of Paramount, in Los Angeles County, California.

Inner-city gangs, their drug use and violence, have presented one of the most difficult problems for prevention. The problems seem overwhelming. Most people feel powerless against the destructive power and influence of gangs. The city of Paramount, however, decided to take some constructive action. In 1981, gang violence was at an all-time high. City officials like Tony Ostos vowed to put an end to the gang problem. By 1982, the Paramount Plan for Alternatives to Gang Membership was underway.

Paramount researched traditional methods of dealing with gangs and found that working with deeply rooted gang members to lure them away was not effective; neither was working with gangs as a group. The longer kids are in, the harder it is to get them out. Researchers then explored at what age the decision was usually made to join a gang, and discovered it to be around age 10 to 11. Thus Tony Ostos and other city officials developed a fifth-grade curriculum to reach kids before they were involved in making this choice; their premise being, "If you stop kids from making the decision to join a gang, eventually there will be no gangs." Kids growing up in gang-infested areas come to believe that gang membership is their only alternative, but it doesn't have to be.

Funded by the city with cooperation of school officials, a 15-week program, taught by city officials, was set up in the elementary schools where gang influence was the heaviest. The curriculum is reinforced by neighborhood meetings held throughout the community to educate families on what will happen to their youngsters if they join gangs. Intermediate school follow-up is also provided, consisting of eight biweekly presentations aimed at reintroducing reinforcing, and expanding the concepts presented at the elementary level.

Studies using pre- and post-tests and control groups, and a one- and four-year follow-up, showed the following results:

- after the program 90% of the students responded negatively to gang membership (compared with 50% of the students who said they were undecided about joining a gang); this remained consistent at a one-year follow-up
- at a four-year follow-up, 98% of program participants reported that they were staying out of gangs

How does it work?

The school curriculum attempts to provide knowledge about what gangs are all about, provide knowledge of alternatives, and strives to prevent gang, involvement. A multimedia approach is used that includes films and videos, slide shows, puppet shows, guest speakers, and interactive cable TV. The written materials and posters are original, designed specifically for the program. Weekly topics are as follows:

1. *Introduction*: This program puts its purpose right up front: to erase gang membership because gangs are destructive. It asks the question, "What are the reasons that kids get involved in gangs?" For every reason, there is an alternative. A gang is defined as a group that involves crime, likes to claim an area as their territory, may wear gang attire or certain colors, fight with other gangs, often writes graffiti, uses or sells drugs, and involves violence. It can start out as a club, but kids are advised to continually check out where the club is headed.

2. *Gangs and Graffiti*: What problems do gangs and their use of graffiti cause for the community? Who pays for it? It causes the community to go downhill. Gangs use graffiti to

communicate messages, issue challenges. There are alternative ways of gaining recognition and getting attention.

3. *History of Youth Gangs/Gangs and Death*: People die, and the number is rising (steadily from 213 in 1984 to 438 in 1988 in Los Angeles County). How gangs are organized: The "hardcores" (5-10% of members); the "regular members" (14 to 17 years old or older, who tend to back up the hardcore members); the "claimers" or "want-to-bes" (average age 11 to 13, not officially members but who act like they are and claim to be, and hang out with them; the "potentials or "could bes" (kids who are getting close to an age where they might decide to join a gang, live in or close to a gang area, or have a family member involved). Gangs try to find "ETs" (easy targets).

4. *Gangs and Violence.* If you're in a gang, violence will find you, even if you're not looking for it. "Drive-bys," when walking to the store, when with girlfriends. The retaliation cycle. How kids start feeling trapped in violence. Who gets hurt? Gang members, their families, and innocent bystanders.

5. *Gangs and Turf.* Freedom and mobility is limited. They feel trapped and restricted in a territory. Most people who get hurt straying into another gang's turf are gang members.

6. *Impact of Gang Membership on Family Members*: The family suffers, from drive-by shootings, from drugs, stealing from parents, causing emotional problems.

7. *Peer Pressure to Be Bad*: Peer pressure is put on you by others to get you to do things, some of which you may not want to do. It is also put on you by yourself to be like others. Once you give in to peer pressure, once you start, it is extremely hard to extract yourself later. Take time out to think before you act.

8. *Gangs and Tattoos*: Tattooing marks you for life. You become a walking target. You can get allergic reactions, hepatitis, even AIDS. You may find yourself being denied jobs. If you want to get rid of it, it's very painful and scars you for life (which the program illustrates very graphically).

9. *Gangs: Drugs and Alcohol*: You are more likely to get involved with drugs and alcohol when you're with a gang. It becomes a stepping stone for later drug involvement and addiction.

10. *Other Opportunities for You*: Everyone has choices. There are career opportunities out there, but you need to stay cool and prepare yourself. Paying bills is hard with a low-wage job. Most gang members are not making a lot of money on drugs, only a few are. To reach that point is to take a lot of risks. That kind of success is short-lived: You can die, get injured, go to jail. There are alternatives. What are their personal interests? What do they like to do? How can they make those things happen for themselves?

11. *Gangs and Crime.* Two-thirds of the people in prisons from Los Angeles County are there as a result of gangs. A film is shown called "Busted."

12. *Gangs and the Police/A Danger to Society*: Police stop gang members more than they stop other kids. They look for a reason to take them in. Girls who get involved with gangs are more at risk for lifelong problems like rape or pregnancy. Gang members use them for whatever they want.

13. *What it Means to Belong to a Gang.* A story of a young man who got involved with a gang. Many kids get involved for protection, but it's a myth: Many more gang members get killed and injured than anyone else.

14. *Alternatives to Gang Membership*: Exposure to many different types of activities to get them involved

15. *The Choice Is Yours*: This title speaks for itself If a kid says, "Why not join a gang, I'm just going to die anyway!" The response is, "Well, why not just go out now and play in the middle of the freeway, if it doesn't matter to you?"

I asked Tony Ostos whether he considered himself in danger from the gangs by pushing this program. He said no, that most of the gangs actually respect what the program is trying to do. They often care about their neighborhood and the people in it, often considering themselves the neighborhood's protectors. Many don't want to see their younger brothers or even other young kids get involved, yet they'll try to recruit others to keep their membership strong.

Other cities and school systems should seriously consider adopting or adapting this curriculum and program for their own use.

Jack Pransky

20. Adolescent/Peer-Focused Prevention

A conversation with a twelve-year-old from the Lower East Side of New York City:

JP: What was your most serious challenge ever?
MC: We had three guys on piggy back, tightrope-walking eleven feet off some water that was only five feet deep. I was on top.
JP: What did you do it for?
MC: For excitement.
JP: What else have you done for excitement?
MC: We went swimming in a lightning storm. I hung out of a twenty-story window. My mother found me skipping school and came after me. I had to make her not come near me—make her afraid. So I headed for the window and hung out. I didn't think of falling. When you do something daring, you don't think of falling. All you think of is getting out of it. (Pransky, 1968)

What makes adolescents behave in such crazy ways?

They're adolescents, that's why. It's tough enough for kids to have hormones and chemicals zipping on an internal roller coaster around their strange, new bodies. To then add to the mix an expanded and exciting world to experiment with, and the breaking away from childhood necessary to be successful in the adult world, it is not so surprising that adolescents behave the way they do.

Adolescence is virtually guaranteed to be a challenging time for everyone: the adolescents themselves, their parents, and anyone who works with them. If teenagers have to go through this internal craziness, they will make sure that everyone else gets dragged in with them.

Yet, adolescence is an experience we've all shared. Each of us should understand perfectly what it's like. The problem is, now that we're older and allegedly wiser, we forget. We think adolescents should behave the way we now think. We create programs for them, but if in our program designs we forget what it is like to be an adolescent, we may be way off base.

When I was a teenager I decided to save all the letters I received from my friends and girlfriends so I would be able to recall a little of what it was like when I had my own teenagers (I didn't know why I was doing it then). I decided to read some of them before writing this chapter. I found-

- an insatiable thirst for fun (or excitement)
- unbounded, uncontrolled energy
- sexual confusion
- constant experimentation
- all-consuming pain, about relationships, about family
- a desperate search for identity

Now the world is frighteningly more complex than it was when most of us were growing up. But it is important to keep things in perspective:

Six thousand years ago, an Egyptian priest carved on a stone, "Our earth is degenerate ... Children no longer obey their parents" (Johnson, in Conger, 1986).

Conger (1986) eloquently describes the plight of adolescents:

Adolescence can be many things: a time of irrepressible joy and seemingly inconsolable sadness and loss; of gregariousness and loneliness; of altruism and self-centeredness; of insatiable curiosity and boredom; of confidence and self-doubt. More than anything else, however, it is a time of rapid changes—of physical, sexual, and cognitive changes within the young person, and of changes in the adolescent's world and the demands placed on the young person by society (p. 101).

Adolescents are in the process of breaking away. Because adults must be independent, adolescents must gradually achieve independence from their parents. Because adults are supposed to be sexually mature, adolescents must begin the process of adjusting to sexual maturation. Because adults must establish cooperative working relationships, adolescents are in training with their peer group, and must learn how to get through without being dominated.

Adolescents are "immersed in a continual struggle to develop a philosophy of life or view of the world, some set of guiding moral beliefs and standards, however simple and basic, that will lend order and consistency to the many decisions they will make in this diverse, complex, often chaotic world" (Conger, 1986, p. 10). But the rapid changes they are undergoing affect teens' ability to think clearly.

How Are Adolescents Doing These Days?

Statistics show that 75% of young people in the 1980s felt that their own lives were going well. What about the other 25%? More than 20% felt their lives were not very useful, that they had few friends with whom they could get together or turn to for help, and that there was little planning for the future because plans hardly ever work out anyway (in Conger, 1986). Such feelings spell trouble for a large number of adolescents.

Conger cites studies that show if we don't emerge from the family with basic feelings of trust, of loving and caring, then we have little chance of developing self-esteem, constructive and rewarding relationships, or a confident sense of identity. Delinquents, for example, are more likely than non-delinquents to have relationships characterized by mutual hostility, family incohesiveness and parental rejection, indifference, dissension, or apathy.

As problem behaviors among young people near their highest rates ever, it is easy to conclude that large numbers of adolescents are not doing so well.

In Search of a Meaningful Role for Adolescents

Our progress and our future as a nation rest upon our children's abilities to become literate, responsible producers in society and literate, responsible participants in governance. But of those who enter high school in Chicago, 58% do not graduate with their class. In New York City, 80% of Hispanics and 72% of Blacks do not graduate. Sixty-two percent of pregnant teenagers do not complete school (Hastings, 1986). Such figures recur all over the country and do not bode well.

Kurth-Schai and Langton and Miller contend that the primary reason for adolescent problems is that "children are excluded from active and meaningful participation in human society;" that "American society provides few meaningful role opportunities for youth, thereby preventing them from assuming adult responsibilities; then society blames them for their pugnaciousness and irresponsibility" (in Benard, 1990, p. 6). As Benard summarizes, " . . . helping professions have often operated from a 'pathology' paradigm in which youth are viewed as problems to be fixed instead of as resources to our communities." For years Bill Lofquist (1983) has been insisting **that young people must be viewed as resources instead of as recipients and objects, if we expect to be successful with them**.

An important longitudinal study by Jessor and Jessor (1977) showed that an adolescent is less likely to engage in problem behavior if he or she-

- values academics and expects to do well academically
- is not overly concerned with independence
- treats society as unproblematic
- maintains a religious involvement
- is more uncompromising about transgression
- finds little positive reward in problem behavior relative to negative consequences
- displays self-control
- is connected with others
- feels social responsibility and social interest
- receives less support for problem behavior among his/her friends

Our job in designing prevention programs for adolescents is to create ways to build such perceptions, skills, supports, and opportunities. Young people themselves should be our resources as we make this happen.

Adolescent-Based Prevention Programming

For prevention purposes at least, we would be wise to keep in mind certain factors in dealing with adolescents:

- Adolescents are still open to change and their defense-mechanisms are not yet hardened.
- As children approach adolescence, there seems to be a progressive decline in parental influence and an increase in the influence of peers.
- Adolescents seem to perceive themselves as invulnerable to the hazards of risk-taking and unhealthy behaviors.

- Profound cognitive changes occur during the beginning of adolescence that significantly alter adolescent thinking and world view. Adolescent thinking is not the same as adult thinking. To effectively work with them, it is important to try to understand their perceptions.
- Adolescents' improved cognitive sophistication enables them to discover inconsistencies or flaws in adult arguments about, for example, potential risks of drug use, and helps them construct rationalizations for ignoring those risks. Thus teens' vulnerability is increased by their growing cognitive skills.
- Adolescents are involved in a dynamic struggle between extremes of dependence and independence.
- Adolescents are involved in increased interpersonal conflict with adults, especially those in authority.
- Adolescents have a tendency to withdraw from high-anxiety situations and to fight back in situations that threaten their self-esteem.
- Feelings are confusing for adolescents, who are often either don't know what they are feeling, or know what they're feeling but are unable to express it.
- Adolescents look up to older kids.
- Adolescents depend on their peer group. Through peers, adolescents gain acceptance and external security. The peer group helps provide a buffer against effects from any earlier destructive patterns. Interpersonal events with peers are far more important than any other events.
- When adolescents are alone, they can feel powerless and isolated. As soon as at least two teenagers get together, they feel more potent.
- Adolescents together often know more than one adult knows alone; they are therefore capable of determining, through group wisdom, what is best in a given situation. Adults should employ teen group wisdom in decision-making. (combined from Conger, 1986; Botvin and Tortu, 1989; and in Quintilliani, undated)

These are key points to consider in designing adolescent prevention programming.

Just Say No?

The "just-say-no" prevention campaign would have us believe that the only skill kids need to resist peer pressure is the ability to "just say no." If it were that simple we wouldn't have many problems.

It is now becoming apparent to many that something is missing in the "just-say-no" approach. "Just-say-no" was invented by adults as an easy and simplistic way out of a complex problem. If adults tell kids to "just say no," adults don't have to take any responsibility, the solution lies solely with the kids. "Just say no" implies that a young person either will want to say no to drugs or sex in the first place or will be easily convinced to say no. The reality of an adolescent's relationship with drugs, alcohol, and sex is not nearly so simple.

Unfortunately, we can't just laugh this strategy off as irrelevant. I believe the "just say no" approach is detrimental to prevention in two ways:

1. The word "just" makes it sound too easy. If a kid believes all he has to do is "just say no" then finds himself unable to say no when confronted with a difficult, high-pressure peer situation, he is bound to feel bad about himself. If he doesn't conform, his friends will call him something worse than a wimp, no longer worthy of their friendship; if he conforms,

he's a weakling who couldn't even perform the simple task of just saying no. What a worthless human being!

2. Projects emphasizing a "responsible decision-making" approach rather than a "just-say-no" or "no use" approach now have very little chance of receiving federal funding. This could be because "responsible decision-making" sounds akin to the concepts of "responsible use of drugs" or "responsible sex"—even though the concepts are entirely different. Community-based projects have become timid about including language about responsibility in their applications for funding, despite that in this time of "research-proven" programs no research has ever shown that a "no use" message produces better results than a "responsible decision-making" approach. It's only a political game, and this paranoia is destructive to the entire prevention process.

So, instead of "just say no," what would be a meaningful prevention strategy? Young people succumb to peer pressure for many reasons. What do they gain? What are they afraid they'll lose? [See Chapters 4 and 5] **Kids need the same things adults do: love, belonging, and to feel important, to feel worthwhile, to feel powerful; freedom, and fun.**

Young people are in a constant quest to meet these basic needs, although kids sometimes put their emphasis in different places. When kids feel pressured to do something they don't want to do, often they give in, hoping they'll meet one of these essential needs. In one way or another, kids will seek to meet their perceived needs. If society wants youths to attain these in acceptable ways, society must offer at least:

- opportunity (education, employment, alternative legitimate ways to have fun and excitement)
- skills and competence to make decisions that reflect self-discipline, responsibility, and good judgment
- open, friendly lines of communication
- enforced standards of behavior
- encouragement toward responsible independence
- an environment with a limited amount of harmful stress
- an environment with limited destructive influences

Youth Development/Youth Involvement: A Key to Successful Prevention With Youth

Often, young people are not so interested in becoming involved with programs conceived and run by adults. Young people are more likely to be active program participants if they themselves are involved in creating and running them.

The *PYD* (Positive Youth Development) *Link* of Wisconsin (1987) listed many ways to best insure constructive youth involvement in prevention programs. I have adapted and embellished this PYD model to yield the following key ideas. **If a prevention program is having difficulty involving its youths, this could be used as a checklist of important factors. Changes in the program could be made accordingly.**

Motivating Factors

- needs that are identified by youths and addressed by the program
- clearly defined goals, obtainable objectives, and realistic expectations that are agreed to by everyone

- activities that are meaningful from the youths' perspective and valued by the community
- shared decision-making in which all have input and everyone's ideas are valued equally, in some cases, adults may be involved; other programs work best if youth alone make the decisions
- so that youth feel genuinely needed at all stages of development, responsibility given
- meaningful roles for youth that are a source of identity and pride
- public recognition offered to youths for their efforts
- new skills taught that youths value and can apply

Communication Factors

- nonjudgmental interactions
- ideas are encouraged and shared; confidence is shown in youths' ideas
- youth are talked "with" not "at" or "down to."

Effective Teaching of Knowledge and Skills

- challenging activities that allow youth to face problems and experience the frustration and thrill of solving them
- youth are encouraged to try new skills
- formal training in leadership skills is provided
- youth are shown how, not told how
- the focus is on building individual strengths
- positive feedback is given on progress over time; positives rather than negatives are emphasized
- opportunities are provided to practice skills
- mistakes are allowed and accepted; perfection isn't demanded; liabilities are turned into assets
- alternative ways of dealing with situations are promoted and encouraged

Types of Peer-Related Prevention Programs

In Tobler's (1986) meta-analysis of 240 drug abuse prevention programs, she concluded that, for the average adolescent, "[p]eer programs are dramatically more effective than all the other programs." Such a strong statement cannot be ignored. Peer-related prevention must be an essential part of comprehensive prevention programming.

The peer group already has a significant impact upon the attitudes and behavior of young people. Often the impact is negative; peer-based prevention programs attempt to change it toward the positive. To help define peer-related prevention programs, four broad categories have been identified:

1. *peer influence*—programs that attempt to influence young people in constructive directions, through group or individual interaction. Examples: life skills training programs, self-esteem building programs, teenage discussion groups.
2. *peer teaching*—programs that use peers to convey information to other peers. Examples: peer tutoring, teenage health consultants.
3. *peer helping*—programs that use peers to counsel or otherwise help other peers. Example: peer counseling, peer mediation.

4. *peer participation*—programs that engage peers in decision-making relationships with schools or other systems. Examples: youth action teams, the school transition environment project. (adapted from Resnik and Gibbs,1988)

There can be much overlap, as with Teenage Institutes [see Chapter 21].

The Life Skills Training Program

Gilbert Botvin's (1984; 1989) APA-approved project focuses on building "life skills" in young people, i.e., "the basic interpersonal skills necessary for initiation and maintenance of friendship and other mutually beneficial relationships." Botvin believes these interpersonal skills are among the most important an individual can learn, for a lack of social competence may mean rejection and social isolation and lead to poor psychological adjustment. Life skills are the skills children need to function well as adults. The Life Skills Training Program combines a Life Skills Training curriculum with peer leadership, and teaches skills through a combination of modeling, teaching, and reinforcement.

Botvin's *Life Skills Training Program* includes five major components:

1. Knowledge and information:
   - focused on any subject of importance to students (Botvin's program focused on substance use, myths and realities, and other topics)
2. Decision-making:
   - routine and general decision-making strategies
   - social influences affecting decisions
   - recognizing persuasive tactics
   - the importance of independent thinking
   - media/advertising influences and manipulation of consumer behavior
   - formulating counter-arguments for resisting pressure
3. Self-directed behavior change:
   - self-image, its importance, and how it is formed
   - relationship between self-image and behavior
   - methods of improving one's self-image
   - beginning a self-improvement project
4. Coping with anxiety:
   - common anxiety-inducing situations
   - cognitive-behavior techniques for coping with anxiety
   - relaxation
   - application for everyday situations
5. Social skills:
   - communication (verbal and nonverbal); avoiding misunderstandings
   - overcoming shyness; initiating social contacts
   - boy-girl relationships and the nature of attraction; asking someone out
   - assertiveness
   - resisting peer pressures to smoke, drink, use marijuana

The Life Skills Training Program begins in the sixth or seventh grade and is taught either once a week or through a concentrated mini-course over three to four weeks.

The 1980 initial pilot study of this program focused on cigarette smoking among 281 eighth and tenth graders in two comparable New York suburban schools and had very impressive results based upon self-reporting. However, the self-reported data was not thoroughly trusted. In 1982, "peer leaders" were trained to conduct the program for 426 seventh graders, and this time results were based, on saliva tests along with self-reports. Results:

- 58% fewer new smokers compared with controls
- after one-year follow-up, 56% fewer

"Booster sessions" are sessions conducted usually at one- to three-year intervals to reinforce the concepts learned in the original training session. The first booster sessions were added in 1983, when the program was run with 902 eighth and ninth grade students from several suburban schools and was implemented by trained, regular classroom teachers. Results:

- 50% fewer smokers than controls, before booster sessions
- after one year follow-up, 55% fewer smokers
- when booster sessions were offered a year after initial training, results improved to 87% fewer regular smokers

The Life Skills Training program design was piloted for alcohol use with 239 students in the New York City Public schools. Results at nine-month follow-up:

- 54% fewer reported drinking in the last month than controls
- 75% fewer reported heavy drinking
- 79% fewer reported getting drunk one or more times per month

In 1984, the study was expanded to include marijuana use with 1,311 seventh graders from ten public schools in suburban New York. Results:

- initial effects evident only through peer-led (as opposed to teacher-led) groups, where there were 40% fewer experimental smokers and 71% fewer marijuana users compared with controls
- after one-year follow-up: "significantly fewer students in peer-led booster groups were smoking and using marijuana"
- after two-year follow-up, the strongest effects over time were for cigarette smoking, but the teacher-implemented program was conducted with less fidelity than the peer-led groups

Since then, Botvin conducted large studies with Black and Hispanic populations in New Jersey and New York City, which show support for the approach's efficacy with urban students in a multi-racial environment. Long-term follow-up results of his research can be found in Botvin, et al. (1995).

Say It Straight (SIS)

The *Say It Straight* Program by Paula Englander-Golden (1986) attempts to build honest, assertive communications skills based on the principles of Virginia Satir. In this school-based program, which runs 50 minutes a day for five days, students' role-play interpersonal situations they may encounter. The students choose the content. For example, they may identify difficult situations like, How do I say no to a group of friends? How do I say, "I don't like what I see you doing," to a friend? How do I say, "I've quit" to a friend? By choosing the questions, the students gain responsibility for and control over the content and are given an opportunity to deal with situations meaningful in their lives.

Results for high school students after a 1 ½ -year follow-up:

- 4.5 times fewer juvenile criminal offenses, compared with controls (in Benard, 1988)

In addition, program evaluators found "not a single alcohol/drug-related school suspension during an entire school year in one middle school where an almost totally trained milieu was attained in the first month of the 1984-85 school year" (Englander-Golden, 1986).

Mentoring

Resiliency research makes very clear the importance of mentoring relationships (Werner & Smith, 1989). **Children from difficult family backgrounds who develop close, caring relationships with at least one other adult was found to be one of the most important factors in turning around their lives.**

Bonnie Benard, in her extensive article on mentoring programs (1992), defines mentoring as a "one-to-one relationship between an adult and youth that continues over time and is focused on the youth's development..." (p.1). While the types of mentoring are quite diverse, the essential components of a mentoring relationship are characterized by-

- personalized attention and caring, leading to a healthy interpersonal relationship
- access to resources—especially cultural and vocational—that they do not often have
- positive/high expectations—conveying the message to youth that s/he can be successful
- mutual respect and liking
- sustained, personal commitment on the part of the mentor

Drawing on the work of Mark Freedman (1988) and others Benard reminds us that for a mentoring program to affect outcomes, the few hours of contact in most formal mentoring programs often do not have the richness, depth or power of naturally-occurring mentoring relationships.

There is no doubt that a close, nurturing relationship between a wise and caring adult and a youth is beneficial to both. However, the 'natural' way for this to happen is that an adult and a youth gradually become close through contact in their daily lives. It is not clear that a program can replicate this process. (p.11)

231

To have the best chance for mentoring programs to make a real difference, Benard extracted *guidelines for planned mentoring programs*. Here these are supplemented by findings from a Big Brother/Big Sister study (reported later):

- a careful program planning process, including volunteer screening that weeds out adults who are unlikely to keep their time commitment or might pose a safety risk to the youth
- energy and commitment of program manager
- institutionalization within a larger organization or integrated into an array of youth services; paid staff
- careful selection and matching of mentors and youth to ensure a successful relationship; includes preferences of the youth, their family, and the volunteer, and analyzing which volunteer would work best with which youth.
- **caring/love matters most; relationships must be the central focus**
- clear and specific, achievable goals
- training and preparation for adults and youth; communication and limit-setting skills, relationship building, best ways to interact with a young person.
- ongoing support for mentors so their needs are met; with intensive supervision by a case manager who has frequent contact provides assistance when requested or as difficulties arise and facilitating support groups when needed

While natural mentoring is one of the most important things that can happen in the lives of young people, mentoring programs, per se, may be only a "modest intervention" (p.18). However, if part of an overall, sustained effort for youth, mentoring programs can be quite valuable. Benard's recommendation is that mentoring be infused into the family, school and community lives of youth to create what Freedman calls "mentor-rich environments" (p.19). Benard and others caution that mentoring programs not divert attention from needed environmental changes such as the restructuring of schools or the creation of more and better jobs.

Yet, even within a single-focused mentoring program it is still possible that any given healthy relationship can result in great value for the young person, even to the point of turning around that life. In my view, this cannot be underestimated.

Since Benard's article, new information has surfaced. In a study of the *Big Brothers/Big Sisters* program (Tierney & Grossman, 1995) where mentors typically met with young people three times a month for four hours each meeting, where the mentor was viewed as a friend as opposed to an authority or teacher, and activities were based on preferences of the youth, the following results occurred 18 months after program implementation, in comparison with controls: Mentored youth-

- were 46% less likely to initiate drug use during the study period (70% less for minority youth)
- were 27% less likely to initiate alcohol use during the study period
- were nearly 1/3 as likely to hit someone
- experienced improved relationships with peers (especially boys)
- experienced better relationships with their parents

Peer Tutoring

Peer teaching programs offer young people meaningful roles and mature responsibilities. At the same time they provide schools with an abundant supply of paraprofessionals.

Peer teaching programs offer instruction in specific content areas. The process can take various forms: one peer tutor with a group of tutees the same age or younger; groups of tutors teaching other groups of students; peer tutors acting as aides to teachers, librarians, and other school staff. The program can also occur outside the school.

An adult oversees the program. Intensive preparatory trainings and group meetings help the peer educators learn positive ways of communicating and interacting. While the adult serves as a monitor and guide, s/he must be willing to recognize that teens may be able to reach their peers better than adults can, and thus be willing to allow the peer teachers much authority (Resnik and Gibbs, 1988).

Peer education has been found to substantially enhance learning (Bruffee, 1982; in Benard, 1988). Peer-focused programs are important; the most effective change agents are people most like the subjects on all variables except for technical competence in the promoted practices.

The *Youth Tutoring Youth* (YTY) Program, originally funded by the Neighborhood Youth Corps in several cities in the northeast, was perhaps the first organized peer teaching program, although the practice certainly occurred often in the old, one-room schoolhouses of the past. The first YTY program, initiated in 1967, paid tutors a small wage for participating. The tutoring was conducted one-to-one, usually with high school students tutoring elementary school students. At that time, only low-achieving alienated youth were chosen for participation. Yet, results "across the board" were "significant, often startling, gains" in the tutors' own basic skills as a result of the experience.

On the rough south side of San Antonio, Texas, where nearly half the young people drop out before they finish the ninth grade, the *Valued Youth Program* of Aurelis Montemaier has made a difference. There, young people are paid a small, hourly wage to tutor others for four hours per week at a cost of $200/year per teen. Besides an improvement in school performance, the dropout rate among tutors dropped to 5%.

Tutors in peer tutoring programs usually make significant gains in knowledge and affective skills. Interestingly, there is less evidence of specific gains among those being tutored (in Resnik and Gibbs, 1988).

The YTY program identified certain necessary *basic ingredients for successful peer tutoring programs*:

- ◆ A climate of acceptance—Active support of the school administration and everyone involved.
- ◆ Adult supervision and training—The adult must be very skilled in preparing tutors to work with tutees and in monitoring their progress, while patiently allowing them enough independence and autonomy to master the task.
- ◆ A convenient, comfortable space where tutors and tutees can work together—Tutors may have to leave their school and go to another place.
- ◆ Regular sessions—Ideally, tutors meet with their tutees on a regular basis.
- ◆ Available materials—Reading materials and other incidentals for learning games and other activities should be on hand. (in Resnik and Gibbs, 1988)

In the *Jigsaw technique*, developed by Eliot Aronson and Associates of the University of California, peer tutoring is transformed into a cooperative learning-type classroom activity. The following process can be used with virtually any subject area:

1. The class divides into small groups of (ideally) six.
2. All groups receive the same specific assignment; for example, "describe the process of growing and harvesting wheat."
3. Within each group, a student is responsible for finding information related to a series of questions developed by the teacher; for example, "How and where is wheat grown? How is it marketed? What is it used for?"
4. All students responsible for the individual topics form into "expert" groups to get information about their topics.
5. After the expert groups have completed their research, each group member reports back to his or her jigsaw group and teaches the particular piece of the lesson s/he has been assigned.
6. The groups are then tested for what they learned. (in Resnik and Gibbs, 1988)

Peer teaching can be particularly beneficial for imparting information about specific content areas like alcohol and drug abuse (Tobler, 1986), teenage pregnancy, sexual issues, and other health-related topics (in Resnik and Gibbs, 1988).

Often, peer education occurs through teen panels around a specific topic. Usually the panelists are quite open and candid about conveying their experiences and in opening up about their feelings. When the panelists do so, I have never seen students with more riveted attention.

Caution must be exercised, however. In teenage pregnancy panels, for example, many of the young mothers may at first convey only how adorable their little babies are, and how thrilled they are to have another life to love and care for. It is sometimes only upon further probing that the panelists will begin to share real problems they are experiencing in dating, continuing their schooling, working, having time to themselves, as well as feelings of exhaustion, despair about welfare dependency, and other feelings about having their lives drastically changed. Effective adult supervision of panel discussions can guide and focus participants' sharing and handle any problems that arise.

Information about drug and alcohol abuse can also be communicated very creatively through teen theater, with students close in age to teens as creators and performers of skits. The most effective teen theater presentation I have seen was with the *Good Clean Fun Youth Theater* of Leonia, New Jersey. Their skit concerned the dilemma of a teenager who wanted to be "known" (accepted by the in-crowd). Without telling her parents, she invited over two girls who were leaders of the in-crowd clique on a night when her parents were to be out at the theater. Her father got wind of a potential party when a nosy neighbor called, and he confronted her. Although they had a family rule that no one should be invited to the house when the parents weren't home, the daughter convinced her father that she was just going to have a couple of girls over to watch videos. As soon as her father walked out the door, a girl walked in with a wild, nearly-out-of-control guy carrying beer and some joints. The frustrated daughter tried to set limits on the situation, but before she knew it, a big party was brewing at her house with lots of drinking and smoking. Things had somehow gotten totally out of control.

The scene set up an instructive dilemma, but that wasn't what made the performance special. In the middle of the play, the performers stopped and posed the dilemma of the situation to the audience, remaining in their roles while responding to the audience's questions and comments, with the lead performer (the father) in and out of role firing provocative questions at the audience. The performers were thinking and communicating as if still in their roles, yet one step removed from the play. If someone in the audience asked, "What would have happened if you did ____," a performer would either discuss the possibility from his or her point of view or-slide back into the scene, playing it out in that suggested way. At one point during the discussion, the daughter turned to the "known" girl and said, "But I invited you over to watch videos, not do this other stuff!" The "known" girl said, "Oh, come on, get real! What does it mean when someone's invited over when their parents are away?" and the guy yelled out, "Party!" Thus, the audience was brought in to participate in solving the problem.

Kathy Renna, also of New Jersey, has been working with *Kathy's Cable Kids* to create a clever Broadway-like musical illustrating the plight and needs of young people.

Peer Counseling

"Peer counseling," "peer facilitation," "peer helping," "peer-to-peer," "peer friends," or "peer advocates" programs, as they are variously called, all refer to a type of (usually) school-based program where young people with leadership or helping abilities are provided extensive training to assist other young people with problems. The trained young people are not really counselors; they are more like structured friends, advocates or conduits of useful information. Caution might be exercised in using the term "counselor" because it can sometimes cause consternation among parents who do not want their child "counseled" by anyone, let alone a non-professional teenager. But many programs do operate successfully under the name "peer counseling."

Effective peer counseling programs have these common characteristics:

- ♦ preparation of the school community, to gain support of all decision-makers and service groups and to control for mistakes that might prematurely eliminate the program; identifying the needs of groups which might avail themselves of services, offering written descriptions clearly defining roles, functions, levels of responsibility and types of intervention that will be used, as well as training curriculum, selection process, safety valves for difficult problems; keeping the program small at the beginning
- ♦ an "adult advisor," serving as program coordinator, who has sufficient experience
- ♦ involvement of a diverse, representative group of students as peer counselors, not an elite group or a group limited to certain types, but a group of students who are most like the students to be .counseled"
- ♦ stringent selection process of counselors who are emotionally healthy, mature, considerate, caring, trustworthy, compassionate, capable, and "trainable"; a process of selection combining recruitment, the use of sociograms (having students write down the names of the students they would be most willing to go to with a problem), and acceptance of volunteers, carefully screened (although some programs take anyone willing to participate)

- ◆ intensive training to enhance trainees' positive helping responses, emphasizing communication and active listening skills, self-awareness promotion, values clarification, and problem-solving and decision-making skills that trainees can share with those they help. An effective training process, which identifies and defines skills in behavioral terms and breaks them down into small steps
- ◆ familiarity with community resources available for problems and needs such as crisis intervention, alcohol/drug information and treatment, sexual problems and issues
- ◆ definition of the peer-counselor role as one who listens, reflects, questions, probes with discretion, and is a friend-not one who gives advice
- ◆ defined, related tasks the peer counselor will do while on duty during times when not specifically counseling
- ◆ referral of serious or urgent problems to a responsible adult ,
- ◆ confidentiality (except concerning suicide or ongoing child or sexual abuse) so peer counselors can be trusted and helpees can feel respected and comfortable in opening up
(de Rosenroll, 1988; Resnik and Gibbs, 1988)

Peer counselors are taught that they are not there to save the world. They are not there even to solve others' problems; they don't have the answers. Instead, they learn to be sensitive to people who hurt and to become more aware of what others might be feeling. They are there to provide a listening ear for young people who need it, especially for young people who will not often turn to adult professionals or adult helpers.

In some peer-helper programs, the helpers have been used in in-school suspension programs or "time out" to help make those students' time more productive. Peer helpers have also worked in community agencies doing outreach with young people who do not attend school or with those hospitalized or institutionalized.

As with peer tutoring programs, in addition to the support they offer others, peer counselors themselves gain much emotional support through their own support group. Significant affective gains have been demonstrated in peer counseling programs (in Resnik and Gibbs, 1988). When a program of combined individual and group peer counseling was conducted with middle-alternative school students labeled as "severely disruptive" and "potential drop outs," despite a disruptive change in administration midway through the school year, the following results were achieved:

- • 14% decrease in school absences
- • 16% increase in self-concept (as measured on the Piers-Harris Self-Concept Scale)
- • 26% increase in school attitude (as measured by the Rundquist-Sletto Attitude Questionnaire)
(Nenortas, 1987)

Many manuals are available to peer counselor trainers. Two of the more widely used are *The Peer Counselor Starter Kit* by Carr and Sanders (1980) and *Curriculum Guide for Student Peer Counseling Training* by Varenhorst (1980).

Peer Mediation Programs

The *SMART* (School Mediation Alternative Resolution Team) program operated in New York City at William Cullen Bryant High School in Queens. Under this program, students and adults who successfully completed mediation training are available throughout the school day to mediate cases referred by the principal, guidance counselors, teachers, truant officers, security officers, students or parents. Typical problems appropriate for mediation include interracial incidents, fights, property theft disputes, serious threats or harassment, and even some student-teacher and student-parent disputes concerning things like acceptable class behavior, teacher fairness, and curfews.

The project coordinator interviews the disputants to determine whether the conflict can be resolved through mediation. When all parties agree to mediation, the project coordinator identifies one or more mediators to hear the case. The mediators hear both sides of the dispute and encourage communication by helping the disputants see each other's viewpoints and overcome emotions that block settlement. The mediation is considered successful when both parties sign an agreement containing the elements of their settlement. Follow-up is provided. SMART also provides classroom presentations to all students to orient them to negotiated conflict resolution and to the school's program.

The Victim Services Agency reported in 1986 that during the program's first two years of operation

- 88 students and 23 adults resolved 260 disputes involving 620 students
- 90% of these agreements were upheld (according to follow-up interviews)
- school suspensions for fighting dropped from 63 the year before to 34 in the first program year and 18 the second year

The school board funded expansion of SMART into other secondary schools at the middle and high school levels. Similar success is reported at the new sites.

The SMART program has also had a profound positive effect on student mediators' self-image and emotional investment in school. Some may not have been successful in class but are successful mediators. Frequently, "such a student will gladly conform to academic and behavioral standards in order to maintain the privilege of being a mediator... Mediation programs enable students who are extremely fearful or angry about a conflict in school to do something productive about those feelings. Otherwise such students would be at high risk for avoiding school or getting into trouble there" (Benard, 1988).

Combining School Improvement With Peer Support: The School Transitional Environment Project

Robert Felner of the University of Illinois is the leading proponent of a brand of prevention that focuses on times of common, high stress when many individuals are vulnerable (Chapter 24), particularly during times of transition, e.g., moving from a secure situation or environment to a new, unknown one. This happens when one moves from the home to school, from elementary to high school, from school to work. Felner says that individuals experiencing major life transitions are at increased risk for psychological and other difficulties, but the transitions can also be "opportunities for relatively rapid enhancement of developmental outcomes and the growth of more adequate coping skills" (Felner and Adan, 1988).

In Felner's APA-approved *School Transitional Environment Project*, he shows that transition to high school is often followed by significant decreases in academic performance and increases in absenteeism, by marked declines in psychological well-being, and by increased potential for substance abuse, delinquency, and other behavioral or social problems, especially among minority populations. Lower grades and absenteeism are related to school failure, and premature school dropout can lead to more serious forms of emotional dysfunction during adolescence and adult life.

A new and more complex school environment contains much disorganization and flux, particularly when students move from small, rural schools to large union schools. This type of school is more impersonal and shows far less capacity to respond to individual student needs. Felner's solution is to reorganize the school's social system, to reduce the degree of flux a student confronts upon entering this new school situation, and to reestablish a stable peer support system.

The School Transitional Environment Program (STEP) from elementary to junior high school consists of two major parts:

1. Smaller subunits (STEP units) formed within the larger school through largely self-contained groupings of students. A group of students is assigned to a homeroom, then generally moves throughout the day as a unit. The homeroom period lasts 15 to 20 minutes. The STEP units meet once every four to five weeks throughout the school year. If the STEP time runs beyond the homeroom period, it is okay to spend the extra time because the STEP units are primarily self-contained and move to the next class as a unit.
2. Homeroom teachers assigned to serve as the primary administrative and counseling link between students, parents, and the rest of the school. The homeroom teachers help students choose classes and provide counseling for school and personal problems. When a student is absent, the homeroom teacher contacts the home and follows up excuses. Prior to the start of the year, the homeroom teacher contacts the parents and meets with them to identify anyone who may need additional help or support. Increased teacher familiarity with students leads to greater teacher satisfaction, because teachers know more about what's going on with their students.

The intent of the STEP program is to increase the amount of support students receive from school, to increase student accountability and to decrease their anonymity, to increase access to important information about school expectations, rules, regulations, and to establish a stable peer support system.

By eliminating a constantly shifting peer group in each class, the program helps students feel more secure. They are more comfortable with each other, feel a greater sense of belonging, and feel more supported. They perceive the school environment as stable, well-organized, understandable and cohesive.

A team is also formed among the teachers through their training. Throughout the year, teachers have on-going meetings for support and to improve their skills.

The results of the initial study (1982) were as follows:

- significant improvements in grade point average (over controls) students absent significantly less often in ninth grade (over controls)

- student self-concepts generally remained stable on self-concept scales (compared with marked decreases in controls)
- students reported higher levels of teacher support, teacher affiliation, and involvement and had more positive feelings about school's climate

Project students were more successful in coping with the transition to high school than controls. A 1987 follow-up study showed a-

- 21% dropout rate (compared to 43% of controls) comparable to the usual rates of this school system
- no placements in alternative programs for failures (compared with several for controls)
- significantly higher grades in first two years of high school*
- significantly fewer absences in first two years of high school*

STEP "helped poorer students remain above their thresholds for failure and dysfunction." The project has been replicated with similar results, including findings of-

- less depression
- less self-reported substance abuse
- fewer delinquent acts
- higher teacher ratings (Felner and Adan, 1988)

Transitions can be a problem in moving from any major life stage to another, and programs can be designed at all stages.

Youth Leadership—The Leadership Project

The Leadership Project of Windham County, Vermont, was one of the four exemplary programs selected in 1989 by the Office of Substance Abuse Prevention. Leadership Project Teams, each with an adult project coordinator, make high schools their bases to work with a community's needs, desires, and strengths concerning the issue of substance abuse. The Teams become "a catalyst for the empowerment of adolescents in the change process." Their philosophy: "Teens know firsthand the impact drugs and alcohol are having on their generation; they want to improve the situation, and they hold the key to any truly effective program."

The project's intent is to develop a comprehensive community approach by designing a program to-

1. Develop positive relationships among the segments of the community
2. Create a greater awareness of substance abuse issues
3. Assemble a team of adolescents and adults to begin to address the problem at the community level

---

* Note: The figures began to close in later years.

239

4. Develop a structure and support within the community so that current and future problems can continue to be effectively addressed.

The teams strive for a cross-representation of all clique groups. Peers recommend their peers for participation, and thus many different types of students come to perceive themselves as leaders. Teachers and influential community members may be recruited for any team. The number of adults per team is limited to approximately three per ten adolescents to preserve the integrity of adolescent contribution and leadership.

Results indicate that it impacted the youth culture with regard to substance abuse, and the young people are excited about their participation in the program.

Prevention of Bullies and Their Victims

Dan Olweus (1984; 1991) has conducted extensive studies of bullies and their victims in Norway and Sweden. In these countries, 7-8% of the school population was found to engage in repeated bullying of others, and 10-11% are fairly regular victims. These figures are significant for prevention because 60% of former bullies had at least one felony conviction by age 23.

Olweus finds bullies are generally aggressive and strong, have a need to dominate, and lack empathy, but are not necessarily insecure and anxious underneath. Four major factors appear to lead to an aggressive bullying personality pattern:

- negative attitude and lack of warmth by mother
- permissiveness
- use of physical child-rearing methods
- an active, hot-headed temperament

The bullies' victims are usually younger children, boys more than girls, who appear insecure, vulnerable, anxious, withdrawn, and physically weak.

In 1983, an extensive nationwide campaign against bully/victim problems was established in the Norwegian primary schools by the Norwegian Ministry of Education. In this eight-month program, 400 students were followed for two-and-a-half years. The program consisted of a three-pronged attack:

- restructuring schools to create, warm, non-hostile environments, including firm limits ('We don't allow bullying here!"), better supervision during recess, class meetings, cooperative learning, and peer involvement, especially involvement of victims
- training teachers in awareness and knowledge about bullies and their victims; how to play an active role in having serious talks with bullies and responding to problems; using classroom meetings to establish clear rules about bullying and determine violations ("Has anyone violated the rules? What should we do about it?'); getting help for victims and including them in activities
- training for parents in a similar vein

Among the materials developed for the program (available, but possibly not yet in English) are-

- a booklet for teachers and school managers distributed to all schools indicating the research and giving practical suggestions about what they could do to prevent and handle this problem
- a brief, similar booklet for parents designed to reach all parents
- a training video showing episodes from the lives of two bullied children ages 10 and 14
- a short inventory (questionnaire) designed to provide measures of bully/victim problems and the readiness of teachers and students to interfere with those problems

Results were-

- a 50% reduction in bullying after two years
- reduced theft
- reduced vandalism
- reduced truancy
- a 75% reduction in new cases of bullying
- bullying was not displaced away from the school or on to the streets.

Opportunities for Meaningful Involvement: Something More Than Survival

In the *Something More Than Survival* program, young people participate alongside adults in making important decisions about how to improve their environment. In one such program in California, students became involved in school climate improvement by helping to develop an assessment process and ensuring that the recommended changes were made. In a follow-up one year later, "significant improvements were shown in most areas" (in Resnik and Gibbs, 1988).

More on meaningful involvement of youth can be found in Chapter 26.

Elements of Model Programs

The Children's Defense Fund identifies 26 "multisite initiatives serving high risk youths" from several states that are funded by private corporations or foundations and considered successful model programs with "replicability potential" (although the Fund cautions stringently against problems of replication). Rather than list all 26 programs, an examination of program elements that might be included in comprehensive prevention programming for "high risk" and other youth. Some of these elements are:

- ◆ GED and academic remediation
- ◆ career counseling
- ◆ job readiness or life skills
- ◆ motivation building
- ◆ planning skills
- ◆ self-esteem building and personal development
- ◆ responsible decision-making skills
- ◆ coping skills
- ◆ higher order reasoning and comprehension skills

241

- ♦ assertiveness and communication skills
- ♦ advocacy
- ♦ health services
- ♦ social activities
- ♦ peer group support sessions and other support services
- ♦ parenting skills (particularly for pregnant teens and teen parents)
- ♦ school improvement
- ♦ improvement of relations with family and friends
  (excerpted from Children's Defense Fund, 1989)

What Teens Want From Adults

Young people from the Alternatives for Teens program [Chapter 22] listed what they want from adults who work with them. Teens want adults who listen, who can talk to kids, who have fun themselves, who are willing to enforce rules, who keep kids under control, who trust kids, who get involved, who have had experiences with teens, who let teens have a good time. Teens want adults who are caring, respectful to kids, strict, patient, friendly, trustworthy, and who have a sense of humor (from Alternatives for Teens brochure, undated).

21. Teenage Institutes

The Green Mountain Teenage Institute (GMTI) *is a week-long summer gathering of peer leaders from different school systems. In a very supportive, informal atmosphere, the youth leaders learn about alcohol and other drugs and their use and abuse. Armed with this information and new skills, they go back to their schools and communities to develop prevention activities for their peers, for younger students, and for adults. As of 1989, GMTI had served more than 1000 teenagers from 60 Vermont high schools who, in turn, have had meaningful contact with over 200,000 others back in their schools and communities.*

Elizabeth Lawrence *was co-founder and co-director of the Green Mountain Teenage Institute. She has that rare combination of administrative ability and an uncanny talent for working with young people. I wanted to learn how she and co-founders Alan Sousie and Peter Vincent managed to take an idea of such magnitude and convert it into one of the most successful prevention programs seen in the North Country. I also wanted to discover the secret of her success in working with kids. She is not nicknamed "The Mother of Prevention" for nothing. Elizabeth is also co-founder and co-director of Prevention Unlimited..*

JP: What made you and others decide that a teenage institute was needed?

EL: In 1981, through a United Way grant, the Alcohol Information and Referral Service hired me to do drug and alcohol education in the schools, but many schools were saying they didn't have a drug problem. They believed drug education would make the kids want to experiment, so their solution was to not bring the issue into school. In their view, drug education consisted of some state trooper coming in with a plastic marijuana plant and a little kit saying, "This is what a joint looks like. These are pills ..."

JP: Boy, times have really changed!

EL: A lot. What happened was, a few area service providers were regularly meeting together, and Alan [Sousie] read an article in the NIAAA magazine about a "Teen Institute." We all agreed that if we could involve the kids in the whole education process, then they could bring the problem to the attention of school authorities. Subterfuge! People were always talking about kids not taking responsibility, and we thought if kids were trained specifically in education/prevention skills, they could not only take responsibility for their own behavior but could also train their peers.

JP: So from this germ of an idea, how did it all come to be?

EL: Our first step was to determine who our allies were, so we held a couple of meetings of interested persons we knew in schools. We tried to get representation from all schools in Chittenden County, and we talked about our idea. Then we held a second meeting to discuss what kind of students should be involved, how to involve them, and how to enlist the schools' support.

We were looking for both positive and negative peer leaders among the kids—some of us had been negative peer leaders in school and we knew we too had had influence. The only criterion at that point was that the kid not have any harmful involvement with chemicals. In some instances, we asked guidance counselors to identify some kids; in others, we conducted informal surveys, asking kids to list the classmates they perceived as having the most leadership. We set up a very haphazard screening process on a half-page application form and got a fair number of interested students. Then we screened them through the guidance counselors.

JP: Why did you decide not to take kids involved with alcohol and drugs?

EL: We knew we wanted this to be more than straight education. We wanted to incorporate a lot of group process skills. We wanted to create a real growth opportunity, so the kids could look at their own issues and take positive steps to deal with problems with family, peers, or whatever. We believed that kids who were harmfully involved with chemicals, or who had been through treatment and had not been sober for at least a year, would not be grounded enough to deal with the stuff we wanted to do. We also wanted the kids to design their own prevention activities when they left the Institute and follow through, and we felt that would be a burden for people having trouble with their own abuse. And, far too often, it is easier to focus on outside activity if you're having a problem with chemicals, so you don't have to face the problem.

JP: At this point did you have a concept in mind of the program you wanted? You didn't think traditional education would work?

EL: Right. I was involved with something in the seventies called the Social Seminar, developed by NIMH [National Institute of Mental Health] to look at alcohol and drug use and abuse. But the focus wasn't on pharmacology, the dynamics of chemical dependency in the family, or the differences between use and abuse; it was on communication skills and values clarification. The idea was to gather together people with different ideas, and lead them to accept each other as individuals and learn to examine and constructively solve problems together. That was my focus. Alan came from a family treatment background and had his own chemical issues. Peter had an extraordinary knowledge of pharmacology. So the three of us combined our expertise. We designed the program to balance experiential learning with didactic. A "family group" was to be held at the end of each day, where the kids could meet in a small group, process what they'd been absorbing, share as they wished, and have a safe place to discuss individual issues and needs around everything happening at the Institute.

JP: Didn't it seem overwhelming to create something of this magnitude out of nothing?

EL: It was incredibly exciting. We knew we could do it. We had no idea of the power of it, but we had a feeling if we were successful with one group, we could have a far-reaching impact on the state.

JP: What did you consider "successful" to be?

EL: I considered successful to be 15 to 20 students who would initially impact on 50 to 60 individuals in the county by the end of the year.

JP: So your intent wasn't so much to help the kids change their behavior while they were there, as having them go back to their schools and communities and get others involved?

EL: It was both. It's always been a two-pronged attack. At first we needed to provide a very safe environment to operate in, conducive to setting up instant trust between teens and the adults working with them. It took some doing.

JP: How long did it take to establish this trust?

EL: About a day.

JP: Just a day? [laughter]

EL: Well, the environment was very important; we took a lot of time to make sure we had the right space. We wanted a place that was both isolated and near the city in case we needed access or we had an emergency. It had to be comfortable. We met in a carpeted living room and sat around the floor—by design. For food, we focused on interesting things the kids wouldn't ordinarily eat: no junk food, a limited amount of sugar, no potato chips; we would instead have rice or home fries. We wanted them nourished, with healthy energy to operate on.

We wanted to get them comfortable looking at issues related to alcohol and drug abuse, not only among their peer group but also in the community. As it turned out, we discovered that a lot of these kids had problems, which surprised us because these were supposed to be "normal" kids. But many had some real issues in their families.

JP: You hadn't anticipated this?

EL: We did feel that one of the results of the Institute would be to have them take a clear look at whatever issues they had and take action if there was a need—because many issues are related to one's own or somebody else's abuse of a substance. We just didn't expect it to the extent that we got it. We felt that teens had to be clear about their own use and abuse or we would be asking them to unfairly approach their peers. If they had a clear understanding of where they were coming from, they would be on solid ground.

We were not from the philosophy that says drugs are bad and shouldn't be discussed with kids because drug use is illegal. A lot of people felt we shouldn't discuss use of substances like marijuana and cocaine, but we believed strongly that to deny drugs existed, or to not teach as much as we knew about chemical reactions in the body and what happens to people when they're under the influence, would be doing these kids a disservice. Our approach has been a real bone of contention, but we knew we'd be setting these kids up to be shot down the first time they tried to do anything if they didn't have accurate knowledge, if they weren't real clear about the difference between use and abuse, and if they didn't understand the dynamics of use. We knew people would try to sabotage them anyway within the school system and community...

JP: How do you mean that?

EL: We have a tendency in this country to assume that unless you graduate from college you don't know anything and can't be a contributing member of society. Our whole focus in public education is to feed kids information and have them spit it back to us in some form that isn't really relevant to their existence. We don't ask our young people to participate at a personal, experiential level in their education. We focus our public education system on keeping kids in line. We expect them to be responsible for their behavior and be responsible citizens, but we don't allow them to participate. It's a double standard.

JP: So you were trying to set up an environment that would allow that.

EL: Absolutely. And we did!

JP: So how could you tell you were successful?

EL: Not only were the kids out making tons of community presentations, but almost 100% of the kids left the Institute on a total high. This is not uncommon when you go through a meaningful group experience, but it usually fizzles out within a couple of weeks. We were really surprised that the high, that level of energy, lasted for months.

JP: Why did it?

EL: Probably because of their involvement in the plans they made, and because of the expectation that they would do something constructive. If they sought our support or found it within the school they were successful beyond even their wildest imaginations. But a couple of groups also died when the administration said, "You can't do this." In those cases, we encouraged them to change their plans and work in the community. Yet, a couple of kids who had no support at all from their school system still did incredibly well; they just forged ahead. We were stunned by this and thought, "Well, it must be due to the particular group of kids we have." But by all reports from both kids and adults, it didn't have as much to do with the kids as with their empowerment—as much as I hate the word. Once they felt they could really make a contribution, that they were respected and knew what they were talking about, they felt very confident and enthusiastic in their ability to carry out their plans.

Even though I remember feeling totally nervous for these kids when we'd go in front of a large group of, say, sophisticated guidance counselors, the kids were on solid ground because they were coming from their own perspective. They weren't expected to be sophisticated; they were themselves. And the adults were flabbergasted with their honesty and the clarity with which they could discuss the issues. After the first couple of questions, the adults would move forward on their seats, and the kids would lean forward over the table, and it would become a real dialogue. We always ran over our time wherever we went.

The first time they gave a workshop at the Vermont Prevention Conference, people signed up in droves to hear the kids' perspectives on what their problems and issues were. When the adults asked what they could do to help, the kids would always say, "Be yourself." I firmly believe that's something they learned at the Institute, or if they didn't, the idea was certainly encouraged and solidified there. We knew we were being successful when kids from the Institute would be on panels with adult experts and the questions were always directed to the kids. The adults learned far more from the kids than from the adults on the panel, because when the kids talked, the adults were really listening.

JP: What do you think they learned from the kids?

EL: That they needed to focus on kids more as responsible individuals and not bracket them into some sort of "wild adolescent" category. That kids are very willing to participate, be responsible for their own behavior, and help others. That adults have to provide an arena that gives kids more responsibility in decision-making. A lot of kids were asked to be on advisory committees for Act 51 [Chapter 17] because they asked for responsibility and were given it, and they functioned very well. I think it made the schools take a serious look at how they were dealing with the alcohol and drug problem within their own systems, and incorporate some more human ways to deal with the problem.

JP: Getting back to the actual Institute for a moment, you might have 40 teenagers gathered together; weren't you nervous that trouble might erupt?

EL: We tried to anticipate teenage behaviors, because we weren't very far away from it ourselves. That's one of the things that I think made it successful: All of us were adolescent to a certain extent. We were adult, but we certainly didn't behave that way, which allowed the kids to treat us like kids while we treated them like adults. We tried to anticipate things like alcohol and drug use. If they used drugs or alcohol, their parents would be called and they would be asked to leave. We had very clear limits around things that would cause trouble for the kids and for us.

Within these, we knew there would be a number of kids with personal problems around their own family's chemical use and abuse, and probably also around physical and sexual abuse. But we figured it was a small enough group that between the permanent staff, assistant staff, and those coming in for presentations, we had enough competent professionals if trouble arose. Peter [Vincent] and I were working for Champlain Drug and Alcohol Services so we had access to treatment professionals if there was a problem beyond what could be handled in a family group. The first couple of years there were no problems.

JP: But there were later. What kinds of problems?

EL: Some serious emotional problems. Originally the schools were too nervous to send any students but solid student leaders. As time went on, as we gained credibility and expanded, we were being referred kids who had a very thin veneer of, "I'm okay." As these kids went through the Institute, we started to uncover many more issues of physical and sexual abuse than we anticipated. One night we had a presentation by a police chief—you were there—who handled the whole issue of sexual abuse and rape very badly in my estimation, by being very graphic and very callous. This happened on the third night of the Institute when people were very emotionally connected with each other and feeling very free to confide. There were also some teens who were not eating—we were not on top of this—and others who were consuming large amounts of sugar. The situation was a powder keg that just blew up, particularly with one or two individuals who'd had to repress, for years, sexual abuse that had happened or was on-going. Then, as is usual in a large group, there were those who wanted attention and magnified their own personal issues around alcoholism and abuse to get attention too; it was just crazed.

JP: I remember that 10 or 15 of them got up and ran out of the room during that presentation-

EL: Large numbers of women in this country have had to deal with physical and sexual abuse. It's far more prevalent than we have ever admitted. We made the mistake of not having a different kind of presentation. Early on, we made lots of mistakes. What we did in terms of follow-up was report what we needed to SRS, and we contacted the families, but unfortunately the individual who was most effected was really a disturbed individual—

JP: She was in my "family group."

EL: That's right! And she had been classified as the most popular, the best cheerleader, the most active in sports, and was considered to be the darling of the school—

JP: She was runner-up in the Miss Teen Vermont contest.

EL: She was! I forgot that. So here was this girl, overachieving like crazy to get attention and have success, trying to cover up what was going on inside—

JP: You know what was incredible? I remember her entire personality changed before my eyes.

EL: And she went home that way! And she stayed that way. And to my knowledge she did not get any help because of her parents, who said we ruined this child, and they were going to sue us. We kept saying she had serious psychological problems that needed to be dealt with. She did begin to get some help, but then her mother forbade her to go back to the counselor, because her mother was in just as much denial as she was. It turned out that we found a lot of troubled young people crying out for help.

JP: Why was it happening at the Institute?

EL: Because they were free for probably the first time in their lives to express what was going on for them, and take a look at some of the personal issues they had been dealing with—
[emotional pause]

JP: Only within themselves

247

EL: (sigh) Yes.

JP: How did you set it up so the kids felt free to express things they hadn't ever expressed? What are the principles behind it?

EL: Well, it's important to understand group process and group dynamics. If you know there are certain stages any group goes through, and if **you start off establishing involvement and trust, you can build upon those to the point where people feel free to share. Environment and the way the group is facilitated are also key factors. We would say to teens at the start, "If you're going to be here, you're going to be involved with this process. You're free to pass, but we're going to encourage you to participate because this process is yours; we're only here to help that out."**

As the kids owned more and more of their experience, which they're not allowed to do in most public school or family situations, they began to experience a freedom and a power that many of them never had before, which accounted for the high they experienced. **As they began to share what was going on for them in their experiences at the Institute—which wasn't forced, ever—they learned that others had similar experiences. There was so much trust and the environment was so safe, they felt safe to talk very honestly about what their experiences were in a way they'd never been able to do before. That's magic if it's done right. But the magic has to have some sort of closure. You have to bring them back to the reality.** We don't live this way. This is not a utopian society. We cannot risk sharing these things with everybody out there. The transition is a tricky line to walk.

JP: So, if I can hone in on some of the reasons this approach was successful, the structure of the environment is one important factor, the way **you set it up so teens had a lot of power to make decisions, within a framework, and you allowed them the opportunity to express their feelings—**

EL: And we provided **a place where people could really be themselves without any judgment**, where they could risk being themselves. They didn't have to be the cheerleader they had to be in school every day.

JP: And the reason they didn't have to be that way was?

EL: Because we didn't have any expectations that they had to be that way. We had expectations that they would be as comfortable as they could be—we provided that—and that they would be loose and relaxed and enjoy themselves and participate at whatever level they could as genuinely as possible.

JP: Besides the structure, what do you do so kids will trust you? What about you or your staff breeds trust?

EL: We made a real effort to **treat each person as an individual and to focus on each of them. We were never condescending.** The first thing we would ask them to do at the Institute was participate in a situation that would normally be very embarrassing and humiliating: they had to learn each other's names in a repetitive fashion around a circle, write on a name tag some personal things about themselves, then mingle around the room sharing nonverbally what was going on for them at that moment. Now, ordinarily those activities would be so threatening that people would refuse to participate for fear of being considered stupid, but we took the nervousness everybody was experiencing and made it fun, so we put it to positive use. The **adult role models participated along with the kids as their equals. The teens knew the adults were the ultimate authorities if anything went wrong**, and if anything got out of control the adults were obviously going to deal with it, but the adults shared the kids' experience with them, and we made that very clear at the beginning. So, instead of being the authority and the "teacher," each adult was a peer. We asked them to call us by our first names; some of them never even knew our last names. We dealt with each other as members of a community with one responsibility, and that was to learn and participate as much as we could.

JP: And you still found that you were respected as the authorities?

EL: We were respected more because we were much more approachable.

JP: Doesn't that go against what most people think authority should be?

EL: Absolutely. But a lot of time authority is based upon insecurity, so those in authority have to build a superfluous barrier. They don't have the freedom to be themselves. When you think of the typical situation in public school, teachers do not have the capacity to be themselves to the extent one would hope because there's always somebody looking over their shoulders determining whether they keep their jobs. In this case, there was nobody looking over anybody's shoulder. We were the authority. Not me, Alan, and Peter, but "we" the community. If any issues needed to be dealt with, they were dealt with as a community, so everyone shared in the authority.

JP: That's important. **When problems came up, the community dealt with them**.

EL: That's right. The community always met first thing in the morning after breakfast to discuss what community issues arose from the night before: people staying up late, people being disturbed, what the schedule was, whether there were there any changes. Everybody had equal opportunity to participate in and make decisions. No one was behind closed doors making decisions except when the community was in no condition to make them. Such times have been rare, but whenever the community has been unable to carry on, they were asked for their input, the actual decisions were made by the adults—as in the night I mentioned.

JP: I remember Alan did a masterful job that night of calming the group down. He knelt in the middle of the circle and talked to the group very quietly, "We've all been through something real heavy here ..., so we're going to forego all activities for the night and just be available for people to talk if they want to or cool out or whatever—

EL: He was incredible! And in that instance they really needed whatever authority adults could provide. Gives me goose bumps just thinking about it.

JP: How would you tell people how to be successful with kids?

EL: I'd say what the kids say: "Be yourself." The second commandment says, "Thou shalt love thy neighbor as thyself." In our society we don't learn how to love, appreciate, and respect ourselves. As I see it, this is the primary reason for chemical abuse and other kinds of abuse. If we learn to feel good about ourselves, to trust our basic instincts and judgments, and to focus more on how we feel and want to feel in a more holistic sense, then we can be ourselves and treat people as equals. If you don't know how to be yourself, start with one or two individuals, start treating them as if they were you. That's how you learn it, I think. But do it with humor, do it with fun, and keep yourself open to new experiences. Then you're being yourself.

JP: Can anybody work effectively with kids?

EL: No. Not everybody can do everything. I don't think anybody can successfully work with kids unless they **treat them as individual, responsible human beings and expect certain kinds of behavior from them**.

JP: You eventually burned out. Did it have to do with dealing with the kids on that level all the time?

EL: No. I got burned out because my job got really divided. I couldn't really be at a Teen Institute as a participant any more because, after the first four of years, I had so many administrative responsibilities and so much to think about, it got to be more than I could handle.

I wanted to be there with and for the kids, but I was always the one that took the responsibility—and I shouldn't have done this—of making sure the kitchen knew we were going to be 15 minutes late, or making sure the people were greeted. It wasn't that it couldn't be delegated, but I had to think ahead to delegate it.

JP: Besides, you have that, "You've-got-to-do-everything-yourself" philosophy because you know you can do it better than anyone else . . .

EL: [laughter] I know I can do it better than anyone else; that is my major flaw, and it's going to be my downfall for sure. I'm often exhausted because of it. We trained almost 400 kids over four years, starting with 20 the first year. Then it mushroomed. It got to the point where I was taking on too much. I couldn't take any more kids into my life. To this day, I have kids who come up to me and I can't think of their names, and I should be able to. Then there are the wonderful surprises. In the airport this Christmas, a kid came up to me and said, "You sure don't look like a teacher." I looked at him and said, "Well, I'm not really a teacher." He said, "You were my teacher," and I thought, who is this kid, he's whacked out, he's on some drug. It turns out he was one of the shyest kids at an Institute. He was home on leave from the Marines, and he told me how the Teen Institute had been great for him. He said it had taken him a couple of years to absorb it, but it had been really helpful for him when he went into the military. Even the military! [laughter].

2/89

22. Alternatives for Teens

Alternatives for Teens, a prevention program that gave teenagers the opportunity to plan and run alcohol- and drug-free events for their peers, provided a forum for teenagers to discuss issues of importance to them. **Sas Carey** *designed the operations of the program and served as its first coordinator, bringing many years of experience running teen discussion groups. This project was selected as a model by the state of Vermont to be disseminated throughout the state because of its success. It was subsequently selected by the Federal Office for Substance Abuse Prevention as an exemplary program. Sas completed a manual that takes one step-by-step through the Alternatives for Teens process. The manual,* Life Skills for Teens: The Group Leaders Guide to Alternatives for Teens, *may still be available through the Addison County Parent Child Center in Middlebury, Vermont. The program is now expanding into other Vermont schools. Sas has a rare talent for getting kids to talk about things that are important to them..*

JP: How did Alternatives for Teens begin?

SC: The original idea, which came from the Children's Task Force and Drug and Alcohol Council of Addison County in 1983, was to have teen advisory boards meet in four schools to plan and implement monthly, county-wide social and recreational activities that would increase self-esteem, communication, and social skills. The program was funded by the Office of Alcohol and Drug Abuse Programs, and they hired me. The program was supposed to meet every other week, but I found out early that the kids needed to meet once a week for continuity's sake.

JP: How did you get the program off the ground?

SC: It varied from school to school. In Middlebury, I talked to the psychological counselor and she said, "It sounds great. I'll give you some kids' names." Some of them had been in the Green Mountain Teen Institute the year before. Then she gave me some other kids that were pretty "at risk." Mount Abraham Union said, "Well, you only have a grant for five months, and we don't like to start things and then stop, so we're not sure." I had to convince them it would be helpful to them, and they finally let me in. An announcement let students know they could come and talk about things they wanted to. In Otter Valley Union, there was a supportive guidance counselor who chose very high functioning leaders for the program. In the end, this worked against us because those kids became active in other things. We were forced by a new administration to meet after school instead of in school, so the program fizzled and had to close down for a few years. It only recently started up again. Vergennes was tricky because the guidance counselor didn't quite get what I was asking for, and suggested we go to the school board and present it. The school board said okay, but they didn't want to give us names of any "at-risk" kids because they said they didn't have any "at-risk" kids in Vergennes anyway.

JP: Didn't some of your toughest kids come from Vergennes?

SC: Yeah. The next day I met with Social Services and told them what I was doing, and they said, "We'll give you the name of every foster kid we have in Vergennes, and all their brothers and sisters." They gave me 21 names, and I called every one at home and asked if they'd be interested in starting a group, and they said yes.

JP: What exactly did you say to the kids?

SC: I said, "Would you like to come and talk about things that are important to you, and set up alcohol and drug free events?'

JP: What was their response?

SC: It varied from kid to kid. "Yeah, all right, I'll come to see what it's like," or "Well, I'm not really sure." So I'd say, "Okay, well, why don't you just stop in and see what it's like." I didn't do any hard sell. I just said, "This is what it is, if you want to try it, come."

JP: What did you do when they got there?

SC: We'd begin with fun ways of doing introductions, like "If you were in a house that was burning, what would you take out?" Ways to get people to open up and say fun things about themselves. Then we set up ground rules. We talk about attendance. If the group meets during school, we say that if you have a test, or your teacher doesn't want you to go, it's okay to miss. We rotate the times around so they won't miss any one class too much. We talk about respect. No put-downs. We don't talk about people who aren't there. We talk about decision-making, and I explain consensus and how that works. Actually, I only have to explain rules the first time; each time afterwards there's usually at least one kid who has been in the group before who can explain them to newcomers.

JP: What's so special about this program?

SC: I think three things make it a little different from most other programs. First, it's primary prevention, in that **any teenager can volunteer to be part of it. Even when I was given names of high-risk kids to begin with, anybody could have come**. School announcements always read, "Open to anyone." I had personal contact with a few before it started, that's all. And not all the schools gave me high-risk kids.

JP: Did you ask for high-risk kids originally?

SC: No. I asked for kids who needed it, who could benefit from it, and who didn't have too much to do. These terms might be interpreted as high-risk, but I also wanted a cross-section of socioeconomic groups. It didn't really work out that way, although there was a cross section across all the schools. Second, **it's a long term program. A kid can be in it for six years, from 7th to 12th grades. Third, everything is designed by the teenagers themselves. They choose the topics to talk about, the way a topic is discussed, and the events. They run the events**. Another thing is, **an adult facilitator serves as a process person, to focus the discussion, throw in facts where necessary, teach life skills, and model appropriate behavior**.

JP: Okay, you've got the kids gathered in one place.

SC: We talk about decision-making and confidentiality. I do this a little differently than most people. I ask questions about what these terms mean to them. "Suppose you said you were upset about something that happened in your family and told the group, who else would you want to know?" I give them examples so they can think about confidentiality and come up with guidelines for the group. Then I ask, "What do you think Alternatives for Teens means in terms of substance use?" and after group consideration we establish a policy. Then we brainstorm ideas and topics. I say, "This group is for you and there are two main things we do here. First, we talk about whatever's important to you. Second, we set up events so teens will have more activities. What topics do you want to make sure get covered this year?" Usually they're not bashful about suggesting topics, so I just write the suggestions on newsprint. If they're bashful, I give them cards to write on.

JP: What kinds of topics come up?

SC: The main topics are drugs, decision-making, friends, conflict-resolution, sex, families, feelings, suicide, spirituality, and leadership.

JP: Are these pretty much what teenagers will come up with in any group?

SC: Yeah. In any reasonably safe group, today in America.

JP: What is their reaction at first?

SC: They usually get pretty excited.

JP: Why?

SC: Because **they know they're being listened to, and that is really unusual. They already can begin to feel that they have some control over what's going to happen, so they begin to feel empowered, especially in creating events**. I ask, "What events would you like to have happen?" and they list all kinds of activities that would be fun. And I basically say that anything is possible, and that it's up to them to make it happen. I write down all their suggestions—even humorous or outlandish ones.

JP: Then the rest of the process is either talking about the things they want to talk about, or planning events?

SC: Yes.

JP: How do you know it works?

SC: One thing is, **they keep coming back**. That's a pretty big test. I also did a research study that had eight questions. One question is the about use of alcohol at teenage parties when others are drinking and adults aren't present.

JP: Referring to their behavior?

SC: Yes. I did it over a two-year period, and although at the beginning for the group I studied there were only 12 kids that ended up consistently attending, **we found no change in their drinking behavior, which we thought was significant because the Swisher study [a Vermont statewide study] showed that normally kids increased the amount of alcohol that they used over two years. In other words, tenth graders use less than twelfth graders; eighth graders use less than tenth graders. The kids that went all the way with this program didn't increase their alcohol consumption, and there were a lot of at-risk kids in this study**. Eight out of 12 came from alcoholic families, and 3 had been abused as children, and about half misbehaved in the school. We also had subjective case studies showing the kinds of backgrounds the kids came from and what happened to them, and **given these backgrounds, you would have expected alcohol consumption to have increased over those years**.

JP: When you were with the kids, how did you know it was working?

SC: For me, the program is worth it if one kid changes or gets it. By "it," I mean those *Developing Capable People* attributes, that they're worthy, important, capable and powerful. If even one kid makes a good decision or follows through on something he or she wouldn't have been able to before ....

One teen, whose brother was in jail a lot, told me he started smoking pot when he was eight and probably did quite a bit of drugs. I met him at an Alternatives for Teens roller-skating trip. He was a really tiny guy in the seventh grade smoking cigarettes, and I said, 'Why don't you join

Alternatives for Teens?' He finally joined by the end of eighth grade. When he was in tenth grade, the bus drivers accused the kids of slashing the seats with knives. I don't know if this was true, or if the seats just had tape on them and the kids pulled it off, but after we came back from a program trip, the drivers said the seats were slashed and it was going to cost us $350. So we needed somebody from Alternatives for Teens to go and talk to the bus owner to see what he would like us to do: fix or mend the seats for him, replace them if he wanted us to give him some money, whatever. Well, this kid said he'd talk to him. I couldn't stop thinking, I wonder if he's going to do it, or if he's going to remember everything, because I authorized him to spend up to $25 without even checking with me. I didn't know whether this kid was even going to show up the next week. I tend not to put a lot of expectations on the kids, because if I do they're usually not there the next week. So the next week I didn't say anything but was just dying to know, and he said, "Oh, by the way Sas, you know, I went to talk to that bus driver." And I said, "Oh yeah, what did he say?" "He said, 'I appreciated your coming over and talking to me.'" The boy told me the whole conversation, and he handled it really well. He remembered to say everything we had talked about. I just about cried because of who it was. It just about knocked me out. And he looked terrific. I just love that! So it's little things like that. I don't care if that's the only thing that happens, that would be enough.

JP: But how many kids do you think the program affects like that?

SC: All of them. It served some function for all of them, because if it didn't, they left. Nobody's making them attend.

JP: So how many kids ended up sticking it out?

SC: Through one school year? Maybe 75%.

JP: Why do you think the other 25% didn't?

SC: Sometimes they got more involved in their academics and didn't feel like they could miss classes. Sometimes they got upset that there weren't enough activities happening, but they weren't willing to make them happen, so they quit. Sometimes they didn't get along with other members of the group, so they just dropped out instead of working it out, because it isn't like a therapy group where you have to do that. We encourage it, but it's not a given that you have to. Lots of times the kids do work things out. In conflict mediation, they work out a lot of arguments with their friends. In the process, I see them start out really at odds, then they come together in the group. I see that learning happen.

One of the first years I saw a ninth grade girl come to a dance—the first dance her mother ever let her go to—and recently I saw her at Middlebury College collecting tickets for an Odetta concert. I see some real active Middlebury College kids that have been in my groups. They're taking charge there now. And I hear about these things all the time. I had another kid from my first group who didn't do that great in high school but came from a really "good family." They sent him to a fifth-year prep school, and he started groups! He even got an award as the most valuable student because of all the groups he had started, and he did it because he was in my group for three years.

JP: Do you think you had more of an affect on their personal lives than in actual alcohol and drug use?

SC: Yes. Because I think drug and alcohol use is a tiny piece of the whole program. Some people see the program as drug-and-alcohol focused but—quote from you [laughter]—it doesn't really matter what you're trying to prevent, it's all the same. That's the basic philosophy I subscribe to. What teens need is to build self-esteem and feel good about themselves, to learn how to make decisions, and to feel listened to. They also need to feel normal, and they don't. The balance between feeling normal and feeling unique is very tricky—maybe for everyone—but especially for teenagers because it's so scary in junior high to feel unique. Feeling unique is the worst thing. In junior high, kids feel like they are the weirdest things on earth, and everybody feels that way. Around tenth grade it becomes okay to be an individual. It's not easy but it's okay. By the time you're a senior, it's almost good to have a few unique things about yourself, but at the same time they all want to feel normal, to have commonalities with the other kids. So by really listening to each other for an hour every week, they get to hear what's going on with others, and come to feel more normal themselves.

JP: How do you talk to kids about drugs and sex?

SC: I don't talk to them. They talk to each other. Unless they ask me questions, I don't really say too much. I just facilitate the discussions.

JP: Okay, let's say sex is the topic. How do you open it up?

SC: I say, "You guys have chosen to talk about sex today. What do you want to talk about?" Sometimes they have questions. After a while, they can lead these discussions by themselves. But whoever the leader is asks the questions. If somebody comes up with the topic, I say, "Would you like to be the leader?" or "Do you have questions?" or "What made you bring that up?" I try to get at what they really want to know about. They may be a little embarrassed to ask factual things and might like those written down, but other things they feel fine about, so they just ask a question and usually have everybody in the group answer. Another way I have facilitated discussions about sex is to break the group into guys and girls, and have them ask questions of each other. They ask things like, "Why do people think it's a sin to be a virgin, and why are you considered to be a whore if you're not?" "What do you like or dislike in a guy or girl?" "What do you look for in a long-term relationship?" "When is it all right to have sex?" "Let's say you really like this boy or girl, but he or she has AIDS and you want to have sex with her, would you?" "How do you tell or show someone you like them?" "What do you want to do on a date?" "Do you have to love someone to go out with them?" In my manual I list some amazing questions kids have asked on all the topics I mentioned before.

JP: Why would the kids trust you?

SC: Building trust is a big challenge in the beginning. It takes time. **You go in and just listen to the kids; you don't judge them. You could shut them off fast if you said, "You shouldn't do that." If you say that, you may as well walk right out the door [laughter] because they won't talk any more. But if you listen to them for weeks, show up, are consistent, care about them, and ask how they are, if you just listen, pay attention and be there with them, eventually they trust you. Plus, I let the group be theirs. You can't just say it's their group; you have to demonstrate by example.**

JP: Hearing all that stuff you heard over those years, what advice do you have for parents in dealing with kids?

SC: Listen to your kids. Give them your undivided attention every day. Not just to get your needs met, but to get their needs met. I think there should be a structured time during the day that you really listen to them, no matter what. Of course, I just finished being a parent of teenagers, and being a parent is much harder than being a group leader [laughter].

JP: Because you're emotionally caught up in it?

SC: Yes. And because it's relentless; you have it all the time, no breaks. You don't get to say, "OK, see you guys next week." [laughter] My own kids put me through everything. I did groups with more than 1,000 kids over the years, and I probably learned the most from my own kids.

But I believe that if kids feel loved, they're going to be okay. The rest is patching it together somehow. If kids feel loved, the rest is easier. It takes a lot to fill an emotional deficit.

JP: What advice would you give to schools? Without somebody running these groups, schools apparently don't allow the opportunity for kids to discuss what's important to them in a formal setting?

SC: **I believe all schools should have groups like this, and all kids should have an opportunity to talk with and listen to each other from seventh through twelfth grade, especially seventh and eighth grade. In those grades, kids are desperate to find out that they're normal.** Those two years are so difficult.

JP: Should schools have these groups as part of their curriculum?

SC: **It's beneficial to have somebody from the community go into the school, because the kids feel more free to talk. But if you can't have that, next best is to have anybody give them that opportunity. Alternatives for Teens provides teens a chance to set up activities so they feel they can really give something to someone else, make something happen for someone else.** This focus differs from that of school guidance groups. When a teen goes to a school guidance group, it's because their parents are divorced, they're involved with drugs or alcohol, or they're feeling suicidal—any of those problem behaviors. They feel those groups have a stigma attached. But Alternatives for Teens is just a positive space to set up events.

I also provide opportunities for different groups to come together. Usually the only time kids can be with kids from other schools is in competition. Over the past six years, Alternatives for Teens has provided the only opportunity for schools to get together on a noncompetitive basis—just to get to know each other. I think that's important.

JP: Let's say a parent wants to allow their kid the opportunity to open up, make a commitment, share things, but the kid doesn't want to have anything to do with it. What should the parent do?

SC: Be patient. Just keep giving the opportunity. Or, have the kid talk to one of his or her friends. Be very open to the kid having another adult to talk to somewhere. Or ask one of your friends to set up teen groups. I really believe in groups. I absolutely believe they're vital.

JP: So **the important thing is that a kid has an opportunity to open up**. The parent doesn't necessarily have to be the one to allow it?

SC: Yes. Sometimes my own kids might not want to talk in my groups but the other kids do because their parents aren't there. That's fine. My own daughter once said to me, in the midst of a crisis, "You can get every kid in Addison County to tell you everything, but I'm not telling you anything!" [laughter] That kind of response is just a matter of pride, as is having to break away from your parents when you're a teenager, having to be involved with your peer group, and having to make your own decisions. That's one of the developmental tasks of being a teenager: self-identity, individuality.

4/89

23. Talking With Kids About Drugs and Sex

The subjects of sex and drugs can be emotion-laden. Talking about sex and drugs with children makes many parents feel squeamish. These topics are difficult for kids, too. Yet these issues often cause the most trouble for young people. Becoming dependent on alcohol or other drugs or having an unwanted pregnancy can ruin a young life. Parents and teachers need to know how to discuss these subjects to help young people avoid such difficulties.

Setting the Tone

Kids usually discuss the volatile issues of drugs and sex with friends rather than parents. What would it take for a parent to be considered "friend" enough for the child to be able to talk with him or her about these subjects?

The first step, as always, is to establish a supportive and caring environment in the home [Chapter 12]. Parents can learn from listening to practitioners who have been successful in working with young people [Chapters 18, 21, 22]. The common theme: **the more that children are loved, cared about, trusted and respected, the more they're encouraged to participate in their own life in a meaningful way, the better off the kids will be and the more open they will be to talking and sharing. The more we provide a nonjudgmental environment where children and adolescents can feel free to ask questions, the better off we will all be.**

Before parents talk to their children about drugs or sex, parents should be sure they have accurate information. This is not the place to specify this information, but every state has an alcohol and drug abuse agency of some kind. Every state has a health department. Planned Parenthood is usually accessible. Information is available through health clinics, doctors' offices, school health curricula, federal pamphlets, and books. Adults can seek out these resources. Two not-so-common perspectives about risks and responsibilities of drug-taking behavior can be found in the article, "Parents as Educators" (Stern, 1989) in the federal Office for Substance Abuse Prevention's (OSAP; later CSAP) *Parenting As Prevention* manual (Cunningham et al., 1989), and in the pamphlet *Deciding About Drugs: Risks and Responsibilities* (Pransky and Chaffee, undated), from the Vermont Office of Alcohol and Drug Abuse Programs.

Social Inoculation

We can improve the chances of helping our children constructively face complex issues such as sex and drugs by engaging in a process called "social inoculation." Most of what follows is based on a segment of *Developing Capable People* (Glenn, 1987).

An inoculation involves receiving a small dose of a disease-causing agent under controlled conditions, causing immunity to build so when the agent attacks our system, we will be resistant. "Social inoculation" applies this concept to social problems. **If we prepare young people to deal with the problems of drugs and sex, for example, before they actually encounter them, they will be better prepared to resist those problems when actually confronted.**

During the teenage years (and certainly earlier in some neighborhoods), whether we like it or not, young people are often forced to make decisions that can affect their minds and bodies. **Kids need to be prepared for the moment they're handed their first joint, first can of beer, rock of crack, or get their first sexual proposition, at whatever age they might be.**

The social inoculation process works best if it begins when the child is very young. Different steps need to be taken at different stages of development, corresponding to what the child is developmentally ready for. Because in the teenage years such rapid growth occurs and because teens are so immersed and emotionally involved in these issues, between ages 8 and 12 it is critically important to provide a nonthreatening time to learn about these issues and to practice how to respond in critical situations.

Consider the example of preparing a child to resist the temptation to drink. We can begin the social inoculation process very early, as soon as the child is exposed to drinking. **Even four to five year-olds are exposed to drinking on TV, the implication being that drinking is the thing to do. At this stage it is important to simply introduce an alternative message.** If problem drinking has occurred somewhere in the family (not just our immediate family), we need to be ready for a moment we see our children watching someone drink on TV and say something like, "Honey, I just want you to know that drinking alcohol is something people in our family haven't been able to handle very well." Or if there is no alcoholism in the family, "When you see people drinking on TV, I just want you to know that a lot of people get into trouble when they drink alcohol," or, "That's something we don't do in this family." All we're trying to do at this point is introduce an alternative message to the "do drink" messages children are bombarded with.

When kids are between five and seven and can defer gratification a little, we might say something like, "When you see people drinking on TV, come and get me so we can talk about it." Or, "Let's remember to talk about this." At that point we can **sit down and talk with them, look at the drinking behavior, discover their perception then share that sometimes when people drink, the drinking causes big problems for themselves and their families.** "So when you see that, you need to think, 'This is not something my family can get involved with.'" If the unfortunate situation exists where problem drinking goes on right in the home, we have more of a problem. If only one parent is involved, we could say, "That's why Daddy (or Mommy) acts like that sometimes." This is not so easy when it hits so close to home, but it still needs to happen or the child is going to learn the modeled behavior.

When children reach ages eight to nine, or even earlier if a particular neighborhood environment demands it, it is time for serious discussion of sex and drugs, before they become personally and emotionally involved with these issues. Between 8 and 12, youngsters are ready to mature in judgment and adult influence is still high in their lives; thus this is a critical intervention period. After 12, adult influence often diminishes rapidly and peer influence increases, just when a kid becomes most at risk.

Here it is important to discuss how the 12-18-year-old period is unique in a person's development. Much of what our bodies grow into is determined during this period. Once maturing starts, all the hormones need to be in very delicate balance. When chemicals mix with this process, they upset this delicate balance. When alcohol or other drugs are introduced into an immature system, the system, like an unstable chair, can be knocked over more easily than a balanced, mature system. From the time we're conceived, we are programmed genetically to grow into a certain kind of adult. If a child mixes chemicals in with the growth process, they may never get the chance to find out what their potential would have been. Our goal at this stage is to help children make a commitment to themselves that they don't want to jeopardize their growth and development and possibly damage themselves, and that they therefore have no intention of drinking or drugging during these crucial years.

We are then ready for the final and most complicated step in the social inoculation process. We can say something like, "Honey, I know you say you're committed to this, and I believe you, but lots of kids say things like that, but then they get a lot of pressure, they end up doing it anyway. I can see a time in a couple of years when you're hanging out at [the favorite local hang-out] and you're with [his best friends], and they pull out a can of beer and offer you a drink. What will you do? Wait! Don't tell me, show me. I'll pretend I'm [his best friend] and I'll try to get you to take a drink." **At this point we start putting the pressure on and try to come up with every conceivable argument a friend could make to try to get the kid to take a drink**, including things like, "You're chicken. You're a wuss!" and, "If you don't do this, we're not gonna be your friend anymore!" These words can hurt. If our kid gets stuck and doesn't know how to respond, this is when we stop and get into a discussion. We would want to find out what he's feeling, help him figure out all the alternatives and weigh them and figure out what he can do, giving him the benefit of our experience, and helping him with refusal skills like "Let's do [something else], instead." Hawkins' (1988) *Preparing for the Drug-Free Years* program provides an excellent model for refusal skills.

Through the social inoculation process, we have better prepared the child for the moment a difficult situation inevitably happens. Thus, he may not be caught off guard and can do the most expedient thing to survive a difficult moment.

Research by the Jessors shows that the longer one can delay the onset of first use, the less likely the young person will be to develop a dependency, and if they do become dependent they'll be able to kick the habit easier than the person who starts younger (Jessor and Jessor, 1977).

If the Child is Already Drug- or Sex-Involved

If the social inoculation process does not seem to be working, it is possible that the youngster has already become involved. **Once a disease comes along, it's too late for an inoculation. It's too late for primary prevention. The child at this point may need intervention,** or if she is heavily involved, she may need treatment.

First, though, it is important to make certain expectations clear. Popkin (in Cunningham et al., 1989) of Active Parenting suggests saying to the teen (paraphrased): "Here are our expectations... We need to be able to trust you. We will. But if you violate that trust, we'll have to restrict you. That means keeping you home more often, checking up on you regularly, cutting down your freedom."

Some believe that if we have reason to suspect that our kid is using drugs, we should love our children enough to search their rooms and personal possessions and monitor their phone calls until we are certain the problem has stopped. Others believe this violates all principles of rights and freedom in a democratic society and presumes guilty until proven innocent, arguing there is never any reason to violate these principles unless one has just cause. This is very tricky business and we must walk a very fine line.

If a parent suspects that the child is drinking alcohol or doing drugs or having sex, rather than accuse, it is best to stay focused on the behaviors one sees and the feelings one has. In other words, what are the specific behaviors that are causing the parent to be suspicious? What specific feelings does that cause within the parent? Keep the conversation focused at that level. "I am seeing you do this... It makes me feel this..." If the parent stays at this level, the parent remains on solid ground. The kid might try to deny that the parent saw whatever s/he saw, but it is not so easy to deny what someone sees with her or his own eyes. It is even harder to deny that a person has a particular feeling.

If the parent sees the child behaving erratically (that is, even more erratically than normal, unimpaired adolescents), the child could be sick or emotionally unstable, and therefore needs to be assessed by a doctor or other appropriate professional immediately. There could be real danger. The parenting is acting as a responsible guardian by seeking help. Without treatment, a sick or dependent person will not get well; he or she will usually get worse.

24. Making Sense of the Literature on Risk, Resiliency, Assets, Competence, Social Skills, Stress, and Supports

When this book first appeared in 1990, much academic preventionist literature was inaccessible to most prevention practitioners. This was unfortunate because the literature contained much of worth that could be translated into effective programming. While they may not have done it in most productive way, in a sense the federal government remedied this in the late 1990s by insisting that prevention funding be based on research-proven programs. A lot of this research falls under the headings of "risk factors," "resiliency" or "protective factors," "assets" "competence," "stress," "social skills," and "supports." These categories contain much overlap. We need to make sense of it all, but a close look will reveal that this chapter really only provides a further breakdown and more detail of what appears in Chapter 5 and throughout the rest of this book.

Since this book was first published the prevention field has been involved in a number of trends. In the 1990s two approaches to prevention rose to the forefront of popularity in the field: a focus on *risk* and *resiliency*.

Risk Factors

The risk-focused approach is based on research findings that certain factors in the social and physical environment, and internal factors, put people at greater risk for developing problems or destructive behaviors.

The literature suggests that there appear to be common "risk factors" associated with a wide range of problem behaviors; a few are also specific to particular behaviors. The following list of "risk factors" is consolidated from work by Hawkins and Catalano (1989) regarding alcohol/drug abuse and delinquency, by Werner (1988), by Loeber and Dishion (1987), by Watt (1986) for psychological disorders, by Spivack and Cianci (1987) for school behavior problems, and by Wolfe (1987) for child abuse and delinquency:

organic factors:

- prenatal stress
- low birthweight
- congenital defect or acquired physical handicap by age ten

behavioral factors:

- very high or low maternal ratings of activity at age one
- distressing feeding or sleeping habits or temper tantrums
- early antisocial behavior and hyperactivity (history of aggressiveness especially when combined with shyness and withdrawal in grades K-2); problem behavior and aggressiveness
- social withdrawal
- impatience: rushing into things before listening or judging, not looking back to reflect
- need for placement in long-term mental health care by age ten
- early first use of drugs (Children who begin use before age 15 are twice as likely to develop problems with drugs as are those who wait. Waiting until age 19 dramatically decreases the risk.)
- favorable attitudes toward drug use (or shift in junior high school), stealing, lying, or truancy

social-environmental factors:

- low standard of living; low socioeconomic status
- violence breeds violence (emotional or physical, direct or indirect); the risk of later violent criminal behavior increases with the amount experienced in childhood)

family-related factors:

- low family stability by age two; separation from parents
- low maternal education
- poor parental family management techniques (by far the most important)
- history of family conflict or early parental death
- family violence (children from abusive families can exhibit adjustment problems and developmental impairments)
- criminality or antisocial behavior of family members
- family history of alcoholism; biological or environmental parental drug use and positive parental attitudes toward use

school-related factors:

- little commitment to school
- early classroom tendency toward annoying social behavior; self-centered verbal responsiveness, interruption of others; negative and defiant behavior with teacher poor educational attainment; need for remedial education
- academic failure beginning in middle to late elementary school

peer-related factors:

- antisocial behavior in early adolescence (in school, get into fights or see selves as standing apart from peers—an "I don't care" attitude)
- association with delinquent or drug-using peers

community-related factors:

- rebelliousness (lack of bonding to society or any social institution)

unhealthy self-perceptions:

- low self-concept
- childhood profile of nurturing and conforming, or unreliable behavior

limited social skills:

- low social competence
- below-average self-help skills

Generally, the greater number of factors present, and the more intense they are, the greater the risk. Speaking personally, I find long lists of risk factors such as this to be generally unhelpful. What is important is that this research conforms with and merely provides more detail on the left side of the conceptual framework for prevention [Chapter 5]. It is also important to note that this is correlational research; it does not suggest direct cause and effect.

The question becomes, what does this risk-focused research suggest about prevention strategies? Here practitioners have to be careful to apply this research wisely.

A risk-focused approach suggests at least three possible points of attack:

1. identifying the high risk conditions in a community and working to change those conditions
2. identifying the communities or geographic areas that have the greatest number or level of risks, and working preventively with everyone within those areas
3. identifying the individuals found to be at high risk and working preventively with those individuals.

Regarding # 3, **even some of the most respected "risk factor" researchers like David Hawkins and Del Elliott warn of the dangers of latching onto identification of "high-risk" young people as a prevention strategy**. In the field of delinquency, for example, predictions to select young people for interventions are likely to miss a number of youths who will become delinquent, and they will overpredict and identify and treat some as "predelinquent" who will never engage in serious delinquent behavior ("false positives"). Elliott (1988) points out that 78% of those predicted to become career offenders did not, at least in the ensuing four years.

Number 2 would seem a wise strategy, except that some people perceive that it is racist or classist to always be singling out certain communities, for example African American communities, to target [Chapter 30].

The most viable of the three appears to be # 1. Yet there are dangers here as well, as we will explore a bit later.

The Trend Toward Risk-focused Prevention and Outcomes[*]

The first, new major directional trend in the prevention field was initiated when the Office of Juvenile Justice and Delinquency Prevention (OJJDP) adopted Hawkins and Catalano's (1992) risk-focused model, *Communities that Care*, on a nationwide scale. This research-based model

---

[*] Note: The following sections contain, among other things, brief, edited excerpts from the forthcoming, *Prevention (II) from the Inside-Out* (Pransky, in press).

put communities through a process where they identified conditions that put people at highest risk of crime and delinquency as a focus for community prevention strategies to reduce those risks. The Center for Substance Abuse Prevention (CSAP) soon followed suit, and many prevention agencies began to pick up on this or other risk-focused approaches. This signaled a new era for prevention, for it was the first time that federally-funded prevention programming became based on research.

This proved timely because soon thereafter a conservative Republican backlash erupted against prevention in the form of "midnight basketball": organized, inner-city basketball games beginning at midnight as an preventive alternative to gang violence. The Clinton Administration had become arguably the first Administration to speak the language of prevention and proclaim its importance, from Attorney General Reno, to Health and Human Services Secretary Shalala, to Housing and Urban Development Director Cizneros, to Surgeon General Elders, to First Lady Hillary Rodham Clinton, to President Clinton himself. Only since the 1992 Presidential campaign had the word "prevention" become an acceptable utterance of politicians as a viable, important and logical strategy to help America overcome its social ills. Previously, with a few notable exceptions, politicians largely had ignored the need for prevention or considered it fluff. When the Clinton administration took it on, Republican backlash was inevitable. Yet, their point was very well taken. Much prevention programming was unable to show results. This led to a new emphasis on the need to focus on "outcomes" (Williams & Webb, 1992; Schorr, 1997). The research-based, risk-focused approach provided an answer.

When states such as Oregon and Vermont began an outcomes-oriented focus, the next logical question was, "What will best work to produce these outcomes?" Most practitioners of prevention had given only lip-service to what truly worked to prevent problems; they simply went about their business conducting programs that appeared logically to make a difference. In the late 1980s-early 1990s this book and a couple of others (Price et al., 1988; Schorr, 1989) appeared which, along with Benard's (1988) translation of research for the substance abuse prevention field, for the first time exposed many practitioners to research-proven prevention strategies. Yet, only since around 1998 have federal agencies in support of prevention begun to insist that their prevention funds be spent on research-proven programs or at least "promising approaches" (U.S. Department of Health and Human Services, 1998).

A focus on outcomes and research-proven programs sounds completely logical. Yet, as some say, "implementation is everything" and, as of the year 2000, effective implementation may not have lived up to intent. Lisbeth Schorr's (1997) very thoughtful analysis provides reasons why. Her main finding is that the very qualities that make effective grass-roots program models effective often run counter to the way bureaucracy works; in other words, when the bureaucracy attempts to replicate high quality models, it tends to implement them in ways that counteract reasons for the originating programs' success. For example, policy-makers try to impose successful interventions from the top-down, when a reason for their success is that they were developed from the bottom-up. Effective programs are characterized by "flexibility, comprehensiveness, responsiveness, front-line discretion, high standards of quality and good management, a family focus, community rootedness, a clear mission, and respectful, trusting relationships...," but those programs have to fight to sustain those qualities "amid pressures designed to move them in exactly the opposite direction" (p.18). Schorr states, "Under prevailing rules accountability is almost always at odds with achieving the mission" (p. 83). To move demonstration programs into the mainstream requires, as Schorr quotes T.S. Eliot, a willingness to "disturb the universe" (p.27), and bureaucratic and political universes and entrenched prevailing ideas in most all fields often do not appreciate being disturbed. Nonetheless, some positive signs have occurred, as the Federal government went from funding what merely sounded good to funding programs proven by research.

Limitations of the Risk-Focused Approach, And a Look in a Different Direction

One difficulty with a solely risk-focused approach is illustrated by this scenario: Suppose a community conducts a "risk assessment" for its community, and the assessment yields "availability of drugs" as the most problematic risk factor. If a strategy is then designed based upon this risk the community logically would attempt to reduce the availability of drugs. To do this the community might ask itself where and when and by whom drugs are most available in this community. Once such answers are known the community might increase substantially targeted police presence in those areas.

Risk Factor⟶*Planning (based on risk)*⟶ *Strategy (based on fixing deficit)*

This risk-based strategy could work in reducing the availability of drugs. However, a problem remains. Some young people in the community have relied on drugs to fill a hole inside them that needs filling. Now that drugs are less available, what will they do? Chances are, they will either go elsewhere to find their drugs, or the problem will show up in other ways. This will then result in a new risk factor surfacing as most important. This suggests that in prevention a community must also plan strategies based upon the resiliency side of the equation to help fill the holes that need filling so young people will not have to rely on drugs or anything else to feel healthy and whole. This suggests an examination of resilience.

Risk Factor⟶ *Resiliency*⟶ *Planning (based on building strength*⟶ *Strategy (based on building strength)* (Pransky, in Wilson et al., 1995)

Resiliency researchers have suggested the limitations of a risk-focused prevention approach. Garmezy and Rutter (1983) stated:

> While certainly a giant step in the right direction, the identification of risks does not necessarily provide us with a clear sense of just what strategies we need to implement to reduce the risks... While a certain percentage of...high risk children developed various problems..., a greater percentage became healthy, competent young adults..., children who are...'resilient,' in spite of severe stress and adversity... Ultimately, the potential for prevention surely lies in increasing our knowledge and understanding of reasons why some children are not damaged by deprivation.

The Trend Toward Protective Factors, Resiliency and Asset-Focused Prevention

Emmy Werner, another of the original resiliency researchers, states:

> When the concept "risk" became fashionable, people looked at the outcomes such as delinquents or ax murderers and they looked back and, lo and behold, they found that they had been abused, they were poorer, and they had alcoholic parents. If you do retrospective research, you conclude that there is a one-to-one relationship between that negative outcome and risk conditions. Resiliency, on the other hand, focuses on the individual differences within these groups. And we

265

know now from the research on resilience that a negative outcome is not inevitable (from interview in Benard, 1995, p.6).

Many prevention practitioners believed the risk-based approach too negative. In response many rebelled, championed by Bonnie Benard (1993). Thus began a re-focus on the notion of "resiliency." Even Hawkins and Catalano (1992), despite their emphasis on risk factors, maintained that "protective factors"—factors that appear to protect people from the influence of high risk conditions—were the means for building caring communities that make a difference.
Emmy Werner (1989) suggested how important resiliency research is to the prevention field:

> If we can determine the personal and environmental sources of social competence and wellness, we can better plan prevention interventions focused on creating and enhancing the personal and environmental attributes that serve as the key to healthy development...

The resiliency-focused approach to prevention grew out of studies showing that many who grew up in communities laden with risks did not appear to develop problems; in fact, they ended up living generally normal lives and doing reasonably well (Werner & Smith, 1982; Rutter, 1979; Garmezy, 1974). The researchers asked what appeared to protect these people from the risks, and they identified factors that appear to make people resilient.
From examining the combined conclusions of Garmezy in his Minnesota Risk Research project, Rutter in his 14 year follow-up study of 94 abused and abandoned children, Werner in her 18-year study of 698 multiracial children on the Hawaiian island of Kauai to determine factors that both predisposed and protected children from delinquency and mental health problems, and other studies of disadvantaged and disturbed children, it is possible to create a profile of resilience. I drew this one from an examination of research by Hawkins & Catalano (1989), Garmezy (1974), Werner (1988), Rutter (1979), Wolin and Wolin (1993), Segal (1986), and Benard (1987).

- Bonding: Attachment & Commitment to Family, School, Prosocial Peers, Community
  1. *feelings of love, care, support*
  2. *opportunities to contribute in meaningful ways*

- Healthy Beliefs and Clear Standards
  3. *high expectations for success*
  4. *clear standards for behavior set and enforced*
  5. *healthy prosocial beliefs*

- Individual Characteristics
  - *positive social orientation*
  - *socially competent/life skills*
  - *problem-solving skills*
  - *a sense of purpose and meaning*
  - *autonomy*
  - *resilient temperament*

If we focus on the five external factors highlighted above **our preventive efforts can be focused on ensuring that these qualities are developed within the family, school, peer group, and community. These can be considered ways to ensure the development of the healthy self-perceptions identified in the conceptual framework** [Chapter 5]. These five external factors bear a close resemblance to the six major factors identified by Henderson & Milstein (1997) in their resiliency wheel:

- Increase prosocial bonding
- Set clear consistent boundaries
- Teach life skills
- Provide opportunities for meaningful participation
- Set and communicate high expectations
- Provide caring and support

The key to effective prevention efforts is reinforcing, within every arena, these natural social bonds...that give meaning to one's life and a reason for commitment and caring... We must work within our families, schools and community environments to build these social bonds by providing all individuals within these systems with caring and support, relating to them with high expectations, and giving them opportunities to be active participants in their family school, and community life." (Werner, 1989)

Again, while I personally do not find long lists of factors very helpful, I offer the following for those interested in the more detailed breakdown of the external factors by immediate environment.

- Bonding: Attachment and Commitment to Family, School, Peers, Community
    - *feels loved, cared about, supported*
        - family: - a close bond with someone who provides stable, appropriate attention
                    - a caring and supportive relationship
                    - at least one warm, affectionate parent (absence of criticism)/enduring, loving relationship
                    - provides a sense of basic trust
        - school: - a positive role model by a teacher providing warmth, caring, compassion
                    - a warm, responsive climate
        - peers: - caring peers in school and community/peer support youth and families linked into network of peer helping
        - community: - close connection with significant other
                    - rich social networks that promote and sustain social cohesion
                    - community organization
                    - availability of resources needed for healthy human development (health care, child care, housing, education, job training, employment, recreation)
- Healthy Beliefs and Clear Standards
    - *high expectations and skills for success*
        - family: - high parental expectations (without pressure or criticism)
                    - build social or life skills

- school:
  - parent/teacher attitudes that see potential for learning, common sense, well-being
  - academic/educational emphasis
  - clear teacher expectations and regulations
  - high level of student participation
  - many alternative resources and opportunities
  - promote social and scholastic success
  - foster high self-esteem
  - build social or life skills
- peers: - (none cited)
- community: - value youth as resources

- *set and enforce clear standards for behavior*
  - family: - clear expectations for behavior, and maintain order
  - school: - clear school rules, perceived as fair by students
    - respect for student autonomy
  - community: - clear community norms such as for drinking alcohol
- *healthy beliefs*
  - family: - adopting prosocial family values
    - religious/spiritual beliefs that provide stability/faith
  - school: - (none cited)
  - peers/community: - peers bonded to conventional (prosocial) norms
- *opportunities to contribute in meaningful ways*
  - family: - see kids as valued participants in life and work of family encourage independence
  - school: - active student participation/involvement in meaningful, valued activities and roles
    - students treated as responsible people
    - access to/interest in/involvement in variety of opportunities
    - opportunities to belong and have a stake in school
  - peers: - (none cited)
  - community: - opportunities for youth to contribute to their community and use their creativity
    - citizen participation

To help ensure that these are created within the family, school, peer group community, or peer group can be some of our most productive prevention work.

Despite that many practitioners in the past decade saw resiliency as a major paradigm shift, none of it was really new. Resiliency studies had been out since the mid-late1970s (Garmezy, 1974; Rutter, 1979; Werner & Smith, 1982). The first edition of this book had even treated the concept of resiliency rather matter-of-fact, only because every prevention strategy suggested by the resiliency literature was what most astute prevention practitioners already considered good solid prevention practice; it was, in essence, what most of this book was (and is) about. Yet, the new emphasis on resiliency breathed new life into these approaches, and interest in resiliency surged. This proved important because resiliency had been probably the least well-practiced aspect of the field.

Rutter (1987), however, reminds us that protective factors per se are of limited value as means to help us find new approaches to prevention. For that, he says, we need to look at the "mechanisms" and "processes"…"to ask why and how some individuals manage to maintain high self-esteem and self-efficacy in spite of facing the same adversities that lead other people to give up hope" (p.317). In other words, **in prevention the idea is not only to ensure that these protective or resilience factors are in place, but to discover how they get there**. In my view, these "mechanisms and processes" are entirely an internal affair and will be addressed later in this chapter [see also Chapters 4 and 42].

Assets

The Search Institute interviewed nearly 100,000 6th-12th graders in 213 towns and cities in the U.S., and identified first thirty, then forty, "developmental assets," half of which they labeled "external" and half "internal." Youth with greater numbers of assets were less likely to get involved in behaviors such as sexual activity, violence/antisocial activity, school failure, illicit drug use, depression and/or attempted suicide, problem alcohol use, tobacco use, vehicle recklessness, volunteer service, and success in school (Benson et al., 1995, p.10). Calling such assets "building blocks of healthy development," they concluded that if communities went out of their way to build a greater number of assets, young people would do better. This reframing of resiliency into assets captured the imagination and interest of the prevention field and began to guide much of its direction in the late 1990s. Unfortunately, this huge study provides no indication whether some assets have more of an influence than others, or whether if certain assets were in place the need for others would be countermanded.

While the Search Institute's research focused solely on the total quantitative number (the more assets, the better), a major national longitudinal study on adolescent health did look in the direction of relative importance. Surveying 12,118 adolescents in grades 7-12 from 134 high schools including feeder schools, eight areas were assessed: emotional distress; suicidal thoughts and behaviors; violence; use of substances; age of sexual debut; pregnancy history. Results showed that perceived parent-family connectedness and school connectedness were protective against every health risk behavior measure (P.=<.001), except history of pregnancy. In conclusion the authors stated, **"We find consistent evidence that perceived caring and connectedness to others is important in understanding the health of young people today"** (Resnick et al., 1997, p.830) **and that it "serves as a protective factor against a variety of risk behaviors"** (p.831).

The above report overshadowed another important finding of the same study. "Individual characteristics"—which in the study included factors such as "self-esteem," "religious identity," "self-report of physical appearance," "repeated a grade," "grade point average," and "paid work"—sometimes proved even more significant. For example, while parent-family connectedness explained 14-15% of the variability for emotional distress and "suicidality" for 7-9th graders, and school connectedness accounted for 13-18%, individual characteristics accounted for 21-22% of emotional distress. Regarding violence, while family connectedness accounted for 7%-5% and school connectedness 6-7%, individual variability accounted for 44-50%. Regarding alcohol and marijuana use, while family connectedness accounted for 6-9%, school connectedness 4-6%, individual characteristics accounted for 5-7% (Resnick et al., 1997).

Despite equal attention paid in the research to both external and internal factors, most resiliency and asset-building approaches have focused on the external. While few question the validity or importance of internal assets or protective factors, the prevention field has been less clear about what to do about them.

Internal Resilience

The initial approaches of most traditional resiliency proponents to the internal was best summed up in the early resiliency work of Benard (1991):

In order to avoid falling into the pathology paradigm and blaming the victim' syndrome with its concomitant focus on 'fixing kids,' our perspective is that personality and individual outcomes are the result of a transactional process with one's environment. To be successful, prevention interventions must focus on creating and enhancing positive environmental contexts—families, schools and communities that, in turn, reinforce positive behaviors (p.3).

While true, this statement leaves out half the equation. Internal, or "personal" factors, as they are sometimes called, are at least equally important. Later we will see how Benard and others championed this new focus in her later work.

Again, while its usefulness may be questionable, the following is a more detailed breakdown of the internal factors or internal characteristics listed earlier in this chapter that promote resilience.

- *socially competent/life skills*
    - positive social orientation
    - has self-control (impulse control) and self-discipline
    - is responsive, flexible, adaptable
    - is empathic and caring
    - has communications skills
- *problem-solving skills*
    - is able to think critically, abstractly, reflectively
    - has planning skills/generates alternatives
    - is able to produce change, even in frustrating situations
- *has a sense of purpose and meaning, and future*
    - has hope (believes in a bright, compelling future)
    - has motivation to achieve, initiative
    - has success orientation/educational aspiration
    - has healthy expectations
    - has persistence
- *autonomy*
    - has self-esteem, self-efficacy
    - a sense of independence, identity, and direction or mission
    - has an internal locus of control
    - able to separate self from dysfunction/adaptive distancing
- *resilient temperament*
    - has an easy temperament and/or disposition
    - has a capacity for intelligence, insight, creativity
    - has a sense of humor

Unfortunately, "developing and enhancing personal attributes" gained a bad reputation in astute prevention circles because of how it had often been practiced in prevention. By suggesting that social conditions are not to blame, the powers-that-be get off the hook; it becomes easy to suggest that the problems lie only within the individual. In other cases genetic factors are researched to explain away both social and personal responsibility (Albee, 1996; [Chapter 31]). None of this is what internal resilience is about.

When resiliency researchers did address the internal aspects of resiliency for prevention, until the late 1990s their programmatic responses fell largely into one of two categories:

1. *Adjusting to varying "temperaments" or "constitutional vulnerabilities."* This recognizes that internal protective factors are more naturally present in some people than in others. For example, prevention researcher David Hawkins has said in his presentations that he can say anything to his son and it rolls off him like water off a duck's back, but he only has to look at his daughter crosswise and she falls apart. He concluded that his daughter is more naturally sensitive to his tone than his son—part of their different constitutional make-ups—and therefore he has to make adjustments. If he is upset with his daughter he has to be more careful about his tone. The implication is, we are either born with internal protective factors or we're not, and we can only adjust accordingly.

2. *Providing ideas for building internal assets.* Peter Benson of the Search Institute offers "Ideas for Building Internal Assets in Youth" (Benson et. al, 1995). A close examination of these ideas, however, reveals that internal assets are built by creating conditions in the external environment. Examples are: "provide a comfortable place for your teen to study without distractions," "include college and career issues in services and programming," "teach students skills in conflict resolution," "give youth opportunities to express their beliefs," etc. While these are fine things to do, all are externally generated; thus, Benson is once again only speaking about changing external environmental conditions to build the internal. (Note: Later we will see a third, more viable possibility.)

The Search institute's (1995) research identifies four major categories of internal assets: 1) *commitment to learning*; 2) *positive values* (caring, equality, integrity, honesty, responsibility, restraint); 3) *social competence* (planning/decision-making, interpersonal competence, cultural competence, resistance skills, peaceful conflict resolution); 4) *positive identity* (personal power, self-esteem, sense of purpose, positive view of personal future). Logically these make sense, despite that a close look reveals that this research yielded these because they were the ones asked about. But the problem lies in Benson's (1995) following statement: "Unless we begin *providing* [my emphasis] all youth with the assets they need to thrive, we will continue to see many children and youth struggling to find their place" (p.4). To Benson, even the positive internal assets inadvertently appear to assume a lack within a young person; the implication is that it is up to others to provide or build what it is believed they do not have. Benson is not alone. **Subtly and unintentionally in prevention most of us act as if we must do something to or with or for the young person in order for her or him to be fully healthy.**

Yet, Emmy Werner (1996) reminds us, "We need to look and see what researchers found in the first place…It wasn't just that the children behavioral scientists studied were empty boxes into which someone poured "resiliency" (p.19).

Again we are reminded of the public health model which requires that equal focus be placed on the agent, the host, and the environment. In prevention, most emphasis on "strengthening the host" has occurred through the teaching [pouring in?] of skills. Werner is pointing to a notion beyond this; something within the host is what makes it vulnerable to the agent or not—if that something is allowed to emerge. "Internal resilience" has been the least understood and least

271

well-practiced aspect of resiliency. I suggest that what internal resilience or internal assets really means is that something resides within the individual that in and of itself makes people resilient.

A New Look at Internal Resilience

Suppose the key to resiliency is that everyone has resilience within them already; that everyone has "innate health" and wisdom, and it can be drawn upon whenever necessary. If true, the job of prevention would be to help people to realize this.

This could be a goal within any of Lofquist's (1983) four "arenas of human service activity": I. community development; II. personal growth and development; III. community problem-solving; IV. personal problem-solving. "Building on people's strengths," then, would mean a lot more than discovering what people already do well and finding a way to capitalize on it to help them get where they want to go. It would mean more than finding what people do best and offering or contributing their resources to others in a creative community development effort, as suggested by McKnight (1997). The greatest, the ultimate strength that people have is what already lies innately within [Chapters 4 & 42].

Thus, resiliency began to point the prevention field in an important direction. However, rather than only take the factors identified in resiliency and protective factor research (Hawkins et al., 1992), provide those skills and supports, build the right relationships, and create the right conditions, it may be even more important to help people recognize their own internal source of resilience.

Wolin and Wolin (1993) began to look in this direction with their resiliency mandala, which included "insight," "independence," "relationships," "initiative," "humor," "creativity," and "morality." People realize these from within.

Werner's (1982) notion of a self-righting ability within human beings assumed far greater importance for the field when the editors of *Resiliency in Action* (Benard, Henderson, Sharp-Light, & Richardson, 1996) took a major philosophical stance by essentially redefining resiliency as "an innate self-righting and transcending ability within all children, youth, adults, organizations, and communities." "Innate" means inherent, possessed at birth, within all human beings.

Resiliency, then, is something more than the commonly accepted definition, "the capacity to spring back, rebound, successfully adapt in the face of adversity." This newer interpretation brings the definition of resilience in closer alignment with the other dictionary definition: "the property of a material that enables it to resume its original shape or position after being bent, stretched, or compressed" (The American Heritage Dictionary). Resiliency is more than a "capacity;" it is inherent within the very "property" of the material—within our very fabric as human beings. The implication for understanding internal resilience is this: We do not have to do anything to anyone to make people resilient; they already are!

Benard and Marshall (1997) and Marshall (1998) speak of tapping the natural, innate health or resilience of people, defined as "the human capacity for transformation and change" (Lifton, 1993). We are all born with the innate ability to transform the way we experience life from the inside-out with our own thinking.

The innate self-righting ability within all human beings appears to be a force that can keep people on an even keel. People need only not interfere with this tendency. To assume this changes everything. To reiterate a very important point: **instead of beginning with an incomplete person who becomes complete if s/he is in the right environment or learns the**

right skills or gains the right supports or gets the right information, we begin with a wholly complete person who has the innate capacity to realize his or her own internal health and strength and how it becomes obscured [see Chapter 42].

Another major theme identified in studies of internal resilience is religion or spirituality or faith (Resnick et al., 1997). Werner (1996) states, "...shortchanged in scientific studies is that these children had some faith that gave meaning to their lives..." (p.24). This does not necessarily mean narrow denominational faith. "The ones that were able to use this faith to overcome adversity were the ones that saw meaning in their lives, even in pain and suffering. It wasn't church attendance, but it was a belief that life, despite everything, made sense and that even the pain they experienced could ultimately be transformed" (p.24).

Both Rutter (1987) and Bloom (1996) state that the actual mechanisms that produce healthy outcomes in the face of severe and chronic stress remain unclear. Bloom guessed that the mechanism for influencing what we call resilient behavior may be the balance between what Hollister termed "strens" (growth-producing experiences) and the stresses one encounters (Bloom, 1996). I submit that it is more likely that the mechanism and therefore answers to effective prevention, protection, and health promotion may be found in these largely untapped, internal realms, and to be wholly effective in prevention the field must find ways to draw upon these or understand how it all works internally. This is the realm in which *Health Realization* operates [Chapter 42].

Detour: The Trend Toward Ecological and Environmentally-Based Approaches

With controversy brewing in the mid-1990s over whether risk or resiliency/asset-based approaches were the more viable direction, some began to recognize the importance of both, and to see the complex interrelationships among all factors. This direction rekindled interest in ecologically-based prevention approaches and in approaches to alter some or all aspects of the community/social/cultural/physical environment.

In a sense the trend toward the popularized African proverb, "It takes a village to raise a child" (Rodham Clinton, 1996) is reflective of this direction. It recognizes the influence and role, and some would say duty, of the entire community to take responsibility for caring for all its children. It recognizes that the influences are so complex that families cannot go it alone. When conservative Republicans began calling this approach "anti-family," use of the slogan dissipated, but the qualities it attempted to portray not only remained but became even more complex. Partly this was due to a growing body of research indicating that most problem behaviors have no single cause and operate "at several levels of the human ecology to create a comprehensive, multifaceted effort" (Bogenschneider, 1996, p.132), and partly due to empirical experience showing that "there is no one 'magic bullet' program or developmental stage upon which one can concentrate all resources and expect spectacular results. Rather, establishing an array of programs over time will meet the needs of different families at different points in the life cycle (Chamberlain, 1992, p.68). Many prevention practitioners began looking to the ecological model to explain and attend to these complexities.

The ecological model has drawn heavily from perspectives developed by James Kelley (1968) and Urie Bronfenbrenner (1977), and brought to the field of child abuse prevention by Belsky (1980). Basic to the model is that the psychical, cultural, political, and social-psychological environment forms a complex network that influences the behavior of the individual. Any change in one aspect of the system has ramifications for all other aspects. When designing an intervention from an ecological point of view, the individual person, social group, organization, community, culture, and their interaction are all considered (McCullough, 1980).

Ecological theory suggests that it is necessary to identify risk and protective processes at several levels of the human ecology, including the individual family, peer, school, work, and community settings (Bogenschneider, 1996, 128). Thus, a program using this model might focus on the physical setting of a specific culture, level of technical knowledge available, political organization, natural resources, primary institutions, social organization, child rearing practices, educational system, peer group practices, social norms, family systems, kinship patterns, settlement patterns, status forms, social groups (McCullough, 1980). Some ecological models also focus on individual as well as social-environmental factors as targets for interventions (McLeroy et al., 1988).

Things appear to be getting mighty complex! Out of this enormous complexity, it is not surprising that the next natural progression would be Chaos Theory; trying to find order at the edge of chaos and discovering the answers to healthy change in living systems (Wheatley, 1997).

Is all this complexity really necessary?

The answer might lie more in the direction pointed to by Tom Kelley (1990) who said this about the proliferation of theories and approaches in the criminal justice field: "...the variation that exists both within and among our theories appears to have become as great as the variety of factors those theories are attempting to explain. Instead of seeking some common factors that would break down the variation into some comprehensible design, it has become commonplace for the field to focus on the variation itself" (p.3). **To find simplicity—boiling down all the complexity to its essence is the direction we might seek.**

This does not suggest that the answer lies in narrowly-focused environmental approaches, defined as "establishing or changing written and unwritten community standards, codes, and attitudes, initiatives that are either legal and regulatory or service and action-oriented" [Federal Register, Volume 58, Number 60, March 31, 1993]. Such approaches include preventing availability of alcohol, tobacco and other drugs to underage youth, raising alcohol taxes and prices, changing the conditions of availability and hours and days of sales, and community-based approaches to create policy, attitude and practice change (Grover, 1999). These may be important, but these practices do not touch the hole inside many young people that creates their need or desire for substances.

The resiliency approach to prevention, then, suggests at least two possible points of attack:

1. creating healthy conditions in the social environment that protect people from the risky conditions and build healthy self-perceptions, thereby producing resilient individuals;
2. helping to unveil or draw out people's innate health or wisdom or strength, their natural resilience [Chapter 42]

Some fine pieces on resiliency (mostly pertaining to #1 above) can be found in *Resiliency in Action*'s compilation of articles from their first two years of operation (Henderson, Benard, & Sharp-Light, 1999). Meanwhile, some other related prevention research terms and approaches are also worth examining.

Competence

Cowen and associates (1973; 1985) found that social competence was inversely related to psychopathology later in life, and positively related to IQ and healthy adjustment in the classroom. But what does "competence"—a term so often used in the literature—really mean? For preventers in the field, the word can be quite confusing.

Some important thinkers like Caplan (1986) define competence as an "internal constitutional and acquired quality of individuals that enables them to withstand the harmful effects of hazardous circumstances." Others, like Botvin and Dusenbury (1989), use the term competence to mean having the "basic interpersonal skills necessary for initiation and maintenance of friendship and other mutually beneficial relationships," and say that people without these skills lack social competence. O'Mally (in Rotheram-Borus and Tsemberis, 1989) says that "social competence" in children is defined by an ability to successfully achieve social goals in a manner that is mutually rewarding to the child and to others. The term social competence is also used to describe someone with the full range of healthy self-perceptions, yet competence is only one of the four critical perceptions necessary for healthy behavior [Chapter 5]. The interchangeable use of this term can be bewildering. If this isn't confusing enough, some people perceive they're competent when they're not; others are competent but may not believe they are.

We could cut through a lot of the confusion if we simply said that people need both strong, healthy internal perceptions and the skills to be socially competent.

In their social development model, Hawkins and Weis (1985) identify three conditions critical for children to develop socially competent behavior:

- They must have the cognitive, affective, and behavioral skills to succeed.
- They must have multiple opportunities for meaningful, positive involvements in which to apply those skills.
- Those with whom they interact must reinforce competent behavioral performance.

Many of the programs cited in Chapters 10-23 serve to build social competence. There are many models. Cowen (1985) defines some ***common elements of social-competence-building programs***:

1. A set of specific skills is taught, preferably an integration of cognitive, affective, and behavioral skills.
2. Structured activities are provided, usually in a group setting, and it is best if they are fun.
3. Social supports are provided where children's strengths are recognized and emphasized.
4. Opportunities are provided for practice in a group setting.
5. The emphasis should be that an individual can actively and consciously think new thoughts, can behave in alternative ways, and can, be effective in changing problematic situations.
6. The aim should be to make the skills relevant and useful to children and adolescents at various stages of development.

One example is Weissburg and Caplan's (in Weissburg et al., 1989) *Social Competence Program*, aimed to help middle school students cope with social problems. Students are taught a six-step process:

1. Stop, calm down think before you act.
2. Say the problem and how you feel.
3. Set a positive goal.
4. Think of lots of solutions.
5. Think ahead of possible consequences.
6. Go ahead and try the best plan.

The process must be coupled with opportunities for reinforcement. For example, Weissburg and Associates created environmental resources in and out of the classroom to support the development of socially competent behavior, using books such as *50 Simple Things Kids Can Do to Save the Earth* (The Earthworks Group, 1990). The students are encouraged to solve problems jointly and to share their achievements. An initial evaluation showed that students' information-processing skills had significantly improved.

Behavioral Social Skills Training (BSST)

If social skills help build "social competence," Michelson's (1987) expansive list of needed social skills can be useful. His view is that children with antisocial, aggressive, noncompliant, and acting-out behaviors have not sufficiently developed the intra- and interpersonal skills to function optimally; thus, they need to be trained accordingly. Among the social skills Michelson helps people gain are-

- empathy
- role-taking
- giving and receiving compliments, expressing appreciation
- participating in conversations, asking questions, dealing with interruptions
- nonverbal behavior
- giving and receiving feedback, complaints, apologies, criticism
- making requests, asking why
- learning to say no; accepting others' saying no
- standing up for one's and others' rights; recognizing others' rights
- dealing with anger; behavioral self-management
- self-control strategies for impulse control, anger, aggression
- conflict resolution training
- dealing with teasing, accusations, rejection, disappointment
- resisting peer pressure
- decision-making
- honesty
- interacting with adults, accepting responsibility
- cooperation
- paying attention
- increasing frustration tolerance and delay of immediate gratification

Michelson's *Behavioral Social Skills Training (BSST)* program teaches these skills to young people, step by step. The behavior is developed through repeated practice, feedback, reinforcement, and modeling across many social problem situations. The youth are encouraged to express themselves, but not in a way that violates others' rights or feelings. They are taught procedures for self-control as a means of deflecting and redirecting anger, hostility, and aggressive behavior. They are encouraged to behave in an honest, positive, nonpunitive, fair, considerate, direct, nondefensive, sensitive, and constructive manner. Aggressive and antisocial behavior that ignores or restricts the feelings, opinions, needs, or rights of others, or uses impulsive, manipulative, punishing, or socially inappropriate strategies to achieve goals, is discouraged.

The BSST approach was compared with the Interpersonal Cognitive Problem Solving approach (ICPS) [Chapter 10] approach and with Rogerian treatments (serving as control). Subjects were child psychiatric patients with marked antisocial behavior, ages 8 to 12, 62% of whom were Black. After one year, both BSST and ICPS youth proved significantly better than controls in adjustment and behavioral problems at home and at school. Several studies showed significant improvements in the following:

- self-concept
- self-control
- hyperactivity
- coping skills
- anger
- problem-solving
- peer sociometric ratings

Results support the relative and (especially) combined effectiveness of both the BSST and ICPS approaches with high risk youth. However, booster sessions are needed to ensure ongoing effects because generalization (across time and across situations) does not naturally occur for most children. To aid in generalization, one should-

- teach a variety of responses
- train loosely under varied conditions
- train with multiple persons and settings
- provide appropriate applications as everyday situations arise
- use peers in training [Chapter 20]

Social Skills and Assertiveness

Sometimes the social skills are broken down so only one of many life skills needed to achieve social competence are taught and tested. One of the most common of these is assertiveness. However, more often than not, a program that bills itself as "*Assertiveness training*" often includes many of the other social skills needed for effective interaction.

Both assertiveness and social skills training sensitize children to their own feelings and thoughts, and increase their awareness of how they and others act and respond to obtain personal goals in a socially acceptable manner. This yields fewer problematic interactions and more social rewards, which leads to better feelings about oneself and others. In turn, this usually generalizes to other areas of the child's life, such as school achievement.

Children are confronted every day with a variety of interpersonal problems that require assertiveness and other social skills. A number of studies with both socially isolated, unpopular children, and aggressive, rejected children, suggests that increasing children's social competence can enhance their adjustment (Rotheram-Borus, 1988).

We exist on a continuum of behavior from nonverbal to passive to assertive to aggressive. Assertive acts are more likely to result in rewarding interaction with others, but it is still important for children to have a range of behaviors from which they can choose, depending on the situation.

Rotheram-Borus conducted an assertiveness skills training program for 343 fourth to fifth graders for 12 to 20 weeks, meeting twice a week for one hour. The program was delivered by undergraduate and graduate students trained in behavioral management and assertiveness. Tokens with no real value were given to children whenever positive behaviors were observed.

The program first consisted of presentations by leaders role-playing situations like "Mr. Mean Machine," "Mr. Straight Arrow," "El Jerko Deluxe," etc. The students were then presented with problem situations and received their own roles to play. Some examples:

- Your parents have not signed a permission slip for you to attend a school function you want to go to.
- A boy crowds in front of you in the cafeteria line and you don't like it.
- How do you tell someone she hurt your feelings?
- A teacher yells at you for cheating on a test when you haven't been.
- You forget your homework and your teacher is angry with you.

The focus is on questions the kids should consider:

- What do you want?
- What can you do?
- What else can you do?
- What is likely to happen?
- What are you saying to yourself?
- What will the other person do?
- When is it appropriate to refuse?

As part of their learning the students-

- define "passive," "aggressive," "assertive"
- use a "feeling thermometer" anxiety scale (from 1-100)
- practice giving and receiving compliments
- practice applying this for purposes of making friends
- practice anger control by taking time out and playing cool
- learn how to accept a negative response from someone
- learn new strategies to solve problems (interpersonal problem-solving)
- receive feedback on how they played their roles.

Program results (compared to controls):

- higher achievement, as rated one year later by new classroom teachers
- significantly higher grades one year later
- students with initial behavior problems improved significantly in comportment one year later
- the quality of alternative solutions improved significantly
- assertive behaviors significantly improved (from self-reports)
- the more assertive trainers had better success with their students

Some *principles of effectiveness* of this behaviorally oriented program are:

- emphasis on rewards and strengths, rather than punishing inappropriate behavior
- use of "successive approximation." (Once someone shows part of a good behavior, it gets reinforced, and another aspect of the total behavior is noted for the student to concentrate on next time. "I like the way you looked Susan in the eye. Next time I'd like your voice to be a little stronger too.")
- social skill behaviors modeled by trainer. ("Johnny is acting up in the group. What am I going to do? I get upset. I take a few deep breaths. I say, 'I can handle this.' I feel calmer. I ask him nicely not to. If that doesn't work, I say he'll have to take a time out if he does it again.")
- independent thinking encouraged (What do you like about your behavior? What one thing would you like to change? What goal would you like for next time? These questions can be asked indirectly.)

Critical Thinking Skills

Critical thinking is "rationally deciding what to do or believe." At its most basic level, this is another name for decision-making or problem-solving skills. At a more complex level it focuses on the actual processes involved in making decisions and solving problems.

Thinking critically is not only being able to assess one's own and others' views according to a standard of appraisal, but being able to make reliable observations, sound inferences, reasonable hypotheses, and to think of alternative courses of action. Teaching critical thinking teaches students to attack problems inductively, to attain concepts, to analyze their thinking strategies, to analyze social issues, situations and problems, to think divergently, to work together to generate and list hypotheses, to reason carefully, to master complex bodies of information, to analyze personal behavior, to set personal goals, to conduct independent inquiry, and to develop flexible social skills (Benard, 1986).

In *A Place Called School*, Goodlad observed more than 1,000 classrooms and found that less than 1% of teacher talk encouraged or elicited an open student response, such as offering an opinion and supporting it with evidence. Most teachers concentrate on trying to get students to recall the contents, which is counter to the research suggesting that the teaching of critical thinking skills pervade the curriculum so that the teaching of thinking is an important component of every school activity (in Benard, 1986).

279

Stressful Life Events

In 1978, the President's Commission on Mental Health estimated that one in four Americans suffers from mild to moderate depression, anxiety, and other emotional disorders at any given time (in Murphy et al., 1986). That's a lot of people! Most of these problems are brought about by stress. We are all subjected to stress, to varying degrees. Stress affects healthy functioning [Chapter 41], but it appears that those who do not have a strong feeling of competence are affected the most.

"Stressful life event" theory says that stressful life events (marital disruption, loss of a job, and so on) have potential for bringing about illnesses among vulnerable people (Bloom and Hodges, 1988) and psychological behavioral problems in children and adolescents (Compass, 1987; Johnson, 1986).

Bloom and Hodges cite studies by Dohrenwend showing that stressful life events predicted self-reported violence, theft, drug use, property damage, and other minor delinquent acts. Children of broken homes, divorce, or separation tended to exhibit more antisocial behavior later in life. The death of one or more parents yielded more depression or severe psychological distress.

Some of the stressful events that appear to cause difficulties are-

- fateful loss events (death of spouse or parent)
- physical illness and injury
- events that disrupt usual social supports (divorce, separation, marital infidelity, jail, being fired from job)
- victimization
- relatively minor events that have accumulated to major proportions

Personal vulnerability to such events, however, is moderated by personal dispositions such as internal locus of control, coping ability, and social supports. An even closer look would show that our thoughts of stress are the ultimate moderating factor [Chapter 4].

Bloom and Hodges suggest focusing on demoralized individuals who may not have yet developed full-blown disorders. In a six-month, APA-approved study, Bloom and partners helped people experiencing distress from marital disruption to resocialize, to resume the world of the single person, and to deal with meeting people, dating, sexual issues, child rearing and single parenting, housing and homemaking, employment and education, and legal and financial matters.

- At six months, the intervention group adjusted, was able to cope much better, and continued this increase through 30 months. Four years later the magnitude of the differences decreased but were still significant favoring intervention.

As Bloom showed, people must be able to cope with and handle stress, and people who don't seem to know how to do so—or those who have forgotten because their stress seems too overwhelming—can learn.

Betty Tableman et al. (1982; 1987) demonstrated this with low-income women in a project that won the Lela Rowland award from the National Mental Health Association in 1985. A ten-session *Stress Management Training program* was developed to improve the coping skills of women on public assistance. The women were obligated as a component of the "Workfare" program to attend stress management training as part of their job training or job search activities. Transportation and child care were provided. The "curriculum" consisted of-

- changing ways of thinking about and perceiving oneself (three sessions)
- life planning skills [where they want to be in life] (five sessions)
- stress management strategies (two sessions)

This was accomplished through experiential activities and take home "self-discovery" exercises to reinforce learning. Results (compared to controls) were-

- significant reductions in depression
- significant reductions in anxiety
- significant improvements in cognitive skills
- significant improvements in a sense of control over their lives
- significant improvements in self-confidence and self-esteem (two studies)

The program is now a standard part of employment and service programs in Michigan. This project was replicated for both Black and White populations, in both urban and rural areas, for women with infants receiving parent aide services, for pregnant teenagers, for men receiving general assistance, and for mental health center clients. Results have been consistent across all populations.

Some ***principles appear to make this program successful***, besides the actual skills learned:

- communicating the strong message: you can take control of your life; communicating that one can do more than simply manage the stress in their lives—one can take control over it
- showing that change can be created one step at a time
- promoting self-discovery through experiential exercises
- exploring a wide array of potential ways of handling common situations
- connecting what they learn to their personal lives
- helping them view themselves in a positive light
- providing a support network they can count on

A "replication manual" for this project can be purchased from the Michigan Department of Mental Health, Lansing, Michigan.

Compas and Associates (1989) conducted a controlled evaluation of a "comprehensive stress management program for children, parents and teachers," to help people better handle common stressors that they experience. For students, this school-based program consists of eight class sessions dealing with a range of topics, such as the nature of stress, stress management as a matter of lifestyle, decision-making, assertiveness, resisting peer pressure, and relaxation training. The program has been delivered to 3,000 students in grades three to eight over the past five years and was rated extremely valuable to participants.

Self-Esteem

"Virtually all maladaptive defense patterns in childhood, adolescence and adult life have at least one major purpose: protection from the pain associated with lowered self-esteem" (Mack, in Benard 1986, p. 38).

Low self-esteem is said to correlate with the existence of most personal and social problems (Vasconcellos et al., 1990). The interesting exception, at least on the surface, appears to be the use and abuse of alcohol. At least one study even showed that the better the adolescent's self-image, the more likely he was to drink and the more often to become intoxicated (Didier, in Benard, 1986). It may be that because alcohol is so socially acceptable and in adolescence so prestigious, that it is only when alcohol intake has accumulated enough to have detrimental effects that the self-esteem of the individual then begins to deteriorate and contributes to further abuse.

Personally, I wish people had never invented the term, "self-esteem." It is overused. It is confusing because of different interpretations. The American Heritage Dictionary defines self-esteem as "pride in oneself." Yet some people can find great pride in, for example, committing a robbery perfectly. Some people liken self-esteem to "self-concept" or "self-image"—I find it more clear to simply say that everyone needs a set of healthy self-perceptions to feel generally whole [Chapter 5]. If one has these, one probably has self-esteem, and a healthy self-concept and healthy self-image.

Health Realization ups the ante by saying that people have innate self-esteem and can only think themselves away from it (Pransky, 1998)

Bonnie Benard (1986) cites a range of self-esteem studies, primarily based on affective education strategies. The problem with building self-esteem, however, is that its process extends far beyond what affective education can accomplish alone, although many such strategies can complement and enhance the process. Nor is self-esteem always apparent on the surface: "A" students and other high achievers who appear to have high self-esteem but really don't can develop emotional disorders, eating disorders, and suicidal tendencies. We develop self-esteem largely by how we are treated in the major environments that affect us. To truly build self-esteem we must treat people in healthy ways during the process of their growth and development. Then we can offer affective education and self-esteem enhancement strategies to add the finishing touches.

In other words, healthy self-perceptions derive primarily from healthy relationships that affect the messages we give to ourselves.

Supports

Individuals exposed to levels of stress who also have social supports have lower risk of subsequent mental and physical illness than similar individuals exposed to similar stress who do not have such supports. Diseases such as tuberculosis and mental illness occurred more frequently in people who, for various reasons, were deprived of meaningful social contacts. If the stress level is high, poorly supported individuals have about three to ten times the incidence of subsequent physical or mental illness found in the well-supported individuals. This could also mean that people who have a capacity to attract and keep supportive relationships are less vulnerable to stress than those without such a trait (Caplan, 1986).

We can gain supports both from formal professional and community caregiving agencies or from informal and natural helping, friends, groups, and networks. The former may only be necessary if the latter are not present.

Where these informal supports are not present, programs that provide such supports have proven very beneficial. For children, such programs are often provided within the school. For example, children of divorce have to deal with many stressful issues, such as what to say when father does not make his Saturday date, or how to handle vacations. If they are not exposed to a variety of options and do not have the opportunity to receive feedback about their feelings and actions in a supportive atmosphere, they are left to deal with the stress of the experience themselves. Often, they're unable to satisfactorily cope on their own. Pedro-Carroll and Cowen (in Compas et al., 1989) found that when children from grades three to six who were suffering from the effects of parental divorce were exposed to a ten-week support and education group, results (compared to a control group) were-

- a reduction in school behavior problems
- a reduction in shyness and anxiety
- improved school learning
- improved sociability with peers
- greater frustration tolerance

This *Children of Divorce Intervention Program* includes-

- focus on divorce-related feelings and shared experiences early on
- provision of emotional support
- problem-solving skill building through discussions, film strips, and role-play of divorce-related experiences

Caplan (1986) outlines some types of supports that can be provided:

- support groups
- mutual help (one to one)
- a network of natural helpers
- mutual-help organizations

Within these structures it is possible to offer-

- nurturant care—concerned, warm, personalized
- mediation (where needed)
- guidance (including what to do about possible sources of stress)
- support for strategic withdrawal at peaks of stress
- assistance with problem-solving at one's own pace
- fostering hope
- fostering mutual support

Caplan also reminds us not to forget to provide support for the supporters.

Many organizations provide supports around various problem issues, among them self-help mutual aid groups, parent aides, Alcoholics Anonymous, Alanon, Alateen, Citizen Action Parent Support Groups, Parents Anonymous, Grey Panthers, associations for retired citizens, and so many more. People are helped through helping each other. It's a nice concept. It fulfills the need for belonging and significance. Besides that, these programs seem to work. Lieberman (1985) examined evaluations of many self-help and support groups, including women's consciousness-raising groups, *Mended Hearts* (after open heart surgery), groups for widows and widowers, *Compassionate Friends* (for parents suffering from the death of a child), SIDS (Sudden Infant Death Syndrome) support groups, young mother groups, SAGE groups (for people over 65). In all but the groups for first-time mothers (ambiguous results), measurable improvement was seen in-

- levels of depression
- self-esteem
- life satisfaction
- social functioning

Regarding first-time and other mothers, elsewhere [Chapter 7] we saw that supports provided by parent aide home visitors can make a substantial improvement in parental capabilities and functioning. We saw also that supports make a difference for young people [Chapter 20].

Success also extends into the area of treatment. For example, alcoholics who attend AA as part of their treatment appear to do better generally than those who do not (in Lieberman, 1985). We should recognize the enormous healing power in the various forms of informal help, and integrate those forms of help into the formal professional helping system (Weissman, 1986).

An update of Emmy Werner's work (1989), after following her study children into their thirties, showed that a majority of the high-risk children who had experienced some problem or troubled behavior by age 18—while still lagging behind their peers in income and achievement—had overcome their problems by age 30. Those who did were more likely to have found along their way someone or something that essentially gave them "a second chance." Most who made it had formed a trusting, supportive relationship with someone who had encouraged them to take advantage of opportunities—sometimes remedial reading, sometimes technical training and educational opportunities, sometimes social skills and problem-solving opportunities. And the earlier the intervention, generally the better the long-term results. This gives further credence to the use of programs that provide remedial, supportive, and mentoring opportunities to young people, and it suggests that we needn't write off those allegedly at high risk.

We should build this kind of support as a normal part of our overall prevention effort, at the earliest stage possible [see also Chapter 20].

25. Making Sense of "Alternatives" and Community Education Strategies

Alternatives

Way back in 1972, the Bureau of Narcotics and Dangerous Drugs of the U.S. Department of Justice published an at-the-time important document called, *Alternatives to Drugs*, that defined the strategy of "alternatives" in this way:

> Alternatives for the community are designed to provide for the needs of young people...during free time [when] the child's boredom and lack of responsibility [will] most likely lead him to drug taking as a way of absorbing his unused energy. Alternative programs should be able to meet...emotional and medical needs..., provide guidance to help young people sort out their problems, and should offer people recreational, cultural, and service opportunities so they can use their time in a rewarding and stimulating manner... (p. 7).

> If we look for the causes of this problem, we find that the use of drugs is a way of life chosen by individuals because they find their world unstimulating, unfriendly, and unattractive, and they find themselves unable to become contributors to the betterment of their world. The alternatives strategy arose from the perspective that drug abuse is a symptom, and from the attempt to discover those underlying problems in our communities which encourage widespread drug abuse among young people today. In what ways are the homes, the schools, and the community failing to provide a healthy world for the young? (p. 9)

Unfortunately, what many people seem to have heard within that statement is that "alternatives" equals "recreation programs," and that if "alternative" programs are set up for young people, they will attend and will stay off drugs. This interpretation could not be further from the truth. Some research has even shown that the frequency of alcohol consumption actually rises with increased participation in recreational activities, because that's how people celebrate afterwards (Perdue and Rainwater, 1984). Use of drugs has skyrocketed since the bureau's report came out.

If we ask young people why they get into trouble, very often they will say, "Because there's nowhere to go and nothing to do." Our logical response is often to try to create a program or "center" where kids can hang out so they won't be out on the streets and where they can engage in constructive alternatives to problem behavior.

There is one problem with this logic. Most research does not bear it out as an effective prevention strategy (Johnson, Bird, Little, 1980). This means that while "drop-in centers" or "youth centers" may be wonderful places for kids to go, and there are many fine alternative programs that are good for kids to participate in that should be available, not much research shows that such alternatives prevent delinquency, drug abuse, or any other problem.

Sometimes only certain groupings or cliques of young people end up congregating in a particular center. Sometimes the kids who get into the most trouble won't show up, or, if the kids who do get into trouble attend, the place often gets a "bad reputation" and other parents won't let their children attend. Kids can also spend hours at a center and still get into trouble or find drugs on their way home.

Even exciting alternative programs that bring kids out to the wilderness and teach them survival skills, where staff observe very exciting progress while the young people are there, at first seemed not to have much lasting value, at least without extensive follow-up (Wright, 1983). It was believed that probably these environments were so different from normal that the skills are not easily transferable, and once back in the familiar environment with everyone else behaving as they always did people have a tendency to revert to their previous behaviors. However, new evidence on adventure education may suggest otherwise. A meta-analysis was conducted on 96 studies of out-of-school adventure programs, involving 12,057 participants (72% male; 28% female, ages 11-42), where usually small groups of students are transported to the wilderness and assigned challenging tasks, such as mastering a river rapid or hiking to a remote point. An example is *Outward Bound*. Overall, students made gains in 40 different outcomes, categorized as follows:

- *Leadership.* Conscientiousness, decision making, teamwork, organizational ability, time management, values, and goals
- *Self-concept.* Physical ability, peer relations, general self, physical appearance, academic confidence, problem-solving, self-efficacy, self-control, family and self understanding
- *Personality.* Femininity, masculinity, achievement motivation, emotional stability, control of aggression, assertiveness, locus of control, maturity, and neurosis reduction
- *Interpersonal* skills. Self-control, cooperation, communication, social competence, behavior, relating skills, and decreases in recidivism
- *Adventurousness.* Taking on challenges, flexibility, physical fitness, environmental awareness.

The researchers believe that adventure programs have positive effects for four main reasons:

- The intensity of the immediate experience allows the participant full involvement in the activity.
- The challenge and specific goals direct attention and effort.
- The large amount and quality of feedback is vital to the experiential learning process: "Feedback is the most powerful single moderator that improves affective and achievement outcomes."
- Mutual group support provides opportunities in which to reflect, dialog, and act, as well as to cope with and understand one's world (Hattie et al., 1997, p.75).

These researchers warn that "adventure programs are not inherently good. There is a great deal of variability in outcomes between different studies, different programs, and different individuals" (p.77).

If "alternative" centers or "alternative programs" have a chance of being effective prevention strategies, first the alternatives must be more attractive than the behaviors they're trying to replace—a tall order. Second, everything about the program must be geared toward helping the young person build healthy self-perceptions and skills. This means that the planning for a "center" and its programs should be done by the young people themselves, with at least one skilled adult offering guidance to help them be successful. This is how the "alternative" takes on meaning. The youth are involved, and through the process they become capable of figuring out how to do things, they take some control over their lives, and they learn a host of skills. This is the type of "alternative" that can make a difference.

The *King Street Area Youth Program* in Burlington, Vermont, was founded on these principles and as a result has been the longest-lasting "center" in Vermont. The parents and community are fully involved in the program. Yet it is still unclear whether even this excellent program reduces problem behavior. What we can say is that the kids keep showing up and that most community people believe this program makes a difference for area kids in helping to reduce area vandalism (Pransky, 1981).

The *Orion Multi-Service Center* in Seattle (Refling, 1989) is another program done right. This drop-in center and related services appears to have made a difference in the lives of nearly half of the young people who attend. In one representative sample of 39 Orion clients, 92% had been institutionalized in detention, mental health institutions, or drug/alcohol rehabilitation centers. In a cross-section of 107 clients, 51 had been involved in prostitution. These are tough kids, and to be able to reach nearly half through an alternative program like this is no small feat. Yet, when they left the program-

- 49.5% "successfully terminated," meaning they were off the streets, no longer involved in prostitution, and had stable living situations

Interestingly, youths who made a successful exit were found to share the following characteristics, compared with those who didn't:

- they had experienced less abuse as children prior to street involvement
- they had spent more time with parents or parental figures
- they had become involved with street life at a later age

Successful "bonding" or "attachment" to a program can enhance this process.
The Orion program consists of the following:

- *street outreach*—a specially trained, highly visible, mobile outreach unit called "the Team Machine" (named by Orion youths) that spends time in areas where youths congregate. Orion young people actively assist with service delivery alongside professionals. Orion counseling staff also conduct regular group sessions at the King County juvenile Detention Center.

287

- *drop-in center*—furnished with couches, tables and chairs, a stereo, and games, where kids can just hang out or talk, and a place for them to get help if they want it. The center has three rules: no drugs, no sex, no violence. Staff people view themselves as the youths' advocates. The first intent is to establish trust. If youths later show a willingness to get more involved, they can meet regularly with a caseworker. The goal is to help youths move out of street-related activities and into a stable living situation. Orion's philosophy is, "We don't take power away from these kids. We attempt to give them power."
- *counseling and advocacy*—not only counseling on issues such as sexual and physical abuse and alcoholism, but in helping them secure medical help, legal aid and other necessary services, and accompanying them to court hearings.
- *hot meals*—six nights a week, provided by area churches. From October to July they often have 50 kids for dinner. The youths often help serve and clean up.
- *medical services*—two free night clinics in collaboration with the Division of Adolescent Medicine at the University of Washington Medical school, plus a licensed health practitioner available during at least part of each workday.
- *other services* include emergency and transitional housing, drug and alcohol abuse counseling and referral, education (GED, for example), and employment services.

New research suggests that that neighborhood centers can make a difference. McLaughlin, Irby and Langnian (1993) conducted a 5-year research study of 60 neighborhood-based organizations serving more than 24,000 youth in 3 urban areas in the U.S. They found that these "urban sanctuaries," as they called them helped at risk youth to develop a positive life trajectory. They concluded that "**a variety of neighborhood-based programs work as long as there is an interaction between the program and its youth that results in those youths' treating the program as a personal resource and a bridge to a hopeful future**" (p. 5). **The critical component of the successful youth organizations was the energy, passion, and mission of the program leader. These leaders saw the young person's potential, held high expectations for them, and focused on their strengths. The researchers found further that the successful leaders had themselves a strong sense of personal efficacy, and a belief in their own ability to facilitate changing a life trajectory from despair to hope and success.** While the programs differed, they shared *important features*. They provided-

- ♦ physical and psychological safety
- ♦ opportunities for youth to have a major voice in how the program worked
- ♦ chances to learn concrete, prosocial skills
- ♦ real responsibilities and real work, and the opportunity for achievement and accomplishment

Their main message is that perspective really matters. **Adults need to stop viewing young people as something to be fixed and controlled and instead help them enable their development.**

So it can be done, but it must be done right. If the family and school and peer group have failed to build healthy perceptions and skills in a constructive way, where else are these young people to gain them?

Where else can a constructive, supportive peer group be found? The more these programs are designed by following the principles outlined in the rest of this book, the more success they will have.

The type of "alternative" that seems to work best is a program that engages young people in meaningful community service [Chapter 26].

Community Support of Teens: The Milwaukee Teen Initiative Project

In a cooperative school truancy prevention program among the Milwaukee public schools, the Milwaukee Police Department and six community agencies under the auspices of Family Services of Milwaukee, this "volunteer incentive program" is designed to meet the needs of at-risk youth, ages 11 to 15, in six Milwaukee middle schools. The program runs for 11 hours each week after school and weekends and focuses on role-modeling, esteem-building, job-skill training and opportunities, tutoring, athletic events, and neighborhood enrichment projects.

A "resource and support specialist" analyzes the specific needs of the community and the kids and develops a weekly set of activities like short-term money-making opportunities, drug and alcohol abuse workshops, volunteer activities, athletic teams coached by volunteers from the police department, and crime prevention workshops conducted by police officers. The youth specialist is in ongoing communication with school personnel.

A program evaluation was conducted in the first year comparing 141 program participants with 50 in a comparison group. The results were:

- 72.4% improvement in program youth's grade point average
- 55.6% decrease in the number of days absent from school by program youth; truancy significantly lower than comparison group; statistically significant relationship found between decline in school absences and high-level participation in the program
- statistically significant relationship found between theft and vandalism and frequent contact with the program (Greater Milwaukee Crime Prevention Project, undated)

Community Education

Something has always troubled me about "community education" as a prevention strategy. It shouldn't be troubling. After all, we know that people need accurate information. We know that many adults aren't aware enough of many prevention-related subjects because they never learned about them from school or from their own parents. Community-wide education is the only way they can receive accurate, up-to-date information. What is there to be bothered by?

My question is, Who decides what information people should have? In our arrogance, perhaps, we decide that people need information about alcohol and other drugs, teenage pregnancy, good health practices, sexually transmitted diseases—even AIDS. We believe we know the "right" information that people should have. Yet some of us then turn around and throw up our hands in despair when we hear about community education campaigns that other groups are conducting—Right to Life, as one example. Who decides what's right? Who decides what people need anyway?

This is the problem with community education. **Rarely is the community asked what kind of information it wants. The providers of information usually decide, then push their decisions on the community. The community education process often undercuts or**

contradicts the community development process. Community education clearly has its place. But it is best if it occurs within a complete, well-planned effort to help a community meet its prevention-related needs.

Community Education in Public Health

Community education has often been used appropriately in the field of public health. For example, in 1973, when 36% of children under age five at Children's Hospital, National Medical Center, in Washington were found to have an unacceptably high level of lead in their blood, a citywide lead elimination advocacy project reduced this figure to 0.9%. Community education was a major part of this effort, but the information was used to generate community concern so that action could be taken.

Another effective community educational effort was selected as an APA-approved prevention program: Maccoby and Altman's (1988) *Stanford Heart Disease Prevention Program.* The question was, how can cardiovascular disease be prevented or reduced in a community?

Key predictors of heart disease are family history, elevated blood pressure, cigarette smoking, elevated plasma cholesterol, obesity, physical inactivity and "Type-A" behavior. All but family history are related to health behavior. The same is true for cancer, lung disease, accidents, injuries, substance abuse, and sexually transmitted diseases. All are related to individual behaviors.

The Stanford Heart Disease Prevention Program assumed that while mass-media education can be powerful, its effects maybe augmented by community development. Needed is active involvement by community organizations in the delivery, reach, and effectiveness of the community education, to increase the likelihood of community adoption and maintenance.

Before embarking on a community education strategy, the designers of the Stanford program believed it was important to gain a perspective on how individuals and groups change their attitudes and behavior. They concluded that the following steps were necessary:

- make people aware, by getting their attention
- increase their knowledge, by providing information
- increase their motivation, by providing incentives
- help them learn new skills, by providing training
- help them take action, by modeling how
- help them maintain change, by providing guidance and support

The Stanford program based itself on the principles of social marketing: that principles and techniques used to market commercial products could be applied to community health behavior change. The focus must be on a transaction where something of value is exchanged. It begins with an understanding of the consumer. What attracts the consumer in terms of price, promotion, and distribution channel? What is "the right product backed by the right promotion in the right place at the right price."

The program also incorporated "diffusion theory": that communication, persuasion, and learning in communities flow through identifiable social networks; therefore, community leaders should be recruited as collaborating educators.

The Stanford program incorporated three elements typically ignored in health (and prevention) campaigns:

- careful analysis of the specific needs and media consumption patterns of the target audience
- mass media materials that teach specific behavioral skills, as well as the usual practice of offering information and influencing attitudes and motivation
- validated methods of achieving changes in behavior and self-control through training

The program selected three comparable communities in northern California, all reasonably isolated by media accessibility. One served as a reference community. Two received health education through the mass media for two years. One also received intensive face-to-face instruction for two-thirds of the group identified as "high risk."

The basic strategy was to-

- present information about behaviors that influence the risk of heart disease (including probable causes and specific behaviors that reduce risk)
- stimulate personal analysis of existing behavior
- demonstrate the desired behavioral skills (food selection and preparation, for example)
- guide individuals through practice of these skills, with gradual withdrawal of instructor participation
- help individuals become self-sufficient in maintaining new health habits and skills

Diverse and integrated health communication messages were seen and heard through a variety of media: television, bus cards, newspapers, billboards, pamphlets, booklets, and radio programs.

Besides "improved health knowledge," results were as follows:

- improved health behaviors in, for example, diet, nutrition, exercise
- reduction in risk factors like high blood pressure, high cholesterol, smoking, and overall coronary heart disease risk

Their conclusion was that the mass media, when used appropriately, can help people improve their health habits. To make the use of media more effective, it should be designed to supplement face-to-face instructional programs in natural community settings (schools, the workplace, and in community organizations). The project should develop and coordinate such programs.

The *Stanford Five Cities Program* was then developed in five larger communities. This educational program was more extensive, running from six to eight years, with two additional goals:

- to increase not only the knowledge and skills of individuals, but also to enhance the educational practices of organizations
- to create a self-sustaining health promotion structure, embedded within the organizational fabric, to continue after the project ended

In addition to using broadcast and print media, community interpersonal programs were established.

Traditional strategies such as classes and lecture were used, coupled with incentive-based contests and use of lay opinion leaders. Heart-healthy items like chicken, fish, and salad were labeled in restaurants and grocery stores, and grocery checkers and baggers were persuaded to add health education flyers to grocery bags.

The interim results available as of the 1988 report were-

- significant reductions were shown in cardiovascular risk factors, including blood pressure and pulse rate
- some environmental change occurred by keeping cigarette machines from minors or abolishing them; smoking was banned in some worksites and public places, cigarette advertising was banned or severely restricted; more healthful foods supplanted disease-promoting ones in schools, restaurants, and food-dispensing machines; exercising opportunities were made more readily available

Community Education to Prevent Social Problem Behaviors

I was unable to find hard data supporting a similar approach for the prevention of social problem behaviors. Perhaps this means only that the type of extensive community education program practiced by Stanford has yet to be tried, or at least extensively studied, within this realm.

The state of Illinois, largely through the efforts of Alvera Stern (1988) formerly of the Department of Alcoholism and Substance Abuse, undertook an extensive media-based approach to preventing alcohol and drug abuse, called the *Families in Touch* program. Their research indicated that if kids had their choice, they would rather get their information about alcohol and other drugs from their parents than from their peers, and they would want to go to their parents if they were in trouble with substances. Yet, most parents do not have the accurate up-to-date information or skills to offer. Stern concluded that if a community education approach were designed to reach the parents, it would ultimately aid families in being more effective at this natural process. Thus a campaign was developed that included "creating awareness" through the media of the power of the family and the dangers of alcohol and other drug abuse, "skills building" through media vignettes of how to change behavior, plus in-depth intensive training provided by community-based programs like family support and education programs.

The media can reach the most parents. The messages have to be presented in away that catch parents' attention. Unfortunately, prevention isn't by nature sexy, yet the message has to be presented in a sexy enough way to grab people. This can sometimes create a conflict between what is healthy practice for prevention and what messages will turn people on. Practitioners may need to walk a fine line. When is the most appropriate time for the message to be delivered? Their conclusion: soap opera time. They drew these and other conclusions from very extensive consultations with a media expert. Next the media had to be convinced to become more involved. Good community organizing practice would suggest that the question should be asked, To whom does the media respond? How can those people be persuaded to become involved?

As of the initial writing, this was probably the most extensive campaign yet developed by any state in attempting to prevent alcohol and drug abuse through the media, complemented by the efforts of community-based groups. It was too early to determine actual results.

Principles of Effective Community Education

Again, it doesn't really matter if people increased their knowledge; what matters is that their behaviors improve as a result. Much more is involved in changing behaviors than merely giving people information, so a broad-based community education strategy needs to take those other factors into account. Wallach and Wallerstein (1987) offer some *principles of effective community education*. These efforts should include:

♦ a broad definition of the problem, so many constituencies will serve as partners to attack the problems
♦ a program based on real, expressed needs to ensure people's commitment
♦ involvement of diverse groups with a stake in the problem, so they win be involved in the solution, and broaden support and impact
♦ a means for people to relate to and become invested in their part in the change process, so they see it as their personal responsibility to improve their lives and the quality of community life; encouragement to take personal action
♦ incentives for motivation
♦ a diversity of approaches for groups with multiple needs, risks, backgrounds, and learning styles to ensure that all groups are reached
♦ policy or community change

Taking Community Education One Step Further

Even given an effective community education campaign, we cannot be assured that all those in positions to give messages to young people will give consistent messages. Rarely are the messages from the many diverse segments of a community similar. This can be quite confusing. This problem was tackled in Chisago County, Minnesota, northeast of Minneapolis.

The program began as an attempt to coordinate *under one roof* existing resources for "youth-at-risk" involvement in a wide variety of social behavior problems. Its intent then expanded to ensure that young people receive the same messages from all segments of the community—from law officers, students, leaders, youth workers, pastors, parents, teachers, and so on. Their belief was, people learn what they see, and most people try to fit in with social norms. Would they be able to create a community norm for appropriate behaviors, and have the various segments of the community give those messages? At the most fundamental level, the messages were:

- You don't have to use chemicals to be who you want to be.
- You can say no to chemicals and still have fun and friends.
- There are people in this community who care about you and what you're going to become.

Community education, then, becomes the first step in changing a community norm. Thus these efforts become what are now often referred to as "environmental approaches" [see also Chapter 24]. In this program, a large number of people have become involved, from police officers, schoolteachers, coaches, activity directors, counselors, administrators, 4-H and other youth organizations, public service agencies, churches, and parents. As of 1989, 500 people from

12 communities had been trained by Hazelden Services, Inc., and each of these has had an effect on many others. After the training the organizations and people design programs to reach the segments of the community over which they have most influence.

While the program admits it has a long way to go to be fully successful, some encouraging changes have occurred in Chisago County, as indicated by comparing a 1985 and 1988 student survey:

- average age of first use of alcohol rose from mid seventh grade to early eighth grade
- self-reported drinking and driving dropped from 60% to 48%
- heavy drinking at a sitting decreased
- decreased use of sedatives and amphetamines

Tackling the Media

Television has become a surrogate parent—the most convenient of babysitters. The messages communicated through television are learned well by the young.

Spearheaded by Max Abbott, the National Mental Health Foundation of New Zealand became terribly alarmed with the amount of violence on television. They found that children were exposed to approximately 10,000 episodes of violence a year, at an average rate of 5.7 episodes per hour on children's programming. Research showed that violence on television was as strongly correlated with aggressive behavior as any factor, that children ages eight to ten were the most susceptible, and that people subjected to violence through repeated exposure became desensitized to violence and were less likely to help victims. The foundation moved into action with a national campaign against television violence. The result was a reduction in episodes of violence on TV from 9.6 per hour at peak to 4.7 per hour (Abbott, 1990).

Whether this actually reduces the rates of violence among young people remains to be seen, but one could say that their community education and advocacy campaign was successful, at least partially so.

Abbott shared a New Zealand cartoon by Murray Bell in *Footnote Flats* where a sheepdog sitting in front of a television says, "When you see how these people behave, it's no wonder they keep them in that little box."

Another Approach to Media: Neutralizing the Effect

Unfortunately, given the saturation of the media in promoting messages contrary to prevention, including "do drink," and "do drug" (through medication) messages, most campaigns to provide alternative messages amount to a drop in the bucket. It's been estimated that children see nearly 1,000,000 television commercials between birth and the age at which they can legally drink, and 10% of those messages are for beer alone (Hazelden, 1989).

With that in mind, Jean Kilbourne of Newton, Massachusetts, developed an approach to counter the messages of the media through her film, *Calling the Shots* (1982), so that when one sees or hears a "drinking-is-good" message, another message will click in that automatically neutralizes the effects of the first. The original message no longer has the intended effect. In other words, if consumers are helped to understand exactly what the advertisers are trying to do to us, how they try to suck us in, and what techniques they use to accomplish it, we will never again look at traditional media messages in the same way, and they will no longer have that influence over us. If we see exactly how they try to get us to connect drinking with high status, with popularity, with an adventurous life, with sex, and see how many of these messages are geared to the problem drinker, we will no longer succumb to that type of appeal. This approach has potential to reach further than any alternative messages would ever be able to reach.

Imagine what it would be like if we had the same amount of money, and therefore access to same amount of time during prime time, as the large corporate advertisers for providing prevention and health promotion messages.

26. Meaningful Work and Community Service

Economic conditions are among the most powerful contributors to "at-risk" behavior. Without basic changes in employment, it's unlikely that other prevention strategies will make enough of an impact (Benard, 1986).

Opportunities for young people to find meaningful work are limited, particularly in low-income areas. Changes must occur in the-

- availability of meaningful jobs
- preparation of young people to successfully attain and retain jobs
- opportunity for meaningful community service

Work obviously provides us only with the means to sustain ourselves physically. If the work or community service is perceived as "meaningful" from the point of view of the worker, it also provides young people with a chance to-

- demonstrate competence
- feel self-worth
- feel and be perceived by others as useful and contributing
- feel a sense of belonging to a community (Clutterbuck, 1984; Beville and Chioffi, 1979)

Delinquency prevention theory suggests that these factors are what keep young people out of trouble. In other words, if work is perceived as available, if the young people are committed to the work and the organization, if they see themselves and are seen by others as useful and contributing, they will be less likely to engage in delinquent behavior. If this is true, why then have the majority of studies examining youth employment programs as a delinquency prevention strategy not been successful?

Hawkins and Lishner (1981) examined findings of 63 employment program evaluations and reviewed 7 of them extensively. The programs did not reduce crime. The researchers concluded that the programs failed to achieve desired results because they contained serious deficiencies. The program designs and staff lacked quality, and federal program objectives were confusing. The programs focused on short-term remedies (for example, providing counseling and income maintenance at survival levels) rather than attempting to alter circumstances in the work place or correct malfunctioning labor market conditions that caused the problems in the first place.

Hawkins and Lishner did identify some ***common elements that showed promise*** in helping to reduce delinquency:

- ◆ job satisfaction, with-
  - the work itself
  - opportunity for promotion and advancement
  - rapport with supervisors and co-workers
  - opportunities to use one's skills on the job
  - opportunities to learn new things
  - job status
  - pay
- ◆ provision of-
  - incremental rewards
  - positive feedback for successful job performance

Romig (1978) reached similar conclusions in his review of 123 employment programs: **"Delinquent acts are reduced when an individual finds meaning, status, and the opportunity for learning and advancement in a job"** (p. 4).

Availability of Decent Jobs

Most young people aspire to have a decent job—it's part of the American dream. Almost everyone shares the same goals; however, inequality of opportunity makes it impossible for some segments of the population to get what they want and still play by the rules. As a consequence, some turn to illegitimate means to fulfill their needs.

For young people who fail in the school setting, the absence of other opportunities may be particularly damaging. Where else can they find legitimate opportunities to prove themselves worthwhile? If they can achieve success at a job, or by providing some meaningful service, it diminishes the impact of a negative school experience. They can still prove themselves competent and useful—somewhere.

If young people aspire to get jobs but can't, or if they're able to attain only menial employment when they believe they're capable of accomplishing more, it can be disturbing to them. When looking for work, many young people experience repeated rejection. They label themselves incompetent and stop searching. Reality, as they perceive it, and their aspirations appear unrelated. Systems must be established to increase access to employment and expand the range and types of jobs perceived as worthwhile by young people.

To increase employment opportunity means-

- eliminating barriers to legitimate work and service
- finding ways to improve young people's abilities to locate work and community opportunities (Beville and Chioffi, 1979)

Developing Effective Youth Employment Programs

Young people are no different from adults in what they need from employment. In 1984, the Canadian Mental Health Association published the extensive report *Work and Well-Being* (Clutterbuck), after surveying 1,218 workers from five different Canadian communities. Their responses can be quite instructive for designing work programs. Workers felt a source of pride in their work when it-

- allowed them to demonstrate their competence, capabilities and knowledge
- related to a sense of purpose, personal accomplishment or achievement, thereby providing inner satisfaction
- gave them a sense of usefulness, of making a contribution, of being productive.

Workers felt good about themselves and felt encouraged at work when they experienced-

- responsibility, freedom, and autonomy on the job
- recognition and feedback
- cooperation among workers
- supportive management

The report also cited other research indicating that high job satisfaction is related to the opportunity to exercise more control or choice on the job.

To make their workplace a healthier and happier place, the workers offered these recommendations:

- better communications in the work setting
- improved relations with employers and supervisors
- more effective management
- reduced workloads

While many people note that some degree of stress may be necessary to motivate and challenge performance, negative stress resulted in "decreased effectiveness and efficiency on the job" and "negative attitudes" that affected job commitment. High stress caused irritability, impatience, anxiety, tension, frustration, anger, exhaustion, and generally not feeling well. The major sources of negative stress were reported to be-

- structure and conditions of work
- interpersonal relationships on the job (with both co-workers and supervisors)

The workers indicated that the following fundamental changes were needed in the organization of work to reduce negative stress and promote positive mental health among employees:

- opportunities for workers to evaluate or give feedback on supervision without fear of reprisal (97% of responses)

- opportunities for workers to learn more than one job and to perform a variety of jobs over a period of time (96%)
- more decision-making responsibility given to individual employees (92%)
- worker participation in the design or redesign of the workplace (90%)
- creation of smaller working groups responsible for completing a whole job (86%)

Other recommended improvements to be made on the job were-

- health and safety programs (93% of responses)
- stress management workshops (90%)
- workplace-based information and referral services (83%)
- personal counseling (81%)
- preretirement counseling (77%)
- addiction dependency workshops (73%)
- fitness and recreation (63%)
- child daycare (51%)
- budget and management counseling (51%)
- cultural activities (49%)
- nutrition workshops (46%)
- childrearing workshops (31%) (Note: this may appear low on the list but it was still desired by nearly one-third of the workforce.)

The workers cited what they believed would help them do their jobs better:

- career education and skills training opportunities (91%)
- problem-solving workshops (86%)
- team-building workshops (82%)
- decision-making skills (80%)

The report concluded that the quality of interpersonal relationships is at the heart of the workplace. The workplace is a social environment. Efforts to create and support positive human relationships will not only benefit the individual but also contribute to the overall quality of that environment. Where there are quality personal relationships between supervisors and co-workers, there is-

- less anxiety and irritation
- less depression
- fewer somatic symptoms
- less job dissatisfaction
- less boredom
- less concern about workload

Young people are "a special sub-group of the working population with a special set of attitudes and opinions about work." The report cited research showing that young people who are new to the workforce have a more positive orientation to work and are more intrinsically motivated than older workers, but they also show much more job dissatisfaction than those older

jobs for young people are generally in lower-status occupations, with little opportunity for training and advancement. When future job opportunities seem discouraging, young people may become disillusioned with the world of work. When young people don't feel like productive, contributing members of society, their normally strong motivation and commitment erodes. Younger workers need a vision of a more promising future, or other more exciting and lucrative (as well as more dangerous and illegal) endeavors will grab them (Clutterbuck, 1984).

Qualities of Designing Jobs Programs for Youth

In a typical job training program, young people are told to report on time, how to dress, and what to do. They are counseled to make their aspirations and behavior fit the reality of the situation. The programs often try to modify the behavior of the young worker rather than modify the design of the work, the expectations of those within the setting, or the manner of integrating younger members into the routine of the organization.

In designing jobs, recruitment and hiring, training and instruction, evaluation and feedback, and support services, if we want the best chance of attaining and retaining youth in employment, and ensuring that the employment has a meaningful affect on their lives, they must perceive the work as useful.

This means, it must be some combination of-

- challenging—requires problem-solving and imagination
- advantageous—expands capabilities; offers knowledge and skills that will help them in the future
- central—directly related to the goals of the organization
- interesting—the nature of the assignment or the people in the organization
- providing an opportunity to be viewed as competent and responsible
- reasonably matching capabilities and requirements
- permission to assume responsibility—allowed to take initiative to solve problems or carry out portions of an assignment
- valued—seeing misconduct as something that would jeopardize their position (Beville and Nickerson, 1981)

To create the best chance for a young person to look forward to going to work each day, employer-employee relationships should be characterized by an atmosphere of-

- acceptance
- support
- caring
- warmth
- availability for consultation about job-related matters and personal problems
- security (i.e., knowing they'll retain their position if they make an honest attempt to do the job)
- trust (i.e., that they will be relied on to do the job without someone continually checking, and they have the support and respect of fellow employees)

Rules should be perceived as consistent, fair, just, necessary, reasonable, helpful, and connected. In developing work programs, some important questions should be asked:

- Do the young people see themselves as important contributing members of the work group?
- Do they have the opportunity to gain skill, knowledge, school credit, adequate money?
- Do they view their jobs as essential to the workings of the organization?
- Do they have a sense of ownership in the creation of procedures for getting the work done, and in the outcome of that work?
- Will the work be perceived as interesting and challenging enough to hold sufficient interest, so that they're willing to give time and energy for the accomplishment of the required tasks? (Menial jobs may promote the belief that they are incapable of achieving anything better.)
- Is there a perceived career ladder to move up?
- Are the skills being developed transferable to other organizations?

Where young people participate in the development of a job and in the evolution and refinement of tasks as the work progresses, they will be more invested. This is not always possible, but where it is it will help.

Where possible, youth-adult task groups should be formed to allow attachments with others, to help in learning what's appropriate and understanding procedures. Performance evaluation should be built in as a routine and frequent part of the job (Beville and Nickerson, 1981).

Pre-Employment Skills

The Vermont Department of Employment and Training, largely through the work of Peter Comart, concluded that many of the young people placed in jobs failed because they lacked skills that would enable them to find and keep jobs. As a result they developed a list of what they believed to be necessary pre-employment competencies and designed a program to train young people in acquiring them.

- **work acquisition**
  - identifying personal interest areas, including occupations
  - identifying and recognizing personal strengths and skills
  - recognizing personal and work-related values
  - identifying barriers to employment (completing job applications)
  - identifying preferred places of work
  - identifying major employers in those areas
  - recognizing the starting wage in local market areas
  - contacting an employer by phone, in writing, and in person
- **work maintenance**
  - maintaining acceptable attendance
  - reporting to work on time
  - completing assigned tasks
  - using appropriate language

- performing work and training assignments without prompting
- personal dress and hygiene
- maintaining a positive attitude
- cooperating with and assisting co-workers
- following instructions
- working under supervision
- accepting constructive criticism
- **life management**
  - participating in the work setting free from substance use
  - problem solving
  (Vermont Department of Employment and Training, 1986)

The Youth Employment Company

70001 Ltd. is a "youth employment company" that includes many of these components. Its intent is to train young people and place them as soon as possible into unsubsidized jobs in private business.

70001 "associates," as young people involved in the program are called, are all high school dropouts, 74% having completed grade ten or less. Their average reading scores are below seventh grade level upon entering the program. Approximately 60% are Black and 25% Hispanic.

The program began in Delaware in 1969 to motivate and employ high school dropouts. In a five-year period, more than 3,000 young persons obtained unsubsidized jobs in the private sector. They earned a total of more than $12 million and paid $2.5 million in federal, state, and local taxes.

The 70001 program includes three essential components:

- GED instruction or work toward obtaining a high school diploma
- pre-employment training
- job placement

The associates also participate in 70001-sponsored youth activities. In 1981, 70001 Ltd.-

- placed more than 2,600 high school dropouts in unsubsidized jobs
- had an average placement rate of 75%
- jobs averaged $3.64/hour for 33 hours a week, earning a total of $4.7 million in wages and salaries, and paid more than $940,000 in taxes

70001 participants fared better in the labor market than the general youth population:

- 39% of program participants were employed full time (compared to 19%); they worked more hours per week and received higher hourly wages
- less need for unemployment insurance and AFDC payments (PPV, 1981)

In a 1980 associated follow-up survey,

303

- 66% of respondents said 70001 helped them build self-confidence
- 53% said 70001 was useful in obtaining their GED
- 52% said 70001 helped them get a job
- employment satisfaction increased

70001 and a similar program studied "are so successful that they can expect to recover operating expenditures in under two years. Much of this success comes from improving the probability that the youths will be employed. Also, the employed youth tended to work longer hours for higher wages (PPV, 1981).

The *70001 J.O.B.S. Program* is designed to assist 16- to 18-year-old juvenile offenders in acquiring unsubsidized positions in the business community. The program consists of-

- 6-8 weeks of pre-employment training
- individually assessed education
- team-oriented motivational support
- intensive individual, group, and family counseling
- job development, placement, and coordination
- follow-up services

Results have been-

- a significant impact on recidivism
- many have returned to public school

To quote a probation officer: "I have had several clients involved in this program. Since their involvement, their delinquency and acting out has ceased" (PPV, 1981).

The 70001 program consists of-

- *Pre-employment training*—4-6 weeks (unpaid) of learning employability skills, including-
  - career awareness
  - job-seeking skills
  - interviewing
  - job retention skills
  - individualized aptitude assessment and skill development
- *Responsibility training*—this training portrays realistic situations in which youth are likely to find themselves, to develop essential life skills:
  - self-awareness
  - goals and values
  - coping skills
  - ownership of action and responsibilities
  - dealing with authority figures
  - communications and listening
  - giving and receiving feedback
- *Education*—Youth are taught in nontraditional settings, consisting of-

- individualized assessment, planning to meet youths "where they are," and allowing them to work at their own pace
- remedial basic education through preparation for GED
- *Youth organization*—The young people learn about-
  - political mechanics, such as
  - voting leaders into office
  - selecting and planning activities
  - building a team
  - recognizing achievements
  (National Youth Work Alliance, 1981)

Upon completion, the young person is placed in the first available position identified as appropriate.

For this type of program to be successful, partnerships need to be developed with business leaders. 70001 originally formed a partnership with the Thom McAn Company. An advisory council of business and community leaders provides guidance and support for each program youth. Community-based organizations raise funds for charitable causes and participate in service projects.

In a world where dropouts have little hope, programs like this provide a way out.

KICS—Kids in Community Service

The best alternative to destructive behavior is a situation where young people can develop a sense of self-worth and a commitment to their community. The more that communities see young people involved in constructive and helpful pursuits, the more the negative labeling will be reversed.

Opportunities for young people to provide meaningful community service go along way toward achieving this end. Such opportunities help young people to feel connected and needed, and to demonstrate their competence. Others begin to see them in these ways. An upward spiral begins, reversing the downward cycle.

KICS was developed by Peter Perkins and based on a program originally created by Lynn Whitlow, both of the Washington County Youth Service Bureau in Montpelier, Vermont. KICS serves "high-risk" youths between the ages of 13 and 15. The program includes:

- weekly educational peer support group meetings
- recreation and challenge activities
- community service to improve both the perceptions and skills of youths

The KICS model-

- provides peer support through the weekly support groups, which address self-concept, empowerment, feelings, clarifying values, problem-solving, decision-making, risk-taking, support, resources, and healthy termination
- develops critical life skills, including communication, decision-making, and judgment

- tests those skills and the young persons confidence through the "challenge activities," which teach that with perseverance, patience and practice, goals are attainable, but experience is needed in how to attain those goals
- prepares them to take their newly developed skills into the community and into their everyday lives
- provides meaningful activity
- provides an opportunity to be of service to the community
- provides referrals for additional service
- encourages parental involvement (for example, permission to participate in youth group activities must be obtained from parents or legal guardians)

The intent is to integrate high-risk youths into the life of their community. When KICS members engage in community service, they are seen as meaningful and contributing members of the community. They acquire and learn to apply skills. They belong to a worthwhile, engaging group and can see their direct (if modest) impact on their surroundings.

Community members are encouraged to actively support the young people and therefore begin to see them in a different light. KICS has come to be viewed by everyone-the community at large, parents, kids, schools, and service agencies-as extremely positive. The intent is for all segments of the community to join together to help prevent young people from becoming involved in troublesome behavior. The community has responded very warmly to the help that this program has provided with thank-you letters and telephone calls to young people who participated in activities.

Based upon 1989 and 1988 evaluation questionnaire results-

- 60-71% of KICS young people increased their self-esteem.

Transition to the World of Work

The transition from school to work is often a high stress time for young people. First, school and work are so different. Second, many young people find that school has not prepared them for their jobs and the responsibilities that accompany those jobs.

To make up for this lack of preparation where schools haven't changed their structures to solve this problem, transition programs are needed that prepare young people for the world of work. The Washington County Youth Service Bureau was funded as a demonstration project by the (then) Office of Substance Abuse Prevention to test the validity of this assumption. Based on the success of the KICS program they predicted that, ***to be successful, the following components were minimally needed***:

- ◆ building young people's self-respect, through supportive, small-group experiences
- ◆ developing young people's respect for the community, and improving perception of the young people, through providing meaningful community service
- ◆ improving their preparation to assume job responsibilities by creating access to educational and vocational opportunities, and by providing job apprenticeships improving their chances of obtaining meaningful jobs by helping connect them to job opportunities improving their chances to retain those jobs by following up with contact and through a continued support system

The Need for Youth Employment and Service

Young people are capable of performing many useful tasks. America is faced with increasing social needs. This would seem a good match. In fact, it could be the basis for providing jobs for young people.

Urban transit and inter-community rail systems are decaying. Large numbers of people (the old, the young, the mentally ill, the handicapped) are being offered inadequate services and, in some important areas, are being totally neglected. National parks and inner-city recreational facilities have few services, and parks are in disrepair. The environment is deteriorating. Instruction is needed in the arts so people can be participants rather than recipients of our culture.

> The list of unmet needs, physical as well as social, is virtually endless—housing, preservation of resources, development and installation of alternative energy systems, reclamation of wastes, beautification of cities—to name but a few. We lack not socially useful things to do but the vision and sense of mission to get them done (Pearl, 1978, pp. 47-48).

We must have the ability to predict where future job opportunities are likely to be, then train young people accordingly to prepare them for those opportunities. Labor market information can be found in publications by the U.S. Department of Labor, Superintendent of Documents, U.S. Government Printing Office, Washington, D.C.

We can even build the concept of community service into intervention and treatment, which would aid prevention endeavors. As Jack Calhoun (1990) says, we've got to change around the system to emphasize how we're all connected with one another. If someone gets something from the system, they have an obligation to give something back. "As part of your treatment plan, you're going to do something for others." A coach or teacher could say, "Okay, I've been teaching you; now you teach what you know to the little kids."

Prevention on the Job/Production as a Result

The work environment can have a powerful affect on one's self-perceptions. On one hand, when people are treated like cogs on the wheel of a machine, simply doing their little part to produce or repair a product or provide a service, they come to feel and work that way. Under those circumstances, it is a rare employee who puts out more than minimal effort. On the other hand, when workers are given a say in how to run the business or operation, and when their ideas are sought and valued, productivity increases, worker satisfaction increases, and the "climate" of the workplace markedly improves. The results are so consistent it's a wonder that more American businesses don't follow suit.

Many of us became awed at the way the Japanese have turned around their own economy and taken over many American markets. We wonder how they did it, and how they run such low-cost efficient plants. Some of the clues came with Ouchi's (1981) book on *Theory Z* corporations, subtitled "How American Business Can Meet The Japanese Challenge." Most corporations in America have traditionally been organized according to what is called "Type A," with the boss at the top and the people at the bottom. Theory Z broadens the base of decision-making authority, bringing more supervisors and employees into the process, creating a team that is focused on the good of the whole. Of course there's more to it than that. For example, many Americans have become less enamored of the Japanese approach as the amount of self-sacrifice involved in their practices becomes more evident. The question, however, remains, "Can we make it happen here (at least the good parts)?" And the answer is, "Yes we can!"

The book on Theory Z cites examples of how certain American corporations like Hewlett-Packard put key principles into effect and turned their corporations around. More evidence comes from two 1989 public television specials by Tom Peters, titled, "The Leadership Alliance" and "Excellence in the Public Sector." Whether they be in a Ford Motor Company plant, the Johnsonville sausage-making company, the Harley-Davidson motorcycle manufacturing plant, the Winchester, New Hampshire school system, the Almeda Air Force base, the Spofford juvenile detention center of New York City, the city of Phoenix, Arizona, the National Theater Workshop of the handicapped, or the National Forest Service in the Ochoco National Forest of Central Oregon, all share some basic principles that turned around their operations and markedly improved their products or services and their worker productivity and satisfaction. Here are some *key principles* the specials identified:

- a driving desire to put out high quality products or service
- creating high standards and measures for those products or services, and holding people accountable for those high standards
- defining the purpose or mission so each employee knows how his or her work relates to the whole
- sharing information
- trusting that those involved in the operation are in the best position to make improvements, giving them the authority and the autonomy to do so, respecting their abilities to come through
- giving people the necessary training and tools to expand their knowledge and skills
- allowing people to learn at their own pace
- providing incentives for people to come up with innovations that will yield higher quality or more efficient and effective service
- encouraging teamwork and partnerships to take responsibility and make improvements
- redefining rules and regulations so only the critical ones remain; having workers participate in developing and redefining those rules
- acknowledging and celebrating small improvements
- demonstrating care about the staff or employees
  (Peters, 1989; 1982)

Whether the intent is to increase profits, cut operating costs, reduce employee or staff turnover, or simply provide the best-quality product or service, putting these principles into effect can make the key difference. In short, given a chance to shine and to take risks, people will come through.

Tom Peters closes with a list of paradoxes that he found in examining these very successful corporations that turned themselves around: fewer inspectors means more control over quality, fewer rules means more control (because it can mean more individual perception of inner control); less control over the numbers means more honest numbers; less goal-setting from the, top down (and more goals set by workers from the bottom up) means tougher goals set.

These contradict the hierarchical management practices by which most businesses have conducted themselves over the last 200 years. Tom Peters paraphrases an unnamed political economist:

> We have two choices as a nation: to be a commodity producer of second-rate products and see if we can match the Indonesians on wages, or...to join the Japanese, the Germans, the Swiss, and others, and become a nation which emphasizes high value added, awesome quality, and extraordinary service. And those words don't come from robots, they come from people. People who are continuously trained. Where training, self-respect, self-development, and teamwork, and partnership, and 'we' rather than "they" become the watchwords throughout the American economy. America has a stark choice: one path or the other (Peters, 1989).

27. Health Promotion in the Workplace

Businesses can make effective use of prevention strategies to improve the health of their employees, reduce absenteeism, and increase productivity. **Madeline Motta** *of Montpelier, Vermont, helped businesses do just that. She authored the state of Vermont's handbook,* Health Promotion in the Workplace.*.*

JP: What is "worksite wellness" all about?

MM: "Worksite wellness" or "health promotion in the workplace," is community organization for prevention within the workplace. It's organizing the workers for healthier lifestyles, emotionally, physically, and, more recently, spiritually.

JP: What's in it for the businesses?

MM: First of all, **it lowers their health care costs, specifically their health insurance premiums. It lowers their absenteeism and the number of disability days an employee will use. It lowers worker turnover rates and the cost of all that's associated, like the cost of temporary workers, retraining efforts when you lose employees...** And that's exactly the point we make to employers to get involved with health promotion. And that's exactly how you put worksite programs together: You assess things like your cost of insurance premiums, the number of hospital admissions, their absenteeism and turnover rates, the cost of temporary workers, and other things like the age and sex of the employees.

For instance, if the factor that's causing the high cost of their insurance premium is low back pain—if workers are ruining their backs and that comes up in different surveys—then you can say, "I can do something about these high disability claims around lower back pain," and if you institute an ongoing training program on how to protect your back, how to lift, and things like that, then you've helped the business. When you look at worksites, for instance a furniture company, their biggest complaint is back pain because they're lifting furniture; they're making furniture. Right then and there you know you've got to do something about it.

JP: So it sounds like you start with an assessment that gets very specific about what's causing whatever problems they have. How do you find out the risk factors in a worksite?

MM: There's a...thing...in business management called "risk management." Basically, someone will go in and assess the risks of the workplace or the employees and then institute programs and insurance policies that would cover those risks. That way, they know how much liability they would have to have. I do a "risk identification screening program," which includes things like collecting and analyzing existing data around their claims, administering an employee

311

health-risk appraisal in which you ask questions of an employee about all the risk factors that the person has in his life, for instance, whether he might have high cholesterol; if it's a woman over 35, whether she gets mammograms or has had a pap smear recently; drinking and driving; seat belt use. A health-risk appraisal is a questionnaire where all these questions are asked of the employee.

JP: And it's given directly to the workers?

MM: Yes, and it's kept confidential. You get a data summary of what all the risk factors are for the workplace, by percentages. To obtain a relevant sample, you try to get about 80% of the worksite employees.

JP: So you get a general reading of what the workplace is like. At that point it moves out of the realm of the individual to become a business-wide health profile?

MM: Yes, what you do is **get a reading of their current risky behaviors. So if 40% of their employees are overweight, and 50% are smokers, and 30% eat fatty foods or meat five times a week, then you look at the insurance claims and you see that there's a lot of heart attacks, and they're all in executive positions, you've got a cluster with respect to heart disease. So if you don't want your insurance rate to go up, you'd institute heart attack prevention programs** because that's what's showing up in the surveys analysis.

JP: So it shows you where the risk clusters are and tells you where to direct your health promotion efforts?

MM: Yes. This is a cost-effective way of providing health promotion programs, because you're targeting risky behavior groups.

JP: Now, does this have anything to do with improving worker productivity, their satisfaction in the workplace?

MM: Some statistics have come out to this effect, but because this has been going on for only the last 10 to 15 years, there have been no major long-term studies. Johnson and Johnson are doing one now, they have a five-year study out that seems to indicate that, yes, if a person is feeling better and healthy in their body, then they're feeling better on the job and performing better on the job, they are more positive and get a sense that the employer is really concerned about the conditions of the employees, and they feel better about working there too. It's just common sense.

The dangerous part of health promotion for businesses is that you start getting healthy employees, and they start looking around at the unhealthy features of their workplace and start trying to change them. That may be upsetting to employers. I mean, if workers are being told that they've got to change their diet, and they go into the cafeteria and find meatball subs every day, then they want to change the food in the cafeteria. Then they notice that they're working among smokers, and they want a smoking policy. Then they notice that they have a lot of single mothers who are stressed, so they, say, "Why can't we have a day care center? That would help." So you start getting these health activists, and that's the only "danger," you start getting healthier people who want healthier things.

JP: So the business might not want to make the changes. But then they have a choice whether or not they actually do, right?

MM: Usually you have to have somebody in top management interested in health promotion. It's crucial to have someone's commitment at the top to help push these things through, or else it's not going to work. When you go into a worksite, you have to look around for individuals who are personally interested in health promotion and lifestyle change. But sometimes you might get people interested in instituting these kinds of programs, when the problem is really the supervisors.

JP: How do you deal with that?

MM: There are a number of ways. One is to try to get a survey out about how workers feel about stress on the job and what's causing it. That's the beauty of it—there are so many different tools out there you can use. Or assessing whether or not they feel happy on the job and why. Basically what you've got to do is to spend some time on-site and interview people and find out what's going on in that environment. It's like any other community. You've got to spend some time digging to find out what's really going on with the members.

JP: So your health assessment form isn't all there is to finding out what's going on.

MM: Right. You have to have meetings. That's why I said health promotion in the workplace is community organizing. That's what got me excited about it in the first place. I was able to do community organizing, and I hadn't done that in years. It's different in that you're going into the workplace and you don't want to be seen as the patsy of management, but you need their support.

JP: You're brought in by management—

MM: They buy your service.

JP: But then you have to make the workers feel comfortable enough with you to tell you what's really going on there—

MM: Right, usually you align yourself with a nurse who is already providing health services, or if they're really going to buy a health promotion program in a large workplace they place you within "personnel."

JP: Does "stress" come up a lot as a worksite problem?

MM: Yes, depending on the type of worksite.

JP: What else comes up?

MM: It depends on the age and sex of your employees. If you've got a worker population of 20 year olds, their major risk factors are usually drinking and driving, use of drugs, smoking, and sexually transmitted diseases. With an older person it's more the risk of heart attacks or, in some environments, the risk of cancer.

JP: And you find this out not only with your assessment tool, but also from meeting with them and pulling it out of them.

MM: The best way to do it is form a coordinating committee of some kind. You usually try to get the union represented, the nurse, and people who are interested and responsible for employee health issues.

JP: Okay, you're sitting with them for the first time, what do you tell them their role is?

MM: You ask them what they want to do in the worksite. You ask basic questions like, **"What do you perceive are the major health problems?" "What would you personally like to see happening?" and they'll come up with their own answers**: "We want to change the cafeteria," or, 'We want to have aerobics on-site at lunchtime," or, "We want to get work time while we're doing aerobics, or running, or something," or "We want to get exercise stations on the grounds." So when you start sitting down with committees you start looking at program development goals.

JP: At what point is that? Before or after the assessment?

MM: After. Or you can have the kind of committee that helps you set up the assessment too. They can become your marketing method. Hopefully you try to get them from every division. I'm talking about large worksites, but the same principles hold for smaller ones, you just have less people and resources to work with. If you're going to do a promotion, you give your committee stacks of paper to post up, and talk it up.

There are usually three kinds of programs you can do in a worksite: health risk appraisals, fitness programs, and lifestyle education. There are two implementation levels for each. In the first year you can go in and do risk identification screening, cholesterol, blood pressure—those kinds of health-risk appraisals, and you give them that information. Just doing that is a lot. And **the first level of a risk identification screening program would be awareness through promotional activities,** like putting up posters, putting out literature, paycheck inserts, getting workers a special deal at a fitness club, that kind of stuff. **Then you could actually get the fitness programs on site, or put together resource guides where employees could go to get the fitness they need. Or, you could sponsor annual fitness runs. Or, you could have lifestyle education programs, self-help kits that you can leave around,** a newsletter about health-lunchtime informational sessions.

JP: All that's at the first level?

MM: Yes. It's essentially health awareness. The **second level is actually establishing the program.** If you start a blood pressure **screening** program, you keep going back to check it again so they can see progress or not. You do that with cholesterol. You not only take the screening, but you also do a **health education** piece with those individuals or with the group as a whole. You might form a heart attack prevention **support group** where you get people who have had heart attacks together with those at risk for heart attacks.

For "fitness programs" you could build in an incentive program at this level, like, you get $100 back if you participate in this fitness program, or you get a day off. Or if you lose weight you get so much money, or if you stop smoking. The management actually puts out money to build in an incentive. Those really work. Or they do incentive programs with contests between divisions. They're all supposed to lose 250 pounds as a total division. That's the goal, so they work together as a group. And those can be great fun if you've got the right people organizing them. They've got scales, charts on the wall, and the last day before the weigh in, one group sends the other group some donuts and cakes and ice cream to tempt them. And the group that actually makes their target gets bonuses in their paychecks, with personnel awarding it to them. The best way to increase participation in these health programs is to make it be fun.

The same is true for the second level of "lifestyle information," although here you would also find **changing worksite policies like vending machines, cafeteria and smoking policies.** The big thing that many businesses don't bother to do is to keep statistics so you can see changes over the years.

JP: Can the businesses take this on themselves or do they need to hire a consultant like you to do it for them?

MM: It depends. Often what a consultant will do is to go in and train someone to do it. If it's a big worksite, they may hire somebody to do it full time.

JP: But the consultant could either start them off or carry them through the whole process?

MM: Usually what they want is a little of both. They want you to come in and start it, but they also want you to train somebody because it would be more cost effective to actually have somebody on site. They don't usually want to put a whole lot of money into this, and **they don't want it to take a lot of their time either, and that's why they hire a consultant. But those are the first people to go if a business gets into hard times. They're seen as luxury. And that's**

really too bad. That's the kind of thinking that has to change for any kind of long-term change to occur, and for employee health to improve.

JP: So ultimately, what's in it for them is their insurance premiums go down, they have healthier workers who are more productive ...

MM: And who want to stay because it's a healthier place and a caring and more satisfying place, and they can get some of their human needs met there.

JP: Do family issues ever come up in the assessments you do?

MM: It comes up usually when we talk about stress. For workers between age 30 and 50, children and teenagers are usually involved. When this is found, a business may want to **bring someone in to teach parenting courses**, dealing with your child or teenager, or even helping your elderly parent; courses to lower stress in your household.

JP: So the theory is, **if there is a lot of stress in the household, they bring it along to work and aren't as productive**.

MM: Of course. Oh, the other person to talk to who I forgot about is the EAP [Employee Assistance Program] coordinator, if there is one. If there is, then you know they're at least somewhat employee-need conscious. They're at least doing intervention for the emotionally troubled employee.

JP: Summarize all this. What do you think are the **most important principles of an effective worksite health promotion program**? For this kind of program to work well, what do they have to have in place?

MM: They have to have **interested individuals committed** to do it.

JP: Does that mean if a business does not, don't try to make them be committed? Start with the ones that are?

MM: Yes. There are a lot of businesses out there. Otherwise you spend a lot of time trying to get them to see it your way and never reach the program level. So that's the major principle. Another is to **determine the need for and employee interest in a worksite health program**. The employees may not want to be involved. That means collecting and analyzing existing data.

Another principle is that there should be some type of **financial commitment** from the worksite itself, not just hiring a consultant but actually willing to do things like put money into incentives, or bring in instructors for lifestyle change courses or even parenting courses, or screenings. These things cost money.

The other important part is to develop an **implementation timetable** that makes sense, either as a pilot, or phase-in approach, or a total implementation. Employers like either a pilot or a phase-in so they can see what you can do.

Another thing is to take the time to **evaluate** these programs, take **pre- and post-tests** on the courses offered, and of fitness levels, how many people are still smoking, how many people have put the weight back on after six months. Those statistics need to be kept so in five years you can say, the reason you're not paying high premiums anymore is that the heart attack rate has gone down, and it seems to have coincided with the instituting of this program. It takes long-term studies, and people don't like to stick with them.

JP: Are some types of employers more receptive than others?

MM: Interestingly, the military and state police operations are becoming more aware of the stress of doing that work, and that they don't have healthy employees. They're even doing things now like demanding fitness tests every year that the employees have to pass. Think about it: In the state police, they have to be incredibly healthy and fit to get in, and they have to pass a rigorous fitness test that's like trying out for a football team. But then, as soon as they're in, their job demands that they sit in their patrol cars and eat fast food and wait for the next speeder to go by, and then their adrenaline hits as they react and jump up, and then they experience chest pain. Coronary disease rates in the police force are incredibly high because these guys actually have very unhealthy lifestyles. But now they're embracing the whole concept because they need healthy men and women to run after the assailant. So they build in incentives and give out bonuses, and hold annual competitions, because the vitality of that whole workforce depends on each individual's vitality and health.

The hardest group to organize around this are usually doctors and nurses. A lot of doctors don't seem to know much about good nutrition and stress today, or at least they don't do what it takes to stay healthy.

12/88

28. Reflections on a Healthy Worksite

David Smith had been trained as a lawyer, worked as a public defender for many years, and helped create the Vermont state prevention legislation. He gave it all up to become Innkeeper of the Highland Lodge in Greensboro, Vermont. But he never forgets from where he came, bringing with him primary prevention concepts and putting them into practice within his own controlled environment. The result is a healthy work environment—particularly for his employees.

JP: What makes this place different in how you deal with your employees?

DS: I'm a humanitarian. Most employers are not. That's what makes this business, and Ben and Jerry's, different.

JP: What exactly is different?

DS: It has to do with how the employees are treated as human beings. I've spent since 1962 looking at the issues of why we're born and what we do while we live and why we die. As a result of looking hard at those issues, I can't help but be a humanitarian. [laughter] That means, although I'm running a business and concerned about the money people bring, and the money I spend to keep the business going, I tend to think of my business in terms of human enterprise, human interests and needs. My guests are treated as humans first, not as open pocketbooks. My employees are treated as potential contributors to a quality of life that I chose when I came here.

I left a profession that works with people in miserable circumstances wanting to hurt each other or being hurt, and infusing me with all that misery. I left with a number-one priority: never again to work in miserable circumstances. So what we've created here is a happy workplace. The people I hire must have the capacity to keep this a cheerful working place for me! [laughter]

JP: What do they feel about being here that would be different from working someplace else?

DS: **They know that they're wanted**. Most of the people who work here are unskilled or semiskilled, and generally, anywhere else they work, they contribute to the income of the enterprise by putting in their hours and doing routine work. I appreciate them before they even walk in the door, because I know they're going to make my life easier, and they're going to make it possible for me to continue living in a cheerful way. I had been a trial lawyer for eleven years and was burned out. Taking over this lodge helped me develop a real appreciation for nonprofessional, simple-minded work, and how satisfying that could be. So I appreciate being here, and that makes it easier for me to appreciate my employees, because if I'm secure in what I'm doing, then I'm secure in the way I handle my employees.

317

So **the first order of business, the first foundation of primary prevention theory in human enterprise, is how well you think about yourself. If you're self-secure and self-motivated, and interested in life generally, rather than constantly worrying about how you appear, what you should be doing, what your goals should be, then you're going to constantly contribute to the character and the atmosphere of your working environment**.

JP: How would you characterize the working atmosphere of the Highland Lodge?

DS: Right now it's wonderful, but it's a constant challenge to keep it that way because new people keep coming in. We started out with maybe 10 to 15 employees and now we're up to 54. We're doing three times the business now that we were when I took over ten years ago. But what we learned in short order was that we were going to have constant high turnover in employees unless we kept them from burning out, so **we increased the number of employees to prevent burnout**. Instead of one chef, we have five. Instead of two chambermaids, we've got four to six. **All these people rotate through the days and weeks to fit their living schedules so they come to work feeling like doing some work, feeling like being here**. Most are part-time employees. People who have to produce perfectly, as often as a chef must, can only do that so many times a week. It's a production every night. So we have others substitute, so our main chef can get a couple of nights off during the week.

Our main chef had a desire a couple of years ago to study with a trainer of professional chefs, so we sent her to France for several weeks. She learned a lot and thoroughly enjoyed it. **As a result we have someone who has an investment in the lodge**. It's her business as well as ours.

A second full-time employee is a chambermaid who, because of family issues, had to work so many hours at an hourly wage that she was going to burn herself out. So now we make it easier for her. We pay her a salary and force her to take two weeks off a year. She had no vacation before that. We tell her, "You have to go somewhere with your family!" And she's now doing that, so she's more rested than she was before.

JP: What are some other principles that make this operation successful in a preventive sense?

DS: In managerial terms, as soon as possible when we hire our seasonal workers we have a staff meeting that includes all the workers, and **we not only talk about their individual responsibilities in their work area, but also about the human side of enterprise and how they should treat each other and us so we have mutual respect**. I want them to be just as considerate of their co-workers as they are of their prospective lovers, people they may be trying to impress with consideration. I want them to be secure in their work, to feel as though we're not looking over their shoulder. **I tell them that we're counting on them to learn and do their work so they don't require constant supervision, so they don't have to feel they're doing it our way, but they're doing it the best way it can be done, defining that as they go along. They are essentially working for themselves.**

We also move people around to different areas of our operation. It's not just that they're learning different working skills, they're learning different ways of relating to each other, they're evolving. We take kids 16 years old from farm families nearby and give them confidence in themselves as they master skills in these different areas. Several kids who started out washing pots and pans and dishes have become waiters and waitresses, have worked on the beach, have painted buildings outside, have helped me gather wood, have learned every aspect of the physical operation of this business, then learned the business skills of operating the office, and now operate this place for us as though it was theirs, because they've incorporated this as part of their life.

JP: Why do they want to become that involved?

DS: I try to be sensitive to their moods when they come through the door. I say something positive to every person that comes in. I notice something about how they look. I catch them doing something good when they don't expect it. I make them feel good about themselves because they're here. And if they feel good about being here, they want to come back. Especially because life is so much harder on the outside working somewhere else. When kids grow up working here and go into the outside world they come back and tell us how much they appreciate the way they were treated here as human beings, rather than as industrial age employees.

JP: Is that all there is to it?

DS: No. We give them direction. **We don't tell them what to do; we show them how to do things** that they don't know how to do, but we don't do it with a supercilious tone: "Don't you know how to do that?"

JP: So it's just like bringing up kids.

DS: No. It's like bringing up someone else's kids [laughter]. **How do you get people interested in learning something? You develop their attitudes first; then you give them the skills.** We're talking primary prevention here. So I concentrate on the attitudes of my employees, and I'm working on that every day we're open.

JP: What if they screw up?

DS: Everyone has bad days. One of the people who works here is going through a divorce. She comes in some days so depressed I think she's going to be crying all morning. She comes in some days so mad I think she's going to rip me apart. She comes in exhibiting every emotion you can think of that would be the result of a breakdown in a tight, human relationship. Life is hard for her. So I have to adjust to her mood of the day. If I think it's going to be damaging to relationships with people she will come in contact with, I don't send her home; I send her outside to work in the garden with the flowers.

I've learned to become more sensitive to the energies of the people I'm working with, and how to direct or redirect them. I've become more intuitive in handling people. That does not mean I'm the perfect intuitive tool [laughter] but rather that I'm less dense than I used to be. I still make some horrendous mistakes.

JP: How do you get your employees to take as much pride in their work as you would?

DS: I don't. They take pride because it is their nature to be prideful. It's their nature to do well. When I look at the beds our chambermaids make, they're perfect. They scrub these rooms cleaner than I would ever scrub them. Obviously they're taking some interest in cleanliness as an art, and doing it from their own resources.

JP: Is it everybody's nature? Or just people who happen to come through the door of your place?

DS: I think everybody's nature.

JP: But a lot of people don't.

DS: Yes. Those are the people who've been hammered on.

JP: But you somehow set up the expectations—

DS: The expectations are that people who come in and stay here expect to find a clean place. And those expectations are demonstrated by what they say as they go out the door: "I've never been in a place as comfortable and clean as this!"

JP: So when a new employee comes on—

DS: They hear that. They hear it from their coworkers. They hear it from me as I hear it through the season. As guests tell me something positive about the way the place is kept, I pass it along at a moment calculated to have the most impact.

319

JP: How do you know when that moment is?

DS: I don't know. Because I've become more sensitive to timing. I think it's because I've learned comedy timing. [laughter] A lot of what I do here is done through humor. I shake people up by bringing fun into some situation. I diffuse tense situations and make a drudge job more tolerable by bringing some humor into it. I want to have fun in a cheerful working atmosphere. I want them to laugh.

JP: If someone were starting a business and they were going to have employees working for them, what would you tell them about how to do it right?

DS: I'd tell them to go out and learn theater. [laughter] Learn how those people are able to work with each other to create a successful production. They would have to work on their relationships with each other, as well as their delivery of lines. They would have to determine how they complement the total cast performance, rather than taking over. They would have to learn that life is theater and we're all playing roles, and the more aware they are of other people's roles, the better they can complement how well those people play their roles. And this can be done without investing any real seriousness. After all, it's just a play, and it doesn't really matter. Everyone's doing what they're doing as well as they possibly can, and you're trying just as hard as you can to complement that performance, so it all comes out well.

I remind myself of this metaphor from time to time so I won't be impacted psychologically and disturbed by what I see. **Let's say I see someone doing something awful. If my immediate reaction were to unthinkingly take over, show how to do it, erase what I thought had been done badly, then I would simply hurt that employee's perception of his or herself. If, on the other hand, I look at that as a performance that needs to be adjusted, then I can figure out: what should I say? what should I do? what should my behavior be? And that's the kind of approach I try to take in my work.**

JP: Is this possible to do in a large-scale business?

DS: Sure, because you're working with one person at a time. And even if you were talking to a cast of dozens, you're still talking to them as if they were one person.

JP: How do you know what you're doing here is successful with your employees?

DS: Because they keep coming back. This is not inherently interesting work. Most of what we do here is dull. The interest comes from interacting with other people in a satisfying way. So we inevitably lose people to more interesting work, or to their continued evolution. They graduate from high school and go on to the real world where they get battered about and most of them come back and express their appreciation for how much better they were treated here. They've gone beyond this work, they have other roles to develop and interests to pursue, but we're always training somebody new. That makes it hard for us, and I don't know how long we can continue training people the way we do and working with them as well as we do. We've done it ten years now.

JP: How does anyone take what they're doing, no matter what it is, even if it's drudgery, and make it a satisfying experience and fun for them?

DS: I do it by taking the time to do the job as well as it can possibly be done; I take the time to do it right. I use the best materials. In our "atmosphere improvement" here we look at how the furniture feels, how the walls look, how the floors are, and my wife and I collaborate in replacing old worn-out unsatisfactory equipment with something so complementary that it's satisfying to be living with. I love to get advice from other people about something and have it work perfectly. I love that. That contributes to my satisfaction as a human being.

Then, **if we're going to consider how I'm going to relate to other people for the day, the most important thing I do is "tune up" almost every morning after I get of bed. I take some time to creatively visualize how I'm going to relate to people during the day**. So the minute I come downstairs I'm sensitive, I'm intuitively awake to what I'm going to say. Am I going to say, "Grrrrr!" or am I going to say, "Wow, what a color combination for the kitchen today!"

JP: Is it real?

D S: Oh, yes; I always feel it. I don't falsify anything. Whatever I say, I feel. **I would just rather be complimenting people than criticizing them. I would rather be noticing what's good about them than bad. I would rather love them than hate them. I would rather be unconcerned about their work because they're doing it for themselves rather than for me**. So I try to relate as well as I possibly can to them each day. You have to be on good terms with everyone. I think that success in the business world depends on an ongoing, studied philosophy of life. I have to have a sound philosophical approach to my day's work.

JP: You seem to tie spirituality into your work.

DS: Spirituality is part of my life. I look for explanations of how things work in life, outside of obvious and surface explanations, and being engaged in this lifelong exploration, I have found that the more sensitive I am to the more spiritual side of our body politic [laughter] the more successful my life is. I'm speaking of success in terms of evolution. If I weren't consciously aware of my spiritual relationship with every other living thing, I would not continually evolve as a human being. Everything living has its own energy, no matter how small or how subtle that might be. So what I'm doing is exploring spirituality at least in part as an energy relationship between humans and the other living things in the environment.

JP: What's the purpose?

DS: My desire to relate better to other people is so life will be more satisfying, more interesting—for me. I find it uninteresting to wake up in the morning, go to work, get tired, find some entertainment, read a little bit, and go to sleep, and go through that same cycle over and over again for a corpusless corporation, a business without a body and brain and spirit that taps into mind. It's more important for me to know what humans are spiritually, mentally, and physically than to just coexist with them.

JP: What conclusions have you come to so far about what we're doing here?

DS: I think Earth is a classroom for Human Life 101, a survey course in all the things we can learn through all our senses. Life on Earth is best lived through the emotions and the senses. We who try to intellectualize our way through life are missing out on the best it has to offer. We have to enjoy all the things the senses provide to their fullest in order to be really living. So what I try to do is salvage some spiritual worth and some continued evolution from the extremely difficult, almost terrible circumstances we as unthinking humans have created as a working environment. Think of all the awful things we do to each other and to our environment every day that make life difficult and almost impossible, and from that I salvage what makes life interesting and worthwhile for me by taking a spiritual approach to it.

JP: What kinds of things have been helpful in shaping your attitude?

DS: I learned how to slow down and turn off my thinking brain and identify thoughts as simply that, as products of the brain. **The brain is essentially a thought-producing machine, and if you can identify thoughts as having no power other than what we give them, then they come up, blossom, and go away. If you observe them as a passing show, then you can slow down their process and gradually stop the brain from producing them**. Now that doesn't mean that's what you want to do all the time. We want to be thinking humans, because it's through our thoughts that we survive, but it is also difficult to be constantly mindful of how we're supposed to be operating in the ordinary world. But if I can realize when I'm being controlled by a thought pattern, the same thought cycling through over and over again, if I appreciate that the brain is cycling through these thoughts, then I can cut the cycle. I can say, stop the thinking, and assign my brain to doing something else more useful, certainly more cheerful than being absorbed with fear and guilt.

Mindfulness means paying attention to everything you do, everything you are at that moment, mindfulness means creating dualism, being an observer of everything. By being the observer, you can, in detachment, learn what you have been. The "Catch-22" is, while you're an observer, you're not entirely a participant, and you're missing out on what you could be right now or in the future. So you have to blend being observer and being a participant, and being mindful and being enthusiastic in life is difficult.

I also cleaned out my body, stopped eating red meat for a while, gave up caffeine, and I guess, sadly, I've given up alcohol for good, after 30 years of learning to appreciate the taste of a really fine ale [laughter]. So as a result of having a cleaner body, I'm more sensitive to the energies around me. So all we've been talking about, all this management-as-prevention strategy, is a consequence of how I am as an evolved human being, rather than what I'm thinking about or how I *should* act. I'm a better businessman now because I'm a better person to work with and be with. But I am constantly struggling with that. My basic degradation drags me down. I'm constantly foiling myself.

JP: You mean you're constantly being human?

DS: Yes. It's my humanity that keeps me from being perfect and I wouldn't have it any other way [laughter]. And if I fuck up, so be it!

6/89

29. Corporate Responsibility for Social Change

Once upon a time back in 1978, two real guys, Ben Cohen and Jerry Greenfield, decided to go into business together but could not afford the machinery to make bagels. So they scrounged up $5 for an ice cream correspondence course from Penn State University, set up shop in an old redecorated gas station, and the rest, as they say, is history. Not only did Ben & Jerry's Ice Cream become a phenomenon in the ice cream business, beating all odds of making it big in the established, competitive, corporate world, but the company has also blazed a remarkable trail in progressive corporate practice for social responsibility.

In 1985, Ben & Jerry's successfully launched a "What's the Doughboy afraid of?" "guerrilla campaign" to fight an attempt by Haagen-Dazs and its parent conglomerate, Pillsbury, to freeze Ben & Jerry's out of key New England markets. In 1988 Ben and Jerry were presented with the National Small Businesspersons of the Year award by President Reagan, and were honored by the Council on Economic Priorities with the Corporate Conscience Award for Corporate Giving, in recognition of the company's policy of donating 7½% of its pre-tax income to social service agencies and community causes through the Ben&Jerry's Foundation (which each year awarded grants totaling approximately $280,000 to numerous organizations). But that's not the half of it, nor is the 31,000 gallons of ice cream that the company has donated to food banks and neighborhood events and organizations each year, nor was their Vermont-only stock offering to reward their supporters, nor was their sponsorship of the Newport Folk Festival, or their Minister of Joy's (Jerry's) attempts to reduce worker stress and increase job enjoyment, and so on. What really makes Ben & Jerry's special (besides irresistible ice cream) is that they remained true to their values and beliefs after becoming multimillionaires, and they continue to put these beliefs into practice. Witness their 5:1 rule, whereby the highest paid employee can't earn more than five times the lowest paid employee or their "l % for peace" campaign that aims to have 1% of the military budget devoted to international peace efforts. And there's much more.

*But now the company has been sold; everyone hopes not sold out. Even before this, all was not completely rosy in Ben & Jerry's land. An interview on CBS-TV's "West 57th Street" in 1989 showed marked philosophical differences between Ben, the company president, and high-level managers of the corporation who complained that Ben was "obsessed with changing the world" at the expense of company profitability, to which Ben replied, "A company, a business, is supporting peace. Why is that so odd?" As I watched, I became so impressed with **Ben Cohen's** corporate social conscience that I knew his mind held great insights for the prevention field. One* *thing for sure is that no one who has criticized Ben or Ben & Jerry's for having "sold out" or not living up to their rhetoric has accomplished a tiny bit of what they have.*

JP: This first question has very little to do with prevention—or maybe it has everything to do with prevention. Why you? A lot of people must have bought that ice-cream-making kit from Penn State, and yet they're not famous guys now, but you are. What did you do differently?

BC: Oh, I don't know. Jerry and I just kinda' worked hard. We opened in Vermont, which is a small state, and it's easier to get recognition here, I think. Also the people in the state are real supportive of Vermont businesses. And we've got some great raw ingredients' to start with in Vermont. Mostly a lot of hard work, perseverance, and a willingness to take a lot of risks. We were never in it to make a lot of money, and because of that, we did things in kind of unusual ways, and those things have kinda' helped to make us stand out.

JP: How would you characterize those unusual ways?

BC: Well, we were making flavors that other ice cream companies never tried to make because they wouldn't really run on the machinery, so we had to do a lot of stuff by hand, and we had to alter a bunch of different machines. People seemed to respond to the unusual chunky flavors, cookies and candies and nuts all mashed up. And when we started off selling pints, I was the truck driver. We were always learning by doing, and we did all the jobs from the bottom up. And our approach to marketing our product is real "down home- and "off beat." We were looking to be honest, essentially, and that was a rare commodity. So while everyone else was trying to make believe that their ice cream was coming from foreign countries, we were saying "Ben & Jerry," those are our real names, these are our pictures, we make it in Vermont. We weren't trying to put on any airs, and I think people responded to that unique marketing.

JP: Now that you have made it, that puts you in a position to do what you want. I first got inspired to interview you after watching that "West 57th" interview with you guys. -

BC: Yeah, it's real interesting being in a position of leadership in a business where increasing profits is not your major motivation. I see this business as a very powerful tool. **A lot of people define business as an entity that produces a product or provides a service. I see a business as a combination of organized human energy and money, and to me that equals power. If you decide to use that power for improving the quality of life for people or for social change, there's a lot you can do with it because it's such a powerful force**. What's happened in our country, I think, is that people have used this power of business pretty much solely for increasing and maximizing profits, and **I think what we're learning and demonstrating here at Ben & Jerry's is that you can combine both missions, a profit mission and a social mission, and we can conduct our business in a way that, as we do things that are profitable for the company, they're also making a major contribution to the community**.

It's also important to point out that the major things a business can contribute are not money. **A lot of times, people define a socially responsible business as giving away money, donating money to this cause or that cause. I see that as a very, very small part of how business can contribute to the community**. Just this morning this thing crossed my desk that there's a new long-distance telephone service starting up whose purpose is to generate funds to support the homeless. So in terms of Ben & Jerry's, if we switch over to using that telephone service, at the same time as we're conducting our business and paying out whatever money we would normally pay to a telephone service, we're supporting the homeless.

We're doing the same thing with brownies. We need to buy brownies for our brownie ice cream sandwiches. We're just starting to use a new secondary supplier, a new Buddhist bakery in

New York City, and the work of this Buddhist community is to provide housing for the homeless, then teach them how to become bakers in the bakery so they can get out of that cycle of poverty. So again, by selecting this particular vendor (and paying the same price that we pay for brownies anyhow), in this case 100% of the profits from this vendor are going back to the community. And we do voter registration at our shops in Burlington, so anyone who comes into our shops any time day or night can get registered to vote, and those are all things that involve virtually no expenditure of money on our part, but those are, I would say, more powerful than the $250,000 to $300,000 a year that the Ben & Jerry's Foundation gives away.

Another example of using the communications power of business is the "1 % for peace" campaign, where we're using the space of our packages to communicate a political action that we believe needs to be taken in order to improve the quality of life for people. We got into "1% for peace" because we took a look at our foundation—we give away our $250-300,000 a year and we realize that it's not even a drop in the bucket in terms of meeting basic human needs for so many people. We asked ourselves why was this happening and we realized that 10% of the entire national budget (of $300 billion) is going to the military. We understand that **the only way we're ever going to get the resources and the money we need to improve the quality of life for people who aren't getting the bare necessities now is to start redirecting some money** out of the military budget and into human needs.

JP: I was both impressed and tickled when I saw your "1% for peace" idea, because when we were putting together the prevention legislation in Vermont in 1983 to become the first state to require state agencies to be involved with preventing the social problems they deal with all the time, we had built into that legislation a requirement of one-half of 1% of state agency budgets to be spent for prevention. But some legislators knocked that out early because they said it would never pass if there was a percentage attached.

BC: Yeah it's amazing that the society seems more than willing to spend money on the symptoms but never to spend money in dealing with the causes. And that's a change we recently made in the **Ben & Jerry's Foundation guidelines. The foundation has changed its guidelines to fund only those programs aimed at dealing with the root causes of the problems, as opposed to the symptoms**.

JP: And that's what prevention is all about, and that's why I'm writing this book, for precisely that reason.

BC: Then you're very much aligned with the foundation.

JP: Is all this just internal to you? A lot of people are simply content to make money and gain power and use it in other ways—

BC: Yeah, it's interesting, making lots and lots of money doesn't really do much for me. I personally don't want to be really wealthy in a world where people can't eat. I don't feel good about that. Of course, you take a look at my net worth, and I'm a very wealthy man. But I guess the way I see it is that I'm using that wealth to affect social change. I remember when I first realized that Ben & Jerry's had the potential of becoming as large as it is today, and of making as much money as it makes, and I felt very strongly that no one person, or no few people, deserve that wealth, and that was part of the motivation for the Vermont public stock offer, where it was a very deliberate effort to make the community the owners of the business, so that as the business prospered the community would automatically prosper, and we had a very low minimum buy, so for $126 you could become a shareholder in Ben & Jerry's, despite all the advice of the financial and legal experts that told us we were crazy to make stock available for that low price. And we deliberately underwrote it ourselves and advertised it to the man and woman on the street. We advertised it in the first section of the newspaper in with the supermarket and clothing ads so we were deliberately targeting the average person, as opposed to the preferred or usual method of financing, and the one that was recommended by virtually all our advisors: to use venture capitalism, essentially, take a few wealthy people and help them to become wealthier. Our philosophy behind our 5:1 salary ratio is the same.

JP: Did your advisors advise you against that, too?

BC: Definitely. And we were very strong in saying that **we don't believe there should be such a division of wealth in the country, and as far as our business is concerned, we don't believe that any one person, no matter what he does, is that much more valuable than another person**.

JP: You started out "doing things for the community" in a small way. As I recall, you put on community events, and I remember thinking at the time that this was great. It made me want to buy your ice cream. Why not buy ice cream from someone who does something nice for us? And I think that may have contributed to the interest in purchasing your product originally.

BC: It's interesting, I'm the same way. I like to support businesses that I feel are supporting me or my community. But, you know, we didn't do it for that reason. We did it because **we felt that business has a responsibility to give back to the community**. So we weren't doing it to get more customers and make more money. I used to speak at Rotary Clubs around Vermont, and at the end of the talk some guy would raise his hand and say, "All those things you're doing for the community, you're just really doing it to increase your profits, aren't you?" And I said, "No, we're doing it because we believe it's business's responsibility to give back to the community." Now when I go around and talk I say, "**Giving back to the community really does end up increasing your profits, because the community ends up supporting you.**" just because the phrase, "the good that you do comes back to you," is written in the Bible and not in some business textbook doesn't make it any less valid. I mean, we believe that kind of stuff when we're outside of the business world, "What goes around comes around," "karma," "As you sow so shall you reap"—all that stuff. Those are the things that all the major religions of the world are built on, I believe the Golden Rule—but somehow the prevailing wisdom is that when you are in the business environment where you spend most of your waking hours, you're supposed to throw those ideas out the window, because that's just church stuff [laughter].

JP: You've evolved from doing nice things for the local community to getting at the root causes, and serious social change. As you kept increasing your profitability did you then come to realize the power of the corporation?

BC: That's part of it. We're all members of lots of different communities. The first one is probably our families, and for a business it's our employees. Then we're members of our local community, our national community, and members of the world community. When Ben & Jerry's was just in a gas station, the only community we really dealt with was our own employees and Burlington. As the company has spread out so that now we're distributed pretty much nationally, we feel like our community starts to be the country, and then the neighboring community down the street happens to be the world. But it's also that as we've grown, as we've developed more resources more people, more money, organization, communications ability—we find that we're able to do more things that affect a wider community. In terms of a percentage of our resources that we've devoted to the community, it's stayed about the same—it's just that we've gotten a lot bigger.

When you look at contributions to the community from businesses, you have to look at it as a percentage of what resources are available to that entity. We look at big

corporations that donate money to community organizations and we say, "That's a really great community-minded organization,," but the reality is, in terms of a percentage of what they could be doing, many of them aren't doing doodly-squat. And the local small business down the street might not be doing as much on an absolute level, but as a percentage of what that business could actually be doing they might be up around 70%. That's the way we've got to start looking at corporate and business contributions.

JP: Would your critics say that you're doing things that just reflect your own political beliefs, and isn't Donald Trump's taking out a full-page ad in the New York Times to reinstate the death penalty the same kind of thing?

BC: It's a really interesting question, when you talk about values and business. Anita Roddick, who runs The Body Shop in England, which is the most socially responsible company in England, talks about the idea of a values-led company. And I really like that idea. But then the question becomes, whose values? Is it the values of the founder? The values of the board? The values of the upper-level managers? The values of the 300 people in this company? I mean, how the hell do 300 people ever agree on what their values are? I don't know. I don't really know the answers.

JP: From the 'West 57th' interview it appeared there was at least some tension between the two.

BC: Yup, there is.

JP: How do you reconcile that?

BC: I don't know. That's where we're at. That's what we're working at now, trying to figure that out.

JP: In that "West 57th" interview, the reporter said to you, "You're in the business of selling ice cream." And you started. to say, "I'm in the business of . . . " and she cut you off and went on to something else and you never finished the sentence. Would you like to finish it now?

BC: **Our company has a three-part mission statement. The first is a product mission: it talks about making the highest-quality product and providing the highest-quality service. The second is a social mission: it talks about the responsibility to the community and acting as a vehicle for social change and improving the quality of life for people. And the third is a profit mission: it talks about making a reasonable profit. So that's what we're in the business of. Those three things, and they're equal missions.** One is not above the other; they're exactly on a par. You think about a family and running a family, and you wouldn't say that family is in the business of making money, you wouldn't say it's in the business of repairing cars, if that's what the breadwinner in the family happens to do. The family is in the business of, I think, creating a good quality of life for themselves and their neighbors. And for this family, the way we make our bread is through ice cream, but I see us as more like that family on a block with a bunch of neighbors, and we happen to be a rich neighbor.

JP: In the interview you likened the growth of this company as going from "your baby" to being an "adolescent" now; that you would like your adolescent to live up to your own values because you believe, of course, that your values are the good ones [laughter], but sometimes they don't. So as a parent, or as a company president, how do you handle it?

BC: Well, you know, you try to talk with your adolescent as much as possible [laughter] and keep the lines of communication open [laughter], try and be constructive, try and applaud their successes and let them make mistakes and try to help them. I really feel like there's no way that Ben & Jerry's can become the business I would like to see it become without the people who work here also wanting that to happen, also believing that. So that's what I have to do—try and work with the people here as individuals. I guess the other way might be to impose my will in an authoritarian kind of way, and I might get a little done, but it's not going to be lasting.

JP: They're saying, "Slow down and let us catch up with you," and you're saying, "I want it to be weirder." There's a big gap between those two.

BC: Yeah, I keep wanting it to be weirder. Yeah, it's so much easier to come up with an idea than it is to actualize it. I think "being weird" means doing unusual things that aren't part of the business mainstream. Doing things in a different way. Being able to look at a situation without any preconceived notions and come up with an answer to it that will many times not be the traditional answer or the traditional solution used for that problem.

JP: Can you characterize where you're ultimately heading? What would make you the happiest in where you would like this company to go?

BC: **I'd like to see Ben & Jerry's be at the cutting edge of finding innovative ways for business to support people. I'd like to see Ben & Jerry's act as a force for social change in trying to help deal with some of the root causes of poverty and starvation and disease and illiteracy**. I do believe that dealing with those problems can be integrated with the day-to-day profit-making business of the company. There's a guy named Bill Norris, who was the head of this company called Control Data, a major corporation, espousing that belief that business is successful by meeting the needs of the society, and if you see society as a lot of social needs, then a business that comes up with a way of meeting those needs is going to be very successful. He started a lot of for-profit undertakings dealing with the social problems I mentioned earlier.

I think it's interesting that people who are humanistically-oriented, who really care about people, who have that as their big focus, don't usually go into business, because they don't see business as a real caring institution. So they end up in nonprofit human services organizations. That's where they're able to do something along those lines, and so they're not in the business community moving and influencing the business community in that direction. So I think the two—for-profit businesses and nonprofit social service organizations—need to start to merge, because social service organizations need to become more businesslike and businesses need to become more social service oriented.

JP: How can social service organizations be more businesslike?

BC: I think there needs to be more accountability in those organizations and more efficient organizational structures. They could probably learn something about management techniques from the business sector. And they could certainly learn a whole lot from business about financing. **I believe it's very possible for social service agencies to be financially self-sufficient, essentially by having a business arm, a profit-making arm, so they wouldn't have to be dependent on contributions and grants and all that kind of stuff**. There are so many businesses around where the person that owns them isn't running them. Some investor has decided he wants to be in this business, and he hires a manager, and the manager runs the business, and the investor makes money. That may be a little oversimplified but, essentially, nonprofits could be the same way. They could be that owner, that investor making that money…

JP: Are you as interested in domestic issues, root causes of domestic problems, as you are in, say, world peace?

BC: I don't know, there's so many things you can be interested in. The challenge for me is to try to be interested in less [laughter].

JP: Is "1% for peace" a pie-in-the-sky idea, or do you really think it can make a difference?

BC: I really do think it can make a difference. I think it's what has to happen. People look at "1% for peace" and they'll say, "Oh that's pie-in-the-sky. It's a good idea but it's never gonna happen; they're never gonna pass that law." But yet people are very free to say, "I'm for peace" and "The government should be doing this; the government shouldn't be doing that." They'll sing songs of peace and put peace bumper stickers on their cars, but in order to actualize any of the things people are talking about, it's got to end up being legislation. So **that's what "1% for peace" is: the legislation that says let's start devoting a very small percentage of our resources toward trying to make friends amongst people instead of trying to make enemies**.

JP: Do you have any advice for the other businesspeople of the world?

BC: I think the traditional wisdom out there is that you cannot retain your values and have a profitable business at the same time. I think what people traditionally do is suspend their values when they go to work and then when they go home they say, I'm going to contribute something here or volunteer some time there. But in the business environment when they could be the most powerful, they suspend those values. What we've learned is, you don't have to do that to have a financially successful business. **You can integrate your values within the fabric of your business**.

JP: Anything else you want to say?

BC: No, I think I've said a lot, don't you? [laughter]

5/89

329

30. Prevention as Social Change

What happens to a dream deferred?
Does it dry up
Like a raisin in the sun?
Or fester like a sore—
And then run?
Does it stink like rotten meat?
Or crust and sugar over
Like a syrupy sweet?

Maybe it just sags
Like a heavy load.

Or does it explode?

(Langston Hughes, 1951)

Despite all our efforts to affect people's lives in healthy ways, to strengthen their self-perceptions, build their skills, provide supports and promote awareness of critical issues, we must face the fact that an overabundance of the problems we seek to prevent come from the poor, high-stress areas of our country. Many of these areas are in large inner cities, some where social isolation abounds, or where people have been torn away from their rich cultures. In areas where there is a staggering sense of hopelessness, and where residents are largely cut off from many of the social advantages other citizens have ready access to, the most significant number of problems lie, including drug abuse, crime, rape, AIDS, school failure and dropping out. As preventers—in fact, as United States citizens—we must ask ourselves why certain social problems are specific to certain areas, then attack the conditions that result in these problems.

It is so easy to "blame the victims," to point to the rare exceptions and say that anyone can "make it out" if they want to. Even if it were true, it would be irrelevant, for we are a nation replete with social problems, suffering because of them, emptying our pocketbooks in an attempt to pick up the pieces through the inordinate costs of our Welfare and Medicaid systems, through crime and our legal and prison systems, and through Special Education. In addition, we've made the horrifying discovery that a decreasing percentage of young people are entering the work force adequately prepared to help us compete economically with other nations. The real relevant question is, "What can be done to change this destructive course?"

This is the most difficult task we face in prevention work. It troubles me for the tiny field of prevention to have to attempt to change the conditions that lead to social problems, although I know that this is where a major focus must lie. So much can and should be done at other levels. I don't want the few of us involved in prevention to become completely overwhelmed and frustrated because we can never do enough.

Therein lies the problem. Social change to eradicate poverty is a bigger job than what preventers and preventionists can accomplish alone. These answers lie in political and economic solutions, in massive national and state policy changes and shifts in priorities. Who are we in the prevention field to try to set such enormous wheels in motion? But if we do not do it, who will?

What Do We Want as a Nation?

The United States of America must decide what it wants to be as a nation.

When we consider conditions in places like China, wherever freedom is denied, we are grateful to be living here. But we cannot allow ourselves to become complacent, because this country is far from perfect. Do we want to continually throw increasing amounts of money to remediate social problems?

Where do we begin? People differ so much in their political views and proposed solutions. Is there any common ground? I believe there is. Most people can usually agree on a desired "end" result. Who would not agree that child and sexual abuse should be eliminated, that the spread of AIDS must be stopped, that crime must be reduced, or that drug and alcohol abuse should not continue to cripple our young? Where people usually disagree is in proposed solutions and methods. Is there any common ground between those who believe increasing punishment is the only way to stop crime, and those who think that changing the socio-cultural environment is the only way? Is there any way to join in working out solutions together?

To complicate matters, many people don't appear to care. Others resist making changes because they believe they could lose what they have. The "working class"—the backbone of this country—may fear that the little they have will be threatened by increased rights and opportunity for those more financially disadvantaged than themselves. The wealthy might fear a more equitable distribution of that wealth. Those who wield power might fear what would happen if the 50% of the population who do not currently vote suddenly began to. These are difficult questions. What would make it worth their while to change poverty-breeding conditions?

So long as people believe that the problem resides only in inner-city ghettos, it doesn't feel close enough to them to matter. But social problems affect us all. Even if we have no compassion, even if we find reasons not to care, we all pay for the results of poverty. Contrary to what many people believe, 66% of the poor in the United States are White, and only 43% of the poor come from central cities (in Huey, 1989).

Until we figure out what will make people care, this country is diminished. So much talent is going to waste; so much money—our tax money—is going to waste. The experiences of people living in African American, Hispanic, Native and other poor communities is not moving enough to people who are not immediately affected. Perhaps if it happened next door, it would be a different story. Perhaps if their own children were suffering, they would rise up in protest.

Something is overtaking this nation so gradually, so insidiously, that we can't readily see how it eats away at us. One day it could overtake us, just as neglecting our garbage or neglecting the global warming can—unless we take action. Too many continue to ignore the condition of our people in poverty, especially in this time of economic prosperity. Economic prosperity and the focus on prevention by the Clinton Administration has helped, but the gap still widens between rich and poor.

Even if one believes that individuals decide for themselves whether to make their way out of poverty, what about their children? They didn't choose the situation into which they were born.

This is not "bleeding heart" thinking. We're talking about our future financial well-being. Having to pay ever-increasing amounts of money to endlessly patch up the problems caused by poverty doesn't make good economic sense. Social change is the pragmatic solution.

Social Change at the Micro (Community) Level

At the community level, the most basic form of social change takes place when individual institutions are changed.

James Comer's *Yale-New Haven Primary Prevention Project* is one example. The project's prime purpose is to stop the cycle of educational failure for "at-risk" youth. When the program began in 1968, its focus was the institutional change of two of the lowest-achieving elementary schools in New Haven, Connecticut—schools that were 99% Black and almost all poor. In a collaborative effort between the Yale Child Center and the school system, a School Development Program Model was established that focused on trying to prevent the underlying problems.

A collaborative mental health team provided school staff with information about child development and behavior. The team also trained school staff members to help students compensate for underdevelopment in social-interactive, psycho-emotional, moral, speech and language, and intellectual-cognitive-academic areas. Parents of students were also enlisted to support the overall work of the school in a climate of mutual respect. Children thus received the message that the expectations of home and school were basically the same.

A comprehensive school plan focused on improving the school's environment and providing adequate focus on academics. The program was designed to teach young people how to use basic social skills in four areas: "business and economics," "health and nutrition," "politics and government," and "spiritual and leisure time." Through simulated and real activities in these areas, students experienced the relevance of basic skills to mainstream work and societal expectations. This served to increase their interest in basic academic work and improved their social interaction skills.

A ten-year follow up study was conducted. Results were:

- highly significant academic gains (the schools went from the lowest achievement, the worst attendance, and the worst behavior records to ranking third and fifth in fourth-grade test scores, with superior attendance)
- "highly significant social gains"
- decreased need for remedial services in school

The project spread to other elementary schools in New Haven.

In another school system, Columbia Park Elementary School in Landover, Maryland, only 50% of the students had been performing at or above grade level and 30 students a year were being suspended. After Comer's principles were adopted, 95% of students performed at or above grade level, and suspensions dropped to two per year (ETV, 1990).

This model recognized the historical conditions that created family and social problems, resulting in children who were underdeveloped by the time they entered school. It encouraged groups to come together in a way that allowed everyone to support the development of students. It provided an opportunity for students from low-income backgrounds to establish relationships with employers, and to learn that mutual respect and responsibility must be promoted—they cannot be assumed (Comer, 1989).

Other impressive feats can be accomplished by local residents like Bertha Gilke or Irene Johnson who organized residents to take over housing projects like Cabrini Green. Accomplishments like these create a sense of pride in ownership and in the neighborhood and drive out drug dealers. Entire neighborhoods can turn themselves around, building by building, block by block. As Irene Johnson says, "Given the same opportunity that I was given, that is, training and support, anyone can do it." Well, maybe not everyone. Perhaps part of their success is due to the forcefulness of their personalities, but certainly many, many others could be trained and supported to accomplish similar feats (CBS, 1989; 1990).

The same can be said of George McDonald and Muhammad Rashid, who offered the homeless of New York City an opportunity to renovate city apartments and to get themselves and their families out of welfare hotels, in exchange for a guaranteed apartment and a full-time job (after a period of time).

This is social change at its most basic, community level. It changes the way important institutions act and interact to achieve a common purpose. With its success it spreads, enveloping other institutions along the way.

The Cycle of Poverty

We can learn much about the need and implications for social change from Comer's (1989) analysis of the three major causes of economic poverty:

1. the absence of employment opportunities
2. the presence of factors that lead to attitudes, values or ways that inhibit employment, employment seeking and job retention
3. limited individual development and functioning needed for success in the modern job market, including social and interpersonal behavior patterns, psycho-emotional and moral attitudes, speech and language skills, thinking and school learning abilities, and others.

When enough families are able to earn a living, meet basic needs, and function reasonably well, then social networks and communities usually constitute wholesome environments in which adequate child growth and development are the norm. Good functioning is most likely when authority figures within such networks are able to influence most people to live by socially desirable standards. This is possible because constructive belief systems—often grounded in religion, but sometimes based on a family, community or national ethos—positively influence the behavior of families involved. But, although minimal income is not an absolute deterrent, desirable family functioning is nonetheless more difficult to sustain without a reasonable threshold level of economic opportunity (p. 110).

Even families with adequate income and education feel stressed by the complexities of...and need help in supporting the development of their children. Despite this need, we have an education system in which a large number of professionals, if not a majority, have not had adequate training in applied child development, and cannot establish and manage schools that support...students... to function adequately...in a competitive, democratic, open, society (p. 113).

When entire neighborhoods are poor and isolated from the mainstream, destructive conditions emerge and a vicious cycle begins. Heads of households who can't find work often lose respect for and confidence in themselves. Families fall apart, yet people still have the same basic needs. Sometimes they try to fulfill those needs by having children, even though they can't provide for them; having them is what seems to provide a sense of personal adequacy and self-fulfillment. Sometimes they try to fulfill their needs through crime. But in areas that outsiders avoid, economic development is less likely to occur, and where there is no economic development, people find other ways to make money. An underground of drug dealing, stolen property trade, prostitution, and gang membership develops to support the need for money and status. Welfare dependency becomes a necessity, particularly for teenage and single mothers. A sense of helplessness emerges because people believe they can't achieve what society says is valued. When people feel trapped they don't act as they normally would. Anger and resentment builds. Even if good education represents a way out, few schools seem to inspire students, particularly in the inner-city. Furthermore, how does a caring parent, who has had no substantial education, provide his or her children with experiences to help them become socially and academically competent in the classroom? When generation after generation of children fail, a so-called "underclass" is created by destructive social and economic circumstances, and reinforced by inappropriate public policies and practices (Comer, 1989).

Lisbeth Schorr (1989) further characterizes the cycle:

Just as high school graduates who are competent and willing to work can't support a family if there are no jobs at a decent wage, so expanded economic opportunities cannot be seized by young people whose health has been neglected, whose education has failed to equip them with the skills they need, and whose early lives have left them without the capacity to persevere and without hope (p. 150).

A few escape poverty under even the most adverse circumstances, but this is not the norm. These are usually people who have somehow been treated in ways that where healthy self-perceptions had been built or who had supports along the way or who have some internal thinking that yields hope and the belief that they can make it out. When many people from a minority population eventually make it out, the social problems of that group substantially decrease. These groups do not create these problems for themselves; the conditions inherent in the way this society works do; therefore this society also has a responsibility to do something about it.

Breaking the Cycle

What, then, needs to be in place to break the cycle?

Besides ensuring that every level of the community prevention pyramid is in place, also needed are:

335

1. jobs—more jobs, jobs that pay better, expanded job training
2. decent housing
3. a welfare system that acts as a safety net and provides adequate income support during those necessary times, while building independence and helping more recipients to become productively employed
4. adequate health opportunities
5. restructuring the human service delivery system toward a family-based approach that can catch family problems early and help families successfully through the serious problems they face

Programs like *Homebuilders* in Tacoma, Washington, for example, deal with families whose children are in danger of being removed from the home. With the hardest-to-reach families, Homebuilders begins by helping to solve the family's immediate crises, by first making friends and by helping to take care of the family's basic needs so they can establish trust and begin to build more lasting skills. The workers have small, manageable caseloads, allowing them adequate time for the most difficult families whose children would continue to cause all kinds of problems. The cost of this program in 1985 averaged $2600 per family served, quite modest compared to dollars spent on out-of-home placements. Homebuilders calculates a return of $5-6 for every dollar invested (in Schorr, 1989). Lisa Kaplan (1986) also offers an excellent model for work with "multi-problem families."

> The more longstanding the neglect, deprivation and failure, the more difficult and costly the remedies. Help early in the cycle is more effective—failure, and despair don't have as firm a grip, and life trajectories are more readily altered (Schorr, p. 151).

One example of how the business community can interact with the community at large to promote preventive social change is an effort that took place in Miami, Florida, after the Liberty City riot of 1980. After pragmatically recognizing that "no one wants to vacation in a war zone," the business community, led by James K. Batten, chief executive of Knight-Ridder, developed the Tacolcy Economic Development Corporation with the help of the Ford Foundation-backed Local Initiatives Support Program (LISP). The effort economically revitalized the area. First they found a highly qualified area resident to manage the program (Otis Pitts). They then found financing to rebuild a looted supermarket at a pivotal corner, and added a shopping center "to provide quality goods and services at competitive prices in a safe and decent environment." The subcontractors and workers hired to complete the work were mostly Black. The organization also added a beautiful, well-maintained and secure apartment complex for low-income tenants. Facades along the streets of Liberty City were refurbished and expanded to aid the nearby Hispanic community. The point was to keep upwardly mobile people from leaving the area, and to draw others back into the community. McDonald's and other businesses have subsequently moved into the area, and Liberty City appears to be recovering economically, providing jobs and a new sense of pride for many community members (Huey, 1989).

LISP has raised more than $200 million from more than 500 corporations and foundations and leveraged over $1 billion of direct investment in more than 500 community development corporations across the country. They are a model of business investment in the fight against poverty (Huey, 1989).

Interventions That Work for Low-Income Populations

Schorr (1989) analyzed many successful programs focused on children and families who live in areas of concentrated poverty and disadvantage to identify common elements that contribute to their success:

♦ A broad spectrum of comprehensive services that meet many client needs: social and emotional support to families, help with food, housing, income, employment, advice on parenting, or anything that seems to the family to be an insurmountable obstacle. Continuity in relationships with services is important. These programs operate at a higher level of intensity than traditional programs.

♦ The child is seen in the context of family, and family in the context of its surroundings.

♦ Program staff are perceived by recipients as people they can trust and respect, and who care about them; staff are highly skilled and well-trained.

♦ Flexible staff and program structures: Program content is adapted to meet the distinctive needs of the people being served. Professional staff are able to redefine roles and escape from the typical bureaucratic constraints. They deliver services where they are needed—in peoples' homes and communities. (Examples: Health care adequate for monitoring the pregnancy of a healthy middle class woman may totally bypass the most pressing needs of an undernourished, depressed, drug-using pregnant teenager. The parent-support component of a preschool program is often essential for high-risk families.)

Schorr speaks of a "fundamental contradiction between the needs of these children and families and the traditional requirements of professionalism and bureaucracy." People who work in the prevention field have known this for years. Others apparently do not, as evidenced by most state systems of human service delivery. This explains why effective programs for these populations are much more rare. Schorr says there is no correlation between the ability of a program to survive and how successful it is in improving outcomes for families at risk. As a result, Schorr calls for a complete overhaul of policy and a change in the administrative context in which programs for disadvantaged families and children are expected to operate.

I have long been troubled about what I call the "add-on mentality" of human services; that is, seeing every new, progressive idea that comes along as adding to everyone's costs and workload and therefore not affordable. What we need is a complete revision of the entire system, with the prevention-intervention end of the spectrum included as an integral part.

The new system must be adequately funded and provided with intensive technical assistance based on effective practices. Society must begin to accord a higher value to occupations that care for the social needs of disadvantaged children and their families. All people who work with these children—school staff, for example—must be trained in encountering all the difficulties they face.

A close examination of the long-term successes achieved by programs and institutions serving high-risk populations clearly demonstrates that children in the greatest danger of later damage need interventions that are more intensive, more comprehensive and often more costly than those needed by families living in less disadvantaged circumstances (Schorr, p. 165).

337

The highest priority in the next decade's efforts to break the cycle of disadvantage and dependence must be to make intensive, high-quality services available early in the life cycles of children who live in areas where the risks to healthy development are concentrated. New funds and sweeping changes are needed in legislation, in procedures for allocating resources, in bureaucracies, and among professionals.

The Choice Is Ours

The young people in these circumstances will become the unemployable, and the parents unable to form stable families of their own. Many will join the ranks of the hungry and the homeless. Surrounded by despair, neglect, and violence, these young people are likely to lack any vision of the future which would inspire present sacrifice. Disconnected from the mainstream of American society, unable to make the transition to productive adulthood, they will get stuck at the very bottom of American society and become part of a growing underclass.

We all pay to support the unproductive and incarcerate the violent. We are all economically weakened by lost productivity. We all live with the fear of crime in our homes and on the streets. We are all diminished when large numbers of parents are incapable of nurturing their dependent young. We have an enormous stake in undoing the bonds that keep children in misery today, and threaten to keep their children even more permanently excluded from America's mainstream (Schorr, 1989, p. 167).

Between 1973 and 1984...[a]s economic opportunity shrank for the less skilled...the many blacks who were in a position to take advantage of expanded opportunities to obtain higher education and enter the professions, business, or skilled trades, moved up and out with devastating effects on the inner-city areas they left behind. Professor William Julius Wilson calls it "one of the most important social transformations in recent U.S. history." Although there are still plenty of people who work very hard, there is no longer the critical mass of stable, achievement-oriented families that once provided neighborhood cohesion, sanctions against aberrant behavior, support for churches and other basic community institutions. Missing are the essential practical connections to mainstream society, the informal ties to the world of work that provide models of conventional roles and behavior that could alert youngsters to job openings and help them obtain employment. In American inner cities today there are too few neighbors whose lives demonstrate that education is meaningful, that steady employment is a viable alternative to welfare and illegal pursuits, and that a stable family is an aspect of normalcy. The vacuum is being filled, says Yale University psychiatrist James Comer, by drug pushers, pimps and prostitutes. They're often the only successful people that the kids see (p. 168).

These young people are surrounded by others like themselves who are poor, alienated, unmarried, unemployed. Single parenting isn't necessarily bad, but when single parenting is a common occurrence and a whole neighborhood of children is growing up without a consistent male presence or a steady income, those children are deeply affected. And when important needs are left unfulfilled, children wind up looking for fulfillment out on the street.

Why Do Many Inner-City Youths React as They Do?

The attitude among many young dope dealers and gang members, when confronted with the inordinate number of killings around them, is,, "Hey, if you're gonna get killed, you're gonna get killed. We're all gonna die sometime." They've lost all hope of anything better. Their economic choice is often 1) to make relatively easy (if dangerous) big money dealing drugs, or 2) to spend many hours sweating it out as a fast food chain employee for close to minimum and poverty wage. But who cares about them?—especially in their eyes. They just get written off.

Yet some of the greatest problems we experience arise from the behavior of young people in low-income, inner-city communities. People are legitimately concerned, but behavior problems among inner-city young people will be difficult to prevent if care is not taken to understand why they act as they do.

Could it be that the behaviors of inner-city, low-income youth interfere with middle-class values precisely because these children are trying to live up to the values of their own culture? I was struck by this in 1968 when, on an independent study from Clark University, I spent six weeks living at the Boys Club of New York on the Lower East Side, studying a 12-year-old boy labeled a "potential juvenile delinquent." My project was to try to figure out what motivated his behavior. I was inspired because Mike Callahan (as I called him in my report) had been my favorite kid when I served as "village leader" at a Boys Club camp for inner-city kids from Harlem and the Lower East Side. After camp ended, I was amazed and appalled to learn that this apparently happy-go-lucky, sharp, tough, friendly, delightful kid had been labeled a "potential delinquent." I was thankful no one tipped me off to this earlier, but I wondered how we could have formed such different impressions.

My first visit to Mike's top-floor apartment in "the projects" showed me how much I didn't know. For one thing, I learned he had an alcoholic father who, after having given me permission to conduct interviews and write a report, eventually tried to grab my "confidential report" out of my hands in a drunken rage. Mike's mother was obese and ineffectual. This boy desperately wanted to respect both of his parents but couldn't because they thoroughly embarrassed him.

What was he to do with these feelings? Mike was intelligent, but he found school terribly boring and thought most of the teachers were either "fools" or "mean." As a consequence, he spent most of his time being truant. The only place he had left to go was the streets, with his friends, many of whom faced similar difficulties at home and school. I observed that they spent most of their time looking for excitement and action.

Mike told me about the kinds of games they played—games such as "chicken," where they would ride the tops of the projects' elevators and see who could be the last one to jump off before getting crushed to death. Then there were mild games like "'knucks"—a card game where the winner takes the full deck and tries to knock the skin off the loser's knuckles or gives the loser a "sandwich" by putting his hand in the middle of the deck and jumping on the cards, sometimes from great heights. These are nothing compared to the "wilding" and "crack" use of today, but the principles are the same.

I asked him what he thought made the kids around there get into trouble.

MC: The older kids are a bad influence. There's good kids around here, you know. They follow one bad apple and they all become bad kids.

Excitement was what he and his friends lived for, and he needed the freedom to fulfill those urges, no matter what form it took, from building fires in salt mines to sending cops on dead calls. If he needed money, that was all that mattered at the moment. If he couldn't get it from his folks, he would whine and sulk at home, but on the streets he would sometimes steal if it was important enough to him. He found it difficult to empathize with his victims, although he did empathize when it came to somebody else's victims. He didn't make the connection—didn't want to even think about it.

> JP: Suppose you were walking along and you saw something you really wanted just lying there. What would you do?
> MC: I would look around and then yell, and then I wouldn't take it because no one would be around. You see, there has to be a catch. But it still wouldn't be right.
> JP: How do you feel about people who are really honest?
> MC: I think they might be afraid to do it.
> JP: Do you think the rules you broke were good rules or bad rules?
> MC: Good rules. There should be laws. Without them there'd be murderers and cutthroats.

Mike did have internal morals. To him there was a big difference between toughness and cruelty. Cruelty was unacceptable, unless Mike was participating in cruelty himself. Most often it was directed toward the weakest link available.

The people he respected most were those he considered to be the toughest. This could mean the toughest physically, the most skilled, the toughest mentally, people who had strong mental images of themselves, or who had a reputation. To Mike, "toughness" meant being in control of the situation. Mike thought highly of those who could control him, and there weren't many who could. He would test people continually to be sure they were worthy of his respect and could be trusted to come through for him. He quickly formed value judgments about a person's relative toughness.

When I asked him why he never gave me any trouble at camp, he said:

> MC: Because I knew you could think of quick punishments, and when I escaped from the infirmary [by crawling out a window so he could go on an overnight camping trip], I thought you'd be real mad, and you laughed.

What he looked for most in a friend was a companion with whom he could share his adventures, and "someone who knows enough to stay out of trouble, who knows when to fool around and when not to, who's fun to be with but knows when to stop." Mike's family said that he never knew when to stop. Virtually everyone I interviewed told me that he got into the most trouble when he was with his group of friends. Many people told me that much of what Mike was accused of was because of his reputation.

I know Mike was a good kid; I spent part of a summer with him. He was just a normal, healthy kid from that part of the city. Walter B. Miller (1958) had pegged it ten years earlier. The reason "delinquents" from the "lower class" behaved as they did was because their culture held certain values, and they were simply trying to live up to those values; namely:

- *trouble:* a person's ability to get in or stay out of trouble at will (which varies according to the individual and circumstances)

- *toughness:* strength, skill, bravery, masculinity (Miller believed this stemmed from the usual lack of a male figure in these families)
- *smartness:* the ability to outfox or con others
- *excitement or thrills:* doing daring things, including drugs, alcohol, sex, adventure, gambling, stealing ("wilding," even killing, these days)
- *fate or luck:* feeling subjected to a set of forces over which they have little control

Today, "drugs" are the number one reason for inner-city crime, but before drugs took over, Miller believed that most lower-class crime was committed to satisfy the values and standards of behavior of that culture, by whatever means available. This still holds today. Those who can't "make it" in that world are considered "chumps," or whatever word is "in" today. Their motivations for behavior are based, not on what middle-class culture believes is acceptable, but by what their peer group on the streets considers to be right. The goal is to secure the esteem and acceptance of one's peers by conducting oneself in a manner acceptable to that group. This behavior might be all a front, concealing considerable fear and caution (which is why street kids often choose easy targets for their victims), but the fact is, if they're not accepted on the streets, they've got nothing, and they might well be the victims. They would be fools to act otherwise. This is where most of their perceptions of belonging, importance, and capability and power come from.

It is practically impossible to live the conflicting standards of two diametrically opposed cultures at the same time. Miller says, what appears to be short-run hedonism is actually rational balancing of the near certainty of immediate loss of status in the peer group, compared to the remote chance of punishment by society.

> JP: Suppose your friends wanted to steal some money and you were slightly opposed to it. Would you go along with it or not?
> MC: I would go, but I wouldn't stay nearby.

After hanging around these streets for a while (I remember feeling a little guilty at the time that I could go back to my middle-class, protected life, but guilt doesn't do anyone any good), I came away with a personal theory: Perhaps the kids who could not succeed in living up to these "lower class" standards, the deviants of their society, were the ones who turned to "middle-class" standards and became defined as "good kids."

A logical answer for prevention would appear to be to help these kids find excitement legitimately–to help them be tough and smart legitimately.

Cultural Aspects of Prevention

Prevention will not have the desired impact—particularly in areas of high poverty, crime, drug abuse and the like—unless we recognize that a homogeneous approach, based largely on White Anglo-European values, will be unable to reach many of the people we seek to impact. How do we connect with people who have been traditionally hard to reach through standard programs?

People are already innately connected to something—to their own pride as a people. We are rooted in our own cultures, which lie deep within us. It is part of our basic need "to belong."

Many of us can find meaning and purpose in our lives through an appreciation of from whence we sprung.

According to Michael Bopp (1987), "culture" is a shared structuring of reality and all that flows from it—ways of knowing, art, technology, institutions, history, a vision of the future—that constitutes a people's unique and all-embracing relationship with the universe. These are what we hold in common with certain others with whom we share a set of experiences.

If we live in an area replete with unemployment, underemployment, low educational achievement, powerlessness, hopelessness, high crime, drug abuse, and if we also feel cut off from our cultural heritage, our roots, we swim helplessly within that tide. With a cultural connection, however, we may be able to better understand—even overcome—our present dilemma. People develop a sense of pride from an understanding of where they came from, what brought them to where they are, and what factors created their type of community. Asking questions like, "Was there a time when we were different?" "Have we been involved in an ongoing struggle for human justice?" "Are there others like ourselves that we can look up to?" can give a group of people a fresh perspective. It helps to feel connected to something significant that is greater than ourselves (adapted from Bell, 1990).

Yet, in many cases, that connection has virtually disappeared. Ancient traditions that have held people together for centuries, passed from one generation to the next are, for many, lost. For those whose cultural perspective has been wiped out, dependencies of any kind might serve as a numbing substitute to ease the pain.

This has happened, for example, in many small Native Alaskan villages where no positive role models can be found—everyone is alcoholic—and this is what's now being passed from generation to generation. Here, babies are continually being born with Fetal Alcohol Syndrome and young people commit suicide with frightening frequency. In the name of prevention, breaking this cycle is one of the most difficult jobs imaginable.

There is an answer. It is not easy. It is not quick. Perhaps one of the only ways to break into this cycle of destruction and despair is for a culture to reclaim its people. Little else might have a strong enough pull. Under any circumstances it is a difficult task, but it can start with one brave warrior.

Long ago, there was a custom among the Canadian Plains Indians to send out a warrior brave before a battle. Out before his enemy, he would draw a circle in the earth around him. He would then tie himself to one end of a stake and drive the other end into the earth. By staking himself down to the ground, he was proclaiming that here was where he would take his stand. Here was where he would confront his enemy.

The enemy would approach the staked-down man, look him over, size him up, look him in the eye. They would prod and poke at him, charge at him, and threaten him, and if the warrior showed any fear, they would kill him. But if he showed no fear in his eyes—if he was strong and steadfast—they would go back to their chief and tell him that their enemy was for real.

Now the enemies are alcohol and despair, and they are killing the Native people. In Alaska, where the alcohol problem is probably greater among Native Alaskan tribes than anywhere in the country, perhaps in the world—a few native warriors like David West, Doug Moodig, and David Sam decided to take a stand. They formed a small circle of warriors, most recovering alcoholics, and declared that they are staking themselves down against the enemy, alcohol. They declared a fight to the death. This small circle of warriors went into Native Alaskan villages, one by one and, with much Native Indian ceremony, invited anyone into their circle who wished to join. The circle gradually grew. Native warriors, a few at a time, began to get sober, expanded the circle, and thereby expanded the influence.

Without that connection to culture, ceremony, and tradition—to a rekindling of the spirit that has been lying dormant but is so deeply ingrained in the soul that, once touched, can have a hold little else is capable of, breaking this cycle would be virtually impossible.

This story and custom was brought to the Native Alaskans by consultant Michael Bopp, who learned it from the Canadian Plains Indians with whom he works. Together, in western Alberta, they are achieving great success in mobilizing people into action. This is how the movement spreads.

And therein lies the message for prevention. If we truly want to reach people from other cultures, White middle-class America can't expect to achieve results with a half-hearted attempt to address and respond to those cultures. Whether they be Native people, African Americans, Hispanic Americans, Asian Americans, Pacific Islanders, or whomever, they each have their own unique, diverse cultural identity. In many places within this country, that culture has been torn away, or has been lost. Without a concerted effort to help build it back, through whatever prevention effort is planned with that community, there will be little hope of preventing problems, for there will be little reason for anyone to move beyond their own plight.

Without it, as Jane Middleton-Moz (1989) says, some people may even develop "cultural self-hate." If some people from other cultures have difficulty understanding the ways of the larger society, they may come to believe there is something wrong with them; that they somehow aren't capable of understanding and fitting in. Some even attempt to deny and repress their cultural roots in hopes that it will help them better assimilate. The trouble is, it doesn't often work.

In the film, *Eye of the Storm,* the controversial 1969 classroom experiment is depicted where the students with blue eyes were told they were superior to those with brown eyes, and the brown-eyed students were told they were inferior. Soon the brown-eyed kids were exhibiting characteristics often displayed by oppressed people; their grades dropped, their behavior worsened. After a time, the experimenter said he'd made a terrible mistake: It was, in fact, the blue-eyed kids who were inferior, and the brown-eyed who were superior, and before long the blue-eyed kids were displaying the oppressed symptoms, decreased learning and worsened behaviors. A "Frontline" ETV show called "A Class Divided" speaks to the participants many years later.

Cultural Diversity

Unfortunately, much prevention programming has been conducted without taking into account the diversity of different cultures. Ed Sanchez (1990) reminds us that our systems, including our government, have functioned to unite a society full of differences under the Constitution (except for Native people and, initially, African Americans), but mostly favoring those having European ancestry. In its attempt to unify, many diverse cultural groups lost their unique identities for the sake of creating a homogeneous society. Cultural diversity has been considered a secondary issue. This attitude has spilled over into most prevention programming, which has lacked the insight and relevance to attract the commitment and participation of various cultures. In the Black community, for example, as Darnell Bell (1990) points out, tactics developed by others, not founded in Africanism, not written from the African American

343

perspective, do not address the peculiarities of the Black experience and will only have marginal success.

Culturally responsive programs build upon the values held dear by the culture they address. In African American cultures, cultural programs could be designed to build from the inherent values of mutual aid, adaptability, extended family, and interdependence, to name but a few. In Hispanic cultures, programs can build upon the importance of family, sincerity, generosity, responsibility, cooperation, and harmony. Each culture has important, innate values and beliefs it holds dear, and which can serve as its springboard (Sanchez, 1990).

The real lesson is in recognizing the importance of and respecting the diversity of different cultures—using it as a guide for programming and ensuring sensitivity to what makes a people unique and special. Many cultural factors need to be taken into account, among them: values, communication styles and patterns, information flow of that cultural system, history, rules and procedures, formal and informal relationship patterns, general feelings and expectations, style of authority, leadership structures, intergenerational patterns and extended family, traditional family roles (for example, the role of first child in the family), the cultural significance of adolescence, role expectations and changes at different ages, the roles of elders, typical conflicts and the ways they're handled, how outsiders are viewed, the value placed on education and work, culturally specific remedies, rituals and traditions, language and the translation of inferences. These are only some examples. It's very complex business (Sanchez and League, 1990).

In designing programs, have we really taken the time to be sensitive to the cultural ways of others? When teaching communications skills, for example, are we aware that in certain cultures it is inappropriate to give "feedback," or to look someone in the eye? When teaching life skills, are we taking into account that many kids have already learned a set of street survival skills that they're very good at, and are we attempting to build upon those and their strengths in applying those skills to other aspects of life? Are we taking into account inferences of translation that may have meanings other than what we intend (for example, in some Oriental cultures, the literal translation of Kentucky Fried Chicken's "finger-lickin' good" slogan means "eat off your fingers," and that's frowned upon). We must be sensitive that most Native people identify themselves as part of a particular tribal group, as opposed to being generally "Indian."

In parenting, do we recognize that hitting children can mean different things in different cultures? For example, Alvy (in Baldacci, 1990) found that, in general, many Whites hit their children as a last resort out of frustration, while many Blacks view hitting as a way of teaching right from wrong and maintaining authority, believing it has many positive purposes. Black historians say this view evolved from a survival mechanism rooted in slavery, when Black parents needed absolute authority to protect their children because any misbehavior could cost their lives. Thus, today the question becomes, "What are other ways to get children to listen, respect, and cooperate?" A culturally sensitive response may be, they say, "We must appeal to children's minds, not their behinds."

Are we aware enough of the importance that certain institutions hold within various cultural communities; for example, the church within the Black community? Whether it be Southern Baptist or the Nation of Islam—whatever it may be—the church has regular contact with at least 60% of the population, holding unique status in Black culture because it is virtually the only autonomous social institution owned and run by Blacks. Its purpose is to nurture and protect its members spiritually—it is a place of both worship and healing—but it also helps to define the values and norms of the Black community. It has traditionally served as an agent of change and has ministered a wide range of needs and thus might be very helpful for prevention. Before plowing ahead, we have to be aware of other subtleties. Consider, for example, a 1986 Gallup poll that showed many clergy members still saw alcoholism as a sin, a character flaw, or a failure of will-power (Prugh, 1986).

The process and patterns of migration often set up conditions that affect how family members perceive the world, and ultimately how they behave. Ed Sanchez reminds us that if we don't take this into account, we can miss many reasons why people act as they do. This is particularly important because two-thirds of the world's immigrants are coming to the United States, and it won't be long before the White Anglo culture is no longer the majority; in fact, there will be no dominant single group. For prevention purposes, when a family has migrated from one place to another, even back a couple of generations, have we taken into consideration the reasons that they moved? Was it because they weren't satisfied where they were? Were they trying to escape a bad living situation? Was it because of work possibilities for the head of the household? Was it to provide more opportunity for the kids? How did those reasons affect all family members involved, particularly if they felt forced to move? Is it possible that they might have denied or repressed their feelings, or even their entire heritage, and idealized the adopted culture, for survival reasons? Is it possible that they will someday feel lost or cut off or have hopes of returning to their country, but find it too painful to talk about? Maybe they have to rely upon those they're close to and distance themselves from others or take out the despair they feel on their kids. Perhaps the absence of an extended family affects them. Perhaps they're having difficulty relating to many things around them, like birth-control pills. What implications do conditions like this hold for prevention programming (Sanchez and League, 1990)?

Are we designing programs that consider the full range of influences acting upon individuals in those communities—powerlessness, discrimination, racism, and the like? While the issue, ultimately, is one of helping people become empowered to take charge of and control their own lives and environment, will that message be heard if the culture is not respected and a cultural identity not fostered? If power is important to a particular cultural group, the connection must be made, for example, between drugs and how their use affects the power of the individual, family, or community to control their own destiny (NIDA, undated).

Every strategy within the community prevention "pyramid" (Chapter 6) could be developed with cultural relevance for specific populations. Within the level of "alternatives," young people could be helped to find meaning in their lives by examining relevant cultural practices, rituals, heritage, cultural values, and reinforcing the concept of perseverance in what one believes in. Legends could be used, not merely as tales, but to help young people explore the meanings behind them, to make connections with their own lives. Natural helping networks could be used to enhance many different strategies (NIDA, undated).

Today, most school skill-building approaches, and most parenting skills courses, are written and taught from a White middle-class perspective. Just because a Black cartoon figure allegedly appears in a film strip as part of the Nurturing Program doesn't make that program culturally relevant for African Americans. Just because a course such as STEP is translated verbatim into Spanish doesn't make it culturally relevant for Mexican-Americans. On the other hand, programs like Effective Black Parenting and Los Ninos Bien Educados have been carefully designed in conjunction with members of those cultural groups, with cultural relevance as a key goal [for citings, see Chapter 12].

To use Effective Black Parenting as an example, a "Pyramid of Success for Black Children" was created and is taught by engaging parents in a call-and-response dialogue similar to minister-congregation exchanges that characterize many Black church meetings. The top of the pyramid considers "life goals" that Black parents believe are important for their children to achieve (good job, good education, loving relationships, helping the Black community, resisting street pressures). The next level considers what the children might need to achieve these goals (high self-esteem, pride in Blackness, self-discipline, healthy habits, good school skills and study habits). The bottom level considers how parents can help their children develop these important characteristics (by modeling and teaching love, understanding, pride, and skills pertaining to the above level). Each time a new skill is taught, the parents are drawn back to the pyramid of success to make the connection.

For Native people, Victoria Graves took the process of parenting a step further (or a needed, basic step back) by dealing with issues that Indian parents need to confront before they could even be open to actual skills of parenting. Many Native parents have permissive childrearing styles. This is part of their culture. Within the context of the rest of their culture, those practices worked fine—there were very few problems. With the rest of their culture now virtually stripped away, permissiveness doesn't work anymore—outside of that context.

The best cultural diversity-related program I have ever seen is also my personally favorite outside-in prevention program, because it has so much heart and truly touches young people's lives. The *Council for Unity* began in 1975 at John Dewey High School in the Bensonhurst section of Brooklyn when then teacher Bob DeSena became deeply concerned about racially motivated gang violence after an incident occurred not unlike that portrayed at the end of Spike Lee's wonderful film, *Do The Right Thing*, and an African American gang member injured an Italian American gang member. The Italian gang, led by Nicky Chiapetta, was after revenge. DeSena pleaded with those gang leaders, plus the leaders of the Jewish, Irish, Asian, Hispanic gangs, to stop the violence and come together to resolve their differences. Prior to that incident gangs ruled, but one by one the gang leaders agreed, and when finally Chiapetta became the last to agree, the Council was formed. [Chiapetta later became the Council's Director of Program Operations]. The Council began to celebrate what made each of their cultures unique and special, and members began to appreciate each others' cultures. After a while, when enthusiasm began to deteriorate, they added small group "sensitivity sessions" where members each began to share personal concerns about their lives, and they began to see the commonalities among all the diversity. This provided the spark the Council needed to blossom. Kids began to join in droves, and the council expanded, eventually spreading into the younger grades in 1987 and throughout New York City. The Council does not solicit chapters, but will consider any school that comes to them. The Council provides a supportive family atmosphere for the youth involved, coupled with community service and racial and ethnic harmony. Council members are also taught how to handle racial and ethnic issues beyond their own school and neighborhood (Maniglia, 1992). When the completely diverse racial and ethnic mix of young people all gather in a circle and sing their theme song, "That's What Friends Are For," it truly warms the heart and is a wonder to behold, especially considering from whence they came.

Another excellent example of a program planned with a multicultural perspective is the *Winners* program of Los Angeles (Bell, 1990). It begins with the premise that much of what people do is influenced by culture; therefore, it focuses on the richness of Black heritage. The program addresses school, family, and community from a "pro-Black, racial-identity perspective." Winners believes in indoctrinating Black youth with African American culture and a Black perspective much as the Jewish community does with its youth within its culture.

The program is based on the following:

1. **Recognition** that drugs and alcohol abuse have always been problems in the Black community, but never more so than today. To resist, people must have a reason for living. To help young people find purpose in their lives, Winners provides them with positive role models, in this case local and national Black role models—individuals who have been outspoken and proud in themselves, in their communities, and in their heritage. The pride and positivity of people like Martin Luther King, Jr., Malcolm X, Huey Newton, Angela Davis, Roy Wilkins, and Jesse Jackson, who have shared the belief that the hope and future of the Black community rests on the shoulders and minds of Black youth, are an inspiration to young people.

2. **Social change.** Social/community organizations can make a difference; for example, the Southern Christian Leadership Conference, Urban League, NAACP, the Black Panther Party, Project Push for Excellence, and the Nation of Islam have played active roles in the community, educating youth and adults alike on matters related to ethnic pride, community service and responsibility. They can teach that when one abuses drugs and alcohol, or abuses others, one has no pride.

3. **Responsibility.** Each person is responsible for doing his or her part within the Black community to improve conditions for residents, and to better the community. When people are on drugs and abuse alcohol, they aren't making a contribution.

4. **Family values and relationships.** These include becoming aware of communication styles, improving communication skills, and accepting family fears about alcohol and other drugs. To deal with this, a core group of parents is trained to serve as catalysts, network-builders, and advocates for community needs.

5. **A sense of community within Black neighborhoods.** Local role models, people who've succeeded, are recognized and honored for their accomplishments, thereby helping to improve the esteem of all community members.

6. **Internship programs** for both high school and elementary school students. Students help other students. Local businesspeople help students. A college community, internship program helps provide positive role models and helps direct energies of students back to the community.

7. **Ethnic identity and self-esteem**, through the development and use of **culturally sensitive and relevant materials and resources**. "Discovery outings" take groups to museums to study historical Black organizations and institutions. After-school and weekend alternative programs consist of drama, dance, arts, crafts, sports, and cultural studies.

The Winners program includes three workbooks, each with many creative activities to help build self-esteem, nurture a sense of Black heritage, and build racial consciousness (Winners, Avalon Community Center, Los Angeles, CA).

Most of the effective programs for Hispanics focus on the family and community as opposed to the individual. They provide face-to-face outreach in Spanish at their homes or in school or wherever they can be engaged. But it is often necessary for program facilitators to make personal contact two to three times a week before people are willing to attend an activity (Nicolau and Ramos, 1990). Effective programs use language-relevant materials that don't require a lot of reading. They use mentors and apprenticeships. The Center for Health Policy Development (San Antonio, TX) has many culturally relevant curricula, and other materials and resources for Hispanics. They offer training and technical assistance for programs from AIDS to drugs. Of particular note is the *Latino Family Life Education Curriculum* series; the *Cultural Pride* curriculum unit, which focuses on Latino history, customs, culture and family, to strengthen students' self-esteem identity, the *La Familla* curriculum unit, which explores the Latino family and its strengths; the *La Comunicacion* curriculum unit, which builds communication skills for bicultural students and their families; and *Delivering Preventive Health Care to Hispanics: A Manual for Providers.*

The Forgotten People - Women and AIDS, is a half-hour documentary that explores traditional roles versus realities by discussing acculturation, assimilation, and relationship in the acquisition of habits, especially among those of second and third generations (available from the National Coalition of Hispanic Health and Human Services Organizations, Washington, DC).

For Native people, many culturally relevant materials are available from the Four Worlds Development Project; University of Lethbridge, Alberta, Canada, including many support materials and curriculum packages. One of these is *The Sacred Tree*, which helps teach young people positive values through basic, universal teachings common to most indigenous people, concerning human nature and the ways and means of living a healthy and productive life. This curriculum uses comfortable, familiar language, helps reconnect native people to their spiritual roots, and helps shed light on the path for a ways out of the alcohol and drug abuse dilemma, especially for young people. Its message is that unless spiritual development is integrated with social development, neither can really advance.

For Native Hawaiians, the Native Hawaiian Drug Free Schools and Communities Program (Honolulu, HI), has developed many culturally responsive materials, including videos made by native young people about their proud heritage and continuing traditions. Here, much emphasis is placed on drawing from the spiritual concept of *lokahi*, which speaks of balance, harmony, and unity of the self in relation to the spirit, the body, and the rest of the world. Among Native Hawaiian youth, it would be quite difficult to prevent substance abuse, for example, without incorporating how drugs may affect the reaching of lokahi.

In testimony before Congress on April 3, 1990, Charlene Doria-Ortiz spoke about the need for policymakers to respond to the cultural strengths and resources found within Mexican-American communities. "If Kool-Aid, Jell-O, Budweiser, and Marlboro can produce culturally sensitive bilingual ads to sell their products," she asked, "why can't our federal and state substance abuse prevention efforts do the same thing to sell health, individual and family well-being, and community unity against alcohol and drug abuse?" Doria-Ortiz testified to the need for culturally focused research, essential for conceptualizing sound prevention programs and strategies and culturally appropriate staff development and board training within community-based organizations. Attention must be paid to the needs of special groups within Hispanic communities: adolescents, refugees, migrants, farm-workers, and women. She also testified that there has been a lack of recruitment and training of Hispanic personnel and a lack of indigenous leadership development; that programs must be not only available and accessible, but also acceptable (culturally compatible as seen by the community); and that programs must be accountable to Mexican-American communities. She said that Hispanics have much to offer as a people, with resilience, strength, loyalty, tenacity, and commitment, and they should be used as such. To do so would help create "our nuestro bienstae" (well-being). The same could be said about most other cultural groups out of the mainstream.

Respect for oneself grows out of awareness of the value and importance of respect for differences among people in general. As Michael Bopp says, cultures really need each other; each has different and valuable gifts that can be shared. Drawing upon Indian traditions, he points out that we all exist within one circle; recognizing this makes us stronger than we would be alone. The fundamental nature of sickness is disconnectedness. The creator has given us the gift of the circle, Bopp paraphrases, so we can discover our identity. In community development work we must create the circle to connect with the spirit and use it to learn from everyone. This is the type of wisdom we can gain by tapping into the ways of specific cultures.

In attempting to respect people of all other races, cultures, and ethnic groups, we would all do well to consider the belief of the Native Alaskans: "We are all relatives."

Poverty and Wealth

For prevention at the macro level to truly make a difference, it is important for this nation to recognize that distribution of wealth affects the problems we're trying to prevent. This is not a partisan political issue as some would have us believe; it is not a conservative-liberal issue. It is not "class warfare," as conservatives like to call it. It is simply a fact. The more that the top 1% to 5% of Americans increase their wealth, the more the bottom 10 to 15% have experienced increased poverty. If a few people have it, most others don't, and many prevention-related problems result from that condition.

Democrats and Republicans alike voted for tax cuts between 1978 and 1988 that dropped the tax rate for the wealthiest Americans from 70% to 28%. The combined share of taxes paid by the top 1% of the population fell from 31% in 1977 to 23% in 1984. I am not sure what it is as of the second edition. During this period, between 1978 and 1988, it is no coincidence that the number of millionaires doubled—the number of billionaires doubled in two years (1986-1988)—while the number of people living in poverty, the homeless and the hungry, also doubled. While the average family after-tax income of the top 10% of Americans increased by 24%, for the lowest 10% it fell by more than 10%. As of 1983, the wealthiest one-half of 1% (420,000 households) accounted for 27% of the total net worth of all U.S. families, the top 10% accounted for approximately 68%, leaving 32% to be divided among everyone else. And now with the incredible stock market gains of the 1990s the gap has gotten even wider. [Is it a coincidence that the stock market falls with low unemployment?] In this time of high economic growth, it is a crime that the gap between the rich and poor is wider than it has ever been. When is it supposed to trickle down?

In prevention and human services we are often told there is no money. We have to suffer budget cuts. But it is not a question of money; it is only a question of priorities.

I reported in the first edition that funding to finance this country's huge debt—federal expenditures on the interest alone—climbed from $96 billion in 1981 to $216 billion in 1988. Now, in the year 2000, with President Clinton projecting record budget surpluses over the next ten years amounting to $2.6 trillion, our national debt is over $5.5 trillion, approximately $28,000 for each person! **From 15-18% of our total tax revenues goes to pay interest alone on the national debt. This is why there is not enough money to fund prevention and so many other valuable programs!**

Our debt is in part a result of combined policies of lowered tax rates for the wealthy and their corporations, increased defense spending, and a purposely devalued dollar (because some major corporations were losing money to foreign corporations). The details can be found in Kevin Phillips's (1990) enlightening and chilling book, *The Politics of Rich and Poor*. Suffice it to say that the reasons for our growing debt are not because of skyrocketing expenditures for prevention and human services.

It is easy for people who benefit from these policies to call this discussion "class warfare" while their wealth is increasing. They keep saying that their increased wealth benefits the economy, creating many new jobs, greater abundance for all, and greater economic strength within the world community. It's a great theory, but the fact is that the gap between rich and poor is the widest in our history. The poor are who suffer the consequences, and hard-working laborers barely make enough to survive with two incomes. This is happening to people whether they are liberal or conservative, Republican or Democrat. As George Wallace said, "The rich get richer, and the rest just get taken." And it's all because of policy!

In 1969 Ferdinand Lundenberg shocked many of us when he wrote in his landmark book, *The Rich and the Super Rich*, that the propertied elite accords itself fantastic tax privileges down to and including total exemption. He cited examples where many with $5 million or more steady income often paid no tax at all for many years while a man with a $2,000 income (in 1968) denied his family medical or dental care to pay tax. In one example Lundenberg showed how it was possible for a person with a $300 million investment on which a $33 million income was gained through investments in tax-free bonds, oil royalties, and growth stocks—to pay no tax (as of 1965); but that same man's chauffeur, if single and receiving $6,000 a year, would have paid a tax of $1,130. Some of the tax loopholes he alluded to in his book have since been closed, but many remain. Who creates this kind of policy?

There is no excuse in this abundant country of ours for any child, or any person, to go hungry. There is no excuse for any person who wants decent shelter not to have it. We live in one of the wealthiest nations in the world, but with that wealth concentrated in the hands of a relative few, the majority doesn't experience its benefits. Somewhere within the vast expanse that separates those who have most of the wealth and those who do not lies a primary answer to hunger, to homelessness, to poverty and its resulting problems. Food and essential items, affordable housing, jobs, health programs, and the essential programs that comprise the prevention "pyramid" all cost money. Who has all the money? The question is, Are the people with the power and wealth willing to do anything about it?

The Need for Social Change

Social change lies at the root of prevention. If we did the rest of our jobs exceptionally well, without social change, we would be left with reasonably healthy, productive young people in all parts of the country except among the inner-city poor, the minority poor, the rural poor. Are we satisfied with a prevention strategy that has little effect on the places that have the most drugs, the most abuse, and the most crime?

If the United States had policy priorities that supported the elimination of poverty, the healthy development of children, and prevention, we would see the results. If the wealthy paid their fair share of taxes or were required to pay for the programs to prevent and intervene in the problems caused by the discrepancies between rich and poor, we would be able to fully support and expand the good efforts already in place. We would see community-wide reductions in problem behaviors and we would be able to substantially reduce poverty.

Instead we have other policies, for example to spend over $2 billion each year to provide water subsidies to farming conglomerates and $800 million to pay for crops we don't need. It is policy to spend now well over $2.5 billion to keep people in prison, rather than spend it on programs that will help prevent and reduce crime. These are examples of our priorities.

350

"We the People" are supposed to hold the power, yet one-half of us do not vote. Why? Independent Congressman Bernard Sanders of Vermont believes it is because the political system is not debating the real issues. If all the people who felt they weren't getting a fair shake got together, the entire political system could be turned around.

After studying the long-term effects of early and sustained intervention in the lives of disadvantaged children, the Committee for Economic Development found that "improving the prospects for disadvantaged children is not an expense but an excellent investment, one that can be postponed only at a much greater cost to society" (in Schorr, 1989, p.162).

One would think this would be a compelling argument. Unfortunately, it has a major flaw. For example, we may get a threefold return on every dollar spent in the preschool period to prevent elementary school failure, but we won't realize the savings within the same budget—it will be seen years later. That the two are not tied together means people do not readily see the connection, and therefore have no vested interest. We do not see politicians pointing this out.

What rallying point could bring everyone together to solve preventable problems? Could it be protecting our children? Could it be supporting families or protecting the future of the American economy? No matter what it is, someone has to take the responsibility.

On the other hand, the few people in the prevention field shouldn't be held accountable for changing all of these conditions. Most of us are involved in prevention on a small scale—our individual programs—and that's good enough. We can't wipe out poverty too—at least not by ourselves. But we might consider joining with whatever other forces also have this as their goal. We need to support each other for the work we are all doing, acknowledging that much more needs to be done.

Ultimately, it takes politicians to make macro-level changes. At present, most appear uninterested. It takes responsive bureaucracies. At present most appear so caught up in perpetuating their own creations that they seem more interested in the means than in the ends. It takes not only grass-roots political action, but the people with the real wealth and power to make such substantive changes.

In the meantime, there are smaller pieces of social change that need to be accomplished—comparatively little things like turning around the way insurance is handled so that people have incentives to stay healthy. Many of these fall under the heading of creating a national prevention policy [Chapter 33].

Jack Pransky

31. Reflections on Prevention at the Macro-Level

George Albee enjoys a wide reputation as one of the founders of the prevention movement in the field of mental health. He has devoted his professional career to the prevention of mental-emotional disabilities. Dr. Albee has served as president of the American Psychological Association and director of the President's Commission on Mental Health Task Force on Prevention. His early prevention formula has been the prototype for many explanations of prevention that have followed. He was professor of psychology at the University of Vermont when I interviewed him. The University forced him to retire at age 70, but it did not slow him down.

JP: You've been around prevention longer than most of us, so you probably have the best perspective on comparing where things are now with the way they were back then. Can you take us back 10 or 20 years?

GA: Well, let me start 30 [now 40] years ago. A major benchmark in this whole field was something called the joint Commission on Mental Illness and Health, during the Eisenhower administration. It was a major effort to examine the nation's needs and resources in the field of mental health. It met for a two-year period, and I was director of the Task Force on Manpower, a term we wouldn't use anymore. The final report of that joint commission was in a book titled *Action for Mental Health.* It was really an attempt to find a way to give the states an out to not build new mental hospitals. You see, in the middle fifties, the state hospitals were absolutely bulging at the seams. So the plan was to do something to keep people from going into the state hospitals, and to discharge as many people as possible into the community. So the joint commission proposed building 2,000 community mental health centers across the country.

One of the requirements for a community mental health center, according to this plan, was "community consultation" and—they didn't use the word "prevention," but—keeping people from becoming casualties. So in a way, "prevention" had its official birth at that time.

Jack Kennedy read the book and almost immediately then became president, and he sent the first message to Congress ever by an American president proposing that federal money be spent in the area of community care. One of the critical elements in Kennedy's message in 1963 was that treatment in the community be available, but also that prevention programs be set up. Now, the Congress was relatively conservative, and—without going into a lot of detail—it decided to build community mental health centers—bricks and mortar—but give no money to staff them, because that was "socialized medicine," and we all know that's like godless communism. So the

353

community mental health center movement began with a handicap that there was no money to staff these places.

Later, when Lyndon Johnson became president and he had a little more clout with Congress, some money was made available to staff them, and there were "community consultation" elements in the community mental health centers. These have since disappeared because they don't generate any income. Today, the only things that go on in community mental health centers are programs that can generate income, because under the Republican administrations the funding for community mental health centers has been very slim.

Jumping ahead, I did the book on manpower and became convinced that we would never have enough professional people to treat all the people with problems, and I learned something about the field of public health, which says, "**No mass disorder afflicting humankind has ever been eliminated by attempts at treating the affected individual...**," so my conversion to prevention occurred during the late fifties and early sixties.

When finally Jimmy Carter was elected in the mid-seventies, he appointed a new Commission on Mental Health, and he appointed his wife Rosalynn an honorary chair of that commission. The other important person on that commission was Beverly Long, who was president of the National Mental Health Association, and a long-time friend of Rosalynn Carter. I was made chair of the Task Panel on Prevention, and there were a number of preventionists whose names you know: Emory Cowen and Bernie Bloom—a lot of people who'd been in prevention for a long while were part of that task panel. We recommended that the federal government fund prevention programs. The psychiatrists on the task panel vehemently opposed that, and sent our report out for a second reading and other opinions. Fortunately, Rosalynn Carter and Beverly Long were dedicated to the concept of prevention, so they overruled the psychiatrists and, as a result, the final report of the Carter Commission strongly recommended setting up an office of prevention at NIMH (National Institute of Mental Health), and a research center on prevention there.

The report of the Carter Commission was during the last year of his administration. NIMH didn't want to do anything about prevention, so what bureaucrats often do when they don't want to do something is appoint a study group. They then study it to death until finally either people forget or the president is defeated. So NIMH made a couple of mild efforts in the last months of the Carter administration. They set up an office of prevention in the office of the director where it could be controlled, and they set up a kind of office of prevention research within NIMH. As soon as Reagan was elected, the whole Mental Health Systems Act, which President Carter had gotten through the Congress, was repealed. NIMH received a message from the Reagan White House saying, "we will no longer support research into the social origins of mental disorder, only research on biological origins."

JP: Did they give a reason?

GA: Well, the Reagan administration was very much opposed to explaining mental disorders as due to social problems. People of that political persuasion don't believe that poverty and discrimination and sexism are the responsible forces. I mean, there's a long history in this field where political conservatives strongly support explanations which find evil inside the person— organic defects. The first three directors of NIMH were all trained in public health. Since that time all the directors of NIMH have been organic psychiatrists who find the cause of mental illness inside the person, so they can say, "Schizophrenia is due to a brain disease." Conservative psychiatrists today explain homelessness as due to some inherent defect in the person. If you blame homelessness on injustice and inequality, then you've got to do something, which is prevention. But if you blame homelessness on a brain disease or a personal defect, then you blame the victim.

JP: Do you think this is a sincere belief on their part, based on one interpretation of the research, or are they believing what they want for a purpose?

GA: I think it's part of an inherent value system that some people apply, not just to this field but across the board. They say there are lots of jobs if people will just go out and look for them. People who are on Welfare are lazy and don't want to work. And there's a value system that says anyone can make it if they try. Others say some people are handicapped through no fault of their own but through social victimization. So it's part of a whole, general value system. Political conservatives often are opposed to spending money on prevention because prevention is an environmental concept: to prevent something you've got to prevent poor parenting, you've got to change discrimination, sexism, all the environmental forces that cause stress.

A long time ago a psychologist named Nicholas Pastore did a study of opinions of world scientists on the nature-nurture question: Is nature (heredity) more responsible, or is nurture (the environment) more responsible. There was almost a perfect correlation between the scientists' political beliefs and their attitudes toward this question. So, efforts at prevention have been held down through lack of funding, based on the political beliefs of some conservative administrations.

When finally the pendulum swings back in the other direction there will be more money for prevention, because the basic structure is in place. It's like building irrigation ditches. When there isn't any water flowing… There's no money flowing now, but hopefully there will be.

JP: Do you think we substantively know a lot more now than we did about prevention in the last 10 or 20 years.

GA: Oh, yes! We know a great deal. We know about preventing mental retardation. We know about reducing stress. We know clearly that social support systems are a major factor in reducing the rates of a whole variety of conditions. We know that there's a high correlation between self-esteem and resistance to stress.

Basic, fundamental, predictable, reliable data suggest that what happens to infants and children has a significant effect on the later rate of distress. There have been so many clear-cut research projects to demonstrate that children who grew up in institutions and without love and affection have a very high rate of later disorder. Joe Hunt, who wrote a book on early environment and intelligence, or the whole series of studies done in Iowa by Marie Skodak and Harold Skeels, where they took kids in institutions for the retarded and placed them in loving, middle-class homes, and the kids blossomed, while those left in the institutions didn't. There are just so many studies that relate bad parenting and miserable home environments to later difficulties.

But now, you see, the major source of opposition to this insight is coming from the National Alliance for the Mentally Ill [NAMI], a very effective lobbying organization with incredible power. They now have a hand in selecting the director of NIMH. They're active in every state. Their basic message is, "Don't blame the parent. Parents are not to blame." Almost all these NAMI families are families with a disturbed teenager or adult. Now you can understand their anxiety, and their resentment, and their problem. It's a tragedy to have an emotionally disturbed child. But the conservative psychiatrists have formed an alliance with NAMI, and they're now working together, and they're controlling the media messages: "All mental illness is a medical disease. All mental illness should be treated by a physician with drugs. Parents are not to blame." This has incredible power. The head of a twin organization called the American Mental Health

Fund, which has all kinds of distinguished public personalities on its board of directors and is raising an incredible amount of money, is a guy named Jack Hinkley, the father of John Hinkley, Jr., who took a shot at President Reagan. Jack Hinkley and his wife Joanne have written a book called *Breaking Point*, which is a major exercise in denial in my view. They're saying, "We were so relieved to learn that it's not our fault that John Hinkley, Jr. became disturbed." They and the organic psychiatrists are gunning for more money for treatment of severely disturbed young people.

One of the interesting sidelights of this is that most of the members of NAMI are White, and they're middle class or upper middle class. We know that schizophrenia, whatever it is, is far more common among the very poor. So in terms of the number or highest percentages of schizophrenics in this country, they're Black and Chicano and Puerto Rican and poor White. So the small group of politically organized middle class Whites that belong to NAMI and AMHF are now opposing money for prevention and supporting money for treatment. Many of them also favor involuntary treatment. They would like to pass laws in favor of forcing treatment on people whether they want it or not; many of them are also in favor of involuntary hospitalization. They want their kids off the streets, if the kids are schizophrenic, drug users, or whatever, and the organic psychiatrists are going along with this.

Now this may seem like a distant consideration so far as prevention is concerned. But there's just so much money in the mental health pot, and the more money you force into the treatment of severely disturbed people the less money you have for other purposes.

JP: Let's take other fields like alcohol and drug abuse and delinquency. Is the same emphasis being placed on organic reasons for their occurrence?

GA: I have a collection of newspaper clippings at home quoting "experts" who claim that crime and delinquency are largely due to genetic factors, that juvenile delinquents have, they say, abnormal brain waves, and that this is an organic condition that is going to be treated eventually with drugs and pills.

Alcoholism is now labeled as a disease. I gave a speech in Texas in which I said that I had asked a distinguished geneticist from the University of Virginia whether he felt the data supported the concept of a genetic base for alcoholism, and he said, "No. The data are very ambiguous." When I said this, a lot of the people in the audience were very upset and angry with me because they want to believe that alcoholism is not a matter of development of a bad habit, but it's a disease. Society is very confused on this issue. If alcoholism is a disease, we don't punish other people for having a disease, but we punish drunken drivers. We say we've got to do something about the problem of drunk driving, yet at the same time, if drinking is a disease, why are we punishing people that have this disease? We don't punish epileptics who accidentally hurt others.

JP: But what about the recent research that suggests that alcoholism is now known to be inherited?

GA: It is far from convincing. If you read the headline in the Burlington Free Press, it sounds as though the issue is closed. But if you read the article itself you find that it was based on a very small sample of very serious alcoholics, and the authors of the study themselves indicate that their findings represent far from conclusive proof. Many other serious alcoholics in their study did not show any genetic factor and so, as usual, they interpret their findings as "tentative."

JP: Why are you so determined to oppose any suggestion of genetic factors in alcoholism and other conditions?

GA: There are several reasons. Perhaps the most important is the fact that **calling alcoholism, or addiction to drugs, or criminal behavior, a consequence of genetic defect lets the perpetrators off the hook of responsibility for changing their behavior**. They claim that their drinking, or use of drugs, or criminal behavior, is a result of forces over which they have little or no control. It also means that the moment someone's job is threatened because of the excessive use of drugs or alcohol they can sign themselves into a treatment clinic and escape the consequences of their behavior. We all read about star pro athletes who are caught using drugs and who immediately sign themselves into treatment centers claiming that they need help to deal with their problem. Even prestigious politicians, their spouses, movie stars, and other public figures, spread the notion that people are not responsible for their behavior. I agree with Thomas Szasz who argued that everyone should be held responsible for what they do. One of my other favorite writers on this subject is Stanton Peele, who has written some very insightful books on the medicalization of addictions.

The same general argument applies to schizophrenia. The diagnosis of this condition is quite unreliable, and we all know there can't be any validity in the absence of reliability. One of our doctoral students at the University of Vermont, Courtney Harding, demonstrated quite conclusively that chronic schizophrenics who were discharged from the Vermont State Hospital back in the 1950s, after some intensive efforts at rehabilitation, blended into the Vermont population and were practically indistinguishable from their neighbors and peers when followed up thirty-some years later. These chronic schizophrenics "recovered" without any drug treatment, and most of them were found to be leading relatively normal lives. One of them even became a millionaire!

JP: But doesn't AA claim that their success results, at least in part, from admitting that one is powerless over alcohol?

GA: Alcoholics Anonymous succeeds with some people because it is a great support group. But many alcohol abusers have quit on their own, just as lots of people have quit other addictions on their own, from heroin to tobacco.

JP: Do some attempt to explain child abuse and sexual abuse as a result of organic causes?

GA: In the area of child and sexual abuse the organic-cause supporters are largely silent. You see, this is one of the most compelling kinds of evidence against their position. Child abuse, physical abuse, child neglect, the sexual abuse of children is clearly a parental, familial problem. We have good evidence that sexually abused children often grow up to be disturbed adults, so we're doing our best to try to educate and curb child abuse.

JP: Do you think that the forces are mounted as strongly against prevention in these fields as they are in prevention of mental health problems?

GA: Justin Joffe and I wrote a little essay—it was really Justin's idea—called, "The Cause of the Causes" (Joffe, 1984). **What we tend to do in this field is to divide up child abuse, elder abuse, juvenile delinquency, psychopathology—all these different conditions—and we treat them as if they each had separate causes**. When we take, say, teenage pregnancy, and we say, "What's the cause of teenage pregnancy," and we study the young women that become pregnant, we find that they're poorly educated, they have relatively little sex knowledge, they're often from the inner city, they're often from welfare families, and we say, the way to prevent teenage pregnancy is through sex education and better casework by the social workers; teach them about contraception and keep them in school longer. We treat that group as if it had unique problems. Now what Justin said is that the same cause is behind many of these different conditions. **It's the economic system that allows horrible poverty in the midst of an affluent society. The**

highest rate of almost all these kinds of disorders exists among the poor and poverty stricken. So broken families and child abuse and delinquency and drug use all are associated with poverty.

Let me take another tack: As each immigrant group arrived in the United States, it occupied the bottom of the socioeconomic ladder. They had the highest rates of every kind of pathology. So in the 1850s it was the Irish. And you read what was said about the Irish: Why do they throw their garbage in the streets? Why do they have such a high rate of alcoholism? Why do they have such a high rate of lunacy? Why do their kids not learn in school? When the Irish moved up into the middle class, all of that ended. But following them came the Scandinavians. So there was a period when the Swedes were the ignorant and the school learning problems and the juvenile delinquents and the high rates of alcoholism. Then they moved up into the middle class, and the Eastern European Jews and Poles and Hungarians arrived. There was a time in England where they didn't want Eastern European Jews coming because they had such high rates of crime and delinquency and alcoholism, and so on. As soon as the Jews made it into the middle class, their rates dropped. Then the southern Italians arrived, and it's so interesting to read what was said about the southern Italians—that they can't learn, and their kids are one standard deviation below the average in the New York City schools—the same things that had been said about the other immigrant groups.

The point of all this is that whoever is at the bottom of the socioeconomic ladder has high rates of school learning problems and mental disorders. When they move up into the middle class, their rates drop. Now if this is a genetic phenomenon, what happened to all those bad genes? Whenever you improve the economic circumstances of a group, you improve their rates of mental and emotional disorders. So now it's the Blacks and the Chicanos and the Puerto Ricans and the Appalachian Whites that have the high rates. Now, if we were to remove the cause of all the causes, we could reduce the rate of all these conditions; that is, eliminate poverty. Do what has been done in many countries, as in Scandinavia, where you cut off the ability of the very affluent to earn great sums through your tax structure. Have a progressive form of taxation so you don't have any poverty and you reduce the rate of many of these conditions. Not all. Finland, Sweden, Denmark, are not perfect but they have much more enlightened social programs than we have.

JP: You've been trying to keep the field honest for years in reminding people that social change is absolutely necessary for prevention. On the other hand, social change as a prevention strategy is overwhelming for people, especially for those who work in the field. I mean, if people who work in the field believe that they have to be eliminating poverty they get very frustrated. Yet you are implying that there's really no hope for these problems to be seriously reduced unless that happens.

GA: No, there's room in the field of prevention for everyone, including political conservatives. There are many, many effective prevention programs that don't require a revolution. Many things that have been demonstrated to reduce mental retardation, for example, don't require major social change. **Requiring seatbelts and motorcycle helmets, eliminating lead poisoning in the slums, changing the gasoline we use to lead-free gasoline–these are all effective prevention programs that don't require major political revolution**.

The same is true in the area of exploitation. I think the civil-rights movement and the women's movement, while they weren't necessarily organized by preventionists, have had a major positive effect. Betty Friedan wrote *The Feminine Mystique* in 1963 and she started the woman's revolution. She's a psychologist. There are so many things that can be done.

The group with the highest rate of every kind of mental and physical disorder are the migrant farmworkers. There have been major efforts at improving the lot of the migrant farmworker, from the organizing of Cesar Chavez's union to improving housing and providing schooling for their children. There are lots of little things that can be done: providing support groups. **If I had to name one strategy in prevention that can be done without requiring revolution, it is providing support groups for people who are at risk.** Lots of people working in the field organize volunteers to telephone elderly shut-ins every day, or to start foster grandparenting programs, or Meals on Wheels. I don't want to give the impression that prevention isn't possible without major social change.

JP: But the reality is that without serious social change it's hard to imagine that those kinds of programs are going to amount to very much on a wide scale.

GA: Well, they have measurable effects. You can certainly demonstrate a reduction in deaths due to auto accidents in states that have compulsory seatbelt laws. We know that people who are socially isolated are at very high risk, so we can develop support programs that reduce social isolation, and we can measure that fewer people with social supports go into institutions. There are so many programs that have been reviewed and are effective. The American Psychological Association published a book called *14 Ounces of Prevention*, a description of 14 prevention programs carefully measured and evaluated that have demonstrated effectiveness.

JP: But the part of prevention that has to do with social change is the part that is really least practiced. So what do you think needs to be done in this area? What can the prevention field do?

GA: If you look at major social changes that have had a preventive impact, they've almost always been mass movements: the civil rights movement in the late sixties, Martin Luther King and SNCC and all the brave Black kids who sat in lunchrooms in the Carolinas and all the people who rode freedom busses to Mississippi had dramatic effects on changing the job opportunities for Blacks in this country. If you read the *Autobiography of Malcolm X*, you can see that we have made a lot of progress since that time. It's a slow and agonizing process. But now you see minority people on television in responsible roles, and you see integration in colleges and universities and there's great pressure to hire more minority faculty and admit more minority students, things that would be unheard of 40 years ago. And the same thing had been true of women's rights. It was the 1960s women's movement throughout the land that reduced the stressors associated with being a second-class citizen. We haven't done enough, but these social changes have reduced stress and increased self-esteem. I don't know what the next social revolution is going to be; certainly the reduction of homophobia would be a major achievement.

JP: There is the Family Support Movement. As a result of it there seems to be more support now for children and family issues, and more happening in the Congress than in recent memory.

GA: Yes, except I keep reading that **there's far more money spent on the care and support of the elderly than on the care and support of children, because the elderly are much more politically organized.** I don't think there's a comparable group to AARP lobbying for children. It's much more haphazard, and the federal money we spend on the elderly is far more than we spend on children. I would just as soon this be reversed, even though I'm a member of AARP and ready to retire.

JP: Do you see that it's possible to have a "movement" for prevention, or is that just too obscure?

GA: Well there are a lot of roadblocks. **I am convinced that the field of public health is far more important to the health of Americans and to the world than the field of high-technology medicine.** High-tech medicine is individual treatment, and individual treatment has no effect on incidence. Public health has been successful in increasing life expectancy in eliminating major plagues like smallpox, by inspecting the foods we eat, inspecting swimming pools, and doing things about pollution in the environment. But public health is not appreciated—it gets no publicity. We have television programs celebrating individual physicians and individual treatment, but none celebrating public health because public health doesn't have the dramatic impact. You keep people healthy and that's not news. If you remove a brain tumor, that's very dramatic. There's so much publicity about heart transplants and artificial hearts and liver transplants. If you stop and think about it, these have absolutely no effect on the general health or life expectancy of Americans, but we're spending more and more money on these high-tech treatments.,

Also, public health and prevention are inevitably tax supported. People won't pay for primary prevention. People don't pay for individual care in the public health area. The American health care system is vehemently opposed to tax-supported healthcare, because this is socialized medicine.

JP: But at the same time, conservatives, as well as liberals and everybody else, are complaining about the fact that there is too much crime, too much drug abuse, too much teen pregnancy, far too much child abuse and sexual abuse—

GA: Well, whenever they claim that, like in the last years of the Reagan administration, **they talk about the problem but reduce the amount of money that goes into the prevention field. There is anger at the high crime rate, but the solution is to build more prisons, bigger prisons, give stiffer sentences**. And you hear this argument all the time.

JP: On the other hand, we're showing that certain programs when done right make a difference in creating less delinquency and other problem behaviors. So why aren't they jumping at the chance to cut down on these rates?

GA: One of the arguments you get is prevention interferes with the rights of parents or it interferes with individual freedom. If you read the letters to the editor in our local newspaper, there are passionate letters, opposing the seatbelt law, passionate letters opposing the requirement that motorcyclists wear helmets. "They're interfering with my individual freedom." But we can demonstrate a reduced rate of brain injury as a consequence of seatbelts and helmets. Why aren't the conservatives more supportive? They say, "Well, people should have the right to be damn fools if they want to be." I don't know. I'm sure you have answers to these questions. I'm just speculating.

JP: I don't have answers. It really puzzles me why there's so much opposition.

GA: There was a famous Hungarian physician named Ignaz Semmelweis. He was puzzled at the high rate of death of women who had given birth to children in public hospitals. He did a lot of observation, and he finally came to the conclusion that if doctors and medical students would only wash their hands before they delivered babies, this would reduce the rate of childbed fever and death. So he ordered his physicians and students and himself to wash their hands for ten minutes before delivering—this was before germs were discovered. He demonstrated conclusively that you could bring the rate of childbed fever and maternal death down to almost zero in comparison with other hospitals where the doctors didn't wash their hands. Now this is exactly the question you asked. Why didn't physicians rush out to wash their hands? Why couldn't he sell this idea? Because other pompous obstetricians around Europe said this was nonsense. They knew the cause of childbed fever, and it wasn't this. He published his data and he showed the curves. He gave lectures, he wrote books. He finally killed himself because he couldn't convince physicians of the truth of his observation. **Often people aren't ready to**

accept something that goes outside what they believe to be true. They just find it very difficult, even in the presence of clear-cut evidence, to change their ways.

JP: So how do we do it?

GA: Well, Freud said, "The voice of the intellect is soft, but it's persistent," so I think you just have to keep on pointing out what you believe to be true. The other thing is to get important political figures to be convinced of the truth of your data. I mean, here in Vermont we have a former governor who became convinced of the importance of prevention, and he introduced and supported, and the legislature passed, prevention legislation stipulating that prevention had to be a part of the ongoing programs of the state government. I think we've had people in the Congress who are convinced that the prevention effort was worth the money. So one way is to keep publishing your data and writing books about prevention. Another is to make sure that people read them. When Jack Kennedy read Action for Mental Health he resolved that when he could he would do something about this problem. He also had a sister who was in an institution, so he had a personal interest and experience with the horrors of institutions.

JP: As you know, for the last few years I've been pushing to get the academic preventionists together with the people in the field. Why is there such a separation? They're not using each other the way they could.

GA: There are very few people who are committed to prevention in the field of psychology and relatively few in the field of social work, which has traditionally been one-to-one case practice. So, numerically, the number of academics committed to prevention still is very, very small. Out in the real world, the money for prevention has been in the drug abuse field, so a majority of the people working in prevention have been concerned with prevention of drug and alcohol abuse. But there hasn't been a meeting of the minds because most academics interested in prevention have been in preventing psychopathology. So we haven't really been talking on the same wavelength.

A...group...originally founded the *Journal of Primary Prevention*... The circulation of that has always been very limited—maybe 1,000 subscribers including university libraries. There just isn't yet a major commitment to prevention in our society, in the same way that there aren't a lot of people who subscribe to the *American Journal of Public Health*. Public health is a very powerful tool at keeping society healthy, but it's not featured in news articles and stories.

JP: Can you think of anything that would move the preventionists to connect better with the prevention practitioners, and vice versa.

GA: I don't know. If you could find ways of getting them together in meetings where they could learn to talk with each other and get to know each other. But there are so few people in the academic world with an interest in prevention.

JP: How many are there?

GA: I would say probably not more than 100 in the whole world of academia [as of 1990]. We're still committed to training one-to-one therapists. I was at Rutgers last Friday giving a talk to the Professional School of Psychology. They're cranking out therapists. Psychotherapy is a major vocational choice these days in psychology, but also in people entering social work. It's fascinating to drive around and see all the signs saying "psychiatric social worker." Social workers used to be organizers of the poor and people who had a conscience in the struggle for better opportunities for the downtrodden. Now they're doing psychotherapy with middle-class neurotics, making three times as much money as their colleagues in the field of social work. We're living in the midst of a psychotherapy boom. There seems to be an almost endless demand for individual therapy. We have a million divorces each year in this country. A very large proportion of people going through divorce seek some kind of counseling. The children of divorce also need help. So psychotherapy has become a major source of support for people. Somebody called it "the purchase of friendship."

JP: You can see where psychotherapists would be against prevention. [laughter]

GA: Well, they are certainly not wildly enthusiastic about it, although their business is so good, they can afford to be tolerant. [laughter]

JP: Anything else you want to say to the prevention workers of the world?

GA: Well, there are some dedicated preventionists who have kept the blue flame of prevention burning over the years. I think of people like Steve Goldston, who, as long as I've known him, has struggled desperately to keep prevention alive. **Logically, it makes sense to spend a significant proportion—I don't care whether it's 20% or 25%—of our mental health budgets on prevention**. This will happen eventually. The term "prevention" wasn't even current 30 years ago. Now every state is talking about prevention, and most states have a person designated as their prevention officer or their prevention program. There are many states that have very effective prevention programs: Michigan for example, California, Georgia have statewide groups concerned with prevention. Oklahoma has been very busy organizing prevention programs. All of this is through mental health, and it's all significant progress compared to where we were 20 to 30 years ago. So the movement is underway.

The few of us who've been in the field for a long time are constantly being asked to come and talk to groups who have suddenly become interested in prevention. So I've been six times to Asia in the past year, because Asia doesn't have any private practice or one-to-one treatment. But they know about public health because public health has been very effective in reducing death rates and helping people avoid all the problems associated with being a third-world country. So now they're interested in primary prevention of mental and emotional disorders because they don't have any prospect of training individual psychotherapists. I think legislation and programs will eventually get underway. It's coming. It's just a matter of our being impatient at the slow pace.

4/89

III. Prevention Policy

Jack Pransky

32. Developing a State Prevention Policy

One of the more important "environmental strategies" is policy development.

Prevention practitioners working in local communities rarely think about policy change. It seems somehow out of the scope of their normal operations. Yet without strong prevention policy the field will be forever relegated to second class status. Without policy, prevention will be limited to efforts conducted out of the goodness of people's hearts. Without strong policy, prevention will not be conducted on a large enough scale to make a community-wide, statewide, nationwide difference in behaviors.

Policy sets direction. Policy guides. Policy specifies what people should do and frames approaches that should be used. To establish prevention policy is to institutionalize prevention.

Policy and Practice

Webster defines "policy" as (1a) prudence or wisdom in the management of affairs, (2a) a definite course or method of action selected from among alternatives and in light of given conditions to guide and determine present and future decisions, (b) a high-level overall plan embracing the general goals and acceptable procedures, especially of a governmental body.

In contrast, "practice" is what actually happens. Schools, for example, have philosophies and mission statements that endeavor to build healthy self-perceptions in students, yet many practices in schools have the opposite effect.

Commonly accepted practices constitute unwritten policy, though they're not often considered as such. Having no prevention policy leaves only prevailing practices to dictate what the policy is unless something makes it change.

Is it policy to spend 0.1% of human service budgets on prevention? This approximates what Vermont was spending on prevention when we first examined it prior to 1983. It has increased markedly since then, perhaps to a whopping 7%. Each state should know what percentage of its budget is spent on prevention and what percentage is supplied by the federal government. Those percentages constitute current policy.

Most prevention programs can barely scrape together enough money to survive. I can think of only two ways that prevention will ever become a priority: those in positions of authority can voluntarily decide to change practices, or a policy must be made that tells people what to do. People will not often voluntarily change practices that they are used to. They need motivation to change. It is often much more realistic to create policy that dictates practices.

State Prevention Policy

States have policies, written or unwritten, that dictate prevention practice.

Each state needs to determine if it has a policy for prevention. Does the state take any responsibility for preventing problem behaviors, or does it spend tax dollars primarily for rehabilitation and treatment after problems have occurred? Are state agencies required in any way to assist local communities in organizing or funding prevention efforts?

If the answers to these questions are disquieting, an attempt to legislate prevention might be in order. The theory is that if a state is not presently taking responsibility for prevention, it probably won't start unless it's required to. An alternative approach would be to help those in power to become so excited about prevention that they will make it a priority. Both approaches have merit, but which is more likely to succeed? Perhaps a combination of the two would be best.

Policy Guidance

The first question in considering prevention policy is "To what end?" What should a policy accomplish? What should be its guiding principles?

The next question: "Is it needed?" Are there people who would benefit from prevention policy? Which people?

These questions are a starting point: "At what level would it be best for policy to reside?" There are many levels at which state policy can occur. In approximate descending order of authority, some of these levels are-

> legislation
> executive order
> agency policy directive
> legislative resolution
> proclamation
> task force recommendation

Consideration of these possibilities suggests another question: "Whom do we most want affected by our policy?" In other words, whose way of conducting business do we most want to alter? Some possibilities might be the-

> legislature
> funding sources
> all relevant state agencies
> an individual state agency
> a coordinating body
> community agencies
> community groups
> schools

Finally, we must consider what we want to affect specifically. For example:

funding
joint sponsorship or collaboration
agency rule definition, clarification, revision
technical assistance or training
planning
implementation
evaluation research
oversight responsibility
input on guidelines, policies, practices
accountability
enforcement

The answers will be different for each state. But it is important to know specifically what we want if we embark on creating prevention policy.

Can You Legislate Prevention?

Some people believe that legislating prevention is like legislating morality. But in cases where existing practices are not always conducive to the best prevention practice, where the health and well-being of citizens is not always promoted by existing practice, or where existing practices don't serve to reduce the problems of concern to society, then prevention legislation might be considered as a practical option.

The state of Vermont was faced with this dilemma. The desired result was for the state to take set policy for prevention. Vermont chose the legislative route. A law requiring state agencies to contribute to a "state prevention plan" and conduct implementation practices consistent with that plan was, to some of us, a very exciting proposition.

The Vermont Story: The First State to Pass Prevention Legislation

In April 1983, the Vermont legislature passed what later became known as Act 79. In April 1986, a Children's Trust Fund provision amended Act 79, and $150,000 was allocated for "community-based prevention programs that have shown to be effective for juveniles." (Note: Many states have "children's trust funds," but few, if any, are attached to other prevention policies.)

Other states may wish to examine Vermont's legislation to adapt it to their own purposes.

Why Legislation? The Function of Law

Webster defines "law" as "a rule of conduct of action prescribed or formally recognized as binding or enforced by a controlling authority." Laws are to be obeyed and followed, but anyone who has ever driven down a highway at the speed limit as other cars whizzed by understands there is a bit more to it than that.

The ultimate purpose of a law is to affect behavior. For behavior to be truly affected, however, three factors must be considered:

1. the law itself
2. enforcement—if people disobey the law and they're not punished, behaviors don't change
3. the perception or beliefs of those required to comply—if people believe they won't get caught, or believe the law is no good, they will not comply and behaviors won't change

The implication is that a law only takes us so far, but it provides us with a solid foundation from which to proceed.

Vermont's Prevention Law

The key sections of Vermont's prevention law (Act 79 of 1983) provide:

- a definition of primary prevention [§3301(2)]
- a description of the state primary prevention plan [§3304(a)]
- responsibilities assigned to state agencies and departments [§3305]; and
- establishment of the Children's Trust Fund [§3305(a)]

The pertinent parts of Act 79 of 1983, as amended in 1986 (33 VSA 3301-3308), read as follows:

Sec. 1. Policy and Purpose [Note: This section was added in 1986]

It is the policy of the general assembly to encourage community involvement in the development of effective primary prevention programs which promote the health and increase the self-reliance of Vermont children and their families. The general assembly recognizes the far-reaching value, both social and financial, of community-based programs which reduce the need for long-term and costly rehabilitation services. These preventive programs seek to eliminate the likelihood of irreparable damage that can arise from interrelated social problems such as child abuse and neglect, domestic violence, alcohol and drug abuse, juvenile delinquency and other socially destructive behaviors. Therefore a children's trust fund is established for the purpose of providing funds for primary prevention programs.

§3301. Definitions

As used in this chapter.
(1) "Council" means the Children and Family Council for Prevention Programs.
(2) "Primary prevention" means efforts to reduce the likelihood of juvenile delinquency, truancy, substance abuse, child abuse and other socially destructive behaviors before intervention by authorities.

§3302. Children and Family Council for Prevention Programs

(a) A Children and Family Council for Prevention Programs is established. The council shall consist of 21 members who shall be appointed by the governor with the advice and consent of the senate for three year terms.... Consideration shall be given to the selection of persons who will adequately represent the interests of the beneficiaries of the primary prevention, programs. .

§3303. Council; Duties

(a) The council shall assist state agencies and the departments in the development, improvement and coordination of primary prevention programs and activities at the state and local levels. In providing this service, the council shall-
    (1) acquire and provide pertinent research data and technical assistance related to the development and practice of primary prevention programs;
    (2) develop a state primary prevention plan that coordinates and consolidates the primary prevention planning efforts of the state agencies and departments specified in the act;
    (3) evaluate and prepare recommendations on the prevention policies and programs developed and implemented under the act and submit such recommendations on or before January 1 to the governor and the senate and house committees on health and welfare and appropriations.
(b) Administer the children's trust fund as provided in sections 1056 and 1057.
(c) ... the council may apply for and receive federal and private funds, or any combination thereof in order to accomplish the purposes of this chapter ...

§3304. The State Primary Prevention Plan

(a) The state primary prevention plan shall provide for the use of state resources in ways that will strengthen the commitment of local communities to altering conditions which contribute to delinquency or other problem behaviors, so that the burden of state-funded treatment and crisis-oriented service programs will be reduced. The plan shall set forth specific goals, objectives, and key result areas and shall include proposals to integrate and build upon successful methods of primary prevention.
(b) ... by July 1 . . . the council shall submit a prevention plan to the governor and to the senate and house committees on health and welfare and appropriations. Such plan shall incorporate and consolidate the proposals and recommendations for primary prevention developed by;
    (1) the department of education
    (2) the agency of human services, including all departments
    (3) the department of motor vehicles ...
(c) (4) the office of the attorney general
    (5) the agency of development and community affairs
    (6) the department of employment and training
    (7) the department of public safety
    (8) the department of forests, parks and recreation
(d) By July 1, 1986, and biennially thereafter, the council shall revise the state primary prevention plan which shall be submitted to the governor and the senate and house committees on health and welfare and appropriations.

§3305. Implementation

The specified state agencies and departments shall formulate primary prevention policies and implementation practices that are consistent with the state primary prevention plan. Such policies and practices shall be targeted to specific goals, objectives and key result areas.

§3306. The Children's Trust Fund

(a) A children's trust fund is established for the purpose of providing funds for community-based primary prevention programs that have been shown to be effective for juveniles. The fund shall be maintained by the agency of human services. -
(b) The fund shall be comprised of revenues from the following sources: (1) any private donations made by individuals or organizations to the fund for the purposes of the act; (2) when authorized by the general assembly, funds appropriated directly or combined with other funds appropriated for services or programs having purposes consistent with primary prevention; (3) funds received from the federal government as matching funds or other funds for the purposes of the act; (4) funds held, donated to or acquired by any state agency for purposes generally consistent with the purposes of this chapter and transferred at the direction of the governor to the children's trust fund. All interest accrued or generated

by revenue in the fund shall remain in the fund and be available for 'the payment of grants awarded therefrom.

§3307. Trust Fund Program

(a) The council shall plan, implement and encourage primary prevention programs. The secretary of human services and the council shall solicit proposals for grant awards from public and private persons and agencies. The council shall evaluate the proposals and submit to the secretary its priorities for awarding and funding grants ...

[Note: (c) and (d) go on to describe the evaluation criteria for grants and the grant awarding process.]

(e) The secretary of human services in conjunction with the council shall develop guidelines for the coordination of programs and the application for the distribution of assistance from the children's trust fund.

§3308. Annual Report

Annually, prior to January 15, the council shall submit a report of its activities for the preceding fiscal year to the governor and to the general assembly. The report shall contain an evaluation of the effectiveness of the programs and services financed or to be financed by the children's trust fund, and shall include an assessment of the impact of such programs and services on children and families.

The key policy provisions of this law are Sections 3304(a) and 3305. These are very carefully crafted statements designed to guide the best possible direction for prevention programming at the state level.

How the Vermont Legislation Came to Pass

The Vermont legislation did not happen overnight. The purpose of detailing Vermont's experience is so that other states can learn what process we used, learn through our mistakes, and to suggest some principles in trying to get legislation passed.

In 1978, a committee of the Vermont Juvenile Justice and Delinquency Prevention Advisory Group (JJDPAG) observed that the state of Vermont had no policy for delinquency prevention and that nearly all state resources were devoted to dealing with problems that arose only after young people had broken the law. The committee concluded it was unlikely anything would ever change unless the state committed itself to a policy that would prevent young people from committing crimes in the first place.

The JJDPAG appointed a prevention policy task force. The problem was that no task force member had enough time to devote to this complex effort. As such, funds were requested to hire someone who could provide the needed time and energy. Before developing policy, the task force believed it should conduct a study to determine whether there was "support for delinquency prevention as a proper activity for state policy and program development." The Vermont Legislative Council, an independent organization with clout and without vested interests, was asked to sponsor this grant.

In April 1979, a joint resolution was passed by the legislature authorizing the council to receive a grant to conduct a study "to thoroughly research who now pays for 'prevention' activities, how much, and specifically for what are they paying. . . ." Resource gaps were to be determined and mission statements of various state agencies were to be examined to see if they should be responsible for any aspect of delinquency prevention programming.

We sought technical assistance from the Westinghouse National Issues Center and the Center for Action Research to help us set goals and develop a work plan. The goal became: "To inform policymakers, funding agencies, supporters, etc., about current views of delinquency prevention in Vermont so that they have more information on which to base their decisions." A major study began.

The resulting report, *Options for Preventing Delinquency in Vermont* (1980), made several recommendations for action, including "gaining an official mandate" for coordination of delinquency prevention at the state level." We then requested funds to hire someone to assist in carrying out the recommendations.

In June 1981, the task force concluded that legislation would "bind state agencies to spend some of their money and time on prevention activities and provide uniform state policy and strategy for implementing theories and programs about delinquency prevention."

Amid a rash of juvenile murders and a panicked special legislative session to make the juvenile code tougher, thoughts of prevention were temporarily set aside. The task force decided to approach the upcoming 1982 legislative session with a legislative resolution on prevention. Others protested that a resolution was nonbinding and wanted it in bill form. The task force drafted the bill and found a friend of prevention in the legislature to sponsor it, Senator Scudder Parker.[*] The bill was redrafted by the Legislative Council who added a "legislative findings" section taken from the *Options ...* report.

There were a couple of sticky points. One provision of the bill called for certain state agencies to allocate one-half of 1% of their total annual budget for prevention activities. After much discussion we were persuaded that the bill (S-255) would never pass with that provision. Being pragmatic, we reluctantly dropped the money provision.

In response to another concern, the legislative council was asked to investigate whether it would be necessary to add an amendment to individual state agency mandates to require those agencies to conduct prevention practices. They concluded that wording in S-255 requiring their action would suffice; therefore, individual mandates were unnecessary.

A third matter also proved troublesome. Federal Law Enforcement Assistance Administration (LEAA) funds were drying up, which meant that "juvenile justice" needed a new home. Recognizing that it could use the prevention bill as an opportunity, the JJDPAG piggybacked a provision renaming the JJDPAG the Delinquency Prevention Coordinating Council (DPCC). The problem was where to house the DPCC and its staff (me, my assistant Brenda Bean, and the person we hired under the grant, Jim Merrill).

Then my executive director jumped in. She wanted juvenile justice to be relocated in the Agency of Human Services (AHS). The JJDPAG disagreed because AHS was one of the agencies cited in the bill as having to comply with the act. Now it would also be serving an oversight function; thus creating an inherent conflict of interest. Shortly thereafter, the executive director told us that the governor opposed bill S.255.

In January of 1982, upon reviewing the annual juvenile justice and Delinquency Prevention Plan, she found with it an article I had written for the Alcohol and Drug Abuse Division prevention newsletter advocating the passage of S.255. She accused me of lobbying, and I received an official written reprimand stating that federal guidelines prohibited me from

---

[*] Note: The bill, S.255, was also sponsored by then-Senator Peter Smith, later Vermont's U.S. congressman, and Senator Sallie Soule, who later became the commissioner of the Department of Employment and Training.

lobbying. I cited a provision that "introduction and support in the state legislature of general statutory reform..." was exempted. In return, I received a memorandum stating that anything I wrote "had to go over [her] desk for approval," and that "failure to comply will result in initiation of suspension procedures." She then struck out all references to S.255 in the juvenile justice plan.

The advisory group and Senator Parker were not pleased. By February, I was prohibited from going down to the legislature because I "represented the Justice Commission and the governor was opposed to the bill." The bill had already passed in the Senate and was heading toward the House. Senator Parker attempted to reach a compromise but the executive director testified that the administration opposed the bill because "making plans with no chance of implementation (no money attached) was a serious concern." S.255 became stalled in the House Government Operations Committee until the legislative session was over. The chairperson of that committee, who had been showered with mail in support of the bill, said the letters had annoyed him considerably. In May 1982, I was given my termination notice, and a new advisory group, called the Delinquency Prevention Coordination Council (DPCC), was appointed by the governor, replacing the members of the old JJDPAG.

I considered this issue far too important to let die, so over the summer I redrafted the bill, expanded it to include prevention of alcohol and drug abuse, child abuse, truancy (because that was a concern of the governor), "and other problem behaviors," and to promote health. I also called together key members of the now-defunct JJDPAG to strategize. Senator Parker was asked to submit a new bill, and in December he brought it before the new DPCC. They agreed to support it. The new bill was numbered S.42. (Note: Bill S.42 was also sponsored by Senator Soule, by former-governor-then-Senator Phil Hoff, and Senator Doug Racine, who later became Vermont's Lieutenant Governor, and George Little.)

The new DPCC chairperson was assured by a key governor's assistant that the governor would not oppose the bill. In the process we learned that the governor had apparently never seen the previous year's bill; that the opposition had come from one of his administrative staff who was a good friend of the executive director. I was asked to testify but declined because I had recently gone to work for the Vermont Alcohol and Drug Abuse Division, although I did encourage other supporters to offer testimony.

Early in the legislative session bill S.42 unanimously passed the Senate (minus the legislative findings section) and was sent to the House. To prevent repetition of the bill stalling in the House Government Operations Committee, after work hours I lobbied key House members extensively, suggesting that S.42 be assigned to the House Health and Welfare Committee, which was chaired by a former member of the old JJDPAG. I met with the speaker of the House and received an agreement to have the bill assigned to Health and Welfare.

That committee's first move was to remove from the definition of "primary prevention" the phrase "and to promote health." Again, some of us were not pleased, but we accepted what seemed to be a necessary compromise.

The committee's second move was to delay the bill. They had been deluged with bills, and S.42 was not their highest priority. I began taking official leave from work so I could spend more time to remind legislators that people were taking the bill seriously. The bill finally came out of committee in March. The legislature had less than three weeks before they would adjourn.

The Government Operations Committee chairperson asked to see the bill. Because I and Brenda Bean, my former assistant (who had taken my former job), were standing in the hallway, we were asked to testify on the spot. During the testimony the chairperson informed us that he didn't like the idea of states getting federal money because they were usually left to pick up the tab. He also didn't like the idea of councils interfering with state government and said he especially hated large councils. For these reasons he intended to kill the bill. We pointed out that no money was attached to the bill, and we gladly offered to cut the size of the council. He said he would think about it. After further crucial negotiations, Bill S.42 came out of committee on the last day bills were allowed onto the floor.

On the next to last day of an extended session in April, Bill S.42 was called to the floor. One House member stood up and gave an impassioned speech against passage. "You watch," he said, "in a couple years they'll be back here asking us for money." A hot debate ensued. It looked bleak. A roll-call vote was called. I sat in the balcony nervously counting votes. The count went back and forth several times. With a surge at the end of the alphabet, the bill passed 74 to 63. The governor signed it reluctantly, and Act 79 of the 1983 legislative session was finally law.

The Children's Trust Fund Provision

Two years later, the Chittenden County Council on Children and Families and the Vermont Children's Forum, a statewide advocacy group for children, undertook to persuade the legislature to establish a children's trust fund, to be financed by taxing pinball and video arcade games. The bill proposed allocating the modest sum of $250,000 to be spent on "effective primary prevention programs."*

When I saw Bill H.561, I panicked, because its provisions were to be tacked onto the statutes established under Act 79, and many of the controversial issues that had nearly killed the original prevention bill were proposed to be put back in—a name change for the DPCC, an increase in council membership, and money for prevention programs. If the key issue was to get a trust fund established, why risk having those other controversial issues jeopardize it, perhaps even risk repeal of all Act 79 statutes? The vote had been close. I protested.

Luckily the prime movers didn't listen to me. Every one of those previously controversial provisions sailed through the legislature with ease, along with a $150,000 allocation for the Children's Trust Fund. By 1986 the legislative climate had apparently changed. Legislators had become familiar with the concept of prevention. A summer study committee of the legislature on "children, youth and families" had recommended a strong focus on prevention. In 1983 we were pioneers. By 1986 our efforts had paved the way for an actual allocation of prevention funds.

Principles to Consider in Setting Policy

Those who wish to pursue the development and passage of state prevention legislation may want to consider the following:

Whether or not it takes the form of legislation, every state needs a policy on prevention. Without policy, prevention is always considered a lesser priority than all the other things state agencies are mandated to do. In Vermont no one had any responsibility for primary prevention. It was occasionally mentioned in a state agency philosophy and mission statement, but never in an agency's "duties and responsibilities" section, and therefore no one took responsibility.

It is unlikely that proponents of prevention in any one field have enough power, resources, or capability to accomplish prevention policy development or change. It takes a

---

* Note: It was submitted to the legislature under the primary sponsorship of Representative Amy Davenport, one of the founders of the Children's Forum, who later became a Vermont judge.

concerted, combined effort from the fields of delinquency, alcohol and drug abuse, child abuse, sexual abuse, domestic violence, teenage pregnancy, teenage suicide, mental health, health promotion and others. Because the same contributing factors apply to all those problems, it should be in everyone's best interests to work together.

Before beginning, it is essential to have data to demonstrate that prevention works. It also helps to be able to say that people want this kind of policy. Prevention is valuable, accountable, and focused; most people just don't know it. We must demonstrate it. Simple before/after evaluation measures of behavior, coupled with testimonials based on the observations of others, can usually convince a legislature of its worth. We now have much national data that can provide a base, but state data are particularly important. In Vermont, because we could demonstrate that school climate improvement reduced vandalism costs in one school from $12,000 to $1,200 in one year, legislators could relate to it.

We should be very clear about exactly what we want the state to do. Decide who should be responsible, if there should be sanctions if agencies do not comply, if funds should be attached. Then draft the concept and shape it into legislation or some other form of policy. This process takes time. Four and a half years passed between the time the Vermont JJDPAG first appointed the prevention policy task force and the time the legislation actually passed.

At least one person must be found who is willing to take responsibility to see the process through to completion. In Vermont, I assumed that role unofficially because I thought it was so important.

A power base must be established. For legislation, the support of at least one legislator must be cultivated. That person can then rally together as many bipartisan sponsors as needed. Outside the legislature it is important to enlist the support of respected community leaders. We were fortunate to have the Chittenden County Council for Children and Families come forward to support and lobby for us at a crucial time. Begin with whatever legislative branch is most responsive.

In preparing testimony, logic is essential, but understand that logic is not what will win over legislators. Impeccable logic must be used because, if it isn't, those intending to kill the bill will use it against us. In the end, though, **it is emotion that usually makes or breaks legislation.** In Vermont the prevention bill nearly got killed because a key committee member did not like large councils. **Remember, even opponents can often agree on overall desired results. Methods and strategies are what people usually disagree on. Everyone wants less crime and less abuse. Points of disagreement should be anticipated beforehand and responses planned.** Much of what happens will be unexpected, so it's best to be prepared for all that's predictable. It's also helpful to decide beforehand what points you are willing to compromise on. In Vermont, we were quick to offer to reduce the size of the council. We even submitted the bill with no money attached—the money came three years later.

A good, crisp show is necessary. There should be no overkill, no wasted words. Legislators are not bureaucrats, and they despise being talked to as if they are. They tend to think more like the average person, the difference being that they are highly motivated by issues that suit their political ambitions.

Another principle is borrowed from Reality Therapy. **Never give up!** If we fail the first time, we must try again. This issue is too important.

Implementation

The Vermont prevention law did not result in overnight changes. Implementation has been difficult.

Authority for implementation was vested in the Delinquency Prevention Coordinating Council (later named the Children and Family council for Prevention Programs). Since our protests about conflict of interest had fallen on deaf ears, the Agency of Human Services became responsible for staffing the council. As a substance abuse intervention specialist, I was out of the picture and could only watch from a distance.

In April 1983, immediately after the law was passed, the Agency of Human Services Planning Division shifted into first gear. How would departments best comply? Two schools of thought emerged: (1) force compliance through gubernatorial or secretarial dictum; or (2) involve and motivate commissioners to respond enthusiastically. AHS chose the latter, along with another idea: human services departments had a poor public relations image; could this prevention stuff be used to build better public relations? Some of us cringed.

Each department was asked to appoint a representative to serve on a Primary Prevention Task Force that would be charged with developing an approach to implement the law. It consisted largely of middle-level managers from the agencies responsible for complying. Their job was to plan how Act 79 should be implemented. Some of us disagreed that the agencies responsible for compliance should determine what compliance should consist of.

An important part of the AHS approach was to hold a large conference for commissioners to excite them about prevention and motivate them to comply. The conference was planned for September, but it never happened. The consultants who were lined up fell through. It never rematerialized and nothing replaced it. Thus the commissioners were being asked to be enthusiastic about something they didn't understand or care about. The task force began working on a philosophy and mission statement. They quickly concluded that they didn't know enough about prevention to even construct a mission statement, so AHS assigned one of its planners to examine the existing research on delinquency, child abuse, and substance abuse. This resulted in a comprehensive report, called "Primary Prevention of Problem Behaviors" (Samets, 1983). The research was exhaustive but the draft report lacked clear conclusions that could communicate what prevention was all about. I decided to take a shot at making sense of the data. This resulted in my "conceptual framework of prevention" [Chapter 5], which became the introduction to the Samets report.

In the meantime, the departments had been asked to submit in writing what they were doing now with respect to prevention and to identify priority problems to work on. A couple of commissioners were overheard saying that they would not comply with the request because they had too much else to do; others said they would just pay it lip service. Some departments complied but many of their goals and objectives did not coincide with the concept of primary prevention. Task force members expressed that prevention was too intangible and that they weren't being provided with enough direction. It was a predictable response. Since the original plan was predicated on an informational-motivational conference that never happened, many departments were left struggling in a vacuum. I was asked to present the conceptual framework to the task force. It at least provided a focus, but it was still not presented to commissioners.

In May 1983, a new statewide grassroots group, called the Vermont Prevention Group, formed to provide support for prevention workers and advocate for prevention concerns. One of the group's first moves was to write a letter suggesting that local input be included on the Primary Prevention Task Force, and that the Vermont Prevention Group should be represented.

Because enthusiastic commitment was not flowing from commissioners, the AHS planning director, Ted Mable, proposed that all federal juvenile justice funds earmarked for prevention be put into one large collaborative "model" prevention project in one community, so people could see large-scale results for the first time. While some of us liked this idea, the council, which had essentially delegated its Act implementation responsibilities to the task force, turned down this recommendation in favor of their usual method of dividing the money into smaller grants to cover more communities.

By January 1984 it was clear that the original approach was not working. Some Primary Prevention Task Force members began to demand a more coordinated, rather than an individual agency-oriented, approach. The task force decided to change its focus.

Three subcommittees were formed. Subcommittee A would **offer grants to local communities** to initiate projects that respected the intent of the act. Subcommittee B would develop the means to **provide technical assistance and training** to state agency staff who, in turn, would provide technical assistance to local communities to initiate prevention efforts. Subcommittee C would **help state agencies and departments examine their own policies in accordance with effective prevention practice and make changes where necessary**.

Results: Subcommittee A increased funding for community-based prevention efforts. This approach was not new—both JJDP and alcohol and drug abuse prevention funds had been supporting community prevention projects for years—but this funding mechanism became the template for awarding Children's Trust Fund grants once those amendments were passed two years later.

Subcommittee B evolved into the *Vermont Prevention Training Team* [later the *Vermont Prevention Institute Consultation Team*], a collaborative state-private effort where, initially, 23 members were selected and trained by Bill Lofquist to provide prevention training to communities and organizations throughout the state.

Subcommittee C tackled what I believed to be the core of the prevention act. Our first mistake was trying to use logic. We devised a series of questions to help guide departments logically to altering policies and practices in favor of good prevention practice. We asked ourselves, Under what circumstances do state agencies have influence over people and local institutions? We came up with three answers:

1. when individuals need or want something from the state (Welfare, driver's licenses, teacher certification, etc.)
2. when individuals fall under the custody or supervision of the state (Corrections and Social Service clients, etc.)
3. when local agencies, institutions or community groups receive funding or certification from the state (community mental health centers, schools, day care centers, and so on.)

We then asked the departments to indicate who fell into these categories, what healthy self-perceptions and life skills they desired to produce among the individuals or institutions listed, and to cite any laws or policies under which they operated that might affect those perceptions and skills. This set of questions proved too cumbersome for most departments and yielded little of substance. At this point, some lost enthusiasm for cooperating.

When that didn't produce what we wanted, we altered our tack. We listed the criteria in the act (in Section 3304(a)) that indicated whether or not an activity fit the concept of primary prevention. Given this criteria, we asked the departments to specify three policies or practices they would attempt to alter, eliminate, or expand over the next year, and to specify steps to accomplish these goals. We received a satisfactory response from approximately half the departments. For example, the Office of Alcohol and Drug Abuse Programs agreed to: (1) spend an increased percentage of its community grants funds to alter conditions of institutions that affect children's self-perceptions, (2) to assist the Department of Education in helping schools comply with the "school climate standard," and (3) to increase the number of Developing Capable People courses throughout the state to better affect families.

I changed jobs again, and the plans were set on the shelf. Subcommittee C had no clout. Those in positions of authority were reluctant to force the departments to comply, and subcommittee members who had stuck with it to this point burned out. The Primary Prevention Task Force disbanded, leaving the authority for implementing the Act back where it should have been, with the council (now called the Children and Family Council for Prevention Programs under the new children's trust fund amendments).

Vermont also had a new governor. In July 1986, three years after the passage of Act 79, the council wrote to the new secretary of administration, stating that it "continues to express frustration with the resistance from many departments to respond, the inadequacy of their response, and the lack of mandate from authority to require prevention policies and practices for primary prevention." We wanted the governor to require additional wording in the Fiscal Year '88 budget planning guidelines corresponding to the implementation section of the prevention law (§ 3305). The budget and management office then asked the Agency of Human Services what they thought of this idea, found an unreceptive audience, and dropped it.

In 1988 I called the new council chair, Guy Fournier, and reminded him of his original idea to use the budget planning process to ensure compliance. I proposed draft wording to the FY'90 budget instructions:

In accordance with 33 VSA 3305 (Implementation of Act 79 of 1983), specify the primary prevention policies and implementation practices your agency/department/office has formulated consistent with the State Primary Prevention Plans since their inception in 1984...

The council turned down Fournier's plan. They said its role should be to exercise the lead in bringing those agencies into the prevention planning process. Frustrated, Fournier told me he would continue to pursue it.

Just as things looked most bleak, the Agency of Human Services planning director, Ted Mable, developed an AHS Prevention Institute [later called the Vermont Prevention Institute], which would include representation from all AHS departments and offices. They revitalized the planning process under Act 79, and a fourth Vermont state prevention plan materialized. A new Child Safety Coalition formed and recommended that Act 79 be amended to remove the conflict of interest within AHS and establish enforcement provisions. This never happened.

Seven years after the passage of Act 79, little behavior change could be observed on the part of state agencies. There were no enforcement provisions in the legislation and no one in a position of authority had taken the responsibility to force or even strongly encourage compliance by state department commissioners. For whatever reasons, most commissioners perceived this law to be one they neither needed nor desired to take seriously. Prevention, law or not, was still one of the lowest priorities of state agencies. The council, with staffing from the Agency of Human Services, had been trying to figure out a viable way of ensuring compliance for years without much success.

And then—

Then an amazing thing happened. Fortuitously, Cornelius "Con" Hogan was appointed Secretary of the Vermont Agency of Human Services. In addition, a new Governor, Howard Dean, who was a big supporter of prevention, came into office. Governor Dean pushed a *Success by Six* effort which assisted communities in pulling together what needed to be done to ensure that children would be successful by the time they entered school. Con Hogan insisted on the development of desired outcomes for the entire range of human services, and in partnership with the Department of Education and other agencies. These were developed by a new State team for Children and Families consisting of membership from all state human services departments and the department of education, and with community input. The outcomes are-

- Pregnant women and infants thrive
- Infants and children thrive
- Children are ready for school
- Children succeed in school
- Children live in stable, supported families
- Youth choose healthy behaviors
- Youth successfully transition into adulthood
- Elders and people with disabilities live with dignity and independence in settings they prefer
- Families and individuals live in safe and supportive communities, where they are engaged and contributing members

Hogan ensured that measurable indicators were developed for all state outcomes, that baseline measures are taken of all important human services-related behaviors, and subsequently that measures were taken every year so the state could always tell how it was doing at any moment, and trends could be observed. Annually, the Vermont Agency of Human Services issues a report titled, *The Social Well-Being of Vermonters* (Murphey, 1999) which graphs trends in all major outcome areas. Over the decade child abuse rates, for example, have shown a dramatic reduction. Through Hogan's efforts, a system of community partnerships developed, with support and oversight provided by the State Team for Children and Families facilitated by Deputy Secretary Cheryl Mitchell [see Chapter 9]. Hogan ended up doing more to create policy-level prevention and guide action of state agencies toward that end than anything the Act 79 legislation was able to accomplish on its own. Hogan actually paid little attention to Act 79 itself, but his efforts resulted in some real accomplishments of that law that helped to fulfill its purpose.

Conclusions

Was the legislation worth it? I believe so. It has generated much discussion, some research and, even without Secretary Hogan, some action. Before 1983, not many in the state were seriously discussing prevention; now it is commonly discussed and commonly accepted. At least, in answering the question, "Does your state have a policy on prevention?" Vermonters can answer "yes." It may not be the best it could be and may have serious enforcement flaws, but it is an important beginning, and it is a reason for the state's continuing involvement with prevention.

Act 79 guidelines resulted in bringing community people together to formulate local plans for the use of prevention grants. It led to a statewide prevention training team to guide state agency personnel and community members in prevention theory and implementation practices. It caused state agencies to examine some of their own policies and practices that might inhibit or contradict good prevention practice. And although this last effort subsequently died, in retrospect some important policy changes were recommended that could prove instructive to other states attempting a similar approach (hopefully learning from Vermont's mistakes).

- The Department of Social Welfare, in collaboration with the Department of Employment and Training, the Department of Education, and the governor's office, began the "Reach-Up" program to provide vocational and employment opportunities to ANFC single parents, to prevent chronic welfare dependency. Later it implemented Welfare reform.
- The Department of Forests, Parks, and Recreation proposed to provide workshops for communities on healthy leisure lifestyles, and assist municipal recreation directors in establishing latch-key recreation programs.
- The Department of Mental Health proposed to continue, with state funding, self-help "mutual support groups" and groups for family members (because federal funds to support their development were drying up).
- The Department of Education proposed to initiate a program of in-service training for elementary school staff on management of student behavior. (Note: In addition, although this was not included in their submission, they passed a set of school approval standards that included a standard on school climate, comprehensive health education, and school leadership. And in 1990, they began a grant program to reinvent schools for very high performance.)
- The Department of Health proposed to institutionalize with state funding the "Healthy Start" Program that provided pre- and post-natal education to all first-time parents-to-be.
- The Agency of Human Services, as part of its reorganization plans, built in community prevention organizing as a major role of a new regional coordinator position [which since disappeared].

Some of these policy changes were actually realized. It is exciting to think how much more could be accomplished if state agencies truly committed themselves to more changes like these.

Here are a few more ideas of what departments might do to improve policies and practices in favor of prevention:

- The Department of Motor Vehicles could add an item to the driver's license exam requiring each individual to calculate his/her own blood alcohol content level, based upon his/her own body weight. As a requirement for passing, the applicant would have to know how many drinks over particular time periods would make him/her first become impaired and then no longer safe to drive under the law.
- The Department of Corrections, in cooperation with the Department of Public Safety, the Court Administrator's Office, the Office of the Defender General, and the Department of Education could develop a law-related education course and promote it in every middle and high school in the state.

- The Department of Education could require, as a condition of teacher certification and recertification, courses in classroom management techniques, creative instructional practices, school effectiveness, and other school climate strategies.
- The Department of Mental Health could require community mental health centers to devote a designated percentage of their time and resources on prevention to receive contract renewal approval.
- The State Economic Opportunity Office could require as a condition of funding for community action programs that a designated percentage of staff time and resources be devoted to community organizing to fight poverty.
- The Department of Social Services could work with school systems to educate and train students in child care, and help create licensed, affordable day care in schools, staffed primarily with student volunteers, as a service to the community. It could also require incentives for foster parents and group home staff to be trained in effective parenting skills, and provide that training.
- The Alcohol and Drug Abuse Office and other agencies that give out grants could do what Colorado ADAP did: require that all grant recipients attend a one-week training on prevention theory and practice as a condition for funding.

These are but a few of many creative things that can be accomplished without budget increases, in the name of prevention policy development. Changes in state government behavior should continue to be realized as new attempts are made to ensure that agencies comply with the law. Legislating prevention can lead the horse to the water which, at the very least, offers the opportunity for drink.

Prevention Policy in Virginia

Other states, like Virginia, began to recognize the importance of having a coordinated state prevention plan as a policy approach.

In November 1986, after consulting with Vermont, Virginia's Governor's Task Force on Coordinating Preventive Health, Education, and Social Programs recommended the enactment of a prevention policy, formation of a prevention council, delineation of individual agency responsibilities, and an analysis of programs to determine their potential to prevent problems.

In 1987, these recommendations resulted in passage of a law titled "Virginia Council on Coordinating Prevention" (Title 9-270(8)-273).

The result of Virginia's effort was an excellent collaborative state prevention plan. Guided by the planning and staffing skills of Harriet Russell, the 1990 Comprehensive Prevention Plan for Virginia lists seven basic goals in the areas of healthy lifestyles, responsible parenthood, healthy mothers and babies, positive child development, positive youth development, positive family life, gainful employment and literacy, independent living, and safe environment.

Results-oriented "objectives" are designated for each goal. Examples:

- To decrease the incidence of suicide in Virginia by 10% by 1994
- To reduce the number of Virginians who are overweight from 22% to 18% by 1994
- To reduce from 6.5% (8200) of total pregnancies in women under the age of 17 to 5% (6324) by 1994
- To increase from 79.8% to 85% by 1994, the number of women who initiate prenatal care during the first trimester of their pregnancy

- To decrease by 50% the number of localities with no licensed child care providers from 22 to 11 in 1994
- To increase the high school graduation rate from 75.7% to 88% by 1994
- To reduce the number of substantiated child abuse/neglect cases by 10% in 1994
  and so on ...

Listed under each objective are the state agencies responsible for spearheading the effort, other key players, a brief rationale, target populations, source of objective, resource analysis, and a range of possible strategies.

As of the publication of the first edition of this book, Virginia's plan was and possibly still is the best in the country—a model for us all. The more states that adapt a comprehensive prevention planning process, the better off prevention will be.

Other Statewide Prevention Policy Efforts

Spearheaded by Betty Tableman of the Department of Mental Health, Michigan established a prevention department, including directives for state agencies, localities, and private organizations. New Jersey developed a state prevention plan, partially based on the conceptual framework in this book. South Carolina established a primary prevention council through executive order by the governor. Rhode Island has legislation that establishes community ("Branley") task forces for alcohol and drug abuse prevention and provides operational funds from fines collected from traffic violations. Oregon, Maryland, and Connecticut have strong state policies for "family support." Other states have more specific state plans for the prevention of child abuse, or delinquency, or other problems. Many children's trust funds now exist in different forms in many states. Delaware and a couple of other states have a cross-disciplinary state office for prevention.

In its document, *The Prevention of Mental-Emotional Disabilities* (1986), the National Mental Health Association Commission on the Prevention of Mental-Emotional Disabilities offered some policy recommendations for states that are worth noting. These include creating a designated prevention unit in each state mental health agency with adequate budget and administrative structure and a legislative mandate; a statewide coordinated plan for prevention that involves citizen participation; technical assistance and incentives to develop, implement, and evaluate prevention programs; a statewide clearinghouse for prevention information and programs; and informing and educating the public.

The state of California had raised some eyebrows with its policy recommendations on self-esteem from the legislatively sanctioned California Task Force to Promote Self-Esteem and Personal and Social Responsibility. In January 1990 they came out with a document titled *Toward a State of Esteem*. Though the concept has been subjected to some ridicule, the report resulted in some excellent recommendations pertaining to prevention. As assemblyman John Vasconcellos wrote in the preface to the report, it is time "...to turn our attention to searching out the root causes of our social problems and to addressing them effectively, preventively."

In the late 1990s, in a collaborative effort among seven statewide prevention-related organizations, the California prevention network developed a prevention platform that is well worth noting. First, they established what they called "guiding principles:"

- commitment to prevention programs and strategies that have proven effectiveness and that are culturally competent

381

- a commitment to science-based prevention
- recognition that the state must include prevention perspectives involving both individual-based strategies and environmental-based approaches
- recognition of the importance of a multiple strategy and comprehensive approach in implementing prevention efforts
- acknowledgement of the importance and primacy of collaborative approaches in planning sustainable prevention efforts at the community level
- recognition of the importance of local determination as the foundation factor for initiating prevention services appropriate to the needs and diversity of the community
- commitment to a results/outcome-based system for delivering and assessing prevention service at the local and state level
- commitment to integrating a linkage between research findings and policy implementation
- commitment to a continuous review of research that will result in a field that responsively learns and changes based on new and changing information

Then they offered these planks as a "framework for the future:"

1. Create a representative statewide prevention collaborative
2. Assert state leadership with a Prevention Services Division
3. Incorporate a youth-development model into prevention and actively engage youth in the decision-making process
4. Ground California State ATOD policies in science-based strategies and programs within an outcome-based system
5. Move toward professional standards in the field of prevention by developing core curriculum and training programs
6. Maintain and expand, as appropriate, contracts to provide technical assistance
7. Ensure appropriate utilization of block grant prevention sources
8. Convene and annual prevention training summit

As of this writing, in one of the most exciting and hopeful efforts to date, the state of Oregon has passed legislation requiring state agencies to collaborate in developing one common prevention plan for each county that encompasses all prevention-related activity across disciplines to foster caring and productive communities.

Each of the different state approaches noted above can be instructive for any state embarking on a prevention policy effort.

Some Summary Process Questions

Before embarking on prevention policy development, however, it would be helpful to ask some important questions to help guide such efforts:

- Who will take the responsibility?
- Which individual will take on the oversight of establishing prevention policy and commit to seeing it through from beginning to end, no matter what? Because something of this magnitude obviously cannot be accomplished alone, what group will champion the cause and commit to taking on the process?
- Who is needed for help?
- What other groups can be brought in to help sponsor this effort? What other fields should be involved?

- Who are the people in positions of power whose support must be cultivated if prevention policy at any level is to be approved? What would motivate them? What would get them interested? What are their major points of resistance likely to be?
- Is technical assistance needed? It is often helpful to bring in someone from outside the state who does not have a vested interest in what happens to objectively help the state frame its direction and consider a variety of possibilities.
- What is the best level at which policy can occur? Is it through law? Through legislation? Would it be better through some other point of authority? Who specifically should be required to do what? What specifically should be affected? Funding? Practice?
- What happens after the policy is passed? Are enforcement mechanisms necessary, and if so, how extreme must they be? Who would specifically be responsible for enforcing each rule and practice? What will happen if organizations do not comply?

The more states that adopt prevention policy of some kind, the closer we will come to the establishment of national prevention policy.

33. Toward National Prevention Policy

The United States of America is one of only two industrialized nations that still does not have a policy for children or families.

If the various prevention fields received merely half of what is spent on enforcement, treatment, rehabilitation and incarceration per year, prevention practitioners likely would be ecstatic. Many would be satisfied with one-tenth that amount because it would be far more than they receive now. Even quintupling current prevention funding would amount to a drop in the bucket of what needs to be done to truly solve those problems. The government of the United States is always demonstrating its priorities in the Federal budget. Difficult decisions need to be made now to change, or it will be too late!

A nation must be strong from both without and within. The Constitution of the United States places equal emphasis on "promoting the general welfare," "insuring domestic tranquility," and "establishing justice" as it does in "providing for the common defense" and "securing the blessings of liberty to ourselves and our prosperity." Yet resources are not allocated equitably to these pursuits. This nation has not appeared as concerned with protecting its society from internal destruction as it has been in protecting itself from outside enemies. The result is that the United States leads the world in military spending, yet ranks only fourteenth in keeping infants alive in the first year of life and fifteenth in the world in infant mortality rate. It is time to even out constitutional intent. It is time to create a national policy for children and families that reflects good prevention practice. How much longer can we wait? How many more lives are we willing to sacrifice, to ruin or to lose?

Prevention is our greatest potential. Prevention is the only cost-effective way to deal with the social problems—such as violence and drug/alcohol abuse—that this nation is so concerned about.

The issue confronting policy makers is not whether the nation can afford health reforms for children, but whether it can afford not to enact long term improvements. Young people between the ages of 16 and 24 comprised 23% of the U.S. population in 1978 but...constitute[d] only 16% [in] 1995. One in three of our new workers will be members of a minority group. As the number of young workers steadily declines, therefore, business and industry will be forced to rely upon workers and potential workers in whom we traditionally have failed to invest. Our future prosperity now depends in large part on our ability to enhance the prospects and productivity of a new generation of employees that is disproportionately poor, minority, unhealthy, undereducated and untrained. Good health can make the difference between a thriving, productive and

385

competitive workforce and one hampered by preventable illnesses and disabling conditions. Our national wellbeing depends on the future of child health policy (Rosenbaum, 1989).

As Congressman George Miller (1989) says, we've got to turn around the argument. We've been playing defense, and it's now time to play offense. We've got to start asking the same questions of other budgets as are being asked of funding to support families, children, and prevention. When a warhead falls off a nuclear missile we need to ask, "Where's the money coming from?" If we do not invest in prevention and take immediate action, here are the stakes we're playing for: we will not have a competitive workforce in the future, and we will be continuing to waste our money. Therefore, let's invest $10 billion over the next ten years in a success story. We've had enough discussion. The evidence is in! We have all these programs that can show a good return on our investment. We could pay for it if we took our budget surpluses now and paid down our national debt of $5 trillion plus, so we could stop wasting 15-18% of our total tax money to pay interest on that debt. And because the gap between rich and poor in this country is the widest it has ever been, have the wealthy pay their fair share. It is time to ask ourselves who is making money off all that interest we pay. They are the ones who should pay us back.

National policy must guide and direct resources toward an effective preventive approach to problems. At present we have none. In 1989, we saw movement toward this end when the Child Welfare League, the Children's Defense Fund, and the Family Resource Coalition all had national conferences addressing national policy within weeks of each other. In 1999 the alcohol, tobacco and other drug prevention field held a "National Prevention Congress." The year 2000 finds Prevent Child Abuse-America involved in a National Call to Action and, picking up on Ben & Jerry's creative efforts [Chapter 29], pushing a 1% (of the budget surplus) for children campaign. Despite these wonderful efforts, we still do not have a national policy for prevention, children, and families.

An Attempt to Create National Prevention Policy

Every once in a while it is expansive to challenge ourselves, to reach beyond the bounds of our own comfort, to reach beyond what we know and what we believe we do well, to step into uncertain realms that have potential to make even more of a difference than what we are already doing.

In 1991 I took such a leap. A friend of mine who is also a psychic [Chapter 43] said something to me that I found incredible. "Envision your perfect job," she said, "then make it happen." What a thought!

Almost before I knew what hit me, I found myself applying for funds from the Ben & Jerry's Foundation to create and establish a national policy for prevention and for the health and well-being of children and families. I had been preaching that we needed to change the way our nation conducts its business with respect to our social-behavior problems. I knew it would take a national vision and commitment to turn this country around. I knew that if we could force the creation of national policy, prevention may be able to rise to the next plane. I decided to stop talking and try to do something about it.

I knew this would be a huge task, but the more I thought about it the more I believed it could be done. With the help of key organizations, I believed we could create the kind of policy that we want and get it passed, thereby guiding this nation toward practices that would promote the health and well-being of children and families and lead to a reduction of problems.

It would not work without collaboration across the different symptom-specific prevention fields. The problem is, even though we now know there is a common core to preventing all these problems [Chapters 5 & 6], little collaboration exists. I am not talking about "networking" in the traditional sense; rather, true collaboration or what Lofquist (1991) refers to as *Level III networking*. If the various prevention fields were to come together, discover the common elements, and pool resources to make a real difference at those common levels, behaviors might begin to be changed on a wide scale for the first time.

Imagine what it would be like if the major advocacy organizations from all related social-problem fields joined together and spoke with one voice. Imagine a written statement of priority direction for the United States, agreed to and signed by all such organizations. Imagine constituencies of all these organizations together persuading Congress and the Administration that these must be the priorities for U.S. domestic policy—to prevent the social problems they claim to be so concerned about. If properly organized and carried out, this approach could yield the kind of policy change that we are desperately in need of.

So I decided to try to bring together the major national advocacy organizations, coalitions, and associations that represent the different problem-based fields (alcohol/drug abuse, delinquency, child abuse, sexual abuse, teenage pregnancy, teenage suicide, etc.), and children and families, each of whom could in turn reach their own wide, respective memberships.

To my surprise I received the Ben & Jerry's grant, albeit for about 1/4 of what I applied for. But supplemented by an anonymous donation and a small grant from the Haymarket Foundation, though I didn't really have enough funds to proceed, I thought I'd jump into the fire.

I failed (or rather, I had an incredible learning experience). I offer this so others can learn from my mistakes.

My plan was to contact these organizations to try to convince them to join together in united action to produce a written policy statement that defined a direction for the nation in support of prevention, children and families. I wanted their pledge that they would agree to sit down together for a week in Washington, D.C. with the intent of reaching agreement on this national agenda. We would then draft a statement of national policy, send it out to those and other organizations for comments and changes, redraft the policy, and have all the organizations reach agreement and "sign on" to the policy statement.

I wrote a letter to major national organizations, with follow-up by phone. Those willing to explore the subject further included the Child Welfare League of America, Children's Defense Fund, Family Resource Coalition, National Association of Prevention Practitioners and Advocates (NAPPA), National Coalition Against Domestic Violence, National Coalition Against Sexual Assault, National Coalition of Children's Trust and Prevention Funds, National Coalition of State Juvenile Justice Advisory Groups, National Committee for the Prevention of Child Abuse, National Committee on Prevention of Teenage Suicide, National Mental Health Association and its National Prevention Coalition, National Minority AIDS Council, National Organization of Adolescent Pregnancy and Parenting, National Prevention Network, and Parent Action.

Though I received no bites from organizations representing various government functions (such as the National Governor's Association) or corporate interests (such as the National Alliance of Business), or from any organization whose purpose is the general concern of various minorities (such as the NAACP and the Congress of American Indians), I was heartened. The organizations that responded also suggested others, among them: the American Public Health Association, American Public Welfare Association, National Assembly of Voluntary Health and Social Welfare Organizations, National Council on Child Abuse and Family Violence, National Crime Prevention Council, Joining Forces. It became clear that the number of appropriate organizations could get out of hand. I had to walk the fine line between being all-inclusive and having a manageable number to work productively. There would be opportunity for other organizations to sign on later, prior to approaching policymakers.

I flew to Washington where many of the organizations are based and met with a number of them. Face-to-face meetings proved far more productive than phone calls. Where over the phone I'd perceived some arrogance (we're-doing-what-we-need-to-be-doing-and-who-are-you-to-suggest-that-we-do-something-differently), in person they were far more friendly and responsive. Most agreed to participate, although in some cases it seemed a begrudging commitment. Before beginning this effort my intention had been to wait until this book was published so I would have some name recognition but, as in the best laid plans of mice and humans, the publication date kept being delayed, so I was forced to begin before the book came out. I had the feeling that many of these organizations were saying, "Who is this guy?"

I found three reactions particularly interesting. The National Association of Hispanic Health and Human Service Organizations said to me, "We already developed a national policy: the National Commission on Children report" (which at that time was due out in one month). The National Mental Health Association said, "We already have a national policy: the Healthy People 2000 Objectives." The National Assembly of Voluntary Health and Social Welfare Organizations said, "We already have a national policy: the new Young American's Act" (P.L. 101-501, Sec. 901-919).

Something was wrong. If we really did have a U.S. policy for prevention, children and families, why didn't I know about it? More important, why didn't other prestigious national organizations I'd spoken with such as the Children's Defense Fund and the Child Welfare League believe that we had such a policy, especially when some of them sat on the National Commission on Children and had contributed to Healthy People 2000? Were any of these so-called policies officially declared by the U.S. government? The last thing I wanted to do was duplicate any efforts, so I thoroughly researched each of these "policies." Interestingly, in the process I discovered other "policy statements," among them the U.N. Convention on the Rights of the Child resolution, which the U.S. was one of only a handful of nations at that time not to sign.

It struck me that while each of these efforts was an important step toward the creation of national policy and we certainly had greater potential for attaining one than ever before, the fact was that we still had no statement to point to as, "the official U.S. policy for prevention, children and families." My purpose was to create such a statement—what we believe the U.S. should adopt as government policy; what the U.S. will commit itself to do. The statement would likely be based upon many recommendations from other related policy efforts, but it would all be set down in one place.

The fact was that the National Commission on Children report, as beautiful as it turned out, was only a set of recommendations—not policy. The Healthy People 2000 Objectives specified a set of laudable desired results for the nation and suggested what one federal department (Health and Human Services) might do to achieve those results; but its use was only "encouraged." Even the Young American's Act, clearly law, contained a provision that the Commissioner of a new Administration on Children, Youth, and Families, and a presidentially-appointed Federal Council, was to set and recommend policies on children, youth, and families. In other words, we didn't have a policy yet. I was reminded of the national energy policy which was considered a joke by energy and environmental experts across the nation. Did we want to wait for the government to draw up a policy that we would then react to after it was too late, or did we want to be proactive and recommend one?

I prepared for the week-long forum in Washington, where we would draft the policy statement. To strike the delicate balance of respecting individual needs and ideas and creating ownership, yet limiting unnecessary floundering, I constructed a fairly simple process that would help it go smoothly. We would first seek agreement on the categories and sub-categories around which we believe national prevention policy should be developed. We would then get only as specific in each as agreement allowed. Sometimes we might only be able to agree on general concerns, sometimes on specifics such as "what must be provided and to what extent?" and perhaps even on "what should be governmental responsibility." We would always aim to reach the most specific position possible, but we would accept wherever we landed, wherever that may be.

Everything was lined up and ready to go for this first, important step. My plan was that after the actual statement was developed and agreed to, we would then create a structure for the organizations to appeal to their respective constituencies, who, in turn, would systematically contact policymakers to get the U.S. government to adopt the policy. Two weeks before the week in Washington I had 15 organizations committed and ready to go. I thought it was a terrific plan—

—until no one showed up on the date scheduled to draft the policy! I shouldn't say "no one": the Child Welfare League, the National Crime Prevention Council, the National Minority AIDS Council, and the National Assembly of Voluntary Health and Social Welfare Organizations— bless their hearts—trickled in at different times during the week. The Child Welfare League had graciously arranged for us to use the National Association of Counties conference room. Picture me sitting alone at a large oblong table in a plush room, with piles of material spread around me. And I was supposed to be there for a week, virtually on my own expense money because I hadn't quite accumulated enough funds to support me while I was down there! Where were they? I phoned them. The reasons they had for not being there were all impressive, and it all seemed like one huge coincidence. At that point I had to admit that my confidence was shaken.

It took me a day and a half to recover. Then I figured, "Well, the intent of this week was supposed to be to draft a policy statement, so I will draft it! I would still be sending it out to them for comments and changes, so why not? Besides, the Child Welfare League lent me an intern. [Thank you, Mary Rouvellas.] What more did I need!

Fortunately, we had access to a wealth of documents to help guide us. Many high powered people through many Commissions had put years of work into making policy recommendations, and we would draw upon this knowledge. I spread around me the National Commission on Children report (1991), the National Commission on Child Welfare and Family Preservation report (1991), The Children Defense Fund's Agenda for the 1990s (1989), the Healthy People 2000 Objectives (American Public Health Association, 1990), the ABA report comparing the U.N. Convention on the Rights of the Child with U.S. Law (American Bar Association, 1991), the Child Welfare League's Comprehensive Child Welfare Initiative (1991), the Milton S. Eisenhower Foundation (1991) report on Youth Investment and Community Reconstruction, the National Governors Association's (1989) America In Transition report (with, by the way, Bill Clinton as Chairman of the NGA Task Force on Children), the Committee for Economic Development's (1991) New Vision for Child Development and Education, the Institute for

Educational Leadership report, the National Mental Health Association (1986) report on the Prevention of Mental-Emotional Disabilities, the National Forum on the Future of American Children, and *Prevention: The Critical Need* (1991).

I started following the procedure I'd outlined. I envisioned the policy statement in the form of a Congressional Resolution. It was tough work, but doable.

It took me about a month to complete it. I sent it out to everyone for comment as if nothing out of the ordinary had happened.

I thought the draft policy statement was pretty incredible, if I did say so myself. If the U.S. government were only guided by this policy, we would have far fewer problems. I felt good about what was being accomplished—

—until the deadline for comments passed with only the Child Welfare League responding, and with NAPPA the only other organization expressing continued interest. Now I was bummed! Where did I go wrong, I wondered? I was at the crossroads. Should I continue the charade and move to the next step? No, I concluded, it just didn't make sense to go further without support.

I wrote a final letter to the organizations explaining that I was forced to conclude that this effort didn't appear to be enough of a priority to them to warrant my continued involvement, and that I turned over the redrafted policy resolution to the Child Welfare League and NAPPA [now defunct] to use however they saw fit.

I admit I may have made mistakes in the process. I probably should have sought written commitments from the organizations that they would attend and follow through. I probably should have spoken to them more by phone, even though many seemed to have difficulty returning my phone calls. I perhaps could have done lots of things differently. But that's hindsight.

I thought the outcome was unfortunate, for I truly believe that a broad-based coalition of existing coalitions and associations, representing all problems we would like to prevent and the health and well-being of children and families—with all their constituencies pushing for the same thing and putting pressure on our political leaders—may be the only way we will see substantive policy change in this country. I am not suggesting that all the related efforts that have been conducted to date and all the legislation and guidelines that have passed and will pass as a result of those organizations' wonderful efforts have not been very important and worthwhile—because there is no question about that. But to take the next step, to reach that next level—to make what we believe actually become what this nation stands for and which if passed could change the entire way the U.S. government conducts its affairs with respect to these issues—we will have to reach beyond the strategies that we are now using.

However, the effort was hardly a total loss. I offer what I consider to be an impressive policy blueprint—albeit controversial in spots—that consolidates many of the recommendations made in those reports and tells the government what it should do with respect to young people and families. It is a statement of policy direction that organizations could use to form a basis from which future legislation and changes in administrative guidelines could spring—so they do not appear piecemeal to the general public, or even to us.

Components of a National Prevention Policy

What should a "National Prevention Policy" consist of? It seems to me that the following components must be in place:

1. A statement of intent or mission, by the United States government
2. A statement of desired results and indicators of success; in other words, What results does the U.S. hope to achieve through this policy?
3. A statement of what specifically must occur for those desired results to be achieved; in other words, What must be in place (that is not now in place), or what must happen (that is not now happening), to realize these results, and to what extent?
4. A statement of agency-designated responsibility: What Federal agency is responsible for ensuring that each stated result is achieved, and with what other agencies must it collaborate in so doing? [Note: This is not meant to imply that Federal Agencies should be the ones to conduct the programs or do whatever has to be done—this is probably accomplished best at the local or state levels—but the responsibility for making it happen and ensuring that it happens lies at the Federal level.]
5. A mechanism(s) of responsibility; or, By what means will these occur? How will each statement be guaranteed? Through passage of law? Through Administrative edict? Some other means?
6. A commitment of resources to make the potential a reality.
7. A mechanism of enforcement; or, What will happen if those agencies do not take their assigned responsibility or achieve these results?

In other words, the government, through such a policy would be using its resources to work with communities to try to prevent these problems before they begin, so we do not have to pay ever-escalating costs to pick up the pieces and patch people up after the fact.

See Appendix for what can be considered a working draft of a national policy that can be altered in any way that allows it to better meet its intent. This policy draft is huge because there is so much to be done, and it is costly. However, it will save money in the long run! And, **it is important for everyone to realize that if the $5.6+ trillion national debt (at the time of this second edition) is paid off forthwith by earmarking *all* budget surpluses toward this end until the debt no longer exists, the United States of America will be able to pay for this entire effort with the interest savings on the debt alone.** To do so would mean paying off the debt no later than the year 2010. That sounds like a very long time. But the longer we wait, the more the debt accumulates, the longer it takes to pay it off, and the less we have available for children and families and prevention.

IV. Behind the Strategies

Jack Pransky

34. Community Organizing for Prevention

Give me a fish and I eat for a day.
Teach me to fish and I eat for a lifetime.

— ancient Chinese proverb

The purpose of community organizing is to bring people together to solve problems. Its premise is that people can shape the conditions that affect them.

Within the field of prevention the various problems and issues around which a community could organize is nearly endless. Some issues are relatively manageable, such as developing community health promotion projects or dealing with student misbehavior on a school bus. Some are as overwhelming as reducing drug-related gang warfare in the inner city, or eliminating poverty.

"Community organizing" is the process of helping people come together to gain the power and learn the skills to make changes they want in their community. It is a process of creating community change. "Community" can be defined however narrowly or broadly a community wishes to define itself.

Why Organize?

Many individuals experience problems, without full knowledge that many others around them are experiencing similar difficulties. Such problems can often be solved better when individuals solve them together. The more people unite to create solutions and share resources, the better the chance of a problem being solved. It is easy for someone to say "no" to one lone voice barking in the wind. It is far more difficult to say "no" to a group of people all saying the same thing.

Power to create change lies in numbers—number of votes, number of dollars, number of guns. It's easy for people with guns or money to become powerful, but those who haven't much more than their own numbers can also be powerful.

In primary prevention we are trying to create conditions that reduce the incidence of behavior-related problems. Often, the best way to deal with these problems is for people to join together to prevent them.

395

How to Get People Together to Solve Problems

A few years before he became cofounder of the politically progressive Liberty Union Party in Vermont, I heard Peter Diamondstone say to a group of prospective VISTA Volunteers that I was training:

There are only three ways I know of to get people together:

1. threaten them (hold a gun to their heads until they do what you want)
2. reward them (pay people to come to meetings, for example)
3. if they feel something deep inside of them that moves them to take action.

I have never forgotten this wisdom. If we don't want to threaten people, if we don't have the money or don't want to give it away, we have only one hope as prevention organizers: to help people find reward for themselves. Only if people feel strongly enough about something will they choose to do something about it.

> ***Principle: People will rarely do what is not of utmost importance to them.***

It is important for community organizers always to keep this thought in the back of our minds: If we have tried and tried, gone through all the right steps, and people are still not coming together, it is probably because of one of two reasons:

1. The people are simply not emotionally invested enough in the issue; they don't care enough about it. They may have said they care, but they don't care enough. Or—
2. The people are emotionally invested but do not have the means or knowledge to accomplish what they want. Why would they want to try if they can't imagine how to make it happen?

Self-interests are usually what motivate people, and once motivated, they have to know how to accomplish what they want. As prevention organizers, our first task is try to help people "feel it" enough to want to take action. This is very difficult. It would be best if people already felt it. If they do, then we can ask the right questions and help them learn the skills to go after what they want. If they don't "feel it" naturally, and we can't move them, all the skills we can teach won't amount to much.

The Attitude of the Organizer

> ***Principle: The purpose of organizing is to help people get what they want.***

This simple statement has profound implications. Suppose we are concerned with poor housing conditions in a rural area. We think to ourselves, "Now here is an issue worth organizing around!" So we start checking the situation out.

Much to our surprise, we discover that what the people in the town really want is to get their church steeple painted. Poor housing is rampant, and all they care about is painting their church steeple!

As organizers, what do we do?

If our answer is anything besides, "Help them get their church steeple painted," we will likely miss the boat. Are we there to do what *we* think is right or are we there to help people do what *they* think is right for themselves?

If we help them get their church steeple painted, they experience the power that comes with working together to accomplish a common goal. They've also gained confidence in us because we helped them accomplish what was important to them. We can then help them make the connection to accomplish bigger (and better) things.

If we had said, "Are you kidding? Look at these terrible conditions you're forced to live in. How can painting a church steeple be as important?" it is unlikely we would have gotten to first base. At the time, those folks weren't interested in anything else but their church steeple. What we think people need is not necessarily what they want.

Suppose we think painting a church steeple is not part of our job or isn't something we care about, or it isn't morally right for us to get involved (which might happen over other issues). If so, we have a decision to make. Whether we go somewhere else to organize, or forget it altogether, it's our decision to do what we think is best for ourselves, just as it is their decision to do what is best for themselves. What is right for the people we are working with is what is best. If we can't accept whatever that is, for whatever reasons, we should be elsewhere.

However, there may be cases where we believe it is through lack of knowledge that people are making certain decisions, and we may want to be sure that they are provided with the right information. Or we may believe that a community wants to do something we think is not morally right, for example, if discrimination is being practiced and everyone is accepting it. We may choose to take a stand and fight against what they are doing. That's great, so long as we understand what we're up against.

Beginning in a Community

Principle: When beginning in a community, meet people on their own terms.

Some prevention organizers may be new to a community they're supposed to work in. What do they need to know before they begin? How do they find out?

Prevention organizers must seek people out to learn what their concerns are. Community and state agencies that serve people have one valuable perspective, and they are easy to find. Those in positions of power have another. How do we find them? We can ask. We can learn who the biggest property owners in a community are and who employs the most people.

We can cross-check boards of directors of various organizations like United Way, banks, appointed commissions, members of the Chamber of Commerce, to find names that keep appearing. In a rural area we can read the telephone book and find the names of the largest extended families.

The most valuable perspective comes from those experiencing problems first-hand—or from those who have the problem, or from those most victimized by it, or from those close enough to be concerned. We can locate these people through referrals, or we can hang out with people to hear their concerns.

When I first served as a VISTA volunteer in Centralia, Illinois, the director of my sponsoring agency pointed to the Black section of town and said, "That's where you work." "What do I do?" I asked. He said, "Whatever has to be done." What a job description! Luckily, this doesn't happen much anymore. But it does illustrate an important point. I remembered from my VISTA training that I was supposed to hang out where the people hang out. I remembered my trainer telling the story of a man who went to organize somewhere on the banks of the Mississippi River to help the old riverboat workers who had lost their jobs because of changing times. They used to sit on benches along the riverbank all day and stare longingly at the river. The last thing they wanted was to talk to a stranger. The only way the organizer could reach those people was to park himself on the other end of the bench, sit there and stare at the river too. The first hour or two, the organizer was completely ignored. By the third hour of just sitting there, the old riverboat men would begin to get curious, wondering why this young whippersnapper was staring at this river. By the fourth hour, they began to think, "This person must care about this river almost as much as I do." Before long they would be telling their life stories. Any other approach would have been unsuccessful.

I remembered that story as I walked into the northeast section of town that first day and saw the open, raw sewage ditches, and the run-down, dilapidated housing, and the kids playing in the pothole-laden streets. I thought of that story as I learned where most of the people hung out: in the taverns. I groaned! I must have been a sight walking into one of those all-Black taverns for the first time, aware of all eyes upon me, hearing some kids mutter half under their breath, "honky," "cracker," while I tried to ignore them. As I reached the bar, Fats the bartender leaned over and said, "Man, you look scared!" I said, "I am scared!" And we went on from there. As much as I hated doing that, I met some of the people most committed to changing community conditions, and my closest friends, from hanging out in those taverns. I never could have won the support of the people had I not overcome my fear and done that.

I don't pretend that times haven't changed since 1968. It is not always the best thing for a White person to try to organize in a Black or Hispanic or Native community. It would be better to help train those folks to do prevention organizing in their own communities. On the other hand, as Native Alaskans say, 'We are all relatives," and wherever people are skilled, have resources that communities need, are sincere in their desire to help solve problems, and are culturally sensitive, it would be inadvisable to make assumptions about anyone's worth for assisting a community before thoroughly checking them out. I think of consultants such as Michael Bopp and Bill Lofquist, among others, who have been extremely helpful to communities outside their race and culture.

As community prevention organizers, wherever we go, if we want to be accepted we must be thoroughly honest and thoroughly real. We can't expect acceptance, but we certainly won't get it putting on airs. We should never force ourselves on anyone; it is almost always best to wait until spoken to.

In prevention organizing these days, it is often easier to break into a community than the way VISTA used to do it. If we are in a community to help prevent alcohol and drug abuse or teenage pregnancy, and we remember that the contributing factors to all these problems are essentially the same, our job is to bring together the people interested in the problem. How do we find the people most committed to taking action? Again, ask! People will refer us to others who are interested. We can visit them and say, "So and so suggested I talk to you." It is a lot easier on the nerves than hanging out. Perhaps the best way to gain acceptance is to visit someone because someone else told us they might be interested or because they're well respected or skilled in a particular way.

We only enter a community for the first time once. Everyone makes mistakes, but if we blow it on entry it is unlikely we'll get much organizing done. We should always try to put ourselves in the other people's shoes. How would we feel if someone were thrusting themselves upon us? In the movie *The Salt of the Earth*, a White organizer asks a Mexican-American if the picture on the wall is of the worker's grandfather. It turns out to be a picture of Benito Juarez, the father of their revolution. That was it for him (Kahn, 1970). We should always study the culture of the area in which we will work—and respect it.

Common Concerns

After meeting the people with whom we need to work, we are ready for the second major step in the community organization process.

Principle: Listen for common concerns and get people with common concerns together, at first preferably in small groupings.

A key to successful prevention organizing is to ask people what they perceive to be the major community problems. Our first task is simply to listen; listen for a lot of people complaining about, fearful of, or concerned about the same issues. Our second task is to get the people with common concerns together.

Many people sit around and complain about what is bothering them, but it's less common for them to do something about their gripes. Every complaint and every concern is an opportunity to organize around, whether it be, "The landlord won't fix nothing!" "Isn't it horrible that my daughter's classmate committed suicide," "We've got to get these kids off of drugs," "The kids are tearing up the school," "The kids are hanging out getting into trouble," or "The rats are driving me crazy." Each presents an opportunity.

When we hear complaints, we shouldn't let people brush aside their concerns too easily. We could acknowledge that we think these are serious concerns, and something should be done about them! Every time we hear about a problem, we should ask questions (without getting obnoxious). "Who is responsible for getting these broken windows fixed?" "Did you know that when a kid commits suicide, other kids sometimes copy it?" "What do you think makes these kids want to do drugs?" "What's going on at the school that makes the kids want to tear it apart?" "Who's responsible for calling an exterminator? What do the housing codes say about rats?" The idea is to help them want to take action on the issue.

Our questions should also direct people's thoughts toward what might be done to solve a problem. At first they may say, "Aw, I don't know, that's just been going on for a long time. There's nothing I can do." Our questions should help them see possible solutions instead of only the problem. "What is causing the problem?" "What are some possible solutions?" "Who might be able to solve this?"

The next task is to begin to get people together. "Hey, do you know so and so? I just met her, and she was talking about the same concern you were. Why don't we go by and see her?" Or, "How about bringing me by to see some other folks who are also worried about this." We could create conditions where people with common problems can appear in the same place at the same time.

If someone says, "I'm concerned about alcohol and drug use among young people. I'd like to try to do something about it," one approach is to say, "Can you find three other people with the same concern? Then we'll all talk."

It may also be helpful to be aware of some small, individual problems that might be easily solved, and help find solutions to them. This allows people to know that we can be trusted and can get things done. The problem could be as small as picking up somebody's groceries, or as complicated as trucking a family to the welfare office to get improved benefits, but it is best to select something where there's a good chance for success.

Once people recognize that others are interested in the same issues, get them together, preferably in small, informal groupings. People talk most freely when they're comfortable, so their homes might be a good place to start. It's up to them.

Many people find safety in denying that they have problems, or by making excuses like "the people here don't care and won't do anything." In my experience, this is simply not true. I have seen people get together and make a difference. It can be fun and gives people's lives renewed meaning in the process. We might show people where it has happened elsewhere, where people started a parent-child center, where people convinced a school board to keep a neighborhood school opened, where people forced an alleged racist out of office, where kids started the alcohol/drug-free "Project Graduation," where a community formed a neighborhood watch organization, where people got a rural transportation route established, where people formed a food cooperative, where people created state prevention legislation and got it passed. Things like this happen all the time, and they can happen almost anywhere. It depends on what people are willing to go after.

As organizers, we can help them attempt to accomplish what they want, but we cannot do it for them. The people decide everything because it is their community and these are their problems. It's their organization. They call the shots. As organizers we don't have the answers. We may know a process to guide them, but in the end, it's their decisions that determine the outcome.

Building an Organization

In one school of traditional community organizing, we would be paying attention to the fact that different groupings of people in the same community may be concerned about different issues, and therefore this process should be occurring simultaneously with many issues. In certain cases the groupings or their leaders can be brought together to talk about the larger, community picture when the time is right. Each group may have been talking about different problems, but suppose each were to help the other accomplish its goals? No matter what the perceived community problem, it can be solved better through united action than it can by people acting separately. In prevention organizing, we may only be concerned with one issue at a time—but maybe not.

Principle: In community prevention organizing, the sole purpose of meetings is to prepare for action; the sole purpose of an organization is to provide a powerful structure for taking action.

Eventually, the point may be reached where it seems wise to hold a large community meeting. There can be some danger in doing this too soon. There must be good reason for it. Some parent-child centers have been started without ever calling a large community meeting, but where numbers may make the difference for a successful organizational effort, a large community meeting is essential.

Depending on the issue, if the idea is to have the biggest turnout possible, the people must be excited and willing to do whatever is necessary to get the word out. As usual, our role as organizers is to ask questions: What do you think is the best way to get people to this meeting? Through word of mouth? Posters at key places? Flyers delivered to people's doors? Radio and TV announcements? Newspaper articles? Phone calls? Should transportation be provided?"

How many people is enough for a large meeting? The number depends on the size and rural/urban nature of the community and what is to be accomplished. One percent of the population with whom we are working can represent an extremely powerful organization. No matter how many, it is best to estimate low, because if large numbers are expected and only a few show it could be devastating to the cause. On the other hand if people expect a gathering of 25 to feel successful, and 40 show up, they will feel fantastic. Some organizers deliberately set up fewer chairs than people expected to make it appear that interest is greater than anticipated.

In most cases people will come out to a first meeting (except perhaps in the most rural areas if the weather is bad) because they are curious. It's a break from their daily routine. Getting a lot of people out at a first meeting feels good, but it doesn't mean that much. To keep them coming out is one of the hardest aspects of organizing.

The group must know beforehand exactly what it wants to accomplish in having a meeting. What should happen there? Who will play what role? How will people be kept on track and the meeting kept flowing so it won't be a drag? (It's best to stay away from Robert's Rules of Order.) How can lots of participation be ensured? What would be the best setting? What atmosphere should be created? Should refreshments be served? Where will the money come from, or can it be done for free?

The main question is, "What should the outcome of this meeting be?" How will the meeting accomplish its purpose? Is its intent to get people to recognize the formation of a new organization that intends to be a powerful force for constructive change in the community? Or, is it to decide whether people want such an organization? Or is it to get people fired up? Or to identify problems and issues that such an organization could take on and prioritize issues? Or to get people to recognize that their strength lies in numbers? If the purpose is to focus on preventing child abuse or drug abuse, for example, what do we want to come out of it?

The true community organizer stays in the background as much as possible. This is not to say we should not speak if called upon or that we can't be built into the agenda to make specific points, but organizers should not be the recognized leaders. We're usually behind the scenes helping to make things happen, as opposed to up front pulling things along. In prevention organizing there can be exceptions if the organizer lives permanently in a community and is already recognized as a leader, but it is still almost always best for that person to help develop other leadership as well. The organization belongs to the people. As soon as it is perceived as belonging to a leader, it will fail.

It is important to keep everyone involved. Uninvolved people will depart. Each problem has many different aspects to keep lots of people active. If the organizer needs to research something, it is best to take someone along. The more members participate in the decision-making process, the more likely they are to understand what is going on and involve themselves in taking action. One of the best things we can do is to train others to be organizers–to know what we know and do what we do.

In a large organization, it is important to promote the "if-you-scratch-my-back-I'll-scratch-yours" philosophy. All issues will not be of the same importance to all people, but it may be necessary for everyone to work on all issues. If they don't, they may not have the power to accomplish what they want. Different committees can work on different issues, but when it comes time for united action, everyone can be there for everyone else.

The Community Development Approach

In *Discovering the Meaning of Prevention* (1983) and *The Technology of Prevention Workbook* (1989), Bill Lofquist shares a variety of strategies and tools for helping a community move from mere concern about a problem to taking constructive action for change.

One of the most effective of these tools is what Lofquist calls the "Elements Of Change," which is, essentially, a very simple planning process that can be used to help communities move from identification of a problem to taking action. The process, briefly, is to help people identify-

1. the current state of affairs (Condition A)
2. where they want to be (Condition B)
3. the most important priorities of B
4. tangible indicators to show progress from A to B
5. strategies and action steps to get from A to B (Note: if in number 1 above conditions that cause the problem are not included on the list, it is critical to identify those conditions before planning strategies
6. needed resources to help get from A to B and how to engage key allies
7. resisting forces and how to counter them

I would add to the process:

8. before leaving a meeting, people should be asked for their commitment to work on the issue, identify what they're willing to do, know what they're responsible for before the next meeting, and know when and where the next meeting will be. It usually takes more than one meeting to solve a problem.

The Community/Team Approach

It is also important to nurture the group of people committing themselves to taking action. One of the best ways to do this is through the "community/team approach," where teams of people—from one community, many communities, from around a state or region, or from across the country—are brought together to receive training about a particular problem or issue. Together they learn how to organize to combat the problem, then go back to their communities and create change. Much excitement and enthusiasm can be generated in the process.

This means for creating change has been used quite effectively as a School-Team Approach, particularly in the state of Maine, where it had an important effect in reducing many problems in many school systems. On a national-regional level, this process was also used effectively by the Southwest Regional Center for Drug-Free Schools and Communities of the University of Oklahoma. Teams from all southwest-region states came together to learn about prevention and how to go back to their states and make a difference.

Some teams, of course, function better than others. The organization that brings the teams together should keep track of each team after they've returned to their communities. Someone must be left in charge of each team, and there should be a contingency plan for what will happen if the person in charge does not come through. In many cases, where back-up plans have not been set, many teams have floundered, breeding frustration among the members who put themselves out to be part of something that was supposed to make a difference.

Nowhere has this approach been used more effectively than in the *Four Worlds Development Project* of Alberta, Canada, under the leadership of consultant Michael Bopp (1988). The Four Worlds Project is a multicultural, multidisciplinary team that delivers technical support and training to native communities across North America. Culture is placed at the center of the development process, which also attends to the psychological, moral, and spiritual dimensions of development. The people are asked to articulate their vision for the future, of possibilities other than current reality. Active participation occurs at all levels of project development—from needs assessment, through planning, implementation, evaluation "and beyond." Their approach can be quite instructive:

> All our findings point to the same conclusion: the core of the change process that must go on in developing communities is learning. People and their institutions need to learn to carry on basic relationships and activities in ways that preserve and enhance life rather than in ways that undermine it. In other words, learning is the fundamental dynamic of human and community development (Bopp, p.7).

> This includes not only learning about an issue or problem, but also learning how to change it.

> Any given people can produce their own list of problems, needs and possibilities. Because everything is connected to everything else in the complex web of a people's development, to begin anywhere is to begin to work on the whole problem of human development. Inevitably, an effective beginning will lead to working on the entire tangle of challenges. Any entry point is a starting place (p. 8).

In other words, whether we start with physical abuse, drug abuse, environmental issues, education, administration, health, economic development, housing, social services, elders, youth, family, women, or anything experienced as a difficulty, or with any state of affairs we want to achieve, they are all interconnected. To learn how to constructively affect one issue is to learn how to constructively affect them all. No matter where one begins a process of change is a beginning that ultimately changes the whole. The process is dynamic, ongoing, and ever-evolving.

Building on Community Strengths

John McKnight (1997) advocates a very innovative, preventive or community development approach that begins with connecting people to their own, internal personal resources (skills) and community resources to effect community change. He says basically that the community itself, between its individual members and service organizations, contains within it almost everything they need to solve their own problems and develop in an optimal way, and if they started with, and relied on themselves, and organized in this way, most of what we now know as the human services system would be unnecessary.[*]

---

[*] Note: What McKnight speaks of as "inside-out" is not what I mean by "inside-out"—Chapter 42.

Combining community development, economic development and spiritual development, Robert Woodson of the National Center for Neighborhood Enterprise (NCNE) champions the fact that all poverty-laden, crime-laden, gang-laden, drug-laden, violence-laden communities are loaded with strengths just waiting to come forth. NCNE has identified and documented successes of hundreds of very effective grassroots groups, has provided mini-grants, and through its Neighborhood Leadership Development Institute has provided training and technical assistance in financial management, organizational development, and leadership skills and links to resources to enable then to continue and expand their efforts. Woodson declares that spiritual and moral confusion, not racism, is the most urgent crisis facing these communities and the nation today. Woodson's wonderful book, *The Triumphs of Joseph* (Woodson, 1998) is an inspiring testament to the "neighborhood healers" who exemplify the imagination, courage, and self-help ethic necessary to turn around communities with problems.

Differences Between the Prevention Organizer and Community Organizer?

The role of the prevention organizer may differ from the role of the traditional community organizer in at least two important respects.

The role of the traditional community organizer is to ally him or herself with the long-term self-interests and goals of that organization. Building a strong organization that can accomplish many different things is the end result. As prevention organizers, our desired result is to prevent problems and promote health and well-being. Prevention of the problem is more important than the life of the organization. In traditional community organizing it is said that single purpose organizations won't last. True. In prevention organizing it is okay to have a single-purpose organization if it accomplishes important prevention results. Also true. But the best organization is the one that can take on many different prevention-related problems and can therefore accomplish many prevention results.

Another critical difference between prevention organizing, at least the Alinsky (1971) school of community organizing, is that in prevention organizing there should be no "we-they." Enemies should not be defined; the lines shouldn't be drawn. The premise is that we will only be able to solve problems and change conditions together—because the problems affect us all.

Helping the Organization Accomplish What It Wants

Principle: The organizer should always know where s/he wants to go and what should be accomplished.

We, as organizers, should always know where we're heading. This may sound like a contradiction. If the people are supposed to call the shots, what business do we have keeping ideas and goals in the back of our minds that we believe should be accomplished?

This really isn't the contradiction it seems. In the back of our minds we might be thinking, "the organization needs to select an issue to work on." The organization selects the issue. In the back of our minds might be, "By the end of this meeting, the group will have to decide on a general strategy, and everyone should understand what the next steps are before they leave." The organization chooses the strategy. We may even have a particular strategy in mind that we think will have the best chance of working, and we can share that with the organization, but the organization ultimately decides. As organizers, we can only help guide the group by asking questions and possibly making suggestions from time to time.

Principle: At first the organization should pick an issue on which it can be successful.

Being successful feels good. Feeling good keeps people around. Seeing tangible results fairly quickly is a big boost. If the organization wants to take on an extremely difficult issue, it is best first to become recognized as a powerful force and this comes from achieving small victories.

If the group insists on tackling the toughest issue first, all we can do is help them consider the pitfalls. If they make an informed decision, and that decision is to take on the biggest, toughest problem imaginable, all we can do is to keep asking them questions that allow them to see all angles. We may be surprised; they may be right. But if we're certain that what they want to do will fail, we always have the option of saying, "I'm not going to be a party to this" as a last resort.

It is usually not too difficult to look good quickly, if the right issue is selected. Getting a street light put in is one example. But the specific achievement may not be as important at this level as having people say, "Hey, we really made a difference! Maybe we can accomplish bigger and better things."

Principle: Highly charged emotional issues often work to fire people up, but they do not often build the longest-lasting results.

Sometimes an exciting or emotional issue will bring so many people out to a meeting we won't know what hit us.

In the early seventies, Alice Taylor, a dynamic woman from a Black housing project in Roxbury, Massachusetts, who had no organizing experience, was trying desperately to get housing project residents to make a strip of adjacent land into a playground. The City of Boston agreed to donate the land to them if they could develop a neighborhood plan. She could generate no interest. Neighborhood folks claimed they were interested, but only three people showed up at a meeting. Then, in an unrelated move, the school board announced that they were going to close down the neighborhood school. Suddenly, 100 people were storming city hall.

During this demonstration, the neighborhood people received a verbal agreement from the school board that they would keep the school open. When I heard what happened I thought of suggesting that the group call a "victory party" to celebrate their role in the school board's decision and, at the time of the victory party, while the spirit was so high, Alice would be able to say, "Look, we can do the same thing to get a playground for these kids." She could use one issue to play upon another and create a solid organization out of it.

There was one catch. The agreement proved false. The school board reneged on their verbal commitment. They had agreed only to get people off their backs. For the group to have called a victory party at that time would have been a disaster. A couple of lessons can be learned from this:

1) It is important to jump on every issue for its potential to pull an organization together, and even use one issue to promote another, but
2) don't jump the gun.

It is important to remember that for people to act for themselves, they must also think for themselves. Rather than suggesting actions for members to consider, we should ask questions so they can think through alternatives themselves. "What has the best chance of succeeding?" "What are advantages and disadvantages of going with this issue." "Are there other ways to accomplish the same thing?"

Principle: Throughout all stages of organizing, the question to have in our minds is, "How does the issue and the strategy chosen build the organization, or accomplish important prevention concerns."

Leadership in a Community Organization

A funny thing can sometimes happen when people get a taste of power. They suddenly want more.

Leadership depends not only on how well a leader can lead, but the degree to which a leader is followed. Followers can learn how to keep a leader honest.

People who lead an organization in the first few months are seldom its leaders after a few years. Different skills are needed at different stages. The organization can be helped to recognize that an effective organization needs different types of leadership. It needs financial leadership (who can get the money); it needs tactical leadership (who can plan and make the moves); oratorical leadership (who can speak well); day-to-day routine leadership (who can take care of logistical details); leadership that can measure community sentiment (who understands what is happening in the neighborhood), and probably more. There is seldom one person who's good at them all. There are many different leadership roles to spread around.

More observation on leadership appears at the end of this chapter.

What to Do When an Organization Is Stuck

Principle: When an organization is stuck, do something—anything!

Every organizer reaches a point when he or she isn't sure what to do next. After the enthusiasm of an initial effort has died down, members can lose interest and everything seems to be at a standstill.

This is the stage at which an organizational effort is usually made or broken. It often happens after an organization has begun to hold regular meetings, elect officers, and become established. To wait for another issue to come along usually spells disaster. Doing nothing is the best way to kill an organization. There are other ways to kill an organization at this stage: holding too many meetings, especially where no decisions are made; allowing in-fighting among members; not keeping everyone up-to-date; not giving credit and recognition when due.

In prevention there is always much to do. The organization should never be lacking for an issue. If the organization cannot come up with anything on its own (which is unlikely), it may be important to examine the levels of the community prevention strategy pyramid (Chapter 6) to see what the community is still lacking.

A lull in activity might be a good time to bring in new blood, or to reevaluate the organization.

Dealing with Those in Power

Principle: The organizer should always attempt to establish partnerships with those in power so everyone feels they are working together.

Principle: Where that fails, remember that the prime purpose is to succeed at accomplishing prevention ends; therefore, use whatever works.

It's always best to attempt to build partnerships first. If that fails, the prevention issues in question are more important than being nice to those in positions of authority. Some people don't like to hear this.

When this happens, an understanding of Alinsky (1971) organizing tactics can be quite useful. Remember, every community and every situation is different. What might work in one place may completely bomb in another. But certain principles can be applied.

The first step in figuring out which tactic to use is logic. This does not mean that the outcomes will be logical. But we must ask logical questions:

- Who is the key person(s) with the power to act on this issue?
- What are the self-interests of the person or group who has the power? What's in it for them? What might make them want to keep things as they are?
- What are the most vulnerable points of those in power?
- Do they have the capability of making the needed changes or are the decisions out of their hands?
- Is the tactic being planned fun, interesting, and exciting for organization members? Do members understand the purpose for the tactic?
- If confrontations are in order, what are all the counter-measures that those confronted could use in response? How will those counter-measures affect community people? In a rent strike, for example, does the landlord have the power to simply kick everyone out? If so, it is not a good tactic.
- Is the tactic legal or illegal? Can anyone be thrown in jail or be hurt?

Again, it is always best to enter into partnerships with people in power or, if not possible, to give them the opportunity to come through when asked reasonably. It is better to organize people for something than against something. It's not always possible, but try to keep things positive. The following section should only be considered if those in power remain unresponsive to people's needs.

The organization could figure out exactly what it wants from people in positions of power who can make the difference in solving a community problem. What is the best way to ask something of them to get results?

Next, the organization could plan out beforehand what all the possible moves a person in authority could make to deny whatever is being asked, and plan beforehand what it will do to counter each of those possible moves. As in a game of chess, those who can think ahead the farthest and best anticipate the opposition's moves are the ones who usually win. For example, what will the organization do if the person in power-

- absolutely refuses to go along with the organization; turns it down?

- won't even talk to the organization in the first place?
- grants the organization one or two minor points but no major ones?
- says that the decision is up to someone else and he will present it to them?
- says, "Okay, we'll give you what you want," then you never hear from him again?
- says he'll get you evicted or ensure that you never get any funding or makes other threats?
- says, "You're right, but I don't know what to do about it"?
- does anything else the organization can think of.

If the organization doesn't have a plan for what it will do if confronted with each of those situations, it may get caught with its collective pants down.

In one effort to develop a rural transportation system, an organization of townspeople needed to approach the local school board to see if they could use their school buses to pick up low-income and elderly people. After considering the above questions, they concluded that the school board could say they couldn't allow townspeople to make use of the school busses because it was against the law. So they decided to check the law prior to the meeting. If they could find no loopholes in the law, the organization could say to the school board, "Okay, we certainly wouldn't ask you to break the law, but if you think this is a good idea otherwise, will you give us your support when we lobby to change the law? What will you do to help us?"

The organization then considered what they would do if the school board said, "No, we won't support changing the law." They asked themselves how the school board members got where they are. Votes put them there! If the school board said, "no," they would be sure to inform school board members, in the nicest way possible, how this issue could influence the voters.

They then considered how to respond if the school board said "yes," but then they never heard from them again, or waited until September to change their minds. The organization decided to give itself a deadline by which time any additional action would need to be taken. If by a certain date they had nothing in writing stating that they could use the buses, they would go back to the school board with demands (and again to remind them that they were voted into their positions).

What if the school board passed the buck? "The decision is out of our hands, it can only be determined by a vote of the townspeople at the next town meeting [eight months away]." The organization decided they would check into how special town meetings could be called, and find out what they would have to do to call one immediately, if necessary.

Asking these questions, anticipating responses, and figuring counter moves is an extremely valuable exercise for an organization before it takes action.

Although a tactic is arrived at through logic, it is based upon the emotions of whoever will be affected. Those in power must understand that the organization is an independent body, that its requests are legitimately those of the community, that it will back its demands with action if it has to, and that it must be dealt with as a collective body (one or two "leaders" can't be blamed for what is happening).

Although we are trying carefully to avoid making enemies and confrontations wherever possible, Alinsky provides a line of thought that could be quite instructive if all else fails. He says, "if you want to win you must attack the enemy in his most vulnerable spot." A landlord in a large housing project was not getting rid of the roaches or repairing the place as asked. It was illegal to withhold rent. The question was, what could be done that was legal? The organization decided to bottleneck the system by having everyone pay their rent with pennies. Imagine a long line of people dropping pennies all over his desk, having to count them one by one. If he started taking the pennies without counting them, the word would go down the line and people would start paying only half their rent. Occasionally they would be "accidentally' spilled on the floor. Usually there is a breaking point where a landlord recognizes everyone is serious, and that if he doesn't give in, he'll back himself up for a year.

Alinsky reminds us that power is not only what we have, but what others think we have. When the Vermont Prevention Group first started, it only had six active members, but it wrote letters to state agencies and the legislature as if it were a large organization, and some changes were made. No one outside the group had to know, and the organization was open to all.

There are at least two serious problems with the we-they approach. First, it is a prevention principle for everyone to cooperate together and treat everyone with caring and respect. Second, if those in power are seen as either "giving" or denying people what they want, nothing substantive will have changed; in other words, those in power still do the giving and taking. It isn't healthy for people to feel that people in power make the decisions. Whatever can be accomplished by people, regardless of how much power they wield, joining together to make a difference is what is best.

Leaving a Community

Principle: From the moment the organizer starts s/he should be preparing to leave. Even if we live in the community, we may not always want to be the one responsible for making things happen.

If the group we are organizing has come to depend upon us for everything that gets done, we have inadvertently (or otherwise) created the same situation many social agencies do—created a dependence upon ourselves for the organization's success or failure. This is exactly what we do not want, yet this is one of the biggest problems organizers face. Without the organizer, nothing gets done.

Sometimes this dependency is created because we have not brought folks along from the beginning. We have done things ourselves, gone places without including others, and haven't made sure others understood why and how we do what we do. If we teach others how, they can do things themselves and, in turn, can teach others. The more people that know how to get things done, the better off everyone is.

We may run into dependency problems even though we have said all along, "Gee, I really have to start getting myself out of doing these things" or, "I can wait a month or two before I need to get out of doing this." If we have been doing our jobs correctly, we have been preparing others to take over from the very start. We have been taking the blame if things go wrong but taking no credit when things go well—the credit belongs to the organization. If we only take responsibility when things go wrong, the organization shouldn't miss us much.

The only thing we should leave behind is a strong organization and worthwhile prevention accomplishments. We know we helped create them. Who else needs to know? A contradiction arises when an agency sponsors the organizer and needs to receive credit so it can continue to receive funds. If no one knows that an agency is responsible for good accomplishments, no one would know that it deserves to keep being supported. I have no good answer for this. It is contrary to good community organizing, but it is necessary for an agency to keep supplying organizers.

Keys to Effective Leadership

Most prevention-related concerns are solved by people coming together to solve them. No matter what our approach, without good individual and organizational leadership, very little, if anything, can be solved or accomplished. Leadership is, essentially, the wise use of power or the capacity to translate intention into reality, and sustain it (Bennis and Nanus, 1985).

We can learn much about leadership by stepping outside the traditional community development realm to learn what constitutes effective leadership in businesses and corporations. Bennis and Nanus did just that. They interviewed 60 "successful corporate executives and board chairpersons," and 30 "outstanding leaders in the public sector." Among those who were most successful, they found many common elements and identified the keys to effective leadership. These are paraphrased as follows:

1. *Vision—the creation of focus.* The focus is on results that are viewed as important. A vision must get people's attention. Results get people's attention. Vision grabs people.
2. *Communicating so others see (or feel) the meaning.* Communication creates meaning for people. It does little good if one has a vision but no one else finds meaning in it. Communication, in this sense, is the capacity to influence and organize meaning for others. This is best accomplished by expressing ideas graphically, in ways that hook people, often through use of metaphor or "synesthesia" (transforming one sense into another, as in the Walt Disney movie, *Fantasia*). Even the best ideas are only as good as their ability to attract attention.
3. *An organization based on trust; positioning oneself so others want to follow.* To implement the vision, one must be in the right position. To be in the right position, one must establish an organization that breeds trust. Trust must start at the top and filter down through the organization. Followers adhere from example. Leaders that can mobilize people to trust them and their ideas are those who have a clear sense of who they are and where they want to go. An effective organizational structure that makes things happen takes place when there is a clear sense of purpose, with a clear direction.
4. *Perseverance—courageous patience.* Any new idea will not be accepted at first. Perseverance is needed. This means keeping at it and at it and at it until the results are achieved. A leader needs courage to pursue the vision at all costs, no matter how long it takes.
5. *Deployment of self through positive self-regard.* Effective leaders know their worth and trust themselves. There is no ego involvement. They are unconcerned with "image." They recognize their strengths and compensate for their weaknesses. They keep working on and developing their talents, with discipline. They have the capacity to discern perceived skills from what is required. They have the ability to induce positive regard in others by emphasizing the positive, not dwelling on the negative. They have the ability to accept people as they are, not as they would like them to be. They have the capacity to approach problems in terms of the present, not the past. They are able to give others courteous attention and to trust others. They don't need constant approval or recognition from others.
6. *No failure—emphasize the positive.* Mistakes are just another way to learn. There is no such thing as failing. One's perception of the outcome of the event is what counts.
7. *Empower others to translate intention into reality, and sustain it.* Others must be attracted and energized to this exciting vision of the future. It is a vision that gives workers the feeling of being at the active centers of the social order. It emphasizes developing their competence and trusting it. The workers experience a sense of "community" or "family" by being part of the organization, and recognize their reliance on others to achieve the end. There is a sense of enjoyment and fun in working toward this end.

Bennis emphasizes the difference between leadership and management. "Good managers are people who do things right and leaders are people that do the right thing." Management is efficiency. Leadership is effectiveness.

This concept of leadership is invaluable for effective community organization and development and for all aspects of prevention work.

Jack Pransky

35. Planning for Desired Results

Planning is often an exercise that ends up on someone's shelf. Prevention workers can't afford to waste time on extraneous activities. Yet planning can be quite useful and helpful to them. Planning should help ensure effectiveness. Effectiveness depends on two things:

1. knowing what we want to accomplish
2. knowing how well we are doing

With respect to what? To what people running a program think is right? To what the clients think is right? To what the funding source thinks is right? To what the general public thinks is right? Each of these may elicit a different response, and thus guide our planning in different directions.

Traditional vs. Nontraditional Planning

Traditional planning essentially asks, "What is the problem?" "What are we doing?" "Where are we heading?" It focuses on goals and objectives, and methods to achieve them. It begins with where things are at present, and from this starting point all further plans are made. Thus, in traditional planning we are limited immediately to whatever we are able to conceive from our starting point. We exist in continual reaction to this starting point.

For example, if I were running an alternative drop-in center for kids, in a traditional planning process I'd look at what the center was doing now and ask, "What is the problem?," then ask, "What goal do I want to set for this center so the problem can be solved?" From my goal comes my objectives. From my objectives come my methods. No matter how elaborate I make this process, I am confined by both the problem and by what I have planned: my drop-in center. No matter what I choose to do, the problem and center are always the basis from which I proceed. My perception is locked into their existence, and my vision is limited.

This is not the only way to deal with change, or with life. This is not the only way to plan. If we step outside our traditional patterns and systems, we can expand our vision. In the mid-1990s the world of prevention began finally to focus on "outcomes" (Williams & Webb, 1992). What follows is an example of one of the first such planning efforts.

If we examine ancient Chinese culture, for example, we learn that others have viewed life differently and have thus engaged in planning differently. Dr. Fred Jervis of the Center for

Constructive Change in Durham, New Hampshire studied ancient Chinese culture and learned its alternative planning approach.[*] With the ancient Chinese perspective, instead of reacting to the way things are, people can envision the changes they desire and move in those directions.

Jervis claims that by asking a different kind of question and changing what we pay attention to, we can come up with information that will provide a different basis for making decisions. Instead of being reactive, people can be proactive.

Instead of asking, What is the problem?—usually the first question asked in traditional planning—we can ask, "What kind of world do we want?" or "What kind of community do we want?" and move on from there.

The kind of information we get depends on the questions we ask and this information yields a new set of questions. If we identify the results we want, our effectiveness will change, aiming us in the direction of those desired results. The entire context in which we operate is changed.

Traditional western culture has taught us to pay attention to what is happening today and thinking about the "right way" or "best method" to reach goals. It has us asking, "How do I know if I am doing a good job?' or "What's wrong with this___?" Results-oriented planning has us attempting to make some desired "end" happen.

This can be a tricky distinction. The end point is not a methodological end—not a traditional goal or objective; rather, it is an "end" condition that we want to see created outside of what we have control over. We can control whether a goal or objective is accomplished by simply following our planning steps. In other words, if we have determined that kids have low self-esteem and that creating a "self-esteem building" program is our goal, if we follow the steps we set forth, we can create that program and reach our goal, but our program may not improve children's self-esteem. We don't have control over someone else's self-esteem. We cannot control what we see happening in the outside world. Seeing some constructive change in the outside world, however, is the desired result we seek. If we want this end reached, we must seek alternatives, change strategies, alter programs, and create something that produces our desired results. The program we set up may or may not get us there, so the program itself is not what's important. Ensuring that self-esteem is actually improved is.

Results-Oriented Planning

In results-oriented planning we ask, "If we were completely effective, or, if everything were ideal with this situation, what would be happening?"

Let's go back to my drop-in center. Suppose I started with a different set of questions, and asked-

- "To what end are we doing what we're doing?'
- "How will we know when we get there?"
- "How are we doing compared to this end?'
- "What might have the best chance of getting us there?"
- "What can we do differently to enable us to get there?"
- "Does this center have anything to do with this, or will some other approach be better suited?"

---

[*] Note: Developed as the Planaging™ process by Dr. Jervis.

I have suddenly changed the whole ball game.

If we ask questions in this way, we are better able to evaluate the ineffectiveness of the methods and strategies we've chosen, and can easily change our methods accordingly. So long as we keep asking ourselves these questions, we will always be in a position to experience our limitations and know if what we are doing is working, and if our goals and methods are appropriate. We are in a position to guide whatever changes we have to make in the direction of our desired results. Otherwise we are locked into our current methods and goals and collapse our expectations.

This process was originally used effectively for businesses to improve their profitability. Later, Jervis adapted it for social service organizations. It is certainly relevant for prevention.

The Results-Oriented Planning Process (the long version)

1 Begin with our presently defined purpose. Ask: "To what end are we doing what we're doing?"
2 Ask: "What would be happening if this end were achieved?" Brainstorm a list. The answers to this question become what we pay attention to. These are our new criteria. These are our new indicators of success-our new framework from which we operate.
3 Pick the three most important indicators from the list.
4 Break down each of the three indicators into the smallest possible measurable terms by asking: "How would 'consumers' or 'the general public' or 'people out there' know that these things were taking place?" or "What would they see happening out there that would tell them…?" Brainstorm a list for each category. (Note: don't worry about repetition.)

By asking what others would see, instead of asking what we would be doing, we remove ourselves from the sometimes tainted perceptions of what we think is "the right way."

5 Examine the three lists. Look for indicators that have all the following qualities:

- those that are most meaningful
- those that are most measurable
- those that overlap on the lists

Select the top three with those qualities. These are our "key result areas" or "key indicators of success." They become the basis from which all our future planning evolves.

Indicators give us a sense of direction and help guide our action, but they must be expressed in measurable and quantifiable terms. This raises an interesting question. Much prevention work is expressed in terms of "quality," like self-esteem, perceptions, feelings. How do we measure quality?

This is not as difficult as it sounds. We simply have to ask the right questions. Let's say an indicator reads, "people will be self-sufficient." Self-sufficiency is a difficult quality to see. We then must ask another set of questions: "If people were self-sufficient, what would be happening?" or, "How will we know they are self-sufficient?" or, "What will we actually see that will tell us?"

The answers to these questions then become our unit of measurement. Our success at helping people become self-sufficient can be measured by the success we achieve with that measurable

415

indicator. For example, if one of our indicators is, "people will have jobs" or "people will be off welfare," those are things we can measure. They will indicate to us that people are becoming more self-sufficient.

6   Take one key indicator and ask of it: "What is happening today with respect to this indicator?" Answer this question in measurable, quantifiable terms.
7   Ask: "If this is happening today, what do we want to see happening one year from now (or by the end of the grant period, or by the end of the fiscal year) to know we are being successful?" Pick a date. Project a realistic number.

In this model of planning, the problem we work on becomes the difference between where we are and where we want to be with respect to our important, measurable indicators. We can measure this difference by counting actual numbers and examining percentage reductions or improvements. Our task is to reduce the difference between the two.

8   Plan backwards from where we want to be: "If we want to have increased [or reduced] this number by 20 percent by the end of the year, then three months before that, what will we have to reduce it by to know we're on track?" Then, three months before that—the six-month point? Then, three months before that? These become our "benchmarks" for knowing whether we are on target.

If key indicators are measurable and quantifiable, this question is easy to answer. If they are not, it is very difficult. The purpose of benchmarks is to monitor progress toward our results. If we have a way of knowing how we're doing at all times, we will be able to alter our methods as necessary and concentrate on areas where we may not be putting enough effort.

9.   Set up a mechanism by which we can receive feedback on what we want to measure.

To know if we're on target, we must somehow receive feedback to know if we're accomplishing what we set out to do. Good feedback usually comes from counting something, or from someone outside the process telling us if we're meeting our benchmarks. By asking, "How can we find out this information?" we may be able to think of clever ways. Who might be able to observe what's going on and then tell us?

10. Figure out what method or strategy we can use to get to where we want to be (as a starting point only, because we may have to change our methods later to stay on track).

To figure out what might be the best method to reach our key indicator, go back to the "What is happening today?' response. Ask something like-

-    "What specifically is happening?'
-    "Where is this thing taking place?"
-    "When does it happen most?'
-    "With what age group?'
-    "Under what community conditions?"

Break the problem down into its smallest possible units. Identify those areas where we may be able to have the greatest impact, and focus energies there.

10a. Ask: -

- "What might be the underlying conditions causing the behavior?"
- "Why are people engaged in behaviors like this?"
- "What can be done to change these underlying conditions?"

I added step 10a to Jervis's process, because I see one major danger in the use of step 9 for prevention. To determine prevention strategies by step 9 alone could be limiting because of the potential to focus only on symptoms instead of the underlying contributing causes. If kids are using drugs during school hours, it is very important to figure out when and where and with whom it most often takes place so that the school can zero in on that particular problem, but it's equally important to try to figure out what might be causing kids to do drugs in school in the first place. Maybe school is not exciting enough for them. Maybe school is too oppressive to them or they're failing and trying to escape. If we just focus on what, where, when, how, and to what extent, and miss the "why," we may be missing the mark with our prevention strategies. This point is relevant for any planning process.

9. Repeat steps 6, 7, 8, 9, 10, and 10a with the other key indicators.

10.

In traditional planning, people often think about methods too early in the process, and decide what they want to accomplish based upon those methods. In results-oriented planning, eight crucial steps occur before mention is ever made of method or strategy. This approach can be used, though, to see if particular methods are working. If people learn through this process that their chosen methods are not producing important results, methods should be altered accordingly. After all, accomplishing important community results is what is important, not the methods used.

See Figures 35-1 through 35-3 for examples of this planning process.

Can This Process Be Shortened?

The entire planning process is excellent for an organization to go through, particularly one that is floundering and needs new direction. If all staff or members of an organization plan together, they will begin to build a common vision and discover new strategies that can give renewed life. When used for this purpose, any attempt at shortening the process would be detrimental.

On the other hand, this planning process can be used simply to identify indicators of success for evaluation purposes. When results-oriented planning is used in this limited capacity, it may not be necessary to follow the entire process from beginning to end. As valuable as it is, much of the process is cumbersome, and there is much repetition. Shortening the process would only be justified if it yielded approximately the same important indicators. I'm not sure Dr. Jervis would like this idea, because shortening it means less accuracy.

Some people don't like to ask, "To what end?" because they see it as too global. They'd rather start from their purpose statement and ask, "How will we know this is happening?" To do so may be limiting and may forever lock us into the methods we have already selected. Sometimes, people have an interest, for whatever reasons, in maintaining the current methodology and programs.

If the idea is to arrive at approximately the same place as if we went through the entire process, we are ultimately looking for key indicators of success that are very meaningful to the organization, that are measurable (countable), and that would probably be repeated on many lists of indicators if we had such lists. Thus, if we wanted to shorten the process, we would-

1. identify our overall, desired result.
2. Ask, "What would we see happening that would indicate that this desired result was achieved?"

On this list would only allow indicators that were measurable in the first place. We might not even have to come up with a whole list. Instead, we could identify three indicators that all meet the measurable, meaningful, and far-reaching criteria.

Some people challenge this planning process by saying, "It seems like you end up measuring only negative stuff, reducing bad things. It should be more positive." In reality, this is a wholly positive process. But it illustrates another danger of shortening the process. Remember, our first question was, "If everything were ideal, what would be taking place?" Few questions could be more positive. From there, all we are asking is, "How would we know that ideal is being realized? What would the general public actually see?" We are measuring what they can see. It may be that they would see reductions in bad behaviors, but this is simply an indicator that we are reaching our positive ideal. We can measure an increase in good behaviors if we want, if that's more meaningful.

The process can be shortened, but only for a limited purpose, and so long as we are not kidding ourselves. I would encourage use of the full process whenever we encounter a floundering organization, or an organization seeking new direction, or if an effort is beginning. This kind of practical planning can be invaluable when all steps are followed.

Combining Results-Oriented Planning with the Logic Model

In 1999 Deb Brown and I, in behalf of the Vermont Prevention Institute Consultation Team, developed a new model of planning for communities that combines aspects of results planning with some aspects of "the logic model" of planning. The Vermont Agency of Human Services had just released some of its "What Works" series (Brooks and Murphey, 1999), and we wanted to be sure that communities would use them most productively, so we called the process, "How to Make 'What Works' Work?" Rather than merely adopt a "proven-effective" program, this knowledge-based program planning approach is worthwhile for communities attempting to discover the best prevention approach to apply in their community. The model has six major steps, with guiding questions or instructions under each.

1. *Desired Outcomes*
   What does the community want for outcomes?
      a. examine "community profile" [in Vermont, this document shows how well a community is doing with respect to state outcomes]
      b. determine what community perceives is most important issue to work on
      c. examine state outcomes [for Vermont, see Chapter 32]
2. *What Works?*

What does research indicate are proven and promising approaches, to achieve desired outcomes?

    a. examine "What Works" series (various combinations of Jimerson, Brooks, and Murphey, 1998; 1999)

    b. examine other research-based sources that show what is known about what works

    c. if possible, visit successful programs or otherwise explore them

    d. determine what percentage of change did the program actually achieve in indicators of outcomes, and how does this compare with other programs

[Note: A Program Effectiveness Work Sheet could be constructed to be used for each program examined. It could ask for each program, Population Served? Urban, Rural or Suburban? Percentage reduction or improvement for each outcome after how many years? (To calculate, take baseline or "before" measure, subtract "after" measure, and divide by baseline measure = the percentage reduction or improvement)]

3. *Critical Elements*

What critical elements of effectiveness must be included to ensure success?

    a. see examples of critical elements throughout this book under each major program cited

    b. examine original research or any good summary of that research to extract critical elements

    c. if possible, conduct interviews with the programs

4. *Community Conditions*

How do local conditions compare with those in the researched sites?

    a. examine character of community in original study

    b. examine own community and compare

    c. examine costs and other resources: How much did they spend? What did they have available?

5. *Reflection*

What conditions will affect implementation?

    a. Look back at desired outcomes, under what circumstances does its opposite occur?

    In this community-

        - Who is most responsible for causing the problem?

        - Where does the problem happen most?

        - When does it most occur?

        - What "root causes" exist locally?

        - What can we realistically do something about?

6. *Selection* – Theory of Change

Given questions 1-5, what might work best; therefore, what approach should we use?

    a. What should the approach selected be based upon?

    b. consider all approaches and critical elements (the approach selected may be a combination of programs and efforts or it may be a newly-created approach based upon the critical elements)

The alternative is to take someone else's word for it and hope the so-called "proven" program works as well in another community. I would rather put the extra effort in up front and have a better chance of getting the right fit for a particular community, based on logic.

Other Planning Models

Many other planning models exist. Most have similar elements. Some are more user-friendly than others; for example, Bill Lofquist's planning model is highlighted in the middle of Chapter 34.

Jane Vella's (1989) *Learning to Listen/Learning to Teach* model, based largely on Paolo Friere's and also Malcolm Knowles's work, is a combined adult education and community development model that can also double as a planning model. Its foundation revolves around the utmost respect for the participant or community member, drawing out their own capacity for learning and knowledge. As a planning model, additionally it follows a who, what, why, what for, where, when, and how process, although simply listing that sequence does not begin to do it justice. This model works especially well when planning for workshops, teaching, and other presentations.

Barry Kibel (1998) developed a *High-IMpact Planning* model to help a group think creatively and smartly to bring about fundamental changes in social systems and human relationships. A couple of nice features of Kibel's model are that it begins with getting the group or organization in the right frame of mind, and focuses people on what the outstanding features of their program would be if it were world renowned, and what qualities would have to exist to ensure that.

MAPS (Making Action Plans) is a planning process that builds in the clarifying and solidifying of group identity, focuses on group strengths, and promotes trust within a group (O'Brien & Forest, 1989). Some nice features of this approach are that it builds into the process common history, dreams, fears, and strengths which help to crystallize group identity, which it accomplishes in a lighthearted way. All this fun stuff is preliminary to what then appears to be fairly typical planning process.

In my experience, it is in the actual making of action steps that the group often loses energy and gets bogged down. Results-oriented planning is less inclined to create that occurrence.

Figure 35-1

Here is an actual example of how I helped one Youth Service Bureau use Results-Oriented Planning as a tool to guide its actions:

1. What is the purpose of the Youth Service Bureau?
   - for the community to be responsive to kids' needs
   - to have a more effective response to juvenile justice problems
   - to assist youth with problems
   - for kids to become an integral part of the community
   - for kids to make informed decisions to make best-possible choices
   - for kids to have fun
   - to promote healthy families
   - to keep kids off the streets
   - to improve kids' self-image
   - for the community to take over YSB programs

To what end are you doing all these things?
   - so kids will increase their sense of self-worth, reach their fullest potential and take responsibility for their own actions; for the community to improve its response to kids

2. How would you know if this end were ideally being achieved?
   - the community would do projects for kids on its own
   - drop in crime rate
   - less dropping out of school
   - less hanging around the streets
   - kids would take more positive action
   - kids would be less passive
   - parents would be assisting kids with projects
   - kids would be helping community members
   - kids would be doing projects on their own
   - there would not be a Youth Service Bureau

3. Choose three on which to concentrate your efforts.
   - kids would be doing projects on their own
   - less dropping out of school
   - parents and community would be assisting kids with projects

4. For each of these, come up with eight or ten indicators. What would be happening if these occurred? What would you see out there to tell you it was taking place?

kids doing projects on their own
   - kids organizing sporting events
   - less complaints about "nothing to do"
   - kids would have more responsibility
   - community would be giving more positive responses
   - less hanging out on streets
   - less juvenile crime rate
   - increased self-worth
   - different clique groupings would be getting together more

Less dropping out of school
   - lower crime rate
   - less hanging out on streets
   - community would feel better about what kids were doing
   - community would help kids out more
   - increased youth employment
   - kids options would increase

421

- kids self-worth is increased
- fewer kids in drop-in center all day long
- schools would be hiring better teachers and administrators
- less school vandalism
- kids would be better educated

Parents and community would be assisting kids with projects

- lower crime rate
- kids would get to use the school gym
- communication would be improved
- self-worth would be increased
- youth center would get renovated
- more community volunteers
- less hanging out on streets
- more things for kids to do outside YSB
- positive newspaper coverage
- parents help their kids stay in school more
- parents help their kids be less discouraged

5. Look over all indicators. Pick three or four from the list with all the following qualities: most meaningful, overlapping, most measurable.

- less juvenile crime
- increased youth employment
- more things for kids to do outside YSB

6. Less juvenile crime. What is happening today? Need to find out the following:

- how many kids were on probation/parole caseload, per year
- how many kids had negative police contact, per year
- how many kids entered the diversion program per year
- how many kids committed "negative acts"

[Note: They had to go out and collect this data, then make projections from there.)

7. Feedback mechanism:

- probation/parole officer report
- police chief report
- diversion coordinator report
- self-report

8. Project a target.

- reduce rate by 10% by end of next year

9. Set benchmarks (plan backwards).

- 3rd quarter rate per month should be down 7% from previous year
- 2nd—down 5%
- 1st—down 2%

10. Determine methods. (Go back to what is actually happening today.) Ask: Where are most of the juvenile crimes being committed? What kind of crime is it? What are the prime crime targets? What time of day are they being committed?

These types of questions helped zero in on where to deploy police officers at what times. In retrospect (this example happened long ago), another set of questions was also necessary to get at the underlying reasons for kids committing crimes.

What kinds of conditions might, be causing these crimes to occur? What can we do about changing some of these conditions?

This battle has to be waged equally on both these fronts.

The process was repeated for the other two indicators.

Figure 35-2

It may also be instructive to see how I used this process to help juvenile court diversion programs focus on what they wanted changed, and how they would measure their success. The information collected through this process generated data that convinced the legislature to create a law that gave juvenile court diversion programs, as practiced in Vermont, the formal authority to operate and be spread throughout the state.

Juvenile Court Diversion

1. What is the stated purpose of juvenile court diversion?
   - prevention of adult criminals
   - minimize penetration into the criminal justice system
   - alternative to the court process

If the above were ideally happening, what would be taking place?
   - immediate action with juvenile offenders
   - an effective response to juvenile crime
   - reduced recidivism
   - fewer juvenile cases on the court docket
   - lower probation caseload
   - community would take a more active role with youth
   - young people would take a more active role in the community
   - money would be saved
   - state's attorneys would have more time

Look over this list. To what end? What is the overall desired result you are ideally hoping to achieve through court diversion?
   - To make the community a more desirable place to live, and where local citizens have a greater respect for others.

2. Given this desired result, what would be happening if this "end" were ideally achieved?
   - reduced crime
   - people would not be afraid of walking the streets
   - people would be more trusting of one another
   - there wouldn't be a need for these kinds of programs
   - insurance rates would go down
   - youth would take an active part in the community
   - no status offenders
   - greater respect for criminal justice system
   - full employment
   - police would be in more of an assistance role

3. Which three do you want to concentrate your efforts on? Which three would most likely indicate that you were achieving your results?
   - reduced crime
   - youth would take a more active part in the community
   - greater respect for criminal justice system

4. Come up with eight or ten indicators for each. If we had [the above] what would be happening?

Reduced crime
   - people not afraid to walk the streets
   - less breaking and entering
   - more respect and trust for each other
   - less quitting school

Jack Pransky

- reduced court load
- reduced probation and parole load
- community alternatives to the traditional court process
- more local control over minor offenses
- court would be freed up to deal with more serious offenses

Youth would take an active role in the community
- kids and adults would work together
- juvenile crime rate would be reduced
- no need for status laws
- more alternative programs in community
- increased participation in programs
- kids give each other positive peer support
- kids have more responsibility in community affairs
- 'trouble' would be dealt with immediately
- criminal justice system would better respond to youth needs

Changed criminal justice system
- more responsive to needs of youth
- more resources available to juveniles
- faster, more effective response
- truly rehabilitative
- more consistent and equitable
- youth would be involved
- more individualized attention
- alternatives to incarceration

5. Pick three indicators from the above list that are most meaningful, most measurable, and overlap.
- faster, more effective response
- reduced juvenile crime rate
- reduced recidivism

6. Pick one key indicator above. What is happening today with regard to response time? What is the response time now? Break it down.
- from point of arrest until it gets into the state's attorney's hands
- from state's attorney until a petition is filed in court from court petition until assigned attorney calls client
- from assigned attorney contact until disposition (estimated total time: six months)

7. Set a target: What do you want to cut it to in a year?
- two months from point of arrest to disposition

8. Back-plan and set benchmarks.
   3rd quarter - 3 months
   2nd quarter - 4 months
   1st quarter - 5 months

9. Feedback mechanism check dates on petition compared with dates of arrest through state's attorney, police, assigned attorney

10. What strategy should be used to change the response time? Where are the key bottlenecks? Why do they occur? Under what circumstances? Do certain types of cases take longer than others? What problems do those responsible see? What can be done differently? Where is it easily remedied? In this way it is possible to pinpoint the problem and concentrate efforts on it.

Go through same process with rest of key indicators.

Figure 35-3 (Example of a Shortened Process)

This example was taken from a process I went through with a school-based prevention program:

1. What is the purpose of this effort?
   - for teachers to spend less time handling discipline problems and more time teaching

2. To what end?
   - so students can learn

   To what end do you want students to learn?
   - so they will act responsibly and with good judgment

3. What measurable, important indicators would indicate that this is happening?
   - reduced office discipline referrals
   - reduced school vandalism
   - reduced drop-out rate
   - improved academic performance

4. What is happening today with office discipline referrals?
   - 50 per day

5. Set a target by the end of the year:
   - 10 per day

6. Back-plan and set benchmarks:
   - By end of 3rd quarter, 15 per day
   - 2nd quarter, 25 per day
   - 1st quarter, 35 per day

7. Feedback:
   - Report from principal's office. Maintain referral log.

8. Determine strategies:

Under what circumstances do office discipline referrals occur now?

   - Kids act out in class and disrupt.
   - Certain teachers are less successful than others at handling discipline within the classroom.

What can be done about it?

   - So as not to single out certain teachers, train all teachers in handling discipline effectively within classrooms. Then, with all teachers trained, if a teacher continues to send students to the office regularly, it is grounds for documenting what that teacher is doing. This could legitimately result in further action.

Repeat steps 4 through 8 with the other indicators.

[Note: the only shortcut is not creating lists upon lists of indicators that are then weeded down to the final three or four.]

Jack Pransky

36. Practical Evaluation

What Is Evaluation?

Without evaluation, how does anyone know prevention programs are effective? How do we even know?

Evaluation is inquiry into how well we are doing, and why. It is an attempt to discover what works, to analyze cause and effect, to ascertain value or worth. Evaluation can help organizations improve their use of resources. It can help people plan and run better programs. It can aid in marketing because it yields results to communicate.

Many are concerned that prevention evaluations have not been adequate. I would ask, "Compared to what?" Compared to evaluation in treatment programs? Compared to evaluation demonstrating that incarceration deters further crime? I'm not so sure the prevention field should be singled out for not having good enough evaluations to guide it. Still, without question, prevention evaluation could and should improve.

Evaluation for Whom?

To evaluate a prevention project properly, we must know whom the evaluation is for. The answer to that question will determine what should be specifically measured, and to what extent.

What is our purpose for evaluating a prevention program? Is it to demonstrate to funding sources that the program is worthwhile and therefore worthy of continued or increased funding? If so, that would dictate a certain set of questions.

Is our purpose for evaluation to convince state legislatures, or the president and Congress, that pumping funds into and creating policy for these programs is worthwhile? If so, that would dictate another set of questions:

Is our purpose for evaluation to demonstrate to ourselves that what we're doing is worthwhile?

Do we want to convince academicians at the university level that beyond a shadow of doubt there is a direct link between our programs and the changes we seek? The purpose of the evaluation determines what the questions will be.

There are good reasons for conducting evaluation for any of these or other audiences. Our evaluation approach depends on what we are after at any given time. This should dictate the kind of evaluation we do, and how extensive it should be.

427

Levels of Evaluation

Prevention evaluation does not have to be a mystery. Prevention programs can be evaluated on at least eight different levels. In approximate order of relative importance (from lowest to highest), these levels are-

1. Did the project do what it said it was going to do?
2. Did participants show up? (And did they keep attending?)
3. Did participants learn what the project said they would learn?
4. Did participants' attitudes change; or, did self-esteem improve?
5. Did "predictors" of future problem behaviors change for participants?
6. Did community or institutional conditions change?
7. Did program participants' behaviors change?
8. Did community-wide behaviors change?

It is worth examining each of these levels with respect to the question, "prevention for whom?"

1. Did the project do what it said it would do?

This is a very common form of evaluation. But even though some funding sources expect projects to follow predetermined steps, this type of evaluation is probably worth very little. A project can set forth the most elaborate plans and follow them perfectly, but still fail to prevent anything. If I implement a "just say no" program perfectly, and those kids still end up on drugs, does it really matter if I've done a perfect job implementing the program? Conversely, suppose in a "canned" parenting course, I leave out a couple of prescribed sessions and substitute a couple of my own. If the behaviors of participants' children improve, does it really matter that I altered the course? Unless a funding source specifies that they require this kind of evaluation, most programs would save themselves valuable time if they omitted it. But it's important to remember, "the funding source is always right!"[*]

2. Did participants attend?

This level asks if people were interested enough in a particular program to show up. This is valuable information for a program to know about itself. If no one is attending, it means people are not aware of the program, don't care enough about it, or don't like it. If people aren't attending, it's a signal that a program needs to do something differently. Most funding sources like to know this information as well. It takes very little time to collect attendance data, and it's worth the effort. This kind of data, however, is not worth much to anyone else. If participants keep attending, it means they like being there, or they believe they're getting something important out of it. Is this important for prevention? The response below may shed some light.

---

[*] Note: Quote from Tom Hahn, former director of the Orleans County Council of Social Agencies (OCCSA), Newport, Vermont.

3. Did participants learn what the project said they would learn?

This level asks if learning took place. Who might be interested in this type of evaluation? Again, a funding source might (if so, measure it), but it's rare for funding sources to ask for this information. More often, those who run a program predict that this information will be important to someone, so they collect it. Would the legislature, the governor, Congress, or the president care? Not likely, at least not in my experience. If a group of delinquents learns how to survive in the wilderness and how to better handle conflicts at wilderness camp, but they then go back to their home communities and commit crimes, does it really matter that they learned those things? It is good that they learned new information and skills, but it has little to do with prevention if it's not transformed into behavior. If, on the other hand, the purpose of a particular effort is "learning," as in school, then it is important for the teacher to know whether or not the students learned what was being taught. This has little to do with prevention unless the learning is translated into action.

4. Did participants' attitudes change, or did self-esteem improve?

Attitude change and self-esteem are lumped together here for two reasons: (1) Many practitioners believe attitudes and self-esteem are important to prevention; (2) Neither can be seen. It is impossible to see an attitude. If we see someone that we say has a bad attitude, we are really observing a behavior or series of behaviors and labeling it as an attitude. The same is true for self-esteem. We are seeing behaviors that lead us to assume a particular level of self-esteem. To purely measure either attitudes or self-esteem, we would have to attempt to use some sort of measurement scale such as the Rosenberg Self-Esteem Scale (1979); that is, responses to a questionnaire or an inventory scale. Who would be interested in measurements on an attitude or self-esteem scale? Funders? Doubtful, unless they somehow believe or can be convinced that this is important. Legislators? Usually the last thing most legislators care about is if someone feels good. Academicians? Probably. They are often interested in scales. (However, Dr. Robert Felner of the University of Illinois at Champaign would likely say that measuring self-esteem says nothing about whether we're preventing a problem; it only tells us whether self-esteem is improving.) Practitioners who run programs? Perhaps. But why not simply measure the pertinent behaviors that can be observed instead? It is a question of where people want to put their energies.

5. Did "predictors" of future behaviors change for participants?

At levels 5 through 8, we reach the point of measuring actual changes that can be seen. Some people consider Level 5 to be essentially a fall-back position if we can't show real results; that is, actual reductions in levels of alcohol and drug usage, pregnant teenagers, emotional disorders, child abuse, delinquency, whatever we are trying to prevent. Others believe that "predictors" or "antecedents" or "precursors" of future behavior are critical, because research says that their presence is likely to lead to the behaviors we want to prevent. If we reduce those predictors or "risk factors"—for example, "associating with delinquent peers," "school failure," "onset (age) of first use of drugs"—it is predicted that we will subsequently be reducing delinquency or the use and abuse of drugs.

Another option, particularly for secondary prevention programs, is to map out a progression of behaviors that people are likely to move through, from totally dysfunctional to completely functional behavior, and measure advancement along that progression. The following example may help clarify this. A "Parent-to-Parent" program trains volunteers to meet with single parents of very young children in their own homes. The director of this program was trying to figure out how to measure its success, for a funding source. The program's stated purposes were to increase the parents' self-esteem, increase their education, help them find employment, and improve parent-child interaction. I asked the staff, "If the program were fully successful, how would you know? What would be happening for these parents?" They concluded that the key results they would see would be: (1) to get these parents off the welfare rolls, (2) reduce the incidence of further pregnancies, and (3) reduce the number of abuse and neglect reports filed with the state. But clearly, these were long-term measures and would not be accomplished in time for their funding source to decide whether to continue funding. We went through the following dialogue:

P-P: We know we're making progress with these parents, but we don't have any way of demonstrating this to others.

JP: How do you know you're making progress?

P-P: We can just tell; there isn't really anything tangible we can point to.

JP: Tell me how you know. There must be something that tells you.

P-P: Well, it's little, subtle things like their acceptance of us, and the way they're beginning to use resources independently that they never did before ...

JP: Then you're actually seeing things. When you see things, and it looks like progress to you, there is a good chance it could also look like progress to others, provided that you can spell out logically the specific steps along the way that you believe are necessary before a parent can achieve the ultimate results. Then you can measure your progress with each parent along this progression. In other words, you have to spell out the stages that you believe from your experience the parents you're working with need to move through before they're fully functional.

They then came up with a list of progressive steps their parent-clients would likely have to pass through before the key results could actually be realized. Some of the steps of this progression were

- initial willingness to let the volunteer through the door
- parent willingness to meet with other service providers
- parents using other resources on their own
- parents using the skills they've been taught on their children (as observed by the volunteer)
- continued use of those skills
- effective response to crisis situations (as determined by the volunteer)
- improved children's behavior

If the intent is for the parents to become employed, some logical steps would be: willingness to look for a job, contacting an employer for a job, or going to an interview, and so forth.

A chart of this type of progression through the key results could be drawn up and each client's progress checked off after each stage is reached. Thus, they would have a running record of their progress with each client.

It is very likely that a funding source could relate to a visual progress report like this if it were presented logically, and especially if presented when funding was first being requested.

There are also specific "risk factors" identified through research in various fields that can be observed and measured (for example, Hawkins and Catalano, 1989) and we would want to reduce these. But for preventionists, it's helpful to keep in mind that we're not fully successful until we reach our ultimate, desired results.

6. Did community or institutional conditions change?

Suppose we're trying to prevent school vandalism, and we operate under the premise that a school climate improvement effort would accomplish this. As a result of our efforts, the school discipline system is changed for the better. Clearly, this is a measure of important results. It is not a measure of our ultimate results (reduced vandalism) but, like the above, it can be considered tangible progress toward achieving that ultimate result. Beyond that, many people believe that changing a poor school condition is a desirable prevention result in and of itself, because it changes a condition that needs to be changed—regardless of whether it ever reduces vandalism. Others would disagree.

If we accept Lofquist's definition of prevention [Chapter 1], "changing conditions," per se, is a prevention end in itself and, as such, would be a desirable state to achieve and measure. Many of us have seen first-hand that changing a school discipline system is likely to affect classroom disruptions, office discipline referrals, suspensions and expulsions, perhaps even truancy and drop outs. Therefore, constructive change of these conditions would be considered a desirable end in itself. Some would argue this point. To help settle the argument (if it is even possible), we should go back to the question, "For whom are we evaluating our project?"

Those who run the prevention program, particularly if they accept Lofquist's definition, may well be satisfied that measuring change of a community condition is a valuable prevention result and would thus be a valuable form of evaluation. Prevention academicians may be skeptical of such an evaluation tool, although in general most would probably see the change as a worthwhile accomplishment. For funding sources, it would depend on what they were funding and who was funding it, but quite often funding sources are very satisfied when observable, tangible changes are made as a result of their funding. The legislature? It depends on how progressive they are. Some legislators would not appreciate such changes, but others would. If changes in conditions were tied to actual behavior changes, legislators would be more inclined to see the value in it.

If the community identifies that parents need more and better skills in bringing up children, and their efforts result in the development of a "parent-child center," is that good? Parent-child centers have been known to vastly increase the opportunity for certain parents to acquire more parenting skills through the variety of programs they run. Because a community resource has been created that did not exist before, a community condition has been changed. It is a substantive result that can be seen, and most people would see this as "good," unless they see only increased costs and higher taxes as the result of any program that serves people. But what if this parent-child center turns out "bad"? What if a day-care center is developed and the staff abuses the kids? Is it good that this community condition was changed? In answering this question, we should remind ourselves of the rest of Lofquist's definition (" . . . that promote the well-being of people"). But it underscores that this level of evaluation can be quite tricky.

7. Did program participants' behaviors change?

Who would be interested in this? Almost everyone. Certainly the program itself would be. Certainly a funding source. Certainly the legislature, governor, president, and Congress, provided the behavior was something they cared about. If it reduced crime or prevented the spread of AIDS they would likely be interested. If it reduced emotional problems, they may not care. They will certainly be interested in whatever is politically hot at the time. Academicians would likely be the most skeptical. They often want proof beyond a shadow of a doubt that the program itself was responsible for the behavior change. Thus they demand technically perfect objective studies, "control groups," and, often, to know whether these behaviors hold up over time (longitudinal studies).

To others, this type of extensive control-group-type evaluation is unnecessary. Instead, the assumption is made that if behavioral results are observed within a program, it means the program is doing something right (at least it's not doing something wrong), and if those results are repeated when the program or a similar program is run again, and if similar results continue to be repeated, one can reasonably infer that the program has something to do with the results. If I run a Developing Capable People course for parents and, through the use of before and after measures, I show that the major problems participants experience with their kids have been reduced by 80%, then I repeat the course again and again and keep approximating those results, I can surmise it had something to do with the course. If other instructors run the course and they demonstrate again and again through the use of the same measures that they reduce kids behavior problems by 70%, 1 can infer that it had something to do with the course, and that possibly the extra 10% has to do with the fact that I might be a more practiced instructor, or it has something to do with the particular parents involved, or maybe I just got lucky. But if the same results are repeated again and again over time, it is an assumption I am willing to make. It is not scientific, but it may be nearly as accurate. Many academicians would disagree.

8. Did community-wide behaviors change?

Prevention is ultimately effective if it creates observable, measurable desired changes in behaviors across an entire community, an entire state, an entire nation. Almost everyone would agree that prevention "worked" if this were the case, although academics would still have the same concerns about evaluation design, as indicated earlier. The flaw here is that it is unrealistic to expect that one small program can be held accountable for all the forces in a community that affect behaviors. Perhaps a program could take on this responsibility, but only if it were funded on a large enough scale to have the opportunity to affect every person in that community.

Who Should Be Responsible for Prevention Evaluation?

As indicated earlier, prevention evaluation depends on what one wants.

Should prevention programs be involved in evaluating their efforts? It depends what one means by "evaluation." Should under-funded programs be responsible for paying for extensive longitudinal, control-group studies? I think not, unless they are also funded adequately to conduct this type of extensive evaluation.

It is equally true that the type of evaluation that can isolate program effects through randomizing or holding constant other factors so the change can be directly attributable to those programs is invaluable. Who should perform and pay for this extensive and credible evaluation? Could this be a logical, legitimate role for universities, and the government? Should they then be responsible for getting that information out to all prevention programs, so prevention programs can improve themselves? Individual programs can't afford to pay for this.

On the other hand, should prevention programs be responsible for monitoring their progress toward identified, desired results, and reporting their relative success to the community and interested others? I believe so. We cannot afford to spend money on programs that do not work. Should prevention programs attempt to analyze factors that cause their relative success? I believe they should. Such an analysis can only be helpful for improving programs. It may not be scientific—leave that up to the academics—but the programs would likely benefit, and better outcomes would likely be observed as a result.

What Type of Evaluation Is Best for Prevention Programs

Should prevention programs be interested in definitive knowledge about what works, or should they be interested in change and improvement? Perhaps both. The question is, for which should prevention programs be held accountable?

When I weigh all the levels of evaluation above, and who should be responsible for what level, I arrive at a very clear answer that I would recommend to all prevention programs. Minimally, prevention programs should:

1. go through the planning process outlined in Chapter 35 (or some similar process) to determine observable, measurable key indicators of success
2. take before and after measures based upon those indicators
3. analyze why they believe they are successful or not
4. report on their relative success or progress

If a prevention program has more time it should:

5. ask consumers and the community (in a systematic way) for their perceptions of the relative success of the program. (Note: This can be done to varying degrees, the most complicated but meaningful way being through "Qualitative" evaluation [Patton, 1979].)
6. arrange (if possible) with colleges and universities to use its programs for more extensive, longitudinal, control-group-type studies

Before beginning any prevention program it would be wise to research the evaluations that have already been conducted on similar programs to determine if the type of program is worth doing, or what parts should be integral or avoided, or what principles should be put into place in program operations. The federal and state governments should disseminate such information to programs upon request, or before any funds are applied for.

In summary, the burden for prevention evaluation lies with numerous sources at numerous levels, depending on the audience for the evaluation. What prevention programs themselves should be held accountable for evaluating is not very time consuming, but it is critical. Jane Vella wrote a book titled, *How Do They Know They Know?* (1997) that offers programs a simplified but useful evaluation process. University-based preventionists and the government should be the ones concerned with developing more extensive evaluations, and they should share this knowledge with the programs. Thus the burden of prevention evaluation lies with all parties.

37. Marketing Prevention

The secret of "marketing" is the ability to put oneself in the shoes of the consumer and deliver a product that the consumer will want enough to purchase—with either money or time. Marketing prevention is the same as marketing any business enterprise. It is important to recognize that the product we are attempting to market is not the prevention program itself, but outcomes of the program. The best marketing strategy for a prevention program, then, is to produce outcomes that are meaningful to people, and to communicate those results.

The first principle of prevention marketing, then, should be: Produce results that people care about! If our programs can produce what people want to see, we're generating what they're interested in, and we're well on our way toward achieving an effective marketing strategy. If we don't have what people want, it will be extremely difficult to market our programs successfully.

To give people what they care about, we could take before-and-after measures on key indicators of success and show substantive change [Chapters 35 and 36] or gather stirring anecdotes of individual successes within a program. In my experience, a combination of these has the best chance of moving people to want what we are offering. Producing results and being ready to communicate them provides a backdrop for the marketing process that follows.

What Do We Want from Others? What Do We Need from Whom?

Once we believe we have what others want, we must figure out exactly what we want in return, and from whom. This set of questions is similar to those we ask about prevention evaluation.

- To whom do we want to market what?
- Do we want people with money to pay for our programs?
- Do we want people to participate in our programs?
- Do we want other kinds of support from the public like donations of various items or services?
- Do we want people to simply appreciate what we're doing?
- Do we want other things?

The answers to these questions shape our marketing strategy.

Principle: Mutuality—We get something; they get something.

We have determined what we want. What specifically do "they" want? This is different than asking if we're producing results they care about. This question is, "What can they personally gain from us by giving to us?" In marketing, there are no one-way deals. The intent is for everyone to walk away satisfied.

Marketing and selling are two different things. If we're trying to "sell" our program, we are essentially saying, "This is what we have. It's good. And you should want it too." The focus is on us and our program.

In marketing, the focus is on consumers and what they may want in exchange. What do people with money or services to offer want in exchange for their money or services? Tax breaks? But why would they want to contribute to our program as opposed to another? Or do they want to feel that they are contributing to something worthwhile?

What might they want to avoid? To do something that will make them look bad, or give them a bad name? To be out on a limb? To feel that what they're doing is meaningless? Again, we are trying to put ourselves in their shoes and anticipate what's in it for them.

Principle: A good marketing strategy asks and answers a series of questions that should be considered before any marketing is attempted.

We have already asked the first question:

- *"Is what we have something people will want to buy?"* This question relates to our specific product. How can we make it exciting enough or moving enough for people to want it? As an example, let's say our program is a teenage institute (Chapter 21). We want to market our programs so that teenagers will want to attend, schools will be supportive, staff will volunteer, and donors will contribute funds. How might we accomplish this, following a set of strategic marketing questions?

- *"What is our product?"* Teenage alcohol and drug abuse prevention.

- *"How can we make this exciting or moving enough for people to want to buy it?* The public would probably like it if the kids who attended stopped using drugs. The trouble is that we cannot guarantee this. The teen institute is not a counseling program. Besides, kids who attend are not necessarily on drugs in the first place. There may be instances where, in individual cases, long-time users would be so moved by the teen institute experience that they stop using or at least publicly proclaim that they decided to give up drugs "as of today." Other teenagers who attend may be so moved by the experience that they feel their lives are turned around.

What else might people care about? We know from research that kids learn best from their peers. The teen institute sends kids back to their schools and home communities to start prevention and education programs, often for younger kids. Picture an army of young people out there trying to stop negative peer pressure and having a constructive, powerful influence on younger kids, some of whom may even be the sons and daughters of the people we want something from. Some of the people to whom we want to direct our marketing may be able to find meaning or pleasure in supporting their children's futures.

- *Is the price something people will be able or be willing to afford?* The cost per student is, say, $500 for one week, with all meals and overnight accommodations included. But the cost of the program is greater than that. There is an overall annual operating budget of, say, $150,000—the amount it costs to keep the teen institute in business. This sounds expensive. Is it worth it?

Can the concept of price be expanded further to include the amount society will save in preventing teenagers from abusing alcohol or drugs? How much will be saved in taxes? For organizations desiring to undertake cost-benefit analysis of their prevention programs, Martin Bloom (1981) offers this formula:

costs in supplying prevention
services per unit served
(minimally including organizational
expenses and costs to recipients
of the prevention service)
--- = a cost benefit ratio of helping
unit benefits derived
from prevention (minimally
including predicted problems
being obviated and resultant
expenses not having to be met)

Bloom suggests that this can be compared (and combined) with a similar formula for treatment services, and results might be presented as comparisons.

- *"How will people learn what the program can do for them?* What type of promotion has the best chance of reaching people? Brochures about the teen institute? Personal appearances and speeches? Newspaper articles? Radio or TV? Personal appeals? Appeals from a celebrity? Some of these have more appeal than others.

- *"Where will the people to whom our product is being directed be most likely to see it or become aware of it?* In what place can these people best be reached? Through teachers or guidance people in schools? Through their peers? In their own homes? In their business establishments? At their service clubs?

- *"To whom, specifically, should the marketing of the product be directed?* This relates to the marketing concept called segmentation. Not everyone is the same, nor do we all hear or see things in the same way. Our message may have to be presented a little differently to different groups. If we want students to attend the institute we may want to use a different approach than the one we would use to receive charitable contributions from the business community. However, the message must be similar enough in both so people are not confused or made suspicious.

- *"How can the message best get across to the different segments?* The message must: (1) get their attention, and (2) speak their language. The recipients of the message should be saying, "They mean me!" To get kids to pay attention to the teenage institute they must believe that this would be a fun and worthwhile thing to do. At least one boy decided to attend because he heard that the girls outnumbered the boys three to one. This is not the language that would speak to a businessperson, who might want to ensure that her business is developing a good community reputation, or to take pride in doing something worthwhile. Yet for both groups, presentations by students who attended the teen institute could be an excellent strategy because often what the students have to say is very real and can tug at the heartstrings. Coupled with slide presentations (preferably set to music) that show what the place looks like and provide a feel for the atmosphere, this can be an excellent approach for both groups.

Speaking someone's language, at least partially, means cutting out all jargon. It means talking to them and appealing directly to their interests.

Much of this material comes from Tom Pierce, former manager of WEZF radio station and formerly of WEZF-TV in Vermont who spoke at a Vermont Prevention Conference. He offered an interesting approach to personalizing a message. He said the most effective personal message delivery system is a one-on-one in-depth discussion between two people, but this is also the least efficient way of getting that message out to many people. Pierce established a matrix of most-efficient to least-efficient means for delivering messages, and the most-personal to least-personal means for receiving messages. The list looks something like this:

least personal/ most efficient
    posters
        newspaper
           television
               radio
                   form letter
                       large group discussion
                         personalized letter
                           medium group discussion
                             small group discussion
                             personal letter
                             phone call
                             one-on-one discussion
                             most personal least efficient

One may disagree about the order of these items, but that's not the point. To reach an equivalent number of people, mass media probably costs least per person, but it is also the least personalized. To speak with people individually is the ideal, but the least practical, costing the most per person. Somewhere toward the middle lies a compromise between efficiency and effectiveness. A combination of approaches is probably best, but the most personal approach will have the greatest impact.

A brochure is very impersonal. No matter how good a brochure is, if people receive one in the mail it means very little to them. But when the recipient can connect the brochure with some other message, it begins to take on meaning by reinforcement. When a teen institute student speaks before a service club, preceded by a slide presentation and followed by a personal appeal by the director for a scholarship so two kids from that particular community can attend, it has a personal ring. After a presentation like this, the brochure becomes a reminder of the message. If they received the brochure before the presentation, they might say, "Oh, so that's what that brochure was about"—unless they threw it away. At first it was a piece of folded paper with some words and pictures on it. Now it has meaning.

Principle: Positioning

The concept of positioning comes from a book of the same name by Trout and Ries (1986). In their chapter titled, "Those Little Ladders In Your Head," they state:

> To better understand what your message is up against, let's take a closer look at the ultimate objective of all communication of human mind. Like the memory bank of a computer, the mind has a slot or a position for each bit of information. In operation it is like a computer, with one

exception. A computer has to accept what you put into it. The mind does not. In fact, it's quite the opposite. As a defense mechanism against all you folks with all your causes trying to get my money or my attention, what does the mind do? It rejects information that doesn't compute, that doesn't square with its past knowledge of life and reality...

The product ladder. To cope with the product explosion people have learned to rank products and brands in the mind. Perhaps this can best be visualized by imagining a series of ladders in the mind and each step is a brand name, and each different ladder represents a different product category. Too many companies embark on marketing and advertising programs as if the competitor's position did not exist. They advertise their products in a vacuum and are disappointed when their messages fail to get through. Moving up the ladder in the mind can be extremely difficult if the brands above have a strong foothold. An advertiser who wants to introduce a new product category must carry in a new ladder. Caveat: The mind has no room for something that's new and different unless it's related to the old. That's why they came up with the "uncola."

We could easily substitute "prevention programs" for "products" and "companies" in this statement.

Principle: Persistence

This is another of Pierce's principles: "Be there. And there. And there. Soon you'll be everywhere. And on a higher rung in your organization's ladder." As radio station manager, Pierce receives more public service announcement requests than he can handle. The announcements he chooses to run are the ones where people come in and make a personal appeal directly to him.

The New Business Perspective

As part of a 1987-88 study conducted for the Center for National Policy, the appendix of *Giving Children a Chance* (Miller, 1989) was devoted to a series of meetings with high-level corporate business executives of the baby-boom generation "who are or will likely be part of America's business leadership." These leaders can be critical players in the fight to reduce poverty and resulting problem behaviors. It's possible they're naturally concerned because they're personally affected—they're likely to have their own young and adolescent children. They represent a prime market for potential prevention support. We might pay close attention to what they had to say. Here were some of their concerns:

- They expressed a deep, underlying concern about the future of this country. They worried about the long-term future performance of the US economy in relation to other nations' economies. But they did not appear to link this concern automatically with what they saw as the problems of poverty; homelessness, poor schools, inadequate job readiness. They viewed poverty as separate from their own lives; as a community issue, but one set apart from business, family, or personal interests.
- They were skeptical about the effectiveness of government programs, although some saw Head Start and WIC as successful.

439

- When presented with data that detailed the extent of poverty, particularly among children, there was a perceptible increase in emotional involvement. For some the information heightened a sense of hopelessness, but for the majority the information appeared to provide a reason to find workable solutions and engender greater motivation to try.
- By the end of the sessions, most expressed support for government attention to problems of poverty. The government was seen as the right institution to provide leadership and financing, while nongovernmental entities or local government were looked upon as the preferred service providers. There was a general belief that the private sector should take on anything it can because it could accomplish things more effectively and efficiently than government. The business world is at its best when presented with a problem, and where they are to find the solutions with goals, strategies, and tactics
- After working through the issue, many appeared to draw a correlation between health and education programs and economic well-being. Day care programs were seen as logical focal points for the long-range objective of helping children do better developmentally. The short-term goal was seen as helping poor adolescents find and keep jobs.

The report states that our basic challenge is to develop a comprehensive approach that enables young business leaders to deal with the issues of the underclass in the United States. We need to both inform and involve them, encourage their input on feasible solutions, and encourage their active implementation of programs. Individual charity or scholarship aid is the route that most of those who care have taken. We must help move them in the direction of a public/private partnership to work out solutions to the problems of poverty and other social concerns.

> The key to communicating with business leaders on issues of the poor is in understanding their perceptions about the origins of poverty. We see two conflicting perspectives. The majority contends that the underclass springs from a lack of education, practical job training or good role models; they believe that the people in the lowest economic sphere would be able to improve their standard of living if they were given the tools and training to meet the current needs of the workforce. The leaders who hold this opinion are more likely to view the poor with compassion. Leaders arguing the less prevalent view believe that people are responsible for their own welfare: if they cannot support themselves it is because of a personal failure or character flaw. These leaders will be persuaded less by compassion and more by practical and fiscal considerations...
> If these leaders are given greater knowledge, a comprehensive picture of the policy options, and a better understanding of past successes—and then are shown that an option will work, they are willing to spend money to implement it (pp. 199-200).

They will only pay, however, if they can be convinced that their support will make a difference. They generally don't care if what they're doing is right; what they're concerned with is that their efforts will be successful and that it can be done economically. Compassion is a secondary concern.

Many businesses have been unwilling to commit resources to problems caused by poverty because they perceive the underclass as having very little to do with corporate success or failure. Until recently there has been little recognition of the connection between the growing number of unprepared, unskilled workers and businesses' need for skilled workers. The only thing we can count on from business is that corporations will act in their own best financial interests. They'd be willing to take on social projects if they were to get incentives from the government. Businesses are also more likely to commit to projects that promise more immediate returns.

Some say that conservative Republicans not only want to cut the fat out of these programs (a noble goal) but the meat as well. What would appeal to them? Perhaps analogies like this could grab them: The way this country has been dealing with poverty and other social behavior problems is like children who are continually tripping over broken bottles and cutting their knees on the glass. We've been spending dollar after dollar for the band-aids to patch up the knees. Instead, we could put some money into removing the glass.

Baby-boomer business support is critical to successful prevention marketing.

Marketing and Politics

Marketing within the political arena has its own quirks. How do we convince a state legislature or the national congress that prevention ought to be supported?

To move effectively within the political arena is an art in itself. If we want to be able to market effectively within the realm of politics it's important to understand what makes politicians tick, or, how to play the political game. Nowhere is this art more effectively depicted than in the book, *Hardball*, by Christopher Matthews (1988). He suggests that there are certain principles of political effectiveness (paraphrased):

- Be willing to focus on other people and their concerns, no matter how small.
- Understand every conceivable source of motivation; learn what they care about.
- To understand how a politician behaves, look at what affects each at home, where the voters are.
- Don't tell others what they should be worried about. Let them tell us, then use this information to chart a course to their hearts and minds; make our cause their hope.
- People like to be asked, so ask for a helping hand; let people do us favors; the more favors asked, the more supporters recruited.
- To quote Lyndon Johnson, "It's better to have 'em inside your tent pissin' out, than outside your tent pissin' in." Understand that "people don't do their best work when they're being pissed on."
- Remain on speaking terms with even the fiercest enemies: it shows strength. "Nothing can be more unsettling than some casual chitchat from a guy whose head you've just tried to tear off."
- A strong leader rejects the path of least resistance—instead of shunning opponents, s/he co-opts them, keeps tabs on what they're up to, and gauges their emotions.
- "Don't get mad. Don't get even. Get ahead." As Ronald Reagan said, "I always throw my golf club in the direction I'm going."
- Rather than a "desperate charge 'over the top', dig the trenches deeper and work the networks wider; rather than try to weaken opponents, strengthen ourselves.
- Leave no shot unanswered: "a lie unanswered becomes the truth in 24 hours."
- It's always better to be the bearer of our own bad news. Admitting we have a problem establishes our credibility and allows us to define it in a way that keeps political damage to a minimum.
- "Only talk when it improves the silence." LBJ: "I ain't never learnin' nothin' talkin'."
- Always keep our eyes on the goal.

I would add to this list a couple of points I learned from Tom Davis, chief aide to Senator Patrick Leahy, at a Vermont Prevention Conference workshop:

- Political gains are made opportunistically, not rationally. Had anyone attempted to build a juvenile jail in Vermont prior to an infamous murder of a young girl by a juvenile, they would have gotten nowhere. After the murder there was a public outcry. Those who wanted a jail capitalized on that emotion and used it to accomplish what they wanted. (This could happen with prevention as well.)
- Understand the concept of "territoriality." Many legislators feel very uncomfortable in the State House. To feel a sense of power there, they have to act tough and not let people get their way. If we meet them on their own home turf away from the high pressure of the legislature, we will usually find friendlier, more receptive people. They have homes and families just like we do. Our everyday concerns are the same as their everyday concerns. They may not agree with our position, but they will usually respect us more for meeting them that way. It becomes more difficult for them to ignore, because they have a face and a person connected with that name, connected with that program

With legislators and others in positions of political power the marketing question is, What can we do to politically enhance their position? Or, to put it another way, How will their giving support to us politically enhance their position? How will supporting us make them look? Before contacting them, this is the first thing we have to think through. This is not bribery; it is political fact.

If we don't like playing those kinds of political games to get ahead, we must also be willing to continue to have prevention treated as a second-class field.

Ronald Reagan taught us that to make it in politics it is not wise to talk doom and gloom. It is important to be upbeat, to appear strong. Politicians like smiling, happy faces (at least on the surface), and that of course is what effective prevention builds. What politician would disagree that better, safer neighborhoods are desirable? Drug-free schools? Schools where more students succeed, fewer drop out, more attend, and all behave better? Families where little children are not abused? Keeping our communities free of AIDS? Programs that can save money in the long run with a small investment up front? These are very hopeful things. Prevention is the only way to preclude new problem cases. It's important to sell the solution, not the problem. "This is the way to be successful. Here's how we know these programs work..."

38. Reflections on Marketing Prevention

Rufus Chaffee has been involved with prevention since the early 1970s, most notably, perhaps, as state prevention specialist for the Vermont Office of Alcohol and Drug Abuse Programs, and director of the Primary Prevention Unit of the Lawrence Psychological Center in Massachusetts. Rufus has enjoyed a reputation, nationally, as being a leader in the substance abuse prevention field. After dabbling in real estate and the limousine business for a while, he returned to Vermont and to prevention armed with principles of marketing that he learned in the private sector.

JP: Let's get right down to it. How do you market prevention?

RC: The same way you market any business. A business needs at least three things when it's thinking of getting people to buy a product. You have to establish that there's: (1) a need, and (2) a marketplace, and (3) a group or a segment or segments of people that you can target that have that need so you can be efficient about your marketing. Then you need to have a line of products. If you have just one product, you're in a precarious position. If you have a line of products that interreact, you can move a customer from one product to another to another, and keep their money flowing into your coffers.

JP: So give me an example of how this works in terms of prevention products.

RC: My reference is drug abuse prevention. If I do a one-shot deal where I want to try to get people's attention—that's an awareness product. I want to move them into a place where they want more, like technical assistance, for example. If they're saying, "God, we need to do something about drug abuse. It's terrible, isn't it?" I move them through that awareness into, "Well, we can do this about drug abuse: We can become informed. We can become community organizers." Then they may need some advanced training.

JP: Something troubles me about what you're saying. You're portraying the products as items you're pushing on people, just like you'd be selling toothpaste or something.

RC: Yes, because I believe in the products.

JP: But your product may not necessarily be the right fit for them.

RC: Well, usually when you establish a line of products, if you're going to start marketing, one of the first steps is to do some "focused research." What you do is find out what is it that people need or want. So in many cases the product is going to fit. If you have a diversified line of products, the theory is that you can find a product to fit almost everybody. And if you're doing focused research, you're always asking, "What do you like about this product? What don't you like about it? What are your needs?' And you can redesign. Or you can make products that are redesignable. When Detroit sells cars, the buyer has a lot of options that fit them. The car almost becomes personalized.

JP: Isn't the product in prevention results? Getting results?

RC: Or wellness. Or the product is "resistance [to drugs]." Or something similar. What results is a bunch of "well" people walking around fully self-actualized.

JP: But isn't that ultimately what we're trying to sell? The products we're pushing may or may not aid people toward that end. It seems to me that what we're trying to market in prevention is the idea that these products are going to help people get those results. If we don't keep that in focus, in terms of what we're marketing, we could really get diverted.

RC: I think that's true. If you're ethical, you're ultimately looking at the "wellness" of the clients, the "wellness" of the customers. The products that we design may perpetuate our role in the business. That's okay. I don't think it helps prevention for prevention experts to be out of a job. I think the prevention experts should be in there. The people who've been doing it for a long time, who are fully conversant with many, many areas of the prevention field, should be working and consulting and helping people design better programs. The alternative is, if we convince the world that we don't need to spend money on prevention, the money is going to go somewhere else like build bombs, or be diverted into maybe not some of the best areas. So we've got to market so we redivert it into prevention. We're a little tiny player in a big game. But we're tied up with it. And we've got to get good at it, if we expect to be seeing some of that money. People in this society, I think, are begging to have experts and worthwhile things to spend money on. That's the way people get involved.

JP: What about marketing from the point of view of the individual programs? What do they need marketing for?

RC: They need marketing because they have to expand-

JP: Or at least survive—

RC: As far as I'm concerned, if they're not expanding they're dying. If they're just surviving, they're dying. It's just a matter of time. They just kind of hang on for awhile.

JP: What do you mean by expand?

RC: Recruit new people to be preventers, and to prevent drug abuse and other problems among their kids and among their families and their circles of friends, always expanding the number of people involved, and particularly the level at which they're involved.

JP: What if the program is just doing a good job with what they're doing, and that's it?

RC: I think they'll die. I think at a certain point the people who fund such things will say, "Let's look for something that's a little more exciting than this old, tired stuff." Even a good program like EDAP [Chapter 18] may face that some day. I don't know that they've got a real planned marketing program for expansion yet.

JP: Okay, take EDAP as an example. What do they need to do to expand, marketing-wise?

RC: Well, they may have done these things and I just don't know about them, but they need to take a look at what their product is, and who's likely to buy it, and where are the new markets for it. It looked like they were surprised at the statewide demand for EDAP; they didn't realize how much demand there was going to be. I think they need to do some focused research to find out where their markets are, and what people are saying they need and want. People are saying, "We need to reach these kids in the third grade!" That's an expression of need for EDAP. Is there confusion about what their product actually is among people in the know? They're playing in the

444

realm of schools. They need to know the language and what motivates people in schools, to have an adequate knowledge of their market.

Things are sold on the basis of feelings, not thought... So if you can reach your potential customer by implying, "You're gonna feel great" "You're gonna feel like a million dollars if you have this," "You're gonna be excited!" "You're gonna be on the edge of your chair—titillated—then you can sell it.

JP: So how do you characterize prevention in a way that will excite people?

RC: Sex and death move people. [laughter] Feeling competent. Feeling important. The first three points on Glenn's seven. If you can make them feel capable, important, and powerful... I do that with people. They think I've given them a lot of inside information, and I know I haven't. All I've done is help them feel capable or powerful... like they're really needed. And I believe they are. That makes them feel energized and motivated.

JP: How do you make that happen? How do you do it?

RC: I'm focusing on their feelings. What would make them feel important? What would make them feel capable?

JP: That's what you ask yourself?

RC: Yeah. Sometimes people will say to me, "I don't really know how to do this." I'm going to help them know that they can do at least a part of it before I'm done with them. It may only be five minutes. But they're going to feel capable at least in that little way through that interaction.

JP: Once you make people feel that way, then what?

RC: I try to hook them in with a network. All those feelings get reinforced by being part of a network.

JP: You mean, support?

RC: Yes, support. They will know how to get hold of a few other prevention people. So they know how to hook up. The message should be, "If you need assistance, call one of these people."

JP: What's the whole purpose of this marketing stuff? Is it to get money for survival or for expansion? Or is it something else?

RC: I think that's a by-product probably. It's to expand the purchase of a product—in this case, expand the feelings that enable people to prevent drug abuse. I guess I'm revising what I said the product was initially. The product is the feelings. The products are the services that professional prevention people provide. But the product in terms of what the general public buys is capability, competence, importance, power.

JP: So how would someone who has money be moved to support a struggling prevention program that doesn't have money? In other words, what would a program have to do to market the interest of that guy who's got money?

RC: Find out what he wants and needs. Talk to him. I'd go to the guy with money and say, "Gee, you know, we're trying to prevent drug abuse . . . " or 'We're trying to help people be well and self-actualized" maybe not those words, but most people are going to buy that concept. They'll say, "Yes, I'm for that, too." Then I say, "Great. I need some help." It's a sales technique that's used in insurance and real estate. I was taught in real estate to say on the phone, "I need help. I need help to make my services as responsive as possible for you and your neighbors." People will give you time if you say it that way, even when they know you're a real estate agent and you're probably trying to list their house for too small a price and for too big a commission. But **we must have confidence that we have what they want. It just needs to be packaged right. What we have to say needs to be said in one and a half minutes, because they have so**

many other things to do. If we're writing a description of our product, whatever has to be said needs to catch their attention in the first sentence or they may not read on.

JP: So if you were going to be really helpful to organizations out there who might need to get more involved in prevention marketing, what might a dialogue be like that you would go through with someone who has money?

RC: To start, I'm going to say, "This is what we're trying to do. We're trying to organize this so it's as responsive as possible, and we value the assistance of important community leaders like yourself in helping us design this from the beginning. I've heard about some of the contributions you've made. I'd just like to ask you for a little help. What should we be doing? Where should we be going? Who should we call? And what you've got at the end of that is a person's investment in the product. You need to see if they have any idea what you're talking about when you say prevention. So you say, "What do you think needs to be done for preventing drug abuse?" And they hem and haw, and so you say, "Well, here are the things we've been thinking about. What do you think?" You can always give your theory and say, "Do you think this makes sense?" Most of the time they're going to say it does.

JP: So they'll ultimately support your product?

RC: Hopefully, but focused research can also have the effect of improving our product to better fit their needs. For instance if I were doing prevention research with someone who has money, my guess is, if I mentioned something like "teen institutes or "peer leadership," that guy is going to buy it. That's one of those products that business people like. There's nothing they like better than to take a "potential youth leader," train him, and set him loose to do the work that used to be done by highly paid professionals. They love it. That may be the ticket into that guy's money. "Well, here's what this peer leadership program needs to expand and improve." He knows what you mean when you say this has to expand. That's what business does.

JP: How did you get interested in the marketing end of prevention?

RC: I guess, beating my head against the wall with advertisements and wondering how come so many people want so many drugs. What's driving this? Why would people drink light beer? Because that makes no sense at all to me. [laughter] I mean, you're either on the bus or you're off the bus. [laughter] Obviously, Spuds McKenzie…made a hell of an impact, probably somewhere in the brain stem of most young people in this country. I mean, they just respond without thinking to a black-eyed dog. It drives me nuts. One other thing that happened was hearing people say, "Prevention isn't effective." I mean, we've put a hell of a lot of brain power into figuring out what will work best, and we're always under the gun for evaluation, more so than any of the other human services. The other human services don't evaluate themselves. They say, "We're doing a good job. Look how many people we've served." If we said that we'd be shot out of the water. "We've served 2000 people." So what? To me prevention works and it is effective. Why aren't more people buying in? I'm happy buying into preventing drug abuse in my kids. Why are all these other people saying, "I haven't got time?" We're just not very effective in motivating people, in moving people to do things. We've got good products, we just need to know how to package it and market it—

JP: —in a way that will motivate people—

RC: —and repackaging them so they'll sell better. I'm not willing to say I want to be the same as Spuds McKenzie. But I do want to motivate people and I do want to capture their resources in the direction of prevention. I want to retake that beachhead.

JP: So have you learned anything about what does motivate people in terms of prevention, besides the feelings we talked about earlier?

RC: Yes, children. People will do anything for children. Energy, that vital source–it's the equivalent of sex in some of the other marketing and advertising efforts.

JP: What are you saying? [laughter] We've got to put sex into our prevention marketing?

RC: Well, I'm a little nervous about using sex because I think it's a cheap shot in many ways. But I'm still wondering about it. Maybe we do. And I've done this in talks with kids. And it does grab their attention.

JP: Like what?

RC: "Do you think it's sexier to be drooling and slobbering and slurring your words and smelling like shit? Here's two guys. Which would you rather kiss?" And that's a sexual reference. I think it's reasonably clean reference, but nevertheless. Most of the time when I talk about health I'm thinking, boy, healthy people are sexy. Wow, I like healthy people; beats the shit out of unhealthy people. [laughter] It's true! And it sells.

JP: Where do you draw the line?

RC: Well, I'd want to tell the truth. And I would not want to use it to motivate particularly young people. I don't want them to start screwing because they heard that I said it was healthy. [laughter] I want to be careful how that message gets out.

6/90

39. The Care and Feeding of Prevention Workers

People enter the field of prevention for many different reasons. Most of these reasons are pure, for there is little financial or prestigious gain to be found.

There are, however, personal rewards. Most arise in the heart, from the personal satisfaction and worth that comes from touching someone's life in a way that makes a difference, from creating change for the better, from seeing lives regain meaning and purpose. It can come from seeing a spark in someone's eyes for the first time, or from helping them to find the strength to go on.

Most prevention practitioners seem to be of a certain character. After all, who would enter a field of such low status, where the hours are long, the appreciation is little, and the pay is even less?

Nearly any group of prevention workers has an indefinable spirit, a sense of collective regard. We know we're in it together. Despite the difficulty of trying to change human behavior, the spirit is high. If the prevention field is attempting to move others toward a state of higher well-being—a noble end—then those who work in the field probably carry with them part of that nobility.

Yet forces exist that make an already difficult job more difficult. Rather than simply being able to work with others in a way that would help them move toward this state, prevention programs are minimally funded, and that funding is often not guaranteed from year to year. As a result, instead of being able to put all our energies into effectively working with others, we are forced to struggle continuously to find money so our programs can survive. This drains our energy and dilutes our work. We are forced to put up with federal and state policies that prevent prevention from becoming recognized as a critical force for constructive change.

Thus, many prevention practitioners become frustrated. In these difficult circumstances, who takes care of the workers? We are left to try to take care of ourselves. The frustrations breed some reactive responses. Some focus on becoming "credentialed" so they can at least achieve some recognition. Others debate whether they should do "generic" versus "specific" prevention.

Credentialing

Credentialing of prevention workers has grown dramatically during the 1990s.

The movement toward credentialing of prevention workers grew out of the frustrations of being overworked, underpaid, undertrained, and underappreciated, at least in terms of the worth accorded the profession by this society. Some believe that if preventionists or preventers were to have credentials for their valuable work, they as individuals and the field would be better recognized and appreciated, which would in turn help stop detrimental practices.

The concept of credentialing of prevention workers arose in the alcohol and drug abuse field, particularly in mental health agencies, where great strides have been made toward credentialing treatment providers.

The purposes of credentialing are worthwhile. The following list comes from a workshop on credentialing conducted at the 1989 NAPPA [the former National Association of Prevention Professionals and Advocates] Conference:

- to provide quality assurance (that is, to establish basic criteria for prevention workers in the alcohol and drug abuse prevention field)
- to help define prevention as a necessity and, in so doing, provide leadership for the field
- to increase the professionalism of the field by providing standards
- to increase the status and visibility of the field
- to help create an enforceable code of ethics for prevention workers

These are worthwhile purposes. I have a great deal of respect for many of the people involved in the move to create prevention credentialing systems around the country. Many of them have been among the top prevention professionals in their various states and have themselves accomplished many worthwhile prevention results. Despite this, and despite these worthwhile purposes, I have yet to be convinced that credentialing is good for the field.

Unfortunately, credentials may not produce what the credentialers want. Bill Lofquist (1983) cites what George Odiorne calls an "activity trap": we become stuck in our chosen activities, perpetuating them, even though they may not help us reach our desired results. Credentialing may be such a trap.

Quality assurance of prevention programming and prevention workers is needed, but even the credentialers admit that having credentials doesn't ensure quality prevention work any more than certifying teachers ensures quality teaching.

Professionalism in the field should be improved. Some say that credentialing will help. But what about the community prevention volunteers who provide extremely valuable services? Can we afford to set up a we-they system in the field of prevention—credentialed professionals and uncredentialed volunteers? Capable prevention workers either have natural talent for helping or organizing people, or they can be trained to be capable. Some community volunteers often do just as well as professionals. Further, many credentialing efforts include written tests that may cut out many people who have difficulty with written tests but who do wonderful work with others. [Note: At least the state of Connecticut had the foresight to develop a parallel credentialing track for volunteers.]

The prevention field does need increased status and visibility. Some believe that if prevention workers had credentials, this status would increase. However, credentialing assumes that others outside the field would take a prevention credential seriously and assign a higher value to the work than accorded now. But who are we trying to impress? Community people? Funding sources? Congress and legislatures? Other professionals? Ourselves? Prevention workers should be recognized for their good works—but recognition comes from achieving results, marketing those results, and demonstrating the worth on a wide enough scale. To achieve this recognition, we may have to join the various prevention fields together for increased efficacy and status.

The prevention field does need to be ethical, as does every other field. Some believe that if workers are certified, this will help. But some credentialed doctors and therapists abuse patients. This abuse can happen with or without credentials.

Most prevention workers are ethical now, or they wouldn't be in this field. The exceptions are few and far between. People enter the prevention field for pure reasons; certainly not because of high pay and status. What if they began to enter the field because there was some status to be gained through this credential? If this were to happen, the type of individual entering the field could change, perhaps even decreasing the likelihood that good ethics would be practiced. If credentialed workers ended up committing unethical practices, the field could even be harmed. There are no guarantees about what people might do.

This is not to say that prevention practitioners should not be trained in ethics; there are many ethical issues to be considered in prevention (see below). Without question training in all areas of prevention should increase and improve. Some believe that if workers have to be certified, training will follow. In some states, this has happened; others not. But just because someone has been through training, or has had many years of experience, there is no guarantee that they have become good practitioners of the craft.

Preventers should make more money. Some believe credentialing will help, encouraging higher salaries. Yet, mental health workers are credentialed, and they don't make good money either.

On the other hand, the notion of credentialing has helped people think through what is needed to become a good practitioner of prevention. For example, the Center for Substance Abuse Prevention (CSAP) extracted six domains in which prevention practitioners should have expertise, and the International Certification and Reciprocity Consortium for Alcohol and Other Drug Abuse (IC & RC), a voluntary membership organization that consists of over sixty alcohol and other drug abuse certifying organizations, is consolidating these into five. They are-
1. Planning and Evaluation
2. Education and Skill Development
3. Community Organization
4. Public and Organizational Policy
5. Professional Growth and Responsibility

[Unfortunately, I don't see "inside-out" prevention here, but that is another story. In fact, it is another problem because some substance abuse prevention summer schools have now designed their programs to only include courses that credentialling systems require, cutting out many other worthwhile and informative courses; for example, "Inside-Out Prevention."] Under each of these categories from five to ten tasks are listed for prevention practitioners to be able to demonstrate their expertise in each area.

Whether or not credentialing is a good idea, it unfortunately divides the field, and this field can ill-afford to be divided. Many expert practitioners who have been working in the field for years are opposed to credentialing and will not become credentialed because they disagree with the concept. Thus there will be credentialed and noncredentialed prevention workers in similar jobs being equally effective and ineffective.

Ironically, none of the extremely effective prevention workers who have been in the forefront of creating prevention credentialing systems had prevention credentials themselves when they were out doing their great prevention work.

451

The goals and purposes behind the credentialing movement are certainly worthwhile. It certainly keeps discussions of quality at center stage. But the activity of credentialing may not help the field achieve its ends. It may even be distracting and divert a lot of energy.

Program Standards

The notion of having prevention program standards also developed out of similar intent. As with credentialing the idea is to improve prevention effectiveness and, in this case, prevention program operation.

Most important is for prevention programs to achieve results or outcomes [Chapters 35 and 36]. Their program operations should be geared to ensuring that these outcomes occur. Some people believe that adherence to program standards will better help that program achieve outcomes.

It is important for prevention programs to set high standards for themselves. The question becomes whether others can set high standards for them.

Standards can help less effective programs become more effective. A model set of prevention program standards is available through IC & RC. These can be used to guide prevention program operation.

When such standards move out of the realm of suggested guidance, however, and become adopted by funding sources or by agencies in a position of authority over programs, problems can occur and caution is urged. First, it is extremely important that rigid adherence to program standards not interfere with program flexibility and creativity in achieving results. We need to be cautious that standards themselves do not become an activity trap (Lofquist, 1983), for once standards become cast in stone they often seem to take on a life of their own and they become difficult to change. Written standards always contain a built-in danger that they will lag behind innovations that continue to occur in this rapidly growing and expanding field. For example, if prevention program standards inadvertently cut out inside-out prevention [see Chapter 42] because it does not easily fit into an outside-in framework, then those standards may do a disservice rather than aid prevention.

Further, perhaps the most important facet of any prevention operation lies in the quality of the relationships of its prevention practitoners to others, to themselves as coworkers, and to program managers and supervisors. Can standards effectively address such relationships? It is my observation that the more an organization and the people in it model the health they are trying to affect in others, the more effective that program or organization appears to be in achieving its desired outcomes. This, then, might become one of the most important standards, and it is rarely considered.

A National Prevention Curriculum?

Should there be a national prevention curriculum? Some people think so. The Center for Substance Abuse Prevention (CSAP) took a shot at one in the substance abuse field by contracting with Macro International and Circle Solutions which together convened an "expert panel" that I had the privilege of serving on. The result was an impressive document, *Background Report for the Development of CSAP's Prevention 2001 Curriculum* (1995), pulled together masterfully primarily through the efforts of Laura Sharon, that was supposed to be used as the basis for a national curriculum. CSAP then contracted with Birch and Davis to put out the actual curriculum, but for some unknown reason Birch and Davis did not include much of what appeared in the Background Report. Then, due to political reasons, the project seemed to die on the vine before it could be published. As of this publication date, IC & RC was negotiating with Birch and Davis to pick up where they left off and put out this curriculum.

Generic vs. Specific Prevention

Another issue being debated within the prevention field is whether, for example, substance abuse prevention practitioners should focus on projects to specifically reduce alcohol and drug abuse, or whether they should focus on more generic primary prevention programs and concerns that cut across many lines? This issue, again, has field-dividing potential. The only logical answer is "both." It doesn't need to be debated at all.

If we look back at the prevention wheel [Chapter 6], we will again recognize that people need information, skills, and supports specific to the problems of alcohol and other drug abuse. But that is not enough. People also need to develop healthy self-perceptions and general skills. They need general supports, opportunity, less stress in their lives, and so forth. To attempt to prevent substance abuse without one end or the other is to do an incomplete and therefore ineffective job. That goes for every other problem-behavior field. Both sides—the specific and the generic—are essential.

Another sub-issue is if, as an example, Health Realization [Chapter 42] does not specifically address substance abuse but demonstrates that it achieves reductions in substance abuse, does that mean it would not be funded by substance abuse prevention sources because it is not substance-specific? Some of these distinctions appear silly, at best.

Prevention Ethics

Barbara Jacobi has been one of the leading proponents of prevention ethics. She developed a course and curriculum, *Ethics in Prevention*, based on the code of prevention ethics developed by the now-defunct National Association of Prevention Professionals and Advocates in 1995 (and now available through the Prevention Think Tank). The course explores ethical dilemmas that prevention professionals may encounter in their work. Connecticut became the first state to mandate that the ethics course be considered an integral part of the prevention certification process.

In 1998 Barbara and I developed a list of some ethical questions that may arise in conducting prevention activity.

- misrepresentation
    - Is it ethical to use someone's material or ideas without giving credit?
    - Is it ethical to use someone's material or ideas without getting permission?
    - Is it ethical to misrepresent one's credentials?
    - Is it ethical not to correct someone when they misrepresent your credentials?
    - Is it ethical to bill a seminar as "educational" when it is really a sales pitch?
- money
    - Is it ethical to go after $ to provide something that you don't have the expertise to do?
    - Is it ethical to go after $ to provide something that is beyond scope or mission of your agency?
    - Is it ethical for a prevention consultant to go after $ for something they don't have expertise in, but by the time of consultation they have schooled themselves in the subject?

- conflicts between personal and agency ethics
    - Is it ethical to choose personal ethics over their agency's ethics if a worker believes parents have a right to information about services provided to their children, but their agency or the law prohibits disclosure? In other words, is it ethical to inform the parents?
    - Is it more ethical to do what the agency says because you work for them, even if you don't think it's right, or is it more ethical to do what you think is right, even though the agency says otherwise?
- potential for greater good vs. potential negative
    - Is it ethical to do a "one shot" prevention seminar, even though you know it is generally an ineffective strategy, if it is the entry into a system where comprehensive prevention can eventually be implemented?
    - Is it ethical to accept "tainted" $ if it provides good programming, regardless of where it came from?
    - Is it ethical for a prevention consultant to help community people get what they say they want, even though you know it's not going to work? Or, is it ethical to try to persuade them otherwise (when, after all, they stated what they want)? What if you see it's purpose as either to 1) advance the cause of prevention in the long run or 2) help the community in the long run?
- discrimination - overt and covert.
    - Discrimination is clearly unethical, but is it ethical to work with a "high risk" population without understanding that population? Is there a difference between ethics and stupidity?
    - Do preventionists have an obligation to continue to learn so they can avoid discrimination?
- pushing prevention agendas
    - Is it ethical for a prevention consultant to push or promote prevention ideas if s/he is only being asked to come in to simply facilitate a group process?
    - Is it ethical for a private consultant or a consulting organization to push its prevention agenda when the requesting agency has only requested a simple facilitation?
- pushing prevention programs
    - Is it ethical for a prevention consultant to push a prevention program that, knowingly, does not have a reasonable amount of research evidence to back it up?
- pushing replication of effective programs
    - Is it ethical for Federal agencies or States or anyone to push replication of existing, effective programs (according to research) without also pushing what factors or principles made those programs effective in the first place (because replication without those principles may not work)?
    - Is it ethical for Federal agencies or States to not approve programs for prevention funding that employ those principles but do not go by the name of the replicable programs?
    - Is it ethical to adopt the principles of effectiveness of a proven-effective program and create a new program using those principles under a different name?
- sexual relationships
    - Is it ethical for a prevention consultant to have a sexual relationship with someone in the agency or community in which s/he is consulting?
- prevention certification
    - Is it ethical for prevention certification to be designed in ways that cut out community volunteers?
    - Is it ethical for the prevention field to be pushing prevention certification without evidence that certified prevention workers get better results than noncertified prevention workers?
- Who decides?
    - Who decides what is ethical and what isn't? and What criteria does one use to decide?

For many of these questions or dilemmas the answers can be pretty murky. There is often no clear right and wrong. Prevention professionals must often create their own answers. But on what should they base their answers? First, it would be advisable to consider these issues within a state prevention ethics code (if a state has one), and one's own agency code (if an agency has one). If such codes do not exist in a given location, one might examine the recommended code developed by NAPPA (through the Prevention Think Tank). But clearly it does not provide answers for all of these issues. The answers really come from—and must come from—one's own wisdom, *if* one can step back enough to see the big picture.

Building Prevention Networks

Because people who are not in the prevention field have shown little inclination to support us in our efforts, we have to support ourselves. This is understandable; it is difficult for others outside of any specialized field to comprehend the special problems one encounters or the special needs one has. For example, in prevention, who else could understand the rewards of prevention work, the frustrations, the skills involved, the critical issues, policies that hamper and support our efforts. Sometimes they're even hard for us to understand. We can help each other out.

Prevention is not the kind of work that is easily accomplished alone. Trying to change behaviors—of individuals, of groups, of communities, of bureaucracies—is difficult. We can help each other out.

In supporting each other, we gain strength in improving our own skills and efforts, through sharing, gaining new ideas, helping to take care of each other, and gaining the political power to change policies toward prevention.

It is unfortunate that when budgets are cut, conferences are the first to go. I shudder to think how much would be left out of this book had I not been exposed to (for me) new ideas that I have gained at conferences over the years I've been in this business, or how much less effective I would have been.

Knowing that we have to take care of ourselves has caused many state and national networks to be formed. California, Wisconsin, Arizona, Colorado, Missouri, Illinois, and other states at one point all formed very strong formal prevention networks; other states have strong informal networks. Some are not so strong. Some of these networks meet with others across many different prevention fields; others only meet with folks in their same emphasis area and could expand to cross fields.

National networks are important as well, such as the National Prevention Network (NPN) (specifically for state substance abuse prevention specialists), the National Prevention Coalition (in the mental health field through the National Association of Mental Health), the National Coalition of State Advisory Groups for juvenile justice and delinquency prevention, and Family Support-America (formerly the Family Resource Coalition). The Prevention Think Tank, truly a cross-disciplinary national prevention organization, now sponsored by ETP, sort of replaced the now-defunct National Association of Prevention Practitioners and Advocates (NAPPA). Many more coalitions and associations exist in specific fields.

Newsletters can help connect people. While there is no official national newsletter for prevention workers, although *New Designs for Youth Development* magazine has re-emerged under the new sponsorship of the National Network for Youth out of Washington, DC, under the editorship of John Terry. *Resiliency in Action* fulfilled a most important role in the mid-late 1990s. Prevention First of Illinois publishes the *Prevention Forum* magazine, which offers many fine articles on prevention. From the federal government, the Center for Substance Abuse Prevention, the National Institute of Justice, the National Institute of Mental Health, and the Office of Juvenile Justice and Delinquency Prevention publish some worthwhile material.

455

Privately, for academic preventionists, *the Journal of Primary Prevention*, the *American Journal of Community Psychology,* the *American Journal of Public Health* and other journals, publish many articles that can keep practitioners up to date on the state of the art. The internet is beginning to be a fine source for prevention.

While a number of colleges and universities now offer courses in prevention, Woodbury College of Montpelier, VT, under the able development of Peter Perkins [Chapter 18] became the first college to offer an Associate's Degree (now a Bachelor's Degree) in "prevention and community development."

What Makes a Good Prevention Worker?

A good prevention worker is one who gets results. What kind of results?

To turn a life around is a beautiful thing. A story I first heard at the 1989 New England School of Addiction Studies in a speech by Neill Miner, now director that school, has now become fairly well known. Here is how I remember it:

An old man who loved the ocean and all its creatures spent most of his time walking around by the beach. One day there was a terrible hurricane, and after it subsided when the old man went down to the beach he found the sand littered with hundreds of thousands of starfish. The starfish were dying, for they were away from their life source, the water of the ocean. So being concerned about all these creatures, the old man began to pick up the starfish, one at a time, and toss them back into the ocean. After hours of doing this, some kids walked on the beach to see what was going on. When they saw what the old man was doing, they began laughing at him and taunting him. The old man was undaunted and continued with his work. The kids laughed and taunted some more and said, "You old fool, look at you, you're trying to do something that's impossible. You'll never be able to make a difference doing that." At that the old man straightened up with a starfish in hand, and looked at the boys. Then he whirled and tossed the starfish into the ocean, and said "It makes a difference to this one."

The old man must have been a prevention worker. There are certainly those who believe that to make a difference in just one life is as pure and noble an endeavor as humans can be involved in.

Are we satisfied with just making a difference for one? Everyone has to decide that for him or herself. For me, it's not enough. But when I see many lives change, or see systems change, I feel that I've accomplished something. But the old man and I are both worthy prevention workers.

Many people have energy and interests in a particular aspect of prevention—some may prefer treatment or enforcement. We all have a choice where we want to spend our energy, but we are all needed. Lives can be changed for the better at any level. If we are pure in our hearts, we may still make mistakes, but we can't go wrong.

Beyond that, the best prevention workers are probably those who have an underlying, driving commitment to truly make a difference, coupled with the perseverance, flexibility, and openness to ride with and overcome any obstacles. It also helps not to take ourselves too seriously in the process, and to keep a sense of humor.

V. Personal Prevention/Health Promotion

40. Children of Troubled Families

[Note: I almost eliminated this chapter in this second edition, because putting any kind of label on people, or putting people in any kind of box that allegedly defines who they are, now makes me very uncomfortable. It makes me even more uncomfortable to potentially give the impression that the way we are or the way we act is determined by any conditions in our environment. Yet, I left the chapter in because a careful reading of it shows what our own thinking can do to us if we don't know what it is doing.]

Many children from troubled families seem to have an overabundance of problems and get into more than their share of difficulties. Because of this, although singling out this group brings us into the realm of secondary prevention, a discourse on prevention seems incomplete without it. Many children who grow up in very difficult family circumstances—alcoholism, mental illness, or child sexual abuse—suffer from a multitude of problems.

The strategies that work to prevent problems in all children–altering the ways they're treated so they develop healthy self-perceptions, or helping them see the true source of their experience [Chapter 4]—also work with children of troubled families. We must first ensure that we've done all we can to correct the destructive conditions. Beyond that, children of troubled families may have special needs.

It has helped many children who grow up in difficult family circumstances to hear special information about how what happens in a so-called dysfunctional family has a tendency to manifest itself, the types of problems it may cause for them, and how those problems may carry into adult life. As Sharon Wegscheider (1982) says, the family system becomes a "sick" system that takes on particular characteristics. Each child's role within the family becomes important for maintaining the system as it is. One child often becomes the hero or "caretaker." Another often becomes the "scapegoat." Another might try to hide. Another might try to lighten things up. But no one wants to rock the boat—change the pattern—because it's safer that way. As Claudia Black (1982) says, the dysfunctional family system maintains itself through three primary rules—"don't talk," "don't trust," and "don't feel." No matter what his or her role, each family member learns these lessons very well.

Whether still children or now adults, these children of dysfunctional families first need awareness about these matters so they can say to themselves, "Oh, so that's why things happened in my family the way they did!" "That's why I respond to situations now the way I do!" After receiving this kind of information about their lives, some begin to do much better. Just knowing means something.

As with any other problem, however, receiving information doesn't necessarily make them able to do change it. They also may need skills to handle their lives; they probably need supports. This can be painful information! What happened can still hurt if it is still carried in one's thinking. For some reason, however, it seems to be helpful to know, "I'm not the only one who's like this," "It's not my fault after all," or, "There are other people around who know what I'm going through and they can help me; we can help each other, we can be there for each other!" After participating in this type of support and education group, many people with these problems—both children and adults—can begin to function better. Such groups could be developed in every community.

To avoid the dangers of negative labeling and reinforcing of each other's dysfunctional behaviors, support and education groups for this population can be opened up to anyone interested, thus creating a primary prevention-like response to a secondary prevention problem. If everyone is invited, the group cannot be labeled because no one from the outside knows who's who. Some may be there because they're curious, others because they want to learn more about their friends' problems. If everyone is invited, the behavioral reinforcement pattern may even be altered. We may have to go out of our way behind the scenes to ensure that those who most need the group get there, but unless a group is mandatory we would have to do that anyway.

Just because people participate in support groups does not necessarily mean their lives will get back on track. For some it makes a huge difference; for others the problems may be severe enough to warrant treatment. For those kids and adults the problems are already so serious that they are no longer within the realm of prevention. Prevention practitioners can perform a valuable service in these cases by making appropriate referrals to treatment.

There are many levels at which people can experience an easing of their pain. They may think they've gotten to the bottom of it, but suddenly find that the old patterns have returned when confronted with new situations. Family sculpturing—which simulates past family patterns so participants can reexperience them and help them deal with their residual feelings—can be a powerful tool. But for some, even though it shakes them to their roots and tries to rebuild their sense of worth and esteem, they still may not know how to handle their continued thinking about it.

Family Patterns That Appear to Contribute to Behavior Patterns

Most of the work in identifying family behavior patterns that appear to contribute to why children act the way they do–both as children and as carried into adulthood–has sprung from the "children of alcoholics" field. Yet the family patterns associated with the development of many difficult behavior patterns are not unique to alcoholism. Any type of dysfunction will often disrupt the family pattern, causing the family members to act in ways that allow them to survive, each in their own way.

We have seen the powerful effects that significant others' behaviors have on our perceptions and therefore our behaviors. Nowhere is this more evident than in the homes of troubled families. It is often difficult to see the pain and other feelings that these children carry around, because what they show on the surface is an often inadvertent attempt to cover up that pain.

A common mistake is to assume that everyone who grows up the child of an alcoholic and who falls in a particular position in a family constellation will necessarily display similar behavior patterns. It isn't so. Not all alcoholics, emotionally disturbed people, spouse abusers or child abusers, act the same, for in no home are the conditions exactly the same, nor is people's thinking about those conditions the same.

It would be more accurate to say that wherever similar conditions exist in homes, it is an observation that similar behavioral patterns appear among its members. There seem to be a few common patterns that, if uninterrupted, profoundly effect a child's thinking and reaction patterns as he or she grows into adulthood. Janet Woititz (1983) characterizes these patterns as follows:

- a crisis-to-crisis existence
- "I need you."/"You can't do anything right!"
- "I'll be there for you next time, I promise"
- "I love you."/"Go away."
- "Always tell the truth"/"I don't want to know"

When these patterns are understood by adults and children and they see the thinking patterns that often develop and are carried into adulthood, it seems to be helpful to them. For young children, many worthwhile activities can be found in the workbook/picture book, *My Dad Loves Me, My Dad Has a Disease* (Black, 1979). In fact, Waterfront Books of Burlington, Vermont, has many excellent books for children that help them deal with difficult subjects like family alcoholism, child abuse, sexual abuse, single parents, divorce and re-marriage, and learning disabilities. For adult readers, *Adult Children of Alcoholics* (Woititz, 1983) appears to be most helpful.

What follows is based upon and takes off from Woititz's (1983) work, and it is a departure from the rest of this book. This information is presented here only because the patterns are so pervasive, and few people outside the field know about these patterns or understand where they come from. The discussion that follows is presented in the second person because when people can make a personal connection, the patterns can begin to change.

Crisis-to-Crisis Existence

If you grew up in an environment where you lived on the constant edge of crisis, always living from one moment to the next-

-You never knew what was going to happen next (for example, you might find your mother passed out in the middle of the kitchen floor, or get beaten for no apparent reason), and you may have felt you were not in control over what was going on around you. You may have felt desperate to have things change, but you didn't want to believe what was happening. So you could either exist in a constant state of anxiety where you couldn't function from day to day or you had to block it all out. You may have begun to have fantasies about things getting better or hopes about getting out. And that way of dealing with life may have carried over through the rest of your life, so you may now exist in a world of fantasy or live on false hope.

-Simply to survive, you had to learn to live with distress, and misery became a familiar existence. Not only did you have to learn how to handle crises very well and not walk away from discomfort, you also may have experienced a certain comfort in living with distress because that's what was familiar. And this may have carried through the rest of your life, so today, not only can you respond very well to crisis situations, but also perhaps, if you find yourself in a

461

situation that appears too comfortable, you may do something to make it uncomfortable because that's what is most familiar.

-You learned that the only thing you could control or rely on was yourself, so you may have learned to trust yourself more than anyone else and structure life in a way you could control. Perhaps you became rather rigid in your approach, so today you may continue to need to be in control and to rigidly stick to your own way of doing things.

-If you were in a constant state of concern over what was happening in your family, if you may have felt you couldn't go anywhere because they depended on you—you were the one who had to take charge, to hold everything together so your younger siblings wouldn't be hurt—you may have felt trapped. You wanted to escape but felt you couldn't. As an adult you may continue to have difficulty seeing your way out of problems and tend to feel trapped, no matter what problem you face.

-Perhaps, instead, you may have felt you couldn't handle it anymore, couldn't take all the responsibility. You may have felt there was no choice but to escape: by denying there was really a problem, by leaving physically, or by withdrawing emotionally. And whichever way you subconsciously chose is the way you may continue to respond to a problem or crisis today.

"I Need You"/ "You Can't Do Anything Right!"

If you grew up in an environment where you needed to take care of many of the things parents would normally take care of-

-You may have believed you had to be the one to take over, to be everyone else's emotional support (for example, take care of your younger siblings and perhaps even your parents). This may have made you feel the need to take care of everything throughout the rest of your life, to give everything to everyone who needs it and forget about yourself. But you may have developed no sense of your own limitations, so eventually you may get sucked dry, because it is virtually impossible for anyone to give all of themselves to others all the time. You may go into overload, and then have to withdraw when it appears emotionally (perhaps even physically) impossible to go on. This may create a situation where you either put every ounce of energy into something, or you have to totally withdraw—no middle ground. To withdraw, especially when things get tough, may be the only way you think you can protect yourself from getting sucked in. The implications for future relationships are acute: In the initial stages of a relationship you might put all your enormous energy into that relationship, but then suddenly you might feel a need for yourself. The only way you know how to cope is to withdraw everything, and that leaves a deep empty hole. (Example: "When the woman child of an alcoholic withdrew some energy, people began to see her partner as shorter. She had given so much that when she withdrew, he was actually shrunken.")

- This also has serious implications for growing up with confusing role models, so that you may not even know what is "normal" in a relationship.

If you then add to that an environment where, even though you were needed, you may have been constantly criticized, told you were never able to do anything right, that what you did was never good enough—

-It may have been drilled into you that if anything went wrong, it was your fault, your responsibility. You may have begun to believe that if you had done things just a little bit differently, maybe they would have worked out better. At the same time if anything went right, you may have believed it couldn't possibly have anything to do with you and you could therefore dismiss it. You may have thought there was only one way to escape the constant criticism and that was to be absolutely perfect—that way you couldn't get rejected. You perhaps began to judge yourself without mercy, measuring yourself against this perfection. That you were trying so hard and were still getting wiped out perhaps led you to believe that maybe you were the cause of all this trouble and maybe your family would be better off without you. You may have constantly sought encouragement, because you never got it. As an adult you may continue to seek encouragement in everything you do, and when you do get it, you may not believe it. And always trying to measure yourself against perfection and failing may have helped you develop a chronically low self-image, which you may have become used to. Now it might even feel safer to keep the negative image—there's a certain amount of comfort in it, because changing, accepting praise for being competent means changing the way you see yourself, and that may be too scary.

The combination of these two patterns may tend to make you see everything as "good" or "bad," black or white, without any middle ground. Either side is an awesome responsibility, so you may feel under a great deal of pressure all the time, making yours a very stressful existence. The black-and-white approach to life also has implications for relationships. You may think the only way to protect yourself is to pick a partner who is "perfect." Because no one is, the unrealistic expectations can cause problems. In addition, any behaviors that show up today that remind you of the old demands that were made on you, have a chance of producing similar reactions as they did while you were growing up. Throughout your life you may react this way.

"I'll Be There for You Next Time, I Promise"

If you grew up in an environment where promises were made but never kept-

-You may have learned that if you did not get what you asked for or what you were promised immediately, you probably wouldn't get a second chance. You may have learned that putting things off only gave you trouble, which led to a great sense of urgency. You must do it now! You must have it now! Instant gratification, impulsiveness, with no serious consideration given to the results of your impatience. This impatience and impulsiveness may have carried into the rest of your life. You may spend a lot of time cleaning up messes made because of impulsive decisions you've made, perhaps even marrying before getting to know your partner well enough.

-You may have learned that wanting things would only offer you pain, if so you learned how not to want for yourself.

-You may have watched yourself be manipulated by being at the mercy of another, by being turned on and off at their will. You may have been learned it was away you were controlled, so you could do the same. You might even become an expert at doing it to others. Besides, you may have perceived yourself as a victim; if it was the other person's fault, you didn't really have to take the responsibility.

Despite the forgotten promises, you probably knew your parent meant to keep them when he or she promised them, and in sober or "right-mind" moments tried to make up for letting you down-

-You may have begun to experience guilt for thinking any bad thoughts about the broken promise, or for thinking about yourself, because you were painfully aware of your parents' struggle. And that sense of guilt, coupled with the feeling that you had to be responsible for everything, may have carried over into the rest of your life.

"I Love You/Go Away"

If you grew up in an environment where you were loved one day and rejected the next-

-You may have believed you couldn't possibly be lovable and gained a low self-image. To feel good at all you may have needed others to tell you that you were okay. As an adult you may give a lot of power to others to lift you up or knock you down.

-When someone tries to love you now, you may think you can't really trust it because you will just be rejected somewhere down the line for not being good enough, thus impeding the development of future relationships. (Example: "I'm rejecting of anyone who's willing to love me. The only way I'm ever going to fall in love with someone is if they're absolutely perfect and we have an absolutely perfect relationship as soon as they walk through the door. Otherwise I don't want any part of it. I'm afraid of knowing love is real, or if love is real, have it taken away somehow.") You may have grown up not being able to trust.

-This, coupled with forgotten promises, perhaps made you grow up fearing that you could be abandoned at any time. When a problem arises, you may panic, certain that you're going to be rejected once again, abandoned once again. Throughout your life, minor disagreements and problems may get big very quickly when the fear of being abandoned takes precedence over the original issue.

"Always Tell the Truth'/ "I Don't Want to Know"

If you grew up in an environment where problems were avoided and not resolved, where everything was covered up, where excuses were constantly made, where you were taught to keep feelings inside and not let them out, where you were only allowed to discuss feelings the parent found acceptable—

-You may have learned that lying was the norm of the house. In fact, there was a payoff for not telling the truth: you wouldn't get wiped out. Keeping feelings to yourself was certainly better than risking disapproval, so even though your insides may have been churning, it was a lot safer than letting them show on the outside. Besides, why burden an already overburdened parent? Non-truth would make it easier for everyone. Besides if they were drunk, or not in their

right mind, their words didn't matter anyway. Since everyone was lying, it wasn't something you could feel too guilty about. Besides, you probably couldn't let the rest of the world know what was going on in your home—it was too embarrassing and if your parents found out you'd told someone you'd probably get wiped out for it. You may have carried this approach into your adult life, seeking safety, finding a way to diminish your feelings, even if it meant being accomplished through non-truth, with denial hanging over everything.

- If you deny your problems—and if you add to that your familiarity with functioning in a problem-laden, uncomfortable environment—discomfort may feel strangely safe. You may tend to remain in relationships that would be better dissolved, denying how much of a problem it is or how severely it is affecting you. If your partner treats you poorly, at least you're used to it. It's the way you've learned to be treated. What is known at least is some security; it is better than the unknown. You may grab for something you can control. One way to maybe feel okay is to stay in a relationship with a partner you consider somehow less than you, with whom you can feel superior. That may be one of the few ways you think you can feel okay, by diminishing others. If you don't really know what a normal relationship is, or that there could be anything better or different, you tend to muddle through, because that's the way it's always been, and for all you know, all relationships might be like that.

-If people like you, you might pass judgment on them as not being worth very much. How could anyone worthwhile possibly care for you?

But suppose, as you make your way through life, someone you could care about likes you. First, you may not believe it because nothing that positive was ever said to you. It's difficult to accept because it would mean changing your self-image—one you feel safe with. Through your life you may continue to find it difficult to accept nice things others have to say about you, so you can't win.

Perhaps you don't really want to believe it yourself. There may be too much risk in sharing too much, so you may share very little, and you could mess up a relationship by not letting the other person in, making the relationship devoid of emotion.

When each of these conditions occurs frequently enough, a thinking pattern may develop. Each of these patterns produces feelings. If the same feelings occur often enough, the person starts acting in certain ways, creating a predictable pattern of response to life now.

It is possible to trace this pattern from the family condition that started it to a likely thought pattern today. It's also possible to begin from today's reaction patterns and trace back to see where the patterns probably came from. To see this in a chart may be helpful [see Figure 40-1]. It may look very confusing and complex (only because the patterns are so confusing and complex), but if one traces in either direction from a familiar pattern, it will fall into place.

If the person can see these now as only thought habits picked up from the past that are only kept alive by one's thinking in the present, and she or he is not locked into thinking that way because thoughts change, that person will be less controlled by that kind of thinking.

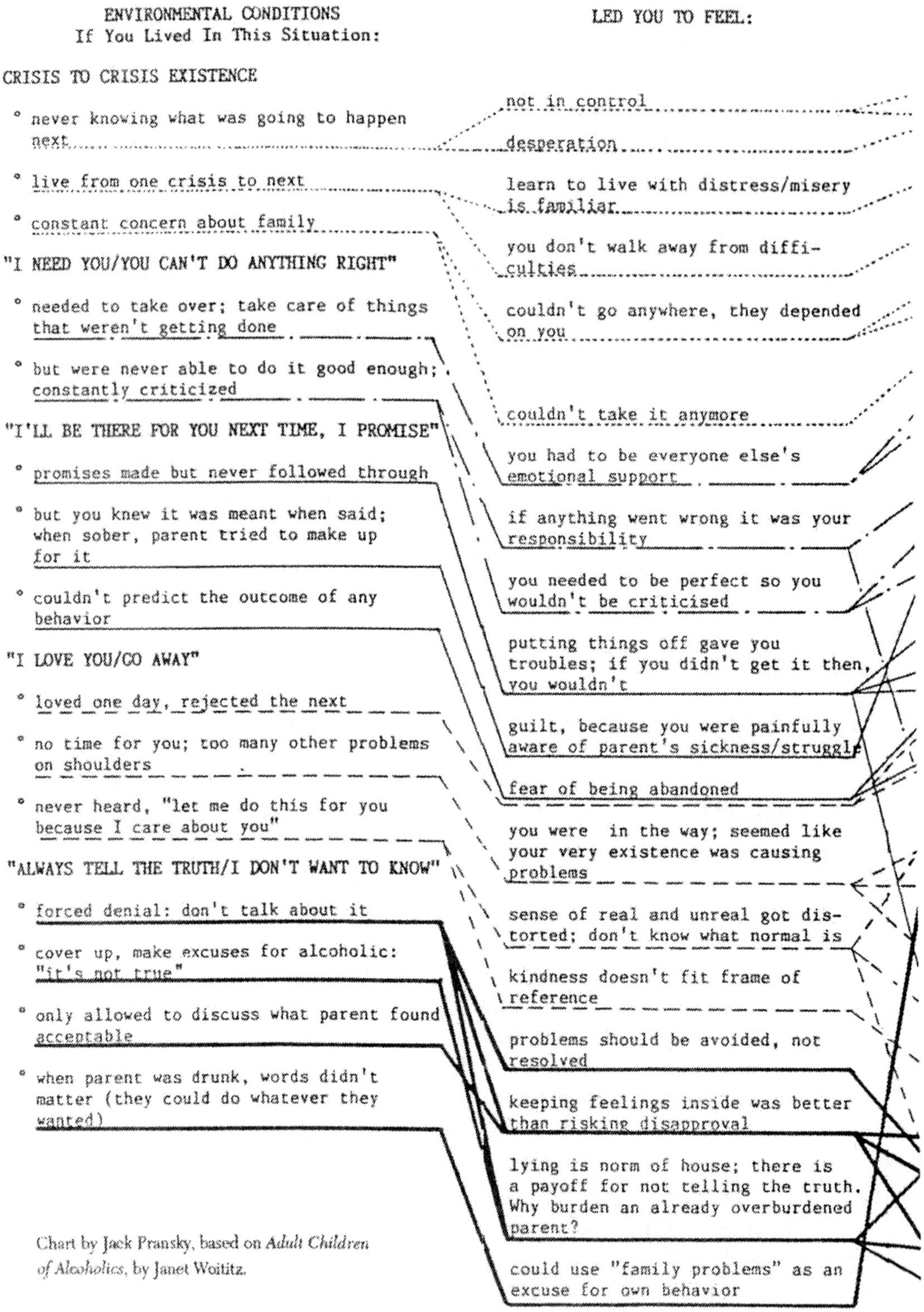

ENVIRONMENTAL CONDITIONS
If You Lived In This Situation:

LED YOU TO FEEL:

Figure 40-1.

Children of Alcoholics Growth Chart

CRISIS TO CRISIS EXISTENCE

° never knowing what was going to happen next

° live from one crisis to next

° constant concern about family

"I NEED YOU/YOU CAN'T DO ANYTHING RIGHT"

° needed to take over; take care of things that weren't getting done

° but were never able to do it good enough; constantly criticized

"I'LL BE THERE FOR YOU NEXT TIME, I PROMISE"

° promises made but never followed through

° but you knew it was meant when said; when sober, parent tried to make up for it

° couldn't predict the outcome of any behavior

"I LOVE YOU/GO AWAY"

° loved one day, rejected the next

° no time for you; too many other problems on shoulders

° never heard, "let me do this for you because I care about you"

"ALWAYS TELL THE TRUTH/I DON'T WANT TO KNOW"

° forced denial: don't talk about it

° cover up, make excuses for alcoholic: "it's not true"

° only allowed to discuss what parent found acceptable

° when parent was drunk, words didn't matter (they could do whatever they wanted)

not in control

desperation

learn to live with distress/misery is familiar

you don't walk away from difficulties

couldn't go anywhere, they depended on you

couldn't take it anymore

you had to be everyone else's emotional support

if anything went wrong it was your responsibility

you needed to be perfect so you wouldn't be criticised

putting things off gave you troubles; if you didn't get it then, you wouldn't

guilt, because you were painfully aware of parent's sickness/struggle

fear of being abandoned

you were in the way; seemed like your very existence was causing problems

sense of real and unreal got distorted; don't know what normal is

kindness doesn't fit frame of reference

problems should be avoided, not resolved

keeping feelings inside was better than risking disapproval

lying is norm of house; there is a payoff for not telling the truth. Why burden an already overburdened parent?

could use "family problems" as an excuse for own behavior

Chart by Jack Pransky, based on *Adult Children of Alcoholics*, by Janet Woititz.

WHICH MADE YOU:

hold fantasies/hopes about leaving, about things getting better

experience simple adjustments as a big deal

handle crises extremely well but find comfort in living with distress

extreme loyalty but its the result of fear and insecurity

have to rely on and trust self more than anyone else

feel trapped

escape by leaving and/or denying

experience confusion about roles

take responsibility for others' feelings

believe you were cause of trouble; if you had just done it differently, it would have worked out / guilt

judge self without mercy

tend to look at things as black-white, good-bad, extremes

urgency: must do it now, no time, no patience instant gratification; impulsive

consider self a victim and blame others/ learn not to confront reality

when a problem arises, you panic

rejecting of anyone willing to love you (unless they're perfect)

tend to pull self back too quickly and decide your instincts are not valid

feel you can't be accepted for who you are

feel its easier to deal with negative emotions about yourself

react to behaviors that remind you of demands

believe you couldn't be lovable, therefore to others to tell you you're ok (gives up power)

fear unknown/don't let someone get too close because might be hurt once again

get angry if someone tries to do something for you, because you don't trust it

learn trusting will only offer you pain, therefore learn how not to want/ seek safety

remain in involvements that are better dissolved (find comfort in distress) (diminish others)

myth that there's something out there called a "normal" relationship

can't let it show to the outside world, even though feelings are bubbling inside

WHICH CAUSE YOU TO REACT TO LIFE NOW BY/WITH:

FANTASY AND HOPE

DIFFICULTY MAKING CHANGES

INDISCRIMINATE EXTREME LOYALTY

RIGIDITY/FEELING THAT YOU MUST BE IN CONTROL

DIFFICULTY SEEING WAY OUT OF PROBLEMS/FEEL TRAPPED

ESCAPE FROM/DENIAL OF PROBLEMS

ALWAYS UNDER STRESS/CREATE DISTRESS

IMPATIENT, IMPULSIVE

UNCERTAIN OF WHAT IS RIGHT, HOW TO BEHAVE

LOW SELF-IMAGE

Do things for others to gain self worth/ give whatever is needed at moment

SEEK CONSTANT ENCOURAGEMENT BUT DON'T BELIEVE IT WHEN GET IT

EXPECT PERFECTION FROM SELF AND OTHERS

EITHER PUT ALL ENERGY IN OR TOTALLY WITH-DRAW IT / BLACK - WHITE APPROACH TO LIFE

DON'T KNOW WHEN TO STOP

DIFFICULTY FOLLOWING PROJECT THROUGH FROM BEGINNING TO END

SPEND EXCESSIVE TIME CLEANING UP MESSES YOU MAKE

Marry without really getting to know mate

DON'T WANT TO TAKE RESPONSIBILITY FOR OWN BEHAVIOR

MANIPULATIVE / SELF-PROTECTIVE

MINOR DISAGREEMENTS GET BIG VERY QUICKLY, BECAUSE FEAR OF BEING ABANDONED TAKES PRECEDENCE OVER ORIGINAL ISSUE

DON'T ALWAYS TELL TRUTH/SEEK SAFETY

LACK OF TRUST

FIND A WAY OF DIMINISHING FEELINGS/KEEP REAL FEELINGS HIDDEN

41. Healthy Lifestyles and Alternative Health Practices

Before discussing "alternative" health practices for individuals who want to improve their general health and well-being, we must consider a far more pressing problem. For a great number of Americans basic health care isn't even an option. Something is wrong when basic health care is considered an "alternative." Every American should have equal access to adequate health care. Unfortunately, many citizens of this country—mostly those who live in poverty but do not qualify for Medicaid, and pregnant teenagers who don't know any better or who don't want others to know—cannot afford or don't have access to basic health care. This is obviously a problem for the state of America's public health. Less obvious, perhaps, it is also an issue for the prevention of social problems.

> [A] growing body of evidence indicates that fewer children are receiving primary health services and that a greater percentage of children are disabled today, perhaps in part because of the greater survival rate of low birth weight babies and the greater incidence of very low birth weight births. A significant proportion of these infants, particularly poor infants, will be left with a disability or impairment serious enough to limit normal childhood activity. Given the higher incidence of death and disability among poor children, these eroding health trends undoubtedly will continue as long as childhood poverty rates remain severely elevated (Rosenbaum, 1989, p. 91).

Rosenbaum also points out that uninsured low-income children with disabilities are significantly less likely to have a regular source of care and only about half as likely to receive medical services than insured poor children. It doesn't seem fair. One of the obvious ways to deal with this problem is to guarantee that everyone is insured at rates they can afford. Obviously, managed care has not done the job. Perhaps a single-payer system is the only way to ensure fair and equitable coverage.

Short of that, or in conjunction with it, another promising strategy is to set up *school-based health clinics* so that school children at least would have easy access to health care. This was done very effectively in St. Paul, Minnesota, where a clinic was set up that offered both sex education and health services (including contraceptives). This program resulted in-

- reduced teenage child bearing by over 50%
- reduced number of second pregnancies before graduation to 2% (in Schorr, 1988)

Health clinics can also be made available in low-income communities. At the O.B. Access Project in Oakland, California, a system of comprehensive nutritional, medical, social, psychological services and prenatal care was offered to the poor, which resulted in-

- a 33% reduction in low birth weight babies born to project participants (in Schorr, 1988)

Individual Health

Beyond that, we do need to be concerned and responsible for our individual health. Each of us is in control over what we do with our bodies.

In the name of prevention and health promotion, controlling what we do with our own bodies and how we treat ourselves should be the easiest aspect of prevention to tackle. Unfortunately for many of us, it is one of the most difficult. Many of us find it difficult to have the discipline to keep ourselves completely healthy, let alone convince others to do the same.

Ironically, preventers give so much to others they often forget about taking care of themselves. Trying to prevent some of the most difficult problems this country faces, with the limited resources allocated, is akin to a middle school basketball team trying to bring the ball up court against the full court press of a National Basketball Association championship team. It can be a highly stress-producing experience. Stress inhibits healthy functioning. The stress produced by prevention work, and many other jobs, is not conducive to living a healthy life—unless we make it a prime focus. Easier said than done.

Components of a Healthy Lifestyle

A healthy lifestyle has at least five aspects:

1. what we put into our bodies—nutrition and chemicals
2. the environment we subject our bodies to—safety and stress
3. the shape we keep our bodies in—keeping fit
4. our attitudes surrounding our bodies—mental and emotional state
5. our perceived connection to the universe/spirituality

To be fully healthy, we should treat ourselves well in each of these areas.

The U.S. Department of Health and Human Services estimates that 50% of all premature illnesses and deaths in this country are related to the adoption of unhealthy lifestyle behaviors; in other words, they are caused by the way we live. We should be able to prevent half the premature deaths in this country, as well as much stress-related disease.

Stress

The human organism has always responded in physiologic ways to the stress it encounters. It used to be pretty clear. When confronted with a saber-tooth tiger, it was either fight or flight, and our body had to physically prepare itself to do either, by pumping adrenaline through our body and getting all systems ready to go. Our basic fight or flight mechanisms haven't changed, but with the current state of civilization, fighting or running away from someone who's causing us

stress isn't always possible. Sometimes the stress necessary for that kind of readiness doesn't get released and thus accumulates.

When we're faced with a stressor in our lives we have at least four choices:

- walk away from it or remove it from our lives
- if we can't remove it, modify the way it relates to us
- if we can't do either, modify the way we respond to it
- remember that stress is really caused by our own thinking and not by our circumstances [Chapter 42]

The field of psychoneuroimmunology insists that the mind, the autonomic nervous system, and the immune system are all connected. If stress is affecting us, and it is not adequately dealt with, it can affect the heart, blood pressure, the breathing mechanism, in fact, nearly all systems, and lead to discomfort and illness. Hans Seyle (1976) said that stress is common denominator of all adaptive reactions in the body. Stress is wear and tear on the body. Too much stress can inhibit the nervous and endocrine systems that are the body's defense mechanisms against illness. It can affect both the structure and chemical composition of the body and its adaptive reactions. It can affect the adrenal glands, the thymus, and the gastro-intestinal tract.

Yet we can recognize early symptoms of stress like irritability, hyperexcitability, depression, pounding heart, dry throat and mouth, impulsive behavior, weakness, dizziness, anxiety, insomnia. The question is, Will we slow down enough to be aware of it, and then will we do anything about it at these early signs?

If we practice stress reduction and stress management techniques on a regular basis, we can build our resistance; in fact, we can control our blood pressure, migraine headaches, and the like (Matson, 1980). Controlling stress is one aspect of a total health promotion effort.

It is not enough to merely manage and control the stress we already have, such as by keeping our bodies active. We must also prevent ourselves from experiencing stress in the first place. This can happen by recognizing that even though it appears otherwise, our stress is caused by our own thinking. For example, the more ego-involved we are, the more stress we experience. The more satisfaction we gain from the simple pleasures of life, the less we experience stress. The less we get frustrated over little things, the less we hate, the less we experience stress (Seyle, in Matson, 1980). The less we take things personally, the less we experience stress.

Health Promotion

Some biomedical researchers, Dr. James F. Files of Stanford University for one, suggest that in the normal course of events, barring accidents or illness, the human body will simply wear out. He suggests that we are programmed to live about 85 years but these 85 years can and should be relatively free of illness and disability. He further suggests that by living the best we know how, we can greatly narrow the gap between the onset of the symptoms of chronic, illness and eventually death…that we should be able to live fully and vigorously almost until the moment of death and we should not be faced with many years of disability, discomfort, or confinement at home or in a nursing home. The end of the period of adult vigor can come much later than it does on the average now. And the only person who can bring this about for you is you. Therefore health promotion is a challenge to you, me, and everyone to stop, look, and listen. . .long enough to assess. . .where we are on the wellness-illness continuum and, most importantly, which way we are moving—toward wellness or toward illness. . .,that each is responsible for the consequences of our own behavior.... [and] that you feel good about [whatever you do to promote your health] because you know you are achieving something which results in a plus, both for you and for everyone around you. This is what health promotion is about–not extensive exercise or quitting drugs per se, but rather the sense of doing something for and to yourself so that you can live a richer, more productive, healthier life (Phillips, 1984).

Our choices determine our lifestyles and our health and well-being, We all have something that we could be working on to improve the quality of our lives. We should not be satisfied with "not sick," and instead choose as a goal the continued growth of the whole self toward realization of full potential. We should act to take control of our health rather than react to illness or stress when it strikes.

Unfortunately, lifestyle-related diseases creep up on us slowly and insidiously. If we smoke heavily, we don't develop cancer immediately; it can build over time until suddenly it is serious, and we notice. The same is true with cirrhosis of the liver, cholesterol build-up in the arteries, emphysema, and hearing and vision problems. Because of this, chronic diseases are approached most effectively with a strategy of "postponement" rather than cure. If the rate of progress of the disease is decreased or slowed, the time at which it becomes threatening or disabling can also be postponed and if postponed sufficiently long the disabling threshold may not be crossed during the lifetime of the patient, and the disease for all intents and purposes has been "prevented." We know that some chronic diseases definitely can be postponed. Elimination of cigarette smoking greatly delays the onset of symptoms of emphysema and reduces the probability of lung cancer. Treatment of high blood pressure retards the development of certain complications in the arteries. There is strong evidence that arterioscelerosis can be postponed by weight reduction and exercise. So can some forms of arthritis. We know that the elimination of smoking may also in some instances postpone the onset of heart disease. Maintaining desirable weight and a proper diet can delay the onset of adult diabetes (Phillips, 1984).

Unfortunately, our "health system" works counter to health promotion. It could be turned around to promote high motivation toward good health. For example, insurance companies could say, "If you lose a certain amount of weight and maintain the loss over a certain period of time, you get part of your money back." (Phillips, 1984).

Programs like *Meals on Wheels* provide proper nutrition to elderly people, plus a shared social experience, that promotes mental health, but so much more could be done. Blighted areas and vacant lots inner-cities could be turned into productive places such as vegetable and flower gardens. Recreation activities could be provided in apartment complexes and neighborhoods, especially for low-income and single mothers, and especially if child care can be provided on site. Such practices are needed if we are to turn around the health of Americans.

Harvey Milkman (1990) suggests that we reach a state of health and well-being when we acquire these "personal skills"-

- the ability to meaningfully engage our talents (when we connect what we do with what we love)
- the ability to attain peace of mind (when we can step out of our frantic space, relax, and appreciate small things; when we're around friendly people in a meaningful way)
- the ability to establish healthy personal boundaries (on the physical, emotional, intellectual, and spiritual levels)
- the ability to engage in healthy pleasures

472

Others have added-

- the ability to have fun.

Milkman reports on the results of a study that says, if we regularly engage in the following seven activities, we live longer and healthier lives; in fact, if we do all seven, we generally live ten to fifteen years longer than if we only do three or four:

1. regular exercise
2. regular meals
3. daily breakfast
4. maintain normal weight
5. no smoking
6. alcohol in moderation
7. seven to eight hours nightly sleep

Alternative Health Practices

Alternative health practices are preventive health practices. Most medical practices today try to fix problems after they've occurred. Many alternative health practices attempt to prevent problems from developing. While some Western-based health promotion practices such as fitness, aerobics, and a balanced diet are accepted by the medical establishment, most Eastern-based health promotion practices are not.

Perhaps the major difference between traditional Western medical practices and "alternative" health practices, particularly those based upon Eastern philosophies, lies in use of the concept, "energy." In physics, "energy" is defined as "the work that a physical system is capable of doing in changing from its actual state to a specified reference state" (American Heritage Dictionary).

Medical scientists would agree that a body or body part capable of or in motion would constitute "energy." Discoveries that the brain discharges electrical-chemical signals sent along the nerves to the rest of the body is now also accepted as "energy." Where Western medical traditions often part company is in extending the concept of "energy" to the belief that-

- energy flows continuously throughout the body, and between two polarities
- the free, even, and unrestricted flow of this energy is what creates a healthy body
- blocks can occur within this energy flow that impede it and cause pain and disease
- our thoughts and feelings affect this energy flow and can create these blocks
- work can be done on the body and mind (and spirit) to balance and harmonize this energy and release the blocks to promote good health

The medical establishment is reluctant to embrace this concept because this type of energy cannot be seen or measured. But many believers say that today's scientific instruments have simply not yet become sophisticated enough to pick up this subtle energy flow. They liken it to the time when scientists believed the world was flat, or when physicians didn't believe in the concept of germs, simply because at the time their instruments were not sophisticated enough to evince these phenomena.

One fact cannot be denied: Many Eastern religions, philosophies, and health practices for thousands of years have operated under the premise that there is a "life force" or energy that flows through the body, that it has positive and negative polarities, and that balancing and, harmonizing this energy is critical in reaching a state of good health.

Whether or not one believes in such alternative health practices, the important question for prevention is, Do they work? For some, they apparently can make a huge difference. The Eastern-based Transcendental Meditation (TM), for example, makes great claims that appear to be backed up by many Western-based scientific studies. TM has been found to-

- improve memory and learning
- improve job performance and satisfaction
- improve reaction time
- decrease oxygen consumption by 16%, thereby changing the metabolic rate faster than sleep;
- decrease heart rate; decrease blood pressure in hypertensive subjects
- decrease reported drug use and alcohol consumption
- decrease crime, even in environments of increasing crime
- increase internal locus of control

(in Denniston and McWilliams, 1975)

- improve self-actualization
  (Seeman et al., 1972)

Even if some of these studies have design flaws, enough studies have shown similar results that we can't afford to ignore TM as a promising health promotion practice.

Other alternative health practices have not been as studied. Some have been studied only by the organization that created or supports them, and other researchers have a tendency not to trust their validity. More independent research is desperately needed. But not knowing enough about them does not make these practices invalid. Ultimately, since these are individual practices, the true test is whether they work for the individual trying them. Different practices appear to work better for some than others. There apparently needs to be a correct "fit" between the individual and the practice.

In examining alternative health practices, it appears that there are at least five major ways to improve the free and balanced flow of energy within the body:

- through the food and other substances we ingest
- through movement
- through manipulation of the body
- through the mind
- through connection to spiritual energy

Most alternative health practices fall under one or more of these categories. It is not uncommon for some combination to be applied within one discipline, particularly if that practice is concerned with full integration of all systems.

It may be incorrect to lump all alternative health practices under the heading of "energy." Some, like standard nutrition and fitness programs, do not apply such concepts. However, whether they believe in them or not, an argument could be made that their practices do affect energy flow. At least they seem to help the body function mechanically in the proper way.

Those who believe in the proper balancing and harmonizing of the body's energy say that energy flow affects all major systems of the body: circulatory, respiratory, digestive, excretory, nervous, endocrine, skeletal, musculature, reproductive, and the senses.

Ingesting Food and Other Substances

Westerners would agree that food is converted into bodily energy. Less common to Western thought is the Eastern belief that different foods are converted into different types of energy. The theory is, if we consider what we eat according to the specific energy produced, we can enhance our health.

According to many Eastern philosophies, all energy exists on a continuum between two polarities: yin and yang (or yin and yan, or ying and yang). All foods we eat carry with them one of these types of energy, to varying degrees. The opposing energies should be kept in balance, and extremes at both ends should be avoided. In Macrobiotics, yin is characterized as acidity; yang as alkalinity. Each of these energies is said to have a particular character.

Extreme yang energy is aggressive energy. When extreme yang foods are digested they are said to produce a surge of aggressiveness, followed by a period of fatigue and drowsiness. The most extreme yang food is eggs, followed by red meat, cheese and other dairy products. At the lowest end of the extreme yang scale lies fish, with chicken and other poultry falling in between.

Moderate yang energy is strength. When moderate yang foods are digested they strengthen the body and build fortitude. Examples of moderate yang foods are grains and legumes (beans).

Moderate yin energy is creative energy. Examples of moderate yin foods are leafy vegetables and seasonal fruits.

Extreme yin energy produces a surge of excitability followed by a longer period of irritability. The extreme of the extreme yin foods are drugs, including alcohol, and sugar. At the mild end of the extreme yin foods are citrus fruits.

This holds implications for what foods we should eat before engaging in various activities. If I am about to write an article, I would do well to eat leafy vegetables or an apple for creativity. If I am about to give a speech or drive a long distance, I would do well to eat grains for fortitude. If I am about to play a football game I may want to eat steak and eggs for aggressiveness. God knows why I would want to eat extreme yin foods like sugar (besides that it tastes so good)—maybe to party! If we desire to be generally strong and creative and healthier, it is apparently wise to ingest as little food from the extremes as possible.

Most of us think of nutrition in the traditional sense, apart from an "energy" framework. From the time we are children most of us hear from our parents or school that we need to eat well-balanced meals. Scientifically speaking, different foods have different nutritive values. Interestingly, many of the foods considered to be the best for us nutritionally are those that also fall within the "moderate" yin and yang brackets. Thus, whether one believes in food energies or not, we would be wise to eat, and stay away from, the same foods as suggested by this model.

We also need an adequate amount of vitamins and minerals. Most nutritionists believe that it is best to get these from the foods we eat, rather than from vitamin and mineral supplements. Unfortunately, unless we grow and raise our own food or purchase our food from organic establishments, we can't really be certain how much of the nutritive value is left in food by the time it gets to us. We don't know what chemicals have been sprayed on our fruits and vegetables. We don't know what has been added to the grains that animals eat, which gets into their meat and milk. Apparently, the Food and Drug Administration doesn't consider it important enough to study and tell us, or they don't want to—not to mention the fruit and vegetables we get from other countries.

Even when they do tell us what chemicals are in our foods, we don't know in what amounts, and most of us don't know which chemicals on the list of ingredients have been found to be harmful, even to laboratory animals. They don't tell us how much cholesterol is in our foods. It wouldn't be difficult to conclude that our government, at least as represented by the FDA, does not particularly concern itself with the health of Americans. At best, they are not allowing consumers to make informed decisions about what they wish to ingest by providing inadequate information about food content.

Various proponents of eating well as a means for health suggest that to be the healthiest we can be, we should-

- cut down on our food intake (eat small portions)
- eat balanced foods
- eat foods high in fiber
- eat foods high in protein
- stay away from fats and oils
- fast every once in a while

Most of us have learned that we can reduce the risk of cancer and cholesterol buildup, which in turn affects heart disease, by eating a diet high in fiber. Colons without an adequate amount of fiber become increasingly susceptible to disease because certain bacteria and bile acids combine to form carcinogens (cancer-causing chemicals). Most of us consume about six grams of fiber per day. Proponents of the high-fiber diet (Reuben, 1975; Galton, 1976) say we should consume 24 grams per day to have the best chance of staying healthy. Foods highest in fiber are bran, whole grains, fresh fruits, and fresh (or minimally cooked) vegetables.

If we're interested in weight loss, some theorists (Stillman, 1974) believe we should eat only high-protein foods and cut out carbohydrates, causing our metabolism and body chemistry to change, which then causes the body to start burning its own fat for energy. Other experts say there is no sure way of reducing weight other than by reducing caloric intake.

The most foolproof way to cut down on calories is through fasting. If one does not eat for two to three days (but drinks two to three quarts of water per day), the body begins to rest physiologically, the metabolism slows down, there is a subsequent decrease in respiration, circulation, temperature, and blood pressure, the stomach can't take in as much food, and the body starts relying on fat deposits and ketone (after glucose is used up). Fasting is believed to cleanse the body. It has been found to remedy some illnesses (Ross, 1976; Cott, 1975).

Many herbs and plants are also believed to contain healing properties, and can help us stay healthy (Davis, 1965; Davis, 1970; Colbin, 1986).

Body Movement

Human bodies are meant to move. If a body lies completely dormant it begins to decay. Simply keeping the body moving is worthwhile. If a body is engaged in free and fast movement for a long enough period of time, the lungs expand to increase respiration, and the heart pumps blood faster throughout the entire body, thereby keeping all systems strong. This is the principle behind aerobics (Cooper, 1968) and the concept of total fitness (Morehouse and Coss, 1975.) The entire system must be stimulated enough and for a long-enough period of time to produce beneficial changes. According to physical health consultant Murray Banks (1990), if you can grab the fat on any portion of your body and shake it around, aerobic exercise is the only way to take it off. Toning muscles through sit-ups or lifting weights or isometrics make muscles stronger, but they don't take off fat. Minimally, to stay healthy, Banks insists that we need at least 30 minutes of aerobic exercise three times a week.

A different type of helpful movement, which is said to produce a different type of energy in the body, is slow and "soft" movement, and stretching movement. This type of movement is believed to increase "centeredness" and suppleness, balance ying and yang energies, increase awareness through attention and intention, promote self-discipline, master the senses, and to allow for the least amount of energy to be expended as possible in movement, thereby increasing energy and strength without fatigue and yielding calmness and clarity.

T'ai Chi Ch'uan (Delza, 1961) is the organized harmonious movement and relationship of the body and mind to achieve health and tranquility. Each movement becomes a part of the next, and all movements are one. The movement is "soft," unrestrained, circular, arcing, curving, light. Attention is paid to every motion to achieve physical and emotional equilibrium. Each motion is evenly placed and "centered" in one's center of gravity. No part of the body is ever in constant motion or at rest.

Hatha Yoga (Vithaldas, 1957) involves the entire body in stretching and holding postures, and integrates the body as a whole, physically attuning it, and strengthening and realigning the body so it achieves a state of unified balance. There is supposed to be no exertion or strain. Quietness or peacefulness in concentration is emphasized. The postures are designed to affect every major system of the body. Yoga has been used therapeutically for relief of nervous disorders, tension, and organic diseases such as anemia, arthritis, high blood pressure, obesity, ulcers. It helps people eat lightly.

Aikido (Westbrook and Ritti, 1971) is a quicker form of movement (as well as a system of physical defense) that is said to help people tap into their center of personal power, which helps them operate from a superior level. From this center, located two inches below the naval, it is possible to absorb and make use of others' force to guide attacks away. Beyond physical defense, the movement in Aikido helps people develop elasticity and suppleness of the muscles, and helps integrate the body and mind.

Other more Westernized approaches are at least related to, if not based upon these Eastern-based concepts. *Feldenkrais* (1975) focused on the correction of movement, concentrating awareness in as many parts of the body as possible, in sensation, feeling, thinking, and movement, thereby improving posture, releasing tension, and improving self-esteem. *The Alexander Technique* (Barlow, 1973) focuses on correct positioning of the body through concentration on particular subtle movements that bring one to various positions and aligning posture, creating a perfectly balanced, tensionless, resting state, leading to increased energy.

477

Movement can also be applied to heal specific systems, as in the *Bates Method* of improving eyesight. Bates (1970) has shown that, often, eyesight can be improved without glasses through a series of exercises for the eyes. Because near- and far-sightedness are related to the shape of the eyeball, Bates claims this shape can be altered through exercise, and that defective vision, even diseases like glaucoma, can be improved.

Manipulation of the Body

We also need to be sure that the body is functioning well from within, so that energy flows unimpeded within us, without restrictions and without blocks.

Some of the principles that drive these techniques are-

- alignment of the body affects functioning, through the skeletal structure, the muscle tissue, the nervous system, etc.
- use of the body and its various parts affect functioning

Our bones need to be lined up and in the right place. *Chiropractic* (Dintenfass, 1970) focuses primarily on the correct positioning of the vertebra. Its belief is that disease is not a thing but a disturbed condition resulting from pressure from a displaced vertebra or another bone on the nerves, causing them to become excited, irritated, and more or less inflamed. This results in nervous tension that can be relieved by the realignment of the bones in question. Body tissue is maintained and controlled by nervous impulses, and when these impulses are disrupted, the result is disease. Chiropractic is said to stabilize the self-regulating systems of the body to allow its recuperative powers to function normally. Strong evidence has shown that chiropractors fared better than physicians in curing arthritis, neuritis, bursitis, and sciatica, and there is some evidence that chiropractic is effective in treating colitis, hypertension, sinus headaches, and constipation (in Matson, 1977). [Note: Chiropractic was vindicated in 1990 when it won a major suit against the American Medical Association for violating antitrust laws by conspiring to destroy the competitive profession of chiropractic in the United States (Natural Health News, 1990), and in the last decade has now become much better accepted by many in the medical establishment.]

Our muscle tissue needs to be in the right place. *Structural integration* or *Rolfing* (Rolf, 1972) contends that our weight should be distributed about a central vertical axis, which leads to good posture. But we have a tendency to put our bodies in unstable positions, either through injury or through birth, or from gravity continually working upon us, so that most of us move away from this axis, causing an imbalance of the body. Once imbalanced, the body has a tendency to remain unbalanced and become reasonably comfortable in these shifted positions. Facia tissue surrounds our muscles and holds them in place, but adapts to the shifted positions, thereby decreasing the body's efficiency and ability to move, increasing stress, and aches and pains. Rolfing is the exertion of force to move fascia tissue back to its original design. Emotional tension is released. Studies have shown that attitudinal changes have occurred in some people who have been Rolfed; they feel lighter and can do more, physically and mentally, with ease (in Heller and Henkin, 1986). Hellerwork is based on Rolfing, but attempts to integrate the systems more by combining other techniques.

We may have other blocks that can impede the free and even flow of energy. Some believe in the Indian-based notion that energy is concentrated in certain "centers" in the body called *chakras*, and that each of the seven chakras corresponds to a different type of energy and body system. Some believe in the Chinese-based notion that energy is concentrated along meridians that run up and down the body, with positive and negative energy. Common to both notions is that energy is concentrated where thought and emotions are focused, and blocks can be created at any of the energy centers or points along the meridian that correspond to different parts of the body. Various forms of "energy work" such as *Reike* or *Zero Balancing* (which combines energy work with subtle manipulation) are said to release these blocks, through healing energy.

Acupuncture (Manaka and Urquhart, 1972; Mann, 1973) is the insertion, and sometimes turning, of very thin needles into the blocked energy points to balance and harmonize this energy, and unify all components, releasing the blocks and restoring energy flow. *Acupressure* and *reflexology* or *zone therapy* (Bergson and Tuchak, 1974; Carter, 1969) are based upon similar principles, the former concentrating on the same points as acupuncture and the latter concentrating on areas of the feet or hands where nerve endings are close to the skin. Each reflex area on the feet is said to directly correspond to the organs of the body. A point of tenderness or pain under the skin is one through which the blood is not flowing normally to the disturbed area of the body. Reflexology can be used to treat a variety of physical problems such as back pain, colds, ulcers, arthritis, chronic fatigue, allergies, and heart conditions. Charts are available showing which spots correspond to which organ systems and parts of the body.

Shiatsu (Irwin and Wagenvoord, 1976; Schultz, 1975), originating in Japan, combines acupressure and massage, concentrating on specific points of the body surface where blood and lymph vessels, nerves and ductless endocrine glands are concentrated or dispersed. The process is geared specifically to diffuse lactic acid and carbon dioxide buildup that accumulate in tissues, causing stiffness or fatigue because of improper blood circulation, abnormal pressure on the nerves, blood vessels, or lymph vessels. The massage works on the skin to stimulate activity of the capillaries, to nourish cells and remove waste. The pressure releases fatigue-causing agents and permits nourishment to reach the bones. It is believed to restore chemical balance regulated by the endocrine glands, and stimulate internal organ functioning.

Other forms of massage also stimulate blood flow to the muscles and reenergize the body.

The Mind

Many of the blocks in energy flow are caused by our thoughts and emotions, and another set of techniques focuses on how to help the mind release these created blocks.

Developing the more intuitive right side of the brain (Ornstein, 1975) and integrating it with the left side is said to help us recognize our capacity to be influenced by subtle sources of energy, from both geophysical and human forces.

Bioenergetics (Lowen, 1975) attempts to bridge the gap between the function of mind and body (structure and movement), their relationship with each other and the outside world. Lowen believes that all energy is interchangeable and can manifest itself either as psychic phenomena or somatic motion. The goal is to reunite the mind and body by getting rid of obstacles that inhibit or prevent the body from releasing tension. By working on parts of the body that are holding tension and putting the body in difficult-to-maintain positions, emotional tension is released and the personality is said to be liberated. It is important to have a skilled person around to help process emotions that arise.

Biofeedback (Brown, 1975; Jonas, 1974) can help us attain conscious control of our brain's alpha waves (relaxed and peaceful state) through self-monitoring. Involuntary functions such as heartbeat, blood pressure, and intestinal contractions can be controlled and modified through viewing external signals on various biofeedback instruments that tell a person what is happening in their bodies from moment to moment. By receiving these cues, we can communicate with our physical self. Migraine headaches have even been relieved by controlling the blood flow.

Hypnosis or *self-hypnosis* (LeCron, 1964) allows people to enter a deep, nonwaking state that allows susceptibility to selective suggestions through the subconscious mind, thereby changing unwanted or undesirable behavioral patterns or habits. Self-hypnosis conditions or deconditions the internal response to situations, and helps adjust and strengthen responses. Suggestions must be positive and results-oriented, and should be repeated three or four times.

Silva Mind Control (Silva, 1977) is purported to allow us to voluntarily enter and control certain states of consciousness or levels of brain function that mostly lie untapped to increase the powers of the mind. If the mind functions from an alpha perspective it can develop controls and it can sense information it does not usually pick up. Some believe that these can even be impressed on the alpha neurons of other brains, regardless of distance. Willful control means a superior mental perspective. It helps people relax and improves one's memory and capacity to solve problems.

Many other practices such as *Psycho-Cybernetics* (Maltz, 1960), and various other methods, have been developed to help us change or improve the course of our lives by changing the way we think and feel about ourselves.

We have not even begun to tap the power and unlimited potential of the mind.

Spiritual Energy

Another set of practices is based on the belief that an individual human spirit can be in communion with or united to a source of "spiritual energy," and that it is possible to reach this state through focused concentration and turning off the mind from worldly thoughts.

Various forms of *meditation*, by disengaging us from superficial mental activity help to produce a state of deep relaxation and wakeful mental alertness, slowing down our metabolism, heartbeat, and respiration, so we use less oxygen, produce less carbon dioxide, and lower blood lactate levels. Brain wave patterns change. The most practiced forms of meditation require a quiet environment for at least 10 to 20 minutes, a comfortable position, a focus on either an object or on breathing or on a repeated word or phrase (mantra), and allowing conscious thoughts to be passively drift from the mind (acknowledged but then "let go").

Of the various forms of meditation, *Transcendental Meditation* (Bloomfield et al., 1975; Benson, 1975) has been the most studied. Maynard Shelley (1972) contends that there is a direct connection between happiness, psychological health, and the ability to maintain an optimal level of arousal, so we enjoy daily activities more. Those who practiced TM were happier, more relaxed, experienced more enjoyment, developed deeper personal relationships, had more of a sense of purpose, and showed more improved performance than those in control groups. TM has been effective in the treatment of anxiety neurosis, obsessive-compulsive symptoms, chronic low-grade depression, and psychosomatic illness.

Many of the "New Age" practices, called by many different names, are adaptations or combinations of these and some other spiritual practices. If nothing else, all can be beneficial to our health—if the fit is right. They can help us relax, ease stress, and release blocks that inhibit healthy functioning.

42. Spirituality as Prevention

The first edition of this book became the first book to give credence to the importance of spirituality in prevention. Unlike the treatment end of the alcohol and drug abuse field where Alcoholics Anonymous long ago had pioneered the use of spirituality as a way of helping people overcome alcoholism, spirituality has been slower in coming to the prevention end of the field.

On a personal level, prevention means attempting to attain a state of personal well-being. Some people have reached such a state through a connection on a spiritual level. There is observable evidence that some people who have had spiritual or religious epiphanies have completely turned problem lives into healthy lives; for example, boxer George Foreman (Foreman & Engle, 1995). As such, it would seem that spirituality could be considered an integral part of a comprehensive approach to prevention.

Is it more than an astounding coincidence that most of the great teachers of spiritual thought reach remarkably similar conclusions about how the universe works and the principles that should be put into practice in our lives?

Joseph Campbell (1989) discovered that every culture on earth has had a connection to a realm that cannot be considered "of this world." While described very differently by different cultures, many of the elements comprising this "spiritual" realm appear remarkably similar, whether they be through formal religions or cultural myths or through other spiritual approaches. The coincidence appears too great to definitively conclude that there is not some form of higher energy or intelligence or power—or whatever anyone wants to call it—than what we can see obviously and measure scientifically.

For prevention, the questions are, "So what if we believe or don't believe in the existence of a spiritual state?" "Is spirituality connected to our daily lives?" "Can a spiritual connection help us to achieve a higher state of personal well-being?"

What Is Spirituality?

"Spirituality" is not easily definable. Dictionaries are not particularly helpful here. There are probably nearly as many interpretations of what spirituality is as there are people. Joseph Campbell said that spirituality is the relationship of the individual to some higher energy/intelligence/power. It is this striving towards, or attempting to reach some relationship with this energy/intelligence/power that embodies the spiritual quest, the same type of quest that characterizes the spiritual quality written about in all religions and individual spiritual journeys, from the ancient to the traditional to the "New Age."

Patricia Mulready, who teaches a course at the New England School of Addiction Studies on spirituality defines some of the elements that constitute "spirituality": Spirituality is a means for giving personal meaning to one's life; a means for feeling interconnected with others and with life; a recognition of personal value; that each of us is an important part of the universe (but not its center). It is the ability to see goodness and attract that goodness to us. It is the recognition that each of us has an important role to play in the universe, that there is a reason each of us is here now, and we will know what that is if we listen to what is going on inside us.

For many, religion may be the means to spiritual fulfillment, but there are other means. Spirituality is not necessarily religion; religion is not necessarily spirituality. Religion is form put around formless spirituality. Spirituality is something that is experienced internally.

According to Mulready, spirituality does not suggest that we must believe in a higher power or supernatural being; in fact, Mulready believes that spirituality can be viewed on a continuum of belief. At one end might be a belief in a defined Supreme Being; at the other end might be nonbelief, or a belief in "humanism." At various times in life we might be at different points along this continuum. There is no right or wrong place to be; what is right is what is right individually. Everyone decides for themselves where they fit. The important thing is not to struggle with it.

If we would like to be moved in the direction we would like to go, we can "ask" (in prayer, in our thoughts, out loud, whatever). Whether we believe that a higher power hears us and therefore moves us toward where we want to be, or that by "asking" we internally drive ourselves forward, is not of much consequence. What is important is whether we end up where we want to be and experience a state of personal well-being in the process (Mulready, 1988).

Whether we believe that our lives are presided over by a Supreme Being, or believe in the formless energy behind life, or believe in a transmigration of souls connected to a higher wisdom, or believe in a particular religion, or believe that all of it is garbage, the universe only works in one way. There is only one absolute Truth. Some may think they know what that truth is. We each may have our own beliefs about it. My own beliefs have changed before and they may change again—such is the power of thought—but the universe still operates according to its own laws, whether we know what they are or not. As Meher Baba (1955) said, absolute truth transcends all "isms."

One of my beliefs (which is also probably of no consequence) is that some people have glimpsed what they believe to be the truth, through whatever experiences they may have had that brought them to their conclusions, but they may have only seen part of the Truth. Yet because they believe what they saw to be the truth, they proclaim that it is. Thus, different paths have been professed as "the way." Whether we believe in the God of Judaism or Jesus Christ or Mohammed or Buddha or Sri Chinmoy or *est* or Kundalini Yoga or Transcendental Meditation or chakras or past lives or crystals or whatever we believe, each may be part of the truth, whatever it is. Some paths may move us closer than others to knowing the truth for ourselves— but who knows? Whatever works for each of us is what's right for each of us. Obviously, some people would disagree with my belief. They firmly believe that their way is the truth, and they may even be right, for all I know. But I am more comfortable believing that I can find a spiritual path that feels right for me. Or maybe it finds me.

When I wrote the first edition of this book in 1990, I would say now, in retrospect, that I was on some sort of spiritual search. When I began to understand the three principles uncovered by

Sydney Banks, my spiritual search stopped in its tracks. I don't know why; I wasn't trying to search or not. It just happened.

Health Realization

Health Realization is a preventive application of understanding how the three principles of Mind, Consciousness, and Thought (Banks, 1998) create people's experience of life. In 1987, Roger Mills applied Health Realization as a community prevention strategy in the low-income Modello and Homestead Gardens housing projects in Dade County, Florida (Mills, 1990).[*]

Of the seven lives chronicled in detail in the book, *Modello* (Pransky, J., 1998)—the story of how Health Realization turned around the two housing projects replete with substance abuse, drug gangs, and violence—one resident was a severe alcoholic who was severely abused by her boyfriend on crack and was abusing her kids. She ended up stopping her alcohol dependency without going through treatment, completely turned her life around and ended her own physical abuse and the abuse of her kids. Another was a crack addict and violent woman who, through Health Realization, came to see enough worth in her life to make the decision to go into treatment and completely turn her life around. Another was an extremely withdrawn mother of the project's main drug dealers and of a daughter so severely addicted to crack that she was prostituting herself to support her habit—her weight had dropped to 80 lbs.—and through her new insights she helped her daughter break her addiction, and she became president of the project resident's council. Another was suicidal with no self-confidence, welfare-dependent, continually being put down by her partner, who through her insights ended up living in well-being and getting her G.E.D. then a good job in which she flourished. Another was a teenage drug dealer whose life turned around to such an extent that he began a crime watch to keep out all drug dealers, graduated from high school (he had been failing and truant) and went on to college. Two other women were beating their children and ended up stopping that abuse and developing wonderful parent-child relationships. These are merely examples of the changes that occurred in people's lives through understanding Health Realization. Further, once a critical mass of residents saw their lives from this new, higher perspective, they worked to successfully drive the drug dealers from their community, to improve their community, and develop productive relationships with the schools and police.

Study results showed that for the 150 families and 650 youth served by the program in the two housing projects, after three years-

- households selling or using drugs dropped from 65% to less than 20%
- the overall crime rate which had been endemic decreased by 70%-80%
- the teen pregnancy rate dropped from over 50% to 10%
- school dropout rates dropped from 60% to 10%
- child abuse and neglect which was endemic decreased by over 70+%
- households on public assistance went from 65% to negligible
- and the parent unemployment rate dropped from 85% to 35%.
  (Pransky, Mills, Sedgeman & Blevens, 1997)

---

[*] Note: It was not yet named Health Realization when the first edition of this book was published, and I had only just been exposed to it then.

The approach was then replicated in other areas, among them the Health Realization Community Empowerment Project at Coliseum Gardens, a 200 unit public housing development in Oakland, California. This project received the California Wellness Foundation Peace Prize and was cited by President Clinton and Attorney General Reno, after-

- a housing project once known as the "murder capitol" did not have one murder in the subsequent five years since the Health Realization program began. This housing project had had the highest frequency of drug-related arrests and homicides in the city of Oakland.
- violent crimes were reduced by 45%
- drug assaults with firearms were reduced by 38%
- gang warfare and ethnic clashes between Cambodian and African American youth ceased
- youth attendance and involvement in Boys and Club increased by 110%
- 62 families members became gainfully employed
  (Pransky, Mills, Sedgeman, & Blevens, 1997).

Further, it was reported that-

- the drug dealers controlling the community have been dispersed
- child abuse/neglect dropped by 60%
- drug and other criminal activities dropped by 65%
- school disciplinary actions dropped by 70%
- 59% of dropouts returned to school and graduated
  (Mills, 1996).

Borg (1997) conducted a rigorous, controlled study of Health Realization that included 124 ethnically and racially mixed residents and service providers (63 in training group; 61 controls) living and working in six low-income housing developments in Fresno, California. Training group participants received training in the Health Realization/Community Empowerment (HR/CE) model over 6 months. A Multi-Variant Analysis (MANOVA) revealed that the HR/CE program, pretest to post-test, showed-

- a significant effect at the $P.= <.0001$ level in decreasing participants' perceptions on all affective scales, such as anxiety, depression, behavioral/emotional control, general positive affect, loneliness, and belonging; no significant changes occurred in the control group on any of these measures.

Health Realization is an inside-out approach because it focuses on helping people understand the inner workings of their minds. With this understanding people come to see themselves and their lives with new, healthier perspective. Their own lives improve, their relationships then improve, and when a critical mass of people have similar experiences, they work together to change their entire community. Health Realization is a spiritual approach because the inner workings of the mind arise from spiritual principles.

Briefly, the Health Realization process begins with workers themselves modeling living in health and well-being. They first try to create a healthy, lighthearted environment that draws out other people's innate health. Health Realization asserts that every human being at his or her core is a healthy, wise, compassionate, loving, individual with natural self-esteem, creativity, common sense, and positive motivation. Health Realization workers create vehicles that community members will be attracted to—such as a leadership training course, a parenting course, a PTA, a tenants council, informal counseling—through which Health Realization understanding is conveyed, where community members are helped to see the principles in action in their daily lives. For example, people are helped to see that is only their learned, conditioned thinking that obscures their health, leading to instability, insecurity, health-damaging and self-defeating behavior, fear, anger, depression, expectations of failure, defensiveness, hostility, etc. They are helped to see that through their creative power of thought the way things look to them continually changes. For example, when people's moods change things look differently to them. When people realize this, they are never stuck with what they now see and experience. Whatever people think they are stuck with in life can be as fleeting as their next thought. Because people's health and wisdom is their natural state, it is buoyant like a cork under water, always trying to rise to the surface, and will when their minds become calm and quiet. Their thoughts are the only things keeping their health and wisdom obscured. But they have the capacity to not take such thoughts seriously or to let them go and thereby regain their natural state.

When enough community people together catch on to this understanding, they become naturally motivated to work make their community a healthier environment for everyone. They begin to invite others (the police, the city council, the chamber of commerce, HUD) to see how they could help make the community a better place to live. People also begin to recognize the power they have over their own destructive dependencies. In the Homestead Gardens Housing Project, when the kids saw their parents involved in improving themselves, they began to get involved. Mills and staff helped people understand how they could use their own higher levels of wisdom for their own good and the good of the community.

When I first listened to Cynthia Stennis and Elaine Burns from the Modello and Homestead Gardens projects—and later when I interviewed the residents whose lives had dramatically changed through this understanding for the book, *Modello*—I realized that I had never seen this level of change in people in all the years I had worked in prevention. This understanding had apparently touched them on a deep, spiritual level—something obviously had connected deep within their souls—and their lives would never be the same. They would never turn back.

Spiritual Principles

The beauty of "spirituality" as prevention is that we do not have to believe in any kind of "other-than-worldly" state to act in accordance with spiritual principles. We can be total nonbelievers. All we have to do is align ourselves with spiritual principles.

A wide variety of spiritual approaches suggests that there are certain common principles that may well move us closer to reaching a higher state of personal well-being.

It fascinates me now to read what I wrote in the first edition, because I researched what I then called "spiritual principles" that appeared to be common to many spiritual teachings and writings. I considered these helpful practices for everyday life. I suggested that, for prevention purposes, it was not important to examine the beliefs that form the basis for these principles—only to live by these principles. When I look at these common principles now, I now realize what

Sydney Banks has been saying since his spiritual epiphany in the mid-1970s [paraphrased]: **If we were to take all the spiritual beliefs and practices in the world and boil them down to their essence, we would come down to the three principles of Mind, Consciousness, and Thought**. This understanding is the basis for Health Realization.

> Mind, Consciousness, and Thought are the three principles that enable us to acknowledge and respond to existence. They are the basic building blocks, and it is through these three components that all psychological mysteries are unfolded… Mind, Consciousness, and Thought are spiritual gifts that enable us to see creation and guide us through life. All three are universal constants that can never change and never be separated… All psychological functions are born from these three principles. All human behavior and social structures on earth are formed via Mind, Consciousness, and Thought. In chemistry, two or more elements create compounds. It is the same with the psychological elements… (Banks, 1998, pp.21-22).

According to Banks, Mind and Spirit are One and the same. People have their own words to describe what Mind is pointing to: God, the energy of All things, the formless, spiritual energy behind life, the intelligence behind life, the Great Spirit, the Creator, Master Mind, etc. The purest part of Itself—pure love—comes to us through pure Consciousness—consciousness uncontaminated by any thoughts. This is, in essence, our Soul, and, as such, it contains pure wisdom. Thought is the creative power that enables us to experience this pure wisdom, or to keep it obscured from view. **The power of thought is a spiritual gift that, combined with consciousness, allows us to have an experience of whatever we think, and we have the free will to think anything we want. Consciousness brings our thoughts to life. Our experience is constantly changing with each new thought.** To Banks, it is that simple. It is also unfathomable. It is impossible to intellectually "figure out"—no one can ever get to the bottom of this understanding; it must be realized from within through insight. Our purpose in life, Banks and other spiritual teachers say, is to find our way "home" to the pure. This is true peace.

To experience this depth of understanding is to see that all the so-called "principles" that I had identified and described in the first edition of this book are merely detail, just as, in my view, the fascinating books, *Conversations with God* (Walsch, 1995) and *A Course in Miracles* (Wapnick & Wapnick, 1995), are merely detail of *the three principles*. An edited version of the so-called "principles" listed in the first edition follow-

- **living in love, loving our neighbors as ourselves**; asking ourselves whether our motives and actions are in or out of accord with the flow of love;
- **the more we dwell on something the more it becomes manifest**; every thought we think, we are either helping or hurting, aiding or hindering.
- **There are no well-defined edges of reality. What appears to us as solid, really isn't.** It is made up of molecules and atoms, each tiny universes filled with space, and smaller particles that make up everything on this earth. Some energy force within this space holds each of these tiny universes together. If our perceptions were impeccably acute, we would perhaps be able to perceive this space as energy force or light, and thereby perceive the world differently. This would open up a new world of possibilities. There are electrical charges in our thought patterns that become part of the spiritual energy surrounding us.
- Look within ourselves by **quieting the mind. Our intuition is infinite intelligence talking to us** between our thoughts. To hear it, we must tune out the noise of the

mind and allow the perfection of the universe to be expressed through us. Each of us has a built-in mechanism designed to guide us toward more perfect responses to all events and experiences. It's what enables a composer to find the perfect pattern of notes, or a professional basketball player to shoot the ball through the hoop perfectly as if he's "unconscious." Conscious mind can interfere with the ability to do a job perfectly.

- Everything has a purpose. Each of us may have a special job to perform that can be done by no other soul. We must be expressing our unique talent to be at peace with ourselves. When we're doing what we love, we know—we can feel it.
- Energy flows out of us like a signal or wavelength from a TV or radio station, We may attract into our lives those people and circumstances in alignment with the energy signals we emit.
- Laugh at ourselves and at life. Life is temporary anyway. **Everything we do—every single act—can be either fun or a drudgery, upset us or not. We decide**.
- Everything that occurs is just another event to be learned from—without judgment or fear. Filling ourselves with love casts out fear.
- **Fear is at the root of most of humankind's ills. If everything is part of us—it's all us—there is really nothing to fear. If we believe our essence and the essence of everything in the universe cannot die, there is total safety.**
- The energy of the universe flows through everything and everybody and "wants" to flow freely. **We interfere by blocking the free flow of energy through our thoughts.**
- Give full attention and appreciation to every moment, no matter what we are doing. What we believe at any time creates a reality for us. Only the present moment really exists.
- Set and accept a standard (an ideal) by which we intend to measure our decisions and actions, then dwell upon the ideal and allow the power of love to flow through us. Have patience.
- **Patience is knowing that things are the way they are for a reason**. Patience is an active force of motivation and purpose—why things are being done at this place and time. Like a flower from a seed, things happen in their time.
- Recognize that the abundance we think we desire we already have, and give thanks for everything we do have.
- Forgive ourselves and everyone around us, no matter what they have done.
- Relinquish attachments. If we are "attached" to anything, it reduces the pleasure we experience from it. The only way to truly enjoy anything may be to let go of it.

This compilation was extracted from combining some principles of Edgar Cayce by Puryear (1982), Seth by Roberts (1972), Emmanuel by Rodegast and Stanton (1985), Millman (1980), MacLaine (1989), Castaneda (1972; 1987), Hay (1984), Gawain (1986), Stevens and Stevens (1988); Levine (1978), Patent (1984), and Keyes (1986). There are no doubt many other so-called principles of this nature, and certainly many, many other great thinkers. These principles of action, if not some of the supporting beliefs, are not dissimilar to many teachings of Jesus, Buddha, Mohammed, Moses, Lao Tsu, and other spiritual giants. Interestingly, most all of the above are similar to conclusions people reach through an understanding *the three principles* of Mind, Consciousness, and Thought.

Spirituality of Prevention

The *Spirituality of Prevention* conference was created by Prevention Unlimited in Vermont. It became arguably the first forum in the country where people gathered together to learn about how these two facets of life and work could be combined, "to learn and share ideas for nourishing the spirit" and explore this new dimension of their work. It met annually on a weekend on or near the Spring equinox from 1992 through 1995 and was rated remarkably well by participants (Namy Dickason, 1993). At its final conference, participants defined principles of applying spirituality in prevention practice. These were synthesized by Jack Pransky and Peter Perkins of Prevention Unlimited, as follows:

- For people to become whole the spiritual dimension of the self is at least as important as the personal and social dimensions; functioning well in each of these dimension is part of an individual's complete health and well-being.
- Spirituality is a connection to something that some people call God/a higher power, deeper or higher consciousness/pure formless energy/soul/spirit/the life force—however people define it for themselves, and however it speaks to them.
- Spirituality in prevention is touching the heart to move people to change and planting seeds of hope.
- Spirituality is connectedness—to one's roots, culture, tradition, church/religion; or to one's own being, one's creative expression; to other beings, humanity, community; to the universe, to nature; to challenge, to hope and possibilities—to discover a state of inner peace, joy, happiness, fulfillment, self-esteem.
- People are already perfect, pure and precious in their essence. Tapping into this essence creates positive change; coming from this core is prevention. Many people have lost touch with this essence [via their thinking]. Spirituality is helping them find their way home.
- Spirituality in prevention is the process of healing oneself and helping to heal others.
- Spirituality in prevention is seeing people seeing the world as capabilities instead of deficit, that everyone has something to offer, to help people feel good about who they are and find their own creative expression. Spirituality is creative expression.
- Spirituality in prevention is loving enough and caring enough to make a difference. Caring is not what you do, it's who you are.
- The more that people are centered and grounded and open to possibilities, the more they come from a nonjudgmental, unconditional place, the more that prevention practitioners model healthy functioning and walk their talk—the more that people will be helped to find their health, well-being, and peace of mind.
- Spirituality is the true embodiment of what prevention really means (the root of the word: prevenire—("to come before"); that is, encouraging and creating healthy conditions up front that preclude problems—creating the good, not just stopping the bad. Spirituality *is* prevention.

We can either become engaged in spiritual practices such as meditation, prayer, visualization, yoga, rebirthing, etc., or for prevention we can engage in Rights of Passage programs for young people which combine adventure-based programs with spirituality, or

we can become involved in religious practices, or we can gain a deep understanding of *the three principles* and realize the inside-out, spiritual nature of life. Through any of these it is possible to achieve a higher state of personal well-being. Out of such a state we tend to treat others and the earth with love and care instead of harm and hate.

Interest in spirituality is growing rapidly, and interest in spirituality and prevention is growing too. Since this book was first published, the Canadian and New Zealand-authored *People-Centered Health Promotion* (Raeburn & Rootman, 1998)—which I highly recommend—posited that the goals of health promotion should be properly concerned with "a better life for as many people as possible, a reasonable level of good health in society, and the enhancement of well-being, life satisfaction, happiness and 'spiritual strength'" (p.38). While the focus is improved quality of life and well-being, they take it further still by boldly stating **the fundamental goal of any true health promotion activity has "something to do with the state or nature of the human spirit, soul, essence**, Buddha Nature, godhead, ground of being, and so on" (p.43). Raeburn and Rootman tackle the issue head on, stating that "numerous health promotion workers, as well as many 'ordinary community people,' have strong interests in this [spiritual] area, but there is not yet the language, the professional permission, or the academic base to put this subject "out there" in the public domain (p.111).

In a review of *Community Building: Values for a Sustainable Future* (Jason, 1997) which speaks of the need to incorporate teachings from "the wisdom traditions" in prevention practice, Berkowitz (1999) states, "What is ultimately preventive and community-enriching is personal transformation, our own transformation, and the full implications of that argument cannot be underestimated" (p.253). This is because "only a transformation of our values will provide sufficient motivation and willingness to work on the forces that cause unequal distribution of the world's resources," and presumably the social problems that accompany them (p.251).

In her review of effective preventive programs Schorr (1997) states, "A growing number of observers and people at the front lines are calling attention to a spiritual dimension to the relationships that seem to foster change" (p.15). Thus, some in prevention are beginning to acknowledge the importance and use of the spiritual realm in effective prevention practice. What we ultimately make of this and where it will lead the field is anyone's guess, but it suggests that Health Realization, which points in this direction, could move the field forward a critical step.

Jack Pransky

43. Reflections on Spirituality as Prevention

Sas Carey is my friend. She also claims to be able to channel spiritual energy. I didn't know this about her until four years before this interview when I attended a workshop she presented at the Vermont Prevention Conference. She began by saying that a few years ago she'd been overcome by horrible migraine headaches. Unable to rid herself of them, she went to a psychic who told her something was trying to come forth, and she should not hold it back. She took the advice, allowed whatever it was to come through, and the migraines virtually subsided. In the conference workshop I witnessed her enter a trance-like state, and proceed from person to person around a circle, spending about five minutes with each, offering the most insightful comments any of us had heard. Despite being my friend, she could not possibly have known what she knew about me. I believed her.

At the time I originally tried to write the previous chapter on spirituality as prevention, I found myself struggling, feeling woefully inadequate to deal with an aspect of personal-level prevention that I believed to be one of the most important and neglected aspects of the field. Suddenly it struck me. Why not go to a source! I decided to interview Sas as she "channelled" this spiritual energy.

She began by reciting a prayer, asking to be a channel of higher love and higher wisdom, having all negativity depart, and summoning all the forces of the universe to come together for peace and healing. She closed her eyes and entered her trance state. Suddenly her personality and voice changed as if she were in another realm of consciousness. She spoke slowly and deliberately. I was thrown totally off guard by her answers to my questions. They were not what I expected, though I'd had no idea what to expect. I found myself feeling completely humbled in this presence, and unable to think cogently.

Whether anyone believes this or not—even if people write Sas Carey off as simply a good actor—the words are what remain, and they hold acute perceptions of others and of the world. No matter what it is she does, she makes an important contribution. Wherever this wisdom comes from, in my view it is worthy of attention.

JP: This is a pretty bold move on my part. I could be subjecting myself to a lot of ridicule by people who think this is all garbage, including at least one of my editors. So why should anyone believe you?

SC: It depends on what you mean when you say "you," for there is no "you." It is only the essence of truth which is inside and outside each of us. This is one means of tapping into truth and simplicity that is available. But if anyone is willing to take the time to meditate and to get closer to their own spirit and inner light, inner truth, or as those in traditional religions believe, in getting closer to God, the same truth is available to them personally.

JP: And what is this truth? What are we here for on earth? What should we be doing?

SC: **Peace is the goal, as nirvana, the state of enlightenment, inner peace, outer peace. And the goal of life on earth is to deal with the various issues that prevent us from being peaceful.** One way to look at it is, if you have particularly strong positive attractions toward someone else, there is something to be learned about love. If you have negative feelings toward someone, there is something to be learned—there is something to heal between the two of you. This, taken on a larger scale, could be looked at as the earth being a chemistry lab to neutralize positive and negative feelings. For in so neutralizing, a peacefulness is reached. As long as there is a strong positive or negative attraction to a person, an idea, a thought, **as long as there is some, as Buddhists say, "desire," either way, it is difficult, impossible, to reach true peace.** So that dealing in prevention with any of the issues helps people focus on the positives and negatives to try to reach inner peace. That is the goal.

JP: I'm not sure I quite followed you. Did you say that if there is a strong positive or negative attraction, either way, then there is no peace?

SC: Yes.

JP: Okay, then, what can we do to better achieve a state of peace, given that we have strong positive and negative feelings?

SC: Yes, that is the part of the earth laboratory, being on the physical plane, that is why we are here. Of course we are not without those feelings. It is actually important to feel them and to experience them and to examine them and to work out especially the negative feelings, so that they can be neutralized, by whatever it takes for the individual situation.

In the drug and alcohol field, people are alcoholics; they are strongly attracted to drinking. They think about it all the time and in their recovery they think about it all the time. That is why they're still alcoholics because there's still a charge between them and alcohol. Then there are people who social drink. They look forward to it. There's still a charge there. There are people who don't care at all. There's no attraction to drugs and alcohol. You understand this, for you, are one. That is where you have come to true peace with that issue. That is not an issue for you, because **it doesn't have a charge to it. It is just something, but it is not yours. It's neutral. This is peace, in relation to drugs and alcohol issues,** that you have reached.

JP: And I take it that some people can be charged about greed.

SC: Everything. Everything. Everything. **All the issues on earth. All the problem behaviors. All the crimes. All the issues that are on the physical plane are because of negative or positive charges toward those issues.**

JP: Why is it important for us to be aligned spiritually in this realm? Won't we know what we're supposed to get to anyway, once we die?

SC: You see, without an awareness of the spiritual aspect of life a person can never really be at peace, a person is always striving for material goals and can never get enough. There is a spiritual reason for each person to be on the earth plane. **There is some—or more than one— but usually one central path for each soul.** There is one reason why each person has made a decision to come to the physical plane, and **the closer that person can be in touch with what that is, the better success that person will have of peace, of joy, of a positive experience** on the earth plane.

JP: How can we know what that is?

SC: [long pause] If I say listen to your inner voice, that might not be clear enough, but that is the real answer. To allow yourself to be so–any word sounds really funny, but—clean or pure; that is, to have dealt with those issues as they come along, so that you're always sensitive and in tune with the things that are coming at you, then you know when things are coming at you or things are coming out of you, you know which are the ones that are in harmony with you, and if you follow the ones that are in harmony, the people who are in harmony, the situations that are in harmony, the jobs that are in harmony, the politics, every single thing that feels in harmony with you and that you're so—sort of—uncluttered that you can be sensitive to that harmony, then you know that you're moving along the spiritual path.

JP: Is there any process that people can put themselves through that will help them be in tune with that?

SC: It is a process of finding harmony, so it's different for each person. Some people might be best to meditate and pray, some might be best to go to church or synagogue, if they feel really in harmony with what's happening there. Some might get it from the earth, working in a garden or being around nature. **Each person needs to examine that place, either inside or outside themselves, that allows them to feel peaceful and at peace with the universe**. Maybe that's not specific enough, but that's what it is.

JP: And the more that you do that, the closer you will get to what?

SC: To peace. To understanding yourself, and your needs, and your soul's path, and you will just sort of move in focus with your goals here, and your gifts, and your reasons for being on this planet.

JP: So it sounds like you're saying that our purpose is to understand our purpose.

SC: Well, that's a part of it, but once you understand the purpose, then you have to move toward it. And also it's important to know that it's a process. It's not any one specific thing. You may be in harmony doing one thing for a specific time, and then you know you've done what you needed to do on that, and then you need to move on to the next piece, and if you're in tune with your soul's path, then you're ready to move through the next. You feel guided, you feel led. The way you're led and guided, even if you don't get it from inside, is to look for harmony in your life, where you feel harmonious.

JP: What stops us from recognizing this?

SC: Being caught up in the physical plane. Daily activities. And the issues that are not clear, but that keep piling up without dealing with them.

JP: What's the ultimate state to be reached? What's the ultimate point to all this?

SC: Peace.

JP: In and of itself?

SC: Yes.

JP: Not love?

SC: All the other issues can be fit into peace. Love and light are the motivating forces, the greatest forces, but there's still a charge with love, and peace is the next step. It is not a lack of love in peace, it is beyond what we see as love.

JP: So peace is the "end." Why?

SC: [very long pause] It just *is*. [pause] I can't get an answer. I just sort of see this light, just sort of this *peace*.

JP: Okay. But I guess I'm troubled by this in terms of what you said before—if I heard you right—that if we feel any charge, including a positive charge, we need to neutralize it, in a sense. That sounds like a pretty dull existence to me.

SC: Of course, so long as we are here in the physical plane, we can never reach true perfection, so we can never be at true peace with everything. So when we feel positively charged it is a signal that there are things to be learned. There are moments that each person making an attempt to move toward this has, who has not clouded their being with drugs and alcohol and other big situations, people who are trying to move toward it have periodic glimmers of peace. These need to be shared with others.

JP: Shared? In what sense?

SC: Described. Taught. **You need to teach each other how it was to reach this peace. How it worked for you**. Communication between people, so that there's a body of information on how it is to get to this point, and what it is like. It needs to be shared.

JP: So learning from each other is how we advance ourselves in that way?

SC: Yes. Of course, it comes from inside, and then you can share it with each other. Inside or outside.

JP: Does each person have a "spiritual guide"?

SC: Oh, yes!

JP: You say it so obviously [laughter], but there are a lot of people who either don't believe it or are at least very skeptical because they can't touch it.

SC: Well, it's just a concrete way of looking at something. It's just one set of beliefs. But it's not vital that everyone believe that. It's more that everyone believes in themselves, whether they have a spirit guide or not, that they themselves have a way of touching the true source of truth and peace—which everyone does—and if people want to say that they have a spirit guide that helps them do this, or they want to say that it's God and it's not within them, or if they want to say it comes from within—however they want to look at it—but **it's important to know that each person has the ability to connect with *truth***, as we call it.

JP: I'm still a little unclear—probably massively unclear—about what this truth is. You just said, peace and truth. I thought before you were saying that the truth was peace—

SC: It's sort of like the truth about peace. It's just all those words, when you get to the top of the pyramid, or whatever, they're all sort of close together: light, peace, love, joy, happiness, sadness, everything. It's just sort of—together. When it's down here it looks like they're all apart, all separate things, but they're very close.

JP: Okay, one way we don't seem to be at peace is in taking care of the earth. We hear from some that we're heading toward the earth's destruction. How seriously are we to take this?

SC: You see, it's the same issue only on a larger scale. And that is the greed and desire of people, the lack of concern for each other, the lack of concern for the earth. **It is time to become aware of the needs of the earth, just as we become aware of our needs and each others' needs. It is time to love your mother—earth**.

JP: And if we don't? If we keep going the way we're going?

SC: It will become more and more unpleasant a home.

JP: What's the most critical thing we need to do now to recapture how we're supposed to be treating it?

SC: Well, the ozone layer is the most important, because without air, without moisture, without cool weather, so many changes will happen on the earth that it will be unpleasant for people to live here—live there.

JP: How seriously are we to take things like eating properly, nutrition?

SC: If you clear yourself, neutralize the issues, then you'll be much more in tune with yourself and your needs. It is the same with food. The more pure, the more focused and centered your food is and your consciousness is about your food, the more you will be in tune with yourself and the world around you.

JP: What is "centered food"?

SC: It is food you're in harmony with, that makes your body feel good—in the long run.

JP: So everyone knows what it is?

SC: Yes.

JP: How should we be dealing with others? How should we be treating other people?

SC: Well, of course, they need to begin by clearing out a lot of things. They need to make a commitment to be the best that they can be, and that's a very difficult point to begin with, but once people will make that commitment to be the best that they can be, then we can help them find what that is for them.

JP: Who's we? What do you mean?

SC: People that care. People that are working with other people can help them find what it means to use their intuition, what it means to become more in tune with their body, what kind of senses they need to use to find what foods are best for them, what issues they need to look at to clear themselves so they can move forward.

JP: The most troubling thing for prevention work is the problems of the inner city, all the gang wars, all the drugs, all those killings. To try to tackle a problem like that just seems overwhelming. What needs to happen to make a difference there?

SC: **Find productive work, using high-level skills, for the leaders and the dealer, with high pay, which of course goes back to the economy spending so much money on defense, so that if there were more money to spend on helping people, jobs for productive purposes could be given to these people, where they would feel more empowered and bring along the rest of the gangs to do productive work.** It is a very long-range answer. It is not simple and it is not short, and it is not cheap.

JP: Are the people in the prevention field going in generally the right direction to prevent these problems, or are there things we could be doing that we're not doing?

SC: Be sure to remind these people to approach the positive, exciting parts of life, and to balance the negative issues with positive exciting situations. The other is taking care of themselves.

JP: All right, let's say our prevention work is driving us crazy. We put out all this energy toward others, and we can feel ourselves draining. We can feel we're not taking care of ourselves well enough, but how can we get ourselves back on track?

SC: So you are asking how these people can be peaceful in their work within themselves. They must not slough over issues that are relevant, that are their issues. They must examine each issue that comes forward as it comes. For example, if a prevention worker has at some time been suicidal, and all of a sudden is dealing with a suicidal person, it is vitally important that that person take the opportunity to examine his or her feelings, thoughts, emotions, body tension, related to that interchange with the person who is suicidal. This means that the worker needs to deal in whatever way with the feelings they are encountering, those buttons that are being pressed, those reminders that are coming. **The problem with people getting very tense in their work is that they schedule too tightly, so that they do not deal with the issue as it comes up**

for themselves. They do not look at the emotions, allow themselves to feel the feelings, and to accept that part of themselves.

Another common problem related to these workers is that they have trouble admitting that they are also on the physical plane to learn the same issues that their clients are here for. They expect somehow to be in a different space. And this prevents them from taking care of themselves in the way they need to be taken care of. So they need to look at the issues, look at themselves in whatever way is best for them, possibly by talking to someone else, possibly by allowing themselves enough time to meditate or pray, or be in touch with their own spirituality, or go to church or synagogue or whatever religious orientation they have, but they need to have some way to balance the onslaught of issues that are coming to them, one at a time, or they'll pile up—

JP: One issue at a time?

SC: Whenever any big thing comes that's been an issue of theirs, they need to deal with it right then, and then it will be easier, and it won't take as much time. You see, the problem is, they just let it go, so that pretty soon they have every single issue that they haven't dealt with, and they have to go to two years of therapy to deal with it, but if they would take one issue at a time, cancel their next appointment, or take a walk or do exercise or just take a break or whatever way they can get in touch with that, and let themselves be with it, then they'll be free to move on to the next situation.

JP: Why hasn't prevention work been taken seriously by those who have the money and authority to really do something about it and make a difference? They claim to be concerned about the problems, they don't like alcohol and drug abuse and child abuse, but they don't do what needs to be done to really make the changes. What's going on?

SC: Two things. Prevention as a concept is not generally understood. And second of all, it is not concrete enough for people to see that it makes a difference. The way it is presented, the way people understand it, is not concrete enough; they do not see that these certain changes happen, with this comes this. It's not A-B-C, it's not scientific enough.

JP: Will my book help?

SC: Yes—a little.

12/89

VI. Conclusions

44. Bringing It All Back Home

The future does not simply happen; we create it.
We can choose our future.

-**Traver Hancock** (Canadian futurist)

Despite the fact that the 1990's generally saw a reduction in a number of problem behaviors, the way the United States has been conducting its business with regard to social problems is not working nearly well enough. Trying to patch people up after the fact is draining our resources and causing us to fall behind other nations. We need a change. We must reduce the incidence of our social behavior problems.

If prevention is the process of creating healthy conditions that come before a problem emerges, research lets us know what should "come before."

We're not doing it—at least not to enough of an extent.

Many people in this country have lost all hope of making it out of their difficult plight. We can say, "That's their own doing." We can say, "They make their own choices." We can say, "It's not our concern." But in fact it does affect us. We pay for welfare. We pay for Special Education. We pay for prisons. We pay for much treatment. We pay for crime. Sometimes we're their victims. We're the ones who might be killed or maimed by a drunk driver. Our children might be the ones coerced by the pushers or by their own peers into taking drugs. Our children might be the ones subjected to someone's abuse.

Even if we don't empathize with the plights of others; even if we can't picture what it would be like to grow up in an inner-city low-income housing project surrounded by crime and drugs and despair or on a reservation, or in rural poverty and isolation; even if we can't imagine what it would be like not to be able to get the food we need, or the shelter, or to have no hope; even if we can't conceive of what it would be like to grow up abused, beaten constantly, put down and criticized continually, sexually abused, sometimes by our own parents; even if we can't picture what it's like for an addiction to grab us and not let go and to have everyone close to us become affected as a result; even if we cannot grasp the horrors of someone else's life; even if we don't care; it is in our best interests to prevent those occurrences, because we're getting hurt.

We wonder why our social problems keep getting worse, or remain the same, or at best show only small reductions, yet we continue to deal with them after they've occurred. We keep pouring in tax money to try to patch up the problems. We're continually dealing with the casualties of our policies. Is this the wise thing to do?

We learned in Chapter 4 that when people are treated in ways that produce unhealthy self-perceptions—especially when difficulties persist over time—they behave accordingly. Drugs are a response. Abuse is a response. Crime is a response. Suicide is a response. Teen pregnancy is a response. Going crazy is a response. Not eating, or purging, is a response. Giving up and not caring is a response, even to the extent of spreading AIDS. Will it ever change? Not unless we work to systematically change the external conditions that affect how people—especially children as they grow and develop—are treated, and not unless we help people realize how to attain well-being. The problems will continue to overwhelm us.

These are the threats to the American dream for us all. We must ask ourselves if this is the kind of world we want our children to inherit. What about our children's children? Or do we believe we might be rich enough, or safe enough, that we and our offspring will somehow be insulated, so we won't be personally affected?

If this nation does not make an investment now, the problems will only get worse. Our resources will only be more drained. But it can be turned around! To quote Lisbeth Schorr (1989):

> The investment and risks are justified by the prospect that fewer children will come into adulthood unschooled and unskilled, committing violent crimes and bearing children as unmarried teenagers. Fewer of the children living in concentrated poverty today will tomorrow swell the welfare rolls and the prisons. Many more will grow into responsible and productive adults, themselves able to form stable families, contributing to, rather than depleting America's prosperity and sense of community. Utility and self-interest, as well as humanity, should move us to apply what we have learned about preventive interventions to change the futures of the children growing up in society's shadows, and thereby to break the cycle of disadvantage (p. 170).

In the meantime, a small band of prevention workers are trying their best, fighting against great odds to make a difference. They are doing terrific work, trying to contribute as best they can. They are making a difference in some people's lives, helping them find a way out of their difficulties, helping to bring communities together to solve problems and create conditions that cause fewer problems. These preventers—along with the preventionists who conduct the research to help us know what works and how to be more effective—should all be commended. But they cannot solve the problems of this society alone. Others need to get on board. We must all join together in a concerted effort for prevention.

Some people think this is "do-gooder" mentality. No! It's selfish! It's survival! It's logic. It saves money in the long run. We're all in this together! This is a purely nonpartisan issue. Some think this is "doomsayer" mentality. No! It's just the opposite—because we can stop it now! All we have to do is join together. All we have to do is learn how to and then treat everyone and our environment in healthy, constructive ways and ensure a decent life for all citizens. That's all! We can make the difference! Prevention is the hopeful way out. Imagine what we could do as a nation if prevention became a priority. Imagine what could happen if this nation began to place as much emphasis on bringing together the best minds in the country to prevent social problems and eradicate poverty as we did in sending people to the moon or in developing nuclear power? Do we really think, under those circumstances, that it couldn't be done? We must make a choice. It's time to stop talking and start doing!

Summarizing the Research

We now know that virtually all social-problem behaviors are related to the same contributing causes, and therefore the same basic solutions apply to them all. We now know what works—at least to enough of an extent. We cannot wait for further definitive proof. If we had waited for definitive proof that treatment works before beginning to treat, we would still be waiting. Prevention can and should continue to be studied while we proceed. We've proven that prevention can be successful on a small scale in select communities all over this nation. We must now ensure that this "pyramid" of effective prevention strategies [Chapter 6] is set in place in every community, not as replicated programs but by ensuring that the elements that made these programs successful are set in place through a solid community development process—and that the pyramid rests on solid ground.

When we compile even some of the research conducted on proven, effective programs and promising approaches, we see a very compelling picture of how to direct our resources toward preventing a wide variety of related problems.

Pre-Post Birth Care
Pre-natal Early Infancy Project (Olds, 1988) (7-year study):

Nurse/Home visitation program, providing health care, immunizations, nutrition; protection from chemicals, STDs, injuries; parental supports and skills; building a healthy emotional climate; reducing stress; providing opportunity.
- 75% reduction in pre-term delivery for very young teenagers
- 6% of fewer mothers abused and neglected their children, compared with 20%
- 50% less public assistance
- 40% fewer repeat pregnancies

Nutritional intervention (in Craydon, 1986):

providing full protein/vitamin supplementation
- 50% reduction in premature births

Attachment and bonding (in Minde, 1986):

promoting responsiveness to infant cues
- reduced dependency, restlessness
- increased empathy, caring

Family Support and Education Programs
Houston Parent-Child Center (Johnson & Breckenridge, 1988) 5-8-year follow-up:

providing pre/post birth care, parenting supports and skills, early ed., etc. through center-based program
- for children: fewer behavior problems (destructiveness, restlessness, attention-seeking, withdrawal, less dependence); 4x fewer referrals for special services
- for parents: increased self-esteem, work motivation, security

Addison County Parent Child Center, Middlebury, VT (Meyers, 1987):
- 5x more parents got off welfare than got on

Parents as Teachers (Missouri D.O.E., 1987):

promoting home-school partnerships from pregnancy through age 2, to improve children's development; providing screening, home visits, group meetings
- higher IQ, comprehension, verbal/language, cognitive, motor, social language ability
- improved parents self-perceptions

Quality Child Care (available, affordable, responsive, well-trained staff, low staff-child ratio; low staff turnover [reasonable pay], high interaction).

Employer-provided day care (in Kuntz, undated) study of 195 firms:
- 65% reduction in turnover
- 53% reduction in absenteeism
- 49% increase in productivity

Early Childhood Education

Preschool (Perry) (Schweinhart and Weikart, 1988) 16-year study:

providing cognitive, social, behavioral, language development; broadening of experience; child-centered curriculum
- 15% mental retardation, compared with 35%
- 31% delinquency and crime, compared with 51%
- 18% welfare assistance, compared with 32%
- 46% less teenage pregnancy
- 33% school dropouts, compared with 51%
- 16 % in Special Ed., compared with 28%
- 61% literacy, compared with 38%

Head Start (Zigler, 1987):
- 59% graduated (compared with 32%)
- 31% were arrested (vs. 51%)
- 18% went on welfare (vs. 32%)

Interpersonal Cognitive Problem-Solving (Spivack and Shure, 1988):

promoting consideration of alternatives and consequences, cognitive skills, planning, and changing behaviors accordingly
- 50% of impulsive children became adjusted, compared with 21%
- 75% of inhibited children became adjusted, compared with 35%
- 86% of adjusted children displayed no behavior problems on entering primary grades, compared with 58%

Early Compensatory Education/Abecedarian Project (Ramey, 1988):

screening all children for developmental, cognitive, motor and language delays, then providing services to those in need through a home- and center-based program; promoting home/school partnership, from pregnancy through age 2, to improve children's development; providing screening, home visits, group meetings
- 12-point IQ improvement
- 8.3% mild mental retardation, compared with 36%
- significantly improved cognitive development, memory; motor; perceptual, quantitative, verbal skills

Family Development Research Program, Syracuse University (Lally, 1988):

Enriched day care and family services, providing education, health, and counseling beginning in last trimester through age 5 and an enriched child care center at age 6
- 6% with delinquency records, compared with 22%
- fewer failures (girls only)
- increase in mothers' responsiveness

Parenting Education

Parenting courses (Alvy, 1987 review):
- some parents dramatically transform relationships with their children; others don't
- parenting practices related to self-esteem and love, acceptance, warmth, involvement, social adjustment, responsiveness, clear standards and rules, high expectations, independence (promoted in courses) are related to reduced delinquency, mental-emotional disabilities, alcohol/drug abuse, abuse/neglect

Developing Capable People (Glenn, 1988) (Pransky data, 409 parents):

Building self-perceptions of capability, importance and power
- 72% reduction in most troubling children's behaviors per week
- 92% believed children's behaviors improved

School Climate Improvement

Champlain Valley UHS, Hinesburg, VT[*]: revising school rules; providing Reality Therapy discipline system, individualized learning styles, accelerated learning
- 85% fewer discipline referrals
- $15,000/yr. to $1,500/yr. less school vandalism costs
- 0.5% dropout rate, compared with 7-8%*

Cleveland HS, Seattle, WA (in Howard, 1978)
providing school assessment/shared leadership, revision of rules, revised school discipline system, revised grading/ranking/tracking systems
- 5.6% absenteeism, compared with 35%
- reduction in drop-out rate
- 50% fewer discipline referrals

Widefield-Security School District, Colorado Springs, CO (in Howard, 1978):
providing school-wide assessment and shared leadership
- 30% fewer discipline referrals ("serious", 73% fewer)
- 55% fewer thefts (during school hours)
- 20% less absenteeism rate
- $19,272/yr. to $365/yr. reduction in school vandalism costs

Colville and Washington Schools, South San Francisco (in Howard, 1978):
providing a financial incentive program (partially paid to students in vandalism savings)
- 78% and 90% reduction in school vandalism

Williamstown junior-Senior HS, VT (in Pransky, 1981)
providing LEAST discipline system
- 53% fewer discipline referrals
- 38% fewer suspensions
- 64% reduction in vandalism costs

Comprehensive Health Education Curriculum (including physical, emotional, mental, social, and spiritual health; alcohol/drug abuse, personal/sexual abuse safety, family life, AIDS/STDs, self-esteem, decision-making and other skills):

Connell (1985) evaluation (grades 4-7, 1,071 classrooms):
- improved health skills and practices
- improved decision-making skills
- 3x fewer smokers at 7th grade
- improved self-esteem

Project STAR, Irvine, CA (in Crime Prevention Center, 1987) grades 7-8:
alcohol/drug curriculum combined with refusal/resistance skills, social skills, assertiveness, personality styles/differences, and stress management
- delayed onset of marijuana/alcohol/cigarette use
- 48-51% reduction in tobacco use
- 22% reduction in alcohol use
- 38% reduction in marijuana use
- improved classroom behavior
- improved school attendance

---

[*] in Pransky, 1981; this volume.

TRIBES (in Crime Prevention Center, 1987): providing social skills plus cooperative learning
  - less disruptive behavior

Ombudsman (Kim, 1981) 5th-6th grades: providing skills, supports, and community service
  - reduction in correlates of drug use

I'm Special (Kim, 1989) 4th grade: similar program to Ombudsman
  - 13% less alcohol users
  - less reported stealing
  - less absenteeism and suspension

Behavioral Social Skills Training (BSST) (Michelsen, 1986):
  communications, values, attitudes, responsibility, problem-solving, decision-making skills
  - improved self-control

Assertiveness Training (Rotheram-Borus, 1988):
  - improved achievement

EDAP (Early Drug Abuse Prevention), Montpelier, VT (this volume) grades 4-7:
  - 73% improved self-esteem

Law-Related Education (NICEL, 1988):
  - reduced delinquency and association with delinquent peers

Gang-related Education, Paramount, CA (this volume) grade 5 curriculum:
  - 98% staying out of gangs, compared with 50% "undecided

Peer-Focused Prevention

Life Skills (Botvin, 1988):
  providing a substance abuse curriculum, with decision- making, self-directed behavior change, coping with anxiety, social skills, peer leadership
  - 58% fewer new smokers
  - 54% less reported drinking
  - 79% less reported getting drunk (87% with booster sessions)
  - reduced marijuana use (peer-led groups only)

Say It Straight Program (Englander-Golden, 1986) high school (after 1/2 yr.):
  assertive communications skills, role-playing interpersonal situations, with students choosing content
  - 4.5x fewer juvenile offenses.

School Transitional Environment Program (Felner and Adan, 1988) jr. hs-hs:
  providing school structure change and peer supports
  - reduced absenteeism (first 2 yrs. hs)
  - student self-concepts remained stable (rather than dropped as usual)
  - 22% reduction in dropout rate
  - 0 failure placements
  - improvement in grades (first 2 yrs.)
  - reduced substance abuse
  - reduced delinquency

San Juan Unified School District, Carmichael, CA (in Crime Prevention Center, 1987):
  a comprehensive K- 12 substance abuse prevention program coupled with community education; providing many health and self-esteem curricula, supports, peer leaders, rap sessions, substance abuse prevention clubs, Developing Capable People, SAP, EAP, etc.
  - 50% reduction in substance-related suspensions
  - reduced discipline problems

Bully prevention program (Olweus, 1984; 1991) (after 2 ½ yrs.):
  creating warm, nonhostile schools with firm limits, better supervision at recess, class meetings, cooperative learning, peer involvement, teacher and parent involvement
  - 50% reduction in bullying (75% in new bullying cases)

- reduction in theft and vandalism
- reduction in truancy

Peer Tutoring programs (in Resnik and Gibbs, 1988):
- gains in tutors' basic skills

Peer Counseling programs (Nenortas, 1987):
- 14% fewer school absences
- 16% increase in self-concept

SMART peer mediation program (in Markwood, 1988):
- 67% reduced school suspensions for fighting (second yr.)

Teenage Institutes (this volume):
- vast increase in meaningful community involvement

Alternatives for Teens (in Carey, 1989):
teen discussion groups plus meaningful community service
- no increase in alcohol consumption from early to late high school

Supports/Stress Reduction

Stress Management Training program (Tableman, 1982; 1987):
   as an obligation of the 'Workfare' program, providing life planning skills and stress management strategies, experiential activities, "self-discovery" exercises, changing perceptions of oneself
- reduced depression and anxiety
- improved cognitive skills
- improved internal locus of control
- improved self-confidence/esteem

*Children of Parental Divorce support group (*Pedro-Carroll and Cowen, in Compas, 1989) grades 3-6:
   promoting sharing of feelings and experiences; providing emotional support and problem-solving skills
- reduced school behavior problems
- reduced shyness and anxiety
- improved school learning

Meaningful Work/Community Service

70001 Ltd. (PPV, 1981):
- job placement rate for dropouts: 75%

KICS (Kids In Community Service) Montpelier, VT (this volume):
- 60-71% increased self-esteem

Health Promotion in the Workplace

teachers in schools (Blair, 1987) *study*:
- decreased absenteeism (1.25 days/yr./employee; less need for subs)
- improved morale and job satisfaction
- improved teaching
- 18% of smokers quit

Alternatives

Orion Multi-Service Center, Seattle, WA (Refling, 1990):
   street outreach by youth; drop-in center with hot meals; counseling and advocacy, medical services; emergency and transitional housing; education and employment services
- 49.5% "successfully terminated" (off the streets; no longer involved in prostitution; in stable living situations)

Milwaukee Teen Initiative Program (Greater Milwaukee Crime Prevention Project, undated):
   11 hr./wk. after school/weekend program) providing community service, alternatives, role modeling, esteem building, job skill training/opportunities, tutoring, athletics, neighborhood liaison with schools, enrichment, drug/alcohol workshops

- 74% increase in grade point average
- 55% less school absenteeism
- reduced theft and vandalism

(The more frequent the program contact, the better the results.)

Community Education

Stanford Heart Disease Prevention Program (Maccoby, 1988):

abolishing cigarette machines in worksites and public places; restricting cigarette ads; providing healthy foods in schools/restaurants/machines; stress management and exercise

- reduced blood pressure/pulse rate in hypertensive people

Alternative Health

School-based health clinic, St. Paul, MN (in Schorr, 1988):

combining sex education with health services (including contraceptives)

- 50% + reduced teenage child bearing
- reduced to 2% the number of second pregnancies before graduation

OB Access Project, Oakland, CA (in Schorr, 1988):

a system of comprehensive nutritional, medical, social, psychological, and prenatal care to the poor

- 33% reduced low birthweight babies

Spiritual Development

Transcendental Meditation (in Denniston and McWilliams, 1975):

- improved memory and learning
- improved job performance and satisfaction
- decreased heart rate/blood pressure
- decreased reported drug/alcohol use
- decreased crime, even in environments of increasing crime

Health Realization:Modello/Homestead Gardens Intervention Program (Pransky, Mills, Sedgeman & Blevens, 1997):

inside-out prevention; understanding spiritual principles that change community members perceptions of their lives, improve relationships, and lead to community change

- 65% to less than 20% drop in households selling or using drugs
- 70%-80% decrease in endemic overall crime rate
- 50% to 10% drop in the teen pregnancy rate
- 60% to 10% drop in school dropout rate
- 70+% decrease in endemic child abuse and neglect
- 65% to "negligible" drop in households on public assistance
- 85% to 35% drop in parent unemployment rate

Social Change

Yale-New Haven Primary Prevention Project, CT (Comer, 1989):

institutional school change and preventing underlying problems by compensating for underdevelopment; providing a mental health team; staff training to promote student growth; a parents program who work with staff, integrating social and basic skills; appreciating the arts; curriculum relevant to work, at Columbia Park School

- 95% of children performing at or near grade level, compared with 50%
- 93% drop in suspensions.

This is but a sampling of many prevention programs that have demonstrated results. It mixes data from both "research-proven" programs and "promising approaches," but the point here is not stringent science but to provide an inkling of what it could mean for a community to have in place a full "pyramid" of effective prevention programs and efforts. If many communities did so, it is not hard to imagine how statewide and nationwide rates of problem behaviors could be changed.

Dollar Savings

As of this second edition in the year 2000, the current major thrust within many federal agencies appears to be to demonstrate saved money as a result of prevention programs, in addition to reduced problems. Money savings have been realized at some levels of the pyramid [cited elsewhere in this book]: For example-

-at the *pre-and postnatal care* level:
- $1 for WIC saves $3 in short-term medical costs.
- $1 for prenatal care saves $3.38 in care for low birthweight infants.
- $1 for prenatal care for Medicaid recipients saves $2 in first-year care.
- $1 for prenatal care saves $4-6 in newborn intensive care.
- $1 for family planning saves $2 in health-care costs.
- each publicly assisted teen birth prevented saves over $7,600 in medical and welfare costs the first year.

-at the *early childhood education* level
- $1 for one year of preschool saves $6; $1 for a two-year preschool program saves $3.56
- Welfare savings of about $16,415 per person plus projected tax revenues generated by increased earnings ($25,948 lifetime) give a benefit to taxpayers of about $21,155. This is equivalent to the cost of a two-year preschool program, which means that two years of preschool pays for itself. [Note: One child-year of Perry Preschool costs about the same as one student-year in special education and less than half the cost of imprisoning a criminal for a year.]

-at the *school climate improvement* level:
- $1 for school climate improvement (mostly for training of teachers, or contributing to student activities fund) can save $1.76 in school vandalism costs.

-at the *early intervention* level:
- $1 for intensive family home-based services (for those in danger of having their children removed) saves $5-$6 in subsequent state services/subsidies (Homebuilders, in Schorr, 1989).

Martin Bloom (1981) cites a few other related findings:
- $1 invested in seat belt installation saves more than $1,000.
- $1 invested in pollution abatement and prevention saves more than $5.

These are only some examples. Cost savings would likely also be realized at other levels. Even if fault could be found with the individual statistical calculations, again the conglomeration of these figures presents a very compelling picture for prevention. It is not difficult to see how inexpensive per person prevention programs are when compared with treatment, rehabilitation, and incarceration. Each is important, but we must restore balance to the other end of the scale-toward primary and secondary prevention.

Effective Prevention Programming

There is one important caution! We can't just plunk these programs down in various communities and expect them to work. We can't replicate programs and expect them to perform as well as the originals. Instead, we need to pay attention to the principles that make these programs effective, and apply principles of effective program development.

Bonnie Benard did more to inform prevention practitioners of research-based knowledge than anyone through her former column, "Bonnie's Research Corner," first in the *Prevention Forum Newsletter*, published by the Prevention Resource Center of Springfield, Illinois, then in the *Western Center News*, then in *Resiliency in Action*. Unfortunately, her audience had been limited primarily to the substance abuse field. I first learned of her excellent work in 1987 during the National Prevention Network's First National Symposium on Prevention in Chicago, where I discovered that much of our work had been paralleling the other's.

Because of her extensive examination of preventionist literature, Benard (1986; 1988) reached conclusions about themes and characteristics of effective prevention programs that, if adhered to, would advance the field. While her work provides the basis for what follows, I also combine insights by Schorr (1989), Musick and Halpern (1989), Lindgren (1988), Price (1988), Bond and Wagner (1988), and myself. Listings such as this, which appear in various places, are not useful unless practitioners can easily use them to guide their preventive efforts.

The pertinent question is, "What constitutes an effective prevention program?" Or, "If people want to design an effective prevention program, of what should they be cognizant?" Outside-In Prevention programming at least will be most effective on a wide scale and in the long run if it has the following qualities: It must-

1. *Affect multiple systems* (families, schools, peers, community, work), and use multiple strategies at many different levels (provide accurate information and supports, build healthy self-concepts and life skills, change environmental conditions, provide opportunity, reduce stress, influence the media, etc.). Since research clearly shows that the contributing "causes" of social problem behaviors are multiple, prevention efforts based on a single strategy will probably fail to achieve meaningful results on any extensive scale. There used to be a myth in this country that prevention meant "education;" that "education is the answer." This myth is slowly beginning to dissipate because it is not true. Education is only one important but small part of the total picture. If we want effective prevention we must look beyond. We need a broad spectrum of coherent and integrated services.

2. *Target all youth* (or all community people), not just those identified "at high risk." While so-called "high risk" young people are most likely to develop problem behaviors, it does not logically follow that those "at risk" should be singled out for intervention. First, we may be wrong. Some people we think are at high risk for developing problems will not develop them; others who do not appear to be at high risk will. Prediction is dangerous business. Second, the same practices that benefit high-risk youth also benefit others. Everyone should have equal opportunity to benefit from primary prevention. Where we have only limited resources we should first institute programs in areas where the greatest numbers of high-risk individuals and problems are concentrated, and offer our programs to everyone within those areas. As David Hawkins (1988) says, programs should target high-risk predictors, not high-risk people.

3. *Change environmental conditions that contribute to social problems*. One of those forcefully advocating this practice is Robert Felner of the University of Illinois (1989), who calls this the "Transactional-Ecological Model" of prevention, a mouthful that basically says stop blaming the victim and instead change the negative aspects of the

social environment to positively affect the individual. Ecology is the science of the relationship between organisms and their environments. It suggests that everyone and everything is connected. We must begin to see young people within the context of the environments in which they find themselves. The social environment is a human creation that can sometimes affect us in unhealthy and negative ways. Since we created it, we also have the power to change it. If we don't, social problems will continue to arise out of our relationships with these destructive environments. We can accomplish this both on a small scale (changing classroom and parent-child interactions) and on a large scale (through state and national policy development). It is important to remember that **the main purpose of changing conditions is to build or draw out healthy self-perceptions**. This is my conclusion from extensively reviewing effective prevention programming research. It is the most important ingredient for success. This must happen primarily within the family, school, and peer relationships, but it can be built within all other environments and programs.

4. *Collaborate with other social problem fields*. Because research shows that many social problems are related, many elements of prevention in many fields are essentially the same. None of these fields alone has the resources to fully prevent their respective problems. To have enough impact, the fields must get together. While a few researchers and students of prevention (Jessor and Jessor, 1977; Glenn, 1983,1987; Joffee (with Albee), 1984; Botvin, 1989; Benard, 1988; Lofquist, 1983; Pransky, 1985; and some others) have noted this connection for a number of years, little progress has still been made in bringing the single-issue, single-focused fields together. They may be talking to each other more now than they used to, but little collaborative program planning and implementation is taking place, and there has been extremely little pooling of resources to reduce all problems on a wide scale.

5. *Emerge from a community development process*. Programs should be developed locally. When we have knowledge of what works, that knowledge should be shared, but the people should decide what programs they want and what shape they should take. Leadership needs to be developed. A wide network should be brought together to make the necessary plans and carry them out. The community development process helps people gain the power to make needed changes. The people assess the need, consider alternatives, and make choices.

6. *Focus on desired results and behavior change*. Changing behaviors is ultimately how we can tell that our efforts are effective, and this is what we must strive for and measure. Just because program recipients increase knowledge or change attitudes or acquire skills, it does not necessarily mean that a real difference is being made in their lives. If we expect to convince policymakers of prevention's worth we must measure behavior change. Every prevention program can take before and after measures of behaviors people care about.

7. *Affect people at all developmental levels and across the life span*, pre-conception through elderly. **The earlier a solid foundation is built, the more that positive outcomes are assured and sustained**. Longitudinal studies such as the Perry Preschool attest to the lasting benefits of early programs in affecting problem behaviors. Instead of waiting for kids to become high risk, **we should be attempting as early as possible to build resilience and reduce stressful environments, so fewer children will emerge at risk**. There are also certain times of high stress in life—during transition times and

traumatic events—when people are particularly vulnerable. We can't always predict trauma, but we can anticipate many life transitions. **Prevention should also be focused during times of major transition**.

8. *Be of sufficient quality and quantity*. If one looks at Olds's Home Visiting Program and concludes that home visiting is the answer and therefore every parent should receive one home visit, it does not make an effective prevention program. The home visiting must be of sufficient quantity and quality—similar to the way Olds designed it—to show similar effects (Schorr, 1997). Prevention has a cumulative effect. Programs should build upon each other. One-shot deals rarely work. Our program designs should be guided by research. But "quality" means that **it is the personal interactions and relationships within prevention programs that primarily decide whether programs are effective or not**. Without constructive relationships between staff and recipients, the programs won't be worth much. We can enhance this by attracting quality staff and by providing quality training.

9. *Be integrated throughout daily life*. Messages across all systems and environments could be more consistent, so that they are continually reinforced. For example, if all people who live and work with children and adolescents were taught similar principles of effective parenting and teaching in all interactions [Chapters 12 and 13], far more reinforcement would take place. America's best resource for dealing with young people is teachers, and most school staff have not been trained to promote effective prevention.

10. *Adapt program content to the distinctive needs of participants*. In other words, to be most effective prevention programs must-
    - **be culturally sensitive, culturally relevant and culturally appropriate**
    - **be developmentally/age-appropriate**
    - **address different modes and styles of learning**

11. *Have appeal to young people*. If we intend to compete with the "high" of drugs, the thrill of crime or the appeal of sex, we need programs that are engaging, extremely exciting, fun, longer-lasting, and don't have negative side-effects. No easy task. We've got to try to put ourselves in their shoes and ask ourselves what would make young people want to be involved? What would motivate them to behave reasonably?

12. *Prove (and proclaim) the cost-effectiveness of prevention*. We have the evidence. We can show results on a program-by-program basis. That is important, but it is not enough to make a difference in the nation's social problems. How can policymakers recognize that investing in prevention is "not only cost-effective, but essential to the economic survival of our nation" (Schorr, 1989)? How can we help them understand that the more longstanding the neglect, deprivation, and failure, the more difficult and costly the remedies are. Besides showing results, we must show evidence that will be convincing to the body politic. We need to effectively compete with others for policymakers' attention. We need policymakers to allocate the necessary resources for large-scale implementation so we can see large-scale results. We haven't yet done it.

13. *Long-term commitment "to a new vision of social change."* According to Jessor, "Failure to recognize the necessity for macro-environmental changes, while at the same time emphasizing personal responsibility for health seems tantamount to 'blaming the victim'" (in Benard, 1988).

Hopes for the Future of Prevention

In one of the best articles on prevention I have ever read, Benard (1996) summed up her hopes for the future of prevention in the final issue of the *Western Center News*. She offers five critical points:

1. *Prevention is positive youth development.* In other words, when youth "get their developmental needs for safety, belonging, respect, accomplishment, power, and meaning met in some way, they are able to successfully negotiate stress and adversity in their lives without engaging in problem behaviors."(p.1)
2. *Prevention is a process, not a program.* We must move beyond seeing prevention as specific programs and content to seeing prevention at a deeper systemic level of creating healthy connections and building healthy relationships.
3. *Prevention must focus on building community*, where youth and the disenfranchised are given the power with guidance to create what needs to be done in an environment that fosters the major external resiliency factors.
4. *The key to effective prevention is the belief in every youth's innate resilience.* Citing the Health Realization model, which she calls "the most powerful prevention model I've witnessed" (p.3) [Chapter 42], this means recognizing that innate health, resilience, and wisdom resides in everyone and can be drawn out, despite any risk factors, and to see how our thoughts, attitudes, and beliefs affect our mental and physical health.
5. *Prevention is inside-out social change to create a compassionate society.* When the health and wisdom that resides within each of us is drawn forth so that it affects the community, nation, and world is when real, lasting change occurs.

See the forthcoming *Prevention (II) from the Inside-Out* in the year 2001 for more on the view and paradigm shift expressed in points 4 and 5 above.

To successfully prevent social problems takes persistent commitment and fortitude over the long haul. We must be committed to fight for as long as it takes, no matter what, and know in our hearts that what we're doing is "right," makes perfect sense, and can be realized. It will take perseverance. It will take many people at different levels of commitment to bring it about. It will take long-term commitment from prevention policy planners, human service planners, and concerned policymakers. This new vision must change the focus from management of problems to leadership toward growth and constructive change, and build on people's strengths. It will ultimately take a complete overhaul of policy. As Schorr (1997) says, we have to allow professionals to redefine their roles and escape the constraints of bureaucracy, because there seems to be an inherent contradiction between the needs of children and families and the traditional requirements of professionalism and the bureaucracy. What is needed is a systematic framework, a yardstick against which to measure the nation's progress.

The Nation's Progress: Prevention in the Public Eye

In the 1990s interest in prevention skyrocketed, compared to what it had been. Prior to October 9, 1990, it would have been difficult to imagine a *Time* magazine cover story devoted to this nation's lack of care for its children, titled, "Shameful Bequests to the Next Generation:

America's legacy to its young includes bad schools, poor health care, deadly additions, crushing debts—and utter indifference" (Gibbs, 1990). Here was a magazine of the establishment lashing out powerfully against United States policies toward children, particularly poor children. First it stated the gravity of the issue:

> Forget the next century, just consider for a moment a single days worth of destiny for America's children. Every eight seconds of the school day a child drops out. Every 26 seconds, a child runs away from home. Every 47 seconds a child is abused and neglected. Every 67 seconds a teenager has a baby. Every seven minutes a child is arrested for a drug offense. Every 36 minutes a child is killed or injured by a gun. Every day 135,000 children bring their guns to school (p. 42).

Then it showed the nation what it could do:

> Spending on children, any economist can prove, is a bargain. A nation can spend money either for better schools or for larger jails. It can feed babies or pay forever for the consequences of starving a child's brain when it is trying to grow ... (p.43).

It even showed a "pay now or pay later" chart similar to the one presented earlier in this chapter. But most of all, it pointed to the blinders worn by our politicians for solving this national crisis: "But somehow, neither wisdom, nor decency, nor even economics, has prevailed with those who make policy in the state houses, the Congress or the White House." It reminded the nation that, "[A] society cannot sacrifice its most vulnerable citizens without eroding its sense of community and making a lie out of its principles."

> With each passing day these arguments become more apparent, the needs more pressing. Where is the leader who will seize the opportunity to do both what is smart and worthy, and begin returning policy to focus on children and intercept trouble before it breeds (p. 45)?

All this was in *Time*! At the same time, the public indicated through a number of polls that it wanted American policy to take a different, constructive course as it moved into the 1990s and beyond. A poll cited in the *Time* article stated:

- 67% say they would be more likely to vote for a candidate who supported increased spending for children's programs, even if it meant a tax increase.

A 1986 Harris Poll showed that-

- 63% believe we spend too little effort on problems of children
- 88% said they want the government to provide more health coverage and daycare services for children of the poor
- 75% said they were willing to increase their taxes to provide more day care and education.

A 1988 Family Resource Coalition poll:

- 80% believed the quality of life for families had deteriorated.
- 80% said they were willing to pay more taxes to support programs to improve the quality of life for families.

We knew, too, that progress was being made when *Fortune* magazine ran an article in April, 1989, recommending a template for rebuilding an effective antipoverty effort, proclaiming that programs would be effective if they worked from the bottom up, were allocated adequate money (to be spent carefully on programs that work), and were partly built with private financing. The article identifies "a set of broad objectives that our finest minds and talents need to assault in as depoliticized and bipartisan an atmosphere as possible," and goes on to recommended many of the practices also recommend in this book. Its concluding paragraph speaks for itself.

> Even if you disagree with every principle and recommendation lad out here, put the poverty issue on your personal agenda and demand that it take its place high on the national agenda. Recognize that by doing nothing to address the blight, we are at high risk of condemning ourselves to a permanent bifurcated society, one whose tensions and difficulties could eventually narrow the scope of our national aspirations and perhaps even limit some of our freedoms, economic, social, and political—that we have long enjoyed (Huey, 1989, p. 136).

The last paragraph of the first edition of this book read, "If we add to this agenda, 'and the prevention issue,' it would seem that we should end on this note. We don't have to hide. We can be proud. Prevention is catching on. It's the only way to go. It is essential for our society. And the people will support it."

In the year 2001, we can go a little further. Perhaps these *Time* and *Fortune* articles and the polls helped to set a spark, perhaps it was merely coincidence, perhaps it was simply the time within the century, but this intent was picked up by the Clinton Administration, which became the first presidential administration to speak the language of prevention. Is it a coincidence that as the second edition of this book is being written a decade later, a front page July 14, 2000 *Washington Post* newspaper article reported that from 1990 to 1998 serious violent crime reduced from 785 to 616 or 21.5% among 12 to 17 year olds, teen pregnancy reduced from 37.5 to 30.4 per 1000 or 18.9%, child mortality reduced from 46.8 to 34.4 deaths per 100,000 or 26.4%, children below the poverty line decreased from 20% to 18%, the lowest rates in 20 years.

But, but, but—it is too easy to become complacent. This Nation could look at this latest data and decide it has done enough, and forget, and if we do so it will not take long for the problems to again reach all-time highs. Yet, to provide perspective with an example, the U.S. still lags behind 20 other countries in infant mortality. Besides, there is another way to look at this new data: What percentage of young people—how many young people—have we still not reached?

Our work has only just begun. To date we have been only so successful. We are learning more all the time, and if we want to continue to truly make a difference we can never stop learning about new ways of being effective in prevention. Until we are 100% successful, we still have so much more to learn.

One of the most promising new directions, in fact an entirely new paradigm, can be found in turning around and conducting prevention from the inside-out. Stay tuned for *Prevention (II) from the Inside-Out*.

Jack Pransky

Bibliography

The following are sources of multiple citings used for this book that again and again are cited below. I offer them here in a separate section so the full citings do not have to be repeated continuously. [Please refer to this multiple source list whenever a reference below ends with (example) "In Bond & Compass–"].

Sources containing multiple citings below

Bond, L. A. & Compas, B. E. (Eds.) (1989). *Primary prevention and promotion in the schools.* Newbury Park, CA: Sage.

Bond, L. A. & Wagner, B. M. (Eds.)(1988). *Families in transition: primary prevention programs do work.* Newbury Park, CA: Sage.

Burchard, J. & Burchard, S. (Eds.)(1987). *Prevention of delinquent behavior.* Newbury Park, CA: Sage.

Chamberlain, R.W. (Ed.) (1988). *Beyond individual risk assessment.* Washington, D.C.: National Center for Education in Maternal and Child Health.

Cunningham, M. et al. (Eds.)(1989). *Parenting as prevention* (draft). National Prevention Implementation Program. McLean, VA: OSAP.

Kessler, M. & Goldston, S.E. (Eds.)(1986). *A decade of progress in primary prevention.* Hanover, NH: University Press of New England.

Miller, G. (Ed.)(1989). *Giving children a chance: the case for more effective national policies.* Washington, D.C.: Center for National Policy Press.

National Mental Health Association (NMHA) Commission on the Prevention of Mental-Emotional Disabilities (Ed.) (1986). *The prevention of mental-emotional disabilities: Resource papers.* Alexandria, VA: National Technical Information Service (1986).

Price, R. H. et al. (Eds.) (1988). *14 ounces of prevention: A casebook for practitioners.* Washington, D.C.: American Psychological Association.

Prevention works in public policy series. Madison, WI: Wisconsin Prevention Network and Wisconsin Clearinghouse.

Other Sources

70001, Ltd. (1982). Corporate report: The youth employment company. Washington, D.C.

Adolescent Pregnancy Prevention Clearinghouse (1986). Model programs: Preventing adolescent pregnancy and building youth self-sufficiency. Washington, D.C. Children's Defense Fund.

A class divided (1969). film. *Eye of the storm.* Frontline ETV program.

Aitchison, R. (1976). Confident Parenting workshop leader's guide. Studio City, CA: Center for the Improvement of Child Caring.

Albee, G.W. (1996). Revolutions and counterrevolutions in prevention. *American psychologist.* 51(11): 1130-1133.

Albee, G.W. (1989). Primary prevention in public health: Problems and challenges of behavior change as prevention. In Mays, V.M. et al. (Eds.). *Primary prevention of AIDS: Psychological approaches.* Newbury Park, CA: Sage.

Albee, G.W. (1983). Psychopathology, prevention, and the just society. *Journal of primary prevention.* 4, 5-40.

Albee, G. W. et al. (Eds.) (1987). Prevention, powerlessness and politics: A book of readings on social change. Newbury Park, CA: Sage.

Albee, G. W. (1980). Social science and social change: The primary prevention of disturbance in youth. Burlington, VT: University of Vermont.

Alinsky, S. (1971). *Rules for radicals.* New York: Vintage.

Allensworth, D. D. and Kolbe, L. J. (1987). The comprehensive school health program: exploring an expanded concept. *Journal of school health.* 57 (10).

Alvy, K. T. (1988). Parenting programs for Black parents. In Bond & Wagner–

Alvy, K. T. (1987). Parent training: A social necessity. Studio City, CA: Center for the Improvement of Child Caring.

Alvy, K. T. (1989). Parent training as a substance abuse prevention strategy. In Cunningham–.

Alvy, K. T. et al. (1987). *Black parenting. Strategies for training.* New York: Irvington Publishers.

Alvy, K. T. et al. (1987). *Los ninos bien educados.* Studio City, CA: Center for the Improvement of Child Caring.

American Bar Association Center on Children and the Law (1991). *Children's Rights in America: U.N. Convention on the Rights of the Child compared with United States Law.* Washington, DC.

American Public Health Association (1990). *Healthy People 2000: National Health Promotion and Disease Prevention Objectives.* Washington, DC: Superintendent of Documents, U.S. Government Printing Office.

Asher, J. (1982). Learning another language through actions: A complete teacher's guidebook. Los Gatos, CA: Sky Oaks Productions.

Bailey, J. V. (1990). *The serenity principle: Finding inner peace in recovery.* New York: Harper & Row.

Baker, L. and Udis, J. (undated). "Naturalistic-Responsive" model of evaluation. Johnson, VT: Larraway School.

Baldacci, L. (1990). Putting parents in control. *Chicago Sun Times*. (July 22).

Bancroft, J. (1978). Caycedo's spohrology and Lozanov's suggestopedia: Mirror images of the system. *ERIC*. ED 183033.

Bandura, A. (1989). Human agency in social cognitive theory. *American psychologist*. 44: 1175-1184.

Bandura, A. (1982). Self-efficacy mechanism in human agency. *American psychologist*. 37: 122-147

Banks, S. (1998). *The missing link*. Vancouver, BC: Lone Pine Publishing

Banks, S. (1987). *Second chance*. New York: Ballantine.

Bangert-Drowns, R. L. (1983). The effects of school-based substance abuse education: A meta-analysis. *Journal of drug education*. 18 (3).

Barlow, W. (1973). *The Alexander Technique*. New York: Alfred A. Knopf.

Barrett, E. R. (1985). Assertive discipline and research. *ERIC*. ED 288875.

Bates, W. H. (1970). *Better eyesight without glasses*. New York: Pyramid Books.

Battistich, V. (1990). Evaluation of the Child Development Project: Summary findings to date. San Ramon, CA: Developmental Studies Center.

Battistich et al. (in press). The Child Development Project: A comprehensive program for the development of prosocial character. In Kurtines, W. M. and Gerwirtz, J. L. (Eds.). *Handbook of moral behavior and development*. 3. Hillsdale, NJ: Erlbaum.

Bavolek, S. and Comstock, C. (1983). *The Nurturing Program for parents and children*. Eau Clair, WI: Family Development Resources.

Belenky, M.F., Bond, L.A. & Weinstock, J.S. (1997). *A tradition that has no name: Nurturing the development of people, families, and communities*. New York: Basic Books.

Bell, D. (1990). Winners: Prevention planning for the Black community. *California Prevention Network journal*. 4 (Fall).

Bell, C. S. and Battjes, R. J. (1985). Overview of drug abuse prevention research. In Bell, C. S. and Battjes, R. J. (Eds.). *Prevention research: Deterring drug abuse among children and adolescents*. NIDA Research Monograph #63, Washington, D.C.: Supt. of Documents.

Belsky, J. (1980). Child maltreatment: An ecological integration. *American psychologist*. 34(4): 320-335.

Benard, B. (1996). Musings II: Rethinking how we do prevention. *Western center news*.

Benard, B. (1996). From research to practice: The foundations of the resiliency paradigm. *Resiliency in action*. 1(1): 7-11

Benard, B. (1995). Interview with Emmy Werner, 'Mother Resilience.' *Western center news*. (March) 6

Benard, B. (1994). The Health Realization approach to resiliency. *Western center news*. San Francisco, CA: Far West Laboratory for Educational Research and Development (December).

Benard, B. (1994). Guides for the journey from risk to resiliency. *Western center news*. 7(4).

Benard, B. (1994). The Health Realization approach to resiliency. *Western center news*. Portland, OR: Western Regional Center for Drug-Free Schools and Communities (December).

Benard, B. (1994). Neighborhood organizations as places of hope. *Western Center News*. 7(3).

Benard, B. (1994). Back to the future: Prisons or prevention. *Western Center News*. 7(2)(March).

Benard, B. (1993). Resiliency paradigm validates craft knowledge. *Western center news*. (September).

Benard, B. (1992). Mentoring programs for urban youth: Handle with care. Portland, OR: Western Regional Center for Drug-Free Schools and Communities.

Benard, B. (1991). Fostering resiliency in kids: Protective factors in the family, school, and community. *Western center news*. Portland, OR: Western Regional Center for Drug-Free Schools and Communities.

Benard, B. (1990). Families: Issues and trends for the 1990's and beyond. *Prevention forum*. 10 (3).

Benard, B. (1990). Youth service: From youth as problems to youth as resources. *Prevention forum*. 10(2).

Benard, B. (1989). Working together: Principles of effective collaboration. *Prevention forum*. 10 (1).

Benard, B. (1989). Moving towards a public policy response to alcohol-related problems. *Prevention forum*. 9 (4).

Benard, B. (1988). The coming crisis: Young people in jeopardy. *New designs for youth development*. (winter).

Benard, B. (1988). Youth at risk revisited: Public policy imperatives. *Prevention forum*. 9 (1).

Benard, B. (1988). Peer programs: The lodestone to prevention. *Prevention forum*. (January).

Benard, B. (1988). Visions into reality: Themes of successful prevention programs. *Prevention forum*. 8 (4).

Benard, B. (1987). Protective factor research. *Prevention forum*. 7 (8).

Benard, B. (1987). A fall review of exemplary prevention programs. *Prevention forum*. 6 (1).

Benard, B. (1986). Characteristics of effective prevention programs. *Prevention forum*. 6 (4).

Benard, B. (1986). The coming crisis: Youth at risk. *Prevention forum*. 7 (1).

Benard, B. (1986). The issue of self-esteem. *Prevention forum*. 6 (3).

Benard, B. et al. (1987). Knowing what to do-and what not to do-reinvigorates drug education. Curriculum update. Alexandria, VA: Association for Supervision and Curriculum Development.

Benard, B. & Lorio, R. (1991). Positive approach to social ills has promise. *Western center news*.

Benard, B. & Marshall, K. (1997). A framework for practice: Tapping innate resilience. *Research/Practice*. (Spring), 9:15. Minneapolis: University of Minnesota, Center for Applied Research and Educational Improvement.

Bennis, W. & Nanus, B. (1985). *Leaders: The strategies for taking charge*. New York: Harper & Row.

Benson, P.L. (1995). Uniting communities for youth: Mobilizing all sectors to create a positive future. Minneapolis, MN: Search Institute

Benson, P.L. (1992). *The troubled journey: A profile of American youth*. Minneapolis, MN: Respecteen.

Benson, P.L. et al. (1995). What kids need to succeed. Proven, practical ways to raise good kids. Minneapolis, MN: Search Institute.

Benson, H. (1975). *The relaxation response*. New York: William Morrow & Co.

Benson, H. and Wallace, R. K. (1972). Decreased drug abuse with Transcendental Meditation. *Congressional record*. 92-1. Washington, D.C.

Bergson, A. and Tuchak, V. (1974). *Zone therapy*. New York: Pinnacle Books.

Berkowitz, B. (1999). Transforming the values of preventionists. *Journal of primary prevention*. 19 (3): 251-255.

Berruta-Clement, J., Schweinhart, L. Barnett, W., Epstein, A., & Weikart, D. (1984). *Changed lives: The effects of the Perry Preschool Program on youth age 19*. Ypsilanti, MI: High/Scope Press.

Beville, S. L. and Cioffi, C. A. (1979). A guide for delinquency prevention programs based on work and community service alternatives: A working paper. Washington, D.C.: U.S. Dept. of Justice: OJJDP.

Beville, S. L. and Nickerson, C. (1981). Improving the quality of youth work: A strategy for delinquency prevention. Washington, D.C.: U.S. Dept. of justice/ OJJDP.

Biddle, W. W. and Biddle, L. J. (1965). *The community development process: The rediscovery of local initiative*. New York: Holt, Rinehart, Winston.

Biendseil, R. (1987). A Sensible approach to preventing delinquency. Prevention works in public policy series. Madison, WI: Wisconsin Prevention Network and Wisconsin Clearinghouse.

Bird, T. D. (1980). So who's interested in results? A skeptics view of evaluation. *New designs for youth development*. (July/August). Tucson, AZ: AYD.

Black, C. (1982). *It will never happen to me*. Newport Beach, CA: ACT.

Black, C. (1979). *My dad loves me/My dad has a disease*. Denver, CO: MAC.

Blair, S. N. et al. (1987). Worksite health promotion for school faculty, and staff. *Journal of school health*. 57(10).

Bloom, B. L. and Hodges, W. F. (1988). The Colorado Separation and Divorce Program: A preventive intervention program for newly separated parents. In Price—

Bloom, B. L. (1986). Preventive intervention in the case of marital disruption. In NMHA—

Bloom, B. S. (1956). Taxonomy of educational objectives: Cognitive domain. New York: David McKay Co.

Bloom, M. (1996) Primary prevention and resilience: Changing paradigms and changing lives. In R.L. Hampton, P., Jenkins, & T.P. Gullota, (Eds.) *Issues in Children's and family's lives*. Vol. 4. Thousand Oaks, CA: Sage

Bloom, M. (1987). Toward a technology of primary prevention: Educational strategies and tactics. *Journal of primary prevention*. 8 (1 & 2).

Bloom, M. (1981). *Primary prevention: The possible science*. Englewood Cliffs, NJ: Prentice-Hall.

Bloomfield et al. (1975). Discovering inner energy and overcoming stress. New York: Delacorte.

Bode, J. (1989). Eating disorders and addiction. Presentation at New England School of Addiction Studies. June 20-22.

Bogenschneider, K. (1996). Family related prevention programs: A ecological risk/protective theory for building prevention programs, policies, and community capacity to support youth. *Family relations*. 45. 127-138.

Bond, L. A. and Wagner, B. M. (1988). What makes primary programs work? In Bond & Wagner—.

Bopp, M. (1987). The Four Worlds Development Project. Towards the year 2000. Lethridge, Alberta, Canada: University of Lethridge.

Borg, M.B. (1997). The impact of training in the Health Realization/Community Empowerment model on affective states of psychological distress. Doctoral Dissertation. Bend, OR: Psychology of Mind Resource Center

Botvin, G.J., Baker, I., Dusenbury, L., Botvin, E.M., & Diaz, T. (1995). Long-term follow-up results of a randomized drug abuse prevention trial in a white middle-class population. *JAMA*, 273 (14): 1106-1112.

Botvin, G. J. et al. (1984). A cognitive-behavioral approach to substance abuse prevention. *Addictive Behaviors*. 9.

Botvin, G. J. and Dusenbury, L. (1989). Substance abuse prevention and the promotion of competence. In Bond & Compas—

Botvin, G. J. and Tortu, S. (1988). Preventing adolescent substance abuse through life skills training. In Price—

Boyer, E. (1983). *High School*. New York: Harper & Row.

Brazelton, T. B. et al. (1974). The origins of reciprocity: The early mother-infant. In Lewis, M. and Rosenblum, L. (Eds.). *The effect of the infant on its caregiver*. New York: Wiley.

Brazelton, T. B. (1988). Presentation at Family Resource Coalition conference. Chicago, IL.

Bronfenbrenner, U. (1977). Toward an experimental ecology of human development. *American psychologist*. 32: 513-531.

Brooks, D. and Paull, R. C. (1985). How to be successful in less than ten minutes a day. Pasadena, CA: Thomas Jefferson Research Center.

Brooks, T, Downey, K., & Murphey, D. (1998). What Works: Keeping youth in school in your community. Waterbury, VT: Vermont Agency of Human Services.

Brooks, T, & Murphey, D. (1998). What Works: Preventing teen pregnancy in your community. Waterbury, VT: Vermont Agency of Human Services.

Brounstein, P.J., Zweig, J.M., & Gardner, S.E. (1998). Science-based practices in substance abuse prevention: A guide. Washington, DC: Substance Abuse and Mental Health Service Administration & Center for Substance Abuse Prevention.

Bruner, C. (1991). Thinking Collaboratively: 10 Questions and Answers to Help Policy Makers Improve Children's Services. Washington, DC: Education and Human Services Consortium, Institute for Educational Leadeship.

Bubl, J. E. (1988). Evaluation of "Here's Looking at You 2000" curriculum in rural Marion County schools. Salem, OR: Marion County Prevention Program.

Bushell, D. (1973). *Classroom behavior*. Lawrence, KS: Allen Press

Burns, E.T. (1994). *From risk to resilience: A journey with heart for our children, our future*. Dallas, TX: Marco Polo Publishers

Burod, S. L., Aschbacher, P. R., and McCrosky, J. (1984). Employer-supported child care: Investing in human resources. Dover, MA: Auburn House.

Cabrini Green Housing Project. CBS-TV. *60 Minutes* (5/13M); *48 Hours* (8/31/89); *West 57th Street* (3/25/89).

Calhoun, J. (1990). Presentation. Primary Prevention of Psychotherapy conference. Burlington, VT: University of Vermont.

Campbell, J. (1989). *The power of myth*. New York: Harper & Row.

Canter, L. and Canter, M. (1976). *Assertive discipline: A take-charge approach for today's educator*. Los Angeles, CA: Canter & Associates.

Caplan, G. (1986). Crisis intervention and support systems, In Kessler & Goldston—

Carkhuff, R. R. (1978). The LEAST approach to classroom discipline. Washington, D.C.: National Education Association, Instruction and Professional Development. Carnegie Corporation (1986). A nation prepared for the 21st century. Task force on teaching as a profession. New York.

Carlson, B. E. and Davis, L. D. (1980). Prevention of domestic violence. In Price, R. H. et al. (Eds.). *Prevention in mental health: research, policy, and practice*. Beverly Hills, CA- Sage.

Carey, S. (1989). *Life skills for teens: The group leader's guide to Alternatives for Teens*. Middlebury, VT: Addison County Parent-Child Center.

Carey, S. et al. (undated). Teenagers need adults: What kind of adult are you? (pamphlet). Middlebury, VT: Addison County Parent-Child Center.

Casteneda, C. (1987). *The power of silence*. New York: Pocket Books.

Casteneda, C. (1972). *Journey to Ixtlan*. New York: Pocket Books.

Cauce, A. M. and Srebnik, D. S. (1989). Peer networks and social support: A focus for preventive efforts with youths. In Bond & Compas—

CBS-TV news special (1990). America's toughest assignment: Solving the education crisis (Charles Kuralt, host).

Cedar, R. B. (1985). A meta-analysis of Parent Effectiveness Training outcome research literature. Ed.D. dissertation. Center for Substance Abuse Prevention (1995). *Background Report for the Development of CSAP's Prevention 2001 Curriculum*. Washington, DC: CSAP, Division of Community Prevention and Training, Training and Evaluation Branch. Chapter III-12 and III-22.

Center for the Study of Social Policy (1986). Preventing teenage pregnancy: A literature review. Washington, D.C.

Centers for Disease Control (1988). Guidelines for effective school health education to prevent the spread of AIDS. Morbidity and mortality weekly report supplement. 37 (S-2). Atlanta, GA: Public Health Service.

Chamberlain, R.W. (Ed.) (1988). *Beyond individual risk assessment*. Washington, D.C.: National Center for Education in Maternal and Child Health.

Chamberlain, R. W. (1988). Community wide approaches to promoting the health and development of families with children: Examples from Scandanavia and Great Britain. In Chamberlain—

Chaffee, R., Simpson, S. et al. (1983). Alcohol and drug education curriculum plan. Montpelier, VT: Dept. of Education.

Chaffee, R., Simpson, et al. (1984). Act 51 Alcohol and drug abuse prevention education: Curriculum plan grade level objectives (K-12). Montpelier, VT: Dept. of Education.

Child Welfare League of America (1989). Children's legislative agenda. Washington, D.C.

Child Welfare League of America (1991). *Comprehensive Child Welfare Initiative: Strengthening Families/Preventing Child Abuse and Neglect*. Washington, DC.

Children's Defense Fund (1989). *A Vision for America's Future: An Agenda for the 1990s*. Washington, DC.

Clutterbuck, P. (1982). Work and well being: The changing realities of employment. Toronto, Ontario, Canada: Canadian Mental Health Association.

Cohler, B. J. (1986). Some reflections on the study of offspring of parents with major psychopathology. In NMHA—

Coie, J. D., Rabiner, D. L., & Lochman, J. E. (1989). Promoting peer relations in the school setting. In Bond & Compas—

Colbin, A. (1986). *Food and healing*. New York: Ballantine Books.

Coleman, D. (1986). Major personality study finds that traits are mostly inherited. *New York Times*. (12/6).

Comer, J. P. (1989). Poverty, family and the Black experience. In Miller—

Comer, J. P. (1985). The Yale-New Haven primary prevention project: A follow-up study. *Journal of the American Academy of Child Psychiatry*. 24 (2, March).

Comer, J. P. (1986). School experiences and preventive intervention. In NMHA—

Committee for Economic Development, Research and Policy Committee (1991). *The Unfinished Agenda: A New Vision for Child Development and Education*. Washington, DC.

Compas, B. E. et al. (1989). Stress and coping preventive interventions for children and adolescents. In Bond & Compas—

Compas, B. E. (1987). Stress and life events during childhood and adolescence. *Clinical psychology review*. 7. 275-302.

Connell, D. B. et al. (1985). Summary of the findings of the school health education evaluation: Health promotion effectiveness, implementation and costs. *Journal of school health*. 55 (8).

Cooper, K. H. (1968). *Aerobics*. New York: Bantam.

Cooper, S. (undated). CAP: The Child Assault Prevention Project: A community prevention project teaching children to prevent verbal, physical, and sexual assault. Columbus, OH: The Child Assault Prevention Project.

Conger, J. (1986). *Adolescence: A time for becoming*. In NMHA—

Cousins, N. (1979). *Anatomy of an illness*. New York: Bantam.

Cowen, E. L. (1986). Primary prevention in mental health: Ten years of retrospect and ten years of prospect. In Kessler & Goldston—

Cowen, E. L. (1985). Person-centered approaches to prevention in mental health. *American journal of community psychology*. 13. 87-98.

Cowen, E.L. (1977). Baby-steps toward primary prevention. *American journal of community psychology*. 5(1): 1-22 *clinical psychology*. 41.

Cowen E.L., Wyman P.A., Work W.C., et al. (1990). The Rochester Child Resilience project. *Developmental Psychopathology*. 2. 192-212.

Cowen, E. L. et al. (1973). Long-term follow up of early detected vulnerable children. *Journal of consulting and clinical psychology*. 41.

Craydon, J. W. (1986). Nutritional approaches to preventive mental health. In NMHA—

Crime Prevention Center, California Office of the Attorney General (1987). Schools and drugs: A guide to drug and alcohol prevention curricula and programs. Sacramento, CA.

Cullen, A., Held, J., Keller, B. (1987). Accelerated learning 1985-1986. New Orleans, LA: Center for Accelerated Learning.

Cunningham, M. et al. (Eds.)(1989). Parenting as prevention (draft). National Prevention Implementation Program. McLean, VA: OSAP.

Cuomo, M. (1989). presentation at Child Welfare League conference.

Currie, E. (1977). Crime and ideology. Working papers. 9(3).

Davis A. (1970). *Let's eat right to keep fit*. New York: New American Library.

Davis, A. (1965). *Let's get well*. New York: Harcourt Brace.

Davis, N.J. (1999). Resilience: Status of the research and research-based programs. Rockville, MD: Substance Abuse and Mental Health Services Administration, Center for Mental Health Services.

Davis, T. and Chaffee R. (1986). Politics and program effectiveness. Presentation at the Vermont Prevention Conference.

De Jong, W. (1987). A short-term evaluation of project DARE (Drug Abuse Resistance Education): Preliminary indications of effectiveness. *Journal of drug education*. 17(4).

Delza, S. (1961). *T'ai Chi Chuan: An ancient Chinese way of exercise to achieve health and tranquility*. New York: Cornerstone.

Denniston, D. and McWilliams, P. (1975). *The TM book*. Los Angeles, CA: Price/Stern/Sloan Publishers.

DePanfilis, D. (1986). Literature review of sexual abuse. Washington, DC: Clearinghouse on Child Abuse and Neglect Information.

de Rosenroll, D. A. (1988). Peer counseling: Implementation and program maintenance issues. *ERIC*. ED 298361.

Developmental Studies Center (1989). Creating a caring school community. San Ramon, CA.

Dinkmeyer, D. and McKay, G. (1976). *Systematic Training for Effective Parenting: Leaders manual*. Circle Pine, MN: American Guidance Service.

Dinkmeyer, D. and McKay, G. (undated). Systematic Training for Effective Parenting: Research studies. Circle Pine, MN: American Guidance Service.

Dintenfass, J. (1970). *Chiropractic. A modern way to health*. New York: Pyramid House.

Dohrenwend, B. P. (1986). Social stress and psychopathology. In Kessler & Goldston—

Dollars and $ense (1987). Columbia, SC: Office of Vital Records and Public Health Statistics.

Doria-Ortiz, C. and Gasco, L. (1990). Testimony to the Congress of the United States Subcommittee on Legislation and Delinquency Prevention. Washington, D.C.: Westinghouse National Issues Center.

Dorris, M. (1988). *The Broken Cord*. New York: Harper & Row.

Dreikurs, R. (1969). *Children: The challenge*. New York: Hawthorn Books.

Dreikurs, R. (1968). *Psychology in the classroom*. New York: Harper & Row.

Dryfoos, J. (1990) *Adolescents at Risk: Prevalence and Prevention*. New York, NY: Oxford University Press.

Durrell, J. and Bukoski, W. (1984). Preventing substance abuse: The state of the art. *Public health reports*. 1.

Dunkelberger, G. E. and Heikkinen, H. W. (1M). Mastery Learning: Implications and practices. *Science education*. 67 (5).

Dunn, R. and Dunn, K. (1978). Teaching students through their individualized learning styles: A practical approach. Reston, VA: Reston Publishing.

Durham, G. (1983). School-prevention skills: How to prevent problem behavior. Presentation at Vermont Prevention Conference.

E arthworks Group (1990). 50 simple things kids can do to save the earth. Kansas City MO: Andrews and McMeel.

Ellas, M. J. and Clabby, J. F. (1988). Teaching social decision making. *Educational leadership*. (March). Alexandria, VA.

Elliot, D. S., Huizinga D., and Ageton, S. S. (1982). Explaining delinquency and drug use. Boulder, CO: Boulder Research Institute.

Elliott, D. S. et al. (1988). The identification and prediction of career offenders utilizing self-reported and official data. In Burchard—

Ellsworth, J. D. and Monahan, A. K. (1987). *A humanistic approach to developmental discipline*. New York: Irvington.

519

Englander-Golden, P. et al. (1986). Brief Say it Straight training and follow-up in adolescent substance abuse prevention. *Journal of primary prevention.* 6 (4).

Epp, J. (1986). *Achieving health for all: A framework for health promotion.* Ottawa, Canada: Minister of National Health and Welfare.

ETV special (1990). Learning in America: Schools that work. (Roger Mudd host).

Faber, A. and Maslish, E. (1983). *How To Talk So Kids Will Listen/How To Listen So Kids Will Talk.* New York: Negotiation Institute.

Family Resource Coalition poll (1988). Chicago, IL: Family Resource Coalition

Feldenkrais, M. (1975). *Awareness through movement: Health exercises for personal growth.* New York: Harper and Row.

Felner, R. D. and Adan, A. M. (1988). The School Transition Environment Project: An ecological intervention and evaluation. In Price—

Felner, R. D., Ginter, M. and Primavera, J. (1982). Primary prevention during school transitions: Social support and environmental structure. *American journal of community psychology.* 10 (5).

Felner, R. D. and Felner, T. Y. (1989). Primary prevention programs in the educational context: A transactional-ecological framework and analysis. In Bond & Compas—

Ford Foundation Project on Social Welfare and the American Future (1989). *The common good: Social welfare and the American future.* New York: Ford Foundation.

Fors, S. W. and Dostar, M. E. (1985). Implication of results: Factors for success. *Journal of school health.* 55 (8).

Four Worlds Development Project (1989). *The Sacred Tree.* Lethridge, Alberta, Canada: University of Lethridge.

Freedman, M. (1991). *The kindness of strangers: Reflections on the mentoring movement.* Philadelphia, PA: Public/Private Ventures

Galinsky, E. and Friedman, D. E. (1986). *Investing in quality child care.* Basking Ridge, NJ: AT&T.

Galton, L. (1976). *The truth about fiber in your diet.* New York: Crown.

Gantrell, D. (1987). Assertive discipline: Unhealthy for children and other living things. *Young children.* (January).

Garbarino, J. (1995). *Raising children in a socially toxic environment.* San Francisco: Jossey- Bass.

Garbarino, J. (1989). Early intervention in cognitive development as a strategy for reducing poverty. In Miller—

Garbarino, J. (1980). Preventing child maltreatment. In Price [see Carlson and Davis, above.]

Garbarino, J. & Kostelny, I. (1992). Child maltreatment as a community problem. *Child abuse and neglect.* 16: 455-464.

Garmezy, N. (1991). Resiliency and vulnerability to adverse developmental outcomes and associated with poverty. *American behavioral psychologist.* 34(4): 416-430

Garmezy, N. (1985). Stress-resistant children: The search for protective factors. In J.E. Stevenson (Ed.), Recent research in developmental psychopathology. *Journal of child psychology and psychiatry book supplement No. 4* (pp. 213-233). Oxford: Pergamon.

Garmezy, N. (1971). Vulnerability research and the issue of primary prevention. *American Journal of Orthopsychiatry.* 41, 101-116.

Garmezy, N. & Neuchterlein (1972). Invulnerable children: The fact and fiction of competence and disadvantage. American Journal of Orthopsychiatry. 42, 328-329.

Garmezy, N. & Rutter, M. (Eds.) (1983). *Stress, coping, and development in children.* New York: McGraw Hill.

Gawain, S. and King, L. (1986). *Living in the light: A guide to personal and planetary transformation.* San Rafael, CA: New World Library.

Gibbs, N. (1990). Shameful bequests to the next generation. *Time.* (October 8).

Gilmore, M. R. et al. (1989). The dimensions of bonding: A confirmatory factor analysis. Seattle: University of Washington: Social Development Research Group.

Ginott, H. G. (1965). *Between parent and child.* New York: Macmillan.

Glasser, W. (1986). *Control theory in the classroom.* New York: Harper and Row.

Glasser, W. (1985). *Control theory.* New York: Harper & Row.

Glasser, W. (1969). *Schools without failure.* New York: Harper and Row.

Glasser, W. and Powers, W. T. (1981). *Stations of the mind: New directions for Reality Therapy.* New York: Harper & Row.

Glenn, H. S. (1988). *Developing Capable People* tapes. Fair Oaks, CA: Sunrise.

Glenn, H. S. (1983). *Developing Capable Young People* tapes. Hurst TX: Humansphere.

Glenn, H. S. (1981). Dealing with the hostile child/adolescent (tape). Hurst, TX: Humansphere.

Glenn, H. S. and Nelsen, J. (1988). *Raising self-reliant children in a self-indulgent world.* Rocklin, CA: Prima Publishing.

Glenn, H. S. and Warner, J. W. (1983). *Developing capable young people.* Hurst, TX: Humansphere.

Gold, S. (1983). Vermont's (Act 51) mandatory alcohol and drug abuse prevention education program: The state Act 51 assistance program. Waterbury, VT: OADAP.

Goodlad, J. 1. (1983). *A place called school.* Boston: Houghton-Mifflin.

Gordon, T. (1975). *Parent Effectiveness Training.* New York: New American Library.

Gottlieb, B. H. (1987). Using social support to promote health. *Journal of primary prevention.* 8 (1 & 2).

Governor's Task Force for Prevention of Teenage Pregnancy (1987). A better future for Vermont teens. Waterbury, VT: Agency of Human Services.

Graves, V. (unknown). The family tree. Bemidji, MN: Bemidji Area Vocational College (attn: Sonia Knapp); or Victoria Graves, Box 335 Highway 1, Redby, MN.

Gray, E. (Undated). What we have learned about preventing child abuse? An overview of the "Community and minority group action to prevent child abuse and neglect" program. *Prevention focus*. Chicago, IL: National Committee for the Prevention of Child Abuse.

Green, F. (1986). Prevention of brain dysfunction after birth. In NMHA—

Green Mountain Teenage Institute (GMTI). Burlington, VT: Green Mountain Prevention Projects.

Greenspan, S. et al. (1986). Diagnosis and preventive intervention of developmental and emotional disorders in infancy and early childhood: New perspectives. In NMHA—

Greenspan, S. (1989). Equal opportunity for infants and young children: Preventive services for children in a multi-risk environment. In Miller—

Gross, G. (1987). Maintaining maternal and child health. In Prevention works in public policy series–

Grover, P.L. (Ed.), (1999). Preventing problems related to alcohol availability: Environmental approaches: Practitioners guide. Prevention enhancement protocol system. Rockville, MD: Substance Abuse and mental Health Services Administration, Center for Substance Abuse Prevention.

Gullotta, T. P. (1987). Prevention's technology. *Journal of primary prevention*. 8 (1 & 2).

Gurdjieff, G. (1975). *Views from the real world*. New York: E.P. Dutton & Co.

Gusky, T. R. and Gates, S. L. (1986). Synthesis of research on the effects of Mastery Learning in elementary and secondary classrooms. *Educational Leadership*. (May).

Guttentag, M. (1975). Subjectivity and its use in evaluation research. *Evaluation*. 1 (2).

Foreman, G. & Engel, J. (1995). *By George: The autobiography of George Foreman*. New York, NY: Villard Books

Fox, R. (1975). School climate improvement. Bloomington, IN: Phi Delta Kappa.

Halpern, R. and Weiss, H. B. (1989). Evidence about the effectiveness of family support and education programs. Paper prepared for the Public Policy and Family Support and Education Programs Colloquium. Annapolis, MD.

Hammann, K. (1972). What structural integration (Rolfing) is and why it works. *The osteopathic physician*. (March).

Harris, L. (1986). Children's needs and public responsibilities poll. New York: Westinghouse Broadcasting.

Hardy, J. B. (1986). Adolescent pregnancy and parenting. In NMHA—

Hastings, M. M. (1986). Policy, prevention, and youth-at-risk for problem behavior. In NMHA—

Haggerty, K.P,, Mills, E., & Catalano, R.F. (1991). Focus on Families: Parent training curriculum (unpublished). Seattle: Social Development Research Group.

Hattie, J., Marsh, H., Neill, J., & Richards, G. (1997). Adventure education and Outward Bound: Out-of-class experiences that make a lasting difference. *Review of Educational Research*, 67(1), 43-87.

Hawkins, J. D. (1989). Parents as consultants and educators on peer pressure. In Cunningham—

Hawkins, J. D. (1981). Student Team Learning: Preventing the flocking and feathering of delinquents. *Journal of primary prevention*. 2 (1).

Hawkins, J.D. & Catalano, R.F. (1992). *Communities that care: Action for drug abuse prevention*. San Francisco, CA: Jossey-Bass.

Hawkins, J. D. and Catalano, R. F. (1989). Risk-focused prevention: From research to practical strategies. *High risk youth update*. (April).

Hawkins, J. D. and Catalano, R. F. (1989). Parents as originators of and participants in healthy family activities. In Cumingham–

Hawkins, J. D. and Catalano, R. (1986). *Preparing for the Drug-Free Years*. Seattle, WA: Developmental Research and Programs.

Hawkins, J.D., Catalano, R.F. & Miller, J.Y. (1992). Risk and protective factors for alcohol and other drug problems in adolescence and early adulthood. *Psychological bulletin*. 112(1): 64-105.

Hawkins, J.D. & Weiss, J.G. (1985). The Social Development Model: An integrated approach to delinquency prevention. *Journal of Primary Prevention*. 2

Hawkins, J.D. et al. (1992). Risk and protective factors for alcohol and other drug problems in adolescence and early adulthood. *Psychological bulletin*. 112:1.

Hawkins J. D. et al. (1988). Changing teaching practices to improve bonding and behavior of low achievers. *American educational research journal*. 25 (1).

Hawkins, J. D. and Lam, T. (1987). Teacher practices, social development and delinquency. In Burchard—

Hawkins, J. D. and Lishner, D. M. (1983). Cooperating to prevent delinquency, A school-based approach. Seattle, WA: U. Washington. Social Development Research Group.

Hawkins, J. D. and Weis, J. G. (1985). The social development model: An integrated approach to deli nquency prevention. *Journal of primary prevention*. 2.

Hazelden (1989). Under One Roof A model prevention program in Chisago County, Minnesota is paying off. *Hazelden professional update*. 7 (3). Minneapolis, MN: Hazelden Health Promotion.

Helfer, R. (1984). A review of the literature on the prevention of child abuse and neglect. *Journal of preventive psychiatry*. 1.

Heller, J. and Henkin, W. A. (1986). Bodywork: Choosing an approach to suit your needs. *Yoga journal*. (January-February).

Henderson, N. and Milstein, M. (1997). *Resiliency in schools: Making it happen for students and educators*. Thousand Oaks, CA: Corwin Press.

Henderson, N., Benard, B, & Sharp-Light, N. (Eds.)(1999). *Resiliency in Action: Practical ideas for overcoming risks and building strengths*. Gorham, ME: Resiliency in Action, Inc.

Henderson, N., Benard, B., Sharp-Light, N., Richardson, G. (1996). The philosophy of Resiliency in Action. *Resiliency in Action*. (summer).

Hersh, R. H. (1981). What makes some schools and teachers more effective? Eugene, OR: University of Oregon.

Howard, E. (1987). Handbook for conducting school climate improvement projects. Bloomington, IN: Phi Delta Kappa Education Foundation.

Howard, E. R. (1980). Some ideas on improving school climate. Denver, CO: Colorado Dept. of Education.

Howard, E. R. (undated). How to conduct a school climate mini-audit. Denver, CO: Colorado Dept. of Education.

Howard, E. R. (1978). *School discipline desk book*. West Nyack, NY: Parker.

Huang, O. J. (1988). An empirical on the applicability of STEP to Korean parents. South Korea: Cuhung-ang University.

Huey, J. (1989). The society and the war on poverty. *Fortune*. (April 10).

Hughes, L. (1951; 1970). Raisin in the sun. In Hughes and Bontemps. *The Poetry of the Negro*. New York: Doubleday.

Hunter, R. M. (1987) Law-related educational practice and delinquency theory. *International journal of science education*. 2 (Autumn).

Hunter, R. M. and Johnson, G. (1987). Law-related education. Boulder, CO: Center for Action Research.

Institute of Medicine (1994). *Reducing risks for mental disorders*. Washington, DC: National Academy of Sciences

Jacobson, M. (1981). Chemical cuisine. Washington, D.C.: Center for Science in the Public Interest.

Jackson, C. (1988). A community-based approach to preventing heart disease: The Stanford experience. In Chamberlain—

Jason, L.A. (1997). *Community building: Values for a sustainable future*. Westport, CT: Praeger.

Jervis, F. (1977). Constructing change: How to plan, manage, and organize results (conference workbook). Durham, NH: Center for Constructive Change.

Jessor, R. (1991). Risk behavior in adolescence: A psychosocial framework for understanding and action. *Journal of adolescent health*. 12 (8): 597-605

Jessor, R. and Jessor, S. L. (1977). *Problem behavior and psychosocial development. A longitudinal study of youth*. New York: Academic Press.

Jimerson, T., Brooks, T, & Murphey, D. (1998). What Works: Preventing youth disruptive or violent behavior in your community. Waterbury, VT: Vermont Agency of Human Services.

Jimerson, T. & Murphey, D. (1998). What Works: Preventing youth substance abuse in your community. Waterbury, VT: Vermont Agency of Human Services.

Joan, P. (1988). *Preventing teenage suicide*. New York: Human Sciences Press.

Joffe, J. M. (1984). Approaches to prevention of adverse developmental consequences of genetic and prenatal factors. In Joffe et al. (Eds.). *Readings in primary prevention of psychopathology*. (76-81). Hanover, NH: University Press of New England.

Johnson, D. L. (1988). Primary prevention of behavior problems in young children: The Houston Parent-Child Development Center. In Price—

Johnson D. L. and Breckenridge J. N. (1982). The Houston Parent-Child Development Center and the primary prevention of behavior problems in young children. *American journal of community psychology*. 10 (3).

Johnson, D. W. and Johnson, R. T. (1986). *Learning Together and Alone*. Englewood Cliffs, NJ: PrenticeHall.

Johnson, G., Bird, T. and Little, J. W. (1980). *Delinquency prevention: Theories and strategies*. Washington, D.C.: Office of Juvenile Justice and Delinquency Prevention, U.S. Dept. of Justice.

Johnson, C.A., Pentz, M.A., Weber, M.D., Dwyer, J.H., Baer, N., MacKinnon, D.P., Hansen, W.B. & Flay, B.R. (1990). Relative effectiveness of comprehensive community programming for drug abuse prevention with high-risk and low-risk adolescents. *Journal of consulting and clinical psychology*. 58(4): 447-456.

Johnson, J. H. (1986). *Life events as stressors in childhood and adolescence*. Beverly Hills, CA: Sage.

Jonas, G. (1974). *Visceral learning: Toward a science of self-control*. New York: Pocket Books.

Kahn, S. (1970). *How people get power*. New York McGraw-Hill.

Kaplan, B. and Heneman, S. (1987). Teen Pregnancy Prevention. Prevention works in public policy series—

Kaplan, L. (1986). *Working with multi-problem families*. Lexington, MA: Lexington Books.

Kellam, S.G., Rebok, G.W., Ialongo, N., & Mayer, L.S. (1994). The course and malleability of aggressive behavior from early first grade into middle school: Results of a developmental epidemiology-based preventive trial. *Journal of Child Psychology and Psychiatry and Allied Disciplines*. 35, 259-281.

Kellam, S. G. et al. (1982). The prevention of teenage substance abuse: Longitudinal research and strategy. In Coates, T.J. et al. (Eds.). *Promoting adolescent health*. New York: Academic Press.

Kelley, J.G. (1968). Toward an ecological conception of preventive interventions. In J.W. Carter, Jr. (Ed.). *Research contributions from psychology to community mental health*. New York, NY: Behavioral publications, Inc.

Kelley, T.M. (1990). A neo-cognitive model of crime. *Journal of offender rehabilitation*. 16: 1-26

Kenyon, J. (1988). Acupressure techniques: A self-help guide. Rochester, VT: Healing Arts Press.

Kempe, R. S. and Kempe, C. H. (1978). *Child abuse. The developing child series*. Cambridge, MA: Harvard University Press.

Kessler, M. and Goldston, S.E. (Eds.)(1986). *A decade of progress in primary prevention*. Hanover, NH: University Press of New England.

Keyes Jr., K. (undated). *Prescriptions for happiness*. Coos Bay, OR: Love Line Books.

Kibel, B.M. (1998). ACTION script for High-IMpact planning. Chapel, Hill, NC: Pacific Institute for Research and Evaluation.

Kibel, B. (1996). Evaluation using Results Mapping. *New designs for youth development*. 12(1): 9-15.

Kibel, B. (1994). Evaluation of local prevention practices: An open systems model in action. *New designs for youth development*. 11(3): 15-22.

KICS: Kids In Community Service project. Montpelier, VT: Washington County Youth Service Bureau (1988; 1989). KICS (undated). Evaluation questionnaire results. Montpelier, VT: Washington County Youth Service Bureau.

Kilbourne, J. (1982). *Calling the shots*. film. Newton, MA.

Kim, S. (1981). An evaluation of Ombudsman primary prevention program on student drug abuse. *Journal of drug education*. 11 (1).

Kim, S. (1983). Short-term evaluation of a national prevention model on student drug abuse. *Journal of primary prevention*. 4 (2).

Kim, S. (1989). The impact of the I'm Special program on student substance abuse and other related student problem behavior. *Journal of drug education*. 19 (1).

Kim, S. (1990). A short-term outcome evaluation of I'm Special. *Journal of drug education*. 20 (2).

Kim, S. (1983). A short and long term evaluation of Here's Looking at You alcohol education program. *Journal of drug education*. 18 (3).

Kitzman, H., Olds, D., L., Henderson, C.R., Hanks, C., Cole, R., Titelbaum, R., McConnochie, K.M., Sidora, K., Luckey, D.W., Shaver, D., Engelhardt, K., James, D., & Barnard, K. (1997). Effect of prenatal and infancy home visitation by nurses on pregnancy outcomes, childhood injuries, and repeated childbearing: A randomized controlled trial. *JAMA*. 278(8), 644-652.

Klagsbrum, F. (1981). *Too young to die: Youth and suicide*. New York: Pocket.

Klein, D. & Goldston, S. (1977). *Primary prevention: An idea whose time has come*. Washington, DC. DHEW

Koerher, M. (1989-90). San Juan Unified School District. Office of Substance Abuse Prevention. Carmichael, CA.

Kotulak, R. (1996). *Inside the brain: Revolutionary discoveries of how the mind works*. Kansas City, MO: Andrews McNeel Publishing.

Kumpfer, K.L. (1997). What works in the prevention of drug abuse: Individual, school and family approaches. DHHS, Center for Substance Abuse Prevention. Secretary's Youth Substance Abuse Prevention Initiative: Resource Paper, 69-105. March.

Kumpfer, K.L., DeMarsh, J.P., & Child, W. (1989). *Strengthening families program: Children's skills training curriculum manual, parent training manual, children's skill training manual, and family skills training manual*. Prevention Services to Children of Substance-abusing Parents. Social Research Institute, Graduate School of Social Work,University of Utah.

Kumpfer, K.L., Molgaard, V., & Spoth, R. (1996). The Strengthening Families Program for prevention of delinquency and drug use in special populations. In R.D. Peters, & R.J. McMahon, R.J. (Eds.) *Childhood disorders, substance abuse, and delinquency: Prevention and early intervention approaches*. Newbury Park, CA: Sage Publications.

Kumpfer, K. and Turner, C. (1991). The social ecology model of adolescent substance abuse implications for prevention. *International journal of addictions*. 25(4): 435-463.

Kumpfer, K.L., Williams, M.K., & Baxley, G. (1997). Selective prevention for children of substance abusing parents. The Strengthening Families Program. Resource Manual. Silver Spring, MD: National Institute on Drug Abuse.

Kuntz, S. (1988). Child care and the workplace. Burlington, VT: Childcare Resource and Referral Center.

Kushi, M. (1977). *The book of macrobiotics*. New York: Japan Publications.

Lally, J. R. et al. (1988). More pride, less delinquency: Findings from the ten year follow-up study of the Syracuse University Family Development Research Program. *Zero-to-three*. 8 (4).

League, V. C. (1991). *The Prevention Planning Manual: A Guide for Developing Successful Alcohol and Other Drug Prevention Programs*. Tucker, GA: Vincente Publications.

LeCron, L. M. (1964). *Self-hypnotism*. New York: New American Library.

Leitenberg, H. (1987). Primary prevention of delinquency. In Burchard—

Levant, R. F. (1983). Client-centered skills training program for the family, A review of the literature. *The counseling psychologist*. 1 (3).

Levin, H. M. (1988). Accelerated schools for at-risk students. New Brunswick, NJ: Rutgers U. Center for Policy Research in Education.

Levine, S. (1979). *A gradual awakening*. Garden City, NY: Anchor.

Lewis, A. (1989). Restructuring America's schools. Arlington, VA: American Association of School Administrators.

Lewis, D. O. et al. (1987). Biopsychosocial characteristics of matched samples of delinquents and nondelinquents. *Journal of the American academy of child and adolescent psychiatry*. 26 (5).

Lewis, D. O. et al. (1979). Perinatal difficulties, head and face trauma, and child abuse in the medical histories of seriously delinquent children. *American journal of psychiatry*. 136 (419-423).

Lieberman, M. A. (1986). An overview of health related self-help groups. In NMHA—

Lieutenant Governor's Task Force on Youth Suicide Prevention in Vermont (1988). Youth suicide prevention in Vermont. Montpelier, VT: State House.

Lifton, R.J. (1993). *The protean self: Human resilience in an age of transformation*. New York: Basic Books.

Lindgren, J. G. (1988). Social policy and the prevention of delinquency. In Burchard—

Little, J. W. and Haley, F. (1982). Implementing effective LRE programs. Boulder, CO: Social Science Educational Consortium.

Little, J. W. and Skarrow, M. (1981). Delinquency prevention: Selective organizational change in the school. Washington, D.C.: U.S. Dept. of justice: Office of juvenile justice and Delinquency Prevention.

Little, R. (1976). QUEST. Columbus, OH: Quest International Center.

Little, T. (1987). Teen suicide prevention. Prevention works in public policy series—

Lober, R. and Dishion, T. J. (1987). Antisocial and delinquent youths: Methods for their early identification. In Burchard—

Lofquist, W. A. (1983). *Discovering the meaning of prevention*. Tucson, AZ: Associates for Youth Development.

Lofquist, W. (1991; 1989). *The technology of prevention workbook*. Tucson, AZ: AYD

Lohrmann, D. K. et al. (1987). School health education: A foundation for school health programs. *Journal of school health*. 57 (10).

Lovell, M. L. and Hawkins, J. D. (1988). An evaluation of a group intervention to increase the personal social networks of abusive mothers. *Children and youth services review*. 10.

Lowen, A. (1975). *Bioenergetics*. New York: Cloward, McCann & Geoghagen.

Lundenberg, F. (1969). *The rich and the super-rich*. New York: Bantam.

Maccoby, N. and Altman, D. G. (1988). Disease prevention in communities: The Stanford Heart Disease Prevention Program. In Price—

MacLaine, S. (1989). *Going within*. New York: Bantam.

MacLaine, S. (1983). *Out on a limb*. New York: Bantam.

Maltz, M. (1960). *Psycho-cybernetics*. New York: Simon & Shuster.

Mann, F. (1973). *Acupuncture*. New York: Vintage.

Manoff, R. K. (1988). Social marketing. In Chamberlain—

Martin, H. P. (1986). Children with special stressors: Abuse and neglect. In NMHA—

Markwood, A. (1988). Negotiated conflict resolution: A neglected element of prevention. *Prevention forum*. 8 (3).

Marshall, K. (1998). Reculturing systems with resilience/Health Realization. *Promising positive and healthy behaviors in children*; Fourteenth Annual Rosalynn Carter Symposium in Mental Health Policy. Atlanta, GA: The Carter Center. (48-58)

Matthews, C. (1988). *Hardball. How politics is played by one who knows the game*. New York: Harper & Row.

Maslow, A. (1968). *Toward a psychology of being*. New York: Reinhold.

Mason, L. J. (1981). *Guide to stress reduction*. Culver City, CA: Peace Press.

Matson, K. (Ed.) (1977). *The Psychology Today omnibook of personal development*. New York: William Morrow & Co.

Maynard, B. (1977). School violence and vandalism: An alternative approach. Seattle, WA: Seattle Public Schools.

McClellan, J. and Turpin, E. (1989). Prevention of psychiatric disorders in children. *Hospital and community psychiatry*. 6.

McCormack, S. (1987). Assertive discipline: What do we really know? *ERIC*. ED 286618.

McDonald, L., Billingham, S., Dibble, N., Rice, C. & Coe-Braddish, D. (1991). F.A.S.T.: An innovative substance abuse prevention program. *Social work in education*. 13(2).118-121.

McGuffin, P. and Katz, R. (1986). Genetics and psychopathology: Prospects for prevention. In Kessler & Goldston—

McKnight, J. (1997). *Building communities from the inside-out: A path toward finding and mobilizing a community's assets*. Acta Publications

McKnight, J. (1992). Mapping community capacity. *New designs for youth development*. 10(1): 9-15.

McLaughlin, Irby, and Langnian (1993). *Urban Sanctuaries. Neighborhood Organizations in the Lives and Futures of Inner-City Youth*. San Francisco: Jossey-Bass.

McLeroy, K.R., Bibeau, D., Steckler, A. & Glantz, K. (1989). An ecological perspective on health promotion programs. *Health education quarterly*. 15(4): 351-377

Meher Baba (1955). *God speaks: The theme of creation and its purpose*. New York: Dodd, Mead & Co.

Meyer, A. J. et al. (1980). Skills training in a cardiovascular health education program. *Journal of consulting and clinical psychology*. 48 (2).

Meyers, H. W. (1987). The adolescent family life project: Addison County Parent Child Center. Burlington, VT: University of Vermont.

Michelson, L. (1986). Cognitive-behavioral strategies in the prevention and treatment of antisocial disorders in children and adolescents. In Burchard—

Middleton-Moz, J. (1989). Presentation at Alaska Prevention Conference.

Milkman, H.B. (1990). Presentation at Roaring Fork Valley Community/School Team Training. Aspen, CO.

Milkman, H.B. and Sunderwirth, S. (1986). *Craving for ecstasy: The consciousness and chemistry of escape*. Lexington, MA: Lexington Books.

Miller, C.E. (1991). Book Review: Prevention: The Critical Need: A User Friendly guide for 21st century parents, practitioners, and planners. *New designs for youth development*. 10(1): 28.

Miller, G. (Ed.)(1989). *Giving children a chance: the case for more effective national policies*. Washington, D.C.: Center for National Policy Press.

Miller, W.B. (1958). Lower class culture as a generating milieu of gang delinquency. *Journal of social issues*. 3.

Millman, D. (1980). *The way of the peaceful warrior*. Tiburon, CA: H.J. Kramer.

Mills, R.C. (1996). *Realizing Mental Health*. New York: Sulzberger & Graham

524

Mills, R.C. (1991). A new understanding of self: Affect, state of mind, self-understanding, and intrinsic motivation. *Journal of experimental education.* 60: 67-81.

Mills, R.C. (1991). The Psychology of Mind applied to substance abuse, dropout, and delinquency prevention: Modello - Homestead Gardens Intervention Project. Paper presented to the Florida Alcohol and Drug Abuse Association Annual Conference, Orlando, FL.

Mills, R.C. (1990). The Modello Early Intervention Project: A model for prevention; A demonstration project based on Psychology of Mind. Presented at the Seventh Annual Conference on the Psychology of Mind. Miami, FL.

Mills, R.C., Dunham, R. and Alpert, G. (1988). Working with high-risk youth in prevention and early intervention programs: Toward a comprehensive wellness model. *Adolescence.* 23(91): 643-660

Milton S. Eisenhower Foundation (1990). *Youth Investment and Community Reconstruction: Street Lessons on Drugs and Crime for the '90s.* Washington, DC

Milwaukee Teen Initiative Program (1987). Pertinent evaluation data. Milwaukee, WI: Greater Milwaukee Crime Prevention Project, Milwaukee Safety Academy.

Minde, K. (1986). Attachment and bonding: Some theoretical and practical implications for the treatment of high-risk caregiver-infant dyads. In NMHA—

Mitchell, C. (1988). Report of the Vermont delegation. In Chamberlain—

Mitchell, S. K. et al. (1988). A comparison of home-based prevention programs for families of newborns. In Bond & Wagner—

Monahan, A. et al. (1989). Accelerated learning for at risk students: Teacher, student, parent empowerment. Tuba City, AZ: Unified School District No. 15.

Morehouse, E. (1979). Working in the schools with children of alcoholic parents. *Health and social work.* 4 (4).

Morehouse, L. and Goss, L. (1975). *Total Fitness.* New York: Simon & Schuster.

Mulhern, S. (1987). Youth involvement: The key to successful prevention. *The PYD link,* 4 (7). Madison, WI: Wisconsin Positive Youth Development Initiative.

Muller, J. & Mihalic, S. (1999). *Blueprints: A Violence Prevention Initiative.* Washington, DC: U.S. Office for Juvenile Justice and Delinquency Prevention, in cooperation with The Center for the Study and Prevention of Violence at the University of Colorado, Boulder.

Mulready, P. (1988). Presentation at New England School of Alcohol Studies. Durham, NH.

Murphey, D. (1999). *The Social Well-Being of Vermonters.* Waterbury, VT: Vermont Agency of Human Services.

Murphy, J. T. (1980). Getting the facts: A fieldwork guide for evaluators and policy analysts. Santa Monica, CA: Goodyear Publishing.

Murphy, L. R. (1986). Evaluation of worksite stress management. In NMHA—

Musick, J. and Halpern, R. (1989). Giving children a chance: What role community-based early parenting interventions? In Miller—

Namy Dickason, C. (1993). Spirituality of prevention: A first conference of its kind. *New designs for youth development.* 10 (3, summer): 27-28.

National Academy of Sciences (1991). *National Forum on the Future of American Children.* Washington, DC.

National Association of State Alcohol and Drug Abuse Directors and National Prevention Network (1989). Prevention in perspective. Washington, D.C.

National Coalition of Hispanic Health and Human Service Organizations (1990). Women and AIDS (film). Washington, D.C.

National Commission on Children (1991). *Beyond Rhetoric: A New American Agenda for Children and Families.* Washington, DC: Superintendent of Documents. U.S. Government Printing Office.

National Commission on Child Welfare and Family Preservation (1991). *A Commitment to Change.* Washington, DC.

National Council for Crime and Delinquency (1972). *Alternatives to Drugs.* Washington, D.C.: U.S. Dept. of justice.

National Governors Association (1989). *America in Transition: Report of the Task Force on Children.* Washington, DC.

National Governor's Association (1987). The first sixty months. Washington, D.C: Committee on Human Resources.

National Governor's Association (1987). The first sixty months: Next steps. Washington, D.C.: Committee on Human Resources.

National Governor's Association (1987). Making America work: Bringing down the barriers. Washington, D.C.

National Governor's Association (1988). Making America work: A follow-up report. Washington, D.C.

National Governors Association, Committee on Human Resources (1987). Missouri's Parents as Teachers program. The first sixty months: The next steps. Washington D.C.: NGA and Center for Policy Research.

National Institute for Citizen Education in the Law (1988). Study reaffirms that LRE can curb delinquency. *Street Law News.* IV (1). NICEL Clearinghouse.

National Institute on Drug Abuse (1998). *Preventing drug use among children and adolescents.* National Institute of Health. www.health.org/pubs/prev.

National Institute of Drug Abuse (1988). A guide to multicultural drug abuse prevention: 3. Strategies draft. Rockville, MD.

National Institute of Justice (1983). Arrest may be the most effective response to domestic violence. National Criminal Justice Association. justice research. (May-June). Washington, D.C.

National Mental Health Association (NMHA) Commission on the Prevention of Mental-Emotional Disabilities (Ed.) (1986). *The prevention of mental-emotional disabilities: Resource papers.* Alexandria, VA: National Technical Information Service (1986).

National Mental Health Association Commission on the Prevention of Mental-Emotional Disabilities (1986). *Prevention of Mental-Emotional Disabilities*. Alexandria, VA.

National School Boards Association (1984). Toward better and safer schools: A school leader's guide to delinquency prevention. Washington, D.C.

National Security of the House of Representatives Committee on Government Operations. Washington, D.C. (3, April).

Native Hawaiian Drug Free Schools and Communities Program. Honolulu, HI.

Natural health news (1990, Spring). AMA-Guilty. Montpelier, VT: Pleasant Chiropractic.

Natural Resources Development Council (1989). Intolerable risk: Pesticides in our children's food. Washington, D.C.

National Youth Work Alliance (undated). 70001 J.O.B.S. program: Employment program completes the puzzle for serious offenders. *Youth alternatives*. Washington, D.C.

National Technical Information Service. Adolescent pregnancy and childbearing. Springfield, VA: U.S. Dept. of Commerce.

Nicolau, S. and Ramos, C. L. (1990). How to build partnerships between schools and low-income Hispanic parents. *California Prevention Network journal*. 4.

Nederhood, B. and Hawkins, J. D. (1986). Effects of a year-long exposure to student-team learning on seventh grade students. Seattle: University of Washington. Social Development Research Group.

Nelsen, J. (1981). *Positive Discipline*. Fair Oaks, CA: Sunrise.

Nenortas, G. V. (1987). A drop out prevention program utilizing peer group counseling with middle school alternative students. Ft. Lauderdale, FL: Nova University Center for the Advancement of Education.

Nerad, A. S. (1986). Mental health education in the schools. In NMHA—

North, S. (1987). Voucher system helps companies administer benefits for child care. *New England business* (March 16).

Nuestro Bienstar. (undated). San Antonio, TX Center for Health Policy Development.

Oberle, K. (1991). A decade of research in locus of control: What have we learned? *Journal of advanced nursing*. 16: 800-806

O'Brien, J. & Forest, M. with Snow, J. & Hasbury, D. (1989). Action for inclusion. Toronto: Fronteir College Press.

Olds, D. L. (1988). The prenatal/early infancy project. In Price—

Olds, D. L. et al. (1984). Final report: Prenatal/early infancy project: A follow up evaluation at the third year of life. National Technical Information Service. Springfield, VA: U.S. Dept. of Commerce.

Olweus, D. (1992). Bully/victim problems among school children. In Rubin, K. and Pepler, D. (Eds.). *The development and treatment of childhood aggression*. Hillsdale, NJ: Erlbaum.

Olweus, D. (1984). Aggressors and their victims. In Frude, N. and Gault, H. (Eds.). *Disruptive behavior in schools*. New York: Wiley.

Ornstein, R. E. (1975). *The psychology of consciousness*. New York: Penguin.

Osofsky, J. D. (1986). Perspectives on infant mental health. In Kessler & Goldston—

Osborn, J. E. (1989). A risk assessment of the AIDS epidemic. In Mays, V. M. et al. (Eds). *Primary prevention of AIDS. Psychological approaches*. Newbury Park, CA: Sage.

Ostos, T. et al. (undated). The Paramount plan: Alternatives to gang membership. City of Paramount, CA.

Ounce of Prevention Fund (1987). Child sexual abuse: A hidden factor in adolescent sexual behavior. Springfield, IL: Illinois Department of Children and Family Services.

Ouchi, W. (1981). *The world of Z*. Reading, MA: Addison-Wesley Publishing.

Pascoe, J. M. and French, J. (1988). The development of positive feelings in primiparous mothers toward their normal newborns: a descriptive study. *American journal of diseases of children*. 14 (April).

Patent, A. M. (1987). *You can have it all: The art of winning the money game and...a life of joy*. Piermont, NY: Money Mastery Publishing.

Patterson, G. (1975). Professional guide for families and living with children. Champaign, IL: Research Press.

Patton, M. Q. (1978). *Qualitative evaluation methods*. Beverly Hills, CA: Sage.

Penn, N. et al. (1982). The interaction of social policy and welfare dependency. La Jolla, CA: University of California, San Diego School of Medicine.

Pentz, M. A. et al. (1989). A multi-community trial for primary prevention of adolescent drug abuse: Effects on drug use prevalence. *JAMA*. 621 (22).

Perdue, R. R. and Rainwater, A. (1984). Adolescent recreation and alcohol consumption. *Therapeutic recreation journal*. 18 (2).

Perkins, P. J. (1986). *EDAP. Early Drug Abuse Prevention: Facilitator's guide*. Montpelier, VT: Washington County Youth Service Bureau.

Perkins, P. J., Stapleton, G. and Lesnak, M. (1989). *DART. Drug Abuse Reduction Training: Facilitator's manual*. Montpelier, VT: Washington County Youth Service Bureau.

Periera, C. (1988). Law-related education in elementary and secondary schools. *ERIC*. ED S088-6 (June).

Perry, C.L., Williams, C.L., Veblin-Mortenson, S., Toomey, T.L., Komro, K.A., Anstine, P.S., McGovern, P.G., Finnegan, .R., Forster, J.L., Wagenaar, A.C. & Wolfson, M. (1996). Project Northland: Outcomes of a communitywide alcohol use prevention program during early adolescence. *American journal of public health*. 86(7): 956-965.

Pert, C.B. (1997). *Molecules of emotion: Why you feel the way you feel*. New York, NY: Scribner.

Peters, T. J. and Waterman, R. H., Jr. (1982). *In search of excellence: Lessons from America's best run companies*. New York: Warner Books.

Peters, T. J. (1989). The leadership alliance and excellence in the public sector. ETV progmms.

Phillips, L. A. (1984). Health promotion: Whose job is it? Kansas Department of Health and Environment.

Pierce, T. (undated). Pierce's Personalization Matrix. Burlington, VT: WEZF-TV.

Pittman, K. et al, (1989). The lessons of multi-site initiatives serving high risk youth. Washington, D.C.: Adolescent Pregnancy Prevention Clearinghouse.

Popkin, M. H. (1989). Parents as family policy makers or rule setters. In Cunningham—

Popkin, M. (1984). *Active Parenting*. Marietta, GA: Active Parenting.

Pransky, G.S. (1998). *The renaissance of psychology*. New York: Sulzberger & Graham.

Pransky, G.S., Mills, R.C., Sedgeman, J.A. & Blevens, J.K. (1997). An emerging paradigm for Brief treatment and prevention. In L. Vandecreek, S. Knapp, T.J. Jackson, (Eds.) *Innovations in clinical practice: A Source Book*. 15: 76-98. Sarasota, FL: Professional Resource Press.

Pransky, J. (1998). *Modello: A story of hope for the inner-city and beyond: An inside-out model of prevention and resiliency in action through Health Realization*. Cabot, VT: NEHRI Publications.

Pransky, J. (1997). *Parenting from the Heart*. Cabot, VT: NEHRI Publications.

Pransky, J. (1994). Can prevention be moved to a higher plane? *New designs for youth development*. (11:2).

Pransky, J. (1990). Skills for parents: A series of five papers. Cabot, VT.

Pransky, J. (1986). Self-concept and school climate. Waterbury, VT: Office of Alcohol and Drug Abuse Programs.

Pransky, J. (1986). Can you legislate prevention? *New designs for youth development*. 7 (2).

Pransky, J. (1986). Excerpts from 1981 juvenile justice and delinquency prevention plan. In *Coming together: Delinquency Prevention*. Washington, D.C.: Westinghouse National Issues Center.

Pransky, J. (1985). Self-concept and school climate. Waterbury, VT: OADAP.

Pransky, J. (1985). Making sense of prevention: A conceptual framework. *New designs for youth development*. 4. Tucson, AZ: AYD.

Pransky, J. (1983). A guide to developing comprehensive K-12 substance abuse education curriculum. Waterbury, VT: OADAP.

Pransky, J. (1981). Delinquency prevention in Vermont. Montpelier, VT: Vermont Commission on the Administration of justice.

Pransky, J. (1975). How to organize communities into action. Cabot, VT.

Pransky, J. (1967). Mike Callahan: The case study of a "potential juvenile delinquent." Worcester, MA: Clark University.

Pransky, J. (undated). Planning for desired results. Montpelier, VT: VCAJ.

Pransky, J. and Chaffee, R. (undated). Deciding about drugs: Risks and responsibilities. Waterbury, VT: Office of Alcohol and Drug Abuse Programs.

Price, R. H. (1988). Integration: The preventionist's craft. In Bond & Wagner–.

Price, R. H. et al. (Eds.) (1988). *14 ounces of prevention: A casebook for practitioners*. Washington, D.C.: American Psychological Association.

Price, R.H., Ketterer, R.F., Bader, B.C., Monahan, J. (Eds.) (1980). *Prevention in mental health: Research, policy and practice*. Thousand Oaks, CA: Sage.

Prugh, T. (1986). The Black church: A foundation for recovery. In Sugarman, B. (Ed.). A think tank. Cambridge, MA: Lesley College.

Puryear, H. B. (1982). *The Edgar Cayce primer*. New York: Bantam.

Qualia, R.J. & Fox, K.M (2000). *Believing in achieving: Eight conditions that make a difference in the lives of all youth*. Toronto: SARS Educational Services.

Quintilliani, A. (undated). Information for parents: Some ways to communicate with your children about substance abuse. Hinesburg, VT: Champlain Valley Union High School.

Raeburn, J. & Rootman, I. (1998). *People-centered health promotion*. New York, NY: John Wiley & Sons.

Ramey, C. T. et al. (1988). Early intervention for high risk children: The Carolina early intervention program. In Price—

Ramey, C. T. and Campbell, (1984). Preventive education for high risk children: Cognitive consequences of the Carolina Abecedarian Project. *American journal of mental deficiency*. 88 (515-523).

RAND Corporation report (1988). Steady work. National Institute of Education. Washington, D.C.

Refling, M. (1989). The Orion Multi-Service Center Seattle's drop-in center for street youth. Champaign, IL: Community Research Associates.

Reissman, F. (1986). Support groups as preventive intervention. In Kessler & Goldston—

Regier, D.A., Myers, Kramer, Robins, et al. (1984). Archives of general psychiatry. 41 (entire issue). Rockville, MD: National Institute of Mental Health.

Render, G. F. and Lemire, D. (1989). A consciousness/spirituality domain based on Maslow's hierarchy. *Holistic education review* (summer).

Resnik, H. S. and Gibbs, J. (1989). Types of peer program approaches. In Office of Substance Abuse Prevention. Adolescent peer pressure: Theory, correlates, and program implications for drug abuse prevention. Rockville, MD.

Resnick, M.D. et al. (1997). Protecting adolescents from harm: Findings from the national longitudinal study on adolescent health. *JAMA*. 278 (10): 823-832

Reuben, D. (1975). *The save your life diet*. New York: Ballantine.

Rhinehart, L. (1976). *The book of est*. New York. Holt, Rinehart and Winston.

Ripley, H. S. & Dorpat, T.L. (1984). Prevention and treatment of suicidal behavior. *Journal of preventive psychiatry*. 1.

Roberts, J. (1972). *Seth speaks*. New York: Bantam.

527

Rodegast, P. and Stanton, J. (1985). *Emmanuel's book*. New York: Bantam.

Rodham Clinton, H. (1996). *It takes a village: And other lessons children teach us*. New York: Touchstone Books.

Romig, D. A. (1978). *Justice for our children*. Lexington, MA: Lexington Books.

Rosenbaum, S. (1989). Recent developments in infant and child health: Health status, insurance coverage, and trends in public health policy. In Miller—

Ross, S. (1976). *Fasting: The super diet*. New York: Ballantine Books.

Rotheram-Borus, M. J. (1988). Assertiveness training for children. In Price–.

Rotheram-Borus, M. J. and Tsemberis, S. J. (1989). Social competency training programs in ethnically diverse communities. In Bond & Compas—

Rowland, L. W. (1957; 1976). Pierre the Pelican. American Medical Association Council on Mental Health.

Rubino, K. K. (1988). The Ounce of Prevention program in Illinois: Empowering at risk families through community based family support programs. In Chamberlain—

Rutter, M. (1989). Pathways from childhood to adult life. *Journal of child psychology*. 30 (1): 23-51.

Rutter, M. et al. (1979). *Fifteen thousand hours: Secondary schools and their effects on children*. Cambridge, MA: Harvard University Press.

Samets, I. (1984). The development and primary prevention of problem behaviors. Waterbury, VT. Vermont Agency of Human Services.

Sanchez, E. (19W). Diversity and the role of prevention. *California Prevention Network journal*. 4 (Fall).

Sanchez, E. and League, V.C. (1990). Planning for diversity. Oakland, CA: Vincente & Associates.

Sanders, B. (1988). Presentation at Vermont Conference of Social Concerns.

Sandler, I. N. (1986). Children of parental divorce and parental death: The prospects for prevention program. In NMHA—

Savage, R. C. and Allen, M. G. (1986). Educational issues for the traumatically brain injured early adolescent. Castleton, VT: Castleton State College.

Scapocznik, J. Santisteban, D., Rio, A., Perez-Vidal, A., & Kurtines, W.M. (1989). Family Effectiveness Training: An intervention to prevent dug abuse and problem behaviors in Hispanic Adolescents. *Journal of counseling and clinical psychology*. 57(5), 571-578

Schaps, E. et al. (1978). Primary prevention evaluation research: A review of 127 program evaluations. Walnut Creek, CA: Pacific Institute for Research and Evaluation.

Schorr, L.B. (1997). *Common purpose: Strengthening families and neighborhoods to rebuild America*. New York, NY: Doubleday

Schorr, L. B. (1989). Breaking the cycle of disadvantage: New knowledge, new tools, new urgency. In Miller—

Schorr, L. B. (1988). *Within our reach: Breaking the cycle of disadvantage and despair*. New York: Doubleday.

Schultz, W. (1975). *Shiatsu*. New York: brake Publishers.

Schuster, D. et al. (1976). Suggestive-accelerated learning and teaching: A manual of classroom procedures based on the Lozanov method. Des Moins, IA: Society for Suggestive-Accelerated Learning and Teaching.

Schweinhart, L. J. and Weikart, D. P. (1988). The High Scope/Perry PreSchool Program. In Price—

Schweinhart, L. J. and Weikart, D. P. (1980). Young children grow up: The effects of the Perry PreSchool Program on youths through age fifteen. Ypsilanti, MI: High/Scope Educational Research Foundation.

Search institute (1997). 40 developmental assets. Minneapolis, MN: Search Institute

Searight, H. R. and Handel, P. J. (1986). Premature birth and its later effects: Towards preventive intervention. *Journal of primary prevention*. 7 (1).

Seeman, W. et al. (1972). Influence of transcendental meditation on a measure of self-actualization. *Journal of counseling psychology*. 19, 184-187.

Segal, J. (1986). Translating stress and coping research into public information and education. In Kessler & Goldston—

Seyle, H. (1976). *The stress of life*. New York: McGraw-Hill.

Shaffer, D. et al. (1987). Review of youth suicide prevention programs. New York: New York State Psychiatric Institute.

Shaheen, T. (1981). Presentation at Westinghouse National Issues Center workshop.

Shure, M. B. (1988). How to think, not what to think: A cognitive approach to prevention. In Bond & Wagner—

Shure, M. B. and Spivack, G. (1988). Interpersonal Cognitive Problem Solving. In Price—

Shure, M. B. and Spivack, G. (1982). Interpersonal problem-solving in young children: A cognitive approach to prevention. *American journal of community psychology*. 10 (5).

Shure, M. B. and Spivack, G. (1979). Interpersonal Cognitive Problem Solving and primary prevention: Programming for preschool and kindergarten children. *Journal of clinical psychology* (summer).

Shure, M. B. and Spivack, G. (1987). Competence building as an approach to prevention of dysfunction: The Interpersonal Cognitive Problem Solving model. In Steinberg, J. A. and Silverman, M. M. (Eds.). *Preventing mental disorders: a research perspective*. Rockville, MD: National Institute of Mental Health.

Siegal, B. S. (1986). *Love, medicine, and miracles*. New York: Harper & Row.

Silva, J. and Miele, P. (1977). *The Silva Mind Control method*. New York: Pocket

Simpson, S. et al. (undated). Framework for the development of a health education scope and sequence, K-6; 7-12. Montpelier, VT: Dept. of Education.

Sizer, T. R. (1984). *Horace's compromise*. Boston: Houghton- Mifflin.

Slavin, R. E. (1987). *Cooperative learning: Student teams*. West Haven, CT: NEA Professional Library.

Smith, D. S. (1984). The effects of Systematic Training for Effective Parenting on natural parents' attitude and communication responses. San Diego, CA: Professional School of Psychological Studies.

Spivack, G. (1986). Psychological competencies in mental health prevention research and intervention. In NMHA—

Spivack, G. and Ciani, N. (1987). High-risk early behavior pattern and later delinquency. In Burchard—

Stern, A. (1989). Parents as educators. In Cunningham—

Stern, A. (1988). Families In-Touch initiative campaign. Springfield, IL: Department of Alcoholism and Substance Abuse.

Stevens, J. and Stevens, L.S. (1988). *Secrets of Shamanism: Tapping the spirit power within you*. New York: Avon.

Stillman, 1. M. and Baker, S. S. (1974). The doctor's quick weight loss diet. New York: Deli Books.

Stoudemire, A. (1986). Prevention of depression. In NMHA—

Straus, M. A. (1986). Prevention of family violence. In NMHA—

Streit, F. (1983). EPAC. Highland Park, NJ: Streit Associates.

Strom, T., Scannell, T., Hill, P. (1988). The first 100 days: A children's initiative. Washington, D.C.: Child Welfare League of America.

Suarez, R., Mills, R. C., & Stewart, D. (1987). *Sanity, insanity, and common sense: The groundbreaking new approach to happiness*. New York: Fawcett Columbine.

Swift, M. S. and Healy, K. N. (1986). Translating research into practice. In Kessler & Goldston—

Swisher, J. (1988). Evaluation of the Philadelphia elementary school prevention and intervention program for at-risk youth. State College, PA: Data Base.

Tableman, B. (1987). Stress management training for women on public assistance: A replication manual. Lansing, MI: Michigan Dept. of Mental Health

Tableman, B. (1986). Statewide prevention programs: The politics of the possible. In Kessler & Goldston—

Tableman, B. (1982). Stress management training for women on public assistance. *American journal of community psychology*. 10 (3).

Tadmor, C. S. (1988). The perceived personal control preventive intervention for a caesarian birth population. In Price–

Tadmor, C. S. and Brandes, J. M. (1986). Premature birth: a crisis intervention approach. *Journal of primary prevention*. 6 (4).

Tadmor, C. S. and Brandes, J. M. (1984). The perceived control model in the prevention of emotional dysfunction for a high risk population of caesarian birth. *Journal of primary prevention*. 4.

Tafoya, T. (1991). Presentation at Please Stop Our Hurting conference. Burlington, VT (March).

Taylor, G. L. (1983). Mastery learning: A prescription for success. NASSP bulletin (September).

Tierney, J.P. & Grossman, J. (1995). Making a difference: An impact study. Philadelphia, PA: Public/Private Ventures.

Title 16. *Vermont Statutes Annotated* §131, 134, 135, 906. An Act relating to comprehensive Family Life Education and appropriations. Montpelier, VT.

Title 33. *Vermont Statutes Annotated* §3301-3308. [Act 79].

Tobler, N. (1987). Meta-Analysis of 143 Adolescent Drug Prevention Programs. *Journal of drug issues*. 3.

Trautz, O. (1977). On desired results and indicators. Montpelier, VT: GCAJ.

Trotter, R. J. (1987). Project Day-Care. *Psychology today*. (December).

Trout, J. and Ries, A. (1986). *Positioning: The battle for your mind*. New York: Warner.

U.S. Dept. of Education (1979). The school-team approach. Washington, D.C.

U.S. Department of Education (undated). Replicable or promising approaches for safe and drug free schools" (undated). Washington, DC.

U.S. Department of Health and Human Services (1998). Science-based substance abuse prevention. Paper prepared for National Prevention Network's conference on Joining Forces to Advance Prevention, San Antonio, Texas. Washington, DC: HHS

U.S. Department of Justice, Office of juvenile justice and Delinquency Prevention. (undated). Law-related education: Making a difference. Washington, D.C.

Vasconcellos, J. et al. (1990). *Toward a state of esteem. The final report of the California Task Force to Promote Self-esteem and Personal and Social Responsibility*. Sacremento, CA: Department of Education.

Vachon, M. L. S. et al. (1980). A controlled study of self-help intervention for widows. *American journal of psychiatry*. 137 (11).

Van Buskirk, W. (1980). A review of current research on school climate. Denver, CO: Colorado Dept. of Education.

Vella, J. (1997). *How do they know they know: Evaluating adult learning*. San Francisco, CA: Jossey-Bass.

Vella, J. (1989). *Learning to Listen/Learning to teach*. Westport, CT: Save the Children.

Vermont Department of Education (1988). Guidelines for the development of an HIV/AIDS education program in the Vermont schools. Montpelier, VT: Dept. of Education.

Vermont Department of Employment and Training (1986). COMPASS. Montpelier, VT.

Vermont Legislative Council (1980). Options for preventing delinquency in Vermont. Montpelier, VT.

Vermont State Board of Education (1984). Standards for approving Vermont's public schools (and self-assessment guide). Montpelier, VT.

Virginia Council on Coordinating Prevention (1989). 1990-92 *Comprehensive prevention plan for Virginia*. Richmond, VA.

Wallack, L. and Wallerstein, N. (1987), Health Education and Prevention: Designing Community Initiatives. *International quarterly of community health education*. 7 (4).

Wright, A. N. (1983). Therapeutic potential of the Outward Bound process: an evaluation of a treatment program for juvenile delinquents. *Therapeutic recreation journal.* 17 (2).

Washington County Youth Service Bureau (1989). Drug Abuse Reduction Training (DART) Evaluation Report. Montpelier, VT: Washington County Youth Service Bureau.

Watson, M. (1982). Classroom control: To what ends? At what price? *California journal of teacher education.* 9(75-95).

Watson, M., Tuck, P., Morris, E. L. (1986). Good books for good kids: A guide to children's literature that enhances interpersonal understanding and concern for others. San Ramon, CA: Developmental Studies Center.

Watt, N. F. (1986). Prevention of major mental illnesses: Risk factors in schizophrenic and depressive disorders. In NMHA—

Wayson, W. W. et al. (1982). *Handbook for developing schools with good discipline.* Bloomington, IN: Phi Delta Kappa Commission on Discipline.

Weaver, C. (1987). Sally Cooper: Children must be safe, strong, and free. *MS.* (July/August).

Weaver, H. (1988). A Generation in despair. A people in peril. *Anchorage Daily News.* (A special report). Anchorage, AK.

Wegscheider, S. (1982). *Another chance: Hope and health for the alcoholic family.* Palo Alto, CA: Science and Behavior Books.

Wegscheider, S. (1976). *The family trap.* St. Paul, MN: Nurturing Networks.

Weingast, D. (1983). Shared leadership—"The damn thing works." *Educational leadership.* (March).

Weiss, H. B. (1989). From grass roots programs to state policy: Strategic Planning and choices for family support and education initiatives. Cambridge, MA: Harvard Family Research Project.

Weiss, H. B. and Halpern, R. (1988). Community-based family support and education programs: Something old, or something new? Paper prepared for the National Resource Center for Children in Poverty. New York: Columbia University.

Wellman, D. (undated). Putting on the poverty program. Boston, MA: New England Free Press.

Weissbourd, B. (1986). Parent education and support. In NMHA—

Weissberg, R. P., Caplan, M. Z., and Sivo, P. J. (1989). A new conceptual framework for establishing school based social competence promotion programs. In Bond & Compas—

Weller, S. (1988). Battered children: How we can save them? *McCalls.* (June).

Werner, E.E. (1996). How children become resilient: Observations and Cautions. *Resiliency in action.* (Winter) 18-28

Werner, E.E. (1989). High risk children in young adulthood: A longitudinal study from birth to 32 years. *American journal of orthospychiatry.* 59: 71-81

Werner, E.E. & Smith, R. (1992). *Overcoming the odds: High-risk children from birth to adulthood.* Ithaca, NY: Cornell University Press.

Werner, E.E. & Smith, R. (1988). *Vulnerable but invincible: A longitudinal study of resilient youth.* New York: McGraw-Hill.

Westbrook, A. and Ritti, O. (1971). Aikido and the dynamic sphere. Rutland, VT: Tuttle.

Wheatley, M. (1997). Goodbye command and control. *Leader to leader.* (Summer) 21-28.

White, M. B. and White, W. C. (1987). *Bulimarexia.* New York: Norton.

White, J. S. and Swisher, J. D. (1989). Vermont schools: Drug and alcohol needs assessment 1988-89 academic year. State College, PA: Data Base.

Wilhelm, R. (1967). *The I Ching or book of changes.* Princeton, NJ: Princeton University Press.

Williams, H.S. & Webb, A.Y. (1992). *Outcome funding: A new approach to public sector grantmaking.* Rensselaerville, NY: Rensselaerville Institute.

Williams, R. (1987). Prevention in the mental health arena. Prevention works in public policy series—

Wilson, S. (1981). Vermont schools tackle discipline problems. In *Coming together. Delinquency prevention.* Washington, D.C.: Westinghouse National Issues Center.

Wilson, S., Simpson, S., Pransky, J., Johnson, S. (1995). From risk to resiliency: A training curriculum developed for the Vermont State Team for Children & Families. Waterbury, VT: Vermont Agency of Human Services.

Wilson, S. and Muraskin, L. D. (1985). Creating Family Life Education programs in the public schools: A guide for policymakers. Alexandria, VA: National Association of State Boards of Education.

Wilson, W. J. (1987). *The truly disadvantaged: The inner-city, the underclass, and public policy.* Chicago: University of Chicago Press.

Woititz, J. (1983). *Adult children of alcoholics.* Hollywood, FL: Health Communications.

Wolfe, D. A. (1987). Child abuse prevention with at-risk parents and children. In Burchard—

Wolin, S. and Wolin, S. (1993). *The resilient self: How survivors of troubled families rise above adversity.* New York: Villard Books

Woodson, R.L. (1998). *The triumphs of joseph: How today's community healers are reviving our streets and neighborhoods.* New York: Simon & Schuster.

Wright, W. F. (undated). Information sheet. Apache junction, AZ: Apache junction Unified School District.

Yahraes, H. (1977). Teaching mothers mothering. DHEW. Pub. No. (ADM) 77-52. Washington, DC: U. S. Government Printing Office.

Yogi Vithaldas (1957). *The Yoga system of health and relief from tension.* New York: Simon & Shuster.

York, P. and York, D. (1980). *Tough Love: A self-help manual for parents troubled by teenage behavior.* Doylestown, PA: Tough Love.

Youngwood, S. (1990). Day care caught in money crunch circle. *Vermont business magazine.* (January).

Zasloff, K. D. (1988). PASA's Bridges to Common Ground. Brooklyn, NY: P. A. S. A.

Zigler, E. (1988). Head Start and legislative approaches to promoting healthy families and children. In Chamberlain—

Zigler, E. (1986). Discerning the future of early childhood intervention. In NMHA—

Zigler, E. (1986). The family resource movement: No longer the country's best kept secret. *Family resource coalition report.* 5 (3). Chicago, IL: Family Resource Coalition.

Zmiewsld, P. (Ed.). East Asian Medical Society (1985). *Fundamentals of Chinese medicine.* Brookline, MA: Paradigm.

Jack Pransky

Appendix

A COMPREHENSIVE NATIONAL POLICY FOR THE PREVENTION OF SOCIAL PROBLEMS AND THE PROMOTION OF HEALTH AND WELL-BEING OF CHILDREN AND THEIR FAMILIES
(Draft)

Preamble

WHEREAS the Congress finds, in Section 902 of the Young American's Act (42 USC 12301), that-

(1) children and youth are inherently the most valuable resource of the United States;

(2) the welfare, protection, healthy development, and positive role of children and youth in society are essential to the United States;

(3) children and youth deserve love, respect, and guidance, as well as good health, shelter, food, education, productive employment opportunities, and preparation for responsible participation in community life;

(4) children and youth have increasing opportunities to participate in the decisions that affect their lives;

(5) the family is the primary caregiver and source of social learning and must be supported and strengthened;

(6) when a family is unable to ensure the satisfaction of basic needs of children and youth it is the responsibility of society to assist such family; and,

(7) it is the joint and several responsibility of the Federal Government, each State, and the political subdivisions of each State, to assist children and youth to secure, to the maximum extent practicable, equal opportunity to full and free access to (A) the best possible physical and mental health; (B) adequate and safe physical shelter; (C) a high level of educational opportunity; (D) effective training, apprenticeships, opportunities community service, and productive employment and participation in decisions affecting their lives; (E) a wide range of civic, cultural, and recreational activities that recognize young Americans as resources and promote self-esteem and a stake in the communities of such Americans; and (F) comprehensive community services that are efficient, coordinated, readily available, and involve families of young individuals; and,

WHEREAS too many American children enter adulthood without the skills and motivation to contribute in a constructive way to a highly skilled workforce or to society and often lag behind their counterparts in many developed nations; and,

WHEREAS the problems of alcohol and-other drug abuse, child abuse and neglect, crime and delinquency, teenage pregnancy, teenage suicide, sexual abuse, mental-emotional disorders, eating disorders, school failure and truancy and dropouts, poverty, hunger, and homelessness, and other domestic problems continue to threaten the health and well-being of this nation's children and youth, limit individual potential, and undermine the quality of life of many families; and,

WHEREAS United States taxpayers must pay for the results and thus assume the burdens of these problems, including treatment of chronic physical and mental health conditions and disabilities, incarceration, foster care, special education, welfare, and other social programs that respond to the symptoms of these problems; and,

WHEREAS many national commissions such as the National Commission on Children, the National Commission on Child Welfare and Family Preservation, the National Mental Health Association Commission on the Prevention of Mental-Emotional Disorders, the Task Force on Children of the National Governors' Association, and many private reports, such as the Ford Foundation Project on Social Welfare and the American Future and the Eisenhower Foundation report on Street Lessons on Drugs and Crime for the Nineties, and the Healthy People 2000 National Health Promotion and Disease Prevention Objectives of the U.S. Department of Health and Human Services, and the United Nations Convention on the Rights of the Child, have all found similarly that preventing problems before they become crises is the most effective and cost-effective way to address the needs of troubled families and vulnerable children, and that an investment in children and families and in prevention would simultaneously reduce the frequency of mental-emotional disabilities, decrease the cost of health care, welfare, crime, and other social costs, enhance family stability, enable citizens to live healthier and more productive lives, increase productivity throughout all sectors of business and therefore prove in this era of increasingly tight budgets

533

to be a very prudent expenditure, and that without such an investment in prevention the United States inevitably will continue to pay ever-escalating human and financial costs of these problems and disabilities; and,

WHEREAS prevention means not merely stopping something from happening but creating positive and healthy conditions and personal attributes that promote the well-being of people so problems do not materialize; and scientific findings have clearly demonstrated the efficacy of primary and secondary prevention strategies, so that every American child can develop his or her full potential;

NOW THEREFORE BE IT RESOLVED AS A POLICY FOR THIS GREAT NATION

THAT the cornerstone of American domestic policy shall be the strengthening of families for the benefit and support of children and the prevention of human behavior problems that adversely affect this society, and this policy shall ensure,

I. PRENATAL CARE

I.1. Prenatal Education through Home Visiting

THAT because every prospective parent needs the knowledge, the skills, the supports, and the desire to provide a sound fetal environment that has the best chance of a producing a healthy baby, (a) every new, prospective mother and every prospective mother at risk of giving birth to a low birthweight or premature infant or infant with other than normal problems, within two weeks of a determination of positive pregnancy, shall have the opportunity to receive a minimum of one prenatal home visit, with additional visits as needed, by a caring nurse or trained, qualified parent aid, and (b) that this visit shall include the provision of prenatal education consonant with educational and language ability, including but not limited to knowledge about nutrition, creating a chemical-free environment, the need for proper medical care and routine check-ups, what to expect from a baby and childbirth, how to handle common situations that might arise, and available resources; and (c) to secure this, the Federal and State governments shall ensure that every community has access to a program of home visiting and maternity care, within reasonable geographic proximity, with guaranteed, continued eligibility throughout pregnancy as needed; and,

I.2. Healthy Fetal Environment

THAT to provide the best opportunity for a fetal environment that is nutritionally sound, free of chemicals such as tobacco, alcohol, cocaine/crack, heroine and other drugs that can damage the fetus, and free of sexually transmitted and other diseases such as AIDS that can harm the fetus, and to provide a fetal environment that minimizes the chance of infant mortality, premature birth and low birthweight, and so that United States citizens do not to have to pay for neonatal intensive services for conditions that could have been prevented; (a) the nutrition program for women, infants, and children shall be provided to every mother and child in need of its service, and the home visiting program [I.1.] shall provide accurate, up-to-date information about these issues, supported by easily understandable and compelling pamphlets written in a variety of appropriate languages, and highly increased and improved media advertising about said issues; and (b) that pregnant adolescents, first-time pregnant women and expectant fathers, shall have the opportunity to attend support groups on said issues in or within reasonable geographic proximity to their community; and (c) the Federal and State governments shall offer tax or other incentives to the media to produce and air, at prime time and at other times when targeted audiences are likely to be watching, messages that promote such information; and,

I.3. Medical Care

THAT to promote the best opportunity for a healthy infant to emerge from the womb, (a) every pregnant woman, within the first trimester of pregnancy where possible, but not later than within six months of pregnancy, shall receive routine, adequate and proper prenatal and pediatric care within a reasonable geographic distance and (b) shall be provided with prenatal screening to detect fetal abnormalities, with counseling and guidance provided as needed; and, to secure this, (c) the Federal Government shall ensure that the barrier of financial constraints be removed for any pregnant woman who would have difficulty paying, such as providing for extension of Medicaid coverage into higher middle-income brackets so undue financial hardship would not be caused; and,

II. EARLY INFANCY CARE

II.1. Attachment and Bonding

THAT because every set of parents of newborns needs the opportunity and adequate time to attach and bond successfully with their newborns with loving affection, (a) hospital or birthing room staff shall provide an optimal birth environment for parents to attach and bond to their infant immediately after birth, and shall provide appropriate and supportive instruction accordingly, and which also includes what to look for and how to respond to and how to appreciate the way a newborn communicates; and, (b) a minimum of one, and preferably both, parent(s) shall have the opportunity to be provided with an adequate amount of protected leave from employment with reasonable compensation while on leave; and, to secure this, (3) the Federal government shall provide tax or other incentives to businesses that establish policies and practices of protected parental leave for its employed parents of newborns for from two to four months, and with further incentives for providing said parents on such leave with an adequate percentage of their salary; and,

II.2. Postnatal Education through a System of Home Visiting

THAT because every parent needs the knowledge, the skills, the supports, and the desire to raise children in ways that will help them have a healthy start in life physically, mentally, emotionally, and socially, (a) every set of parents that gives birth to a child shall have the opportunity to receive at least one home visit with more as needed extending through the first year of life, by a caring nurse or trained, supportive parent aid, and (b) this visit shall include but not be limited to education and skill-building and providing assistance where necessary with attachment and bonding, breast feeding, proper and effective child care, nutrition, healthy parent-child interaction, consistent emotional nurturing, promotion of reasonable expectations of the child at various developmental stages of early life, sensitivity to individual temperaments, cognitive stimulation, situations to avoid such as shaken babies, health and safety information, appropriate and regular health services, stress management, assistance in resolution of conflicts, referral to services when needed, and help in providing emotional support where needed; and to secure this, (c) the Federal and State governments shall ensure that local communities have an organized system for and the means to provide this system of home visiting; and

II.3. Routine Medical Care and Immunizations

THAT (a) every child shall be provided with, or where preferable parents shall select, an identified primary care giver who provides routine medical care at appropriate and regular intervals, a basic series of immunizations, and screening for genetic disorders and other disabling conditions, except upon objection by the child's parents, and (b) where a child tests positive for a disease or condition that child shall receive appropriate treatment, with referrals as necessary, and such service shall be provided at affordable costs to parents consonant with their ability to pay; and, to secure this, (c) the Federal and State governments shall ensure that local communities have proper medical facilities within reasonable geographic proximity, and have a reasonable number of primary care givers to provide this service; and, (d) the Federal government shall provide incentives such as forgiving or reducing student loans, per year, to medical doctors, physician's assistants, and nurses for serving in areas lacking an adequate number of primary care givers, and (e) shall provide incentives to private enterprise for establishing medical facilities at reasonably low costs per patient in undeserved areas; and,

II.4 Tracking "At Risk" Infants

THAT because infants determined to be at high risk of developing illnesses or behavioral problems often overburden the health and human services system and require high costs to the American taxpayer, and because many of these disabilities and problems can be overcome through a system of early identification and intervention, (a) the State system of human and social services shall identify infants determined to be at risk of developing illnesses, disabilities, or other problems, such as Fetal Alcohol or cocaine/crack Syndrome babies, and shall develop a tracking system to follow such children throughout their childhood through age 18 where determined necessary, for the said purpose of providing them and their parents with assistance at the earliest signs of a problem and so that case managers can effectively ensure appropriate preventive services for these children; and, to secure this, (b) the Federal government shall ensure that States establish adequate and responsive tracking and helping systems; and,

III. PARENTING EDUCATION AND SUPPORT

III.1. Parenting Skills

THAT because all parents need the information, skills, and supports to raise their children in ways that promote their optimal health and well-being and that develop healthy self-perceptions and life skills, (a) every community shall provide parenting skills education in a wide variety of forms on a coordinated, systematic and regular basis, covering all levels and aspects of child development, with such education beginning during early childhood and reinforced at significant points of transition during the child's life, such as when a child begins to walk, enters school, becomes an adolescent, enters high school, and enters the world of work; and (b) that this education shall promote positive, loving parenting, open channels of communication, enforced standards of behavior, encouragement toward responsible independence, and shall provide an understanding of disciplining children in ways that build healthy self-perceptions and intrapersonal, interpersonal, systemic, and judgmental skills, coupled with parental support and assistance to help them nurture their children and strengthen their families; and (c) that this education shall be provided in a variety of learning formats, such as parenting courses and home visiting that respect individual learning styles and cultural diversity, and which provide opportunities to learn and practice new skills and provide follow up at reasonable intervals; and, to secure this, (d) the Federal and State governments shall ensure that every community has at least one community-based organization designated with the responsibility to provide for or coordinate parenting skills education, and (e) shall ensure that adequate funding be provided for such efforts; and,

III.2. Family Support and Education Programs

THAT because all parents need opportunities to gain knowledge, skills, and supports, and the opportunities to successfully raise their children and promote strong, stable families, and have opportunities for their own growth (a) every community shall have access, within reasonable geographic proximity to families served, to a center-based or coordinated program of services, offered to any family that wants to participate, which builds on family strengths, enhances parents' capacities to meet children's needs and be supportive and nurturing, ensures healthy child development, and builds on the capacity of families to fulfill their responsibilities in raising children, and (b) such programs shall provide a range of services voluntarily selected by families to meet their individual needs and interests that include but are not limited to providing information about available services, assessing the developmental needs of children and families, identifying families that need services and either providing said services or referring people as needed, building culturally responsive family support networks, creating a range of activities and programs that support prevention and early intervention, and advocating in behalf of families, and (c) which is staffed by trained, committed, caring, adequately paid staff; and, to secure this, (d) the Federal, State,, and local governments, in partnership with private community organizations, shall develop and expand community-based family support and education programs and ensure the provision of adequate funding to provide all essential core services; and,

III.3. Family Planning

THAT because both parents and prospective parents need to share the responsibility for planning their families and delaying pregnancy until they are capable of assuming the obligations of parenthood, and although decisions concerning family planning are and should continue to remain a private matter, (a) every community, within reasonable geographic proximity, shall have access to family planning services to ensure that all families, regardless of income, can plan responsibly for parenthood; and to secure this, (b) the Federal government shall ensure that adequate support is provided for such services; and,

IV. CHILD CARE

IV.1. Child Day Care and After School Care

THAT for single parents or both parents to work and to secure the income needed to adequately live without having to depend on public assistance, and to ensure that when a child is cared for away from the parents said child is not harmed and is enhanced by the experience, (a) all parents shall have the opportunity to obtain accessible, safe, affordable, high quality child care, both day care and after school care where needed, either center or family-based, available in a range of settings such as those operated by non-profit and for-profit organizations, employers, schools, nursery schools, religious institutions, community-based organizations, group homes, neighborhood family day care providers, relatives, or other flexible arrangements, with full-time, part-time, evening, and weekend care options which permit parent choice; and, to secure this, (b) the Federal and State governments shall provide incentives to private providers and to school systems to improve the availability, affordability, and quality of child care services for all children and families that need them, except that where no private provider or school system within a reasonable geographic distance is willing or able to provide enough available, affordable, quality child care opportunities, public-operated centers shall be developed and provided; and,

IV.2. Child Care Subsidies

THAT (a) all families with the desire to take advantage of child care shall have equal opportunity, regardless of means, to choose among quality child care options on the basis of their children's needs, depending on available openings, and (b) child care programs shall be provided with adequate funds to pay child care staff adequate wages and benefits to reduce staff turnover which may be detrimental to the stability of the child care programs and to the children; and, to secure this, (c) the Federal and State governments shall ensure that all families have adequate resources for child support, including those families who do not qualify for public-supported child care yet who cannot afford private care, and shall provide adequate child care subsidies to needy families through refundable tax credits or other means, while assuring that the subsidy brings the total reimbursement up to the market rate of care; and, (d) the State government shall withhold or withdraw child care licenses and renewals for those centers that refuse to take subsidized children; and, (e) the Federal and State governments shall provide adequate child care resources for children with special needs and for families who may need supportive services such as transportation; and, (f) the Federal and State governments shall provide incentives for child care operations which adequately design and operate programs to meet the early childhood educational needs of children under 5; and,

IV.3. Licensing standards

THAT to secure safe, quality child care centers and programs, (a) the Federal and State governments shall establish national guidelines and state licensing standards or regulations that require consistent, supportive, quality care, and which protect children from harm, and which enhance the children's learning and healthy development and (b) that such standards shall include but not be limited to (1) proper siting of centers and family day care homes (2) group size and a reasonable ratio of children and infants to caregiver, (3) minimal health and safety standards, (4) staff training on topics such as parenting education, child development, effective and supportive discipline, and building social competence in children, and early childhood education, (5) encouragement of parents to monitor their children's child care settings, (6) except that such standards shall not include regulations extraneous to the purposes stated in this section and shall not include regulations that would require a prohibitive financial or paperwork burden on centers or operations, unless the Federal or State government also provides adequate grants or low-interest loans to child care operations for this purpose, and that such standards shall remove unnecessary barriers that may prevent child care operations from taking place in safe settings such as homes or churches; and, (c) the State government shall provide certification and monitoring mechanisms that are rigorous in enforcing safety standards with an adequate number of trained staff available to monitor child care programs and help them meet State standards; and,

IV.4. Employer-supported child care.

THAT the Federal and State governments shall provide tax or other incentives to employers who provide at least one reasonable child care option for their employees with children up to age five, or that include adequate day care assistance in their benefit packages; and,

V. EARLY CHILD EDUCATION

V.1. Preschool and Head Start

THAT because every child needs to be prepared to enter school ready to learn and to achieve success intellectually and socially, (a) every child shall have the opportunity to attend a high quality and developmentally appropriate preschool or Head Start program with stimulating learning opportunities provided in a supportive caring atmosphere that enhances children's intellectual and social development and helps prepare them for school, and that such early childhood education shall be considered an integrated, essential part of the formal educational process; and, to secure this, (b) the Federal, State, and local governments shall ensure that in every school district there is access to universal, high-quality early childhood education, either through, or a combination of, publicly supported preschool education such as expansion of Head Start to include all eligible children, and private programs; and, (c) the Federal and State governments shall offer financial incentives to local school districts that provide such preschool programs, and (d) the Federal and State governments shall offer financial or other incentives to public or private early childhood education programs that include interpersonal cognitive problem-solving skills or other programs showing promise to be equally effective and demonstrating such as a portion of their curriculum; and,

V.2. Early Compensatory Education

THAT because children who have developmental or learning delays often have many learning and other difficulties when they enter school, and they need the opportunity to overcome or compensate for those delays so they present minimal difficulty as the child progresses through school, (a) all preschool age children shall have access, in every community within reasonable geographic proximity, to universal screening for developmental and learning delays designed to catch potential problems early, coupled with (b) early compensatory educational opportunities designed to help children overcome or compensate for these delays, except that where feasible these programs shall be provided in conjunction with the programs specified in section V. 1 (a)., and that (c) such programs shall include "center" or "playgroup"-based learning and social opportunities where parents can participate, combined with home-based learning experiences where needed designed to compensate for the child's learning difficulties; and, to secure this, (d) the Federal and State departments of education and local school boards shall ensure the provision of programs specified in (a), (b), and (c) of this section in every school district, by ensuring that adequate funds are provided to school districts for this purpose, where needed; and,

VI. SCHOOL IMPROVEMENT

VI.1. School "Climate" Improvement

THAT for schools to continually improve their ability to enhance student learning and student desire to attend school and to reduce student discipline problems, (a) all school personnel in every school system shall receive training in how all aspects of the school environment affect how people learn, feel, and act, and in how to develop a school and classroom climate conducive to building healthy self-perceptions and improving learning in all students, and (b) that this training shall include but not be limited to developing and implementing an effective school climate improvement process, effective discipline systems and practices, effective instructional practices, integrated learning and curricular relevance to life and work outside school, building a school structure designed to enhance the success of all students, school and student governance, building student supports, reducing status differences among all persons in the school, understanding applied child development and social and human behavior, and improving the involvement of parents and the community; and, to secure this, (c) the Federal and State departments of education shall ensure that school administrator and teacher certification and recertification is contingent upon the receipt of successful completion of experiential training specified in (b) above; and, (d) the Federal and State governments shall provide financial and other incentives to school systems that demonstrate their intent to design and implement an effective school improvement process, and further incentives upon demonstrating school improvements that result in improved learning and discipline, and that (e) the Federal and State governments, in conjunction with local school boards and private organizations or citizens, shall provide incentives to teachers who demonstrate improved student learning and behavior, (f) shall provide financial incentives for college to students who would not normally have the opportunity to attend college, provided that they agree to have their learning monitored, obey they law, shun drugs, avoid early pregnancy or parenthood, not drop out, and where the school offers these students special help as needed to help them achieve this success; and (g) the Federal and State departments of education shall remove all unnecessary regulations and restrictions and paperwork that may get in the way of schools and teachers providing the most effective learning environment; and,

VI.2. School Restructuring

THAT because the United States educational system needs to yield high school and college graduates capable of and motivated to become productive citizens and self-sustaining adults, and who can provide businesses with trained, qualified individuals who enhance the capacity of U.S. business to compete successfully in the global economy, (a) every school system shall seek input from business leaders and the community to develop its mission, goals for education, and measures of performance, and to change school regulations to provide for greater flexibility and accountability with respect to its mission and goals, and to allow the opportunity for flexible school-based management to achieve these results, and to provide incentives to students that encourage them to work harder, learn better, and take greater responsibility for their education, and (b) that the school administration and school teachers unions shall provide for more flexible arrangements to recruit and retrain skilled, quality teachers, and to remove teachers and administrators who, after retraining, demonstrate that they are unable to perform at a level of proficiency that helps students improve their learning and their desire to learn; and to secure this, (c) the Federal and State departments of education shall remove unnecessary regulatory barriers and provide for greater flexibility in the use of Federal and State funds for education, with increased accountability based on student outcome measures but that are not based on biased forms of testing or testing of retention of unnecessary facts; and, (d) the Federal and State governments shall provide incentives to local school districts that allow teachers and other school personnel and parents to have a greater say in school site improvement toward this end, and shall provide incentives to businesses and volunteers that participate in school enhancement and restructuring activities that aid in schools achieving such results; and, (e) the State departments of education or district supervisory unions shall close down or reorganize schools that are clearly not making substantial progress in achieving these desired results; and (f) the Federal and State governments shall ensure equitable and adequate funding across all school districts per pupil expenditure so that every student has equal and broad-based educational opportunity; and,

VI.3. Transition Programs

THAT because students often suffer from stress upon moving from a reasonably secure, familiar situation to a more complex, stressful one, to achieve this, (a) all junior high schools and middle schools shall provide a structure or program that helps students entering and about to enter such schools to make the transition between childhood and adolescence and also from middle school or junior high school to high school, and (b) that larger schools, where feasible, shall reorganize internally into smaller, more manageable units where students can gain increasing independence while remaining in a personalized environment and where they can feel supported; and to secure this, (c) the Federal and State departments of education shall provide incentives to school systems that create effective structures and programs to help ease this transition and that reorganize into said smaller units; and,

VI.4. School-Home liaison

THAT because some students need supports over and above what is necessary for most students to achieve success in school, such students need a personal connection with someone who takes a special interest in their needs and their families needs, and to achieve this, (a) school systems shall provide a home-school coordinator for every reasonable number of such students for the purpose of designing creative multi-disciplinary initiatives to help students with serious and multiple needs reach their academic potential, and to help provide support systems and needed resources linked to schools for these students and their families and (b) that the home-school coordinator shall provide services that include but are not limited to meeting with truant students and their families, establishing and maintaining an outreach system for parents, linking them with needed resources for human services, health care, nurturing, education, career and family counseling, and working with teachers to provide special school or community based education activities based on the students special needs, identifying and facilitating use of support services, providing orientation and training for individuals and organizations serving schools, acting as a liaison and advocate for students with these special needs; and to secure this, (c) the Federal and State departments of education receive adequate funding from federal and state governments to provide financial incentives for school systems to establish and maintain said position(s) and for student assistance programs for students with special problems such as alcohol or other drug abuse and attempts at suicide; and,

VII. SCHOOL CURRICULUM

VII.1. Comprehensive Health Education Curriculum

THAT, in addition to reading, writing, mathematics, science, social studies and the arts, every child needs the opportunity to acquire accurate, up-to-date information and develop the skills to make responsible decisions about all issues that young people are likely to encounter in the process of their growth and development, and, to achieve this, (a) a comprehensive, sequential, K-12 health education curriculum shall be provided to every student in every school system, and (b) that this curriculum shall cover at appropriate age and developmental levels all subjects of potential concern to young people, including but not limited to personal health, healthy lifestyle choices, fitness, nutrition, substances and abuse, sexual issues and pregnancy, sexually transmitted diseases including AIDS/HIV, family life education including preparation for future parenting roles, managing interpersonal relationships, personal safety, injury prevention, adolescent depression and proper handling of suicide, eating disorders, adolescent stress and management, cognitive and interpersonal skills such as communication, cooperation, problem-solving, conflict resolution, assertiveness, resistance or refusal, responsible decision-making, skills for adequate socialization, and understanding of how thinking leads to creation of experience and behavior; and (c) this curriculum shall be connected to other health-related aspects of school such as school lunches, physical education, and school nursing activities, and shall be culturally relevant and sensitive to community values and diversity; and (d) to secure this, the Federal and State departments of education shall ensure that such a curriculum is adequately provided for in every school system; and,

VII.2. Law-Related Education

THAT every child needs the opportunity to explore issues related to law-related behavior and the legal system, and to achieve this (a) a law-related education curriculum and, where appropriate, a gang-related education curriculum shall be provided in every school system to every student, at age and developmentally appropriate levels, and (b) that this curriculum shall include but not be limited to issues such as the function of law in society, justice, rights, the legal system, gangs (where appropriate), moral and ethical behavior, and aspects of decision-making that are not covered in a comprehensive health education curriculum, and (c) this curriculum shall include input and teaching, where possible, from members of all levels of the legal system; and to secure this, (d) the Federal and State departments of education shall provide incentives to school systems that encourage the development and teaching of law-related education courses; and,

VIII. TEEN/PEER PROGBAMS

VIII.1. Youth Service System

That because adolescents are continually seeking ways to meet their physical, emotional, and social needs, some of which change considerably during the course of adolescence, and because the way that these needs are met depends in large part on the direction and strength of the influences in their lives, (a) all adolescents shall have access, within a reasonable geographic distance in their respective communities, to a peer-related program, or a coordinated set of programs, that provide supportive, positive direction and help them meet their multiple needs, and that are designed to help young people build competencies, foster healthy and positive development, enhance their ability to contribute in a meaningful way to the community and society, develop a personal sense of achievement, broaden opportunities for success, aid in developing close healthy relationships and positive peer influence, and that involve of youth in the development of programs that provide a broad array of preventive services to young people, and (b) these programs shall include but not be limited to providing opportunities for tutoring and academic enrichment, supportive interactions with both peers and adults, peer discussion groups on issues important to their lives, peer counseling or peer helper programs, big brother/big sister-type programs, arts and recreation, comprehensive health services, life skills building, meaningful community service [VIII.3.], group counseling, job readiness and job training, life option counseling, leadership development, efforts to delay the onset of first use of cigarettes, alcohol and other drugs, and creating positive incentives for motivation to succeed in school and work; and to secure this, (c) the Federal and State governments shall ensure that every community has access to an adequately funded system of youth services which provides services consonant with (a) and (b) above; and (d) each State government shall establish an interagency youth council composed of senior officials from educational, job training, and human service agencies, business, community-based youth service organizations, and youths, that is charged with developing strategies to coordinate youth services delivery, fill gaps where needed, share information, maintain community and quality control in local programs for all youth particularly those at risk of engaging in socially disruptive or other problem behaviors, and assessing each community's resources and opportunities for young people, and developing an action plan to deal with deficiencies, and that shall coordinate all other State planning efforts with respect to youth, and that shall explore the use of schools as centers for delivering integrated services to youth; and, (e) the Federal government shall establish a federal Office of Youth to provide for the coordination and oversight of duties described in (d) above; and,

VIII.2. Adolescent Pregnancy Programs

That because many adolescents are sexually active and are in positions to become pregnant or contribute to pregnancy and to have children before they are emotionally and financially ready, (a) every community shall establish, within a reasonable geographic distance, and where feasible in combination with the programs specified in VIII.1., 11.2., or 111.3., a program or coordinated set of programs designed to assist adolescents to delay the onset of sexual activity, pregnancy, and parenthood, and to support and assist adolescent parents in helping to raise their children in healthy ways, and (b) this program shall include but not be limited to counseling, support groups, discussion of human sexuality and values surrounding sexuality and what it means to bring a new life into the world, and the full range of family planning services for both potential parents which includes but is not limited to a range of options for and the means to avoid sexual activity, avoid sexually transmitted diseases including HIV/AIDS, avoid pregnancy, and avoid adolescent childbearing, and to provide teenage parents with a range of comprehensive services that help them become self-sufficient and ensure a good start in life for their children; and to secure this, (c) the Federal and State governments shall ensure that adequate funds are provided for the purpose of this section to achieve the results of reduced adolescent pregnancy and reduced adolescent parenting; and,

VIII.3. Meaningful Community Service

THAT because all young people need opportunities to see themselves and have others see them as worthwhile, contributing members of the community, (a) every community shall establish a program of meaningful community service with incentives for participation, in coordination with and developed as provided for in VIII. 1., and (b) that said community service shall provide or coordinate opportunities such as tutoring adults with literary deficiencies, working with low income children, working with mentally retarded children or adults, assisting child care providers, refurbishing public housing, working in public parks, providing companionship and chore services to elderly shut-ins; and to secure this, (c) the Federal and State governments shall assist local communities in establishing and providing needed funding for such programs; and, (d) the Federal government shall establish a program of incentive options for participating in designated meaningful national, state, or community service efforts, such as forgiving or reducing amounts owed or to be owed on federally-provided college loans, on a graduated rate based upon length of service; and,

IX. EMPLOYMENT

IX.l. Job Availability

THAT because all able United States citizens need the opportunity to become productive, self-sufficient, contributing members of society, every citizen must have the opportunity for full employment at a reasonable living wage, except that the child shall be protected from economic exploitation and from performing work that is likely to be hazardous to or interfere with the child's education or physical and mental health or spiritual, moral, or social development, and to achieve this (a) an adequate number of jobs shall be made available through the combined efforts of private business and through the public sector in areas where private enterprise is unable to provide enough jobs to serve everyone willing and able to work; and to secure this, (b) the Federal and State governments, shall provide tax or other incentives to businesses that provide or increase the number of available jobs in geographic areas of job scarcity, and for opening plants areas of high unemployment, and for providing measures that allow workers to change jobs without losing pension and health benefits; and, (c) the Federal and State governments shall provide tax disincentives to U.S. businesses that choose to open manufacturing plants outside the boundaries of the United States except as part of an overall, Congressionally approved administration plan to enhance the development of another country; and, (d) the Federal and State governments shall ensure adequate jobs through public employment programs where incentives for private businesses have not yielded an adequate level of employment in a particular geographical area; and, (e) the Federal government shall establish a Federal National Youth Investment Corporation office responsible for overall policy and direction of government youth employment efforts and shall provide seed funds as incentives for operating in the private sector, leveraging public against private monies, to fund programs adhering to the program elements that have made successful youth employment programs effective, and expand the number of community organizations that can implement such programs, and this program shall be designed to encourage non-profit organizations to create or strengthen for-profit entities to generate income streams that can at least partially finance operations of apprenticeships or nonprofit social development and youth empowerment activity; and,

IX.2. Worker Preparation and Skill Training

THAT because jobs need to be filled with trained, qualified workers, young people as prospective employees need to be provided with the education and training necessary to qualify for and meet the skill requirements of needed jobs, and those who are disconnected from educational and work institutions need motivation to attain goals in life beyond what they can immediately see, to aspire to success, and to overcome problems of dependency, and to achieve this (a) every community, within reasonable geographic proximity, shall provide a job skills program that draws out the inner strength and motivation of young people and includes but is not limited to remedial or basic education, occupational training, support services such as child care and transportation, and real job placement assistance to young people, including school dropouts, through community-based organizations, Job Corps centers, vocational schools, community colleges, and business apprenticeships, and (b) that these opportunities shall be linked closely with schools which shall help young people become aware of employment and career options, help them to acquire the skills, knowledge and experience for their chosen fields, and help provide transition programs to the world of work; and to secure this, (c) the Federal government shall ensure that adequate funds are provided for this provision including Federal jobs programs, and shall alter such Federal jobs programs to operate by the principles that made effective the Job Start demonstration program funded by the Ford Foundation, and shall implement this program in ways that benefit families and provide long-term investments in education and training, such as providing child care to families in need as a means to help them become independent in accordance with Section IV. A.; and, (d) the Federal government shall ensure that adequate funds are made available for intensive remedial education and long term vocational training and other support services for young people for whom the services of current programs are not enough, and for apprenticeship and other structured training programs that move non-college bound young people into clearly defined career paths with opportunities for advancement, and more effectively link such training with private placement; and,

IX.3. Healthy Worksites

THAT because employees deserve to work in a healthy environment, and because employers have a stake in the health and well-being of their workers due its effect on productivity and because employers pay a major portion of health care costs, (a) employers shall provide work environments that are not detrimental to the physical and emotional health of its employees and that also enhance their physical and mental health, and to achieve this, (b) employers with work forces of reasonable size shall provide through the worksite at lunchtime or at other times activities and other opportunities, such as help with stress management and reducing job-related stress, teaching coping skills and what to do when confronted with a stressful event or life transition, exposure to topics related to personal and family health and well-being, physical fitness opportunities, support groups, job enrichment activities, worker participation in decision-making, career sequencing, and opportunities to assist with community and school improvement projects or participate in learning activities; and to secure this, (c) the Federal government shall expand responsibilities of the Occupational Safety and Health Administration to assess the work environment with respect to its effect on the physical and emotional health of its employees, and it shall do so by developing a rating scale measuring same using a reasonably simple form designed with consultation from health promotion and business experts so that only essential questions are asked, and which shall include but not be limited to an assessment of the physical characteristics of the work environment as they relate to effect on workers, levels of worksite stress, stress management and other prevention-related opportunities, and the extent of worker participation in decision making, and shall then allow businesses the opportunity to apply to receive a health promotion index rating, the top levels of which shall make businesses eligible for graduated tax and other incentives, and shall publish its requirements for same to ensure that all businesses have equal information about this process, and shall also publish annually by state a listing of those businesses that fall into various categories of rating, and where any misuse of ratings is determined severe sanctions shall be imposed both to OSHA and to the offending business by the Attorney General of the United States; and,

IX.4. Family-Oriented Policies

THAT because families need to be preserved and supported even as they work to make a living, and healthy child development depends on parents and children having adequate time together during the early months of life to foster the formation of close, bonded relationships in accordance with Section II.1, (a) employers shall provide a full range of family-oriented benefits to employed parents, and (b) these benefits shall include but not be limited to options for flexible management of working hours, options for permanent part-time and job-sharing arrangements, options for child care (IV.4.), and options for adequate job-protected leave for medical problems and for the family responsibilities of childbirth or adoption to aid in raising infants for a reasonable period of time to gain a solid footing in life, and for dependent family care, with prorated benefits for part-time workers, and to secure this, (c) the Federal and State government shall provide graduated tax or other incentives, based on the extent of family-related benefits, to businesses that engage in such practices designed to enhance and support the family; and,

X. SUPPORTS AND STRESS REDUCTION

THAT because the chance of developing mental-emotional problems increases during or after times of acute stress and, often, this stress can be alleviated through supportive interactions with helpful others, (a) every community within a reasonable geographic distance shall have a coordinated system of services and other options where those who are faced with an abundance of stress or a critical life event can receive social and emotional support from others or the spiritual support that comes from religious or other spiritual beliefs, and (b) this system of supports and services shall include options such as the means to receive information on stress and its sources and symptoms and predictable patterns of behavior associated with high stress, how to see a situation in ways that do not foster stress, or ways to manage stress; and to secure this, (c) the Federal government shall ensure that every community, within reasonable geographic proximately, has access to a coordinated system of well-publicized community-based services and other options that help people reduce and manage the stress in their lives; and (d) the Federal and State governments shall provide tax and other incentives to health and life insurance companies that offer stress-reduction and stress-management and other-related health promotion benefits (XIII.5(d).) to their subscribers, based upon the extent of those benefits; and,

XI. POVERTY and INCOME

XI.1. Adequate Living Wage

THAT because in the United States of America no child should have to grow up in conditions of poverty, (a) all citizens with full-time employment shall be provided with a wage that provides an income sufficient to support a family above the poverty level, and to secure this, (b) the Federal government shall ensure a comprehensive income security plan for all its employed citizens based on fundamental American principles of work, family, and independence, and (c) this plan shall include but not be limited to establishing a base "family wage" that allows parents to earn enough to keep their children out of poverty, and expanding the use of the Earned Income Tax Credit by varying its benefits with the size of a recipient's family to encourage low-income parents to enter the paid workforce and strive for economic independence; and (d) the Federal government shall establish an adequate, refundable child tax credit for families of all children through age 18, and with the requirement that these funds shall be spent to help meet the child care needs of families or otherwise meet the needs of their children, and shall eliminate the personal exemption for dependent children, or the Federal government shall provide that families with children shall be eligible for adequate, refundable child tax credits on a sliding scale according to need; and,

XI.2. The Welfare System

THAT a system of government that provides a base living income for families needs to be structured in ways that both support the healthy development of families and encourage employment for recipients who are able to work, and therefore (a) the Federal and State systems of welfare shall [continue to] be overhauled to support families and emphasize work instead of long term dependency; and to secure this, (b) the Federal, and State governments shall establish a system that includes but is not limited to (1) improving work readiness through education and training in conjunction or in cooperation with Section IV.2., (2) limiting the time that those determined able to work are entitled to welfare benefits by reorienting welfare as short-term relief in periods of unanticipated unemployment, disability, or other economic hardship to provide a safety net to poor families with children who through no fault of their own would otherwise not get the help they need, (3) providing a public-sector job as a last resort for those who have exhausted their benefits but cannot find work, (4) providing adequate child care benefits to working parents in conjunction with Section IVA. so that employment becomes financially beneficial, (5) eliminating narrow categorical restrictions on two parent families or otherwise finding ways where both parents or partners can live in the same home without having families penalized, and (6) for those still remaining on welfare establishing a national minimum benefit standard equal to 2/3 of the federal poverty level, including provisions such as AFDC and its equivalent plus food stamps, which sets benefits at levels that allow parents to live in their own homes with dignity and security and where they can meet common needs for food, shelter, and clothing; and,

XI.3. Food Subsidies and Food Stamps

THAT because in the United States of America no child should have to grow up or live in hunger, (a) the federal government shall ensure that food subsidies and food stamp benefits allow low-income families to purchase or otherwise obtain an adequate, nutritious diet after meeting the costs of other necessities such as rent, and to secure this (b) the Federal government shall establish a system that includes but is not limited to (1) eliminating government programs that pay farmers not to plant crops or otherwise produce goods that could be consumed by low-income families and, instead, establishing a system to pay farmers, at a reasonable market value, for foods that can be allotted to and consumed by low-income families, and (2) revamping the food stamp benefit computation to take into account not only households headed by elderly or disabled Americans but the high housing costs of other poor households, and (3) ensuring that all eligible families are aware of and have the opportunity to apply for food stamps, (4) removing unnecessary administrative barriers to participation in the food stamp program such as monthly reporting requirements, and (5) enlisting the help, through providing incentives, of social service agencies, community groups, and religious institutions to get eligible families and children the food they need; and,

XI.4. Child Support Payments:

THAT because many children are poor because wage earner parents who are no longer custodial do not pay required child support even though they are financially able or will be able in the future, (a) the Federal and State governments shall require that for noncustodial wage earner parents who do not pay their required child support said child support payments shall be directly withdrawn from their paychecks and be so distributed, and (b) shall require identification of both parents' Social Security numbers at the birth of a child, and (c) shall base collection of child support payments on uniform guidelines across states; and (d) where the parent who would provide this support is physically or emotionally unable to, the Federal and State government shall provide a government-insured minimum child support benefit when absent parents do not pay their full obligated amount; and,

XII. HOUSING

THAT because United States families deserve to live with adequate shelter, every family shall be ensured an affordable home that meets reasonable living standards and which will prevent unnecessary placements of children in out-of-home care due to homelessness or other housing problems, and to secure this (a) the Federal government shall ensure that an adequate supply of affordable housing units is provided for by means such as ensuring adequate funds for low-income housing assistance, ensuring an adequate number of new and existing subsidized housing units each year, and providing incentives to expand public and private partnerships such as low interest loans for new construction and housing improvement programs; and (b) the Federal and State governments shall ensure that families are provided with adequate income to pay for housing that meets reasonable standards, and shall provide when necessary supplemental rental or other housing assistance to families prior to eviction, and shall ensure that targeted funds are available to help maintain and expand where necessary effective programs that prevent low-income families in crisis from losing their housing, and help already homeless families find permanent housing; and,

XIII. HEALTH

XIII.1. Promotion of Physical and Mental Health

THAT all children and their families have the right to enjoy the highest attainable standard of health, and no child shall be deprived of access to adequate, affordable health services; and, to secure this, (a) the Federal and State governments shall ensure that every community within reasonable geographic proximity has or develops a system whereby all families are equally informed of and are provided with an easy-to-follow system of family health care guidance that begins with preventive health care and health promotion, and which, if followed, would likely lead to healthy lifestyle choices, and which includes service delivery by health care and public health providers, and (b) that this system shall include but not be limited to education about and use of basic knowledge of child health and nutrition, the advantages of breast feeding, hygiene and environmental sanitation, the prevention of accidents, ways to promote healthy lifestyles, and other public health concerns, and (c) the Federal and State governments shall ensure that effective health care programs are provided to undeserved populations by (1) providing incentives for the development of low-cost private and public community health centers for low-income and migrant populations, and of primary care clinics that are school-based or located near schools, and (2) by providing incentives such as forgiving or reducing repayment of medical school loans for the purpose of deploying on a continuing basis health care professionals in areas of the nation that suffer a shortage of primary health care services for families with children; and, (d) that the Federal and State governments shall ensure a healthy living environment for all children by providing testing for and cleaning up of environmental hazards such as lead-based paint and asbestos in homes and ensuring clean drinking water; and,

XIII.2. Nutrition

THAT because all children deserve to be provided with adequately nutritious foods that promote their healthy growth and development, (a) all schools shall provide a low-cost school breakfast and school lunch program that provides nutritious foods to all students that want it; and, to secure this, (b) the Federal government shall provide incentives to school systems that operate such programs, and (c) shall ensure that and these and child care food services are consistent with the nutrition expectations depicted in the Dietary Guidelines for Americans; and,

XIII.3. Screenings/Community Health Promotion Programs

THAT because it is best for potential health problems to be caught at the earliest signs of occurrence, (a) every community shall have access to a program or coordinated system of services that provides to all infants and children at appropriate age levels routine health screening, oral health screening, and screening for impairments of vision, hearing, speech, and language, and assesses other developmental milestones as part of general well-child care, in conjunction or in cooperation with Section V.2(a)., with referral and follow-up as necessary, and (b) all parents and children at appropriate intervals shall be regularly provided with blood pressure and cholesterol checks, and HIV testing for the potentially HIV-infected, and (c) all family planning clinics, maternal and child health clinics, and other appropriate clinics and that screen, diagnose, treat, counsel, refer, and other appropriate primary health care and mental health care providers shall offer age-appropriate information and counseling on the prevention of HIV/AIDS and other sexually transmitted diseases, and shall offer partner notification services for HIV infection and other sexually transmitted diseases; and, to secure this, (d) the Federal and State government shall ensure that screening clinics serve all communities within reasonable geographic proximity, and that said clinics receive adequate funds to provide screening services at low cost, commensurate with patient ability to pay; and,

XIII.4. Immunizations:

THAT because the spread of many dangerous infectious diseases can only be prevented by a thorough system of immunizations, (a) all American children, except upon objection by parents in writing to the state department of health, shall be fully immunized by being provided with a basic immunization series at age appropriate intervals, to be offered through schools, preschools, day care centers, clinics, and other appropriate means, and shall be provided with information about the reasons for and the need for immunizations; and, to secure this, (b) the Federal and State governments shall ensure adequate financing of and effective delivery of immunizations so no American has a financial or access barrier to receiving recommended immunizations; and,

XIII.5. Health Insurance:

THAT because all children need adequate health and medical care, and because United States citizens must either absorb the costs of medical care for uninsured pregnant women and children, or their families must experience extraordinary financial hardship to purchase care, or families and children must forego health care services because they are unable to pay for them, (a) the Federal and State governments, in conjunction with the business community, shall develop a universal system of health insurance coverage for pregnant women and for children through age 18 that includes a basic level of care, and which includes provisions to contain costs, and which improves the quality of care, and shall provide a combined system of employer-provided and government-provided care to fully cover all children and pregnant women, until such time as the United States develops a system of universal health insurance for all American citizens; and, to secure this, (b) the Federal and State governments shall expand Medicaid to include full coverage for all children and women eligible to receive the supplemental nutrition program for women, infants, and children who are not fully covered, and shall extend the program for early periodic screening and diagnostic testing to all persons through the age of 18, to adequately provide health coverage to all children and their families, including pregnant women, and (c) the Federal government shall ensure that employers provide either a basic package of health insurance coverage to workers that includes all needed child and family health and medical care costs, or that employers contribute a sufficient amount per employee to a public fund that will finance low cost coverage for uninsured workers to fill the remaining gap between private insurance and Medicaid; and, (d) the Federal and State governments shall provide tax or other incentives to employers and insurers that include preventive health care maintenance and health promotion coverage such as preventive mental health services, home health visitors for new parents in conjunction with Section 11.2., parent support and education program for health,, and preventive health care services; and, (e) the Federal and State governments shall develop a process and formula so that tax dollars for health services and research are allocated in rational alignment to the amount of disability and lost productivity caused; and, (f) the Federal government shall provide incentives to, or otherwise ensure that, the health care systems and health insurance systems economize and reduce health care costs; and,

XIV. FIREARMS

THAT because children and parents deserve to be in a safe environment without danger of getting killed or maimed by firearms and deserve to be able to walk safely on the streets of their neighborhoods without getting shot, robbed, or otherwise threatened by firearms, and to ensure this the Federal and State governments shall ensure that (a) all firearms shall be registered; (b) all people possessing any firearm shall be licensed; (c) no person with a criminal record that includes any criminal offense for which a firearm may be used, and no person with a mental health record that indicates gross instability or where indications of attempts at suicide are evident, shall be allowed to purchase or possess any firearm; (d) thorough background checks for criminal records shall be conducted within an adequate time period wherever firearms are sold and whenever they are given as gifts; (e) no person prior to age 21 shall be allowed to possess or purchase any firearms, and appropriate and severe penalties shall be determined upon violation, and (f) the design of all newly manufactured firearms shall be modified to prevent inappropriate discharge of said firearms by children; (g) the sale or use of all automatic, semi-automatic, and high-powered weapons that are beyond the scope of normal recreational use shall be prohibited, and a buy-back program of automatic weapons at a twice the average, current, retail price of a particular model shall be instituted to last for one year, and after that time shall increase the penalty to life imprisonment for possession of such firearms and for anyone illegally selling such firearms, and (h) the Federal government shall provide financial or other incentives to States that adapt the buy-back approach depicted in (g) above for handguns, and,

XV. MEDIA/COMMUNITY EDUCATION

XV.1. Media Messages

THAT because so much time is spent by children and family members as consumers of media programming and commercial advertising, (a) children and family members shall receive media messages supportive of the healthy development of children rather than counter to it, and to secure this, (b) the Federal government shall provide tax or other incentives to media and businesses on a sliding scale based on categories developed by the Federal Communications Commission with input from children and family advocacy groups such as the Children's Defense Fund and the Child Welfare League of America, and from mental health groups such as the National Mental Health Association, and from media executives, which substantively reduce the amount and type of programming and commercial time devoted to messages counter to the healthy development of children, and increase the messages supportive of the healthy development of children and families, and (b) which includes but is not limited to programming such as portraying constructive ways of dealing with stress, of resolving interpersonal problems, of showing caring and kindness toward others, of emphasizing the personal rewards and long-term benefits of academic and intellectual achievement, of promoting cultural enrichment and diversity, of hard work and perseverance, and advertising such as aiding in public awareness campaigns educate the public about preventing violence, alcohol and other drugs, teenage pregnancy, child abuse, sexual abuse, and other public health problems, and helping to create citizen and community action and participation in preventing such problems, and promoting cultural beliefs that are supportive of families and intolerant of interpersonal violence, and that raises the visibility and status of child and family concerns, and in strengthening families and supporting parents in their dual roles as wage-earners and parents, and the acceptability of reaching out for help and that resources for help are available; and, (c) the Federal government shall provide tax and other incentives to the mass media to disseminate information and material determined to be of social and cultural benefit to the child, especially those aimed at the promotion of his or her well-being and physical and mental health, and to provide such programming in geographic areas of particular linguistic needs; and,

XV.2. Recording Industry and Computer Games Industry

THAT while recognizing the right to free speech it is also important that those exercising this right exercise it responsibly, (a) the Federal government shall communicate to the recording industry and to its artists and to manufacturers of computer games a reminder about the responsibility that need accompany free speech in a democratic society, particularly with respect to the healthy development of children, and (b) the Federal government shall provide tax and other disincentives to recorded music production and distribution companies and artists and computer game manufacturers that use lyrics or depictions which assault any cultural, racial, or ethnic group, or which promote or otherwise glorify rape or other sexual abuse, violence, or Satanism; and,

XV.3. Community education

THAT because communities interested in preventing the problems that may impede the well-being of children and families often need assistance in so doing, (a) the Federal and State governments shall provide incentives to communities that develop teams of representatives from various government agencies, elected officials, community leaders, service providers, and citizens, which work to combat such problems and which provide training for its physicians, nurses, social workers, law enforcement officers, and others in matters involving such problems and their prevention, and which develop a multidisciplinary, interagency team to assess, plan, and design the best prevention approach for that community, and which enlist the mass media in such an effort, and (b) the Federal government shall provide tax and other incentives to TV network affiliates that become partners with such community teams to promote the health and well-being of families and prevent the problems addressed in this policy; and,

XVI. THE HUMAN SERVICES SYSTEM

THAT because the current system of human services must serve the best interests of families and children to meet their needs and help solve their problems so that society does not have to suffer the consequences of unmet needs, and because human service-related problems can never be eliminated by treating or rehabilitating those already displaying the symptoms, (a) all levels of government must direct resources toward building and enhancing family strengths rather than focusing solely on family and dysfunctions; and to secure this, (b) the Federal and State governments shall subject all governmental administrative and policy regulations pertaining to the system of human and social services to a complete overhaul in support of effective practices for families and children that meet actual needs to constitute a fundamental change in the governmental approach to family services in favor of coordinated and collaborative efforts that are flexible in design and administration and that encourage creativity, commitment and a sense of shared goals, and which remove rigid funding and organizational structures dictated by Federal and State governments that often prevent them from meeting the complex needs of children and families they serve, and (c) shall ensure that all communities, within a reasonable geographic distance, shall have access to the full range of services found to be effective prevention and early intervention, and (d) shall ensure that staff and management resources are adequate to provide effective services to families, and, (e) shall establish benchmarks for the Nation against which each community, state, and the nation as a whole can measure its progress; and (e) shall deliver services wherever possible through a community-based service mechanism, either one centralized agency or multiple agencies, and which provide for (1) common intake and comprehensive family assessment that includes family problems, needs, and strengths that reflects social, community, and individual changes, and information about the full range of available services, (2) uniform eligibility criteria and consolidated, streamlined application processes that use brief, easy-to-understand application forms and expedited processing, (3) case management by a single provider or who coordinates with and collaborates as needed with other providers of services to meet that particular families' needs, (4) advocacy for development of the most effective and appropriate services for a particular family, (5) referral to and follow up with services where needed such as income maintenance, education, health, mental health, youth services, substance abuse and family planning services, employment, economic and social supports, housing and social services, crisis and early intervention services, and preventive services that offer practical solutions to the problems and needs faced by families; and, (f) the Federal and State governments shall ensure coordination and collaboration of child and family policies across the executive branch, and decategorize selected federal and state programs to bring greater cohesion and flexibility to programs for children and families; and (g) the Federal and State governments shall ensure by whatever means necessary that salaries and training opportunities in the early childhood, child welfare, youth serving, teaching, and prevention fields are increased to levels that attract the best such workers, except that pay structures and incentives shall be linked to demonstrated competence; and,

XVII. GENERAL

XVII.1. Resources

THAT (a) the role of the Federal and State governments, except as specified otherwise in this policy, shall be to ensure that adequate financial and other resources are provided for effective programs that prevent domestic human behavior problems by strengthening the commitment of local communities to altering conditions that contribute to these problems so that the burden of national and state funded treatment and crisis-oriented service programs is reduced; and that not less than 20% of all grant funds allocated to combating substance abuse, juvenile justice and delinquency prevention, mental health, teenage pregnancy, AIDS, and other related issues, shall be used for proven or advanced techniques in developing, maintaining, and expanding programs and services designed for the primary prevention of such problems, and ensuring that a solid funding base is provided to all community-based organizations found to be providing effective services to children, youth, and their families; and, (b) the Federal and State governments shall provide appropriate and adequate resources for coordinated prevention research, training, and evaluation functions related to such problems and issues;

XVII.2. Training

THAT the Federal and State governments shall ensure that training for all human services professionals, including mental health professionals, social workers, teachers, physicians, and other professionals whose work significantly affects the welfare of others, includes training in prevention principles and practices as an integral part of their regular training and professional education, both preservice and inservice; and,

XVII.3. Research

THAT (a) the Federal and State governments shall ensure that adequate and coordinated research is conducted on what works to best prevent, reduce or eliminate provided to human behavior problems and how to enhance constructive behavior, and (b) that such information is disseminated on a regular basis to all community-based organizations involved with these problems or involved with promoting the health and well-being of children and families; and,

XVII.4. Governmental Practices

THAT (a) the Federal and State governments shall ensure that its own policies and practices best meet the needs of the people being served and conform with effective prevention practice, and (b) shall promote in other institutions healthy environments in which children can best grow and thrive at home, at school, at work, or wherever they may be; and,

XVII.5. Oversight and Monitoring

THAT the Federal government shall appoint an ongoing, representative national council, to monitor, evaluate, and provide oversight of this Policy in accordance with its specifications and against the achievement of behavioral and financial results; and,

XVII.6. Financing

THAT because various national commissions cited in the Preamble of this Policy have estimated that it will cost minimally from $10 billion to $56 billion per year to adequately fulfill the intent and finance the provisions of this policy, but that the United States is also likely to see reduced future costs to the taxpayer for costs associated with welfare, vandalism and other crime and incarceration, special education, and other related costs, (a) the Federal government shall consider implementation of and financing for this Policy to be as critical to national security as national defense emergencies, and (b) to fulfill the intent of this policy and not contribute to a Federal deficit, the Federal government shall ensure that adequate resources are provided through immediately and forthwith applying all budget surpluses to paying off the national debt [Note: $5.6+ trillion in the year

2000] until the debt no longer exists, and applying future savings of annual interest payments to pay for this policy.

Index

CPSIA information can be obtained at www.ICGtesting.com
Printed in the USA
LVOW032320040412

276190LV00002B/19/A